Washington Is *Like* That

Washington Is *Like* That

By

Willard

W. M. KIPLINGER

Harper & Brothers Publishers

New York *London*

Contents

v

Washington Is *Like* That

I

City of Power and Glamour

IN THE firmament of the East, along the Atlantic seaboard of the
United States, is a constellation of five cities, which are, from north
to south,

> Boston,
> New York,
> Philadelphia,
> Baltimore,
> and
> WASHINGTON.

Each has its own peculiar quality, temper and personality. Each is a
star in its own right, luminous for its own reasons, shining bright in its
own region, visible to the entire country. Washington, farthest south, is
not the biggest, not the oldest, and not necessarily the best, but it is the
brightest. It shines farthest. It is the star city which attracts the most eyes.

It has power and it has glamour.

Now, glamour in cities is like glamour in girls. It brightens them in others'
eyes. It makes them dress up and perk up to act the part. They dare not
relax and be natural. They are admired, but it's questionable whether they
are deeply loved.

It's that way with Washington. Washington dresses well to keep up a
front. Everyone is looking, and everyone is saying that here is a beautiful
glamorous city. But behind that front and beneath that glamour, a discern-
ing eye can see that Washington is a lonesome gorgeous creature who
yearns for understanding which she does not always get. Kleig lights are
blinding. They shine at, but not into. They make a grand spectacle, but
they also make illusions, and however pleasant illusions may be, they do
not pay. Far better is understanding—of the good and the bad, the bad
and the good, the reasons why, the strong points and the weak.

Excessive awe is a bad thing for human institutions. It puffs them up
in their own estimations, and it makes people stand aloof from them. You
can rub off the awe and the glamour, and still maintain the proper amount
of respect, without descending to the poverty of cynicism. You can do this

I

with Washington, and thereby do a good service both to Washington and to yourself.

If it develops that Washington is not a god or a hero on a pedestal, but that it is earthy, with common faults and common virtues, it is well that this be known. If illusions fade, so much the better, for they will be replaced by sympathetic appreciation, without any kowtowing worship.

The life and affairs of Washington are closely integrated with the lives and affairs of people everywhere. Washington is both servant and master of the people, both follower and leader. The people have made it what it is, and it helps to make them what they are. When Washington dawdles, it is the people's fault. When it gets pompous, the whole nation is to blame. When it buckles down to hard work, as during a war, the credit belongs to the people. When it suffers under strain of war emergency, the strain is transmitted to the public. In all these things it needs understanding, without the cluttering of glamour and awe.

Washington is called the capital of the nation, but it is really more than that—it is the capital of a World in the Making, for through it flow the forces which will help to make a new world when the forces of war are spent. This capital has power in war, power in peace, but the power does not belong to Washington. The real motive power is what the people think. As one basis for their thinking, the people of the nation and people of the world need to know Washington as it is, internally, inside out, honest to goodness. They need to know what's what about it.

Here Are the Internals

Washington is a city built upon a piece of land called the District of Columbia, a piece of land which is subject to federal government. The District of Columbia originally was ten miles square, but now it is only two-thirds of a square, a mutilated square, for the Virginia third was given back to Virginia nearly a hundred years ago. The remaining two-thirds is merely a bite out of Maryland. Here lies the city of Washington, on the southern edge of the North and the northern edge of the South. Past it runs the Potomac River which supplies the city with water and boating, and then goes down to Chesapeake Bay, toward Hampton Roads and Norfolk. To the east, 36 miles across country, is Annapolis on Chesapeake Bay. To the northeast, 38 miles, is Baltimore. New York is 233 miles away, north and slightly east. Richmond is 109 miles south. Battlefields of the Civil War are within an hour's drive. Sixty miles to the west are the Blue Ridge Mountains of Virginia. Built in the bottom of a shallow bowl, but now spilling over the hills which surround it, lies Washington.

Nearly a million and a quarter people live in Washington and the immediate environs, and more than a fourth of them are Negroes. Individually the people of Washington are very much like the people of any other city, but in the mass they are different, and this makes the story of Washington different.

It is a single-industry city, and the industry is government. It is the only large city in the world devoted exclusively to government, without the leavening of other normal human occupations.

The customs are not northern, not southern, not eastern or western, but a conglomeration of all of them, with some of the merits and faults of all.

Not long ago Washington was a "big small town," and very sleepy. People tossed off light remarks about "Main Street on the Potomac." But in the years when people were not looking, Washington grew to be a very large city, which it now is. And it is growing faster than any other big city in the nation because it has the growingest industry—government.

Before the Civil War, Washington was a sink hole of a city, with stray pigs running loose in muddy streets in front of the few imposing public buildings. During and after the Civil War, it was like a booming western mining town, all helter and skelter. Around 1900 it began to take itself seriously, in the manner of a youth who has donned long pants. World War I shook it out of its lazy lethargy, and gave it a bit of the air of a cosmopolitan city, but during the 20's it went back to basking in the sunshine. In the folds of its neck was perspiration from its own humidity, but no sweat of toil was upon its brow. Then came the Great Depression, the expansive New Deal, and the idea that the interests of the people lay in bigger government. It was in this period that Washington grew out of adolescence, and became an adult among the nation's other cities. There is much about the Washington spirit that is small-townish, but in size and physique it is grown up, even though still a bit youngish.

People of Washington boast of how grown up it is, and in their boasts you can see how recent this new stature is. They proudly say that it is "culturally more sophisticated" than a decade ago, and the pride which is taken in the assertion betrays the thinness of it. They point to the fact that it has a symphony orchestra "all its own," and that it even supports public chamber music concerts. They speak of its entrance into big time sports of ice hockey, boxing, midget auto racing, and professional football. Self-conscious Washingtonians are proud of these great achievements.

Washington in the past ten years has taken to dressing up. Its new public buildings cover acres of city blocks, like monumental mausoleums. Its parks are greener and smoother, its squirting fountains more numerous, its hotels more elaborate, its cocktail lounges more splendid. The old place

3

is spruced up like a home before the company comes. And now the company is coming in droves—tens of thousands to help run a war.

One odd thing about Washington is that most people who live in it were not born in it and they do not have any deep inherent pride in it. In a way they regard it as "their city," but only as the people of the whole nation regard Washington as "their city." There isn't much concrete local enthusiasm, compared with most other cities. Most people who live in Washington do not think of it as their home. They are merely living here. Their homes are back in Ohio, or New Hampshire, or Texas, or California. This city has been bestowed upon them, and they accept it, but they did not struggle to build it, and so it is not spun out of them, not a part of them. And they do not even run it.

As for the Great Men with whom Washington abounds, the typical attitude toward them is that they come two-for-a-nickel. Senators can eat in privacy in any restaurant. The Secretary of State can walk to work without being asked for an autograph. Joe Louis draws as big a crowd as any President ever did. And only a visiting movie star, or Winston Churchill, or the Duke and Duchess of Windsor are mobbed.

In Wartime

Wartime has not changed Washington as much as you might think. The city bustles under the emergency, and it takes on new surface appearances, and the spirit is more electric, but deep down underneath, the life of the city rolls along about as usual. It is more spectacular to call attention to the differences in wartime, but it is more accurate to note the samenesses which exist under peace and under war.

True, the surface is hectic. There's an influx of war workers, both high and low. Offices are crowded. People scoot up and down halls, running into each other at corners. People telephone to other people who aren't in. Everyone works harder, both in office hours and in off hours. Especially the top men work hard, in long hours at the desk. Hotels are full, and boarding houses are jammed. People open their homes and "take in roomers." Streetcars are packed, and taxicabs are hard to get. Movie houses are thronged. On the streets, in the hotels, in the cocktail lounges, there is "more life." Seldom is it glum, in spots it is gay. Government moves some agencies to other cities, but the city seems more crowded after they move than before, for hordes of new workers still come.

Of such is the surface of Washington in wartime. But the war does not make a wholly new Washington. What was true before the war is still essentially true. Only the emphasis changes. Even after the war the story of Washington will be merely more of the same.

Partisan politics have not been adjourned, as many like to think. Partisan politics go on forever, and both major parties play politics even during war. Their immediate aims are the same—to win the war. In this sense there is unity. It dulls the cutting edge of partisan politics in Washington, but it is a temporary, not a permanent change.

It's a Cross Section

Washington is a cross section of America, with some of the best, the worst and the average. It is a composite or synthetic expression of American life and ideas. What you like about it can be found elsewhere, and what you don't like about it can be found elsewhere, for practically everything in Washington has been brought in from elsewhere. As a county fair represents the county, so does Washington represent the nation. The products and qualities on display here were grown out in the states. They were shipped in, and they took root. They may be good or they may be bad, but they will wither and dry up and blow away again unless they are fed and nurtured by forces which originate outside Washington.

It might be a good thing if Washington and everything in it could be put aboard a train and hauled on display up and down and across the land, and stalled on sidings for people to handle and inspect, with a banner reading,

HERE'S WHAT MOST OF YOU VOTED FOR.

Writers write that "Washington thinks this," or "Washington thinks that." Yet Washington has no body of cohesive thought which stands alone. Its voice is the voice of the nation, and as for its ears—they are elephant ears, and they are always cocked toward the nation to catch all the big and little whispers. If Washington had a motto, it would be— "How'm I doing?" It may face the world foursquare, as a pitcher does a batter, but always in the corner of the eye is the grandstand, with 50 million voters, and every voter is a coach. This is what makes Washington a self-conscious city.

Not purely a leader, not purely a follower, but a bit of both. A leader who often looks behind to see whether there is a following, and who changes direction if there isn't. A follower who often fails to follow the will of some of the people because of fear of some of the others. Damned always by those who disagree with the course. Praised at times by those who are temporarily in accord, but denounced a little later by the same people. Thus Washington is always in step, and always out of step—with some portions of the public. The standard attitude of the public toward Washington is, "Yes, but . . ." The "yes" betrays the approval, and the

5

"but" betrays the qualification, and the two flow from the same mind and the same tongue at the same time. This phenomenon is called "the democratic process."

Behind the Front

Perhaps the most notable thing about Washington is the multitude of contradictions within the body and the spirit. These are the contradictions which spoil the common illusions about the nation's capital, and which rub off some of the glamour.

Washington is a city all green and white, with hovels where the sightseeing busses do not go.

It flaunts its tremendous government buildings which house clerks who shuffle papers at monotonous jobs and who watch the clock for the closing hour. Some work harder during war, but some do not.

It is a city of magnificent distances, and these distances sometimes seem to visitors to be symbolic of spiritual distances from the common affairs of ordinary folks out around the country.

You see here a clean city with gleaming fronts and unlittered gutters, without the smoke and grime that come from factories, for Washington is determined not to tolerate those sordid plants which turn out things for people to use.

Undoubtedly it is the gem city of the nation, and it ought to be, for it is a kept city, kept by the nation.

You know Washington mainly because it is a city of the dateline, with a reputation built upon the dateline, advertised at home and abroad by columns of daily dispatches, which play the city always up. The whole publicity mechanism is geared to make the capital appear as the dwelling place of either arch-gods or arch-devils, and in the dispatches there often is no room left for the more realistic fact that the capital is also the working place for thousands of ordinary mediocrities.

A prosperous city without deep depressions, for government is an always-growing industry and it thrives on depressions.

A lovely city to live in, for the normal working hours are short and the social hours are long, and the working hours are short in order that the social hours may be long. Even under war the city does not work quite as hard as do most other cities.

A stimulating city, with its sets of interesting people who have interesting ideas on how people should live in the less-enlightened hinterlands.

A city of public servants, serving their masters, the people, and telling the people what to do.

On the streets you see well-dressed women, and many of them work for

6

the government at good pay to help support their husbands in better manner than the husbands alone could afford. Forty-five per cent of the women work outside their homes at wage-earning jobs, and this is a far higher percentage than that of any other comparable big city in the nation. It may be a city of dignitaries, but it is also a city of working women. The women outnumber the men by the ratio of 10 to 9, and this is why in the city of Washington there is such a scramble among the unmarried working women for eligible males. (And even, sometimes, for the males who are married.) The birth rate is not low, as you might expect in a city of working women. It is about average, which seems to prove something or other about working women.

The Big Name Men—you can see them on the streets, or in the hotels, or at the baseball game, or scurrying into a store to get a clean shirt for tonight's affair. And yet you *don't* see them, for you don't know them by sight, and by and large neither does anyone else in Washington.

Here in this capital city originate the public statements, the ringing speeches which sound the clarion call, which summon all right-minded citizens to battle for the righteous cause, to defy with indomitable will those unspeakable forces which would undermine the unchallengeable rights of the people to work out their inalienable destiny in the light as given by Almighty God—the speech written by a $60-a-week publicity man.

Here you see a city of people whose daily work is to govern others, but who have no local vote on the local officials who govern them.

Up the political or social ladder which leads to this glamorous city of Washington, millions aspire to climb. And thousands who make the grade find themselves wishing in later life that they had chosen to stay in their own home towns and home states, and do their climbing there. The backwash of this war will leave thousands of such persons on the shores of Washington.

Halos are things which are manufactured out around the country and shipped to Washington, where they are worn a great deal. Many persons in Washington own them and wear them on occasions. There are little cheap halos, and big expensive ones. The little halos are worn by government employees, who have licenses to wear them, the license being based on the awe and respect which is felt by ordinary citizens of Bellefontaine or Mt. Sterling for anyone who has a job in Washington. The big halos are worn by the public men who get publicity. Some halos are gold-plated, and some are tinsel, but all of them glitter. They tarnish when left in the dark, without the light of publicity, and that is why their owners cultivate

7

the newspapermen, who can turn the light their way. Out of this war will come some solid halos, but it's hard to tell precisely who will wear them.

Washington is not exactly like your own home town. Of course there's some distant similarity between the President and your mayor, or between Congress and your city council, or between the city hall gang and the federal politicians. The forces and the influences are pretty much the same, and the motives behind them are similar. But the difference lies in that quality known as prestige. Now, prestige increases by the square of the distance. If it weren't for the distance, there would be a little less awe of the gorgeous city of Washington, and also a more wholesome attitude toward it. It's a sort of official secret, but still a fact, that much of the prestige is false, and that many a good man or good woman goes soft under the intoxication of it.

Washington is a place where reputations are made, and sometimes lost. A place where back-home nobodies can become Somebodies, of Washington, D. C., and where people who were Somebodies back home may shrink into nobodies.

Many men make their money elsewhere (or let their fathers make it), then bring it to Washington where they buy big houses and settle down for the winter season, perhaps to bring out their daughters and make the next generation a social improvement over the past.

It's relatively a wealthy city, with most of the wealth imported. Only a few fortunes have been made out of local Washington business, mainly out of real estate, and one of the largest was started on beer.

You can see multitudinous mansions in Washington, lining some of the older streets. But in streets and alleys to the rear are huts of Negroes, sleeping four to a room, breeding tuberculosis.

WPA does a big business among the Negroes of Washington, for the colored population is proportionately the largest of any city of its size in the United States or the world. But domestic help is scarce, and white women talk incessantly of the shortage of maids.

Here in Washington is the Negro intellectual capital of the nation. Here is the focal point for all movements to achieve advancement for the Negro race, with the ultimate goal of something approaching equality. Here are the movement's leaders, an earnest band of Negro doctors of philosophy, and the movement's potent backers, the President and Mrs. Roosevelt.

Here is the city of history. Of course the history does not run so far back as that of New York, or Boston, or New Orleans, but there's a greater quantity of it in a single heap than anywhere else in these United States. The men of history walked these streets, spoke in these chambers, lived in these houses, drank in the taverns which stood on these spots.

The history and the physical beauty of Washington are profitable local resources, for millions of visitors come to look upon them, and the visitors leave much money behind. Only in wartime does sight-seeing drop off. There are still sights to see, but there are fewer available places for sightseers to lay their weary heads.

Despite the wealth of national tradition attached to Washington, there is very little native culture. The city has never been a notable breeding place for art, or music, or literature. Unlike other great capitals of world thought, such as prewar London and Vienna and Paris, where the native-born leaders of the cities shaped the intellectual patterns which influenced the nation, Washington as a city has no home-grown culture. Its influence in cultural matters is not "by Washington," but, rather, "via Washington." Whatever culture there is here was started elsewhere and brought in and pasted on.

Washington is the place where all sorts of causes are promoted—through Congress and through the Executive agencies of government. It is the greatest cause center of the nation. Special interests pull a lot of wires, and whether they are good special interests or bad special interests depends upon your point of view.

The greatest special interest in Washington is Government Itself. It works in its own behalf to develop a government which is bigger and more powerful. Of course the government promoters believe in their causes, but they are not oblivious to the fact that more government makes more jobs for government workers, better opportunities for advancement of those who already have jobs, and more political plums to toss to deserving party workers. Washington as a community has a well-developed habit of not resenting the expansion of federal government. There is never any careless overlooking of the fact that as government grows, so grows Washington, and that as federal pay rolls expand, so do retail sales expand.

Washington seethes with advanced thinking on social and economic reforms, and this is the city's most important contribution to our times. It is the thing which makes Washington a dominating influence. "Doers of good" abound. They attach themselves to government or to the fringes of government, and they pry loose the great reforms with a federal crowbar. Also sometimes in the doing of these good deeds and the cultivation of influence for their causes, they win good jobs for themselves, and these jobs pay better than the jobs back home, which makes the doing of good all the sweeter.

Within the hurly-burly of government, with all of its personal self-seeking, are some of the world's greatest unsung heroes. They are not known to the millions, they do not bask in publicity. They are the plodders,

9

the career men and women of government service, who embarked upon the ship of state because they had ambitions to do certain jobs, and who stick to the ship because they have a zeal for the jobs, regardless of the political administrations which come and go. Some of these men and women reject fancy salaries in private employment, and prefer to work for the government because they feel deeply that they have missions to fulfill. This is true especially of the scientists. Some of the Big Men, too, are heroes in their own way. Some are truly statemen of either the political or the economic variety. They have a passion for contributing to the welfare of the people, and the way is hard, and the pay is small, and the buffeting is very great.

War brings many self-sacrificers to Washington to work. They range from $1-a-year men who can afford it, to $1-a-year men who cannot afford it, and a multitude of others who take whatever jobs are offered at whatever pay is offered, regardless of the higher pay of the jobs they quit in order to do war work in Washington. But, despite the self-sacrificers, Washington does not suffer materially during wartime. It is twisted, strained, and gorged with excess population, but it is very far from broke. Many other cities suffer more.

Power

The one big thing which must stick in the mind about Washington is that despite its human frailties, it is powerful. Although honeycombed with faults and inconsistencies, Washington still remains a vibrant influence on the lives of the people of the nation. It does things to them, it changes their mode of life. Some of them like it and some of them don't, but all of them admit that the governing city cuts quite a bit of ice.

Some think this is due exclusively to Roosevelt and the New Deal, but that is a short view. The influence is deeper than that. It springs from the ascendancy of politics over the other great forces, which we call "economic" or "social." This ascendancy doubtless would have come regardless of the vicissitudes of parties, and it doubtless will persist far into the future.

Capital and City

Washington is two things: It is a capital, and also a city. As a capital it has a spirit and a reputation, but the city is the body, and the two cannot be separated. To understand the capital you must see the city and the people. To know government you must know the people who run government, including the small fry. Principles and policies must be seen in conjunction with the men and women who make them—the spirit and the flesh. If the two seem all mixed up together, well, that's the way it is. Not in a logical pattern, for government is not always logical. See Washington not as you think it ought to be, but as it *is*.

See how a day runs. See the big men, and the little men. The President, keeping physically and mentally fit for the war jobs at hand. The Army men, the Navy men. The men who manage the foreign relations. The managing of the war economy. The sustenance of civilian morale.

See the government workers, and the rest of the people who make up the city. The boomtown atmosphere. The newsmen at work. Members of Congress in the shadow. See the politicians who make a business of politics. And take a look at the growing influence of women in Washington.

See how the farmers get what they want, and how labor advances step by step. See the great dispensers of money. Government the great social worker. Government the great builder of things. The Supreme Court with its nine men who are not so very old. The G-men and other government sleuths. See the thinkers, thinking up a new social and economic order, planning for postwar. See the scientists, the trade association men, the lawyers, the private girls' and boys' schools. See Society, working hard, even during war. See the tons of pamphlets from the government presses. People and principles, all mixed up. Public life and private life go side by side. The unusual and the ordinary. A peaceable city directing a war. A place where a multitude of influences crisscross and meet. Disorderly and orderly, both, for Washington is *like* that.

2

The President

ACQUAINTANCE with Washington requires first an acquaintance with the President of the United States, for he is the biggest man in the town.

Here is the background of Franklin Delano Roosevelt:

He comes from the gentry of New York and New England, and was reared to follow his father's life as a country gentleman who managed his investments wisely. His forebears—chiefly of English origin, despite his French and Dutch names—had been solid folk who prospered as farmers, sea captains, merchants, and bankers. They lived well, sent their children to good schools, and constituted themselves as Society, but rarely attained distinction.

He was born January 30, 1882, the only child of his father's late second marriage. He was hand-raised by his parents, governesses and tutors until he was 14, then sent to Groton, an exclusive preparatory school, and later to Harvard, from which he was graduated in 1904. He was a quick-minded student, but neither thorough nor brilliant enough to win academic honors. At his father's Hudson River estate and summer home in New Brunswick, Canada, he learned to ride, shoot, swim, sail, play tennis and handle an iceboat. He tried his hand at football, rowing and track, but he excelled in none. His traits best remembered by his school and college mates were: vigor, range of interests, personal charm, and ability to infect others with his enthusiasms. At Harvard he showed some political aptitude. As editor of the Harvard Crimson, student newspaper, he campaigned against the political machine of the select social clubs—to one of which he belonged—and got himself elected permanent chairman of his senior class.

At least two known special influences on his early life now seem significant: frequent trips to Europe and the seafaring tradition of his mother's family (mainly in the China trade). From the age of three he was taken almost every year to England, France, Germany, or Switzerland. Thus he learned the psychology of the chief European peoples and got a sense of close ties between that continent and the United States. (In a German school he learned military map-making, although the significance of this curricular novelty did not strike him until later.) He was taught to be proud that his ancestors, unlike many of their class, had supported the Revolution, had not been Tories. By the age of twelve his interest in the sea and ships was already pronounced, and he was an intense Navy fan, reading avidly about John Paul Jones and other American heroes.

His mind was turned toward public life by the success of his distant cousin, President Theodore Roosevelt, whose favorite niece he married. She was a shy, homely girl who had had a strait-laced upbringing and a finishing school education and, as she wrote later, did not know the difference between the federal and state governments. (Later she learned.)

He attended Columbia Law School for three years, did not graduate, but took the bar examination in 1907 and passed it. Later he practiced law in New York in a desultory sort of way, but he never made much money out of his law practice.

His political rise was rapid, but orthodox. He was elected twice to the New York State Senate, first in 1910 at the age of 28. He supported Woodrow Wilson for the presidential nomination in 1912, and was rewarded with the Assistant Secretaryship of the Navy. The first World War made this a big job—which he filled creditably for seven years, from 1913 to 1920, while he was still in his thirties. In 1920 he was nominated for the Vice Presidency on the ticket with Cox, and the ticket was defeated.

A year later, he was stricken with infantile paralysis, and he spent the next seven years in recovering from the illness. During this period, he had plenty of time to read, muse, and meditate. It was a spiritual opportunity, and doubtless it contributed to the growth of his philosophical roots.

After the seven-year interlude he was elected Governor of New York in 1928, and two years later was re-elected by a record-breaking plurality. It was Al Smith who persuaded him to run for Governor, somewhat against his will, for his intention had been to continue in private life until he had regained his ability to walk.

Certain practical political circumstances favored him. He was a Democrat (by inheritance) when a split in the Republican party put the Democrats in power. He lived in the state with the largest electoral vote, and became highly eligible politically for the presidential nomination in 1932 when a severe depression almost assured a Democratic victory. His surname had been made an asset by his celebrated cousin. He was a rare variety of Democrat: a Protestant rural northern Democrat of impeccable social background. He was independent of the notorious machines, but had won the affection of rank-and-file Democratic voters of the northern cities by his efforts to put their hero, Al Smith, in the White House.

His political thinking grew out of the ferment of the early 1900's, was shaped chiefly by the "progressive" or "liberal" ideas of T. R. and Wilson. His own 1932 slogan, "a New Deal," was a conscious union of the New Freedom and the Square Deal. His practical aim was to make the Democratic party dominant by combining the western progressives and farmers with the working men and the old South. This was revealed in his policies as Governor of New York.

He entered the White House, not as a Messiah, but as an experienced public officeholder and skillful politician. People looked to him more with hope than with assurance. Two terms seemed certain from the beginning of his first term. The margin by which he was voted a third term (the first third term for any President) was due largely to the oncoming threat of war.

In his pre-White House record, only one thing was unique. Infantile paralysis deprived him of the use of his legs. He surmounted that handicap by developing a dogged will power, which persisted into his later life.

What He Is Like

He is an unusually complex man, in whom petty and strong traits come out in unexpected combinations. His closest friends and aides, men who have seen him almost daily for years, often diagnose him differently. His most outstanding characteristic is an air of supreme self-confidence. He always gives the impression that to him nothing is impossible, that everything will turn out all right. The war has subdued, at least temporarily, his cocksure manner but not his natural optimism or sense of effortless superiority. He shows strain at times, but never despondency, frustration, or even deep perplexity.

This comes partly from his exceptional vitality, probably also from the triumph over his physical handicap, from his family background, and from his long success in politics. He is always "the boss." Without saying it, he imparts the impression that he knows he has had broader experience in public office, borne heavier burdens, and made graver decisions than any other living American citizen.

He has many friends and many critics, and most of his true friends are also critics in some degree. Here are set down the criticisms which are most commonly heard within the New Deal, together with the comments that are usually made by persons who have tried to understand and appreciate him, without necessarily worshiping him.

Makes mistakes, but doesn't admit them. True, he seldom acknowledges an error. His psychology is that of a general who knows he will suffer setbacks and losses—some due to his own mistakes—but who is determined to deny comfort to the enemy and to win the ultimate victory.

Resents criticism. He takes much of it in private from sympathetic sources, and also from the outside when politically necessary. But he seldom forgives criticism of his *motives*. Oddly enough, he often distrusts the motives of his friendly critics, and rates them as "destructive" when they are trying to be "constructive."

Is stubborn. True. He admits it and even boasts a bit about it. It is both a good and a bad trait.

Is a compromiser. Is not a compromiser. Both complaints are heard, and both are true. The practice of compromise is inescapable in democratic government. When he has been uncompromising—as in the Supreme Court fight—he has usually been licked. But in the end he gets his way, in most issues. His lack of compromise seems more notable than his occasional inclinations to compromise.

Is vain and feeds on applause. This is admitted by all who know him. Reverses upset him, make him feel depressed, sometimes even make him ill. He does best when he is in the center of the limelight, and when he hears the cheers of the public. Then he is warmed, and he rises to heights. These are qualities which are normally developed in any occupant of the White House. The love of adulation by a President is an occupational ailment. (Coolidge was the only President in recent years who did not suffer from it.)

Prefers weak subordinates; can't get rid of incompetents. This is only partly true. He likes strong subordinates if they are in harmony with his views or if he trusts their judgment. (Note Wallace as Secretary of Agriculture, Douglas as SEC Chairman, Henderson as Price Administrator, and Nelson as War Production Administrator.) It is not quite true that he dotes on yes-men. Some of his closest advisers have not been yes-men. But he dislikes subordinates, weak or strong, who try to frustrate him or who don't translate him and try to understand what he is driving at. As for firing incompetents who have been loyal to him, he is just plain chicken-hearted. He hates to hurt their feelings. He has a great sense of personal loyalty, and it often interferes with the impersonal conduct of public affairs. Rather than fire incompetents, he prefers to submerge them under a layer or two of additional personnel and functions, and thus let a situation "work itself out," which it sometimes does, and often doesn't.

Is vindictive. Yes, he has a long memory, especially against aides who he feels have turned against him, although since the war began he seems honestly to have tried to wipe the slate clean.

Acts on the advice of the last man he listens to. This is true on many minor decisions. He has the habit of "yessing" callers, just to be amiable, to take on their color, as many impressionable persons do. And he has a

15

penchant for snap judgments. This is encouraged by the tremendous load of responsibilities imposed on a President by the necessity of making quick decisions, by overcentralized administration and consequent lack of time to explore all questions thoroughly. On big decisions, he is not influenced by the "last word." He weighs important decisions carefully. As he gets older and more experienced, he is influenced less by the "last caller."

Distrusts men who have made a success in private life. He respects private achievements in some fields, but is notoriously prejudiced against financiers and big industrialists. Formerly he complained that they misunderstood him, as they did. Then he came to regard them as unconvertible political enemies, unwilling to understand his reforms. Since the war started, he has earnestly sought their help, however, and has used their ideas to check the more extreme New Dealers. But he is firmly convinced that business experience ordinarily is not good training for public administration. Some of his associates feel that he has carried his distrust of businessmen too far, and has alienated them when he might have cultivated their cooperation on the work for which they are suited and trained—the production and distribution of goods.

Never had to meet a pay roll. This is a figure of speech or symbol which is often used against him. It is true that his experience does not include that brand of material competition which involves "making a living," either for one's own family or for the families dependent on the pay roll. He has not had the benefits of the emotional experiences which are represented by figuring closely, to meet the pay roll or to pay the monthly rent. He was born with wealth, and thus was endowed for public service. His lack of opportunity for rubbing elbows with ordinary people in the competitive business of working and earning a living sometimes makes him idealize excessively those classes with which he never had contact in everyday life. But there's no doubt that his sympathies are with the working people.

Embraces every new idea he hears. No, not every one, but he does have a soaring imagination which is not excessively earthbound by details. He is an artist, not an engineer. As an artist he dreams great dreams, and makes some of them come true. He is always inclined to think that the details will adjust themselves.

He is not frank, does not take the public into his confidence. This is true in some cases, especially during the election campaigns, and during the year preceding the war, when he tried to do double talk—to the effect that we would get into war, and, simultaneously, that we could avoid getting into it. In arrears, it appears that he was not frank and blunt enough. This is said in the light of hindsight, and with this light it can also be seen that millions did not accept even the degree of frankness which he did show, did not believe, for example, his talk of the need for a larger Navy. A popular leader cannot always leap too far ahead of his people, lest they fail to follow. Doubtless he was influenced by this thought during the year preceding war, and he compromised cautiously on the extent to which he told what he believed to be the full truth.

Is not a good organizer or administrator. Basically this is true. He improvises, he plays by ear, he thinks in terms of persons, friendship, loyalty, intentions. He does not understand the fundamental hard principles of organizing or administering. He hates to delegate authority, likes to keep the strings in his own hands, and often creates complications with tangled lines of responsibility. This weakens the power of subordinates to make their own decisions. Since the war he has shown improvement.

A common denominator in these comments is a trait which many persons, even in Washington, have been slow to recognize: As a public man he is highly competitive, a fighter. His gaiety and political flexibility have been misleading. They are on the surface. But deep down he is at his best when he is fighting. In the period after Pearl Harbor he was in good health and functioning efficiently, despite his strain and fatigue.

He is history-minded. He felt during his first two terms that he was the agent of a readjustment which would be compared to the Jeffersonian and Jacksonian revolutions. As war approached he lifted his sights to cover the whole world. He assumed, almost as a matter of course, the world democratic leadership.

He is opportunistic, but his record shows an underlying consistency of philosophy and purpose, which revolves around his idea of welfare for the masses of people, to be achieved by reorganization of the social and economic order—through democratic processes. He rises to big challenges better than to the small ones. With all his faults he is a strong, thoroughly seasoned man, still vigorous at the age of sixty.

There's one more thing: People like Mr. Roosevelt. Many disagree with him, many criticize him, many vote against him, but nearly all like him when they meet him face to face. His manner is more pleasing to more people than that of any President since Teddy. This is a personal attribute of public importance.

The President's Work Day

Here's what Mr. Roosevelt does in a normal day:

Has breakfast in bed or in his room around 8 o'clock. Reads the morning papers. Looks over the day's list of engagements. Dictates memos and

17

perhaps some letters to a secretary who lives in the White House. Confers in his bedroom with close advisers, usually with Steve Early, the press secretary, Rear Admiral Ross T. McIntire, his physician, and his military and naval aides.

Gets to his desk in the oval office of the west wing around 10 o'clock. Starts on the scheduled callers, usually 15 minutes each. Some run longer, especially in wartime, and the schedule for the day is often disarranged.

Takes an hour for lunch in his office, at his desk, and almost always has a guest or two. Food is brought over from the White House kitchen in a "wagon," like a big tea cart, with electrical apparatus to keep it warm.

After lunch, more conferences, and much telephoning. He spends about a fourth of his working day on the telephone.

Leaves office around six in the evening. Stops off for a swim in the White House pool about twice a week. (Once this was daily, but he doesn't have time for that now.) Sometimes gets a quick shower and a muscular massage.

Dinner with the family, and usually there are guests. Doesn't mind donning a dinner jacket, but hates to get all dolled up in white tie and tails.

After dinner, he occasionally watches a movie (he especially likes newsreels and light screen stories). But usually he goes right to work again in his bedroom on a pile of papers brought over from his office in a wire basket. He makes notes on "tabs," which swing the office staff into action the next day. Sometimes he dictates letters. Sometimes he reads a relaxing book, or works over his stamp collection. Emergency calls are taken on a phone at his bedside. Sometimes they come after he has gone to sleep. No matter how late he works, he is always awake by eight in the morning.

The Job of Being President

It's a hard job, a work job, a grueling job, a long hours job—to be President. Often it is tedious, often it tries the patience. It requires a combination of show-off and labor. There may be roses and palms on the platform where the President speaks, but there are thorns in the seat of his office chair.

It is one of the four most powerful jobs in the world—the Dictator of Germany, the Dictator of Russia, the Prime Minister of Britain, and the American Presidency. Probably it is the most powerful of all four—the next few years will tell.

All Presidents in recent years have had to work hard (except perhaps Coolidge), but the current President, Roosevelt, is the hardest worker of all. His job is bigger, broader, more complicated, because government has grown bigger, broader, more complicated. It is a job for ten men, and yet

18

it is encompassed by one. He must shift from phase to phase, and play every position on the team. The grandstand is full of rooters, and also booers. It's a rough job, and it takes a tough man.

The Constitution gives a wrong steer on the duties of the Presidency, because it sets them down all nice and orderly, like a blueprint. You can read a thousand laws without finding out what the President does. He is not merely an individual, he is a complex institution.

Here are some of the things the President does as part of his official job:

He is leader of his party, the in-power party. He runs the party policies through the National Chairman and the other political workers, and the chairman is usually designated by him. He tries to dictate the party platform, and usually succeeds (Roosevelt certainly does). He runs the quadrennial election campaign by telling subordinates generally what to do.

He is the boss of the executive machinery of the government. He appoints the men who run it, and he has something to say about the men whom they appoint as their subordinates. They are not always like-minded men, and they do not always agree with their boss or with each other, but somehow they get along, and he mixes in with almost everything they do.

He issues executive orders which are cooked up for him. These are the equivalent of "decrees." They have the force of law, because they were authorized under general laws passed by Congress. More and more the tendency in law-making is to lay down general principles and policies, and assign the working out of them, the application of them, to the President. He, then, with the advice of his appointees, determines what many laws shall mean in practical operation.

He does not vote the laws, but actually in many cases he makes them. The first drafts of bills in Congress are often written by technicians in the executive branch, with the President's approval, either specified or implied. Then the President turns the heat on Congress, and often gets them passed substantially as he wishes them.

Turning the heat on Congress is a job in itself. It is done by direct conferences with the leaders in Congress, usually the party leaders. It may be done by telephone. Word goes around Congress by grapevine that "the Boss" wants this bill. It is an "administration bill." Members who "vote right" are rewarded by patronage, by appropriations for their districts, by promotions, by social invitations. Members who "vote wrong" run the risk of being passed over in the distribution of plums. For the President to "speak a good word," or to refrain from it, on behalf of a member of Congress sometimes makes all the difference between that member's reelection and his defeat at the polls.

The President makes up the budget for government, through his budget director, attached to his office. It runs into billions, and it contains hundreds of thousands of items, too many for any member of Congress to read in full. Congress may change, trim and buck on some items, but the budget as a whole is usually approved in approximately the form in which the President submitted it. Newspapers make much of the "fights on the budget," but they are merely skirmishes on the fringes.

He may veto any bill which Congress has passed, and usually the bill stays killed, for not often does Congress muster the two-thirds vote to pass a bill over the veto. Sometimes the whispered threat of a veto is used by a President to "persuade" Congress to follow the line of the President's wishes.

He appoints all justices of the Supreme Court, and other federal judges, subject to Senate approval, which is usually given. Over the long pull the President determines the general brand of thinking by the courts.

He runs the foreign relations. True, the Secretary of State is supposed to do this, but it is the President who fixes the broad outlines of policy. It is to the President that the other big nations look.

He runs a war. He is Commander in Chief of the Army, the Navy, and the home front. Actually he signs many orders which determine the conduct of a war, the strategy. He delegates many war duties, of course, but he is still, literally, Commander in Chief. Most of the operations on the home front, the manufacture of munitions, the planning of the economy, the regulating of prices, are done under the President's order or authority, directly or indirectly. During war he is, frankly, a dictator, and the laws of Congress make him that. He is chief supply officer for the United Nations. Materially, he is the most dispensing man in the world.

The President is the top publicity man for the United States. He does the most uttering, the biggest and loudest uttering. The press is his megaphone. The radio is always at his right hand, and hundreds of millions in the world may listen. This brings the President into the homes of the people as a vocal visitor, and it is one of the reasons why the current President is the most potent President this nation has had. He can deal directly with the voters, if he wishes. He does not have to go through the channels of the politicians.

Any President is the chief silk hat wearer, when occasions require it. He is the greeter, the glad hander, the No. 1 "appearer" for the government and for the nation. In England the King does much of this burdensome work, but in America it is one of the flashy duties superimposed on the other big duties of a President.

Any President is a prisoner of his bodyguard. He can't go anywhere in public, or even sometimes in private, without the presence of the men who are told by law, by Congress, to guard him. This is one of the most inconvenient things about being President.

He passes out billions of dollars to the people by telling his subordinates where to pass them out, after the billions have been voted to the President in a lump sum to be spent as he decides, within certain specified broad limits.

He selects the men to be appointed to head big private business corporations which are really subsidiaries of government, chartered or financed by government. He is the top man of the biggest holding company in the world, which the United States government has become.

And, above all else, the President is Chief Citizen. He can say anything about anything, and millions will listen to what he says, and think like him if they choose, and often they choose. His is the power of prestige.

These are not all of the powers of the Presidency, but they are some, and they are enough to suggest that the Presidency is quite a big job—and a hard job.

Presidents Seem to Like It

It's work, not play, and you might think that men wouldn't like it, considering all the beating they have to take. For years I have been curious about this, just humanly curious. I have known six Presidents, not intimately, but at close range, seeing them at their work, and I know some of the things they thought. Only Harding didn't like the job. All the others did.

One President who had his share of troubles said something like this: You work hard and are never free of responsibility. Prayerfully you do what you think is right. It involves balancing the interests of some sets of people against other sets of people and doing the best you can for all. People often misunderstand you. They say you are partisan and political, and you may be, but usually you are not. They give you too much credit when things go right, and too much blame when things go wrong. It is hard, but it is exciting.

And he added, "I am grateful for the experience."

One evening I picked up Mr. Taft at the door of his church and gave him a ride to his home, and we gossiped about things. He was then Chief Justice, and I asked him how he felt when he looked back on his term as President. With a heaving belly-chuckle he replied: "I liked it—even if it did cut down my weight a bit."

Men who missed being President always say they are relieved. I heard one such man explaining to a group of friends how glad he was that he was not nominated. Later I asked him in private whether he had meant

21

what he said. "No," he replied, "I was lying like hell. I wanted to be President so bad that my teeth ached."

Presidents lose their youth, sometimes their health. They are cut off from ordinary normal friendships. They must watch sharp to avoid being sold down the river. They acquire bitter enemies. They lead a life which is not their own. And yet, there's something about the job which stirs the blood of men, and they really seem to enjoy it.

3

White House: Office and Home

THE White House is a house with a big front yard and elm trees, and a big back yard with a place to hang out the wash. In ordinary times you can walk right up to the front porch. The address is 1600 Pennsylvania Avenue, Washington, D. C., and the telephone number is National 1414, listed in the phone book in small type like any other, preceded by "White Horace H".

The name had a practical origin. Once it was the President's House, but marauding young fellows from England, dressed in red coats, marched into town one day in 1814 on what seemed more like a picnic than a war. They piled up the furniture in the President's House and set fire to it, and the smoke made the outside walls dirty, so the government had to paint the President's House white, and it became the White House.

The President lives at the White House and works there, but most of his public work is done in the offices of the low wing which extends westward to West Executive Avenue. Mrs. Roosevelt lives at the White House, and makes it her base of operations for goings and comings. Official callers come there. Personal callers come there. It is the social tops of the capital. To visit the Capitol Building means something, but to visit the White House means much.

Since war started, the streets that separate the White House from the State Department on the west and the Treasury on the east have been closed to traffic. The bordering sidewalk of Pennsylvania Avenue is closed, and pedestrians must walk on the opposite side of the street. Soldiers and policemen are all around. Only one gate in the fence enclosing the grounds is open and you have to have credentials to get through it.

The Offices

The regular White House office staff consists of approximately seventy members. About a hundred others are borrowed from federal agencies under authority of a standing provision of law. At the head are the three secretaries to the President. One of the secretaries, Brigadier General Edwin M. Watson, known familiarly as "Pa," arranges appointments for the President. Another, Stephen Early, is in charge of press relations. Duties of a third secretaryship consist mainly of supervising office operations. Marvin McIntyre holds this post. William D. Hassett, assistant to the press secretary, is another member of the secretariat.

On the main floor of the office structure (the west wing) are the offices of the President and his secretaries, the room in which the Cabinet holds its meetings, quarters for the Secret Service men, newspapermen, photographers and radio reporters and commentators. On the floor above are offices for stenographers and clerks, also the "communications room" in which are located the telephone switchboard and telegraph instrument which link the President and his staff with the outside world. The telephone switchboard has 16 trunk lines and about 150 extensions. Direct lines lead to living quarters of a few high-ranking government officials. Operators know by heart the list—on which are about 100 names—of people who are to be put through directly to the President when they call. Facilities for handling the large volume of White House mail are on the basement floor.

The offices are equipped with indirect lighting, cork and rubberized flooring and air-conditioning apparatus. An electric communication system enables each presidential secretary to summon armed guards at a moment's notice.

Space for White House offices has increased steadily since the turn of the century, reflecting the growing accumulation of work with which Presidents have been burdened. In Theodore Roosevelt's administration, the office section was built and the working offices were moved from the White House proper. The office building was enlarged to twice its original size in 1909-10. Additional working space was gained in 1927 by converting the attic into a third story. And, in 1934, the space was tripled, by enlarging the former attic, extending the basement by excavations and making an addition to the first floor. The building was badly damaged by a fire on Christmas Eve, 1929.

Before the war, the U.S.S. *Potomac*, naval vessel assigned to the President's use, was a sort of "floating office," almost an adjunct to' the White House offices. The President was fond of taking intimate advisers and ponderous problems "down the river" on week-end cruises.

Expenses

You've probably heard it said that it would take an annual net income of a million dollars a year, after paying taxes, to "live as well" as the President. That's putting it on a bit thick, but it would take about half a million. The annual appropriations by Congress for the White House and the Executive Mansion these days run about $450,000, divided as follows: For the Executive Mansion and grounds, about $150,000; for the White House office, approximately $300,000. This is in addition to the President's annual salary of $75,000.

Still, it's evident that the presidential family is housed, tended and fed in a good style. They occupy the most famous residence in the United States without paying rent, and without having to meet bills for heating, lighting, and repairs. All the servants in the White House, the gardeners, and the other workmen are paid out of the public funds. White House automobiles, with chauffeurs and gasoline, also are supplied without drain on the presidential salary.

The White House food bill is split, however, part of it being paid by the President out of his pocket and the rest being met by the government. Two sets of books are kept on expenditures. One carries notations of money spent for strictly family purposes. These bills are paid out of the President's pocket. The government pays in full for expenditures connected with the President's official functions.

Of the $150,000 appropriated annually for the upkeep of the Executive Mansion and the grounds surrounding it, approximately $100,000 goes to pay salaries of the staff of more than sixty persons. Here are the breakdowns of estimates for the fiscal year beginning July 1, 1942: Fuel, $3,000; electricity, $11,670; laundry, $5,528; repairs to building, furniture, etc., $9,572; supplies and materials, $13,542; and "special and miscellaneous current expenses," $5,570. Estimates, prepared more than six months ahead of the fiscal year to which they apply, go through the Bureau of the Budget and the congressional appropriating machinery just like any other federal expenses. Budget officials and congressional committees do not question proposed White House expenditures as they do nearly every other contemplated federal spending.

The greater portion of the annual appropriation of $300,000 for the White House office goes for salaries of the regular staff and working force, totaling nearly a quarter of a million dollars a year. The secretaries to the President get $10,000 each, as also do each of the six administrative assistants to the President (the "assistant Presidents" who have "a passion for anonymity"). Twenty-nine persons, exclusive of the President, draw more than $3,000 a year. Personal secretaries to White House officials get $5,000 a year; private secretaries get $2,600. The salaries of employees borrowed from other government departments are not included in this figure.

The $300,000 includes $50,000 "for contingent expenses of the White House office, including stationery, record books, telegrams, telephones,

25

books for library, furniture and carpets for offices, automobiles, expenses of garage, including labor, special services, and miscellaneous items to be expended in the discretion of the President." White House office telephone and telegraph bills run around $15,500 a year. Letterheads and envelopes come to more than $2,000.

Also included in the annual White House appropriation is $30,000 for traveling expenses of the President. After the coming of railroads, and until Taft's time, Chief Executives rode around the country free of charge. Then a scrap between Congress and the railroads brought a law forbidding issuance of passes to federal officials. It was then that Congress voted travel money for the President, the amount originally being $25,000 a year. President Coolidge figured that the cost of hiring a special train to haul him and a retinue of Secret Service men, newspapermen and others, whenever he made a trip, was too much money. So, one time when he was going out West, he just took a drawing room on a regularly scheduled train.

That gave fits to a lot of people, particularly the Secret Service men. It did not take the Interstate Commerce Commission very long to rule that the railroads, in the interests of the President's safety and their own peace of mind, could provide the President with a special train free of charge. Under that system, which has been in force ever since, the White House appropriation pays for accommodations on the train used by the President and his personal party. The Treasury Department pays for the Secret Service men's transportation, and the employers of newspapermen and news photographers pay for theirs. Politicians and other favored citizens who climb aboard en route pay their own way; and that has led to many an argument with train conductors who asked them for money when they thought they were riding "on the house."

The House

In the midst of 16 acres of well-kept terraced lawns, the mansion with its portico and columns ordinarily looks much like the manor house of a southern colonial plantation. But today, in wartime, the house and grounds are shrouded in a net of war precautions. There are squads of soldiers with fixed bayonets on constant patrol along all sides. There are uniformed police and plainclothes Secret Service agents.

The White House is a three-story home with a basement and an attic. Extending east and west, the central portion is 170 feet long, 85 feet wide and 58 feet high. If you were a social guest at the White House, you would enter through the north portico (on the Pennsylvania Avenue side) into the broad reception hall. There you would see in the floor the President's

26

seal, made of bronze and about three feet in diameter. Visitors used to get a thrill out of walking across it. Now it is fenced off with fancy red cords.

If you were to turn to the left, you would go into the East Room, 87½ feet long and more than half as wide, the scene of a variety of historic assemblages, ranging from grand receptions to weddings and funerals. The room was "done over" not so long ago. New draperies, costing $4,000, probably will remain in service for a quarter of a century. The principal feature of the room consists of three giant crystal chandeliers. The famous "gold piano" placed in the East Room in 1902 has been hauled away to the National Museum, and has been supplanted by one of more modern design. At the other end of the east-west corridor is the State Dining Room, second largest in the building. Formal dinners are served here. When one is scheduled, carpenters bring up a lot of plain wood units which are fitted together to form the large horseshoe table, capable of seating more than one hundred guests. A private dining room, in which most Presidents have had their family meals, adjoins the State Dining Room. It is comparatively small, with a vaulted ceiling. The Blue Room, elliptical in shape, is where state receptions are held and where foreign ambassadors meet the President to present their credentials. The remainder of the main floor is occupied by the Green Room, opening on the south portico, and the Red Room, now used as a reception room for small dinners, and by the office of the chief usher.

A wide stairway, with a wrought-iron gate at its base, and a small elevator, with oaken panels cut from rafters of the Old South Church in Boston, lead to the upper floor and the presidential family's quarters. On that floor are located seven bedroom suites, a library, and a study, all opening on the wide hall extending the length of the building. The most spacious suites are those located at the four corners of the building. Each of these has a large dressing room adjoining the bedroom. Suites on the north side of the second floor are those used by guests. One is decorated in rose, another in blue, and a third in gold.

A large room used by wives of former Presidents as a bedroom has been used by Mrs. Roosevelt as a sitting room and workroom. She made the smaller dressing room, which adjoins it, her bedroom. The west end of the second-floor corridor is screened off and furnished for use by Mrs. Roosevelt for conferences and small teas. The President's bedroom is small. It has a plain bedstead, chest of drawers, and bedside table. The President's study, the one in the main section of the White House, is a large oval room. The table, presented to the White House by Queen Victoria, was made of wood from H.M.S. *Resolute*. The chair, a duplicate of one designed by Thomas Jefferson, is upholstered in red leather, has a

27

high back, long footrest and a swiveled seat. The walls are full of paintings and prints of historical naval scenes. The "Monroe Drawing Room," long used for cabinet meetings, now is a sitting room. And a room once used by President Lincoln as a study is now a bedroom.

The basement floor is put to good use. It houses the library in which are kept the books presented by American publishers in recent years. President Roosevelt regularly receives catalogues from more than thirty booksellers who cater to his interest in ships and oceans. Throughout the President's collection, a visitor might see the monthly issues of the United States Naval Institute Proceedings, of which he has a complete file. Other favorites are a large accumulation of the works of Oliver Hazard Perry, U. S. Navy officer during the War of 1812; Lovette's *Naval Customs, Traditions and Usage*; Riesenberg's *Log of the Sea* and *The Fighting at Jutland*; Spear's *History of Our Navy* and *Log of the Constitution for 1813-1815*.

Across the corridor from the library is a room in which is displayed china used by Presidents, their families and guests since Washington's day. A third room is the one from which President Roosevelt has delivered his "fireside chats" over the radio. A fourth contains furniture used during the Johnson and Arthur administrations. A corridor reaches from this area, open to tourists during peacetime, to the west terrace, beneath which is the swimming pool where President Roosevelt takes a dip when he has time after leaving his office. The corridor is flanked by service rooms.

On the top floor, or attic, are servants' quarters, storerooms, a sewing room, and the housekeeper's cedarized storage room.

Housekeeping

A close official watch has been kept over the White House furniture for many years to make sure the place doesn't get cluttered up with articles left behind by outgoing Presidents and their families. No piece of furniture or equipment may remain permanently in the White House without approval of the Fine Arts Commission and the consent of Congress. This gives each newcoming First Lady opportunity to fix up the family quarters according to her own liking.

The Executive Mansion staff consists of the chief usher and his assistants, the housekeeper, ladies' maids, the President's valet, doormen, engineers and maintenance men, butlers, cooks, chambermaids, gardeners and house men.

Mrs. Henrietta Nesbitt, the housekeeper, has her office in the basement. She supervises the servants, plans meals, purchases food—in short, runs the house. She and her husband, Henry D. Nesbitt, joined the White

House staff when President Roosevelt took office. When Mr. Nesbitt died, his widow—with the aid of an assistant—took on his work of checking all purchases and gifts, keeping inventory and checking everything that goes out. When Mrs. Roosevelt is in Washington, Mrs. Nesbitt confers with her daily about menus and other details. Mrs. Nesbitt has said that her job is pretty much like running an average house, except that the work is on a larger scale. Ordinary home economies are practiced, such as turning of curtains and repairs by darning. The mansion furnishings get a thorough dusting and vacuum cleaning each day, with the real house cleaning awaiting times when the President and his family are absent. Back in the days when tourists were admitted to the lower floors, their habit of sliding their hands along banisters was a factor in an official request to Congress for an appropriation to hire an extra man. He was hired to go over the banisters every fifteen minutes and otherwise to keep clean the areas through which the throngs of visitors moved.

The White House kitchen, which is down in the basement, was remodeled and stocked with new equipment in 1935. New underground storerooms were constructed under the west driveway to the north portico. The old kitchen was divided into three rooms, with glass walls and working surfaces of stainless metal. Equipment includes a huge electric range and these electrically-operated devices: Stock kettle, food chopper, meat grinder, batter mixer, dish washer, and thirty-gallon storage box for ice cream. The kitchen is arranged so that it can function efficiently for the preparation of everything from a small tea to a state dinner. A dumb-waiter lifts the food to the butler's pantry between the two dining rooms on the main floor.

The top kitchen staff consists of the chief cook, two assistants and a dish washer. The "downstairs staff" totals twenty-five. Running from the kitchen are passages that lead to cupboards, refrigerators, storage rooms, a small wine cellar and a room for reception of packages. When a large state dinner is being prepared, thirty chickens or ducks go through the culinary plant, with everything else being handled on the same scale. All food, except bread, cakes, ice cream, candies and some desserts, is prepared in the White House kitchen.

The food generally is simple and almost entirely American, provided in good variety. The President's favorite dish is scrambled eggs. He never seems to tire of it, as he has—at times—of liver, string beans and one or two other such bits of fare. Whitefish, another of the President's favorites, comes from Lake Superior. Fruits often are ordered from California or Florida. Canned goods may be purchased from an out-of-town dealer if his quality and price are reasonable, but most of the provisions are bought from local dealers. The only article raised for table on the White House grounds is mint from a bed originally planted by Theodore Roosevelt and recently increased by transplantings from Wakefield and other historic places in Virginia. Food given to the White House is distributed to local hospitals and charitable organizations.

President Roosevelt and Mrs. Roosevelt notably have been more active socially than any other occupants of the White House. Or they *were* until the emergency came along to bring a canceling of the big dinners and receptions. The food bill usually ran about $2,500 a month in normal times when social functions were not curtailed.

Typical state dinners, such as one for the diplomatic corps which brings about 165 guests when conditions are normal, are set up something like this: Crabmeat cocktail, calves' head soup, celery and stuffed olives, broiled filet of flounder with mushroom sauce, broiled duck, green peas, sweet potatoes, brandied peaches, toasted cheese crackers, salted almonds, ice cream, petits fours, and coffee. State dinners include white and red wine. The Roosevelts rarely dine alone. When they do, a Sunday dinner may include a jellied bouillon, fried chicken, corn on the cob, potatoes, Stilton cheese salad, caramel ice cream, and coffee. Other "regulars" on the menu are: "Kedgeree"—flaked whitefish—rice and hard boiled eggs, all mixed and browned in the oven; Italian rice, which is a mixture of browned rice and onions, simmered in chicken broth; and pecan or walnut pie.

Formal luncheons at the White House often are as elaborate as dinners. This is a typical line-up for such an occasion: Creamed pea soup, celery and olives, capon, cubed sweet potatoes topped with toasted marshmallow, string beans, salad avocado, rum parfait and little cakes, candies, nuts, coffee, and cigarettes.

The gold table service, purchased in France by President Monroe, is reserved for state occasions. Its central feature is a gold plaque—mirrored and about four feet long—and gold figurines, vases and comports. The flat silver—engraved with the words "The President's House"—is "gold washed." The dinnerware design was adopted when Mrs. Roosevelt found it more economical to buy a new set of china rather than attempt to fill in missing pieces of the old set. It is a modification of the motif of the Roosevelt coat of arms.

. . . . . .

Foreign visitors are always amazed at the "smallness" and "simplicity" of the White House. By foreign standards it is no palace. Even by American standards it is not a rich mansion, but, rather, a comfortable big house. As government buildings go, it is one of the smallest structures in Washington. And yet it packs a punch, for from the White House, more than from any other place, is run the government, the nation, and a war.

4

Producing for War

THE personal affairs of yourself, your children and your grandchildren are wrapped up intimately with the story of what is being done these days to produce the goods that are needed for war, and here's why:

First, the materials of war have a greater relative importance in this war than in any previous war. The factory comes first in point of time, and the battlefront second, in deciding the question of whether you, your children and your grandchildren are to live under our own system, or under a German-Japanese system. And the factories, fields and mines, which produce the materials of war, are directed from the top—from Washington.

Second, if the planned economy of war works reasonably well, it undoubtedly will be changed over and adapted for peace. If the unified methods of directing the whole economy are successful in producing more total goods, even for destructive war, the chances are that similar methods will be used to produce more total goods after the war, for the constructive purposes of peace.

Third, the success of the system of production for war depends largely on whether people understand it. People deliver more goods and services when they know what a system is all about, when they are not merely mechanically-driven cogs.

If you start at the top of the pyramid of war arrangements, you run into a jumble of alphabetical agencies in Washington. You encounter such terms as priorities, conversion, price control, rationing, economic warfare, and excess buying power. It is better to start at the bottom, out around the country, and to work up to the dizzy top in Washington. For a moment forget the boards and alphabeticals, and look at a few general but basic facts.

In peacetime there are about 185,000 manufacturing plants in the United States. Some are big and some are little. Each finds its own niche. Each makes things because people will buy them. It is not a haphazard system, but it is a private system, with private initiative and private ingenuity, devoted to satisfying private wants. The factories depend on customers at the outlet door, and supplies at the intake door. In normal times the supplies and raw materials are plentiful.

But when war comes, the government becomes the big customer, and this customer wants from factories a lot of war things which they formerly didn't make. They must convert their plants to new products. That's *conversion*, which you hear so much about.

More and more of everything is needed, not only for the normal civilian requirements, but for the new war purposes. So certain industries are urged to enlarge. And that's *expansion*.

There aren't enough raw materials for the increased needs. It takes time to dig them out of the earth, to grow them in the fields, to haul them from other lands, and ships are scarce. War needs come first, and so the government sets up a system of laws and regulations by which factories making war goods get first or "prior" call on raw materials, supplies, anything they need. These regulations are *priorities*.

Other nations which are fighting on our side need things, too, in order to do their best fighting. So through lend-lease their requirements are balanced against our own requirements, and they get what our government decides they must have. Their priorities are mixed in with our own priorities.

There isn't enough stuff left for the normal needs of civilians. Yet civilians must not freeze or starve or go without clothing and shelter, partly because they have human rights and partly because they are the people who are making the things for the fighting and fighters. Some things civilians must have, and some things they can get along without. So it is up to government to draw lines, and define *civilian essentials*, or *less-essentials*, or *non-essentials*. The lines between these groups shift from time to time, depending on the pressure from war needs. Factories making non-essentials, or less-essentials have their supplies cut down, or cut off. Thus develop *shortages*. These shortages are not accidental, they are planned. Government shuts off things which people can get along without, and this forces the closed factories to convert to war production.

Then there develops a shortage of necessities. It may not be an absolute shortage. There may be enough for all, if all will be thoughtful of others, and not grab more than they need. But individuals often are not like that, and so there must be a system of apportioning out what they need—not what they can afford to buy, but what they need. This is *rationing*.

On top of that, there's *price control*. Most things become scarce, and buyers always bid up the price of things which are scarce. If this were allowed, the supply of scarce goods would go to the relatively well-to-do, and the relatively poor would have nothing. Besides, the whole economy might go to pieces under runaway prices and inflation. So the government sets up a policing system, and this is price control. All prices aren't *frozen*, but sellers are told they may not charge *more* than they did at a certain time in the past, so prices are restrained, regulated, controlled.

There comes a shortage of workers, of man power. There aren't enough workers to make and do all the things that are needed, including the fighting. So government sets up a system for encouraging the flow of workers into essential work, and discouraging the flow into non-essential work. In this way arise the *labor priorities.*

Then come the taxes, which serve several purposes. First, they get money to pay part of the costs of the war. Second, they take away part of the money which otherwise people would spend for things which they could get along without. This lessens the pressure for higher prices. Also the government must borrow to pay the greater part of the costs of war. Borrowing becomes a sort of bookkeeping transaction between current generations and future generations. The scarcity of things which are available for people to buy helps to route excess money into savings—in the form of war bonds. Also there's a current scarcity of enterprises in which people can invest, and this scarcity helps to route more savings into war bonds.

One more activity: To have the material resources needed, our government sets up a system by which it gets all the materials it can for ourselves, our allies, and our friendly nations, and helps to keep their economic health good. It also tries to keep as many materials as possible from the enemy nations, and to undermine their economic health as much as possible. This is *economic warfare.*

That's the a-b-c of war economics, of planned economy for war.

The planning and execution of war economy has not been done as well as it should have been done. It is now apparent that at a thousand points in the development there was "too little too late." The delays, it now seems with the benefits of hindsight, were stupid. The faults were numerous, both within government and in the thinking of the people. There are still faults, plenty of them. But in the over-all picture, with allowances for errors in calculations which were general on the part of the public and the government, it now looks as if the whole system, the machinery, the factories, and the people both within and without government, are doing a good job. Our economy, hastily planned for war, is on the march.

How the Job Is Done

What the umpteen thousand people in Washington do to arrange for and to speed up production is not a mystery, if you forget the names of the agencies and look at what they do. The troubles involved in the big airplane program are a good case history.

The President decided that 60,000 planes should be built in 1942, and 125,000 in 1943. In the background of these figures were calculations by such agencies as the Army General Staff, Navy General Board, Lend-Lease Administration, War Production Board, and others.

Manufacturer "A" is building military planes for the government, and doing a good job of it, so the government asks him to take a contract for some more. He quickly sees that he will need a new building and more tools and materials and workers and houses for his workers. To build his new building, he gets financial help from the Defense Plant Corporation of the Reconstruction Finance Corporation. As the building starts, there is a question of getting steel for it. A government man in Washington gives Manufacturer "A" a high priority rating for the steel, which means that "A" will have first claim on scarce steel ahead of thousands of others.

"A" also knows that he will need so many hundred or thousand trained workers, so he starts training some in his present plant and he gets another man in Washington to scout the field for trained men and to arrange training courses for others so they will be available when the time comes.

"A" can tell how much aluminum he will need. He gives his figures to a government man in Washington who is dealing with all aluminum users. The government man adds up his figures for all aluminum users, finds there won't be enough to go around, and begins arranging for increased production. That, too, means new plants and a repetition of the priority problems involved in steel for "A's" building.

It takes a lot of electric power to make a little aluminum. That means more dams, and more generating machinery from factories which already are struggling under huge orders for military generating and propulsion equipment. The power takes copper, extracted from a supply already inadequate for shells and other military items. More copper means more mining machinery in the United States, and more ore hauled to the United States in scarce ships. More ships mean still more generating and propulsion machinery, more steel, more copper, more of everything.

The men who work for manufacturer "A" have to be housed, and someone has to decide how to get scarce materials and man power to build shelter for them. The workers also have to have food, and besides that the United States is trying to supply its allies with food now and to build up a reserve for postwar feeding of the world. It takes plows and tractors and scores of tools to produce the food. Most of these are made of steel, just as are the girders in "A's" new plane plant. So somebody in Washington has to decide how much steel shall go to the manufacturer of farm equipment, how much to manufacturer "A," how much to the aluminum producer, how much to railroads, to ships and tanks and guns and shells.

34

Obviously, manufacturer "A" couldn't solve all these problems. And there are hundreds and thousands of manufacturers like "A," each with similar problems. Naturally, there is frequent conflict between government men who make the decisions. Before the War Production Board was created, many things got tied up in knots because there was no one but the President who could be the umpire, and he had lots of problems besides production to worry about. Now, however, Donald M. Nelson, Chairman of the War Production Board, can make the final decision on most production issues.

Preliminary Fumbling

There was pulling and hauling and fumbling and politicking before America got down to the plain fundamentals of producing for war. Until after Pearl Harbor, there was not even any definite program of what should be produced for war. The President had never told the country publicly what it would have to do. The 1940 political campaign was a restraining factor, for many people thought the war would never be brought to this country and the politicians had to appeal to the people to win their votes. So there was talk about "no expeditionary force," and "keeping the enemy away from our shores," and "neutrality" and "defense," and so on. And most of the tough talk that came from the top was directed at the enemy— calling them back-stabbers and scoundrels and other dirty names. But there was little pressure for the sticks and stones with which to really hurt the enemy after the words rolled off his back. It was two years and a half after his first timorous move before the President worked himself up to creating a machine which looked as though it could do the job.

The first move came in August 1939, when the President appointed a War Resources Board of businessmen, headed by Edward R. Stettinius, Jr., of U. S. Steel, to study plans which the War Department had been making for 15 or 20 years for mobilizing the nation's productive resources into war production. The War Department's Industrial Mobilization Plan had been redrafted from time to time, and the Stettinius board looked it over and suggested more changes. Even as the Stettinius board began its job, the public howled against warmongering, and the New Dealers objected vigorously at putting control of the program into the hands of businessmen. The Board lasted only six weeks. Before the Board's report was submitted to the President, he publicly and nonchalantly waved it aside as something that perhaps had better be forgotten.

Not until Hitler's mechanized army blitzed the Low Countries in May, 1940, did even a semi-serious production set-up emerge from the White House. Then the President appointed an Advisory Commission to the

35

United States Council of National Defense, and the new agency became known as the Defense Commission or the NDAC. The NDAC had no authority. It didn't even have a home. Its seven members, with differing ideas and philosophies, had offices at various places, and some of them worked at two jobs at once. They held their infrequent meetings in the impressively sedate Federal Reserve Building, certainly not an atmosphere conducive to the speed and hustle and bustle necessary for all-out war production. When the NDAC did meet, the members talked and debated and argued, and issued unanimous statements about inconsequential things —not because the individual members were incompetent, but because of their varying views and because they were trying to do a job without any authority. But the people were still anti-war—and it was election year.

In January 1941, after the election, came OPM, the Office of Production Management, that two-headed institution run jointly by Director General William S. Knudsen and Associate Director Sidney Hillman. The idea was to create a labor-industry partnership, but these partners fumbled and fussed. Although Knudsen and Hillman never came to open conflict, their subordinates were in constant battle, and labor and industry each maneuvered for ascendancy. Industry fought expansion, New Deal "theorists," curtailment of civilian output, and closed shop. Labor fought for labor and not for war. When the peak of the strike wave was approaching, Hillman issued a pamphlet called "Labor Speeds Defense."

Seven months later, in August 1941, the President made the mess messier by creating still another agency on top of those already in existence, a sort of holding company, the Supply Priorities and Allocations Board, known as SPAB. Because of the President's distrust of businessmen, even this agency was subject to political leadership—Vice President Wallace was its chairman. SPAB's members were heads of agencies involved in defense —Knudsen and Hillman of OPM, representatives of Army, Navy, and so on. Donald Nelson, director of priorities in OPM under Knudsen, was made executive director of SPAB and was supposed to run the show, more or less. But again there was no centralized authority. Nelson of SPAB was superior to Nelson of OPM; Nelson of SPAB was also superior to Knudsen of OPM, but Nelson of OPM was subordinate to Knudsen of OPM. SPAB bogged down before it got started.

It was six weeks after the attack on Pearl Harbor before the President created a really effective agency. In mid-January 1942, he set up the War Production Board and made Nelson its chairman. One reason he chose Nelson was that Nelson for months had been battling through the reluctant Army and Navy a "Victory program" calling for huge quantities of ships and planes and tanks to win the war. When, after Pearl Harbor, the public finally demanded action, the President could present the "Victory program" as the answer. If Nelson had not been so farsighted, it would have been weeks or possibly months before the President could have arrived at any program.

Nelson's first assignment was to decide how much authority he should have in the new job. He wrote a wide-open ticket, leaving no real doubt in anybody's mind that he had the final say-so on everything concerning war production and procurement. He could even overrule and direct cabinet members. And the President OK'd Nelson's ticket.

Nelson Gets Tough

Donald Marr Nelson is a big man, a pipe-smoker, a steak-for-breakfast eater, an expert who did all the buying for Sears Roebuck, of which he was executive vice president. He isn't a desk-thumper, and above all he hates to be called a superman. He looks upon himself as a fairly good business-man who just happened to have the right experience inside and outside government to let him know a little something about what he is doing.

Nelson rarely raises his voice, and he never shouts. Cold logic, he thinks, should be presented coldly. When he had trouble buying things for the Army in early OPM days, he would simply call a meeting of the industry involved, tell its representatives what the government wanted and the price which it thought would be fair. Then he would turn the meeting over to Milton Katz, his favorite government lawyer, and let Katz read and explain sections of the law empowering government to seize goods and materials and plants. Never a shout or a threat—but his listeners got the idea and Nelson got the goods at his price.

One of Nelson's toughest problems was small business. Many wanted to take scarce material away from war and essential civilian plants and give it to others so they could keep going. Jewelry makers used "just a little copper and tin and employed a lot of people," so they should be allowed to have the metal—so said some. But Nelson decided that small business should be used, not saved, and that if small business was allowed to keep on with its usual business it would not try hard enough to shift into war business. He refused to complicate his own No. 1 job of getting every available ounce of war production by stopping to figure out how to save small business.

Nelson's weakness was that when uncertain of his authority, he hesitated to exercise it. For months, he let Knudsen block plans for expanding pro-duction—because he wasn't sure of his own authority, and besides he hated to hurt Knudsen, a friend for whom he had great respect. But after Nelson became chairman of the War Production Board, he surprised a lot of people who thought it would take glandular injections to make him tough instead of easygoing. One subordinate complained that the production job which Nelson had fixed for the subordinate's industry was impossible. Nelson listened to the wails, then told the subordinate to write a long memo citing all the reasons, keep a carbon copy for his own record, tear up the original addressed to Nelson, then "go ahead and do the job." The subordinate now is well on the way toward achieving the "impossible." Other subordinates who couldn't do it are back home.

The characteristic that really makes Nelson a good executive is his ability to delegate authority. He picks his men with care, gives them hard and then harder jobs to do. If they come through, he gives them more authority and responsibility, backs them up if they run into trouble, and looks for new fields upon which he can concentrate.

Politics baffled Nelson when he came to Washington with the NDAC. He was a businessman babe lost in the vote-getting woods. Some of his businessman elders were not impressed with his ability, and when they formed little cliques of their own they left him out. Like any man, Nelson needed companionship, people with whom he could talk frankly. Only 52 himself, he turned to the younger men and, strange as it may seem for a businessman, he turned to New Dealers, too. Among the latter group was Leon Henderson, who comes pretty close to being as good a politician as the President and a better one than most members of Congress. With Henderson and young businessmen to help and advise him, and by using his own ability to figure out new and tough problems, Nelson became a pretty good politician. He learned a lot about the philosophy of the New Dealers and found out that they all weren't revolutionists after all.

When conservative business groups began to notice Nelson, and wanted to cotton up to him, it was too late. He had surrounded himself with what his industrial elders called "young squirts." They were businessmen and economists and engineers and college professors and military and naval experts, usually in their forties and sometimes in their early fifties, who were not afraid of a new idea just because it was new. From them Nelson expected and got results.

Bill Knudsen was a production miracle man, a Danish immigrant who got his start in the bicycle business and became the outstanding mass-producer in a mass production nation. He knew and cared little about dividends to stockholders, about finances, about strikes. At putting labor and materials and machines together and getting production he was a whiz.

Knudsen's name was well known to the public, so when the politically-minded President looked around for somebody the public would believe in, he found "The Great Dane" and called him to Washington. The job turned into a policy-making job, the kind of thing that Knudsen couldn't do and didn't even want to do. He wanted to produce, and people wouldn't let him. He would not prod the Army and Navy for a bigger war program because he said his only job was to produce what they decided the country needed.

His transfer to the War Department with a lieutenant generalcy made him happy. His friends who had tried to force policies and politics upon him advised against it, but Knudsen jumped at it because he saw a chance to concentrate on assembly lines and wrenches and nuts and bolts instead of labor relations, and what the public thinks of this and that, and whose toes are being stepped on. There is already ample proof that his ideas have had much to do with the fact that the nation is now really producing war goods. And it isn't his fault that he didn't get down to that job long before he did.

Henderson Gets Loud

Leon Henderson, boisterous, big-bellied and bellicose, stands way out among the men in defense, for he did much toward getting the nation's war producing machine into order. Early in the prewar period he spotted Nelson as a man who he thought could do the job, he helped him learn his way through the Washington maze, and he plugged and plugged to get him made the production boss.

Henderson is a Swarthmore graduate, a former employee of such opposites as Governor Pinchot and the du Ponts, a man who somehow can find fifteen fingers to put into fifteen different pots at once. Even in high school at Millville, New Jersey, he worked 14 jobs at the same time. He probably has more friends among newsgatherers than any other top official in Washington. He is a sucker for hard-up acquaintances and is constantly passing out 5's and 10's to the down-and-out. He used to be able to find time to play bridge at the National Press Club. His unchallenged boast was that he was "the best damned no-trump player" in the Club.

He is an omnivorous reader. He will subscribe to anything, whether it be "Tory" or "Communist." He sets aside most of his Sundays to get caught up on his reading. In summer, he puts on his oldest clothes (which are very old indeed), takes his boat out into Chesapeake Bay, thinks, reads, and fishes a little. If a bottle happens to be around he will not throw it away. At 46, he's still part boy—and very human.

NRA brought Henderson into the official eye. When NDAC came along, there he was—an economist of considerable ability who, for fun, had carefully studied World War I, and a man who well knew and agreed with most of the President's basic philosophies. Price control was turned over to him.

For months he had no real authority. All he could do was bluster and bluff about what government "might" do to those who violated his price ceilings. He astounded some industrialists who had thought he was a left-wing, production-for-use advocate by fixing price ceilings high enough to permit a profit. His biggest complaint is that businessmen still don't understand him—that they think he is anti-business when actually he is anti-big-business. He feels that if big businesses, "monopolies," are allowed to grow up and freeze out all the little fellows, they are really endangering the capitalistic system because it is much easier for government to take over and run a few big businesses than a lot of small ones.

Henderson's idea when he took over the price job was to hold prices together, not down. He had no hope that the end of the war would find prices where they were at the beginning. He said inflation comes in 5 per cent doses, and he knew there would be plenty of such doses before peace. What he wanted to do was keep some from profiteering at the expense of others. He didn't want farmers to get low prices for their products and to pay high prices for their tools, or vice versa. He watched the relationship between prices, and when some started going up faster than others he smacked them back into line—or tried to.

It was more than political necessity which made Henderson shy away from wage control at the start of the wage boom. He thought the workers should have more money if they could get it. He even said it might be all right for them to earn enough money to buy silk shirts—for he knew there wouldn't be any silk shirts, and he knew that taxes would hit the workers just as hard as any others—or harder. Of course he recognized that something would have to be done later on about wages.

One of Henderson's biggest fights was for expansion of production, on the theory that if raw materials were not greatly expanded there would not only be less than enough for military needs but also such a ravenous demand for the inadequate supply that no power on earth could stop inflation. When he had won his uphill battle, with Nelson's help, he was afraid the victory had come too late for complete success.

Henderson has often been described in congressional corridors as a "red" or a "pinko" or "another New Dealer who never met a pay roll." When he went before Congress in 1941 to testify for his price control bill, a lot of people who didn't know him thought he was putting his head on the chopping block. By the time he got through, everybody on Capitol Hill respected him.

Henderson took on another job which a timid and less earnest man would have ducked—cutting civilian production, rationing the reduced supply. He saw that civilian production would have to be cut or war needs endangered. Nobody else was showing any interest in the cutting job. With the help of able aides who figured out months ahead where and when the pinch would come, Henderson ordered cuts in civilian production and battled them through OPM. He fought Knudsen for months to stop automobile production and won only after Nelson became boss.

As chief rationer, chief civilian cutter, Henderson stands to have a lot of enemies before the war is over, but as price-holder-downer he will make just as many friends. And will he have fun when postwar reconstruction time comes!

Labor's Contribution

Sidney Hillman, the erstwhile Lithuanian rabbinical student, had a tough time in the defense machine. His first job with the NDAC, theoretically, was to see that there was a supply of labor available to produce war goods. For every one man who pulls a trigger in a modern war, eighteen others are engaged in the war effort—either aiming the gun or bringing up the bullets or food, or bridging rivers, or running trains, or working in factories or mines or on the farm. For defense industries alone, Hillman had to count on using half the workers normally engaged in all industry. That meant transfer and training and putting more Negroes to work, and more women, and getting older people back into harness. Hillman did not only what he and his labor associates thought could be done about these problems, but he also called in scores of businessmen and manufacturers to help with his program. He ran into lots of trouble, but he did a creditable job.

At the same time, he stuck his oar into another turbulent pool—labor relations. Early defense activities were guided largely by businessmen, or by Army and Navy officers who generally were unfriendly to organized labor. Little attention was being given to keeping peace between employer and employee. The National Labor Relations Board was in pretty general disrepute, and no other agency was worrying much about problems which would arise later when workers had enough money put aside to quit work if they wanted to, and to demand more money for overtime and to meet increasing living costs.

Attention to these things was imperative, Hillman felt. He foresaw the strike wave long before it arrived, and tried to work out wage stabilization agreements, calling for upward adjustments to offset cost of living rises. In this, he was not completely successful, but he did make some progress.

He went into other fields, such as the placing of contracts, and finally forced through a government policy which in effect required every government contractor to sign a stipulation that he would bargain fairly and collectively with his employees. He set up special committees of employer and

41

union representatives around the country to route workers into war plants and to watch for embryonic strikes, and he employed a staff of industrial and labor experts in Washington to handle strikes when they arose. Some of these experts did more harm than good, but many of them did good, and at least Hillman made the effort.

One of his major worries was caused by the AFofL-CIO split. Off and on, each suspected him of secretly favoring the other, and both frequently criticized him because they thought he was not serving the cause of organized labor. But Hillman explained that the defense program came first, and the interests of any group, including labor organizations, came second. If he could serve both defense and labor at the same time, as he frequently did, so much the better. Few of the impartial observers think that he often put the interests of labor ahead of those of the rest of the nation.

Conversion to War

Hillman's job of shifting workers to war production was part of a bigger job, generally called conversion. This shifting of men and machines from peacetime to war production was not an overnight task. Machines make machines, and these in turn make other machines which men ride or fly or shoot. It was necessary to convert some of the machine-making machines to the production of things for which they never before had been used, and it was also necessary to make lots of new machines because some of those already in existence could not be adapted to war work. It took Henry Ford months to shift from his old Model "T" to Model "A," but that was a comparatively simple task.

A leisurely shift can be made in peacetime, but war can't wait. Still, it does take time to get industry into war. Before World War II began, the War Department had surveyed some 20,000 plants to see what tools and facilities and men they had. Yet after two years of contracting, Army and Navy had given 75 per cent of their business to only 56 firms, and the remaining 25 per cent had brought the number of prime contractors up to only 6,000. Before the subcontracting pressure on the 56 really got strong, there were many thousands of the total of 185,000 manufacturing plants which had no war business at all.

Manufacturers also were reluctant to upset their normal business, and desired to keep on making the things they always had made, if they could. If forced to take war work, they wanted new tools instead of having to destroy the usefulness of their old tools for civilian goods.

Government was slow in getting around to it, but it finally took care of both the subcontracting and the business-as-usual reluctances. It piled orders so high upon some plants that they had to go out and scurry up subcontractors in order to deliver the goods on time. It sicked the little fellows who wanted work on the big fellows who had too much work. Once government got around to it, business-as-usual was easy to overcome. Government just ordered cuts in normal production, told some industries they would have to stop production altogether. Owners and managers, facing the prospect of money tied up in idle tools and idle buildings and idle trained men, got busy and dug up war work.

Economic Planning

Add up all the things government is now doing in war production and the total is "economic planning." Whatever you may think of it, economic planning is here. Government is running business and industry and agriculture and labor. It starts at the farm and tells the farmer what to produce and what price to expect for it. It decides what shall be brought out of mines by controlling metals used for machinery. It tells a manufacturer what he may make with raw materials, how long his workers shall work, what he shall pay them, what his relationships with his employees shall be, what price he shall charge for the things he sells, where and on what terms he shall borrow money for his operations. As of today, government is doing the planning and getting by with it for the sake of war. The ideas are getting a tryout, a test under emergency circumstances. The machinery will be eased here and tightened there as war progresses, but the prevailing assumption in Washington is that centralized economic planning in some form will continue permanently after the war.

5

Army at the Desk

THE United States Army is manned by soldiers all over the world, but it is run from desks in Washington. The fighting is not done in Washington, of course, and the tactics of any single fight are not settled there either. But in Washington the grand strategy is laid, and the levers are pulled to put this or that campaign in motion. Washington is the control center not only for the U. S. Army, but for the whole fighting organization of the United Nations. It is the main headquarters of the Super Staff in the world battle against the Axis. It is the place where British and Dutch and Chinese and Free French and the North and South Americans get together to coordinate their plans. Valor goes on in the field, but the ability of the men in Washington to get the soldiers their planes and tanks and guns—and more soldiers—is what makes the final difference.

There are a lot of things which, taken together, make the U. S. Army different from any other army in the world:

It is new, this army of today. We were late getting it started. It has been put together in just two years, since the Nazis blitzed Holland and Belgium and France. For twenty years it starved—and was kept that way by the people, who were afraid of a big army, afraid of a push toward war.

Until several years ago it was the smallest "big army" in the world. On July 1, 1939, it had only 174,000 men, fewer than the Japanese shipped to the Philippines just to start their first attack. Then it grew apace into the approximate 2,500,000 that it is now, and toward the 3,600,000 planned by the end of 1942. When it is full-grown, it will be the biggest army ever amassed by a democratic country.

Its early tardiness, its troubles of having "too little too late," were a result partly of the temper of the American people. The U. S. Army is a creature of the American public and the public's representatives and their political officials, as well as of the Army technicians.

The Army worked in the dark while it grew in size. It was not told where it would have to fight, or whom, or when. The politics of democracy were an accepted burden to the technical planners, who could not always tell what kind of an army to plan. There was no one man to tell them.

44

It is predominantly a non-professional Army, composed mainly of men who were recently civilians. This is true not only of its privates and non-commissioned officers, but also of commissioned officers. Of the more than 140,000 commissioned officers in the Army today, only 14,000 are "regular" officers who make the profession of war their steady job. They are just yeast in a mass of civilian dough.

The Army is a whole society in itself. It must do all the things that a normal society does—feed its men, clothe them, transport them, exercise them, minister to their spirits. And on top of it all, it has to fight the enemy.

The Front Office

The control men of the Army are housed in three buildings in Washington. The Munitions Building, which was practically the entire headquarters for twenty years, is a long, squat, three-story concrete building on Constitution Avenue, within sight of the Lincoln Memorial. Along its low halls, adorned with old paintings of Secretaries of War in civilian clothes, are the utilitarian-looking offices and the plain-looking desks of the chiefs of this-and-that, and their multitudinous aides. But the miles of corridors and hundreds of offices and wings in this big building were not enough for the requirements of wartime. So the Army put up a New War Department Building, a block north, which looks from the outside like a modernistic theater. Even this was not enough for the demands of war, so there is another, bigger, newer New War Department Building across the Potomac River, in the flats below Arlington Cemetery, where the shades of General Lee and the Unknown Soldier can keep watch on the modern men who run this modern war.

The topmost of the men who direct the machinery of Army war for the United States is the Secretary of War, who is boss of the War Department, including the military men who run the Army and the mixture of Army-and-civilians who run the procurement. When Henry L. Stimson took over the Secretaryship in September of 1940, he had already been Secretary of War once before (under Taft), had served as colonel in the Field Artillery in the last World War, and had been Secretary of State (under Hoover). On him, a man past seventy years old, fell the job of running the mechanism that was to get the men and equipment for the country's new Army.

The direct head of the Army, the boss of the "military establishment" of the War Department, is the Chief of the General Staff. He is the top soldier, and is responsible to the Secretary of War, and the Commander in Chief—the President. General George C. Marshall became Chief of Staff at a time when all the major countries of the world except the United States were getting ready to fight. In the several years thereafter he followed the ticklish course of preparing for war without seeming to prepare for war. In Washington he was characterized as "a good technical soldier but a poor politician," yet he survived the chaotic political situations of 1941 and the impact of Pearl Harbor.

The job of getting the materials made for the fighters to use is turned over to the Under Secretary of War. Modern war has become more and more a thing of machines with the men to run them, so the job of the Under Secretary has become more and more vital. In the first World War, it took five men (some of them soldiers, and some civilians) working behind the front to keep one man at the trigger. Today the ratio of 5 to 1 has changed to 18 to 1. The task of the Under Secretary of War is big, whoever does it, and 51-year-old Robert P. Patterson, who stepped from the U. S. Circuit Court of Appeals to become Under Secretary in July 1940, has done a spectacular job of rushing appropriations into equipment.

These three men—the Secretary, Under Secretary, and Chief of Staff—are the War Council. When they get together in the office of the Secretary, they are the top Army advisers to the Commander in Chief in the White House, eight blocks away. They are the men at the desks, who make big decisions affecting millions of soldiers, thousands of miles away.

Expansion

Back in 1924, when Secretary of War Weeks spoke at a West Point graduation, he told the graduates that they could expect to be nothing more than a police force for the United States and possessions. Most Americans agreed with him then and for a good many years later. They were leery of another AEF. They were still leery when hostilities opened in Europe in September 1939. Even at the end of March 1940, when the Army asked for money to buy 1200 planes to keep its supply at the same level, Congress appropriated enough for 59.

Then in May 1940, the Nazis tore through Belgium, Holland and France, and Congress asked for action. The Army that for twenty years had been held with a tight check rein was suddenly asked to gallop. Congress came running with the checkbook open. The Army was astounded by the change of heart. It was like asking a man to leap from the ground to the top of a tree. It was a new "Reveille in Washington."

In the Army boom that followed, the War Department staff in Washington grew to the size of a small city. From less than 5,000 civilian employees in 1939, it expanded to 50,000 by spring of 1942. War Department offices spilled out of the Munitions Building, which was a "temporary" building put up during the last war, and moved into eighteen other buildings. Stenographers and typists and clerks arrived so fast that a special

War Department agent was put on duty with the Travelers Aid at Washington's Union Station. The Department's telephone switchboard (number, Republic 6700) grew until it was as big as branch exchanges for whole sections of Washington. Mail came in faster and faster. When war broke on December 7, 1941, the Department was almost inundated. People out around the country wanted to know what to do about everything, and they figured the Army would know. Manufacturers wrote for contracts. Mothers and fathers wrote to ask the whereabouts of their sons. Young men wrote for commissions. In one bureau alone, where the total list of officers came to 60, applications for commissions rolled in at the rate of 100 a day. Everything was hectic, but the work was going ahead. The Army was dressing and rushing to the fire at the same time.

Relations with Congress

If Congress had ever believed that a big peacetime Army was a good thing, the United States might have had a big Army in the days between World War I and World War II. For Congress controls the Army's size and set-up. It votes the money for equipment. When any expansion is needed, Congress must vote it. Congress even passes on the transfer of a function from one part of the War Department to another. In 1941, when the Army wanted to take the building functions from the Quartermaster Corps and give them to the experienced constructors of the Engineer Corps, Congress had to say the word.

But Congress never was convinced, by anyone, that a big peacetime Army was a good thing. At least, not through the 20's and 30's. And yet the relations between the Army and Congress were cordial on the whole. Congress did not see the need for increasing the military appropriations, but it did not pare down the estimates very much. Most of the paring was done by the Budget Bureau (at the behest of the President) before the appropriation estimates ever reached Congress.

The tightness of peacetime appropriations continued in the face of one of the closest relations that any department has had with Congress—the relations of the Engineer Corps with individual congressmen. The Engineer Corps is the outfit which in peacetime supervises river and harbor improvements and flood control projects, which traditionally have been one of congressmen's pet ways of getting "pork barrel" appropriations for their communities. And the Engineers are required to consult members of Congress on projects in their districts, so the relationship between the Engineer Corps and Congress was extremely cordial. But even with this tie-up, the Army didn't get any open-handed appropriations throughout the peacetime 20's and 30's.

47

Under the threat of war, of course, the Army can get as much money as it asks for. Beginning late in 1940, Congress was so anxious to appropriate the wherewithal for the weapons of war that it built up a large backlog of appropriations which the Army could allocate almost according to needs.

War Department

The Secretary of War has two Assistant Secretaries, in addition to the high-ranking Under Secretary. One of the Assistants is in charge of general administration of the War Department, and the other is an Assistant for Air. All four of these officials are civilians—the Secretary, Under Secretary, and two Assistant Secretaries—and they are the highest policy officials within the Department. They rank ahead of the Army, ahead of the Chief of the General Staff. Only one official stands above them on questions of Army policy. He is the President of the United States, the Commander in Chief of the Armed Forces, who frequently calls upon the Chief of Staff to work directly with him on questions of strategy, tactics and general operation of the Army.

The Chief of Staff is aided by a compact staff, whose members are his principal counselors. So that the Chief of Staff may be free to attend to the broader questions of strategy, the operation of the Army is delegated to three generals, who command, among them, all the functions of a working Army. One heads the Ground Forces, another the Air Forces, and the third, the Services of Supply. "Task forces" fighting abroad are headed by special theater commanders, and may include soldiers from all three parts of the Army, as well as units from the Navy.

The Commander of the Ground Forces has direct charge of all men and officers involved in ground fighting, including the Infantry, Cavalry, Field Artillery, Coast Artillery, and the Armored Force. The Commander of the Air Forces is head of all aerial fighting units, whether they be pursuit, interception, bombing or observation. Under him also is the program of training new pilots. And the Commander of the Services of Supply deals with all agencies in the Army that handle supplies, wherever they may be. It is his job to take over materials and equipment, after they have been produced, and to see that they are delivered to the men who are to use them.

Procurement

The rise of mechanization has made the Army put more emphasis on equipment than it once did. In this sphere, the Army is getting more and more like the Navy. Once upon a time it was possible to grab a rifle off the wall, sling some powder and shot around the waist and go out to fight.

The Minute Men of Concord didn't spend long months building and smelting and lathing for war. But their Navy did. The Navy had to have ships, and it took time to build ships. Now modern war is bringing the same thing to the Army. The amount of equipment and apparatus per soldier in the Army is going up and up. A single soldier is not always a complete fighter. Often he is the operator of a bigger piece of fighting apparatus. It takes tanks and planes and guns, and it takes time and planning to build them.

The ordering and expediting of the manufacture of Army equipment is supervised by the Under Secretary of War and his staff, who are quartered in one of the three main buildings—the gleaming New War Department Building at 20th and C Streets in Washington. The building was put up to house the Secretary of War and his General Staff. It was constructed with private corridors for the Secretary, and elaborate buzzer systems, and indirect lighting, and colorfully painted walls. But Secretary Stimson didn't want to move into it from his plain offices in the old Munitions Building. Some say he didn't think he would feel comfortable in the new building. It was too doggy. So the Under Secretary took it over, and now it houses the 2,000 officers and civilians who handle the central office of procurement.

The Under Secretary's office works directly with the Ordnance Department, the Engineer Corps, the Signal Corps, the Medical Corps, the Chemical Warfare Service, the Quartermaster Corps and the Air Corps. They take orders from the Under Secretary on everything involving procurement. The Under Secretary's office is in charge from the time an appropriation is passed on Capitol Hill until the time the goods are in the Army's hands. (The estimates which went into the appropriation were made up earlier, of course, by the General Staff.) If a bill is passed providing money for tanks and gas masks and shoes and radio equipment and gauze bandages and propellers and truck parts, the Under Secretary's staff takes it over immediately and adds the figures to the already gathered statistics on total appropriations. Then it gets in touch with the field offices of the supply arms and services, and allocates the orders to the factories and firms in the various regions.

The New Army

In March 1942, the War Department was reorganized. Everyone agreed that it was the most complete housecleaning the Army had had since the World War, and some called it the most drastic since the Civil War. The President's reorganization order followed a study which he had been making since the outbreak of the war. It abolished the positions of the Chiefs of Infantry, Cavalry, and Field and Coast Artillery—fighting "arms." It made their functions part of the job of the Commander of the Ground Forces. It put the Air Forces on a par with the Ground Forces. And it created the Services of Supply under a single head. As a result of the general order, there was reshuffling all down the line. Officers were reassigned to new jobs. Old jobs were pruned out of the mechanism. Lines of responsibility were sharpened.

Previously, the lines of authority had been baffling to some observers outside the War Department. And sometimes they stumped even experienced Army men, too. General Johnson Hagood, who was Chief of Staff of the AEF in France, once said: "The present organization of the War Department . . . is so involved that no Secretary of War has ever been able to understand it, and no Chief of Staff, however well qualified, has ever been able to keep it under control or to know just what was going on among his subordinates. . . . The chiefs of the supply services are directly and entirely responsible to the Assistant Secretary of War in some matters. In others, they are independent of him and responsible to the General Staff. . . . In certain undefined routine matters, the chiefs of services are responsible directly to the Chief of Staff. . . . In some other matters the determination of policy lies, in effect, with the chiefs of the arms. . . ."

Before the March reorganization, the chiefs of the "arms" had been advisers to the Chief of Staff on their kind of fighting, and in peacetime had tended to stress their specialties against others. Because the Army was small, there were no maneuvers, and the "arms" had no opportunity to work with one another. And because the Army appropriations were small, the different chiefs had to struggle against one another to get money for their own "arms." The competition sometimes developed into a clannishness. The battle to get mechanized units included in the Army on a large scale was prolonged by the entrenched advocates of mounted Cavalry. And the Army was slow to adopt what is now known as the "panzer division," because the advocates of Infantry maintained that no position could really be taken and held by anything except masses of Infantry. The competitive attitude of the "arms" was given a shock when maneuvers of the growing Army brought the "arms" together. The necessities of outright war hit it again, and the March reorganization delivered the knockout punch.

The reorganization also brought about a reduction in the average age of some of the top officers. The age trend already was downward, for General MacArthur had promoted a group of youngish officers in the Philippines, and a 36-year-old staff captain had been elevated to the rank of temporary brigadier general in Washington. But to many onlookers, the reshuffling was a distinct relief, for they had watched the average age climb during the peacetime 20's and 30's. Even as late as 1941, out of sixteen major generals, five (aged 62 to 64) were ready to retire in 1941, two in 1942, three in 1943, and four in 1944. The youngest on the list was 58. Of the brigadier generals on the list, all were over 50, many approaching 60, and the youngest temporary brigadier was 48.

This was in contrast to the situation in the German Army, which was expanding through the 30's, and had more positions at the top than the U. S. Army did. Under the Nazi regime, brigadier generals of 42 have been numerous, and there have been a number of major generals who were only 48. The United States did under pressure of war what the German Army had done in advance of war, in preparation for the war that it knew was coming.

In pulling down the age statistics, the Army repeated the experiences of the Civil War and the first World War. In the Civil War, Grant was a general at 39, Sheridan at 33, and "Jeb" Stuart at 28. In the first World War, Pershing made an effort to have young officers. The five chiefs of section at AEF headquarters were commissioned brigadier generals in the summer of 1918: Nolan and Fiske were 46; W. D. Connor was 44; Fox Conner and Moseley were 43. Frank R. McCoy was a brigadier general at 43, and B. D. Foulois and Douglas MacArthur were brigadiers at 38.

Army Officers

Officers of the Army are about a cross section of the American populace, and are, therefore, mainly middle-class. The war has drawn them from every trade and profession and business in every part of the country. Most of them are recently from civilian life. Out of the 14,000 who are "regular" Army officers, only 6,000 are graduates of West Point. So even if there is a bit of the "old school tie" feeling among West Pointers, it cannot and does not dominate the whole Army. Many top-ranking officers did not get their training at West Point. General George C. Marshall did not. He graduated from Virginia Military Institute.

Even the West Pointers are mainly middle-class. A recent survey of the backgrounds of candidates for admission showed that on an average their parents were 33 per cent businessmen, 20 per cent professional men, 15 per cent farmers, 9 per cent skilled laborers, 6 per cent unskilled laborers. This does not represent the Bronx or East Side, and neither does it represent Newport or Tuxedo Park. There is no "officer class" drawn from the highest social caste, as in some European armies. You can read through the Sunday society sections of all the Washington papers and

51

you will not see a large number of Army officers listed among the guests. Except for the occasional men who have married wealthy women, Army officers are not found very much in the gatherings of "the four hundred" in the salons of Massachusetts Avenue. In the society sphere, the Navy far outweighs the Army.

Selective Service

One of the Army's biggest problems—that of getting masses of men for its ranks—is not in its hands. The drafting of men for military service is carried on by the Selective Service System, which is an independent agency, not a part of the War or Navy Department. Every one of the approximately two and a half million men called into military service has been called according to the rules laid down by the National Headquarters of the Selective Service System. But the men of the National Headquarters, who are housed in a former apartment house at 21st and C Streets in Washington, do not do the actual inducting, and they do not have jurisdiction in any single case. If Joe Hamilton in Cedar Rapids thinks his local board "done him wrong," he goes to the appeal board, not to National Headquarters. The National Headquarters set up the system, and now prescribes the rules by which it works, but it doesn't turn the crank. It is the planning agency for the calling of men, a sort of general staff for the mobilization of man power.

In its planning today, National Headquarters is trying to see that men are apportioned among all the needs, industrial or civilian as well as military. One of the most troublesome problems of the Selective Service planners in 1941 and into 1942 was how to prevent the drafting of men who were necessary to industry. Selective Service does not consider itself an adjunct to the Army and Navy, but rather as an impartial allocator. And it considers itself primarily civilian in its outlook. When you walk down the halls of the National Headquarters, you see many Army and Navy uniforms, but practically none of them is on a regular Army or Navy officer. Nearly every draft official is a recent civilian, a former Reservist or National Guard officer, who was detailed to Selective Service. Practically the only regular officers are the Army and Navy liaison men.

The Army and Navy deliberately planned this civilian flavor for the Selective Service System. In 1935, after the Joint Army and Navy Selective Service Committee had been studying draft plans for nine years, the committee went out around the country in search of civilian collaborators. It got 80 young men from all professions and businesses, and it made them into study committees. These committees, plus National Guard officers, were the nucleus of the present state Selective Service set-ups.

They studied past experiences—in the Civil War and World War. They drew up plans, tore them apart and put them together again, over and over again. In September 1940, Congress passed the Selective Training and Service Act, and two months later the first trainees were on the way to camp.

Unity of Command

Modern war is no respecter of arbitrary divisions between the Army and Navy, and so the two armed services have joint boards to make sure they will work together. The first of these boards was created nearly forty years ago, and was called the Joint Board of the Army and Navy. Its members are eight high officers of the Army and Navy, who have at their assistance a subordinate Joint Army and Navy Planning Committee. Another two-way agency, the Joint Army and Navy Munitions Board is one of the most vital joint agencies in this war, because it advises the civilian War Production Board on the military needs for various weapons, and on its advice the priority ratings of materials are usually based. In addition, the Army and Navy have an Aeronautical Board, a Joint Economy Board, Joint Merchant Vessel Board, local joint planning committees, and all sorts of temporary and sporadic joint boards.

With all these joint agencies, most people assumed before the war that the Army and Navy cooperated as closely as a pair of adagio dancers, so it was a rude shock when they found that at Pearl Harbor there had not been complete cooperation. In other places, however, cooperation was better, as in the Caribbean theater, where an Army air officer was made commander of all forces. And in other theaters, "task forces" were put together out of Army and Navy units, with a single officer in charge.

But the over-all unity of command since the nation entered the war has come through the higher channels of the Commander in Chief, the President of the United States, and through the councils of the United Nations. There has been full recognition that this was not an Army war, or a Navy war alone—that it was not a "private war" of the generals and the admirals. The leaders have known that it was a total war of civilians against civilians, with the Army and the Navy providing the hitting force. So the plans have been coordinated, the fighters with the producers, the United States with the other anti-Axis Nations. The war-making is coming from a team of forces—the people, the industries, the Army, and the Navy.

6

Navy on the Land

A NAVY, compared with an army, is a very small thing. In man power, it is relatively a pigmy. Even the United States Navy—the biggest in the world today—is only about one-sixth as large in man power as the United States Army, which is far from the largest in the world. The Navy has around 400,000 men and 32,000 officers, compared with the Army's nearly 2,500,000 men and 140,000 officers. The place where the Navy is large is in equipment—in ships and planes and bases. And ships take longer to build than average army equipment, so a navy cannot grow as fast as an army.

But in the last several years, the U. S. Navy has grown tremendously, according to Navy standards. When the European war started in September 1939, there were approximately 11,000 Naval officers on active duty. Now there are nearly 32,000. You can see signs of the growth around Navy headquarters in Washington, where the Navy is controlled and run. When war broke out in Europe, there were 3,000 civilian employees of the Navy Department in Washington. Today there are 13,000. Now there are nine buildings housing the Navy Department offices in Washington. A year and a half ago, the whole Department was in one building—a long, three-story, white-painted concrete building on Constitution Avenue, overlooking the traffic of Washington rush hours and the green grass of the Mall, and far from the white caps of the sea.

All this growth has come about because the Navy, like the Army, has its ups and downs, its spurts and lags. Before its recent expansion, it had been going through one of its lags. After nearly every war in the history of the United States, part of the Navy has been scrapped or put to peaceful work. It happened after the Revolutionary War, the War of 1812, the Civil War, the Spanish-American War, and the first World War. The scrapping program after the World War was the biggest, because, first of all, we started with a big fleet—the biggest fleet in the world when the shipbuilding came to its peak just after the war ended. And it was the biggest scrapping program also because we trimmed that huge fleet on a huge scale, in accordance with international agreement. As a result of the

Washington Naval Treaty of 1921, we put out of commission three quarters of a million tons of fighting ships. We agreed to keep our Navy in line with a 5-5-3 ratio—5 for Britain, 5 for the United States, 3 for Japan. Then as a result of the London Naval Treaty of 1930, we scrapped another third of a million tons. To top it all, we didn't even keep our fleet up to treaty strength, and not until 1934 did Congress authorize the full strength, which the Navy finally reached about 1938.

In 1938, Naval building began in earnest. Some ships had been built after 1933 out of funds included in the National Industrial Recovery Act, but the building had not been on a big scale. A 1938 act of Congress allowed the Navy to exceed treaty tonnages by 20 per cent, after the treaties had been renounced by other signatories. In early 1940 it was authorized to increase by a blanket 11 per cent. Then, later in 1940, after Hitler blitzkrieged the Low Countries and France, Congress went whole hog. It put on paper its authorization for a "two ocean Navy," which was to be the biggest Navy in the world, the biggest in history. It was planned for completion in 1946, with 32 battleships, 18 aircraft carriers, 91 cruisers, 364 destroyers, and 185 submarines. The program got under way, keels were laid and ships launched, but on December 7, 1941, war struck the United States, and the Navy bore the first brunt.

The People and the Navy

The basic reason that the U. S. Navy remained below the allowed treaty strength through the 20's and early 30's was that most people in the United States didn't see any need for building a whopping big sea force. Most Americans were landlubbers in spirit, and didn't think of themselves as belonging to a seagoing nation, as the British did. As landlubbers, Americans liked to watch movies of big ships plowing through the foamy seas, and read recruiting posters about joining the Navy and seeing the world. But they didn't think their safety depended on building up the Navy beyond what already seemed like a fairly large fleet.

Congress in Washington took its cue from the people out around the country. Congress members were impressed by the Navy. They were sure that the officers knew their business, that it was the best Navy in the world, that it was unsinkable and unbeatable, but they still thought that it was big enough. With this attitude in Congress, it was no wonder that the Navy courted Congress. Congressmen were taken on inspection junkets out to sea, and received complimentary tickets to the annual Army-Navy football game. The Navy had on its side the shipbuilding and steel interests, who were glad to lend a hand. But altogether, the cause of a bigger Navy didn't get very far in Congress.

Neither did Congress get very far in finding out things about the Navy. The admirals from the Navy Department have been traditionally tight-lipped. And they always became especially so when they were asked to appear at a committee meeting on Capitol Hill. Congressmen complained wistfully that they "just couldn't get anything out of them." One time, for example, when a congressional committee was investigating the causes of the S-4 submarine disaster, the questioning of an admiral ran like this:

Q. Why did it take so long for air to be started into the compartment?

A. I just can't be positive about such things. I just can't remember. Ask the technical people.

Q. Why was not the salvage line constructed to send breathing air into the torpedo chamber connected?

A. Well, I don't really know. I can't answer that question. My impression is the divers did all they could do. As to details, I can't tell you. You'll have to ask the technical men.

So it went, in hearing after hearing. Members of Congress acted as if they were asking questions of God, and when they didn't get an answer, they merely shrugged their shoulders. Congressmen knew their place where God and the Navy were concerned.

With the rise of the totalitarian powers in Europe and Asia, Congress and the people changed their attitude toward the need for a bigger Navy, but they maintained their reverence for the Navy's technical ability to build and operate a top-notch fighting fleet. Only one serious blow has ever been dealt to that reputation, and that was the damage done to the fleet in the surprise attack on Pearl Harbor. It was the most serious blow ever suffered by the U. S. fleet, and in the public mind, it pulled the Navy off its pedestal. After Pearl Harbor, when the Navy confronted the biggest task in its history, it also confronted an American public in whose eyes the Navy's prestige was lower than it had ever been before. For the first time, Americans had some doubts about the Navy. It appeared that the Navy could err, just like ordinary men. Navy men felt the change in attitude, and it was reflected around the Navy Department in Washington by a change in naval usage. The colloquial term for the Commander in Chief of the United States Fleet was switched. Officers began to refer to him as "Cominch" instead of using the traditional term, "Cincus" (pronounced "Sink Us"), which apparently seemed too much as though it really meant what it sounded like.

Washington Headquarters

The city of Washington is 150 miles by water route from the Atlantic Ocean. It can't be attacked by warships directly from the sea. A battle-

56

ship would get stuck in the brown mud of the Potomac River long before it got up to the capital. Nevertheless, Washington is a notable Naval center. It has its Navy Yard, which builds big guns, and the Naval Air Station on the banks of the Anacostia River. It has the Naval Observatory, which regulates time for the whole United States and ships at sea. It has its Naval Hospital in the city, and the new one on the fringes of the city, at Bethesda, Maryland. Across the Potomac River, in Alexandria, Virginia, is the factory of the Naval Torpedo Station. Up the River, on the Maryland side, is the new model ship basin that looks like a giant shed. And only 36 miles away at Annapolis, Maryland, is the Naval Academy, whose midshipmen in natty blue uniforms are seen from time to time on the streets of Washington and in the capital's ballrooms.

But the most important of all the Naval establishments in Washington is the Navy Department, which is the nerve center of the Navy, the conning tower on land of all the ships at sea. You may think of the Navy in terms of a flotilla of warships cutting through the swells, with guns ablaze, and with planes zipping up from the deck of a carrier, like a swarm of yellow jackets. It's true. That *is* the Navy—part of it. That is the Navy's fist. It is the fleet, for which everything else exists. But in order to have the fleet at large, there must be unromantic office work in Washington.

Even though the offices of the Navy Department look like the plain offices of any plain business corporation, you can tell you are around the Navy, because there is something of the tang of seafaring. Officers' winter uniforms are of dark blue, gold-braided; new summer ones are of khaki. Lower officers answer superiors with "aye, aye, sir." And in the press section of the Office of Public Relations, the officers (many of whom are newly-recruited ex-newspapermen) "stand eight hour watches"—the word is definitely "watch," not "shift."

The Department

The Navy at the top is commanded by civilians. There have been times in history when the Secretary of the Navy was an admiral, but they have been very, very few. The Secretary is appointed by the President, of course, and is responsible to him. In time of war, he is even more closely responsible to him, because the President, as Commander in Chief of the Armed Forces, takes a closer interest in the affairs of the Navy. This is especially true today, for President Roosevelt was Assistant Secretary of the Navy from 1913 until after the first World War, and has had a lifetime fondness for ships and the Navy. When Frank Knox became Secretary in 1940, he had had no special experience in Navy matters, but his record as a publisher had given him the reputation of being a good administrator, and his Republican politics made the appointment a symbol of "national unity."

Assisting the Secretary in the running of the Department are an Under Secretary and two Assistant Secretaries, one especially in charge of aviation. The Navy has nothing exactly comparable with the War Department's General Staff. The Navy's General Board, which formulates broad policy, is not the twin of the Army's General Staff, because the General Board is purely advisory, and it was set up by the Department rather than by Congress. The Board has great influence, however. On it sit six or eight admirals, who are sometimes called to it from retirement, and who are often referred to around the Department as the "Elder Statesmen." They deliver their experience and judgment without being hindered by administrative duties.

The closest counterpart of the Army's General Staff is the Office of the Chief of Naval Operations, which is charged with coordinating all the agencies that provide the fleet at sea with the things it needs. In supervising this job, the Office supervises the Navy's seven Bureaus, which are the agencies that actually perform the different duties. The Bureaus are:

Navigation (which carries on all personnel work, and keeps all personnel records).

Ordnance (which gets arms and ammunition).

Ships (which does the designing of ships, installing of engines, and experimenting).

Yards and Docks (which includes the Navy's Corps of Engineers, the men who construct all the Navy's buildings, drydocks, ways, harbor works, etc.).

Supplies and Accounts (which is the Navy's storekeeper and bookkeeper).

Medicine and Surgery.

Aeronautics.

Until March 1942, the Chief of Naval Operations and the Commander in Chief of the United States Fleet were different men. But at that time, the posts were merged so that the Commander in Chief became also the Chief of Naval Operations, and the previous informalities and overlapping of authority were eliminated. Now the Commander in Chief of the Fleet is the very highest Naval officer. He is in charge of all the Navy's operating forces, including the Coast Guard (when it is attached to the Navy in time of war) and the Marine Corps. By the terms of an executive order issued by the President in December 1941, shortly after the war broke, the Commander in Chief of the Fleet is responsible directly to the President, "under the general direction of the Secretary of the Navy."

To make it easy for the different Navy high-ups to confer, all their offices are in Washington. This includes the top civilian officials, the Bureau chiefs and their staffs, and the Commander in Chief of the Fleet (who is also Chief of Naval Operations), though he may go to sea when he thinks he is needed more there than on dry land.

Relations with Civilians

An admiral who did not graduate from the Naval Academy is a rare bird. There are no independent naval schools which contribute young officers to the Navy as military colleges sometimes contribute to the Army. Hence the high-ranking Naval officers are more likely to be cast out of the same mold. Their standards of technical knowledge, seamanship and courage are high. They have an esprit de corps which is bred out of close association with Navy men and Navy matters all their lives, for in times of peace, the Navy is concentrated at a relatively few stations along the coasts of the United States and possessions. This esprit de corps, however, sometimes turns into a cliquishness which is directed toward civilians and officers who have come into the service other than through the Academy. A Naval Reserve officer always retains the word "reserve" in his title, even when he is on active duty. He is "Lt. John R. Smith, U.S.N.R." (United States Naval Reserve).

High Naval officers in Washington have little enthusiasm for sharing their Naval knowledge with civilians, and this sometimes hampers even such civilians as Secretaries and Under Secretaries of the Navy. When Secretary Knox and Under Secretary James V. Forrestal took over, they found the admirals rather uncommunicative about some things that were important to the efficient running of the Navy Department. So in the winter of 1941, Secretary Knox hired an efficiency expert, who was chief method statistician for the American Telephone and Telegraph Company. The expert was placed in the Bureau of Supplies and Accounts and told to explore. He reached a point at which he was able to begin drawing conclusions from the information and figures he had gathered. But at this point, Knox and Forrestal left Washington on an inspection trip. The admirals took the opportunity to dismiss the efficiency expert, and to draw their own conclusions from the material he had gathered. When the Under Secretary returned, he found the expert gone, but he was not discouraged. He proceeded to rehire efficiency experts gradually, and to put them into various bureaus, making it difficult for bureau chiefs to conduct a mass purge. Today, as a result, the civilian officials of the Department

59

have a better picture of the inner operations of the Navy Department than almost any of their predecessors.

When the U. S. started building warships on a big scale, differences arose between civilian and Naval technicians. A common complaint of the civilians was that the Navy men were too much connoisseurs of fine ships, that they were more interested in the absolute perfection of their beloved ships than they were in efficient production methods. The civilian engineers grumbled that the Navy specifications didn't fit mass production, that Naval experts clung too long to riveting in the face of newer welding techniques, and that the Navy tests of performance were unnecessarily stiff. The Navy replied that it was adopting the new methods as fast as it should, and that for Naval warfare the performance tests had to be as stiff as they were. The civilians, nevertheless, pointed out numerous places where corners could be cut, the cost lessened, and an equivalent job done. As the building program progressed, the pressure of necessity forced a speed-up in the Navy's traditional ways of building and outfitting ships. Early in 1941, Secretary Knox said, "In an emergency like the present we'd rather have a good ship today than a better one six months from now."

Air Power

Naval warfare today is as different from the strategies of 1917-18 as the land blitzkrieg is from old-fashioned trench warfare. The distances to be covered in this war are greater than they were in the first World War. Now we are fighting enemies on both sides, in two oceans. The fleet must operate over great distances, and in small units. There is no massing of the whole battle line for a final fight to the victory. The necessities of global war make it impossible to concentrate our forces, and we need more than we have—more of everything.

Especially we need more airplanes to protect our heavy battleships. The large-scale use of air power in this war did not take our Navy by surprise, for airplanes have been counted into the naval equation for many years. The Navy used airplanes in the last war, and set up its Bureau of Aeronautics in 1921. Its research and experimentation in the use of the fleet air arm was widely regarded as up-to-date and progressive. It was even regarded that way by the Germans, for they borrowed dive-bombing, which the U. S. Navy originally developed. The Navy also developed the long-range flying boat, the PBY. And the fleet developed the naval novelty called the "carrier striking group," composed of an aircraft carrier and several fast cruisers, which were intended to strike behind the flanks of the enemy fleet and destroy its lines in the rear.

The major use of air power was counted on, but the extent to which air bombardment could put battleships out of commission has been something of a revelation to some Naval experts. The U. S. Navy relied heavily on armor on the decks to protect against bombs carried by planes. As Secretary Knox said in April 1941, "A ship will not be essentially injured until the deck armor is penetrated. No armor as thick as that borne by our battleships and heavy cruisers has yet been penetrated by an airplane bomb. Nor is it very likely to be."

It was one of the major naval controversies of recent years—whether or not a plane could sink a battleship. The question has been answered now, and a number of battleships have gone below the waves. The battleships *Oklahoma* and *Arizona* were struck from a clear sky at Pearl Harbor— and they went down. The British battleships *Repulse* and *Prince of Wales* were not adequately protected in the air—and they were sunk. The German battleships *Scharnhorst* and *Gneisenau* and the cruiser *Prinz Eugen* were accompanied by hundreds of planes—and they got through the English Channel. The necessity for a heavy air escort for a battleship is as axiomatic now as the invincibility of a battleship used to be. It has never been a matter of battleships *or* planes, but rather battleships *and* planes, with the question mark hanging over the issue of how big a part the planes would play. Now it is known that their part is large— larger than it used to be thought—and the Navy is making its plans to fit.

Officers and Men

If you ask a Navy officer about the quality of the sailors and non-commissioned officers in the U. S. fleet, you get a glowing answer. Officers are taught from their first days at the Naval Academy that the enlisted men are alert, intelligent, loyal, and game in the fighting. The Navy has always taken particular pains to keep the quality of its sailors high. It has stressed the training which Navy men could get that would stand them in good stead if they left the service later. Even when the service was not expanding, the recruiting offices kept hammering away, selling the idea of the Navy as a career, keeping the opportunities always in young Americans' minds. As a result, the Navy's "gobs" or "bluejackets" live up to the officers' estimations of them, and in every naval engagement of the war, they have shown that they are intelligent and tough.

The same is true of the commissioned officers. The Navy has a promotion system which depends on examination by a special board, and if an officer is "passed over" by the board too often, he is retired. The result is a residue of qualified officers. And whatever their faults of traditionalism may be, no one has intimated that they are shirkers. Part of their devotion to duty is a consequence of their strict training, and part comes from their lives in compact Navy circles. There is another influence—one that has no exact counterpart in other types of military affairs. It is the love of the sea. Many officers choose the Navy as a life's profession because they love the sea itself.

And yet, some of the officers have to spend much of their time on land. Around Washington, you encounter men who love the sea but who must sit at desks far from the sea. Down at the headquarters on Constitution Avenue, and over at the annex on the Arlington Heights, you can see them doing the desk work that is necessary to keep a fleet at sea. You can see them helping to get the ships built and outfitted and armed and manned and fueled. You can see them getting the men clothed and fed. All these things have to be taken care of in order that the fighters can be free to fight. And also, someone has to stay at desks to see that the fighting is coordinated, and that the fleet works smoothly with other fleets, and with armies, and with politicians and statesmen—who have much to say about the things for which the Navy is helping to fight. The Washington chores are not always attractive to the seafaring officers of the Navy, but they are all a part of the job of running the Navy from the land.

7

Department of State at Work

THE ponderous, sleepy-looking building of the Department of State is awake today with anti-Axis diplomatic maneuvering. In its serene and peaceful rooms are heard the courteous phrases used by diplomats for centuries, but now these phrases have new bite and meaning. They are used by earnest representatives of all the United Nations who are trying to figure out how best to meet a common enemy on the six continents and the seven seas—how to make war instead of peace.

It is natural that the State Department should be the gathering place of these diplomatic plotters. Among other things, it saves time, for when they agree on a program they have only to scoot across a narrow street to the White House to present it to the President of the United States.

In the State Department the traffic is heavy, with more comings and goings of more diplomats than any other national capital, not even excepting London. Here the dispatches pour in and out, telling what each nation expects to do about war. Here the deals are made for war—and for after the war.

All day long, all night long, every day and every night, our State Department talks with foreign capitals. The telegraph wires and sometimes the overseas telephones are busy with messages. It takes only a few hours to send a message and get an answer—anywhere in the world except the war-ridden countries and the enemy countries. Communication with London is by direct wire, as quick as a telephone call to your next-door neighbor. The State Department is a nerve center.

In the old-fashioned office of the Secretary of State hang eleven maps. They show big and little countries with their boundaries that were. They show foreign capitals, provinces, islands, peninsulas, oceans, and inland seas. Charts show the products that come from these foreign lands, and where the products fit into world commerce. The whole political and economic world is shown there—in a single room.

The world is the work field of the Department of State. London, Moscow, Rio, Buenos Aires, Melbourne and Madagascar are at the finger tips. It is the work field of world politics, the relations between nations and nations.

63

The dealings are channeled through diplomats and foreign offices, and the most important foreign office is the U. S. Department of State.

It is an odd department, as government departments go. It is the highest ranking of all, and the Secretary of State is traditionally No. 1 cabinet member, and yet it is the smallest department of all, by the standard of taxpayer cost. It has expanded since the new world war started, it has more than doubled in size, and yet it is still relatively small. Its dealings are largely secret, and yet no other department in government hugs as close to the press. It is essentially nonpartisan in its handling of foreign relations, and yet it keeps its ear close to the ground to catch the murmurs of public sentiment within the United States, and is extra careful to be not too far out of line with public feelings about foreign affairs. In these days of war, it buzzes with activity, and its windows are often alight at night, yet its halls are always quiet. There is no rushing and loud talk, no bumping at the corners, no external appearances of bustle and rush. It is a sedate department, and everyone in it is sedate.

The State Department Building is one of the oldest and ugliest in Washington. It was built in the 1870's, in a style of architecture based upon the idea that the more pillars could be piled atop of other pillars the better the effect, and is an architectural atrocity. It looks like a ponderous old-time frigate. The halls inside have floors of shiny black and white squares of marble, and diplomatic callers often skid on them and nearly break their legs. The time used to be shown by grandfather clocks, which are still around in some private offices, but electric clocks are being used more and more. The furniture in the principal waiting rooms is old, and blackish, and very comfortable to sit in. Offices are equipped with swinging shutter doors, which somehow create the impression of old-fashioned saloons. New modern buildings have sprung up in Washington like mushrooms in recent years, and even the State Department has had to supplement its solid antique by putting some of its wartime overflow in a temporary building on the Mall, that smells of new lumber and plaster.

The men who run the State Department are, somehow, individuals. Each is a Somebody who is a specialist in Something, enthroned in his own Private Office. There isn't any such thing as a big workroom, with dozens of workers in it, as you will find in most other government departments. The personnel of the State Department is hand picked, and this applies to both the high and the low. This is necessary because they handle state secrets, and it is possible because relatively there are so few people in the small department.

Some years ago State Department men and diplomats in general were regarded as "cookie pushers." In the average Washington mind they were

64

associated with teas, receptions, dinners, pin-striped trousers, cutaways, and high hats—both literally and figuratively. Other government officials, perhaps out of a bit of jealousy, regarded State Department men as "too lofty for any good use." There was more than a trace of truth in it, for in Washington and elsewhere there has been a tradition that diplomats and those who spoke to diplomats were distinctly above the common herd. But this is disappearing, and State Department men are now pretty much down to earth. They have become "practical working men." They do not dawdle around as much as they did some years ago. They haven't time, they must work, and their jobs are hard.

The high hat has been replaced by the Homburg, which is several rungs down from the high hat, although still a few rungs up from the common fedora. Pin-striped trousers are standard uniform for Occasions, but now many a State Department man wears plain pants, and sometimes the pants have only the faintest trace of an old and well-worn crease. The wealthy wife, who a few years ago was standard equipment for any diplomat who wanted to get anywhere in diplomacy, is not yet extinct, but there are fewer of her than formerly. The wife now is more likely to be from the same state university where the young man went before he took the examinations and got a job in the State Department. The whole average level of State Department men has come down in the money scale in recent years. This means that the men come nearer to living within their government salaries, they are less swank, and they are a little closer to the average lives of average people. Super-snootiness has not entirely disappeared from the shelves of the State Department, but now it comes in pounds, and formerly it came in tons.

The "Department of Peace"

"It was whispered in the corridors today" is a phrase with which many Washington newspaper correspondents would like to begin dispatches from the State Department. The phrase would tell the truth, for diplomacy is conducted behind closed doors. Diplomacy is technical, involved, often indirect, and has a language all its own. The word "no" is seldom spoken, and "perhaps" may often mean "yes."

The State Department's importance was recognized by the First Congress which created it in 1789 as the first executive department. The Secretary of State is the highest ranking member of the Cabinet, and if anything should happen to the President and Vice President, he would succeed to the Presidency. The Department's influence is great enough to tip the scales for peace or war, although in peacetime it annually spends only $22,000,000—just chicken feed to the Department of Agriculture—and cuts that gross outlay by nearly $5,000,000 through fees received.

It operates under the protection of a tradition that "there shall be no domestic politics in foreign affairs." At least that's the tradition. But no department keeps its ears closer to the ground to detect home political sentiment, for nothing would more weaken a policy abroad than knowledge that it lacked public support at home.

It likes to be known as the "Department of Peace." Yet in wartime its activities increase greatly, because of contributions to the war effort. The German attack in September 1939 set off the current expansion, and within two months after we became involved in hostilities the Department had a staff of 2,000 in Washington, more than twice the number three years earlier. All told, including Foreign Service officers, clerks, miscellaneous employees and the Washington staff, the total now is well over 6,300.

This increase resulted despite the closing of many foreign offices, for new consulates have been opened in far-off places, and in economic and technical fields the Department is a key war agency. It is not only a funnel through which negotiations are arranged between foreign technical missions and other branches of the government, but it is also the negotiating agency itself. It originates many of the projects for purchase of strategic and critical materials abroad. It conducts negotiations with which to win support for the United States against the Axis. It issues visas for refugees to come to the U. S. It arranges for the return of Americans from hostile countries. In the background, it constantly studies postwar problems, for war aims can never be dissociated from peace aims.

Washington is the diplomatic center of the world. Not only are foreign missions arriving almost daily, but the regular foreign diplomatic colony is the biggest in the world. There normally are 57 embassies and legations in Washington. This number has been reduced by those that used to represent the now enemy powers, but it includes the diplomats of refugee governments and overrun countries and the total is still the world's biggest.

It is in this setting that the State Department operates—like a hen sitting over baby chicks. Its eyes are watchful. It is jealous of its prerogatives. It is careful of the proprieties. But in its own ponderous and careful way, it speeds up for war.

It's a Homey Place

The State Department has a more personal air than any other in the government, despite the tag of "stiff necked" officials. The feeling probably comes partly from the Department's relatively small size, and from the

66

careful selection of its employees. When a man or woman goes to work for the Department, he has had personal contact with at least several persons in the Department. In most cases, he has talked at length with many. The Department follows the "know thyself" edict.

Another reason for the homey feeling is the comfortable building which houses the State Department. The drab structure is four stories, filling an entire block, and its gingerbread style was borrowed from the Paris of the Second Empire. It was begun in 1871 and completed in 1888. Like the White House and the Treasury, it fronts on Pennsylvania Avenue. Antiquated cannon captured in previous wars are picturesque guardians at either side of the broad steps. But the Secretary, foreign diplomats, and other callers use the smaller side entrance on Executive Avenue between the State Department and the White House.

Within the building are police and uniformed soldiers, now that war is on. Sight-seers are no longer admitted, and even officials must show passes. But Negro messengers still saunter, unhurriedly, with books and papers through dimly lighted corridors tinted yellow. Original portraits of former Secretaries look down from the corridor walls. They are all there, beginning with Thomas Jefferson who was appointed in 1789.

The Secretary of State occupies Room 208, the center of an extensive suite in the south wing. He sits at a great flat-topped desk in a high back, blue leather chair, with his back to the windows. If he turns around, he can look out on the Washington Monument and the new Jefferson Memorial.

There are bookcases and inviting chairs along the walls. A prized possession is the desk on which John Quincy Adams drafted the Monroe Doctrine, and another is a valuable marble profile of James Madison. The office has ceilings some 15 feet high, and several fireplaces that once actually served for heating. The lighting is indirect, from conservative bowls hung from the ceiling. The floors are covered with dark blue rugs. Adjoining is a private washroom. The total effect isn't doggy.

An ordinary caller waits in a long conference room where the Secretary meets the press daily. Then the visitor walks through the office of the Secretary's three secretaries, through a small anteroom, and into the main office. Diplomatic visitors wait across the hall in a special reception room.

On one side of the Secretary's office, to his right as he sits at his desk, is the Under Secretary's office. To the left is the office of one of the Assistant Secretaries.

What It Takes to Be Secretary

A long line of distinguished men have occupied the Secretary's office. Many previously held elective office. Some later became President, though none since James Buchanan. Several came to the office after having been candidates for the Presidency. Two subsequently became Chief Justice— John Marshall and Charles Evans Hughes. A number were diplomatically as well as politically trained. John Hay, long a Republican spokesman, was called to the office from London where he was ambassador; so was Frank B. Kellogg in the Coolidge administration. Buchanan had been minister to England, and John Quincy Adams was deeply versed in diplomacy.

Other Secretaries have been successful corporation lawyers and leaders of the bar. Only a few have been international lawyers. Many have had previous cabinet experience. But political experience is almost a must, for the Secretary is a political as well as a foreign policy adviser to the President. Of course, the President doesn't have to listen to the advice, and no department can be more ignored if the President decides to conduct foreign affairs through personal confidants. Woodrow Wilson had his Colonel House. Franklin D. Roosevelt has at times inclined toward being his own foreign minister. But these are exceptions, not the rule. Much depends upon who is President and who is Secretary of State.

The Secretary's day almost never ends. He usually has work to do at home in the evenings and early mornings. He reaches his office about 9 o'clock and, with time out for lunch, leaves after the day's grist has been disposed of, anywhere from 5 to 7. He receives important foreign diplomatic callers, senators and congressmen, visiting dignitaries who wish to pay their respects, and personal friends.

Atop the Secretary's desk are piled sheaves of telegraph and cable dispatches from around the world. The important ones are put to one side for discussions with experts in the Department, and possibly for a report to the President.

Several times each week the Secretary walks across the narrow street to the White House to confer with the President on major problems, or to acquaint him with developments. In order to provide speedy communication, a telephone on the Secretary's desk leads directly to the White House switchboard. The Secretary can also reach the Chief of Staff of the Army, and the Chief of Naval Operations, who are similarly connected by direct phone with the White House.

Tennessee Mountaineer

Cordell Hull climbed the political ladder to the Secretaryship of State. He assumed office the day President Roosevelt was inaugurated on March 4, 1933, and stayed on with his Chief into a third term. He was not particularly trained in diplomacy when he became Secretary, but his political experience and instincts enabled him to apply a keen mind to diplomatic problems which were essentially political and to rely upon others for the technique while he learned the art of diplomacy.

A soft-spoken man of placid exterior, Secretary Hull hides furnaces that belch forth at times around the conference table or in private conversation, as could be expected of a man sprung from the mountain folk of Tennessee. Tall and angular, 70 years of age, his hair is white and his classic features set in a Grecian mold.

Hull spent all his adult life in politics, first in his native Tennessee where he became a judge, then entering the national House of Representatives in 1907. The Harding landslide of 1920 retired him temporarily, but he served several years as chairman of the Democratic National Committee before being elected to the United States Senate. His basic belief in a low tariff probably shaped his thought through the years more than any other single factor. On tariff as well as internationalism, he found himself in harmony with President Roosevelt—and the first result of this was the reciprocal trade agreements program.

The Nonpolitical Politician

Unlike the Secretary, the Under Secretary of State never comes from the political ranks. Sometimes he is drawn from law, but more often he is a trained man who is a diplomatic and not a political adviser to the President. He is chief of staff to the Secretary and acts as Secretary during the absence of the boss.

Professionally trained in the tricks of his diplomatic trade, the Under Secretary is usually familiar with foreign countries because he has lived in many of them. He runs much of the machinery of the Department and is the day-to-day contact point for foreign envoys. He deals with major diplomatic problems and is almost as frequent a caller at the White House as the Secretary. His fortunes depend not only on his relations with the Secretary, but on the confidence reposed in him by the President. If successful and politically lucky, he moves up into an ambassadorship rather than into elective political office. He serves until the administration changes, for although he is a professional diplomat he is also a political appointee.

Sumner Welles' story is like that of a lot of his predecessors—a professional diplomat, trained in the techniques, scion of a wealthy New York family, graduate of Groton and Harvard. On the surface, he is unbending, meticulous. His suits are from a London tailor. He swings a cane and wears a top hat and striped trousers with comfort. Yet he is a free and frank talker, a hard worker.

Welles' professional manner, knowledge, and competence made him a first-rate man to deal with foreign diplomats. In his forties when he became Under Secretary, he had traveled a long way, beginning as a junior diplomatic officer in the Foreign Service soon after finishing Harvard in 1914.

Entrusted with important jobs in Latin America by President Coolidge, he entered the Roosevelt administration as Assistant Secretary of State, was Ambassador to Cuba during the overthrow of the Machado regime, and not long after his return to Washington was made Under Secretary.

The Upper Stratum

The upper stratum of the Department is made up of political appointees —including not only the Secretary and Under Secretary, but four Assistant Secretaries of State. They serve during the pleasure of an administration, and are the nerve center of the Department. The Secretary is in general charge, aided by the Under Secretary. The Assistant Secretaries direct various activities, such as administration, legal affairs, economic arrangements with foreign governments, and the like. They are not free lances with independent authority, but reach final decisions only with the approval of the Secretary or Under Secretary.

Below the upper stratum stretches the permanent organization, which serves under laws safeguarding personnel against the political spoils system. This expert staff, years ago, was drawn largely from the wealthy and leisure classes, because Congress did not provide adequate salaries. Today, in a great majority of cases, staffers manage to live off their salaries, although they do keep up the social end, too.

The experts are specialists in every field of foreign affairs, graduates of American colleges in every state. They are geographers, economists, lawyers, historians; experts on shipping, communications, aviation; suave interpreters of the diplomatic thing to do—protocol.

Many of these men as well as those who serve in foreign posts are "career men," and early in life they start to make a profession of diplomacy. Many do special Foreign Service work in post graduate schools, for they have to take a stiff entrance examination to get a career appointment in the Foreign Service. The examination requires expert knowledge of diplomacy, foreign languages, history, geography, economics, and international law.

After an applicant is accepted, he is put through more special training in the Department's own Foreign Service Officers' Training School. Thereafter, the rise of the career man depends upon merit until at the top he may become a minister or ambassador. But if he does become an Assistant Secretary or minister or ambassador, he must resign from the nonpolitical Foreign Service.

Naturally the caliber of career men varies. Some have native ability, others are mediocre. Some are daring. Others are "yes" men with no initiative. Some have made names for themselves.

There was young Willard D. Straight who, during the Russo-Japanese war, won fame by daring the Japanese to haul down the American flag on his consulate at Mukden. There was George C. Hanson who served so long and efficiently in Harbin that he became known as the Emperor of North Manchuria. There was Cornelius Van H. Engert, Charge d'Affaires in Addis Ababa during the Italo-Ethiopian war, who held his legation calmly in the face of stampeding natives.

Many have died violent deaths through assassination, earthquake, war, flood, and disaster. A tablet in the Department honors their memory.

The Organization

Underneath the Secretary, the Under Secretary and the Assistant Secretaries are three professionally-trained diplomats who serve as political advisers to the Secretary on matters pertaining to other nations in certain parts of the world. James Clement Dunn advises on Europe, Dr. Stanley K. Hornbeck on the Far East, Laurence Duggan on Latin America.

Then come a number of divisions, each headed by a chief with several assistants. There are four geographic divisions, one responsible for diplomatic and consular activities in the Americas, one for the Near East (the Asia Minor area), one for the Far East (generally, the Orient), and the fourth for Europe, including all the British Commonwealth of Nations.

Other divisions have charge of special subjects—a legal division staffed by a score of international lawyers, an economics division which follows international trends. Still others are concerned with trade agreements, communications, cultural relations, commercial affairs, historical research, and so on. The Passport Division is the office with which American citizens have direct dealings more than with any other office.

The chiefs of division are permanent officials, most of them career men from the foreign service. They are appointed after competitive examinations and promoted on merit determined by boards and committees in the Department.

The Department at Work

War has made all-important one job of the officers in embassies, legations and consulates all over the world—that of gathering and reporting accurate information to Washington. Their information flows in through a telegraph section in a dozen barred rooms on the fourth floor of the State Department Building.

Each day the Division of Communications and Records, headed by the

71

veteran David A. Salmon, receives or dispatches some 600 messages to officials outside of Washington. As soon as the messages are received, they are decoded, routed, recorded, and dispatched throughout the Department. A message usually is on the Secretary's desk within half an hour after it is received.

If a report from an ambassador, minister, or consul is urgent, it comes by cable to New York, and is then sent to Washington on a special leased wire. There is instantaneous communication with the embassy in London, through a special printer telegraph wire.

Unimportant messages are sent in plain English, but most are confidential and in code. These are unscrambled in the code room, one of the most carefully protected. There are eighteen telegraphers, cautiously selected. One has been with the Department 18 years.

Several copies of each message are made. The copies are classed as "action" and "information." The "action" copy goes to an expert who knows most about the subject. He annotates it with everything that is necessary as background and suggests the proper official for handling the matter. "Information" copies go to officials throughout the Department. The Secretary gets a copy of every official communication. All official messages are addressed to him, and all outgoing messages are signed with his name even though prepared by other officials.

Telegrams and reports are distributed with many safeguards to assure secrecy. Negro messengers take them from the code room in locked boxes to which only the receiving officials have a key. Sometimes, things slip a little. One day a sleepy-eyed messenger wandered into the press room, mistaking it for the Under Secretary's office, and left his box on a table in the middle of the room. A newspaperman, audibly chuckling, gave the box to the Under Secretary.

If an official message is not urgent, it is often sent by mail, or by courier, in a diplomatic mail pouch. Follow-up reports on telegraphed messages also are sent by mail.

The Division of Communications and Records is open day and night. It has not been closed in more than 20 years.

The Department and News

The Department maintains regular relations with the daily press. Correspondents occupy a room in the building, and the Secretary receives them every day at noon. Then he makes announcements and submits to questioning. The attendance runs from a handful to fifty or more, depending upon the urgency of problems at the moment.

This conference is used for extremely important pronouncements of policy. These are made either through oral or formal statements. Or the Secretary may disclose the text of a diplomatic note. And, finally, the give and take of question and answer between the Secretary and correspondents provides means for filling out details that otherwise might be lost in the formal language of a note or public statement.

Many Secretaries have used the conference for expounding and defending policy to the American people and foreign governments. Only a few, through timidity, have not done so. No Secretary approached the conference more seriously than Henry L. Stimson. He would often hold forth for an hour. Secretary Hull employed the conference for many of his most important announcements, but not frequently for explaining and defending.

Another source of day-to-day news is the official press relations office of the Department. Its chief is Michael J. McDermott, astute veteran with a keen news sense. Most announcements come from his office. It also will answer inquiries at any hour of the day or night.

In peace times the press room is the hang-out of many war correspondents. They have reported World Wars or South American revolutions or even the China Relief Expedition of 1900 and the Spanish-American War. Now that war grips whole continents, most of the correspondents are at work in far-off places, but a few return temporarily from time to time to recuperate from strenuous campaigns. Others have not had this field experience but are veteran specialists in diplomacy. One of these a few years back was Edwin M. Hood of the Associated Press, who began his Department reporting in the 1870's and became the confidant of a long line of Secretaries. There are others today like Hood.

There also are the correspondents of foreign newspapers: Sir Willmott Lewis of the *London Times*, Laurence Todd of the Soviet Union Tass Agency, and representatives of press associations and newspapers in France, Argentina, China, and other countries. At press conferences, these foreign correspondents ask no questions because it would not be appropriate for them to cross-examine the Secretary of State.

Press relations are important for the Department, not only because of their influence on public opinion, but because they can smooth the Department's relations with Congress. Money to run the Department is appropriated by Congress, whose committees hold hearings before it passes bills involving foreign policy. The Senate must approve, by a two-thirds majority, treaties and conventions, and it can modify them by attaching reservations. The Senate confirms appointments of Secretaries, Under Secretaries, Assistant Secretaries, Ambassadors, Ministers, and others. And the press

73

is often a good way for the Department to get its case to the whole Congress, as well as the committee involved, on matters in controversy.

The State Department is nearly always expert in its handling of the press.

Planning a Better World

The United States is in a dominating position in the anti-Axis world. It has the greatest industrial resources, it can give the most, or it can threaten to take away the most, and it can even offer to buy the most.

When the war is over, the United States will still have the world's greatest industrial machine. It will have developed sources at home for many raw materials which it formerly imported. It will have been supplying most of the anti-Axis nations with war goods, and its industrial machinery can be geared back to peacetime production so that it can supply much of the world with peacetime goods.

The United States is wealthy. It has most of the world's gold. Nearly everybody owes it money. If the United States chose, it could pinch down on its allies and enemies after the war and cause them plenty of economic trouble.

The flaw in such a policy, as Washington now sees it, is that the world has progressed to such a state of internationalism that if the United States pinched other nations it would pinch itself, too. If the United States wants to sell its products to other nations after the war, it must work out some way to let them sell things to us, or trade will stop.

So, all policies are designed to help the United Nations now, and to be prepared to help even the people in the Axis nations after the war. Such policies call for intricate and continuing planning and negotiating. The State Department is a potent influence. Much that is now talked and planned is under the hat, for that is the way of diplomacy.

But the net of it is that the best diplomatic brains in America and the rest of the Allied world are spending almost as much time figuring out what to do after war as during war. The chances are that the result will be better for everybody than if each nation were left to scramble for itself when the treaties are signed. Thus the State Department is helping to plan for a future that is worth fighting for.

8

Morale, Propaganda and Censorship

PEOPLE have different ideas about what will win the war. Some say "Food Will Win the War." Some say "Ships Will Win the War." Some say "Planes Will Win the War," or "Tanks Will Win the War."

And some say that "Thoughts Will Win the War."

To regulate the thinkings and feelings of people is always a delicate job, but government did it under pressure of war, and is doing it now. The problem was, and is, to propagate the thoughts which help to win the war, without going so far as to regiment the thinking and destroy the freedom of individual minds.

Before the nation got formally into war, Washington started to build the machinery for putting some strings on people's thinking at home, and for war propaganda abroad. Since then the activities have grown, until now there is a well-developed system for cultivating our own war morale, for undermining morale in the enemy nations, and for censoring any information which would aid or comfort the enemy. It is called the "intellectual phase of war."

Here's what was done:

In the fall of 1941 the Office of Facts and Figures (dubbed "OFF") was created to coordinate the various news and information agencies of the government, and to determine basic policies for maintaining the public morale. At the head of the OFF was placed Archibald MacLeish, a soft-voiced poet, lawyer, intellectual, Librarian of Congress, and a former editor of *Fortune* magazine.

For foreign propaganda, excepting in Latin America, government created another office, the Coordinator of Information, headed by Colonel William J. Donovan, who had been a lawyer, a soldier-hero (who disliked his nickname of "Wild Bill"), and a Republican. He set to work on systematic propaganda directed against the Axis nations.

For Latin American relations, government had already created the Office of the Coordinator of Inter-American Affairs, under Nelson A. Rockefeller,

75

the hardworking young grandson of the original John D. Rockefeller, and he went to work to cultivate "good neighborliness" with all Latin American countries.

For the home front, the Office of Civilian Defense was established under bumptious Fiorello LaGuardia, mayor of New York City, with Mrs. Roosevelt as co-director. This was to organize for the physical safety of civilians under raids, and in its early stages it was also supposed to cultivate civilian culture and happiness as a part of the building of morale. Mrs. Roosevelt plugged hard for culture and happiness, but finally ran into a storm of public indignation over these activities, and was forced out, along with her nominal boss, Mayor LaGuardia. James M. Landis came in as director of OCD, and started to clean up the mess and to devote more effort to the physical welfare of civilians.

To keep valuable information from the enemy, an Office of Censorship was set up after the United States got into war. Heading this was Byron Price, executive news editor of the Associated Press. This office proceeded to organize a system by which each writer, editor and radio broadcaster would attempt to withhold certain specified classes of information—on a voluntary basis.

In addition, a number of intragovernmental committees or agencies were set up to coordinate or supervise activities on health, welfare, motion pictures, and other phases of the broad and somewhat vague subject known as "morale." Then, as the nation got deeper into war, the morale and propaganda agencies were reshuffled and realigned, some policy conflicts were ironed out, and an over-all reorganization was effected for the purpose of coordinating war information.

The propaganda involved in some of these activities is not of the German style. Our government took note of what Adolf Hitler had written in *Mein Kampf*: "By propaganda, even heaven and earth can be palmed off on a people as hell, and the most wretched life as paradise." In contrast, our government set out to adopt a policy of disseminating facts and of regarding them as the best propaganda. Archibald MacLeish put it this way: "Democracy is based on the proposition that the government can trust the people and that the people are entitled to all the facts and figures necessary to enable them to make up their own minds." President Roosevelt himself laid down the themes to be followed in the propaganda:

1. The policy of isolationism has failed. We are fighting one indivisible war against the entire Axis, and shall continue to fight until total victory is attained.

2. We are not fighting for material gain, but to establish everywhere in

the world the four freedoms—freedom of speech, freedom of religion, freedom from want and freedom from fear.

3. The war will be hard, but if we remain unified at home and cooperate with our Allies, we shall win not only the war but the peace after the war. In that peace we shall attempt to establish a liberal international economic system based on freer trade and freer access for all nations to the essential raw materials of the world.

These three themes now dominate our propaganda everywhere.

The Home Front

On the home front, the machinery for presenting the government's case to the people is founded on the various press divisions of the main government departments and agencies which functioned for years before the war. When the United States entered the conflict these press divisions were well staffed to do the job. In all, there were 34 separate press departments and before any of the war emergency press divisions were added, the Bureau of the Budget estimated that the information services of the government were costing in the neighborhood of $10,000,000, not counting the $13,000,000 spent annually on publications.

This was in contrast with the set-up in the first World War. At that time, the Committee on Public Information, under George Creel, a veteran journalist, was the sole official mouthpiece of the government for the duration of the war.

President Hoover and President Roosevelt, who were the first to organize anything like a systematic government information service in Washington, decentralized their press divisions. When President Roosevelt came to Washington, Stephen T. Early, his secretary, was assigned the job of establishing in all the main government departments and agencies press divisions which would be staffed by trained, skilled newspapermen.

After war broke in Europe in September 1939, the government's press divisions worked independently, each deciding for itself what information to release and what to suppress. And each of them thought up its own ideas on what could or should be done to furnish public information and to bolster the public morale. There were contradictory statements by the various departments, which led to much criticism and even some confusion as to the government's defense program and foreign policy.

It was as a result of this situation that President Roosevelt organized the Office of Facts and Figures. This office organized the Committee on War Information, staffed by high representatives of the War, Navy, Treasury, State, Interior, and Justice Departments, the Lend-Lease Administration, the Office for Emergency Management, the Office of Civilian Defense, the

77

Office of the Coordinator of Inter-American Affairs, the Office of Government Reports, and the Office of the Coordinator of Information. The function of this committee was to "call signals" for the other press divisions, which actually carried the ball. The completely centralized system of the last war was rejected.

The operation of the Office of Facts and Figures and the Committee on War Information illustrates the government's machinery for watching and bolstering the nation's morale. Trained public opinion experts all over the country report on the morale of the people, on what they are thinking, what they are worrying about, whether they understand the government's policy, whether they are being affected by enemy propaganda, and other things.

At the same time, a scientific check is made on the use being made of official information by the press, radio, newsreels, and commentators, and a study is made of the total output of all the government press sections to see how well they are doing their job. On the basis of these studies, programs are prepared by the OFF for all the departments to carry out, suggestions are made to the President about points he can usefully make in his press conferences and in other ways the policies are amended to make sure that the government's case is clear.

Thus, when at one point it was determined that the people were not clear about the necessity for the United States to contribute to all the theaters of the war at once, the President asked that everybody get a map out on a certain night at a certain time and at that time he explained over the radio in a "fireside chat" the interrelationship between the various battles.

Again, when one or two cabinet members made speeches outside their own field which tended to confuse both the people at home and our Allies abroad, President Roosevelt ordered all cabinet members to clear their speeches through the Office of Facts and Figures. The OFF is also the clearinghouse for all posters, and the coordinator of radio programs. Government motion pictures are coordinated by the Office of Government Reports, under Lowell Mellett, who is responsible for advising the newsreel and motion picture companies what they can do to aid the understanding and morale of the people.

World Propaganda

One of the ironical facts of the world propaganda picture is that while the Nazis got their idea for the propaganda offensive from United States propaganda against Germany and Austria-Hungary in the last great war, the U. S. government was the last of the great powers to get into the international propaganda race in this war.

German propagandists already had proved what could be done with what they termed the three-dimensional war. They had broken France's will to resist; they had undermined the political structure of Norway; and without striking a blow, they had taken Hungary, Rumania, Denmark, and Bulgaria. On propaganda alone in 1941, the Germans spent something like $230,000,000—$130,000,000 on foreign propaganda, and $100,000,000 on "preventive" propaganda on the home front. They maintained 40,000 paid propaganda agents abroad, owned and controlled 300 German language papers in foreign countries, and maintained some 40,000 German societies outside their Reich.

With this situation facing the United States, President Roosevelt sent Colonel William J. Donovan on a special mission to Europe in the early phases of the war. When Donovan returned he told the President that his foreign policy would be more effective if it were backed up by a systematic propaganda campaign. As a result, Colonel Donovan was given the task of carrying out his own suggestion, and in the summer of 1941, the position of Coordinator of Information was announced. Although Colonel Donovan went to work immediately in the international propaganda field, the executive order merely authorized him to coordinate all information coming into this country from abroad. The authorization to conduct propaganda against the Axis all over the world was contained in a private letter from the White House. Thus for months there was secrecy over the foreign propaganda activities.

Even after it was generally known that Colonel Donovan was in the propaganda business, he did not have full say about what could or could not be sent out of the country. The final decision about what should be broadcast abroad remained for months in the hands of the private radio companies. Not until after we had been in the war for some time was the Coordinator of Information able to prepare broadcasting material with any assurance that it would be sent out.

Colonel Donovan used the technique of "making news." After the full force of the Japanese assault fell on the Philippines, General Douglas MacArthur reported to the War Department that the morale of the Filipinos was being affected by the Japanese propaganda broadcasts. The Donovan office immediately got in touch with the White House. Three hours later, the COI broadcast from the three stations on the West Coast a message from President Roosevelt assuring them that they would be avenged and that their independence would be restored.

This same technique was applied in many ways to fit the requirements of the counter-propaganda service. Some officials in the capital liked to point out that the United States was not putting out propaganda, that the administration was not sitting down and writing propaganda as such. This,

79

in the main, was true, but they adopted the much more effective method of having cabinet officers or even the President make comments or remarks which had no other purpose than to counter some particular piece of Axis propaganda somewhere else in the world.

Although most of the effort to break through the Axis wall of censorship is concentrated on the short wave transmitters which are available in this country, the Donovan office also makes use of pamphlets and of certain "tourists" traveling in foreign countries. After each major speech by President Roosevelt, the Donovan office prepares pamphlets containing those excerpts from the speech which are barred in the enemy and occupied countries and these are dropped by the hundreds of thousands from bombers in enemy-held territory.

To direct any counter-propaganda operation, it is naturally necessary for the COI to know precisely what the enemy propaganda broadcasts are saying to the rest of the world and to analyze these broadcasts for any indication of the Axis plans or problems. The job of monitoring all these foreign broadcasts is carried out by the Federal Communications Commission, which established four "listening posts," and hired around 350 persons to translate, monitor, and analyze the various stories.

A translation of the broadcasts is sent with considerable speed over teleprinters to Colonel Donovan's office 24 hours a day, and his staff then analyzes it, decides what, if anything, has to be countered, prepares the copy and puts it out.

To do this job, the Donovan office has a large staff of experts both in Washington and in New York. Some 215 persons were on the staff early in 1942, 75 in the Congressional Library producing background material for both the incoming and outgoing reports, and the rest mapping strategy or writing and moving copy to the short wave stations.

Chief assistant to Colonel Donovan on this work is Robert Sherwood, the playwright, and he in turn is assisted by Joseph Barnes, former cable editor of the *New York Herald Tribune*; Wallace R. Deuel, former Berlin correspondent for the *Chicago Daily News*; and Edmond L. Taylor, former Paris correspondent for the *Chicago Tribune*, and others who are added from time to time.

One of the main problems faced by the Donovan office was that of getting powerful stations to carry the news into the heart of the continent of Europe. Attempts were made to meet this problem by increasing the volume of stations here, but it was finally decided that the most effective medium of transmission was over one of the British Broadcasting System's medium length transmitters in England.

In his broadcasts, especially to Europe, Colonel Donovan's main theme is: You Can't Win. Germany's experience of holding a great part of France for most of the last war and other allusions designed to induce a feeling of frustration and hopelessness within Germany and Italy are emphasized, but in the main, the COI concentrates on getting into the enemy-occupied countries all those ideas and facts which are not permitted to pass through the totalitarian censorships.

Latin America

Difficult as this task has been, however, it is not so complicated or delicate as the problem faced by Nelson Rockefeller in propagandizing Latin America. There is nothing to prevent Colonel Donovan from carrying on any kind of propaganda he likes in the rest of the world, but other more delicate questions arise in sending news and other information below the Rio Grande. That is why the task was not thrown in with the Donovan organization but placed in the hands of a specialist in the Latin American field.

Rockefeller faces many problems. For over 100 years the Latin Americans have suspected our motives and resented our imperialistic ventures. They remember only too well the policy of many U. S. governments which have used the Marines and foreign policy of the United States to further the interests of American business in Latin America. They recall the promises we made them during the last war—promises that were hard to keep when the war was over. And they are very much aware of the fact that their best customer in time of peace was Europe, not the United States, and that, whether they liked it or not, they were bound to cooperate in the future with the dominant power on the European continent.

In meeting this problem, it was as obvious to Rockefeller as it was to the State Department and the other agencies dealing with the Latin Americans that it was no good merely to conduct a propaganda campaign below the Rio Grande. The Latin American countries had been cut off from their European markets by the war, and they needed commercial, military, naval, and financial help more than accurate news.

So the U. S. propaganda took a different turn in Latin America. We poured money into the various countries. We bought all the strategic raw materials we could to provide for our war program, to keep them away from the Axis, and to provide the Latin American nations with exchange. We gave them high priority ratings on the prefabricated goods they needed to keep their factories going; we planned ways of increasing their exports to the United States. And it was only in connection with this practical program of assistance that we conducted our propaganda campaign to convince them that the hemisphere could and should operate as a unit in

81

peace as well as in war. The Rockefeller group was engaged in this propaganda long before the Donovan agency did it, and was a pioneer in the advocacy of systematic activities abroad.

To do this job, Rockefeller hired one of the ablest publicists in the country, Francis A. Jamieson, former Associated Press star reporter and Pulitzer Prize winner, who did an excellent job of increasing the distribution of U. S. news in Latin America. By cooperating with the United Press and the Associated Press, which already enjoyed a great measure of confidence in Latin America, by the adroit use of the short and medium wave radio and by the creation of a direct mail service to newspapers and special subscribers, Jamieson has done much to break down the Latin American prejudices against the United States.

One of the main problems facing him was the fact that the Germans were supplying free news to the impoverished Latin American papers, of which there were several hundred. In the better and more prosperous Latin American papers, the UP and AP were more than holding their own, but these two agencies were covering only about one-third of all the papers in Latin America and the Rockefeller office set out to get objective news in the other two-thirds.

A special picture and feature service has been introduced. Photographs are radioed free of charge from the United States to Latin America. These pictures are "matted" and mailed altogether to more than 500 papers. The office also publishes a regular large monthly magazine, *En Guardia,* and puts out a periodic news letter. The Rockefeller office thus secures a large field for information about the extent and progress of the U. S. war effort.

Coincidentally, the Rockefeller committee arranged for the production of a weekly newsreel on the U. S. defense effort to be distributed in Latin America. It also sends to all U. S. missions in Latin America sound equipment for the showing of these motion pictures. And it cooperates with Hollywood in the production of films which are welcomed in Latin America —full-length entertainment films and documentary films for schools and other groups on U. S. life designed to increase the understanding of the Latin Americans of our way of life and our military, political and social objectives.

To support the policy of giving more commercial support and more accurate news to Latin America, the Rockefeller office promotes a long-range educational program designed to provide more adequate instruction all over the hemisphere in the languages, history, jurisprudence, art, economic and social backgrounds of the various countries. The fact that the Latin American nations cooperated with us when the test came at the time we entered the war is perhaps the best evidence that at least in this field the coordination of our diplomatic, commercial and propaganda campaigns was successful.

Censorship

The last of the four agencies established to deal with information-in-wartime was the Office of Censorship. It was put together after the United States entered the war in December 1941, and as Director of Censorship, the President drafted Byron Price.

The Office of Censorship now is the smallest of all the war administrative agencies in Washington. As long as three months after it was established, it filled only nine offices of the Apex Building, in the Federal Triangle. Its Washington executive and administrative personnel came to the censorship job direct from the newsgathering or broadcasting field, and none of them was interested in impressing any particular ideological pattern on the people of the United States.

As Assistant Director of Censorship in charge of Press, Price called in John H. Sorrells, who had been executive editor of the Scripps-Howard Newspapers. Sorrells selected Nathaniel R. Howard, editor of the *Cleveland News*, as his right-hand man. In charge of radio censorship, Price appointed John H. Ryan, head of the Fort Industry Company of Toledo, Ohio, which operated six radio stations. Stanley P. Richardson, from the office of the Coordinator of International Broadcasting, in New York, became assistant to Ryan.

The press staff was filled out with William Steven, managing editor of the *Tulsa Tribune*; Frank Clough, managing editor of the *Emporia Gazette*; Jack Lockhart, managing editor of the *Memphis Commercial Appeal*; Frank Tighe, editor of the *Automobile Trade Journal*; William Mylander, Washington correspondent for the Paul Block newspapers, and some others, subsequently appointed.

All censorship of publications and radio stations is centered in these men. The job can be done by a compact staff because the government has adopted a system of "voluntary censorship." What it amounts to, in actual operation, is that the job of censoring is distributed among all the writers and editors in the country. Every writer or editor is his own censor. In January 1942, the Office of Censorship sent radio stations, newspapers, magazines and other periodicals mimeographed copies of a "code of wartime practices." It asked that the specified information be withheld unless it were given out by "an appropriate" government authority. It laid down the rules, and left individual writers and editors to apply them, with the help of the Office of Censorship.

The actual censoring, therefore, is not done by government agents who stand at writers' elbows, or look over their shoulders, or blue pencil their copy. The Office of Censorship is not a sieve for information, but rather like a clearinghouse of judgment on all censoring matters. Its members are on hand to advise the headquarters of the major wire services in Washington, and the other writers in Washington, and writers and editors all over the country. And they do as much of their work as possible by telephone.

In addition to advising on censorship policy, the censors try to read a cross section of newspapers to see that the policy is understood and applied. In this, they get the help of the clipping service of the Office of Government Reports, which forwards to Censorship anything which seems censorable. The same kind of cooperation comes from the Federal Trade Commission, which has a crew that reads advertisements, and passes on any that may contain censorable material. When Censorship sees something out of line with the code, the office gets in touch with the publication and tries to straighten out the policy for future reference.

Censorship of mail and cables that go outside the United States is done word for word, unlike the policy on radio and publications. Cable censorship is directed by Capt. H. K. Fenn, a Navy officer detailed to the Office of Censorship. Under him are censors at every outgoing cable point. Mail is handled similarly by "border censors" under the direction of Col. W. Preston Corderman, an Army officer detailed to the civilian job of Chief Postal Censor.

The Shaking Down

This, then, is the brief outline of the U. S. government's experiment in propaganda as a means of sustaining public morale at home and in Latin America and in breaking the enemy's morale abroad. It was a new organization full of personal conflicts and divided authority but also full of talent and full of ideas. It was to be expected that the nation which had developed the art of advertising beyond the level attained by any other nation should show a great aptitude for propaganda. It was also to be expected that the aptitude would be developed rapidly in time of war.

The main trouble seemed to be the division of authority to do the job. Too many people seemed to want to beat Hitler provided he, personally, could do the job. Through the early part of 1942 there were all sorts of conflicts between the Office of Censorship (Price), the Office of Facts and Figures (MacLeish), the Office of the Coordinator of Information (Donovan), the Office of the Coordinator of Inter-American Affairs (Rockefeller), the Office for Emergency Management, and even the Office of Civilian Defense. Some of the conflicts and overlappings were eliminated

84

by reorganization of war information machinery in the spring of 1942, and this helped to clear the decks for a more consistent program.

The true test of public morale and the governmental morale machinery will come later in the war, when the going is tougher. The test will involve the public willingness to buckle the mind down to the hard facts of war. Also it will demonstrate whether the authorities can resist the intra-government pressures to crack down on criticism which is meant to be constructive, and to go too far in regimenting the minds of the people of the United States. It is one of the great tests of democracy.

9

Officials on the Job

BENEATH the President is a thick layer of officials who make the government run, and it may be worth while to see what manner of men they are. Not what they have for breakfast, not the petty details of their personal lives, but their work and how they do it, their jobs and how they manage.

The facts about officials are not sensational. The big shots are men of flesh and blood and ordinary habits. They are not of a different breed. They were not born to be great men. They are not necessarily the pick of the nation, but there's some reason why they are where they are. To understand government, you must have a general understanding of these men.

I have known public officials in Washington for 25 years. I like them—most of them—and so would you if you were to get behind their fronts. They aren't fearsome, they aren't super-special. They are human, and most of them work hard. Those who are truly statesmen don't regard themselves as statesmen, and they are likely to grin a little sheepishly when they hear someone call them that. They have wives who complain that they work too hard. They have children who are forever needing new clothes because the old ones are worn out or too small. They read their names in the newspapers, and say to themselves, "Look at me!" They do and say and think all the things which any other group of people do and say and think.

The term "officials" means "executive officials," the men who execute and administer the laws, rather than the congressmen. The term loosely lumps together a lot of officials of all grades—high, medium and low. It even includes the high-rank employees, the advisers who advise the officials, for in ordinary usage there isn't any sharp line which differentiates civilian "officials" from the civilian "non-coms" and "privates." The officials are the men who are appointed, rather than elected. (The President and the Vice President are exceptions.) The officials are the men who get most publicity in times like these, for they are always doing something or saying something that makes news. And they are the most powerful group in government, for they administer the laws, and the way laws are admin-

86

istered is more productive of either good or bad results than the laws themselves.

It is a government of men. You can philosophize all you like about government of laws, but when you get right down to actual operations of government, you find that the things which touch the lives of millions of people are the decisions made by men who occupy the executive chairs. They interpret laws in order to administer, and often they twist and bend the laws to make them mean what they wish them to mean. This is particularly true under the New Deal, whose executive branch has almost pushed the legislative and judicial branches out of bed.

These executive officials also *make* laws. They don't actually vote them (that's for Congress to do), but they often initiate them, and they often help to make the pressures which make the votes to get the laws enacted.

Most officials who get in the news are amateurs in public office. Most have recently been in private life, and are serving their term in government, and will go back to private life. Most are not lifelong practitioners of the art of government. They just do what they think best, or what they can get away with, and they don't read a lot of books on how to govern. Critics of government often try to smear it by calling the officials "amateurs," but it's doubtful whether the people would really like to be governed by professional governing men. Such men are all right in career jobs, below the top. They produce a balance, and protect against impulsive shifts in policy. But at the top, where the policies are passed upon, we have amateurs because we insist on amateurs. Under our two-party system we throw out one set of amateurs every few years and put in another set of amateurs because we didn't like the way the first set was doing. In the course of time, if they stay in office long enough, they may acquire the status of professionals, simply because they become more experienced, but very few regard themselves as professionals.

New Dealers were notably amateurs in government, and some of them still are (even in the worst sense of the word), but three consecutive terms in office tend to make a considerable proportion of them into "professionals." They learn how to manage laws, administer laws, and wangle public opinion to permit them to do what they think ought to be done for the public. This has both merit and danger. The merit is that the officials are less clumsy as time passes, and they learn how to do their jobs—"professionally." The danger is that they become powerful, and drive the people, instead of having the people drive them.

Mr. Roosevelt is a "professional"—not because he is President, but because he has spent most of his life in the political governing business. Mr. Wallace was distinctly an amateur when he first came in, but he learned the trade tricks of government, and now he is well on his way to being a professional official.

Good and Bad Qualities

In the business of gathering news from officials over a period of years, through many administrations, a person acquires impressions of the qualities which make a good official, and the qualities which are not so good. All generalizations have their exceptions, but the emphasis must be on the generalizations.

Officials are a hard-working lot. This has always been true, even under the easygoing administrations of Harding and Coolidge, but it is especially true now. Officials work long hours and under pressure. They lead tough lives, and those who are not physically or mentally tough soon pass out of the picture. Right now anyone who knows Washington can count at least a dozen high officials whose weakness as officials is that they are permitting themselves to be overworked, approaching the breaking point. If you want a soft job, don't accept appointment to public office.

Officials are underpaid. This is contrary to the common public view, which is that public office is a "sinecure" or "reward" for something or other. But the fact is that in most cases, the salary is not as much as those same men could make in private jobs, and is not even enough to pay their abnormally high expenses while serving in public office. Many of them live on what they have previously saved. A few go into debt and mortgage their futures. The pay of high officials is such that often only men of means can afford to hold office. Poor men can't. When emphasis is on money rather than on brains and ability, something is likely to be wrong in the system which permits it, and that is one of the things wrong with government. Some officials plan secretly to "cash in" on their knowledge and reputations after they have left government. It is a bad practice. It would be economy for the government to raise its official salaries, both at the top, and down to the grades paying around $4,000, for these are the public policy makers, and policy makers are worth more salt than they get.

Congress fixes salaries, and Congress is jealous of salaries which are higher than its own, $10,000 a year for members of both House and Senate. Members of Congress would like to raise their own salaries, but they fear public reaction against what might seem like a "money grab." Yet it might be a good thing for Congress to raise its own pay, regardless of whether its members are worth more, as a means of raising the roof for the pay of executive officials. This would attract better men, make it worth their while to give up private jobs, and it would produce better government.

Retirement pay for members of Congress probably would be a good thing, for it would let them devote their minds more freely to their duties when they are in office, with less fretting and less currying of favors for the sake of their futures when they get out of office. The recent rumpus over the bill to provide "pensions for congressmen," which first was voted, then retracted, was due not so much to consideration of the merits of the proposal as to the rush in putting it through, without adequate public discussion.

Officials who are not "politicians" usually make poor officials. This doesn't mean that a man must have "run for office" in order to be a good official, but he ought to have had some training in dealing with the public. He must understand public feelings and prejudices, and know why masses of people feel the way they do about public questions. The man who is advertised as "not a politician" sometimes makes good, but usually he doesn't—at least until after he has learned to be a bit of a politician. Previous training in the hurly-burly of political strife usually gives a man experience in wangling his ideas through Congress, or in dealing with the blocs and lobbies, or in knowing how to pick his way through the mazes of public opinion. He learns what is feasible and expedient, as distinguished from the full program which he might prefer. Political background or aptitude makes a man flexible, able to compromise, and one of the essential qualities of a good public official is the know-how on compromising.

Sometimes the most experienced can *appear* to compromise, and still have their way. That's one of Mr. Roosevelt's qualities, best known to his opponents. Mr. Morgenthau is an example of a man who was never a skilled politician, but he has learned how to "play politics," and it has improved his work. Some politicians do not make good public officials, but this proves nothing. By and large the officials who have "political sense" make the best officials.

Most businessmen do not make good officials at first, although they soon learn. They have been trained in taking direct cuts, in ordering things done and expecting them to be done as ordered, in pushing a button and looking for results. Government does not work that way. The governing business requires patience, slow approach, persuasion, and unlimited knowledge of the sore toes which are always around, waiting to be stepped upon. It is nice to talk about "direct action," but in government the most effective processes are often by indirection, by going 'round Robin Hood's barn to get where you want to go. Even in wartime this is true, although less true than in ordinary times. Jesse Jones is an example of a blunt businessman who did poorly at first as an official, but who really began to accumulate power when he learned to "play politics," which he now does for a fare-ye-well.

Most newspapermen do not make good officials at first, because they have been trained to do quick thinking, and to have all the answers on the tips of their tongues. Thus, they don't make good team workers in jobs which take the judicial temperament (as many policy jobs do), and which require that the subject be inspected from every angle before a decision is made. Newspapermen make good snappy administrators in public office, however. They take direct cuts and get things done. Herbert Gaston, Assistant Secretary of the Treasury, is an exceptional example of a newspaperman who has learned to deliberate before acting, and he is one newspaperman who has made good as a government official.

The "professors" in government are both good and bad. Normally they have the same faults as businessmen, in that they are inclined to think things out and then try directly to have them done, without adequate understanding of the complex processes of government, and without understanding of public opinion. They think that things which are "theoretically" good are "practically" good. True, they may be, but there is a lag, a gap, a necessary transition, and academic folks often make inadequate allowance for these. Furthermore, the theory is sometimes the result of dreaming, without enough study of the practice, the machinery, the mechanism of the thing about which the theory is held. This applies to some, but not to all of the theory men. In time they can learn to be "practical," just as "practical" men can learn to be broad and philosophical. Also the "professors" can learn to be "politicians," as many of them have done, and these make effective officials.

My observation is that the "professors" in the New Deal have been a good influence net, regardless of the many cases of dreamy incompetence. They have been the social engineers who have brought in new ideas, and even though many of these new ideas were raw and clumsy at the start, they have ripened and shaken down into something workable. Some theoreticians have even developed into good administrators. For example, there was William I. Myers, a Cornell professor, who was head of the Farm Credit Administration, and who did a clean smooth job, and who was entirely "practical." The dean of all the professors in the beginning was Raymond Moley. He was essentially the "idea architect" of the New Deal. But he brought in many other academicians who tried to soar to heaven in a single year, who lost their moorings on earth, and who thought that a new Rome really could be built in a year.

Officials who want the "honor of the post" are usually flops. There are plenty of men, past and present, who wiggled their way into public office for no other reason than that they wanted the "honor." In practically every case they did not make good, and most have gone out without honor.

Officials who set their eyes on publicity are half sunk before they start. In every administration there are examples of "publicity hounds." They play to the press, to get their names in the papers. Now it is no sin to play to the press, and it is often helpful to the job, but the error lies in the practice of putting the thought of publicity *first*. Officials who do so betray themselves, and soon do not have a "good press." Furthermore, they get rattled when it comes to doing a job which ought to be done, but which is "unpopular." The craving for publicity makes them soft-headed in their critical decisions. The best practice is to consider publicity a by-product of the office.

New officials are often more afraid of newspapermen than newspapermen are of them, but most of them soon get over it. Andrew Mellon was an example of a man who quailed in his early press conferences. Herbert Hoover, the same, when he was food administrator in the last war. Both never quite got over their fear. Mr. Roosevelt is a skilled "handler of the press," but often his decisions are excessively influenced by his own pre-determined desire to "make a good story."

The formal rank of officials doesn't have much to do with their effective influence. Under protocol, which is a code of official etiquette, some officials rank high, some low, but they make their own places by their own brains and personalities. Vice Presidents never ranked very high in actual influence within government, but Mr. Wallace is different. He is a Somebody, "even if he is Vice President." Jesse Jones as Secretary of Commerce is just a cabinet member, but as chief dispenser of government loans he is a Big Man. The only Secretary of Commerce who ever amounted to anything on the job was Herbert Hoover, and that was because he made it into a big job, and from it stepped up to the Presidency. Miss Perkins, who was the lowest ranking cabinet member in official protocol, also was lowest ranking in actual influence, due solely to her personality and temperament, which always seemed to rile those with whom she dealt. Felix Frankfurter may be an Associate Justice of the Supreme Court, but his major influence is as a semi-secret adviser of the President on all sorts of public policies. Those who wear the biggest and shiniest public badges don't always cut the most ice within government.

Backslapping is an activity which everyone pretends to disdain, in private life as well as public. And yet, if you stand around for a few years and watch the political officials at work, you acquire a great respect for the skillful practice of backslapping. It is an art, and it can be overdone, but those who figure out the right backs to slap, and who set themselves on a course of doing it, develop a lot of grease which makes the machine run smoothly. Calling people by their first names is one method. Mr. Roosevelt has a system of keeping on record the first names of people he wishes to flatter. On one occasion he held up a telephone call for ten minutes until he could find someone who knew the first name of the man he was calling. He often woos a stubborn man by piling on the honeyed words.

Wives can be of great help to officials. Some wives have political sense, and act as balance wheels to their husbands. Mrs. Hull always had political sense. Mrs. Morgenthau, the same. Mrs. McNutt has horse sense, and understands public reactions to things. But it is mainly as hostesses that official wives have influence. Many a smart wife knows her husband's list of friends, lukewarm associates, and enemies, and she often does wonders in warming up relations by little social courtesies. Some official wives work harder than their husbands at this delicate business-on-the-side.

Working Habits

People ask a good many plain down-to-earth questions about how officials do their daily work.

Telephones are much used. The average cabinet member, for example, has a telephone call to his office at least every five minutes but all calls don't get through to him. Usually women secretaries listen in on all calls, and make notes to remind the boss. Some officials have installed systems for automatic recordings of telephone conversations. These may serve merely as records, but sometimes they serve as espionage, for a department head in a few cases has used the device to check up on conversations of some subordinate all unbeknownst to the subordinate.

Officials get to their offices around 10 o'clock in ordinary times, and around 9 o'clock in extraordinary times such as these. A few come earlier. They leave at all times—5, 6 or 7 in the evening. Recently it has become the custom to burn the midnight oil. War has added many burdens.

Official automobiles and chauffeurs are provided for the higher officials, the heads of departments, and the assistant heads. Some of them have cars at their disposal 24 hours a day. Lower officials use "department cars," which are kept ready, like high-grade taxis, to take them to hurry-up conferences in some other building. Some of the official government cars are very old, and taxicabs are often newer and faster.

Lunch is where they find it. Some eat it off trays brought in to their desks by colored messengers, and invite in visitors to share their sandwiches. Some go to the non-doggy lunchrooms in their buildings. A few walk up to the swank Metropolitan Club, at 17th and H Streets.

The daily job of newspaper reading is done largely by proxy. Most officials have professional readers to read the news, clip it, digest it, and route it around the department. But officials read their own pet newspapers or magazines, just as others do. Wives often watch the news about their husbands, and one of them often has opportunity to say, "John, you *must* read this. It says you are good."

The limelight is always a personal nuisance. High officials are always compelled to be on the lookout for chance acquaintances who turn out to be grinders of axes.

Teen-age children of high officials carry the burden of being pointed out at school as the children of So-&-So. Fortunately for the kids, Washingtonians are blasé about The Great in their midst. Even at that, a lot of official kids get spoiled in Washington by the fixed idea that their dads are something special, and that therefore they are, too . . . but the other kids usually knock it out of them.

Social drinking is a problem for officials. They are always being invited. They must go, but they have learned that other guests go away and report what dropped from the loose tongue of the official, and so they must be careful. A gossip column one morning carried a verbatim report of what Under Secretary X had said at a party on Tuesday night. It was damaging, and it was accurate. Under Secretary X denied it, and since then he has had a drink only in his own home.

Some officials don't travel much. They are stuck to their jobs. They say that if they travel they are criticized for deserting the job. They really ought to travel more, for they are serving their country when they get away from Washington and renew their spiritual energies by talking to people in the hinterlands.

Neither Dumb nor Omniscient

The general public suffers from two extreme viewpoints about government officials. One is that officials are dumb. As in all generalizations, there's some truth in this. Some officials are a little bit dumb about some things, and very dumb about other things. Usually they know it and stay out of the fields in which their knowledge is deficient, and if they don't stay out they are soon forced out. They don't last long. Those citizens who go around raving against government officials in general usually tell a few specific stories involving unfortunate experiences, and spread these out to cover all.

But the public impression that does the most damage is the other extreme that officials are all-wise or omniscient. There are people who look through spectacles of awe at government officials and their decisions. This awe is the product of advertising and publicity, which puffs up great clouds of prestige about big names, and which obscures the natural human fallibility of these men. The quality of brains in government officials is not of any superior brand. Most are good men in their ways, but they are not

Great Men. True, some make themselves into Great Men, but that is due to a combination of a certain amount of ability, plus opportunity.

Very few officials at the top are what you would call brilliant men. For one reason or another brilliant men do not get along with other men who are not so brilliant. The really brilliant men are likely to be found farther down in the ranks, as advisers in the back rooms, not as front men in the main office.

Top officials are not usually the pungent decisive individuals which they appear to be from all the publicity about them. They do not make all the decisions attributed to them in the press. Instead of being individual they are institutional. They are the heads of organizations of men, and the whole organization does the thinking, planning and administering. The Secretary of This-or-That announces a policy, and it bears his name. But he alone didn't think it up and work it out. It is likely to be the product of a score of minds in the department beneath the Secretary. Coworkers on a policy may be high officials, or low officials, or men with no title except that of "adviser." In the New Deal government the advisers are a powerful lot. They work behind the scenes, seldom get out in front, but government policies are made and steered very largely by them.

In official conduct, one of the most important qualities is breadth of viewpoint. One of the first things a man learns when he enters public office is that no longer can he permit himself the luxury of looking at a problem from a single angle, as he may have done formerly. He must now look at how the problem affects a dozen or more different classes and interests. That is the one quality which public men have, and which private men often do not have. It takes training and experience to acquire. It is the quality which some businessmen develop after they have served in government. NRA gave it to many businessmen. NRA may have been a flop in some ways, but it was a good school of experience for businessmen, and when they returned to their private jobs they were better businessmen, and better citizens. The war emergency is doing the same for many businessmen today.

In the working out of broad social problems in the future, the best machinery will be combinations of government minds and private minds. Government minds can contribute the breadth of perspective and interest. Private minds are likely to be more competent in working out the practical details. There is a good chance that such a combination will be worked out successfully for the direction of the new economic and social order which will follow this war.

10

People of Washington

YOUR home city is made up of many different kinds of people, not just merchants, manufacturers, city officials, and early settlers. In the same way Washington is made up of people who do various kinds of work. They are not just statesmen, politicians, officials and bigwigs. Most don't even work for the government, but they are the warp and the woof of Washington. Individually they are ordinary people, in the same sense that each individual thread of a great tapestry is an ordinary thread, not unlike the thread which is used to sew on pants buttons. But these people of Washington, when woven together and seen as a whole, make a community fabric which is different from the fabric of any other community—anywhere.

The street-corner method of looking at people is never exact, but it is always interesting. At the corner of Fourteenth Street and Pennsylvania Avenue, Washington, across from the Willard Hotel, I stood one day and asked twenty people who they were and what they did. Here they are: A high school girl coming from the Census Bureau where she got some figures for a term paper. A Negro dishwasher. An elevator operator who worked for the Farm Credit Administration. A bookkeeper in a department store. A housewife who had bought four sunsuits for her 3-year-old Bonnie Sue. A radio engineer from station WINX. A government stenographer who had been getting her hair set. A taxi driver who was shopping for his wife. A messenger in the FBI. A real estate salesman who had been looking up a title. A Negro woman who worked as a charwoman in the Department of Commerce. A teacher who was going to the National Theater to get a block of tickets for her class. A young man just out of high school, who worked for a window washing company. A Negro yard man who had come from Bolgiano's where he "got a poison stick to kill dandelions with." A linotype operator going to work on the *Post*. A young woman file clerk who worked at the Department of Labor. A woman who kept war boarders and roomers, and who had just bought a preserving kettle. A telephone man, hurrying to a number that reported always busy. A colored man who was a waiter during the week and preached on Sundays. A tailored woman who said it was nobody's business who she was or what she did.

95

That street-corner census proves nothing. It may not even be a typical cross section of Washington people. But anyway, there are twenty Washingtonians, and not a senator, not a congressman, not a bureau chief among them. And not one of them ever gets his or her name into the newspapers of other cities.

They Live, They Breathe, They Breed

The vital statistics about Washington people contain some notable superlatives which might be suitable for a chamber of commerce booster booklet except for the fact that a few of the notable points are superlatively non-booster. For better or for worse, here are some of the facts:

Population is about 1,150,000. This includes about 825,000 within the boundaries of the District of Columbia, and about 325,000 in the Maryland and Virginia suburbs, which immediately adjoin the District and which for practical purposes are integral parts of the city. At the time of the 1940 census, it ranked eleventh in population among American cities, and thirteenth among metropolitan areas. Now it ranks eighth as a city, and eleventh as a metropolitan area. Thus it is what is called a "large city."

Whites number about 600,000, Negroes about 225,000, in the city proper. The proportion of Negroes is approximately 28 per cent. This is the highest percentage of any large or comparable city in the United States. Washington is the fourth largest Negro city in the world. Only New York, Chicago, and Philadelphia have larger aggregate numbers of Negroes, and they are much larger cities. Some cities of the deep South have higher percentages, but they are smaller cities. Washington is proportionately "blacker" than any such large city in the world.

There are more women than men in Washington—ten women to every nine men. The "man content" of the population is the smallest of any big city, for in most communities the men outnumber the women. Thus Washington, statistically, is "womany." It contains a higher-than-normal proportion of women who once would have been called "old maids" and who now are known as "bachelor girls." They are numerous because of the large number of young women who come to Washington to take clerical jobs with the government. Many of them find husbands here, but many don't.

Divorced women are a higher percentage of the population in Washington than in most cities, but this is not the fault of Washington, for they come from elsewhere to get jobs, when the husbands, elsewhere, pass out of the picture.

Women work in Washington—45 per cent of all the adult women work at jobs outside their homes, and make money to bring to their homes. The streetcars in morning and evening show more women than you will see

96

in the streetcars of any other big city, for the women are going to work, or coming from work. Even the work is "womany."

The birth rate is about average for big cities.

The foreign born? Consider that Washington is an eastern city, and that in most eastern cities the foreign born are numerous. Guess on Washington, and you are likely to be wrong, for the foreign born population of Washington is only 6 per cent. This is a lower percentage than in such typically interior cities as Des Moines, Salt Lake City, Denver, and Lincoln, Nebraska. Washington is predominantly a city of native Americans, counting in its black natives.

Illiteracy is only 1 per cent, as compared with 4.3 per cent for the whole nation. Even the illiteracy rate among Negroes of Washington is only 4 per cent. Whatever else may be said of Washingtonians, it may truly be said that a phenomenally large proportion of them can read and write.

As for health, the records show one superlative blot. The tuberculosis death rate is the highest of all large cities. This comes from the Negroes in their crowded alley dwellings. As for white people, their health is normally good, or normally bad, with nothing noteworthy except the larger-than-average amount of sinus trouble which is supposed to come from the hot humid climate of sea level.

So there you have some of the facts of life about Washington.

They Work, They Earn, They Spend

See what the people of Washington do for a living, how much money they make and how they spend it, and how much better off they are, on the average, than those millions who live elsewhere than in the lustrous city on the Potomac.

If you should happen to think that Washingtonians appreciate their economic good fortune, put the thought out of your mind, for it's a false thought. If you would understand these Washingtonians, you must understand their great ingenuity in grumbling about the jobs, the wages, the traffic, and the living conditions in Washington. Of course, their cost of living is high. In normal times, it is neck and neck with New York's as highest in the country, and even during the wartime price rise throughout the nation, it stays in the top brackets among big cities. Still Washingtonians have more of the material things than the average people of most other cities. They have more, but they yell more.

One-third of the people who work in Washington work for the government, and most of the other two-thirds work for the people who work for the government. There are 275,000 government workers, and they are one-third of all who are gainfully employed in and around the capital. The

97

two-thirds are butchers, bakers, store clerks, truck drivers, charwomen, maids, lawyers, motormen, newspapermen, doctors, dentists, nurses, teachers, taxi drivers, street sweepers, telephone linemen, policemen, fish peddlers, janitors, chair menders, and followers of all the other miscellaneous occupations which go to make up the work of a city. It is often thought that most people in Washington work for the government, but most people in Washington do NOT.

Still, the biggest single block are government employees. They dominate the city. The business of the city is run for them. It hangs on them and their pay rolls. It is government pay that supplies the blood which courses through the business veins, and which supports, directly or indirectly, the greater part of a million persons.

The average family income in Washington is higher than the average for most other cities, big and little, and it is double the average for the country as a whole. Washingtonians file more income tax returns, in relation to the population, than the people of any other big city. This record is maintained despite the statistical drag of the large Negro population, whose income is relatively low. Most people live in good houses in Washington. Sixty-seven per cent of the homes are estimated to be worth $7500 or more, whereas the average value of homes in your own city is probably not anywhere near as much. Of course, real estate values are high in Washington, so that a $7500 house in Washington is not as good as a $7500 house in the average city. Many people in Washington live in row houses, built solidly together like books on a shelf, as in Baltimore or Philadelphia. But even these row houses have one or two bathrooms, and rank as "middle-class."

Retail sales are the highest per capita of any large city. And bargain days are popular. Friday, with store-wide markdowns, is the biggest buying day. Wednesday is second, because of its special bargains advertised the day before. And Saturday is always good. But on any day, you'll see plenty of women barging up and down the main shopping thoroughfares of F Street and Seventh Street, or bustling through the smaller stores of Connecticut Avenue or the outlying neighborhood shopping centers.

Telephones per capita are second highest in the whole world, and the per capita volume of phone calls is highest.

There is one passenger car to every four persons (or *was*, just before the war), which is the second highest rate among the big cities of the nation. Los Angeles, which is first, has one car to every three persons, but Los Angeles is a sprawly city, where the distances are greater and the business less concentrated than in Washington. Many smaller cities have more automobiles per capita than Washington.

People of Washington are clean in their clothes. This may sound like a puffer, but it's a fact. First, the city has practically no factories which make smoke, and the streets are kept exceptionally clean. Second proof is that laundry and dry cleaning businesses flourish in Washington. Most workers are office workers, not factory workers. Standard uniforms of male Washingtonians are two-pants suits, not overalls. No wonder the laundry and cleaning industry regards Washington as its prize city. Even the diaper wash laundry business in Washington is good, for women who work don't have time to wash their babies' diapers, and they send them to the special diaper laundry, for a dollar or two per week.

Some people say that the women of Washington are the best-dressed women in the world—on the average for *all* the women in the city, and not merely as applying to the concentrations of well-dressed women such as those seen on Fifth Avenue, New York, or Grant Avenue, San Francisco. Not having seen all the women in all the cities of the world, I am in no position to say that Washington women rank first, but here are a few facts which seem to support the theory: Women in Washington make their own money, in high proportion. Their husbands or fathers make more than the average. The women are office workers, whose standard attire is on the dressy side. In their daily office work they are associated closely with men, and women dress up for men. Furthermore, their advancement in their work always depends to some indeterminable extent on how they look in their clothes. And, finally, the women workers are mainly young women, who are often inclined to spend more on their backs than older women.

When you think of labor unions, you normally think of mills and factories. Inasmuch as Washington has few of these, you might think that Washington would be a non-union town. But it isn't. It's a strong union town. Labor unions have 160,000 members in the District of Columbia, and this is high for a city of its size. The AFofL unions have 140,000, the independent unions, 10,000, and the CIO unions, 10,000. Of the total of 160,000, the largest numbers are in the building trades. Nearly one-third, or 50,000, are in unions of government workers, mainly white collar workers. The remaining union members are in miscellaneous occupations.

The upper-income classes of Washington seldom dream that their city is so strongly union. They think of unionism as something to be studied from afar, in other cities. They do not know that their own city is more highly unionized than many mill towns. In normal times, they do not see many local strikes, for there are no strikes against government, and the building trades unions seldom need to strike.

Drinking of hard liquor is a more important avocation in Washington than in most cities. The per capita consumption of alcohol is high, and it probably is the highest in the nation, although actual statistics by cities are not available. Washington liquor stores sell more distilled spirits than are sold in the entire state of Maryland, which includes the big city of Baltimore, and one-fourth as much as the whole state of California, whose population is seven times as great as Washington's.

There are reasons why Washington is one of the drinkingest of all cities. First, income is relatively high and people can afford their liquor. Second, there is a fairly high per capita rate of that commodity known as leisure. This promotes sipping, and in the long run more alcohol is downed by sipping than by gulping. Third, there is a great deal of sociability in Washington. People flock together in parties, big and little, as a regular feature of their lives in getting along in a governmental city, and where there are parties, there is apt to be liquor. People do their drinking in homes and hotels, more than in night clubs or bars. There are very few night clubs, and there are no bars of the stand-up variety, for they are prohibited by Washington local law. You can sit down and buy a drink, but you cannot stand up at it. This is supposed to promote temperance, although a good many people of Washington are confused over the theory, for they find they can sit longer than they can stand.

Gambling is practiced regularly, daily, by a very high percentage of Washingtonians of all classes. Most of it is by the "numbers" game. A penny, a nickel, a dime, or quarter will purchase a "ticket" from any of the thousands of "runners" who are the retail agents for the numbers business. You pick a three-digit number out of your mind or the air, and if this number comes out in the payoffs at the race track, you win. You have one chance in 999 of winning, but, still, enough people hit the winning number every day to keep some hundreds of thousands of Washingtonians on edge and in the game from time to time. Whites play the game, but Negroes are the mainstay. Negro maids sometimes get fired for being too much preoccupied with their prospects for luck, but they also often get their mistresses to playing. The numbers racket and horse race betting are big business in Washington, although undercover.

Prostitution is not conspicuous in Washington, because there is no segregated district. But it flourishes just the same, in a number of houses and freelancers' apartments.

The People Play

Movies are No. 1 form of indoor recreation for Washingtonians. It is a "good movie town." The taste and demand are relatively high grade. No double bills or bank nights or premiums are needed to whet the appetites, as in some towns. The big downtown movie houses are usually jammed inside, with waiting lines outside, despite the fact that Washington is not a "night life city." People don't ordinarily flock to the bright lights, for there aren't many. After the movie, people yawn and go home to bed.

As for legitimate theaters, there is only one, the old National. Yet theater men regard Washington as a "good show town," for a play never folds up in Washington, and nearly all are box office successes. Washingtonians grumble at length about their legitimate theater opportunities, for they contrast themselves with New Yorkers. But the truth is that Washington has more and better shows than other cities of its size, and most of its plays come directly from New York. Among stage people, Washington audiences are known as notoriously cold and clammy. They are stingy with their hand clapping, and they don't whoop and holler as much as audiences in other cities. It isn't because Washington people are cool and reserved, but because they think they are sophisticated.

There's one burlesque house, the Gayety, located on Ninth Street, Washington's frowzy imitation of a "gay white way." The Gayety dispenses the usual legs, busts, navels and off-color jokes, plus the strip-tease techniques of such artists as Ann Corio, Margie Hart, Renee, and Hinda Wassau. There's no audience timidity here, and many a public man has done his full share to contribute to the stamping of feet and the whistling through the teeth. After the show you can find a near-by eating and drinking joint, or step up the street and improve your aim at a shooting gallery, along with lonesome-looking soldiers and sailors on leave who are trying hard to have a good time, and not succeeding very well.

As for sports, there are two kinds in Washington, as everywhere: The pay-sit-&-look kind, and the play-it-yourself kind. Both do well, but pay-sit-&-look does better.

There's baseball in the afternoon, and some evenings, at the stadium in the heart of the black belt of Washington, with Clark Griffith's American League "Senators," who are usually well down toward the cellar. The fans do their share of griping, and every few years you hear them complain that Washington is "first in war, first in peace, and last in the American League." But they continue to pay and go. Washington is a good baseball town. A good way to see a real live senator or congressman in the flesh is to go to a baseball game on a peak day, for they slip away from the sessions of Congress like boys playing hookey from school, sometimes leaving behind them the word that they have "gone out of town for the day."

There's professional football in the fall, with the "Redskins," whose owner is George Marshall, who also owns one of Washington's biggest laundries, and who has Corinne Griffith of movie fame as a wife.

There's horse racing at four major Maryland tracks—Laurel, Bowie, Pimlico (Baltimore), and Havre de Grace—and at some minor tracks.

From Washington at noon on racing days flocks of men and women go out —on special trains, in special busses, and in long lines of private cars. There's boxing on Mondays, with a normal number of bouts between punch-drunk punks, and an occasional good fight. Washington fans got a look-in on the big time when they watched Joe Louis knock out Buddy Baer (the first time). There's wrestling on Thursday nights, sometimes at the Uline Arena and sometimes at Turner's Arena, affectionately known as "Arnica Hall." There's professional ice hockey, and basketball, and midget auto racing. As a town for the sports business, Washington is improving, even in wartime.

Among the amateur sports, golf comes first. Washington has so many country clubs that in times of even slight depression they have trouble supporting themselves. Practically anyone who owns a $5.95 sweater and a pair of sport shoes can belong to a country club. And there are a great many sweaters and sport shoes in Washington, although few of their owners belong to anything so swank as the Chevy Chase Club.

Water sports come second. There's the annual President's Cup Regatta for speedboats and small sailboats (now called off to conserve gasoline). In the months that the champions are not racing there are small motorboats that putt-putt on the Potomac. And there are canoes that make a good cheap ride for anyone. As for swimming, it is done in pools with which Washington abounds. The Potomac River has its place in the history books, but it does not do for Washington what the Thames does for England, or the Seine for Paris, or the Rhine for Germany, or the Danube for those countries in the Balkans. To Washingtonians the Potomac is noted chiefly for being "too dirty to swim in."

So the swimmers and the boaters and the summer cottagers flock across country to the Chesapeake Bay and its multitudinous inlets, thirty or forty miles away. There, in the neighborhood of Annapolis, they boat, and swim, and fish and fight mosquitoes, and trail back home on Sunday nights in a traffic line that inches along, with the wife who got sunburned and cut a finger while scaling the fish, and the kids asleep on the back seat.

Baseball is so popular in the sandlot government leagues that a good player is sometimes given a soft stockroom job so he can play for the team and keep its league standing high. There's bowling, too, for Washington is one of the bowlingest cities in the entire nation. The city supports more than 800 alleys, at 20 cents a string, and thousands of Washingtonians get so good at bowling that they don't have cramps in the calves the next day. For people of the upper crust, or people who aspire to the upper crust, horseback riding is common, especially in Rock Creek Park.

Collegiate football and other sports are plentiful in and around Washington, for there are teams from Georgetown, George Washington, American, Catholic, and Maryland (in a suburb of Washington). Technically the college sports are second rate, and some alumni of the big universities of the East or the Middle West call them third rate. Lacrosse is an exception, for at near-by University of Maryland, St. John's, the Naval Academy, and Johns Hopkins is the best lacrosse in the world. One of the biggest sporting events of the year for Washington is the annual Army-Navy football game. It is a classic which belongs to Washington, because of the presence here of the high Army and Navy officers, but it is never played in Washington.

As for winter sports, there are none to speak of, for the climate is too seldom wintery. About once a winter the reflecting pool between the Washington Monument and the Lincoln Memorial freezes tight, and for a few days the town's good skaters (and also the town's weak ankles) can get their cheeks red without necessarily reflecting upon either Lincoln or Washington.

And then, too, there's cheap tennis, cheap golf on municipal links, free playgrounds for children, free parks, free picnic grounds, and free courses for bicycling and roller skating under the Japanese cherry trees. Tens of thousands of Washingtonians play. By play standards, it's a wholesome city, and the playing goes on even during war.

Also Culture—of a Sort

If you are from a small city or a town, you doubtless feel that Washington has that vague and intangible quality known as culture. Certainly it looks polished on the surface, and the people of Washington are exposed to the opportunities which make for culture. Yes, there *is* culture here, big blobs of it, but it is of transplanted varieties. It has been carted in from someplace else. It is watered and cared for, and it grows a few roots, but it doesn't take deep root, and it doesn't produce an abundance of bloom and fruit. What there is seems of the hothouse varieties. The city does not grow much native culture of its very own.

Take Art, for example. There are quantities of famous paintings made by artists of other lands, and of other American cities, and they are on view in the National (Mellon) Gallery, the Corcoran, the Phillips and the Freer. But do Washingtonians flock to the art galleries in great droves? They do not. The visitors are mainly the out-of-towners, who are "doing" Washington.

There's an Arts Club, and its members are artists or would-be artists of one variety or another. It holds minor exhibitions, but has been noted chiefly for its annual Bal Boheme.

Literature is read in Washington, but not produced in any notable quantities. Of course the city has writers galore, but they are largely craftsmen, writing of politics, or economics, or journalistic observations—subjects that are not usually included in the rarefied realm of "literature." Only a few persons in Washington are currently among the literary noted. The other writers out of Washington, the journalists and economists and social philosophers, don't turn out much art, but occasionally produce some thinking. David Cushman Coyle is doubtless the best-known provocative social writer of the New Deal brand.

In music, the city is outgrowing its old reputation of a "cultural desert." There are concerts of the National Symphony Orchestra all year round, outdoors and indoors. And there's summer chamber music, put on by C. C. Cappel, and week-long stands of first-rate ballet and second-rate opera. There are concerts all winter in Constitution Hall, and special programs put on by small groups in other halls. At the Library of Congress, there are the Elizabeth Sprague Coolidge chamber music concerts, that used to be "veddy veddy exclusive," but now draw many music lovers who ride the streetcars daily. Washington's music isn't world-beating, and it isn't third-rate. It's somewhere in between.

As for amateur drama, there's plenty of it—in school and college auditoriums, in fraternal halls, and at the open-air Sylvan Theater on the Washington Monument grounds. And there's semi-pro drama, by the Civic Theatre and the two summer barn theater groups.

They Go to Church

People of Washington are just average churchgoers. The attendance record compared with that of many other cities is no better and no worse. It is a well-churched city, for many denominations have taken pains to build noble edifices for display in the nation's capital.

Look first at the whites: Catholics are strong and numerous. Their churches have 155,000 members. Methodists are second, with 25,000. Baptists are third, with 19,000, a large proportion of whom are up from the South. Episcopalians are fourth, with 18,000, which makes a higher ranking for Episcopalians in Washington than in most cities, and which seems to indicate that the social respectability of the Episcopal church has a special attraction for the old-time residents of Washington. Presbyterians are fifth with 13,500, and the Jewish synagogues bring up the rear with about 10,000 members.

Negro churches have more drawing power than white churches. About half of all the 225,000 Negroes go to church at least once a week. Some churches have services every night. At Elder Michaux's neon-lighted

Church of God, the congregation can sing "Happy Am I" and whoop it up in the amen corner any night of the week. And at Bishop C. M. "Daddy" Grace's church, on the order of Father Divine's "heavens," there are nightly "praise services." But most of the Negro congregations are more staid, and meet for Sunday services. Baptists are biggest, with 50,000 members, and 127 congregations. Methodists come second, with 22,000 members. Third, with 10,000, are the colored Catholics, whose masses are celebrated by white priests. Presbyterians are fourth, with 3,000 members, and the Episcopalians fifth, with 2,200. The rest, the strays, worship in offshoot groups like the Fire Baptized Holiness Church of the Americas, the Love Ye Christ Spiritual Temple, and the United Holy Church of America, Incorporated.

Washington Is Middle-Class

The people who make up Washington are largely middle-class, with merely a few upper-class dignitaries in the show window. To say that Washington is a middle-class city is neither an apology nor a boast. It is merely one of those facts to be absorbed by anyone who would understand the city and its people. It is not proletarian—it is middle-class. It is not rich and swanky—it is middle-class.

Middle-class in average income, but bordering on the upper middle. That makes it prosperous.

Mainly middle-class in temperament, in habits of thinking, in spiritual approaches to life and ways of living. The people go to church but tolerate widespread gambling, so long as it is kept beneath the surface. The people have nice little yards, and bits of lawns, that are well kept. They send their children to schools which have few frills. They like an extra bathroom, or at least a lavatory. They prefer movies to art galleries. They shy at modernistic houses. They would rather have their children wholesome than intellectual. They read the *Saturday Evening Post* much, and the *Nation* a little. They own their homes and keep them painted.

They come to Washington from everywhere, and that is the reason why Washington people are typically middle-class. The really forceful leaders of communities out around the country don't gravitate to Washington to any notable extent in normal times, for they have positions built for themselves at home, and they are needed in the community. The lower-class people don't come, for they are mainly people who work with their hands, and Washington has only limited opportunities for people who work with their hands. So it is the middle-class folks who come to Washington, mainly to get jobs with the government, and they make Washington. Naturally they cling to their middle-class ways.

Native Sons and Daughters

At parties, or wherever people meet in Washington, the standard question asked of strangers is, "Where do you come from?" The per capita sale of out-of-town newspapers in Washington is largest of any city in the United States. People tend to keep their roots, their votes, their sentimental attachments in their own home towns, whence they came. And so the native Washingtonian, the man or woman born and reared here, is an object of affectionate jibes. He or she is looked upon as a rare specimen.

The native sons and daughters in turn look on the influx of newcomers as a nuisance and a blight. They resent the intrusions of "outsiders," who complain about the city. For example, there's John E. Ryerson, a lawyer-reporter, a native son. He helped work on this book, but he disapproved of some of the things said about Washington, so he wrote a dissent, in which he said:

"Sure we have our shortcomings and troubles in Washington, just the same as other places. But most of our troubles are made by the outsiders, and we take the blame. We don't have it soft, for we must try to run our city and do our job while impeded by outsiders, who say so much and do so little. You can't convince us that their complaints don't come a good deal from downright jealousy. They wish their home town were as good as ours. It frequently occurs to some of us Washington natives that if this city does not please some of the outsiders (I mention no names), we would be happy to have them go back where they came from."

Some Go Soft

Life in Washington isn't exactly a feather bed, and it isn't a Garden of Eden, but somehow it is easy. The average income is high—a gift from the people of the nation whose average income is lower. Life and living habits are grooved. There are few social or economic earthquakes, or torrents, or tornadoes. Existence for the average citizen and government worker is placid, like a smooth-flowing river. The community never girds itself for great emergency tasks, such as meeting tremendous problems of local unemployment, or getting new industries to move to town, or reforming the local school system. Jobs are never hanging on bushes, but they are usually more plentiful than in other cities, because the main industry of government never shuts down, and never precipitates a truly great crisis. Most people who work for government are protected by civil service. It is hard to fire them. Some can and do soldier on the job and still hold the job. Life is regularized, and sometimes monotonous. There is a lower degree of struggle than prevails in most other cities.

Perhaps prestige has something to do with the habit of coasting. Every person has a certain measure of proper prestige, but Washington people have a little extra measure added on, merely because they are from the great city of Washington, D. C. This is flattering, and a little slice of it may be warranted, but the trouble is that Washingtonians are apt to take the added prestige at face value. Many a young Washingtonian, visiting or going to school elsewhere, entitled to two bits' worth of personal prestige, actually gets four bits' worth for being from Washington. This does something to people, old and young alike, but especially to the young whose sense of values is flexible.

Washington as a city has produced few notable citizens from its natives. There's John Philip Sousa, and J. Edgar Hoover, and Al Jolson, and Helen Hayes, and Duke Ellington, and that's about where the list ends. Kate Smith is also considered a Washingtonian, although she was born in Virginia. Other widely known men and women of whom the city boasts were adults when they came here. They were not indigenous.

．　　．　　．　　．　　．

Your impression of a city often depends upon what you look for. When people come to Washington, they usually look for big men, and big buildings, and big events. They pitch their gaze on that plane, and so they don't see some of the littler things, or if they see them, they don't remember them. But it is not the parks that make the city of Washington. It is not the pillars of stone, or the monuments to the dead. It is not even the living statesmen. They may be the luminous ornaments, and they may make the reputation, but they are not the body of Washington. The body consists of the people you have just met, the people who live and work at jobs, and go home at night to their families or boarding houses. People who save up for vacations, and work in offices, and run streetcars, and look around for better jobs, and go to movies and church, and know someone who knows someone who is Important. These are the people of Washington.

II

Log of a Day

I T TAKES a lot of goings on to make a day for Washington, and most of them are chores. If you could stay awake around the clock, and be here and there and everywhere at once, you would see the goings on as recorded in this log. You may find them the same as in your own home town, or you may find some of them different, but in either case you will see that the chores are real, and that the town is not made of cake.

5:00 a.m.

Watchman at water-front fish market sees first buyers arrive from the city restaurants.

Charwomen who clean congressmen's offices start toward Capitol Hill.

6:00 a.m.

Representative Graham (Pa.), earliest of the early birds among members of Congress, arrives at his office.

Street cleaners with tank washers finish work after being on the job since 11 p.m.

Hotel day clerks come on duty to cope with droves of people trying to get rooms in Washington.

7:00 a.m.

Veterans at Soldiers' Home sit down to breakfast.

First commuters who travel to work by train from homes in Virginia and Maryland start pouring through Union Station.

Staffs of afternoon newspapers begin the daily grind.

8:00 a.m.

Last bit of free parking space along streets of the Mall and the Ellipse is taken by the shift of government workers who start work at 8:15. (Parkers find space more plentiful as tires wear out.)

Capital Transit Company's streetcars and busses go all out to handle rush of traffic which continues until about 9 o'clock.

Distribution completed of overnight accumulation of mail addressed to senators and representatives.

Vanguard of members of Congress arrive at offices: Senators Reynolds, Austin and George; and Representatives Doughton (N. C.), Ludlow (Ind.), Moser (Pa.), Plumley (Vt.), Cannon (Mo.), Knute Hill (Wash.), and Lewis (Colo.).

Government workers pile into drugstores and cafeterias for quick dabs of breakfast.

Donald Nelson on his way to office for a day of 37 interviews.

Mail carriers have half an hour's work behind them.

Rehearsals for stage shows begin at the Capitol and Earle movie houses.

Federal building guards change shifts.

Day shift of city firemen goes on duty.

Mailing of *Congressional Record* is completed at Government Printing Office.

Taxi drivers who regularly haul federal employees to work in groups of three and four pull up in front of rooming houses.

President Roosevelt opens his eyes, no matter how late into the night he worked.

Long strings of busses move across Highway and Key Bridges, loaded with workers who live in Virginia.

Day shift on White House telephone switchboard goes on duty.

9:00 a.m.

Washington Monument opens to tourists. (The phone is Republic 1820.)

National Museum and Corcoran Gallery of Art open.

Secretary Hull arrives at office.

President Roosevelt's working day gets under way in his bedroom, with dictation and conferences with members of his immediate official family.

Operators of big outdoor parking lots hang out their "all full" signs.

Washington correspondents representing afternoon newspapers start pounding out their "by-line" stories.

10:00 a.m.

Traffic Court opens.

President Roosevelt goes to his office desk in west wing of the White House.

Morning rubberneck tours start.

Charles Evans Hughes starts out on his daily constitutional along Massachusetts Avenue near Sheridan Circle.

Board of Commissioners of the District of Columbia meets in the District Building.

Treasury Department issues its daily statement on financial condition of the government.

Steve Vasilakos, the peanut man, wheels his cart into position near the northeast corner of the White House grounds.

A scientist-physician at the National Institute of Health checks to see how his experiment is coming along.

Rush of morning's incoming air traffic from New York ends.

Steve Early, presidential secretary, meets newsmen following his early-morning talk with the President.

Meetings of Senate and House congressional committees start. Some members are late.

President starts on schedule of appointments, each caller getting fifteen minutes or perhaps a half hour.

11:00 a.m.

Weather Bureau makes forecast based on 8:30 a.m. observations.

First shows at downtown movie houses begin, and lines of early patrons move in from the sidewalks.

Government workers' half-hour lunch periods start.

Staff meetings convene in emergency units of government.

First editions of afternoon newspapers hit the streets.

12:00 noon

Washington Stock Exchange closes after a 45-minute session.

White House kitchen prepares luncheon for President and guests.

Naval Observatory gives time signal for the whole United States and ships at sea.

Guard changes at the Unknown Soldier's Tomb on heights of Arlington.

Senate and House sessions open.

1:00 p.m.

President Roosevelt and luncheon guest sit down to noonday snack in Chief Executive's office.

Usual hour for "off the record speeches" at National Press Club lunches.

Lions, tigers and wolves at zoo start looking for the keeper who brings their food.

Cars of mid-day shoppers fill the few remaining spaces in retail district's parking lots.

2:00 p.m.

Rubberneck busses get going for afternoon tours.

Cabinet meeting (Friday).

President Roosevelt gets started on afternoon of conferences.

Banks close. (Except on government pay days, when they close at 5:30.)

Oyster boat from Chesapeake Bay arrives at dock and starts unloading.

3:00 p.m.

Batches of federal workers who came to work at 7:30 in the morning under the staggered system are beginning to get ready to quit at 3:30.

Distribution of mail to homes is nearly finished.

4:00 p.m.

Outpouring of homeward bound clerks blocks all exits from government buildings.

Public clinic at health center clears last of the day's patients.

Policemen change shifts (other changes come at midnight and 8:00 a.m.).

Government clerks who play the numbers game ask messengers, "What was the number today?"

Newsmen gather at White House for one of the President's two semi-weekly press conferences.

Federal building guards change shifts.

Washington Monument closes to tourists.

Sales office of Superintendent of Documents makes last over-the-counter sale of the day.

5:00 p.m.

Busses line up end to end for two blocks in front of Munitions Building (War Department) on Constitution Avenue.

Cocktail parties get going.

Rubberneckers begin returning from their tourings.

Outgoing air traffic to New York reaches afternoon peak.

Evening meal at Soldiers' Home finds old-timers arguing over war strategy as revealed by afternoon papers.

Evening students grab bites to eat before going to first class.

Washington radio news commentators whip notes into shape for early-evening broadcasts.

House and Senate get ready to quit.

Commuter trains pull out of Union Station with Washington workers who live in Virginia and Maryland, some as far away as Baltimore.

Newspaper carriers wind up distribution of home editions in suburban areas.

6:00 p.m.

Cocktail party late arrivals get under way.

Attorney General finishes dictation and signing of mail, starts for home.

Steamer for Norfolk gets ready to pull out.

President Roosevelt leaves office, passing swimming pool, and sometimes takes a dip.

Night shift of city firemen goes on duty.

7:00 p.m.

Secretary of Agriculture is on way home from office after having been at work since 8:30.

Line-up of criminals and suspects starts at police headquarters.

Phone calls hit peak, with local callers making dates and long-distance callers taking advantage of cheaper rates.

8:00 p.m.

Meetings of citizens' associations, businessmen's groups and civilian defense bodies convene all around the town.

President Roosevelt starts on his home work of correspondence and reports brought over from his office in a big wire basket.

9:00 p.m.

First editions of morning newspapers hit the street.

Fashionable dinners wind up, making late arrivals at theaters and concerts.

Rep. Cannon (Mo.), who got to office around eight in the morning, closes up and goes home.

10:00 p.m.

Liquor stores close (hour set by law).

Employees in Division of Loans and Currency of the Treasury Department change shifts on work of counting, mailing and distributing war bonds.

Senator Mead (N. Y.), late worker of the Senate, calls it a day.

11:00 p.m.

Sidewalks on F Street fill up with crowds from last shows in movie houses.

President Roosevelt clears up last of home work, gets ready to spend an hour in reading or arranging stamp collection before going to sleep.

Street cleaning department's flushing tanks start washing the streets.

New shift at Bureau of Engraving and Printing settles down to extra work on defense bonds, government checks and warrants.

12:00 midnight

Federal building guards change shifts.

Hotel doormen take off their fancy uniforms, yawn, go home.

Shifts in War and Navy Department offices quit for the night.

1:00 a.m.

Night's last busload of soldiers returning to Fort Belvoir, down the Potomac River in Virginia, leaves Tenth and D Streets, NW.

Charwomen finish their work.

2:00 a.m.

Sale of liquor in night clubs comes to deadline set by law.

Man who controls streetcar switches at Fifteenth Street and New York Avenue climbs down ladder from control house and goes off duty.

3:00 a.m.

Night shift in offices of United States Conciliation Service, Department of Labor, is still in middle of a batch of work.

Morning newspapers' staffs leave offices as presses roll off home editions.

4:00 a.m.

Cab drivers who started cruising around in mid-afternoon knock off for the night and go home.

And so another day.

12

The City Civic

SHIELD your eyes from the dazzle of national affairs in Washington and you see a city which has much in common with any city of a million population. It has tax problems, dog catchers, public band concerts, gambling and street parades. Also police department shake-ups, church socials, garbage collectors, parking troubles, and community chest solicitations. It has traffic jams, crowded schools, anti-noise crusades, prostitution, sewage disposal difficulties and businessmen's clubs. It has almost everything, but not quite.

It's what you *won't* find in Washington, though you search from the White House to the slaughterhouse, from the water front to the thresholds of embassies, that makes you sit up and take notice. You won't find a ward heeler—not even a ward. There's nothing that comes close to being a municipal "machine." No city hall gang. No big-time local graft. Nothing of that sort which marks the ordinary American city with hair on its chest. And all because the government of the District of Columbia—synonymous with the city of Washington—is a political freak, the like of which never again will be born in this country. It's a three-in-one affair—a federal unit, a state and a city all wrapped up in one administrative bundle. Congress, in making appropriations and taking other legislative action, deals with it as though it were a unit of the federal government. It is a sort of "lean-to" on the federal government. It operates as a state in having its own public utilities commission and other gearings of a commonwealth of communities. Finally, and most obviously, it has the general set-up of a municipality. All of which leads to some strange situations. For instance:

Four separate police forces operate within the District, plus the FBI, the Secret Service and special guards for government buildings. A privately-operated hospital stands on ground owned by the federal government, with the cost of its buildings having been shared equally by the federal and District governments. Speed limits for motoring in some of the parks are set by the Secretary of the Interior, while limits elsewhere in the city are established by District authorities. The officials of national parks within the city are not attached to the regular city government and, during an early war blackout, the park road lights burned brightly because city officials forgot to notify park officials to dim them. The zoo is under direction of the Smithsonian Institution. The Acting Director of the Botanic Garden is the Architect of the United States Capitol. Names of streets in the "old city" (planned by L'Enfant) can be changed only by action of Congress.

The District government cannot add a $30-a-week clerk to its working force without getting specific approval of Congress. Ordinances which would scoot through the city council of a regular municipality take the form of bills which have to be enacted by Congress and approved by the President. When the second lend-lease bill was going through Congress, appropriating billions, the District Committee tried to attach an amendment to provide 100 more Washington policemen, and no one thought the rider was funny. The superintendent of the city's schools is named by a school board which is chosen by a set of federal judges, and he is not responsible to the city authorities, although they and the federal budget officials control the school system's purse strings. Control of the water supply is divided between the Chief of Engineers of the Army and District officials. The District Attorney, who handles local criminal cases, is a federal official. These are only a few of the administrative oddities in this municipality which is not a municipality, this state which is not a state, this federal unit which is not a federal unit.

The District Government

You might think this strange set-up would be certain to produce an impossible tangle. But it doesn't. The intricate and involved administration of District affairs moves along with a fair show of efficiency. The District government is headed by three commissioners, appointed by the President for three-year terms, each drawing $9,000 a year. Two are civilians, the third is an Army officer appointed from the Engineer Corps. The civilian commissioners must have maintained bona fide residence in the District for three years immediately preceding appointment. This keeps Johnny-come-lately politicians from grabbing the jobs. Since 1908 the commissioners' offices have been in the District Building (Washingtonese for "city hall"), which is located three blocks from the White House. The future will find them quartered in a new structure built to house the District government offices, closer to the Capitol.

Socially, the commissioners rank fairly well up, but nowhere near the top of the official ladder. At formal dinners, established practice gives them a rank equal to the brigadier generals of the Army, just below the governor of the Federal Reserve Board and just above the vice-governor and members of that agency. They outrank the heads of independent commis-

sions and the secretaries of embassies and legations. But as official glad-
handers, they take a back seat when top-flight notables are guests of the
city. Then the White House and the State Department usually take charge,
especially if royalty is putting in an appearance. (They still talk about the
time a commissioner decked himself out in top hat and claw-hammer coat
when the King and Queen of England visited the capital, only to be shunted
neatly to the fringe of the reception group.)

Holding down a commissionership used to be pretty much of a snap.
One gentleman who had the job a few years ago used to do a lot of his
work on the golf course, discussing public matters while playing with
members of Congress and other officials. In those good old days, the three
District chiefs would meet twice a week and do a lot of lolling between
times. Now they hold regular meetings three times a week, with special
sessions in between. Public meetings are held on matters of high importance to the citizens. The most important discussions do not always draw
the biggest turn-outs of the citizenry. Consideration of a proposed law to
ban jay-walking, for instance, packed the chamber.

New Problems

Washington's tremendous population boom in the last several years, and
especially in the early months of 1942, has brought a mass of new problems
that swarm over the commissioners' desks in the daytime and molest their
minds at odd hours. On top of that they have to deal with a wide range of
national officials, many of whom feel that, as temporary residents of the
District, they have to horn in on the running of the city. The town is full
of important tender toes which it is not wise to step upon. Also the commissioners have to give personal attention to large numbers of citizens who,
in a "normal" city, would just tune in on their aldermen or ward bosses.
There's a powerful reason for the consideration the citizens receive from the
city's heads. Washingtonians don't have the right to vote and don't have
at their disposal the usual means for bringing pressure to bear. The commissioners, recognizing this, make every effort to be fair and responsive.
And there's always the possibility that a chagrined or disgruntled individual
will hop up to the Capitol and prod a senator or representative from his old
home state to pour powerful words over the phone to the District Building.

The course which a proposed law for the District has to follow in reaching
enactment is long and full of twists and turns. Originating with a District
bureau chief, for instance, it has to get the commissioners' approval by a
majority vote, obtain the OK of the federal Bureau of the Budget (even if
it is not a "money measure"), become the object of a lengthy consideration

by congressional committees, go before the houses of Congress for a vote, and, finally, get the President's signature.

Congress—in reality the District's city council—has to pass upon small details of municipal matters. Just to give you an idea, here are some of the measures introduced during the last session: Authorizing a railroad company to build an underpass beneath New York Avenue; providing for issuance of a license "to practice the healing art"; setting aside the trial-board conviction of a policeman; requiring theaters to sell special tickets when only standing room is available; enlarging the powers of the property clerk of the police department; and repealing the provision that one member of the District of Columbia Boxing Commission shall be a member of the police force.

With the determining action on matters of large and small consequence so centered at the Capitol, the District Building is singularly free from crookedness and graft. It may not be as clean as the famous hound's tooth, but it certainly harbors little municipal "dirt." Once in a while, however, the effects of "pull," influencing the "right people" and similar factors are seen in the handling of District affairs at the Capitol.

Members of the congressional committees which are assigned to direct consideration of District legislation sometimes act—or fail to act—on District matters in the light of what voters back home may think. Example: A congressman from the deep South a few years ago narrowly escaped defeat because his political opponent made a campaign issue out of his vote in favor of better living accommodations for Negro inmates in a District institution.

Handling the Money

When it comes to deciding how District money is to be spent, a subcommittee of the House Appropriations Committee does most of the heavy work. Printed hearings on the 1942 District budget filled more than 1,000 pages. Almost a full year usually elapses between the time bureau chiefs at the District Building make up their annual estimates and the time the President signs the bill which authorizes the expenditures.

District officials, under the law, cannot transfer funds from one unit to another, except where loss of life or property is imminent. As a result, men in charge of units whose funds have been unexpectedly drained—particularly the agencies which feed and house inmates of penal and welfare institutions—sometimes have to go to Washington merchants as the end of the fiscal year approaches and ask for supplies "on the cuff."

The cost of running the District government comes to about one million dollars a week. Congress chips in six million dollars a year to offset a vast amount of federal property in the District which is not taxable and to compensate for water supplies, fire protection and other city services for which no direct charge is made. The federal government used to split the cost on a fifty-fifty basis. Later, it reduced its contribution to 40 per cent. Then it adopted the fixed-sum policy, which the taxpayers don't like and against which the local newspapers editorialize. This year Congress is making extraordinary grants of funds to provide additional community facilities required to take care of the wartime influx of population.

The taxes of Washingtonians are about average, and yet they are higher than they would be if the capital did not draw so many national headquarters of large organizations which go tax free because they are non-profit outfits. Most recent figures show property with a total assessed value of more than $112,000,000 was exempt from taxation under those provisions. A weeding out has put a lot of the exempted properties back on the tax rolls, the official action in each case being subject to protest and court decision. Among the institutions which have been reviewed are the American Pharmaceutical Association, National Academy of Sciences, Brookings Institution, American Chemical Society, American Forestry Association, Carnegie Institution, National Geographic Society, the Women's Army and Navy League, and scores of others.

More than two-fifths of the $2,000,000,000 of property in the District is tax exempt. Approximately one-third of all the property in the District, in terms of valuation, is owned by the federal government.

In ordinary times, the city's regular functions roll along like those of any other city. Washington cleans its streets, builds new ones, looks after the public health, educates its children, locks up its criminals, and dishes out relief. But now, in war times, Washington's public services are being strained by the great influx of newcomers, and District officials are tearing their hair over the problems of running a boom city.

The Cops

The District's main law-enforcement body is the Metropolitan Police force of more than 1,600 men and a couple of dozen women officers. It came in for a tremendous amount of local attention in 1941 when a "crime wave"—notable for the number of rapes—and a reorganization of the force splattered over the front pages of Washington newspapers. After it was all over, the force had a new boss, Edward J. Kelly, holding the title of Major and Superintendent, and a new chief of detectives, Richard H. Mansfield, who is also a cartoonist. His drawings of the nostalgic "good old days" have been a Sunday feature in the *Washington Evening Star* for years.

Kelly, a handsome Irishman known for his photographic memory, is a "cop's cop" who set about breaking up "office politics and drag" in the department soon after taking command. The members of the force are civil service employees and supposedly are under the federal merit system of promotion. But in past years the ranking of individual officers has been strongly affected by the favor or disfavor of high government officials.

This has been responsible in large degree for the inefficiency which has plagued the force. Another factor contributing to inefficiency is the presence in the capital of large numbers of high-ranking officials and diplomats with whom policemen hesitate to lock horns. The "sacred cows" have had a way of putting in a display of power at headquarters, to the "embarrassment" of the officer involved. Under the Constitution, no member of Congress, going to or from a session, may be arrested for anything except treason, felony or breach of the peace. Foreign diplomats, their families and employees, similarly are immune. Although they may not legally be arrested, minor officials have sometimes been taken into custody when their identities were not clear. Transgressions can be reported to the State Department. Most officials and diplomats obey the traffic regulations and other minor requirements of the law. Some of them, however, appear to delight in disregarding parking rules and placing their immunities on display.

Washington's crime record is nothing for the city to brag about. But the blame cannot be placed entirely at the door of the police department. For one thing, the capital attracts more than its share of criminally-inclined "floaters." They are harder to detect than the home-town criminals. Also, many crimes are invited by people who come from small communities to government jobs in Washington and who do not realize—until something happens to them—that they cannot trust everybody and suspect nobody as they did back home. Officers attribute many of the sex and assault cases in a recent crime wave to the fact that young women among the newcomers to Washington retained their home-town friendliness.

Veteran police reporters and others in a position to know what they're talking about say that the Washington police force is singularly free from graft. Old-timers in Washington cannot remember a single honest-to-goodness graft probe in the long history of the police department.

Gambling

The gambling situation boils down to this: The city has a great many small-time gamblers but no great rings such as are to be found in other cities of comparable size. Still the volume of gambling is great and, in the middle of 1941, a former head of the Metropolitan Police Department's vice squad placed the total "play" by Washingtonians on the horses and numbers at $15,000,000 a month, or nearly four times as much as it takes to run the city during the same length of time. Numbers "runners" have even been arrested for plying their trade among high school pupils.

The main field for gamblers is federal and District employees. The get-it-easy gentry have a plan which extends credit to such employees up to half of what they make.

Not so very long ago, a map of the District of Columbia was hung on the wall at police headquarters. In it were stuck more than 1,300 pins. Each of those pins represented a building in which it was known there was gambling. The downtown section was covered with pins, and even the swankiest residential sections were not clear. "How come the police know where all those gamblers are operating and don't arrest them?" Here's the official answer as it comes from those who are in the middle of that kind of goings on: The Supreme Court's ruling that wire tapping is illegal as a means of gathering evidence greatly increased the difficulties of the police in "making" gambling cases. Police are forced actually to make a bet before they can make a case stick in court, and the gamblers know how to avoid placing bets for policemen.

The largest gambling house around Washington is "Jimmy La Fontaine's," just over the District boundary in Prince Georges County, Maryland. For many years, it has opened, closed and reopened as conditions well known to Jimmy dictated. One of Jimmy's most cooperative acts has been to close periodically during the Maryland racing seasons so as to avoid competition with the state-taxed tracks.

Prostitution

Prostitution, gambling's twin in big-city vice, flourishes in Washington. Much of it is under a well-organized inter-city "ring" control. A rather recent police estimate set the prostitute population of the capital at 2,000 in the organized trade, exclusive of the free-lance "loners," many of whom are here today and run out of town or in jail tomorrow. The top-notch women operate out of the better hotels and apartment houses and established centers in swanky residential districts, such as upper Connecticut Avenue and Chevy Chase. These aristocrats of their profession rarely, if ever, seek business on the street. They leave that to the lower-caste, free-lancing and unorganized "loners," drawing much of their own high-class trade from the great numbers of men who come to Washington on business.

It has been nearly thirty years since Washington had a segregated "red light" district. That was abolished in 1913 by an act of Congress called the Webb-Kenyon Act. The district was located in the area now covered by the federal triangle of government buildings, between Pennsylvania Avenue and the Mall and extending from Tenth Street to Fifteenth Street, Northwest. It was known as "Hooker's Division" because some of General Joe Hooker's Civil War soldiers had been bivouacked in the area. Some say the women who catered to Hooker's men stayed where they were when the war was over and thus gave the area its start.

Members of the vice squad say they can't break up prostitution in Washington, and that the best they can hope to do is to wage a constant campaign of harassment. When they raid a house of prostitution, the well-financed "ring" sets up another to take its place. Most of the prostitutes who are hailed before local courts are the "loners," who solicit on the streets. Many of them are found to be health menaces. They are jailed or run out of town. The girls who get caught usually are picked up by young police officers just out of training school who ride around the downtown section of the city in the evening, in plain clothes and unmarked autos with Maryland or Virginia tags.

The War Department last year gathered information on prostitution, with the idea of establishing patrols of military police along the streets on which the commercial women solicited most frequently. Many of these streets, however, were in "good" residential areas and the citizens protested against having them placed on display as "infested" areas.

Traffic

Gambling, prostitution and such other problems as may bother Washington all give way to the Great Big Problem of the nation's capital: Traffic. Washington has more automobiles per square mile than any other big city in the United States. And, at the beginning and closing of the working day they all seem to be milling around in the several square miles in which most of the governmental and private office buildings are located. Outdoors, Washington has become a nerve-racking mixture of tooting horns, traffic lights and signs that work at cross purposes, scared pedestrians and auto owners who wonder why they don't leave their cars at home but never do. On the fringes of that mess are perplexed officials and a host of expressive citizens who average at least one alleged solution per head. For the past year, the problem has engaged the energies of the President of the United States, congressional committees, the District commissioners, advisory boards, District traffic officials, the police, leaders of citizens' associations, and all four local newspapers.

Hapless officials long have blamed much of the trouble upon a man who died a century or so ago and whose tomb overlooks the capital from a serene prominence across the Potomac: Pierre L'Enfant. It was he who designed the city and rigged up the unorthodox street system—thoroughfares meeting at strange angles and intersecting by threes, fours and fives at circles.

Late last year, the President and the ranking member of the Board of Commissioners raised their voices almost in unison, calling to New York, almost begging the nation's metropolis to send some experts to untangle the mess. And the citizenry, noting an official inclination to straighten things out, began to take heart.

Civic Washington

When you look around you for what might be called "Civic Washington," you find the usual crop of businessmen's clubs, organizations like the Chamber of Commerce in your town, dozens of citizens' associations, and the venerable Association of the Oldest Inhabitants of the District of Columbia.

Home-grown Washingtonians, though a minority, are more than a sliver of the population. In their civic life, these natives join with the long-time residents who were born elsewhere in following the tried and true American formula. They have their civic leaders who showed a lot of business enterprise and to whose hands may come invitations to serve on the Greater National Capital Committee of the Washington Board of Trade. They have their Prominent Personages who graduated from committee obscurity into the full glow of running the Cherry Blossom Festival or the Fourth of July celebration at the foot of the Washington Monument, or the community Christmas tree lighting. Without fail, they all read the *Evening Star*, the mother hen of all things civic.

Thus, when you shield your eyes from the dazzle of national affairs in Washington, you see a city which has many of the earmarks of the average American municipality of its size. You see a city which was brought into being to serve as the home of the national government and which does the government scrubbing on the back stoop, while the rest of the capital sits out on the front porch and waves at the nation.

13

Business Boomtown

YOUR city has its ups and downs, but Washington has only its ups. Or, at least, its downs are slight and insignificant. Washington grows most in periods when other cities are growing least, and as a business community it thrives best on wars, depressions and other national disasters. In those periods the federal government expands and pumps more money into the business body of the city.

It was the Civil War which transformed Washington from a sprawling town into a swarming city. In our times it was World War I which awakened the city from its sleepiness and set it on its way to being a big city. It was the depression of the 30's, when other cities languished, which made Washington what it is today, a center of more than a million people, with prosperous local business. Now World War II gives a surge to the city and brings still more money to the tills of Washington business. In the grievous decade of the Civil War, Washington's population grew 74 per cent. In the recent decade of the 30's and the Great Depression, it grew 36 per cent. And in the past two years, since the census of 1940, it has grown by nearly another third, almost as much as it did in the whole decade of the 30's.

Disasters pull the heartstrings of people of Washington, but they do not disturb the business purse strings, except to loosen them for the new inflow of wealth. Words of sympathy and deeds of correction flow out from Washington during wars and depressions, but the more they flow out the greater grows the government machinery, and the more purchasing power the city has for its own internal purposes. You do not hear the business voice of Washington raised on behalf of decentralization of a cumbersome and overgrown government. The thought that government might shrink its bureaus, commissions, agencies and personnel becomes a fear-thought, and it makes Washington businessmen shudder.

The local Washington fear of shrinkage of government is usually a false fear. Government these days does not shrink, especially in wartime, when, for every worker shifted out of town, a half a dozen move in. Government never has shrunk materially, except after the first World War, when the spirit was the "return to normalcy." Occasional tries at "economy" have been short-lived, and always accompanied by much publicity and many gestures which make headlines in the hinterlands. When these little spells of temporary shrinkage end, as they always do, new growth starts in government. The new wood becomes permanent. Names of agencies may be changed, functions may be shuffled, but in one way or another the volume of the governing business grows greater, and that means more retail sales, more money in the collective pocket.

Two things make the ordinary business of Washington extraordinary, and in many ways superlative:

1. It does not make, but it buys. The symbol of Washington business is not the smokestack, nor the grease on the arm, nor the callus on the hand. The symbol is the ink stain on the finger, the office desk, and the sales counter in the store.

2. It has high income, and steady income.

Easy Come, Easy Go

People in Washington spend their money as they make it, quite like people everywhere, but there's this difference: People in other communities are always more conscious of material ups and downs in life, and this has a tendency to restrain them in their spending, even sometimes when the earning is "going good." They have in the backs of their minds the rainy day. People of Washington, on the average, have less acute fear of the rainy day, because of stability of their jobs and their incomes. So they spend. (Why not?) Per capita income in Washington was $1,022 a year as compared with the national figure of $573 in 1940, most recent year for which reliable figures have been computed. The capital, having few factories and not being a distribution center, is essentially a "retail city." It is a leader, year after year, among the nation's big cities in per capita retail sales. Pay days are boom days, and every week brings a pay day for some groups of government workers. Thus every week is a boom week, a plateau week, and nearly every year a boom year, a plateau year. The seasonal dips are like seasonal dips everywhere; but they are less consequential. The steady rain of pay checks on the broad field of government employees produces a continuing harvest of prosperity for Washington merchants.

The nature of a city can often be determined by those of its businesses which are particularly good. They show what people buy, and, after all, what people buy is a reliable index to their culture. Here are some business lines which are far better in Washington than in comparable cities:

Liquor, jewelry, objects of art, cosmetics, books, tailored clothes.

Here are some other badges, in the form of businesses which do well in comparison with other cities:

Dance orchestras, caterers, dress suit renters, florists, dance academies, music instructors, portrait photographers, beauty shops, barber shops, laundries, cleaning and dyeing establishments, camera dealers, typewriter dealers, public stenographers, bowling alleys, automobiles, hotels, restaurants, and groceries.

Beauty shops, including shoppes, have doubled since 1933 (Beautiful people). Barber shops have increased by 40 per cent (Haircut city). Chain restaurant systems, with parking alongside, have grown prodigiously (Eating-out people). Bookstores sell a high proportion of non-fiction (Serious thinkers). Taxicab fares are cheap, with 30-cent base rate (Scurrying people).

Few Factories

As for factories, there are a few: The Government Printing Office, near the Union Station. The U. S. Naval Gun Factory which makes big guns, in the southeast quarter of Washington. The U. S. Naval Torpedo Station in Alexandria, a Virginia suburb six miles down the river. All big, all government owned and operated. Of private industries, there are also a few: A paper company, a sand and gravel company, a flour mill, all in Georgetown, along the river front, where switch engines bump cars within sight of the Washington Monument, and within smelling distance of the gas works. There are also small factories which make soda straws, artificial legs, workmen's clothing, precision instruments, bottle caps, and brassieres. There are three big private print shops, Judd & Detweiler, which prints the *National Geographic Magazine,* the National Capital Press, and Ransdell Incorporated. There are also a lot of smaller print shops, for Washington is quite a publishing center.

Washington's No. 1 commercial export is waste paper, which pours out of the government offices and private offices of the capital. Every day, outgoing freight trains carry about 25 carloads of 16 tons per car—a daily total of 400 tons. It was the city's greatest export even before the defense boom started, and in the past year or so the volume has doubled.

Washington's building and real estate business is big, as would be expected in a city of boom, and most wealthy men who made their wealth in the capital are mixed up in the real estate business in some way. Government construction and housing for war workers brush right by priority rulings which would impede building elsewhere. It is a city of good houses, on the average. Comparatively few houses are built for rental purposes. Houses for rent are scarce! Apartment houses are full up. Vacancies are reported at one-fourth of one per cent, but apartment hunters are convinced that even this rate of vacancy is entirely theoretical. Leases, under custom, run for a year. They carry the "Army-Navy clause" which permits service men's families to move out, irrespective of the lease, when they are called to duty elsewhere. Government employees also benefit by the clause. The turnover of apartments from one end of the year to the other, is very high but doesn't produce long vacancies, because somebody is ready to dart into an apartment the moment somebody else leaves it. The city has been on a building spree for several years—a continuing boom. New apartment houses went up fast in 1940 and 1941, both in the middle of the city and in the suburbs. New houses were constructed by the thousands— by the acres—in Maryland, Virginia and the remaining vacant portions of the District of Columbia. Mainly middle-class houses, ranging in price from $6,000 to $12,000. Lower-cost houses, too, around $4,000, suddenly appeared in outlying areas which had been farmlands and woods. This was a super-boom, piled above the previous boom, from 1936 to 1940, when Washington added 31,425 home units. That was twice as many as were added in San Francisco, the second biggest builder among nine cities of comparable size.

Washington builders are both big and little, but most of them are not big. The large federal structures built in the capital during recent years were put up by large out-of-town concerns. Several of these have permanent offices in Washington.

Retailing

The retail store business is the biggest class of business in the nation's capital city. In volume of retail sales it annually leads all cities of its size. It is ahead of Baltimore, Buffalo, Cincinnati, Milwaukee, Minneapolis, New Orleans, Pittsburgh, St. Louis and San Francisco.

The reasons are various. In addition to the high and steady income is the fact that at least one-fourth of the city's residents are young unmarried men and women, "away from home," serving the government as clerks, making more money than they made back home, spending it freely as people do when they are away from home, and spending it especially freely because they have recently come to what seems to them a grand city. They want to keep up appearances, or lift up appearances. Miss Stenographer, with $1440 a year, perks up and buys new clothes. Young Joe Clerk finds himself in a city where every night can be Saturday night, where there are new faces, new girls to be dated. He goes out to enjoy the new life and he spends in a hurry what he makes in a hurry.

On pay days all stores do a big rush business. Between times they do just a rush business. Nick the Greek, who runs a hole-in-the-wall shop near the State Department, gets business in reverse. He sells four dozen sandwiches a day, except on pay day and the next day, when his sandwich sale is cut to one dozen. "When the clerks get paid," he explains, "they go down to Casey's and get a hot meal, but two days later I get them back for a sandwich, a coke and an apple."

Sales on the installment plan form much of the retail business in Washington. The city has the reputation of being a "credit town." Almost any store will extend installment credit to almost anyone for almost anything. Many government workers get deep into debt, but eventually they pull out. Stores find that they can be easy on credit, and still get their money, because Washingtonians are average or better in meeting their obligations. In some high-grade Washington stores, it is a practice for a salesgirl to try to talk a customer into not paying cash for a sizable purchase, but to open a charge account instead. One low-price store advertises that it sells nothing for cash. Newcomers to Washington are always flattered to discover that the stores are anxious and willing to extend credit, and they often assume that they have been "looked up" back home.

The central shopping district consists of F and G Streets, Northwest, from Seventh Street to Fifteenth Street. This is north of Pennsylvania Avenue, eastward from the Treasury and the White House. These are the streets which come in for the biggest rush on pay days. Seventh Street has some large first-class stores, where the patronage ranges from middle-class down. Here in the Seventh Street region are also the homes of the "bargain sales," and the stores that are glad to take a "dollar down." Connecticut Avenue, running northwest from the White House, is the shopping street which likes to be regarded as "Washington's Fifth Avenue." Its shops are small and "exclusive." Outlying shopping streets have built up fast to serve the families of the neighborhood, and to escape downtown congestion. M Street in Georgetown. Fourteenth Street, Northwest. Georgia Avenue, Northwest. H Street, Northeast. Pennsylvania Avenue, Southeast. And some downtown stores are moving far out on Connecticut and Wisconsin Avenues, near the city's "better districts," to get away from the traffic.

The big department stores are Woodward & Lothrop, Hecht's, Lansburgh's, Kann's, Palais Royal, and Goldenberg's. Garfinckel's is a big specialty store, with a reputation for being exclusive, and Jelleff's is a smaller store of similar class.

Washington is not a notable wholesale distributing center. Neighboring Baltimore takes the play away from it on that score. But it is the funnel through which railroad traffic flows between the northern and southern sections of the Atlantic seaboard. Large switching yards fan out just across the Potomac River, between Washington and Alexandria. It is also on U. S. Route 1, main highway between New England and Florida.

For its population, Washington sells more liquor and wine and beer than any other city in the country. More than 17,000,000 gallons of alcoholic beverages were purchased in 1941, a jump of almost 3,000,000 gallons over the figure for 1940. Some of it goes to people who live in near-by Virginia and Maryland, and some to temporary visitors, but most of it goes to people who live in Washington the year around. It is a city of much champagne drinking, too, as a result of the hundreds of society dinners that are given every year. The sales of alcoholic beverages are made by privately-owned stores and bars and restaurants, with the local Alcoholic Beverage Control Board looking over their shoulders, issuing the licenses and collecting the taxes.

Portrait photography does an especially rushing business among celebrities. One particular door handle in Washington is handled personally by more big-name men and women than any other door handle in the whole world. It is the door handle of Harris & Ewing, photographers. Sooner or later, it is gripped by all of the great and many of the would-be great.

The business of the printed word is large in Washington, and it consists of the magazines which are published here for reading elsewhere (the export business), and the local newspapers (the domestic business). Of the two the export business is more important.

First among the exports of reading matter comes the *National Geographic Magazine,* with a circulation of 1,165,000 readers who are so loyal that they resubscribe each year at the record-breaking rate of more than 90 per cent. It is truly a "local enterprise," for it is printed in Washington, and it was conceived in Washington about fifty years ago. The president of the National Geographic Society and editor of the magazine is Gilbert Grosvenor, who married the daughter of Alexander Graham Bell, also of Washington. The *National Geographic* is one of Washington's biggest businesses. Another large magazine is *The Nation's Business,* published by the Chamber of Commerce of the United States, and edited by Merle Thorpe. Its circulation is 370,000. *Pathfinder Magazine,* weekly news magazine, goes from Washington to 534,000 small town and country subscribers, and does for them what *Time* does for their more sophisticated brethren. Its publisher is Emil Hurja, who burst upon the Washington stage early in the New Deal era as a professional Democrat of the conservative variety. The *United States News,* published by David Lawrence, with a circulation of 170,000, is a weekly chronicle of governmental activities. These are the big four of Washington publications for the "outside world."

Newspapers

The local Washington newspapers are four. The *Evening Star* has the largest afternoon circulation, 174,000 daily, and is known as the "family newspaper." In advertising volume, it has been No. 1 in the whole nation for ten years, and it is a notable money-maker. It is owned by the families of Noyes, Kauffman, Howard, and Adams, all old Washington families. Frank B. Noyes, president of the *Star*, was also president of the Associated Press for many years.

The *Washington Post* is morning, daily circulation 150,000. It is owned and actively operated by Eugene Meyer, who made millions in the investment business, and who has been in and out of government for the past two decades, serving in the War Finance Corporation of World War I, later in the Reconstruction Finance Corporation, and as governor of the Federal Reserve Board.

Both morning and evening is the *Times-Herald*, with daily circulation of 220,000. It was formerly Hearst, but is now owned and published by Mrs. Eleanor ("Cissie") Patterson, of the Chicago and New York newspaper families of Medill and Patterson.

Smallest is the *Washington Daily News*, circulation 91,000, afternoon tabloid, of the Scripps-Howard chain. It covers the main big news of the day, and carries some of the columnists who are most prized by Washingtonians.

Average Washington folks read the *Star* most of all. Intellectuals and internationalists dote on the *Post*. Sensation lovers find the *Times-Herald* most satisfying. Streetcar riders like the easy-to-fold *News*, and a lot of fancy intellectuals read it, too.

Washington is a great hotel city because so many visitors come to see the sights, or to do business with the government, or to attend conventions. (The convention business dropped off when the hotels became congested with war visitors, and convention managers were asked *not* to bring their groups to Washington.) Twenty-eight hotels with about 7,000 rooms are "first rate," by the standards of the Hotel Association of Washington, D. C.

Oldest and traditionally best known is the Willard, downtown, but it is like a man a bit past his prime. Newer and bigger is the Mayflower, where many of the newest of the big public men live, dine, and wine. Outlying, overlooking the treetops of Rock Creek Park, is the Shoreham, big, sprawling, swanky, with the residential air. Close by and of the same general class, but with a little less cost and swank, is the Wardman Park Hotel. Downtown, central, is the Carlton, quiet and dignified, which seems to be preferred by many wealthy $1-a-year men. Downtown also is the Washington, middling new and one of the best by service standards. The Raleigh is old enough to have tradition, and is preferred by Southerners. Across the park from the White House is the Hay-Adams House, small, quiet, ultra-genteel, with the air of an English hotel. Dozens of other hotels, mostly good, both medium and low-priced, do big business with the millions of sight-seeing tourists, and with some Washington people who live in them the year 'round. The big Statler, three blocks up Sixteenth Street from the White House, which has been touted in advance as the swankiest of all, is under construction. Its opening date has been set back by a fire which damaged the partially-built structure in February 1942.

Apartment houses are more numerous in Washington than in most cities of its size, because they make easy living for families in which the woman works as a wage earner. Some are high-grade, but most are middle-grade. Rents of both apartments and houses in Washington are higher than in comparable cities.

The rooming and boarding house business in Washington is something special. Within a mile of the White House are hundreds of good rooming houses, and many of them are old mansions. Girl workers live in them, have breakfasts and dinners, with lunch downtown. The houses are run usually by women of ability and character, who mother their girls and look after their moral and spiritual needs, as well as their rooms and meals. The good rooming houses are little businesses, and are bought and sold as other businesses are.

Rush Movie Business

The night life business of Washington is middle-grade. There are plenty of cafés, dance floors and juke-box joints, but they don't do the business which comparable places in comparable cities do. The reason is that Washington people are not notably night life people. This is changed a bit by the wartime, but even with the new hordes, the downtown streets of Washington are not thronged after 10:30 or 11.

Movie houses do the big business. Attendance is around 500,000 a week. Many people go to a movie once a week, and some go several times a week. The downtown movie houses are always crowded, and so are many of the outlying neighborhood theaters.

Clairvoyants, astrologers, psychics, palmists, fortune tellers, and other seers do a good business in Washington, and some of them have special patronesses among congressional wives, wives of high officials, and society women. By an Act of Congress passed in 1932, they are required to register with the District of Columbia government and pay an annual $250 license

130

fee. This applies to every kind of professional seer, including "tea leaf readers." Licenses can be revoked, but they rarely are, because the authorities seldom receive complaints about flimflamming of customers.

Small loan agencies do a big business with government employees. Those charging high rates of interest which are illegal under local law have their headquarters in Maryland and Virginia suburbs. The pawnshops are there, too, and many a diamond, a watch, and a fur coat finds its way in and out of them. Cooperative credit agencies are growing among government employees to fill the need for consumer credit.

The Washington banks are like banks everywhere, except that they do little industrial business. Their loans are mainly to merchants and real estate people. They have many wealthy depositors who have moved to Washington from other cities, and also more than the usual proportion of small depositors whose balances are so low that they involve service charges. Washington people do business more by check, less by cash, than people of most cities. Riggs National is the biggest and best-known bank—across the street from the Treasury. Its president, Robert V. Fleming, is an active civic leader. Second largest, abutting Riggs, is the American Security & Trust Company. The Hamilton National is third.

The securities business is not exceptionally large in Washington, and yet in 1941 the local stock exchange doubled its 1940 volume at the same time that the New York Stock Exchange had its worst year since 1918.

Per capita life insurance in force on Washingtonians is higher than that of any other city except New York, and it might be even higher except for the fact that wealthy residents who have made their money elsewhere often buy their insurance elsewhere. The high insurance record is made mainly by the middle-class families whose jobs and incomes are stable. The insurance habit of Washingtonians does not lessen the fact that on the average they are great spenders. They get enough to spend and save—both.

Housewives do their daily marketing in the local neighborhood stores, as in any other city—at the chain stores, or the independents. And scattered through the city are a dozen consolidated markets which sell meats, fish, vegetables, fruits, and bakery goods, and they are like the markets of other cities. Food prices are generally about the same as in other cities, although in some cases a little higher. Fish lovers go to the fish wharves to get their sea food, which comes up the river in quantities from the lower Potomac and Chesapeake Bay. Near the fish wharves and the water front are most of the meat and provision houses, with the common nationally known names. This is the kitchen door of Washington, within sight of the great Department of Agriculture building and the Washington Monument and the gorgeous new Jefferson Memorial.

Washington businessmen and merchants are pretty much like local businessmen everywhere, except that they tend to be more satisfied with things-as-they-are than other big city businessmen. Most of the big storekeepers are from old Virginia, Maryland or Washington families, and some are now second or third generation. There are few "new families" or "outsiders" in business in a big way.

Prominent among representatives of old-time Maryland, Virginia or Washington families whose names are identified with successful Washington businesses are these: The Heurichs, makers of beer and owners of real estate. The Noyes and Kauffman and Adams families, owners of the *Evening Star*. The Corby brothers, who founded Washington's largest bakery business. The Corcoran, Glover and Riggs families, of Washington bankdom. The Carrys, who started on beer but switched to ice cream. The Fishers who developed Chevy Chase. The Kanns and Lansburghs who have been department store owners for generations. The Woodwards who stem from a founder of the Woodward & Lothrop department store. The Goldenbergs, who are also store owners. The Hahns, of shoe store note. Malcolm Gibbs, druggist, who established the Peoples drug chain. John Letts, who set up the first local chain of groceries called Sanitary, later absorbed by Safeway.

Some of the leading businessmen are wealthy, and some are not. They all show the inclination, however, to gang together in the usual business associations—in the Board of Trade and the Merchants & Manufacturers Association (with emphasis on the merchants). These are rustling and bustling outfits. But their rustle and bustle is different from that of local business groups in other cities. There's not so much tub thumping, almost no campaigning for big business and manufacturing enterprises to "come to our city." That would be out of character—really useless—in the capital, which doesn't need advertising and is uninviting to enterprises for which other cities clamor. The Board of Trade devotes itself largely to handling businessmen's problems—the peculiar problems which arise in a city which has no vote, no city council, few of the means which businessmen elsewhere utilize to get things straightened out. Activities are not spectacular and results come slowly. With the increase of problems caused by the jamming of the city with war workers, organization membership is zooming. The Board of Trade had 2,500 members ten years ago and 3,500 last year. Today it has more than 4,500.

Higher and Higher

The years 1940 and 1941 were boom years for Washington, and 1942, with its influx of war workers, is topping them both. New telephones went in so fast that by the start of 1942 there were 41 sets for every 100 people. It was second in the U. S. only to San Francisco, which had 45½ per 100, but the per capita number of calls in Washington was first. Long distance tolls soared, as officials talked to people out around the country about war business. Streetcars and busses became overcrowded. Traffic became a notorious tangle. The electric company and the gas company expanded their business tremendously. Automobile dealers sold all the cars they could get before the war, and when the war broke Washington streets were filled with shiny new models. Hotels turned away guests. Apartment houses had no vacancies. Families began to double up. Private families took roomers as a community duty. Domestic help became scarcer because Negroes took jobs with the government. Washington tourist camps were filled with trailers, used as living homes by newly-arrived workmen, until the Army began taking them over for guard camps. Lines of people waiting on the sidewalk to get into movies became longer. Department store sales hit an all-time high, and stores kept open evenings to sell to new crowds of buyers. Pay rolls were highest in history. People rushed to the city to take war jobs. Accommodations of all sorts became full up.

The city was bursting at the seams. Boom on top of boom.

Sometime the war will end, and the reconstruction will set in. That will cause a great shifting in Washington, for some workers will pour out, but others will pour in. There will be a temporary "depression," which means that business will be only super-normal, instead of the recent super-super-normal. At that time there will arise a further movement to decentralize government, to take parts of it to other cities of the East and the Middle West, where routine clerical operations would work quite as well as in Washington, and perhaps better. But it is doubtful that decentralization will go far. The power of Washington is too great to permit it. The newspapers will fight it. Officialdom, while not particularly interested in Washington as a community, will cry that they must keep their administrative machinery within close range of their supervision. They will want their employees close at hand. The employees, rooted in Washington, will want to stay here and will raise a great cry against shifts to other cities. They will organize pressures on Congress not to move government. The combination of forces will succeed.

And so . . . Washington will continue to grow, will always be a boomtown . . . with the nation to support it on the scale to which it has become accustomed.

14

Government Workers

THERE are a half dozen reasons why people like to work for the government.

In wartime it is considered "patriotic." Some work for nothing, some work for $1-a-year, and some quit good-paying private jobs to take low-pay government jobs, and the main compensation they get is self-satisfaction over doing their civilian bit in the emergency. Some young men think they can be exempted from the draft by holding government jobs, but that is not true, for few government workers are considered "essential."

The starting pay for young men and women is high, and that is always a lure.

There's a chance of getting a lifetime job, which means security. Applicants talk of "getting a government job and settling down." They think that when once they land it, their job worries are over.

Also there's glamour in a government job, and perhaps an item in the home town paper that So-and-So has been "accepted by the civil service," and "called to Washington." It makes a great hit with the friends and the neighbors, and the lucky person acquires a temporary prestige.

A few youngsters like jobs in Washington so that they can go to night schools and get a college education while holding down government jobs.

Government service is attractive to certain classes of specialists, such as agriculturalists, statisticians, economists, and scientists, because it is the natural outlet for their special talents.

Those are the reasons people apply for work with the government.

Jobs in Wartime

Millions try to get government jobs in peacetime and there are only tens of thousands of jobs available. In wartime it is a different story. The government combs the country for eligible government workers. Some that it gets are eligible. Some have to be trained. But in either case, it gets new workers, and the government rolls swell.

When the war broke, new employees flooded into the capital. In January 1942, the government roster in Washington grew by 15,000 new workers, with 85 per cent of them women. It was the biggest growth-month in the history of the government. The Budget Bureau estimated that 45,000 new employees would be added from January 1 to July 1, 1942. And in the first four months of the year, the new employees (not counting their families) averaged well above 7,000 a month.

Wartime plays hob with the fixed policies and routines of the Civil Service Commission, the central recruiting agency of the government. Less emphasis is placed on competitive examinations, more on recruiting people fast. The government hires more young people, more old people, more women, more Negroes, more physically disabled people. Fewer competitive tests are given. More weight is put on education and experience. And the applicants are rated in one of two classes—"eligible" or "ineligible." The state quota law is suspended for all practical purposes. In wartime the Commission will take people from whatever states it can get them. Only in those classifications where there are a surplus of workers does the Commission make any pretense of following the state quota law.

The Commission goes in for direct hiring in wartime, and thereby abandons another age-old regulation—the so-called "rule of three." Under this peacetime rule, an agency was permitted to select people from the Commission's eligible register, and the agency was supposed to take one of the first three eligibles. But now agencies are required to give general orders for personnel, and the Commission fills the order. The agencies must take the people supplied by the Commission, regardless of race, color, creed, or looks.

Wartime places a new burden on government—the training of people to qualify them for federal jobs. Many of these newcoming thousands are not trained, and qualified people just aren't available. People are trained, at government expense, for jobs ranging from skilled mechanics to stenographers, and from personnel technicians to meteorologists.

War workers now hired aren't given full civil service status. They get temporary appointments. They are eligible to be transferred, raised in pay, and they are covered under the civil service retirement system. But the theory is that they will be much easier to lop off the pay roll during the postwar readjustment period.

Actually, even though most war workers consider their jobs temporary, for "just a year or two," the greatest number of them will get the government habit and will regard themselves as permanent. This is also true of the majority of workers who come to government in ordinary times. So the fact is that people often determine the course of their whole future lives when they decide to try for a job with the government. Any light that can be shed on government service as a career ought to be useful light. Any questions which an applicant may ask himself in advance may serve the purpose of vocational guidance.

Some Questions

Here are a few questions, and even if they do gum up a pretty imaginary picture, they are good questions:

Why is it that government workers, on the average, lead such humdrum lives after the first enthusiasm wears off, which is usually in about a year? Why do average government workers soon sink into ruts of dull duties, and yawn over their work, and complain about their lot in life? Why do such a large proportion of middle-aged men and women who are firmly fixed in government jobs in the beautiful city of Washington say that they wish they could get back to private employment? Why do they strive to make contacts with private employers, and talk about those few who succeed in breaking out of the government as the "lucky ones"?

Among government employees of the average class—not the exceptional highest—there is a state of mind known as "Washingtonitis." It consists of being resigned to the job, without being satisfied with the meager opportunities for advancement. It is a "settling down" into the groove. It brings a severance of home ties. Old acquaintances become dim memories. The federal government is not as desirable as it seemed, and advancement does not come along. And yet there's a fear to break away from it. The job has the "security" which was originally sought, so it seems dangerous to kick over the traces. Through the placidity of existence on the secure government job, however, there are streaks of yearning for the private job that might have been, and a deep turbulent boiling about the "unfairness" of government employment practices. The surface of government employees may be calm, but the depth often is not. The security turns sour, and brings a spiritual retching. There are exceptions. There are many cases in which government jobs open up vistas for service and grand opportunities for useful careers, and these are the opportunities which get the advertising, while the humdrum lives do not. Yet the latter are more numerous and more typical. They are closer to the average.

The Main Facts

For the benefit of aspiring applicants, the main facts about government employees in Washington can be stated.

There are about 275,000 of them, and they are about one-seventh of all federal government employees in the entire country.

The average pay of government workers in Washington in late 1941 was $2,066 a year, or around $40 a week. (It is slightly higher since recent

136

war raises.) The average pay of federal workers in the entire country was around $1,800 a year, or $35 a week. (This, too, is now slightly higher.) The average in Washington is higher partly because of the presence here of a number of high-pay experts, whose incomes bring the average up, and partly because Washington pay must be higher to cover the higher cost of living, even for average earners.

The cost of living in Washington is highest in the nation, about the same as New York, due to a variety of circumstances, but mainly to high rents in the city, which even in normal times is crowded.

The entrance pay is good, ranging from $1,260 a year for typists, many of whom would work back home for $900 or $1,000, to $2,000 for young professional men and women, many of whom would get less than that in the first phases of private jobs.

Advancement is ordinarily slow. Advancement depends on the "grades" through which employees are lifted from one pay scale to the next. These promotions depend on a combination of proven merit, personality, and personal or political pull with the government supervisors, who are like foremen or straw bosses or office managers in private employment. Only 6 out of every 100 government employees ever reach $3,200 a year, and 85 per cent get less than $2,000.

Most are under civil service, which means that it is hard to hire and hard to fire. Civil service status does not protect an employee in his job absolutely, but it means that he cannot be fired without some good reason, and a whim of the boss is not a good reason. If there were great shutdowns and mass unemployment in the industry of government, civil service rating would not keep a job. But these vicissitudes, common in private employment, do not occur in government to any great extent.

"Once a government job, always a government job" is not quite true, yet in the main it is, and it is probably the luscious bait which makes so many people take the hook.

Vacations and sick leave are liberal. For vacations, 26 days a year, nearly a month, double the usual two weeks' vacation in private jobs. Today, in wartime, vacations have been cut throughout the government, but mainly in the war agencies where only a few days are given officials. Employees are allowed an average of two weeks. The vacation period, called "annual leave," may be split up and taken piecemeal, a day at a time, or even an hour at a time, if desired. For illness, 15 days off are allowed in any year, with pay, and the leave is cumulative over six years. Thus some government employees accumulate their illnesses until they need a good long dose of time off, and, with the aid of a certificate of an accommodating physician, they go and get "good and rested." In these matters, government is a thoughtful employer.

In peacetime the working hours are short—39 hours per week. This means seven hours a day for five days, and a half day on Saturday. But in wartime the hours are lengthened by the heads of agencies to 44 and 48 and even then overtime is required.

Working hours are staggered. The starting hour ranges from 7 to 9:30 a.m. and the quitting hour from early to late afternoon. Hours are staggered to relieve Washington's frightful traffic problem. Many agencies now work night and day shifts to ease traffic and to conserve office space.

Through the wage and hour act the government requires private employers to pay time and a half for overtime over 40 hours a week. But the government pays very few of its employees overtime and plenty of overtime is worked in wartime. Skilled workers are paid overtime but only a handful of "white collar" workers are treated similarly.

The competition for employees, however, has forced the government to raise the salaries of many of its employees through the device of advancing them to the next highest grade. And it is probable that the government will either pay overtime to all employees or else give them a bonus as was done during World War I.

Overtime and hard work and inadequate pay are the rule, even in normal times, among the top 10 per cent of government workers. They are the professional men, the lawyers, the statisticians and economists, the scientists and policy makers, and also the clerks and stenographers who are attached to their offices. This grade of upper-crust workers are truly "public servants," and they are overworked and underpaid. Regardless of what may be said about the lower salaries in government service, it is undoubtedly true that the highest salaries are not high enough. The same quality of services would bring many times more pay in private employment. A $4,000 man in government is apt to be worth $8,000 in private work, and a $6,000 man in government is usually the sort who would be a bargain to the right private employer at $10,000. The upper grades are underpaid, and that is something to be remembered by the young man who aspires to climb to the upper grades.

Each worker is paid twice a month, by greenish-blue checks bearing the words "Treasurer of the United States" in solemn Old English type. No other workers in the world get paid by such impressive looking documents. Pay weeks are staggered by departments, so as to spread out the payments over the month for the benefit of Washington banks and stores. Government workers, like many private workers, rush to spend, and then comes a period of expert skimping, until the next pay day. Sending money to the folks back home also marks pay days. The Washington post office does much more business in money orders than any other city of its size in the United States, due to the fact that a large number of Washington workers help to pay the expenses of father or mother, brother or sister, or aunt or uncle or cousin back home. Thus, while Washington is supported by the nation, its pay roll also helps to support the nation.

Government wages may not be garnisheed, like private wages. Government workers pay their bills, but often they are a little slow. Washington stores grant retail credit freely, but they make allowance for the statistical record of slowness.

Seniority in government service counts heavily in pay raises. Men between 50 and 60 get the highest pay, by average levels.

Retirement on part pay in old age is allowed for all permanent employees. Formerly the system covered only about 65 per cent of all federal workers but in January 1942 it was extended by Congress to cover nearly every employee. Beginning July 1, 1942, 5 per cent will be collected monthly from the employees as a contribution toward retirement. The government adds its share so that many government workers can look forward to a comfortable old age—on a reduced scale of living.

Women Workers

Women workers are about 50 per cent of all government workers in Washington. The war has greatly increased the number of women in government. The women are mainly clerks, typists, stenographers, and the operators of office machines and elevators. Women are supposed to get the same pay as men for the same services, but they do not get advancement as men do, and so their average pay is less than the average pay of men. Women workers are younger, on the average, than the men. Also there is a larger proportion of them unmarried. This fact makes for keen competition among the unmarried girls for the eligible men who are coworkers in government service, the object being (usually) matrimony. Many find their mates, but many don't, and the proportion of "old maids" among government workers is higher than the percentage of "old bachelors."

One reason women get less pay is that the supervisors usually prefer men, except for the jobs of typists and stenographers, which have become specialties of women. Supervisors say that men are more dependable through the entire month, and are never off the job for many months while having a baby. Supervisors have no objection to maternity, but they are inclined to prefer that class of workers, men, who are exempt from this particular cause of absence.

Women workers are incapacitated more by love troubles than men are, say government section bosses. Women-in-love seem to take it to heart more than men-in-love—at least during the working hours. As for married workers, it is common observation among government bosses that both married men and married women are temperamentally more stable. There is no tendency to fire women when they marry—rather the contrary. Whether a man or a woman is married is noted on records of job applicants, but it is supposed not to have any influence on the appointment or on maintenance of the job.

Young unmarried women live usually in boarding, rooming and apartment houses. Many girls live two-in-a-room, three-in-a-room, or even four-in-a-room. They may be crowded, but they live generally well. Morals are like those of any other city, neither better nor worse. Girls away from home for the first time do in Washington what they would do if they were away from home for the first time in any other big city.

Monotony

Most government jobs are monotonous jobs, handling papers of one sort or another, much like the clerical jobs in other offices in other cities. Perhaps it is necessarily so, and yet government as an employer has never tackled the problem of monotony to the extent that it urges private employers to do. Day in and day out, month in and month out, year in and year out, the same job, under the same system, without sharp competition, often without zest—this is the routine of tens of thousands of government clerks. War adds temporary excitement, but the routine always returns to monotony. The result is an occupational ailment which is both mental and physical and which is frankly recognized by Washington doctors.

One well-known Washington physician, whose practice is four-fifths government employees, says that 60 per cent of the women who come to him and 40 per cent of the men are suffering from the mental and physical effects of frustration in their work and lives. They complain of fatigue, lack of endurance and upset digestions. Almost invariably, he says, they have been doing the same government work over and over, all day long, all year long, without much necessity for devoting their minds to the routine. Their minds wander, go into circles, and they become mentally ill. Many other Washington doctors observe the same about government workers, and charge it to the average monotony of the jobs.

These are not the normalities of government workers. They are the abnormalities. But they exist in a large number of cases, in sufficient volume to constitute a note of caution to those who want to know the bad as well as the good about government service as a life career. They raise a question, without giving the answer, about the long-range value of exchanging the vicissitudes of life, such as are supposed to be inherent in private employment, for the reputed safety, security and snugness of government employment in Washington. Security is desirable, but when it leads in so many cases to a mental dry rot, it may be a doubtful bargain.

How to Get a Job

If you want a job under civil service, this is the way to go about it: First of all, you decide what "classification" you belong in. The government does not hire just good all-around people. It hires filing clerks, and stenographers, and information specialists, and typists, and so on. You've got to have a classification. Then, when you have made up your mind what classification you want to adopt, you find out where and when an examination will be given by the Civil Service Commission for the kind of job you want. One good place to get this information is the high school, business school or college you attended, because the Commission keeps in close touch with such quarters. Or you can go to the civil service secretary in the federal building of your home town, unless it is a very small town. Another thing you might do is to watch the announcements of examinations as they appear on the bulletin board of your post office. Another suggestion is to write the Commission giving a detailed description of your background and the Commission will let you know when an examination is announced for which you can qualify. When you find an examination coming up for your kind of job, you write to the Civil Service Commission and ask for an application blank. Then you show up at the place where the examination is to be held. Examinations out around the country usually are conducted by the local superintendent of schools or some other educational official with questions provided by the Commission.

Now that thousands of new employees are being hired every month, examinations are being given as soon as a sizable number of applications is received. So in wartime, it is worth while filing an application blank as soon as you decide you want to apply for a government job. And if you have no special training, it would be well to write the Civil Service Commission to find out about jobs you could qualify to be trained for.

In many cases now the Commission holds "unassembled examinations," which usually involve professional and scientific jobs and the like. In that case you are not required to meet with your competitors and take an examination as they do. You just fill out blanks with a lot of questions about your experience, whom you have worked for, how much money you made and all that, enclose samples of your work, and send the whole batch to the Commission.

Whether the examination was an assembled or an unassembled one, when it is over you wait for the Commission to let you know what your rating is. If you are a war veteran or the widow of a veteran, you are credited with extra points. That pushes you closer to the top of the list, called "the register," and gives you a better chance for the job. If you have a passing grade, then you just wait some more, until the Commission sends you your rating. If you are near the top of the list, you are in line to get a telegram from the Commission offering you a job. You can turn down the offer twice and remain on the register, but your name comes off if you decline three times.

These days, if you come to Washington to look for a job, go first to the Civil Service Commission. It is the clearing house for all government jobs, administrative as well as clerical. If you have special leads, you can follow them up later. But first clear with the Civil Service Commission.

When you present yourself for the job, you are fingerprinted (which is the Commission's assurance against accepting criminals for positions), and given a thorough physical examination (which serves to keep the service from being cluttered with workers who may break down and overburden the retirement fund).

When you get on the job, you are placed in a "grade" which has several steps of promotion and salary increases in it. Length of service works you from one step to another and from one grade to another. You can make a jump ahead of time by getting your job reclassified, and it's here that personal favoritism and political favoritism can come in handy.

The so-called "merit system" means that normally it takes some merit to pass the civil service examinations and to get on the list of eligibles from which appointments are made. From there on, the process of getting a job may be pure merit, or it may be a combination of merit and pull. The pull may come from knowing some politician or political organization that will speak a good word, or from having a first-hand or second-hand acquaintance with the appointing officers. Personality, looks and acquaintances are among the "merits" of the merit system.

After you've been on the job a few years, you'll begin to give serious thought to the retirement system. Latest figures show the smallest retirement annuity was $64 and the largest was $1,900, the variation being due to difference in salary and the length of service. However, under the more liberalized retirement act passed in January 1942, annuities will be somewhat larger. An employee must have worked five years before he can draw an annuity under the retirement system. Compulsory retirement age for all employees is 70, though employees who have had 30 years' service can retire at 60.

Women don't get the breaks for higher jobs in government service as the men do. But they fare a lot better than they used to. Time was when they didn't have a chance to get a government job. Some women were given government work in the early 1850's, but they were not recognized on the official rolls. This first work was the copying of patents in the Patent Office and land warrants issued from the General Land Office. It was done on the "put out" system by which women received the work by mail, and always in the name of some male relative, so that women would not appear as government employees. Later in the 50's the first woman clerk appeared in the Treasury, working at the desk of her husband during his illness. After his death she remained in the position, but registered in the name of her brother. Women were not hired "as women" until the pressure of Civil War work hit the government and General F. E. Spinner, Treasurer of the United States, asked permission to hire them openly for the Treasury. The practice of hiring women then spread throughout the wartime government, and was finally recognized by congressional authorization in March 1864.

Down through the years repeated attempts were made to drive them out. "Women's place is in the home"—was the chant raised in the open. But the anti-feminists used more than a slogan in their efforts to clear government offices of skirts. Stories began to be whispered about the pioneer women who defied convention by living unchaperoned in Washington rooming houses. The tales included the names of members of Congress and other federal officials who were instrumental in getting women jobs under the patronage system.

Then, in 1869, the attack shifted from charges that employed ladies were making use of their charms to charges that they were dishonest. Paper money was missing and suspicious officials, who wanted the women out of there anyway, said they figured the females were hiding the bills in their hoop skirts and making off with it. Things reached the point where the women were ordered to take off their skirts and shake them each day before they were permitted to leave the building.

The battle against femininity in the federal service became less vicious as the years passed by. It was beginning to die down by 1911 when John C. Black, then Civil Service Commissioner, demanded that no more women stenographers be hired. "The blondes," he thundered, "are too frivolous and the brunettes are too chatty."

These many years since Mr. Black cut loose with that generalization, blondes, brunettes, redheads and women whose hair has grown gray in the service are on the federal pay roll in great numbers—more than 125,000 of them in Washington. But, though some of them have managed by sheer display of merit and length of service to rise to some of the top jobs, the majority are on the lower levels of responsibility and pay.

Unions and Cooperatives

Working conditions and salaries in the federal service have been greatly improved for men and women workers alike through the organization of the government employees into unions. These unions are unique because they don't use strikes as means of getting their members what they want. All union constitutions contain a statement of policy against strikes. But unions have served to reveal conditions to policy-forming and law-making officials, have done much in suggesting how those conditions could be improved. The National Federation of Federal Employees, oldest and most conservative of the white collar unions, originally was affiliated with the American Federation of Labor, but split away. The American Federation of Government Employees, also fairly conservative, is lower in prestige. United Federal Workers of America (CIO) is farther toward the left. It is doubtful whether members of these unions form a majority in any federal agency's white collar force.

All three organizations have their headquarters in Washington. Also headquartered in Washington are many unions of federal employees in the postal service. They are responsible, to large degree, for the development of efficiency in the largest government-run business in the world. Much of the credit for the manner in which that business clicks goes to the close relationship between the unions and high postal officials. It is a long-established practice of the postal workers themselves, through their unions, to help effect reforms in the operations of the postal machinery.

Federal employees have a medical cooperative, the Group Health Association, which they can join for a nominal fee. It had its origin when officials of the Home Owners' Loan Corporation took stock of the operating losses caused by illnesses of employees. The cooperative was established with the object of reducing the volume of sickness by making proper medical attention available at low cost. Soon after its inception, the organized medical profession showed fear that the new group was an advance toward socialized medicine. A bitter legal battle resulted, but GHA has survived and has been gradually expanding. It was serving more than 7,000 government workers and their families by the middle of last year.

Career Men

When you get around to looking at successful careers in the government service, you'll find several that would make Horatio Alger and Oliver Optic sit up and take notice if they were on the scene. They are the careers of men who began at the bottom when the going was tougher than it is now and worked themselves up. In the Washington lingo the men are "career-ists." They hold positions just below the cabinet officers and other officials who are political appointees. When the "peepul" rise in the might of their voting to turn out the "ins" and turn in the "outs," the careerists welcome the new set of bosses and tutor them along.

Here are some of the outstanding career men: Daniel W. Bell, Under Secretary of the Treasury. William H. McReynolds, one of the President's six "anonymous" assistants, in charge of personnel problems. Ebert K. Burlew, First Assistant Secretary of the Interior. Harold N. Graves, Assistant to the Secretary of the Treasury. Alvin W. Hall, Director of the Bureau of Engraving and Printing. J. Edgar Hoover, Director of the Federal Bureau of Investigation. W. A. Jump, Director of Finance and Budget Officer for the Department of Agriculture. Alton P. Tisdel, Superintendent of Documents. Elmer L. Irey, Chief Coordinator of Treasury Enforcement Agencies. And Malcolm Kerlin, Administrative Assistant to the Secretary of Commerce.

Nearly every one of these men started as a clerk, studied law in night school, and worked slowly up through the ranks. These cases are exceptional, of course, because there isn't room at the top for more than a few. But the few who do make the grade show that it can be done.

The government today contains a number of employees whose aspirations and training are aimed at policy-making jobs—jobs which require some special education. And the government has ways of helping its ambitious clerks to shoot at these jobs. Those who want to "better themselves" can go to classes sponsored by the governmental departments, with high federal officials as instructors. The largest of these schools is run by the Department of Agriculture, and students can take courses in any of the subjects offered in an average college curriculum. Also, many agencies have adopted the plan of assigning new employees to training courses to give them an idea of what it is all about before they settle down into some special groove.

In the government ranks in Washington are a number of "apprentice administrators," who have been specially trained for their jobs. They are the products of colleges and universities which used to ignore government service as a career for their students, but which now push some of their most alert graduates toward Washington. In their classrooms they studied the problems of taxes, budgets, personnel, bureaucratic organization, government publicity. Then, through the National Institute of Public Affairs (Rockefeller-endowed), they became "internes" of government, working in

145

a federal agency and studying its operations, later becoming full-fledged employees.

This group follows in the footsteps of a fraternity of young administrators and policy makers who came into prominence in Washington early in the New Deal. The earlier bunch was composed mainly of "bright young men," graduates of Harvard and Columbia law schools. The Harvard men, brought in under the influence of Felix Frankfurter, then professor of law at Harvard, soon became known as "the Frankfurter boys." The group played a big part in the drafting of early New Deal legislation.

Today every scientist and technical specialist in the whole country is a potential federal employee. The government has them all listed in a National Roster of Scientific and Specialized Personnel, which was set up in the middle of 1940 to help the government put its finger on technicians for special jobs. On it are the nation's scientists, doctors, cost accountants, engineers, etc., who may be called at any time for a "command performance" in Washington or somewhere else.

A Word to Applicants

(1) If you want to do war work, all right. That's often a matter of inner conscience and feeling. If the government needs you, of course you will work for it gladly. But try not to be a square peg in a round government hole. Try for a job that you fit, and that fits you. If this doesn't show up, perhaps you are contributing most to the winning of the war by doing your own civilian job, in your own way, in your own locality.

(2) Look beyond the starting salaries. These are often higher than in private employment, but remember that advancement in government is ordinarily slow.

(3) Don't forget that living costs in Washington are high.

(4) The scope and variety of private jobs will always be greater than the scope and variety in government, even with the prospect that some form of socialism is ahead—with larger government.

(5) It is often good for men and women who are well advanced in their occupations to "take a turn" in government for a year or two. They bring in points of view which are good for government, and they acquire points of view which help them when they return to private life. The danger is that such persons often "get stuck" in government, as they had not intended.

(6) Private employment, too, has its blighted careers, thwarted ambitions, and occupational ruts. In private jobs or government jobs, you are taking a chance, for that's the law of life. But before taking a government job, strip off the glamour, take a long look ahead at the prospects, and *then* take your chance.

146

15

Negroes and Equality

TWO situations make Washington the No. 1 Negro city of the United States and the world. First, it has a large Negro population, and this is mainly a matter of local interest. Second, it is the center of a new push for Negro equality, and this is of great national significance for whites and blacks alike. The Negroes of the United States are lifting themselves and are being lifted from Washington, and the facts are not generally known.

As for the Negro community of Washington, it consists of 225,000 Negroes within the District of Columbia, as compared with 600,000 whites. More than one in every four persons in Washington is Negro. The population is about 28 per cent Negro, which is a higher percentage than that of any other large city of comparable size in the United States or the world. In actual numbers it ranks behind New York, Chicago and Philadelphia, but these cities are larger and the Negro percentages are smaller. No southern city has as many Negroes, and no northern city has as large a proportion. There's plenty of poverty, but on the average the Washington Negroes are middle-class, and they are schooled, for most of them brought up in Washington have been through high school.

The Negroes have no local vote (and neither do the whites). They have no local politics on which to coalesce as they have in New York's Harlem, or Chicago's or Philadelphia's South Side. They are not a social unit. They are not homogeneous. The masses of Washington Negroes are not even notably zealous for race equality. They go along in their placid course, lulled by a certain security which comes from the government pay checks that trickle down through the Negro population as they do through the white. The Washington Negro community does not supply the driving force for the equality movement.

Equality

Within Washington, however, is a colony of national Negro leaders, highly intelligent and educated men, and they are the "brown brain trust" of the Negro equality movement. Most of them seek, first, economic equality and a chance to get a proportional number of government jobs and private jobs for their people. In the backs of their minds, for the long-range future, is something like social equality, but they differ among themselves as to whether they ought to strive for this over many generations, or to try to get it within a single generation. In the government in Washington they are making great strides. It is really a revolution in Negro relations, accomplished with a minimum of publicity.

The stature of Negroes in government has grown more during the New Deal than in all the previous years since Reconstruction days. Formerly Negroes were expected to be content with three political jobs in Washington—Register of the Treasury, Auditor of the Navy, and Recorder of Deeds for the District of Columbia. Of these three only the Recorder of Deeds is a Negro today, but more than one hundred other Negroes hold down positions of authority within government as executives or influential advisers. The number of Negro employees of the federal government in all parts of the country has tripled from 50,000 to more than 150,000. The number is steadily increasing, especially in Washington, and especially since the beginning of the hiring boom brought about by the defense program and war.

In civil service tests and on civil service records, no longer is any mention made of race or color (or national origin). Photographs have been banned from the records. There is nothing on civil service records to show that an applicant for a job, or an employee of the government, is a Negro, although personal interviews bring it out, and some individual departments and bureaus still have the race question on their application blanks. In some portions of the government segregation of whites and blacks has been abolished. Many of the government cafeterias have been opened to Negro workers.

The three persons in government most responsible for the rise in position of the Negroes are President Roosevelt, Mrs. Roosevelt, and Secretary of the Interior Ickes. Ickes has taken the lead, while the President has followed through with the necessary executive orders to give Negroes equal status in many government agencies. Mrs. Roosevelt has mingled socially with Negro groups, kept in touch with their thinking, reported this to the President, and furnished a number of examples, by her own conduct, of the acceptance of Negroes on the same level as whites. She has been influential in making Negro groups welcome at the White House.

Ickes

One of Ickes' first steps as a trail blazer on behalf of better treatment of Negroes in government was the hiring of racial advisers in the early days of the New Deal. The first was Clark Foreman, a white Atlantan who had been employed by the Julius Rosenwald Fund, and who was familiar with all the Negro advancement causes. Through Foreman, Ickes proceeded to hire many Negroes. In the offices of the Public Works Administration, then under Ickes' wing, they worked alongside of the whites. Foreman also got Ickes to insert in Public Works contracts a provision requiring contractors to employ Negroes on PWA projects in the proportion they represented in the local community.

Foreman was transferred to another part of the government, and all of Ickes' succeeding racial advisers were Negroes. The Department of the Interior became a conduit through which Negroes spread into other government agencies. Many of the current crop of Negro advisers were originally brought to Washington by Ickes. And he later helped them along in their climb to better jobs.

Ickes has also helped Negroes in his capacity of boss of national parks. In Washington, the National Park Service includes a number of public golf courses and tennis courts. Formerly these were used exclusively by whites, but all of a sudden one Sunday morning in the summer of 1941 some Negro players appeared, accompanied by word from Ickes that Negroes were to be allowed to play, and accompanied also by park policemen (also under Ickes) to enforce the order.

Mr. and Mrs. Roosevelt

With the Roosevelts' appearance in Washington, Negroes got a large-scale entree at the White House for the first time in history. The President's calendar was opened to a number of Negro leaders, and Mrs. Roosevelt brought her sympathy for the Negroes out into full view. She entertained the National Council of Negro Women on several occasions. She championed Marian Anderson, the Negro singer, in the squabble with the DAR over whether the singer should be allowed to appear in the DAR Hall in Washington. She often had her picture taken with Negro leaders, which is something that First Ladies might be expected to do with any portions of the citizenry, but which no other First Lady had ever done with Negroes. And she talked Negro problems frequently—especially with two white officials, Wayne Coy, the President's liaison with OEM, and Dr. Will Alexander, WPB consultant on minority groups in defense industries.

The President's part has consisted mainly of issuing executive orders against discrimination—and following them up to make them stick. He has been particularly impressed by stories which Negro leaders have told him about the inroads which communists have made among the Negro people. And several of the steps he has taken have been attributed to his desire to scotch the communists' progress.

Two Pushes

The President's first notable push was against discrimination in factories which had been given defense contracts. It was in the summer of 1941. Negro leaders complained that skilled Negro machinists and other expert workmen were idle while less competent white workmen were hired, and while many factories suffered a labor shortage. Several Negro organizations banded together for a Negro job march on Washington. Then the President ordered that defense factories hire Negroes, and the job march was called off. Part of the executive order read: "All contracting agencies of the Government of the United States shall include in all defense contracts hereafter negotiated by them a provision obligating the contractor not to discriminate against any worker because of race, creed, color, or national origin." Under pressure of the contracts, many defense plants subsequently hired more Negroes.

The second big push, made later in 1941, was for equality of treatment of Negroes within government. It followed a long series of protests by Negroes that discrimination in government service was giving private employers an excuse for discriminating in their own businesses. The President first ordered a Committee on Fair Employment Practice to be set up within the government. Two Negroes were appointed members of the board of six. And the executive secretary, Lawrence W. Cramer (white), former governor of the Virgin Islands, immediately employed two Negro girls as his secretaries.

Then the President issued an intra-government letter which ordered discriminatory practices abolished. The letter was given very little publicity at the time, but it became known in Negro circles as the strongest pro-Negro document issued from the White House since the Emancipation Proclamation. It read:

THE WHITE HOUSE

WASHINGTON

September 3, 1941

To Heads of All Departments and Independent Establishments:

It has come to my attention that there is in the Federal establishment a lack of uniformity and possibly some lack of sympathetic attitude toward the problems of minority groups, particularly those relating to the employment and assignment of Negroes in the Federal Civil Service.

With a view to improving the situation, it is my desire that all departments and independent establishments in the Federal Government make a thorough examination of their personnel policies and practices to the end that they may be able to assure me that in the

Federal Service the doors of employment are open to all loyal and qualified workers regardless of creed, race, or national origin.

It is imperative that we deal with this problem speedily and effectively. I shall look for immediate steps to be taken by all departments and independent establishments of the Government to facilitate and put into effect this policy of non-discrimination in Federal employment.

(Signed) FRANKLIN D. ROOSEVELT

The President's letter galvanized the personnel administrators of all government departments, commissions and agencies. Word was passed down the line, and immediately things began to happen. More Negroes were hired. They were given better jobs. Previously Negroes had been hired largely for menial work, such as janitor service and messenger service. Many Negroes holding these jobs felt that they were qualified for better work in the clerical forces, and many of them got these better jobs. Negro girls began to break into federal service as stenographers instead of charwomen. A few white officials acquired colored secretaries.

White help became scarce at about the same time, due to the growth of defense agencies, and many whites refused to accept low-pay clerical jobs because they could get something better. This made it possible for some government administrators to hire whole groups of Negroes for such jobs as office machine operators. Thus Negroes acquired a toe hold on thousands of jobs in the government clerical field. In the Department of Agriculture a Negro was appointed in the personnel office to spot jobs which Negroes might well fill. A similar practice was shortly thereafter adopted by several departments, and other new jobs were opened to Negroes. The Civil Service Commission adopted more vigorous policies on behalf of Negro applicants, and this resulted in more jobs.

"Rule of Three"

When vacancies occur in the government in normal times, the Civil Service Commission transmits three names of persons who passed the examination with high marks. The government administrators are supposed to take one of these three. Sometimes it occurs that all three are Negroes. In these cases the administrator is often inclined to circumvent the "rule of three" by promoting a white employee from within the organization, or by transferring a white person from some other agency. Thus discrimination against Negroes goes on despite the President's order, but gradually there is less of it.

Late in 1941 and in the early months of 1942, the "rule of three" faded into the background, as the urgent demand for war workers made speed more and more important. By agreement with the agencies involved, the

Civil Service Commission informally shelved the rule. Instead of giving a choice of three eligibles for each position, the Commission made the selections itself, notified the persons of their selection, weeded out those who declined, and sent the final list to the agency which needed the new employees. The agency, by prior agreement, took the workers regardless of their color. During December 1941, out of 3,700 clerical employees hired by the War Department, approximately 300 were Negroes.

Negro Leaders

Most of the Negro leaders within the government have similar backgrounds—"intellectual" or "social worker." Only a few of the Negro advisers and officials within the Roosevelt administration are fraternal leaders. Still, there are enough differences among the current Negro leaders to produce a split in their ranks in Washington. It runs generally between the college-bred "intellectuals" and the "practical men" who have pulled themselves up by their bootstraps. One Harvard-trained lawyer is referred to by the practical clique as "one of the Frankfurter boys."

The number of Negro officials is constantly increasing, so a roster of them would soon be out of date, but here are some of the most prominent:

Judge William H. Hastie, civilian aide to the Secretary of War, a graduate of Amherst College and Harvard Law School, and the first Negro ever given a federal judgeship. He was brought into the government by Ickes to be an assistant solicitor in the Department of the Interior. Ickes later backed him for the job of federal judge in the Virgin Islands.

Dr. Robert Weaver, another Harvard man, first Negro to get his Ph.D. in economics from that institution, now adviser to Sidney Hillman and the War Production Board on Negro labor. Was brought into the government by Ickes.

Earl Dickerson, member of the Committee on Fair Employment Practice. He is a Chicago lawyer and politician, a friend of Mayor Kelly.

Milton P. Webster, of Chicago, the second Negro member of the Committee on Fair Employment Practice, and international vice president of the Brotherhood of Sleeping Car Porters.

Mary McLeod Bethune, director of Negro activities for NYA, and president of the National Council of Negro Women. She struggled to educate herself, founded a school which has become Bethune-Cookman College, and is now president of it.

William Pickens, a Phi Beta Kappa graduate of Yale, who is on the Treasury Defense Bond Staff.

Lorimer Milton, the only Negro $1-a-year man in the government, and a graduate of Brown University. He flies up to Washington from Atlanta, where he is a bank president.

Ira DeA. Reid, a consultant in minorities in the Social Security Board's Bureau of Employment Security in Atlanta. He studied at Columbia University and the London School of Economics.

Edgar Brown, adviser to the Civilian Conservation Corps, and president of the United Government Employees, Inc., a union of low-paid government workers, mostly Negroes.

W. J. Trent, Jr., racial relations officer in the Federal Works Agency. He was brought into the government by Ickes, and served for a while as his racial adviser.

Crystal Bird Fauset, in charge of racial relations, Office of Civilian Defense. She is a former member of the Pennsylvania State Legislature, and was an assistant WPA state administrator.

Robert Taylor, housing consultant in the office of the Defense Housing Coordinator. He is a member of the Chicago Housing Authority, and managed a set of apartments built by the Rosenwald Fund to demonstrate that low-rent properties could yield good returns.

Dr. Booker T. McGraw, assistant to Taylor at the office of the Defense Housing Coordinator, and formerly under Leon Henderson handling war finance. He is a professor at Lincoln University at Jefferson City, Mo., and is an expert on French monetary policy.

George M. Johnson, assistant executive secretary to the Committee on Fair Employment Practice. He is a Howard University law professor who formerly was tax counsel for the California State Board of Equalization.

Thomas N. Roberts, special assistant to the personnel director of the Department of Agriculture. He formerly worked on a Farm Security Administration land utilization project at Tuskegee Institute.

Major Campbell C. Johnson, executive assistant to Brigadier General Lewis B. Hershey, head of Selective Service. He is a former YMCA worker.

Dr. Channing Tobias, member of the Selective Service Board, also a former YMCA worker.

Frank S. Horne, special assistant on racial relations at the United States Housing Authority.

W. Robert Ming, member of the staff of the Office of Price Administration. He is a Howard University professor, and a graduate of Chicago University.

Dr. Ralph Bunche, expert on native problems in the British Empire Section of the Library of Congress.

Charles Franklin, economist for the Social Security Board. He took his Ph.D. in economics at Columbia University.

Truman K. Gibson, Jr., assistant to Judge William H. Hastie, who is civilian aide to the Secretary of War. Gibson is a University of Chicago Law School graduate.

Dr. William H. Dean, Jr., consultant on locations of industry for the National Resources Planning Board. He is a professor at Atlanta University.

Dr. Rayford Logan, member of the Advisory Committee to the Coordinator of Inter-American Affairs (Nelson Rockefeller). He is a professor of history at Howard University, and took his Ph.D. at Harvard.

A number of other Negro leaders are influential within Washington without being government employees, or official advisers of the government. Here are some of them:

Walter White, executive secretary of the National Association for the Advancement of Colored People (NAACP). He is a graduate of Atlanta University, and was a special student at the College of the City of New York. He is a large part white, and is a powerful force in all Negro affairs.

A. Philip Randolph, president of the Brotherhood of Sleeping Car Porters. He is an influential leader who has access to the President, and who organized the job march which was called off after the President's anti-discrimination edict of summer 1941.

F. B. Ransom, an Indianapolis lawyer and politician, and a frequent adviser to the President on Negro matters.

Lester B. Granger, executive secretary of the National Urban League, and another White House caller.

Dr. Frederick Douglas Patterson, president of Tuskegee Institute. He is a veterinary graduate of Iowa State College, and received a master of science degree there and a Ph.D. from Cornell University.

Organizations

The National Association for the Advancement of Colored People is the largest of the "big four" of Negro organizations, it has a record of success in its Washington dealings. Its national legal committee, which consists largely of Washington lawyers, has won many notable victories before the Supreme Court. The National Urban League is interested mainly in industrial employment for Negroes, but it has been powerful in agitating for a better break for its people all along the line. The National Council of Negro Women is the most powerful women's organization and has received much attention through Mrs. Roosevelt's friendliness. The National Negro Congress is usually considered the most leftish of the four. A fifth organization, the New Negro Alliance, with its movement to "Buy Where You Can Work," operates in a number of cities, but is not organized on a national scale.

Differences in aim and method mark the "big four," but in recent years their platforms have become parallel. The NAACP is fairly typical of them all. It fights for equal treatment "wherever this is feasible." This means eventual equality on the social plane. Equal political and civil rights. Equal representation on juries. Equal treatment from police. Equal educational and health facilities. An end to exclusion from political parties. An end to segregation, with its jim crow ramifications. An even break all around, to be obtained by gradual transition, not sudden revolution.

The equality program does not include intermarriage of blacks and whites. Most leaders consider a certain amount of race purity as an indispensable basis for race pride, and race pride, they say, is a "must" for raising the level of Negro achievement. (Furthermore, as one Negro leader put it, "if the whites could see some of our beautiful Negro girls out at Howard University, they would understand why we Negroes are perfectly happy to forget about intermarriage.")

The Negro organizations are influential with the executive branch of government, and have received what they call a square deal from the Supreme Court, but they do not do well with Congress. The mass of southern members of Congress block many measures on the floor and make use of committees for pigeonholing legislation which the Negroes seek— such as the anti-lynching bill. There is one Negro congressman, Representative Arthur W. Mitchell of Chicago, but he cannot do much by himself.

Complaints Remaining

The Negro organizations now have three main complaints about government, and these indicate their immediate objectives:

Complaint No. 1 is that although Negroes have 150,000 jobs in the federal government service, this still is not as many as their proportion in the population entitles them to. (They are approximately 10 per cent of the population.)

Complaint No. 2 is that the average income of Negro government workers in all parts of the country is only $1300, instead of $1871 which is the national average for all government employees. The leaders claim that Negroes are held to the bottom jobs, without adequate chance for advancement.

Complaint No. 3 is that the "rule of three" still is on the Civil Service Commission books, and still allows some administrators to avoid hiring Negroes. Negro leaders would like to see a ruling which would make it

155

compulsory for an administrator to take the first name on the eligibility list for any particular job.

There is no serious complaint about the postal service, which is the government's largest hirer of Negroes. It has at least 7,000 Negro carriers, 6,000 clerks, 1,000 railroad mail clerks, and 6,000 custodial employees.

The Negroes have made tremendous progress toward equality of opportunity under Roosevelt and the New Deal. They have gone further and gained more than most of their leaders ever thought they would get from government at this time. They have given President Roosevelt a secure position as the greatest patron saint of Negroes since Lincoln. And they have gained all this without much publicity, without much attention from the bulk of the press of the nation.

Whether the ultimate departure of Mr. and Mrs. Roosevelt from the White House will mean the end of the game or just a seventh inning stretch, no one knows. But one thing is sure—the Negroes are piling up the score while the going is good.

Home Town Negroes

The local Washington Negroes, the home folks, are distinct from the national leaders and their push toward equality.

You cannot know San Francisco without knowing its Chinatown, you cannot know New Orleans without knowing its French quarter, and you cannot know Washington without knowing its black islands. These are the places where Negroes live, and they are everywhere, in all parts of the city, islands in a sea of whites. They are inhabited by the 28 per cent, the 225,000, who might be called blacks except for the fact that one-third of them have white blood from generations back, and their colors range from black, to brown, to tan, to yellow, to almost pure white. They are "the colored." Many a debutante pictured in the Negro newspaper looks like a white debutante.

Negrodom of Washington has its castes and its levels, as does all of whitedom. At the top, the upper crust, are the aristocratic colored gentry. At the bottom are the peasants. In the middle are the yeomen who do much of the menial work of Washington. There is as much difference between the classes as between upper-upper-whites and poor trashy whites.

Among the top "400" are the government leaders, the professors, the teachers, the doctors, and a few well-to-do businessmen. Some of them are moneyed, and some are not. Some are newcomers, and some are "old Washington families," and proud of it. Most live in comfortable homes with one or more bathrooms. They drive good cars and dress with taste.

156

They shun low-grade stores and make slighting remarks about neighborhood eyesores. They have been to college, or at least through high school. They know what grammar is and they use it. They don't say "yassuh," and they don't shuffle their feet. They are tolerantly amused by the hallelujah churches and mystified by boogie-woogie. They are the uppest class.

The middle classes form the big bulk of the population. They are middle-class in the same sense that most white Washingtonians are middle-class, except that middle-class black income is lower than middle-class white income. A high percentage are high school graduates—practically all of those who were born here.

The bottom fringe Negroes are poor in pocketbook and spirit, and they wallow in the cores of rotted city blocks.

Making a Living

Of the 225,000 Negroes in Washington, more than 35,000 work for the government. Most are janitors, charwomen and messengers. A few are middle-grade clerks and technicians. One group, discussed previously, hold important administrative posts. About 1,500 Negro Washingtonians are teachers in the public schools or night schools, in Miner Teachers College, or at Howard University. A few men are doctors, dentists and lawyers for the Negro community, and they are college educated. The great bulk of the 225,000 work in one way or another for the whites—as chauffeurs, maids, cooks, janitors, barbers, bootblacks, taxi drivers, hod carriers, caddies, bellboys and waiters. (Many a Washington waiter is a college graduate.)

As for Negro-owned businesses, there are few. Stores run by white men cater to the Negro trade, and Negro businessmen can't compete. In the deep South, white families often help their pet Negroes to get toeholds on businesses of their own, but in Washington the whites don't have this paternalistic inclination. Only one type of Negro-owned business thrives notably. It is the undertaking business, and two sizable local Negro fortunes have been built upon elaborate funerals. Negroes may have entered this world unobtrusively, but they do not intend to let the error be repeated at their exit.

The numbers racket is another business which provides a living for thousands of Negroes. There are many jobs as runners or collectors of the pennies, dimes, quarters or dollars which probably half of the Negroes pay daily to gambling in hopes of riches. In one suburban community of 2,200 middle-class Negroes, fifteen runners collect an average of $60 a day each, and make at least $6 a day as commissions. But the numbers game at the top is run by whites.

Taken altogether, Washington Negroes are the best educated single group in their race. Only 4 out of 100 are illiterate. Their public schools are on a level with those of the whites. Their Howard University, which sits high on a hill in the middle of Washington, overlooking a water reservoir and the ball park, is called the "Negro Harvard." It has 268 professors, and 2,173 colored students, and is the leading Negro college in the world. It lifts the social and intellectual tone of the upper crust, but exerts only a faint pull on the middle and lower classes.

Washington is not a garden of the Negro arts. Educated Negro Washingtonians tend to be social or political doers rather than aesthetic creators. There is no Negro drama in Washington, except for some amateur performances cultivated by Howard University. The Howard Theater, which is No. 1 Negro theater, tried running plays, but gave them up for hot trumpets. But even in the field of hot trumpets, Washington Negroes have never been world beaters. The city has contributed a handful of colored singers and tap dancers, and two well-known bandleaders, Duke Ellington and Claude Hopkins, but the city has few joints where hot jazz ensembles are incubated. As a cradle of the blues, jazz and jumping jives, Washington can't compare with St. Louis, Kansas City, Chicago, New Orleans or New York. The hepcats complain that Negro Washingtonians are too highbrow to appreciate good jive. For movies, however, Washington has more Negro theaters than any other city in the country.

The one local Negro newspaper, the *Washington Tribune*, was a staid publication, and folded up late in 1941 because thousands of Negroes preferred to buy the snappy Washington editions of the *Pittsburgh Courier* and the *Baltimore Afro-American*.

Segregation

The jim crow policy does not prevail on Washington streetcars and busses. Negroes can and do take any seat, front or rear. But that's about where the equal privileges end, for in almost everything else Negroes are reminded daily that Washington is south of the Mason and Dixon's line. They have their own hotels, their own schools, their own restaurants. (Exceptions are the Union Station restaurant and some government cafeterias.) They are not admitted to regular theaters and rarely to music concerts. (The upper classes usually go to New York for these.) There are occasional rumblings of dissatisfaction with the unwritten rules of segregation, especially as to movie theaters, concerts and public gatherings, and the time doubtless will come when the Negroes will demand admission.

Today a few light Negroes slip into the theaters, and a few eat at white restaurants, undetected. And every now and then, a very light Negro stays at a white hotel. The most famous example was that of Walter White, executive secretary of the National Association for the Advancement of Colored People, who used to stay at the swanky Hay-Adams House, across Lafayette Square from the White House. Being very white in appearance, he was not recognized until *Time* magazine featured him in a story and on the cover, and he was forced to leave the hotel.

The Negro population, although large, is isolated from the whites. The two may live within the same city block but they do not ordinarily mingle, except in the relation of superior and inferior, employer and employee. In a few civic organizations, such as the Community Chest, they may sit together, but this is the exception, not the rule. In some white newspapers Negro news appears now and then, but it is not much, and the white population does not know a great deal about the black population. The aloofness of the whites is matched ordinarily by the aloofness of the blacks. They keep themselves apart, and in most things they are on the alert to avoid any conduct which would feed a Ku Klux spirit.

Racial feeling between whites and blacks in Washington is ordinarily a negative sort of thing. They get along because they have to get along. White women complain about their Negro maids, but that's more or less personal, not racial. Employers complain that some Negroes don't come to work Monday morning, because they are recovering from the week-end on the bottle, but that, too, is like a phonograph record, and there's nothing racial in it. Once, in 1919, there was a near race riot in Washington, when a white mob formed downtown and moved in mass toward the Negro center at Seventh and U Streets. But serious bloodshed was averted, thanks to the advance warnings given by the "white Negroes," who had mingled with the white mob, and to the vigilance of the police, and to an act of God in the form of a thunder shower which wet the whites and dampened their lust.

In 1941 a series of rapes of white women by Negro men raised the racial temperature. Some of the cases got into the newspapers. Many others were "accidentally" omitted, but got into the underground channels of gossip. This caused some white muttering and brought to the surface the word "nigger," which is not a common term in the Washington vocabulary. Police were extra cautious, and a new tension was present in Negro-white relations.

Homes and Social Strata

Most Negroes of Washington live in areas of many city blocks which have been taken over by the Negroes from their former white residents.

These Negro zones grow, a block at a time. The whole street may be white, but a real estate man negotiates a sale of one house in the block for an unnamed buyer who later turns out to be colored. The price for the one house may be high, but thereafter the other houses fall like dominoes in a row, at whatever price they will bring. Thus the neighborhood shifts from white to black, and the whites move out, and the Negroes infiltrate into the secondhand houses of the whites. Most Negroes live in such houses.

The upper classes of Negroes live in suburbs of their own, on the outskirts of the city. Some of these suburbs are "exclusive," for the black blue bloods of the city—the old residenters, the well-to-do businessmen, and the parents of the colored girls who furnish the annual crop of colored debutantes, and even the black numbers racket barons. The upper-crust Negroes go in for inaugural balls in a big way. They have their very special cabarets, where the cover charge is stiff. They have their select resorts near Annapolis on Chesapeake Bay. They have their swell apartment houses.

There are lofty Negro clubs, just as there are lofty white clubs. One of the best of these is Mu-So-Lit (Mu for music, So for society, Lit for literature). The What-Good-Are-We Club is fashionable, and its dance bids are prized. Once upon a time there were the Bluebirds, the Back Biters, the Earls, and the Buggy Riders, but their place has been taken by the Guardsmen and the Blackfriars.

There are national college fraternities and sororities, and the fact that one is a "brother Kappa" or a "sister Delta" helps many a young colored man or woman to make the social grade in Negro Washington.

Negro society has everything that white society has in Washington except a congressional set and a diplomatic set. It is hard to build a congressional set on one lone Negro congressman. And a whole diplomatic society structure is not quite possible when there is only one Negro diplomat, the Minister of Haiti, who prefers the white rendezvous to the vastly more lively neighborhood of U Street, where pool rooms and "hot licks" make more merriment than diplomats ever know.

Slums

In Washington, if you know where to look for them, you can find Porksteak Alley, Pig Alley, Goat Alley, Tin Can Alley, Coon's Alley, Tiger Alley, Moonshine Alley, Louse Alley and Chinch Row. These are Washington's Negro ghettos. Most of them are the back lots of the white residents of seventy years ago, and they were built on to take care of the influx of refugee Negroes after the Civil War. The construction of alley dwellings was ended by law exactly fifty years ago, but most of the original shacks remain today.

The occupants of these alley shacks are a special breed of people, with their own customs, their own superstitions and a notorious suspicion of outsiders. Marriage is not the rule. More than half of the children born in the darkest alleys are illegitimate. Men often loaf in one house or another, leaving the breadwinning to the women. When you go to look for someone in an alley, you ask for the house by the woman's name. It's Mamie Smith's house, not John Smith's. John is likely to be just temporary equipment. He may be the father of one or two of Mamie's children, but it's likely that she is just keeping him. If he gets tired of her, he may move down the alley to some other woman's house. These men are called "lovers," and are considered a normal complement of alley life. The women may say "Dey ain't no count, no how," but they like them, and they keep them on. Illegitimate children, rather than being a disgrace, are considered a sort of badge of pride for the unmarried mother and are sometimes referred to as "engagement babies." Professional prostitution never has flourished in the alleys, but bootlegging was a favorite occupation during prohibition.

Churches Multitudinous

Washington Negroes go to church more than Washington whites. Most go to the organized churches of Baptists, Methodists, Catholics, Presbyterians, and Episcopalians. The rest go to the independent denominations and to the more spectacular churches run by ministers of God who promise "pie in the sky when you die," with a token slice right now. The best-known of these is the church of Elder Lightfoot Solomon Michaux, who outshouts the devil regularly, and whose choir swings "Happy Am I" on the radio to white listeners all over the nation. The elder's Church of God is located in a neon-lighted building across the street from the baseball park.

Another of the spectacular religious conjurers is Bishop C. M. "Daddy" Grace, founder of the House of Prayer and the Family Aid Society, which operate from a temple with a mansard roof at 6th and M Streets, NW. "Daddy" specializes in a Negro uplift program which includes watermelon parties, mass baptismal wettings with an efficient fire hose, and daily services. He has a sharp mustache, a dagger-point beard, and is an impressive figure about town. Such Negro preachers as Elder Michaux and "Daddy" Grace are better known to most Washington Negroes than is the president of Howard University.

Whites

The 72 per cent of Washington whites would not know how to get along without the 28 per cent of blacks. They rely on them to help them do the drudgery work in homes, stores and offices. They sell them groceries, rent them houses at extra high rents, pay most of the social costs which go along with Negro disease and Negro crime, and complain always about them. The whites are less patronizing than whites of cities farther south, but also less helpful than the whites of most northern cities. They have heard vague rumors about the equality movement but they think it is just a passing phase. They have not yet learned that it isn't.

16

The Press Corps

I F YOU happen to be walking along the sidewalk in front of the White
House some Tuesday afternoon or Friday noon, you will see a hundred
or more men scurrying along in twos and threes, and you will think some
important meeting has just let out. It has, for these are news correspondents
and they are hurrying away from the President's press conference. They
must get to their typewriters to write what the President said . . . and
didn't say.

Listen to the scraps of conversation: "He said off the record . . ." "I'm
going to write the lead and let them pick up the rest from the AP."
". . . but he didn't deny it outright." "That laugh didn't sound to me as
if he planned to do anything about it right now." ". . . gives point to what
Hull said yesterday." "I wonder why he ducked your question . . ." "He
was in good form today . . . feeling good . . . can't be too much worried . . ."

Follow these men as they scatter to their offices. You will hear the typewriters pound, see copy boys scram, messengers hurry, telegraph instruments click, automatic printers busily engaged in sending out words. Even
while you are watching, newspaper offices from coast to coast have the
story, the headlines are being set, and people on the streets or in their
homes can soon read what the President said and how he said it.

All over the city of Washington this news activity goes on hourly,
through the day and night. News, words, dispatches. People talk, say this
and that, and disagree, and meditate on what they read. All the great volume of chatter and thought throughout the land about Washington starts
with the news which flows through a few hundred men, the newsmen of
Washington. They are pipe lines through whom you learn what you learn
about Washington.

The 700 or more men, and several dozen women, who work at writing
news out of Washington are an important lot. Add the radio newsmen who
voice the news to your ear, add the magazine and other writers, add the
photographers, and you have a group of Washington workers who have

great influence on your own affairs. You think what you please, but you think it largely on the basis of what they tell you.

Their work may seem romantic to you, but they don't think so. They yawn when people talk of "the power of the press." They are too busy to think of the power they hold, and sometimes too busy even to think. They wear out a good deal of shoe leather, as well as the seats of their pants, and most of them have wives who grumble that newspaper husbands think all the time about their work. They don't refer to their work as a "game," but secretly and all unbeknownst to themselves they really think it is. They wouldn't miss it for anything.

Who They Are

The men who come out of the President's press conferences are, in general, the most important correspondents reporting or commenting upon the broad aspects of political, national or foreign news, but they are less than a quarter of the whole group of Washington news writers. The others are busy elsewhere. Some are working in the press galleries of Congress. Some are watching constantly the most important of the departments and agencies of the government. Some are searching out feature stories or running down miscellaneous news events of the day. Some are digging up the "home town angle" of the story "breaking" here. Some work at desks, especially in the larger bureaus, sitting at the neck of the funnel through which all news flows.

Take a brief look at these men themselves and see who they are, where they come from, how they got their jobs, their income, education, background and mode of life. The most exhaustive and authoritative study on that subject was done five years ago by Leo C. Rosten* on the basis of elaborate confidential questionnaires from 127 men carefully selected to form a representative cross section of the group.

He discovered that more than half of this group of newsmen were college graduates with scholastic records well above the average. Sixteen were Phi Beta Kappas. Ten won scholarships. Two were graduated *magna cum laude*. Eight held higher than baccalaureate degrees. Four were Rhodes scholars. Four had received honorary degrees.

The average income level then was $5,987 a year. (It is probably a little higher now.) Top incomes were above $20,000 a year. The lowest were around $1,500, but 41 per cent were between $5,000 and $7,500 and 22 per cent were over $7,500.

Their average age was 41.7 years. Almost half of them were sons of

* *The Washington Correspondents,* Leo C. Rosten, Harcourt, Brace & Co., New York, 1937.

professional men. More than two-thirds came from families accustomed to incomes above $2,500 a year. They were and are distinctly a middle-class group.

They are experienced. They have been working on newspapers an average of 18.8 years, and in Washington an average of 9.7 years.

From their answers to Rosten's questionnaires, it seems plain that they like their jobs, get a kick out of being in the thick of things, don't want to be editors or editorial writers. They call themselves reporters; the word journalist they seldom use. Practically all of them are honest and most of them try to be fair in what they write. Not one in a hundred could be bribed—crudely by a direct offer of money—but they are human beings like everyone else and many of them can be influenced over a period of time in their attitudes and opinions by skillful flattery, attentions, or official and social favors.

Most of them take a drink when they are on a party, and sometimes when they're not. There are few teetotalers among them, and among the successful correspondents even fewer who drink to excess. The day when a red nose and whisky breath were the mark of a newspaperman has long since passed in Washington.

Most of them come from a small-town background, are married and have families. Almost half told Rosten they were born in localities having less than 10,000 population. They are not much on church attendance. Over half never go to church and less than 10 per cent go regularly.

Nearly all of the special correspondents were sent to Washington from the local staffs of their papers. Some came through the route of state political writer, but in most cases they got their jobs because of outstanding qualities on their home papers—trustworthiness, keenness, discretion, good judgment and ability to write reasonably well. Personality—general likableness, ability to mix, a certain degee of *savoir-faire*—is more generally characteristic of the group than bookishness or studious application.

Handouts

There are three basic sources from which the Washington reporters obtain the news you find in your daily paper. They are the "handout," the press conference, and the personal interview.

"Handout" is newspaperese for the vast number of press releases which are distributed daily in Washington. They come from both government and private sources. Practically every government agency of any consequence has one or more individuals all or part of whose time is devoted to preparing these handouts. Some of the more important or more publicity-minded departments and agencies have large staffs of a hundred or more devoted to information work.

Every lobbying organization starts off with a publicity man, a mimeograph machine, and a *Congressional Directory* containing the names and office addresses of the Washington correspondents. Many handouts come in daily from private companies with information they want to get to the public, from organizations of all kinds, and from individuals.

Most speeches of any consequence which are made by government or private figures are distributed in this way in advance of delivery.

From these handouts comes much information. The facts in them are usually accurate. They may not be the full facts, or they may be the facts presented in the most favorable light, but they are not incorrect as far as they go.

A great deal of official information is given out through formal announcements of this character. Any newsman would be lost without them. Yet anyone who depended upon such news too much would be worth only a pinch of his salt. The smart ones take the handouts as a beginning and start digging to see what is behind them, what pertinent facts have been left out and why, and what is likely to follow.

Press Conferences

The formal announcements of action or opinion by handouts constitute the basic news available to all. The next stage is the press conference, which is an outgrowth of American journalism and is not even known in many other countries.

Most famous and most important of all the press conferences are those of the President. They are extremely productive, not so much for the information he volunteers (which would be obtained anyway through White House announcements) as for the opportunity to ask questions on almost any subject.

Even though it is a matter on which the President does not wish to talk, his reaction to the question, his manner, the way in which he dodges, often give definite impressions of his viewpoint. The mere fact that he does not wish to discuss certain questions at certain times is frequently illuminating to those who know the ins and outs.

The chance remarks, the repartee (of which there is much), the smile or frown, all give a valuable insight into the presidential mind, especially to those who know Mr. Roosevelt best. Not infrequently, to those who can recognize it, he wears his heart on his sleeve.

There are scores of other press conferences each week. Stephen Early, secretary to the President, holds one or more daily. On the stroke of twelve every day Secretary of State Hull sees the press, or in his absence, Under Secretary Welles conducts a press conference. Other cabinet officers schedule one or two a week and hold them with varying regularity. There are many more by foreign ambassadors or visiting dignitaries, political leaders, businessmen, organization heads, and many government officials below cabinet rank.

No one correspondent could possibly go to all of them. Each goes to the ones which he feels will be productive of most news in which his paper is interested. No official would have the time to see individually each of the correspondents who come to his press conference. But by seeing them in a group he can afford time for leisurely and informative discussion, if he is so disposed.

Private Interviews and Pipe Lines

The personal interview system is a major part of the newsgathering system. It is the means by which a correspondent goes beyond the routine of official announcements.

There are two types of personal interviews—those in which the official is quoted directly or indirectly, and those in which he is not quoted at all. In the second kind, much information is obtained which is never attributed to the person giving it, but is written under such protective phrases as "learned in reliable quarters," "obtained from the highest authority," "learned authoritatively," and "this correspondent was informed."

Many officials will talk much more freely to one man whom they know than to a group. A correspondent who is known as reliable and trustworthy can do much of this by telephone. He may make as many as 50 calls in one day. Most officials are much more accessible for the short telephone conversation which they know they can terminate at will than for the direct interview which runs into time.

The "pipe line" is a variation of the personal interview technique. When a correspondent says he has a "pipe line" into a specific department or agency, that is newspaperese for saying that he knows some high official there so well that he can find out, either on or off the record, almost anything this official knows.

Only reporters with judgment and discretion can establish pipe lines or maintain them long. In the long run they mean exclusive stories, accurate forecasts, illuminating comment, authoritative writing.

Black Sheet Swaps

"Black sheet" is newspaper slang for a carbon copy of a story. One man gets a story of general interest. He writes it and gives carbons to several other correspondents. They rewrite it and file it to their papers. Next day they may give him a story.

The system is most frequent among the independent correspondents and smaller bureaus. It has been much criticized but, provided the original writer has done a careful reporting job, there is really nothing wrong with it. The evil of it exists only where a poor job of reporting is given much wider circulation by this means, but reporters soon find out whose black sheets are reliable and whose are not.

The gossip exchange is the unwritten variant of the black sheet system. News writers who do not compete with each other exchange information and gossip freely. A standard greeting when they meet is "Whadda ya know?"

The Senate and House press galleries, the National Press Club, and the White House press room are the scenes of most of this exchange of news and ideas, but it occurs wherever newspapermen meet. It is most prolific, perhaps, at luncheon time in the Press Club.

The Press Associations

Most of the stories that you read under a Washington dateline will be either by the Associated Press, the United Press or the International News Service, for these press associations are the main disseminators of the spot news. Each keeps men at all key points in Washington all day long. It is their job to report all news as speedily and factually as possible. Much of it is telephoned in to central news desks where dictation men take it down.

Speed is essential. Five minutes is a long time for one press association to beat another on any news break of consequence, and is certain to bring demands for explanations from the slower service.

Except for a few large ones, the newspapers of the country generally depend on these wire reports, which run to thousands of words daily, for the actual news developments. There are only a few papers which make an effort to cover with their own men all important news stories of Washington.

The Independents

The independents are the most diverse group in the corps. Some get high salaries, some very low. Some write only the news which has an interest for their particular locality. Some are among the best and keenest observers in Washington and write illuminating interpretation of what events mean, and what they are likely to lead to. Some are in bureaus of three, four, and five, where a high degree of specialization exists, and some serve a number of papers, each of which pays only a comparatively small amount.

Since Mrs. Roosevelt arrived on the scene, started her regular press conferences, and made the rule that they might be attended by no one but women, there has been a constantly increasing number of women in the Washington press corps.

Mrs. Roosevelt's press conferences occur at 11 o'clock on every Monday that she is in town. From 25 to 35 newspaperwomen assemble in the Green Room at the foot of the staircase leading to the living quarters of the White House on the second floor. Chairs are placed in a semicircle before a davenport upstairs. The girls are gushing and eager for the front seats, and they run up the stairs when the usher opens the gate at the foot of the staircase. The day that Mrs. Roosevelt had as a guest the Princess Juliana of Holland, the Princess was really frightened when they came dashing into the room, so since then they have made a more decorous entrance.

Mrs. Roosevelt shakes hands with each one and then produces a little black book containing her appointments for the week, which she reads off. At the conclusion of that she answers questions. Frequently she brings in some woman in the government who talks about things in her particular field. The press conferences usually last about an hour, sometimes longer. Mrs. Roosevelt talks off the record a good deal but has a rule against discussing pending legislation (even though she sometimes relaxes it a bit). The women never get as tough with her in their questions as the men do with the President, but she will answer almost any question that is asked.

The women have their own organizations, the oldest of which is the Women's National Press Club, which has 120 active members. Some are publicity women and society writers. It holds frequent luncheons at which distinguished guests speak off the record, and once a year it gives its annual stunt party, for women only.

Another is the Newspaper Women's Club of Washington, which has 50 active members all of whom are women writers regularly paid by newspapers. This club has three honorary members—Mrs. Roosevelt, Mrs. Calvin Coolidge, Mrs. Herbert Hoover.

A third is the Mrs. Roosevelt Press Conference Association and was set up to administer somewhat strict rules to forbid any but actually working newspaperwomen to attend Mrs. Roosevelt's conferences.

The Columnists

No group is more distinct than the columnists, and there are as many varieties of them as there are of chrysanthemums. As a group they are the highest paid and best known of any section of the press corps.

The Washington column as it is known today was really started by Paul Mallon in the early 30's. It was so successful that many others flocked into the field. Mallon's is distinctly a news column. So is Ray Tucker's "National Whirligig," and in the main the "Washington Merry-Go-Round" of Drew Pearson and Robert S. Allen.

Classed in the purely commentator variety of columns are those of Mark Sullivan, Frank Kent, Ernest Lindley, Walter Lippmann and David Lawrence. Kent is a cause columnist for the conservative viewpoint. Mark Sullivan is similarly inclined, but seeks objectivity and is writing for history. Lawrence represents a viewpoint usually in line with orthodox business views, while Lindley and Lippmann have strong inclinations toward the New Deal.

Raymond Clapper's column is really a daily editorial on some news subject, but he packs a lot of information into it. He is an influential columnist, and still a good reporter. In all the Washington press corps there is probably no person more highly respected than Clapper.

General Hugh Johnson is always fighting some cause or Harold Ickes. Pegler's campaign against racketeers in labor unions has a big following in Washington officialdom, although his is not essentially a Washington column and is not written here.

Radio, Magazines and Trade Press

The broadcasters form another group. Several of them are as much reporters as any writers for the newspapers, but their transmission medium is different. Albert L. Warner of Columbia, Fulton Lewis, Jr., of Mutual, H. R. Baukhage, Earl Godwin, William Hillman and Raymond Clapper of NBC, all gather their own information and write their own broadcasts, containing a strong analytical quality. They are to be distinguished sharply from radio news announcers who simply read a few press bulletins from the press associations or Transradio news, the organization providing news direct to radio stations.

Still another group in the Washington lightshedders are the magazine men. The *Time-Life-Fortune* bureau is large and elaborate and headed by Felix Belair, former *New York Times* man. *Newsweek,* headed by Ernest Lindley, is smaller. *The United States News,* a weekly published by David Lawrence, has its own staff of newsgatherers. There is also a sizable list of writers who work regularly from Washington for magazines of a more general character.

A rapidly growing group is the trade press. Largest of this type is the McGraw-Hill office headed by Paul Wooton which serves all the many McGraw-Hill trade publications, including *Business Week,* whose Washington news is excellent. There are many other smaller trade news bureaus which pay little heed to the headlines of the day, but which follow closely any developments regarding aviation, engineering, motor vehicles, highways, the oil industry, railroads, radio, and numberless other special interests.

The business or trade press correspondents are usually skilled economic writers and analysts. They know not only what the news is, but what it means when applied to a particular business, or to business in general. Often they get certain news well ahead of the regular newspapermen, so that when the news breaks in the newspapers it is old news to the readers of the business journals. The trade news men have time to do deeper digging on fewer subjects, while the newspapermen wait for it to come to the surface and break in some formal press conference.

News Letters

Washington news letters are a development of the past 25 years. They are relatively small, but they are potent beyond their circulation, because they are read avidly by the hundreds of thousands of upper-crust citizens who can afford their relatively high subscription rates. They are printed or mimeographed, usually four pages, but sometimes more, and they look like typewritten office memoranda. Most are weekly. Some sweep up the news, some analyze it, and some give forecasts or projections of the news.

They are usually specialized in subject matter, and each news letter builds a circulation of persons interested in that special subject. They assume that readers have too much to read, and that a proper function of writers is to boil the news down, point up the significance. They carry no advertising, and are supported solely by subscription fees. They are staffed largely by men who have been brought up in the newsgathering business, and they also have research staffs, economists, and specialists in this and that. They do not have full press status in Washington, but they observe all the regular press rules. They regard themselves not as substitutes for the news, but as supplementary services.

There are a dozen or more letter services dealing with Washington news, but three of them have about 90 per cent of the total circulation. Whaley-Eaton, established in 1918, is the oldest. Kiplinger, second oldest, established in 1923, is the largest. Both Whaley-Eaton and Kiplinger are located in Washington. The third, Research Institute of America, newest and youngest, is located in New York but has Washington correspondents.

Photographers

One of the least noticed but most active press groups in Washington is the photographers. They are everywhere that pictures might be caught. The movie newsreel men, the princes of this group, appear only on the biggest occasions. But the "still men," the representatives of the news picture services, of local papers, and of picture magazines, are around whenever anything worth while is happening. Few pictures are posed. The best ones are caught by patient waiting for a speaker to show just that expression of anger, disgust, or elation that typifies what he says, waiting sometimes sitting on the floor or even under tables to get unusual angles or to be close enough without being in the way of officials or spectators. No group in the whole sphere of keeping you informed works harder or endures more physical discomfort than the photographer in doing his job, and nowhere does perseverance pay better.

Because they may work with mechanical devices within a few feet of the President, the rules of the photographers' association (which has 80-odd members) are far more rigid than the rules of any of the other Washington news organizations.

National Press Club

There are four major organizations of Washington correspondents—the National Press Club, the Gridiron Club, the White House Correspondents' Association, and the Overseas Writers. Each fills a specific function.

Largest and most important professionally is the National Press Club. It occupies the thirteenth and fourteenth floors of the National Press Building in the heart of downtown Washington. The building was put up by the club through one of its members, James William Bryan, and was completed in 1927.

The club itself has 60-odd employees and does a gross restaurant, bar and other business of about $300,000 a year. It is managed entirely by its more than 500 active newspapermen. Once a year the active members fight fiercely over the elections, which are like club elections everywhere. Its non-active and associate membership totals some 2200 and includes former newspapermen, publicity men, government officials, lawyers, labor leaders, lobbyists, trade association executives, and some businessmen. There are no honorary memberships. President Roosevelt is a dues paying member, and so are all but two of his cabinet.

This is the only Washington newspaper organization which operates actively 365 days in the year, and 24 hours of the day. Here every day among the 200 to 300 members who come for lunch may be seen many of the top newspaper figures of Washington. Here the "gossip exchange" operates at its best. Here come all visiting editors, most of whom are non-resident members.

Once every week or two the club holds a formal luncheon which has developed into a national forum of such importance that the club is able to command speakers almost at will.

To the National Press Club are sent most of the handouts which are distributed. Here also many newsmen keep in touch with city-wide developments by frequent access to the ticker, operated by the United Press. This ticker carries a brief summary of all UP world news, and of Washington news in more detail.

Gridiron Club

The Gridiron Club is the oldest, smallest, most exclusive, and most luminous group of Washington newspapermen. It is essentially a social club, like a fraternity, and its main claim to fame arises out of its two dinners a year, at which public men and distinguished guests are roasted on the gridiron of non-venomous satire. The Club was founded in 1885, and its dinners have formed a thread through the history of the times since then. Three books have been written about it.

Out-of-towners often confuse the Gridiron Club and the National Press Club. The Press Club is the bigger, for almost any newspaperman may belong to it, and it plays a practical part in the news scheme of things. But the Gridiron Club is small, with only 50 members, and by somewhat vague social standards they are the cream of the cream, thirty-third degree.

Every President since Grover Cleveland has attended Gridiron dinners, though some have skipped occasionally. President Roosevelt has given the impression of some impatience toward the club, kids it because it requires full dress instead of black tie, and arranged his schedule so as not to be in Washington for the December 1940 dinner. That was the first time in 26 dinners that a President had missed. Since that time, however, the President's cordiality toward the club has increased. But few Presidents, including Mr. Roosevelt, have ever really enjoyed the lampooning of their policies, although most of them enjoy the skits in which the opposition is satirized.

The Gridiron Club's guest list, limited to about 400, undoubtedly is the most distinguished of any dinner in America. People come from as far as the West Coast for it. Some men spend years angling for an invitation to a Gridiron dinner.

All skits are written and acted by members. The planning and writing begins about five weeks ahead of the dinner, and rehearsals about three weeks in advance. Popular songs are parodied freely. The two speeches at each dinner, usually made by the President and a representative of the opposition party, are off the record, but a detailed summary of the skits is given out for publication.

Membership in the Gridiron Club is by election as vacancies occur, and it is a rare thing for more than three or four new members a year to be elected. They are mostly bureau heads, representatives of leading newspapers, or outstanding writers.

There is no country in the world except the United States where such a thing as the Gridiron Club exists, or where lampooning would be tolerated by the government. Some people point to it as a symbol of free speech and a free press.

White House Correspondents

The White House Correspondents' Association is run by the group of newspapermen who are assigned to cover the White House every day, but its membership is open to any bona fide Washington newswriter who wants to pay a dollar. The membership list runs into the hundreds.

The Association controls, subject to White House approval, admission to the President's press conferences and the conduct of members in respect to them. Aside from that, its function is chiefly social. It gives one dinner a year, does not go in for skits like the Gridiron Club, but makes a movie which kids the President and other public figures.

Overseas Writers is a much newer organization which has come into prominence with the increasing importance of foreign affairs. Its membership is limited to those who have, at some time, been foreign correspondents. In general, it is a group that knows something about foreign affairs and writes regularly on that subject.

Off the record luncheons are held every Monday at which some individual who has just returned from a country in the news, or who knows particularly well some field of foreign affairs, speaks and answers questions. Possessors of information are sought, rather than big names. The luncheon group is small, and the discussions are informative. Professionally, it is a valuable and useful group.

Press and Radio Galleries of Congress

Though not in any sense a club, the press galleries of the two houses of Congress are a leading place of congregation for members of the press. Members of the press gallery must be bona fide working correspondents of daily newspapers, and great care is exercised to bar writers who are not actually members of the fast-working daily press. The press gallery list is the master list of qualified newspapermen. The authority for their admission flows from Congress itself, although in actual operation the newsmen make their own rules and do their own policing of membership. It is the nearest approach to a body which can pass on ethics of the news writing profession, but even its machinery is lax and its standards variable.

Radio reporters and commentators have their own galleries, alongside the press galleries, and organized on the same lines.

A visitor in the public galleries of the Senate or House sees in the press gallery only some seats very similar to his own, except for a desk in front of the seats. Most of the time these seats are rather sparsely populated unless something extraordinary is going on. Then they fill rapidly.

But the real press gallery is in the rooms behind the walls on that side of the chamber. Here are batteries of typewriters, rows of telephone booths, press association wires with their operators, offices of both telegraph companies, and lounging space where correspondents may relax and exchange information. These rooms are the centers for the gathering of news at the Capitol, or by telephone anywhere in town. Many of the news writers spend a large portion of the day in the press galleries and write and file much of their copy there.

Press Sidelights

Ickes. He is the chief official critic of the press. He conducts a campaign of lambasting newspaper publishers. He thinks newspapers should shift their editorial policies to accord with elections. Newspapermen point out that Ickes' policy would tend to produce a one-party system. The attack on newspapers as a business doubtless will be resumed after the war, if the New Deal is in power then.

Bias. Among Washington news writers there are some examples of bias, but on the whole the news is straight or factual. Generally, the New Deal has gotten the breaks and has had what is called a "good press"—*net*. The great volume of news out of Washington originates largely with the administration in power, and the net effect of the news is usually on the side of whatever administration is in power.

Sensationalism. This is the curse of the news writing business anywhere, including Washington. Many writers feel the urge to dramatize whatever they are writing, to play it up, to make it exciting, to build it into a "big story," perhaps in the hope that it will make the front page and give them a "by-line." This yields a form of distortion. The facts may be accurate, but the *perspective* may be distorted. One common result is to exaggerate natural differences which exist within government, and to present them to the public as a "clash," a "row," "quarrel" or "feud." It's a basic trait of human nature to love the sensational, and the press out of Washington does its share of feeding the appetite for sensationalism.

Pinks. The proportion of news writers who are "liberal" in their personal views has increased tremendously in the past ten years, but the increase is no greater than the swing in any class of citizens or in the public-at-large.

Guild. The American Newspaper Guild, a trade union of newspapermen, is strong within Washington local papers and in the press association staffs, but is weak among the correspondents, most of whom regard themselves as too lofty and too well paid to stoop into labor unions. The Guild has done a good job of raising the pay of young newspaper reporters. "Guild bias" in the writing of news is a rare thing.

Overwork. Most Washington correspondents are overworked. They do not have adequate time to cover all the news they are expected to cover, and they have even less now that government has snatched scores of the best men out of many private offices to do government war information work. The result is often a thinness of the news, a lack of digging beneath the surface, an easy acceptance of the "official version" because there is not time to check it up. The fault is in the system, rather than in the individual reporters. Essentially the fault is that of the newspaper owners and managers, some of whom expect the impossible of their Washington men. The remedy lies in the assignment of more man power to the Washington bureaus.

Fresh men. For every news job available in Washington there are a hundred newspapermen throughout the United States who would like to get it. Washington news offices are besieged by applicants. There is no one sure way to get a job and a toe hold in Washington. Some do it by busting in, cold turkey. Most do it by working up. The best general advice is to get newspaper grounding on a paper in a normal community, and then work on to Washington. The trouble with many newspapermen who start their careers in Washington is that they have no roots elsewhere. They develop the habit of thinking that Washington is pretty much the whole universe. Such men are apt to become superficial, their work is apt to show it, and they are apt to slide. The man thoroughly trained in some natural community usually goes ahead of the man who got his "breaking in" in Washington.

Wives. Some newspaper wives ruin their husbands professionally, without ever meaning to do it, without knowing they are doing it. They get "social ideas," they want to climb, and they play on the husband to write the sort of stuff which will aid the climbing. He does. It works. But the readers back home may get gypped.

Newspaperwomen. Most of the working women in the Washington press corps are not as good as the men, because they are newer at the business, and because they do not have adequate training in objectivity. (There are a few exceptions.) The fault is temporary, and there is no basic reason why women eventually cannot become as good reporters as men.

Columns. Newsmen are always arguing among themselves as to whether the "columns" are superior to or inferior to the "straight news." Neither of these views is correct. Columns are not a substitute for straight news, but they give readers supplementary insight into the news. They add sidelights which the formal news often misses entirely. The columnists dig behind an announcement, beneath it. They show up reasons, motives, contributory influences. Some columns are very good, and some are really very poor, full of sensational inaccuracies, but the general function of columns is in the right direction.

Straight news. The White House and most other officials prefer this, and they don't like columnists and commentators. The reason is that the officials can pretty much control the "straight news." They make it, they hand it out, it is theirs. The original digging and thinking which is done by columnists, commentators and some of the more vigorous of the newsmen is discommoding to the officials, because it shows up their own weaknesses. It gums up the nice pretty picture which they would like to present to the public as "straight news." There is no substitute for "straight news." It is the most valuable of all. But there is a great need for supplementary writing—explanation, interpretation, analysis, comment. Some news writers give this, but most do not do it adequately.

Off the record. There is a growing tendency in Washington for dignitaries to tell writers things "off the record." The writers may write the facts or the background, but without attributing them to the source. This is convenient, and useful. It is good for the news business. But there's a danger: The official source can and frequently does use this "off-the-record" practice to get news writers to convey information or plug a cause which helps the cause of the official himself.

Same as home town. Practically all of these observations about Washington newsmen also apply to newspapermen in your own home town. The good qualities and the bad qualities are essentially alike.

The lure. Washington newsmen don't go around talking about their public responsibilities. They are more inclined to grouse about their jobs, but the truth is that they love their jobs. Henry L. Mencken once explained why: "It's because they get front seats."

17

Farmers Go to Town

IF YOU want to see a revolution, here it is. A revolution by and on behalf of a class of people who have always been known as "conservatives," even "capitalists." A revolution which has regimented the nation's largest single industry in less than a decade, and which furnishes a general pattern for efforts to bring about an integration of other industries in the future.

The revolutionists are the farmers. They have organized their empire and put the strings of control in Washington. They are supposed to pull the strings which control them, but actually, in practice, they only acquiesce. It is really the government which controls them, their plantings, their harvestings, their marketings, their prices, their income. It has been very profitable. They have been well paid for the revolution they started.

Look at the evidences in Washington, and don't wince at the superlatives, for every one is warranted.

The Department of Agriculture is the biggest peacetime agency of the government. Its two buildings on the Mall are so big that it takes as long as fifteen minutes for some officials to get from their offices to the Secretary's office. It has the most employees. It spends more money in peacetime than any other department. It does the widest variety of things. The agricultural bloc in Congress is the strongest of all blocs. The farmers' lobby is the most powerful lobby. (Organized labor is merely runner-up, and veterans are third.)

The farmers' department of the government in Washington is really "Everybody's Department." It does a vigorous job for farmers, but it is not "just for farmers." Most food and most clothing come from materials grown on farms, and the government regulates them all, for farm people and for city people.

The agricultural sphere of influence in Washington is unquestionably the most virile of all spheres. It is tied in with everything. Before the war it was an active breeding ground of reform causes, many of which bore only indirectly on farmers. In peacetime, it had its fingers in many

178

policy-pies of the government, and it has carried its power over into war-time on a big scale.

When the history of our times is written, a phrase that will stand out is "social revolution." And it will appear that the farmers' revolution was the spearhead of other segments of the revolution that came along after it. It will be recognized, after World War II, as the first example of an accomplished *integration* of an industry. These observations may seem like writing history prematurely, but they give a hint as to the future meaning of the agricultural movement.

Even in normal times, the story of the farmers' push is a story for all. But in war times it is more vital, for the war will speed the coming of the second phase of the farmers' revolution. The first phase was for farmers, national recognition of their rights as producers of the nation's basic necessity—food. The second phase will be for consumers, national recognition of the right of all the people to have plenty to eat—of the right kind of food.

What Farmers Wanted

The first thing that farmers as a class got from government was the Department of Agriculture, third youngest of the family of departments. It was organized in 1889, under the first major piece of class legislation. Up to the time of World War I, it was engaged largely in bettering farming, in making two blades of grass grow where one grew before.

Then came World War I. Government urged farmers to expand production, especially of wheat. They did, and there was a boom of farm prices and land values. Then came the postwar depression, the collapse of prices and middle western land values, and the piling up of unsold surpluses of wheat, and corn, and cotton. Farmers—midwestern farmers particularly—were in trouble. They wanted higher prices. And, during the 20's, all they got from the government was a system of mortgage and crop loans, and a little assistance for their struggling young cooperative marketing associations. Both were considered "radical" in those days. They helped some, but they didn't boost prices or eliminate surpluses.

Politically powerful farmers of the Middle West shifted in the 20's from their traditional hostility to the tariff, and got tariff protection for their products. But the tariffs were ineffective. The muttering that prices were too low became a great howl. Republicans under Hoover tried an experiment, an appeasement—the Federal Farm Board, which gave the farmers' co-ops a big boost, and bought up surpluses of farm crops so as to raise prices. At price boosting it was pretty much a flop, because farmers grew more surpluses than it could buy with the 500 million dollars it had to spend. And because its beginning coincided with the beginning of the nation's worst depression.

When the depression struck, farmers of the Middle West revolted against Republicanism in 1932 and their votes helped to elect Roosevelt, and brought the New Deal and Henry Wallace. The New Deal's aim was to raise farmers' prices. So it scrapped old ideas of farmers' "individualism" and banded farmers together in a great collective effort under government management to control and reduce production, reduce or eliminate surpluses, and boost prices. Regulation was required. Regimentation. Coercion . . . sugar-coated, but coercion nonetheless. New social machinery, not only in Washington, but out around the country—committees of farmers to do the local planning and the policing. It also required public money to pay subsidies to farmers for doing the controlling. It also involved shifting the old mortgage loan system to make it serve the ends of crop control. It also caused shifting of the whole Department of Agriculture to promote the ends of crop control. Dozens of schemes to raise farm prices and farm incomes—and garner farm votes. The lure of government checks was strong, and the lure of higher prices was stronger, and farmers fell in line with the new order.

In these ways the integration of the farming industry was accomplished. And Washington became the center of agricultural power in this country.

Wallace

For every revolution, a leader emerges. In the farmers' revolution Henry Wallace emerged—Henry Agard Wallace, whose father before him had been Secretary of Agriculture. Henry A. sat himself down in his cabinet chair with the tag "Young Henry" upon him. But eight years later, when "Young Henry" moved up to the Vice President's chair, he had taken his father's place as the Department of Agriculture's legendary Secretary par excellence.

"Young Henry," as a Republican-turned-Democrat, had railed against Republican pussy-footing on the farm problem. As Secretary, from 1933 until 1941 he was considered a "mystic," a philosophic dreamer, a poor administrator, and a political tyro—a curious sort of man with a great curiosity. Yet it was he who personally thought up many of the vital mechanical details which made the farm program work.

Inasmuch as Wallace may some day reside in the White House, it is worth while, for practical reasons, to consider his ideas about the farm problem, for they may be translated into government management on *other* industries.

As a farm reliefer, Henry Wallace was an opportunist. He administered government policies which pointed toward food scarcity, but with a heavy heart. Willful destruction of crops and deliberate underplanting seared his soul. The public criticism arising from such actions intensified his natural shyness. Yet he went through with it because he considered such policies the only way of making a start toward solving the farm problem—treatment of symptoms until treatment for the malady could be devised. As a result he spent his eight years as head of the Department of Agriculture with his mind mainly on the future.

Wallace considers agriculture the nation's indispensable industry, the nutritional fountainhead from which flows all sustenance, and, therefore, all health and prosperity; the industry to which all other industries are attuned. Despite his reputation for political ineptitude, he saw that unless the farm program was eventually expanded to aid *all* farmers without hurting consumers, it would be voted down at the polls, or crumble with its own internal weaknesses. He shifted emphasis from "scarcity economics," which were of most benefit to the midwestern and southern one-crop farm gentry, to policies of plenty, which would benefit the more numerous growers of diversified crops.

Wickard and Another Revolution

In the latter part of his tour of duty, Wallace laid the cornerstone of the farm program of the future by setting up a new division of the Department of Agriculture. It is now the Agricultural Marketing Administration, and already it is making progress toward government sponsorship of the *second* agricultural revolution.

· From that revolution will come the farm program, and perhaps even the industrial program, of the postwar tomorrow. It will be based on the philosophy of abundance, at prices which all can afford. It will aim to avoid the American anachronism of bread lines in the midst of food surpluses. A major objective will be high *income* for farmers, resulting from volume sales at reasonable prices. And another objective will be full bellies for all, a higher average of health, and a higher standard of living.

Claude R. Wickard, Wallace's successor as Secretary of Agriculture, will administer the second agrarian revolution—or at least much of it. Wickard is the first bona fide dirt farmer to be Secretary of Agriculture, and he still operates his Carroll County, Indiana, corn and hog farm from his heavily-draped dark red and blue office in the Department of Agriculture. He is a big-looking man, with a ready grin, slow and deliberate, and adamant—after he makes up his mind. He has a deep determination to help the little fellow, the underdog.

Wickard's approach to the policy of plenty is relatively simple. He is de-emphasizing polices which curtail production of wheat, cotton, corn, and tobacco—crops no longer needed in such volume by the American people. And he is expanding the policy of buying up surpluses of the fruits and vegetables and meats and dairy products which Americans could, would, and should consume more heavily. He is telling farmers to produce more, more, more. And he is promising to buy, if prices get below the profitable level.

That is the program Wickard calls "Food for Freedom." Instead of bemoaning our lost European exports of wheat and cotton, Wickard is exporting fruit and vegetables and meat and milk instead—to feed and strengthen our friends, to dangle as a promise before the hungry eyes of our enemies. Wickard says food will win the war and write the peace, food which can be rushed from the well-stocked U. S. larder to the one-time aggressors and to oppressed and starving Europeans when arms are laid down.

And what of after the war—in our own country? If it's a long war, the second farm revolution will be well under way. Commercial production of fruits, vegetables, meats and dairy products will have spread to farm lands once devoted to cotton, and wheat, and tobacco. The South will be able to feed herself and her growing industrial population, instead of "importing" most of her food from the North. The long, highly expensive cross-country hauls of perishable foods will be reduced. Some of the toll of food speculation will be eliminated. The private system of food distribution will be adapted to volume at low cost, perhaps regimented and integrated under government direction.

If the war is not long, then progress will be somewhat slower. Then government will buy heavily while continuing to urge heavier production. The food government buys will be diverted into the mouths of people who can't afford to buy enough to eat, and given to those who can't buy any. And integration of the food industry will be pressed harder.

That is the vision of Wickard and Wallace for the future of agriculture—based on a past which has seen about 6 million farmers integrate their operations into a unified national policy in the short space of a decade —a policy in which government is the manager, and the financier. A policy which, although founded on theories of scarcity and high price, is really aimed at plenty for all at a reasonable price.

That, in brief, is the policy which now seems likely to be followed by government for other major industries, for the whole national economy, after the war is ended—mass distribution of mass production.

You may complain about food prices, but when you sit down to a meal you give no thought to *why* the food costs what it costs. The farmer does. And so does the Department of Agriculture. For when you spend a dollar for food, you pay not only the farmer, but also the butcher, the baker, the miller, the broker, the railroad man, the truck driver, the grocer, and the long, long list of others who work on it after it leaves the farmer's hands. A relatively *large* proportion of your dollar goes to pay those people, and a relatively *small* proportion goes to pay the farmer. And that small proportion of your food dollar is the farmer's "price." The farmer wants a higher "price." There are only two ways he can get it. One way is for him to get a bigger share of the dollar you spend, and the other is to make you spend more dollars (a higher price) for the food you get. Or both. And it is both that the farmer is doing, for that is the farm program as it is operated from Washington today.

Mainly the system operates to make you spend more for your food. It is done several ways. The first way is simply a matter of growing less, of artificially preventing a surplus, of permitting each farmer to plant so many acres and no more. Originally this was called "the AAA program," but back in 1936 the Supreme Court said certain phases of it were unconstitutional. So now it is called "soil conservation," and it *is* conserving the soil to a large extent. But it is mainly federal control of crop production. Not all crops. Just wheat, cotton, corn, rice, and tobacco (and now peanuts), for it was the prices of these crops which were low and surpluses high in 1933.

Here's how it is worked: Before farmers start planting, Department of Agriculture experts figure out just how much can be sold at prices which will satisfy the farmer. And they decide how many acres will produce that much. The total acreage figure is prorated to each of the states, and to each county, and finally, through county committees of farmers elected by their neighbors in the county, to *each farm* in each county. About 2,500 farming counties and almost 6 million farmers are involved, so the allotting alone is quite a job. That is part of the reason why the Department of Agriculture has to employ, full and part time, more than 250,000 people in Washington and out around the country.

It usually happens that the individual farmer's "allotment" of acreage is less than he would like to plant. So the government has to make it worth his while to plant less. Making it worth while consists of paying the farmer in cash, by government check. And the checks come from your tax money . . . more than five billion dollars in the last ten years. Nature may play hob with this part of the farm program by combining sun, rain and temperature in such a way that heavy crops are produced, making still too much to sell at good prices. But when heavy crops are produced the farmer doesn't have to sell his crop, for the government will make him a loan in cash, and take his crop as security for the loan. In such years, his cash loan and his cash crop-control payments together make a pretty good return for his crop, so he lets the government keep it until the government can sell it without losing too much money. The government keeps the crop, on which it has made loans, in bulging government and private warehouses, and even under seal on farms where it was grown.

Sometimes nature has a tantrum and ruins crops. For such calamities, the government has provided insurance, "crop insurance." It's working now on wheat and cotton. The government pays the farmer his insurance as well as his control checks. So that you will not have to pay too high a price for wheat or cotton if a serious scarcity develops, the government is always ready to sell some of the surpluses it has collected previously. It is all rather finely adjusted so that the farmer gets about the same amount of money every year, and you pay about the same, either directly or in taxes. This part of the system, really the safety valve for both farmers and consumers, is called "the ever-normal granary."

Obviously a majority of farmers have to cooperate or the system would not be fully effective. And minorities must be coerced into cooperation to keep them from crippling the system by overplanting. So the farmer is given a choice, and a chance to vote on it by secret ballot. He can vote for crop control, or he can vote to have no control whatever. Of course if a majority of farmers vote against control, no benefits—government checks, loans, and crop insurance—are paid by the government. Consequently, farmers have rarely voted against the controls. And after control has been voted, farmers rarely overplant, because, if they do, they must pay heavy fines on stuff they sell in excess of quota.

All these plans are carefully worked out to appeal to a majority of the farmers involved. So the Department of Agriculture insists that the whole scheme of crop control is "voluntary," or as Wallace called it, "democracy in action." Some farmers call it "dictatorship," on the ground that they have no *real* choice. The practical, non-ideological point is, however, that most farmers find it good for them. The end results are what they wanted.

Surpluses to the Needy

There are many crops for which this system will not work. For several years the farmers who grew such crops got very little from the government, so they squawked, and a system was devised for them. It has the same objective as the crop control plan, to make you pay more for your food. And it works the same way, by artificially preventing a surplus. It is called the "surplus marketing program," and is applied mainly to fruits and vegetables. It consists of buying up the surpluses and giving them away to people who can't afford to pay prices high enough to suit the farmer. The food stamp plan is merely a variant of that basic idea. By food stamps the government simply gives the cash, in the form of stamps, to the needy and lets *them* buy up the surpluses of crops whose prices are too low to suit farmers. In either case, as a non-stamp-user you pay more for the food *you* get. The scheme works because it doesn't take much buying of surpluses (only about 5 per cent of the total) to boost the price of the bulk of a crop.

A third scheme is available for still other crops, and it is widely applied to milk. It is a system of "marketing agreements," and if you live in a sizable city, the price you pay for milk may be determined by such an agreement. The marketing agreement is a government-sponsored monopoly, an agreement in restraint of trade, in which dairy farmers, the dairies, and even the milk wagon drivers "conspire" to make you pay a higher price. They only let you have so much milk. The rest, which must be taken from the cows anyway, is sloughed off by making it into ice cream, or cheese, or canned milk, or dried milk, or butter. In the case of butter, the government had to set up a corporation to buy up the surplus and store it so as to make a market price for butter high enough to suit farmers. Some of the surplus milk reaches school children free, and, at a low price, city people on relief.

Parity

The yardstick of crop prices which will suit farmers is called "parity." It is the relationship between prices farmers get for their crops, and prices they pay for city goods. It is the price for a crop that will give that crop the same buying power it had in 1909-14. Farmers insisted on the 1909-14 basis because they could buy more city goods with their incomes from crops in those years than at any time before or since.

There are many farmers, of course, who haven't been able to make the grade on their own steam. They are the farmers who have had bad luck, or who aren't very good farmers, or who happen to have farms which aren't very good. There are upwards of two million of them. For these "needy farmers" the Department of Agriculture has operated the rural equivalent of government relief for needy city people, through the Farm Security Administration, which you knew first as the "Resettlement Administration," the name it had when it was run by Rex Tugwell.

185

Farm Security handles each farm family-in-trouble on an individual case basis. It may move the family to a new farm, lending the money for the purchase and for the buying of things needed to make the farm pay—a mule, fertilizer, seed, etc. A complete and detailed plan for operating the farm is then worked out for the farmer, and the farmer's wife is told how to do her share, by canning and preserving. The local agent of Farm Security sees to it that the plan is lived up to completely. Several hundred thousand farm families are being rehabilitated that way—and they are paying back their loans on schedule. (See Chapter 19, Money Shovelers. Also Chapter 20, Government the Papa.)

Squeezing Middlemen

The other major phase of the government's farm program, getting for the farmer a larger share of the dollar you spend for food, forms a more difficult job for the Department of Agriculture than making you spend more dollars. The only way the farmer can get a bigger share of the consumer's dollar is to squeeze it from the people who buy his crops from him—the middlemen. So the Department is working away at squeezing them for the benefit of farmers (and for the protection of consumers).

This squeeze consists partly of government harassment of operations, and largely of government regulation. Farmers generally have a deep distrust of all the private trade lines with which they deal, and consequently farmers applaud every government attack on such groups, which they call "the interests." Thus the policies make farm votes.

Chief among "the interests" are the "grasping middlemen." The Department of Agriculture controls their operations with about 20 laws, administered by the Agricultural Marketing Administration. It regulates weights and measures, business practices, provides grading and inspection, keeps middlemen from cheating farmers (and each other) and sees to it that they are truly competitive so they don't gouge the farmer by making too much profit themselves.

"Wicked speculators" are next on the farmers' list. They are controlled, more and more rigorously, through the Agricultural Marketing Administration which has steadily expanded its controls into all fields of speculation in farm commodities.

Also, farmers don't like the "big eastern bankers." So the Farm Credit Administration, another part of the Department of Agriculture, competes with the private bankers so as to force them to keep down their charges. In effect, the Farm Credit system is the farmers' own banker, for it provides a complete commercial banking service, at low interest and long terms of repayment—first and second mortgage loans, loans for producing crops, marketing crops, and processing crops. In addition, Farm Credit will help a farmer get out from under private lenders through a scheme of "debt adjustment."

The "utility crowd" is another bane of farmers. So, in the Department of Agriculture, is the Rural Electrification Administration. Its job is to get "the lights" to farmers by helping them organize into small groups and lending them the money to put in the lines and wire their houses.

Science Works for Farmers

The scientific side of giving farmers what they want goes on its unspectacular way in the Department of Agriculture year after year. The Department is a beehive of laboratories and experiments. Many renowned scientists work there now, and many others worked there in the past. Their fundamental job is to increase farmers' productivity, lower their costs, so their net profits will be larger. They also aim to find new crops for farmers to grow, and new uses for crops already grown, especially industrial uses —Chemurgy. And they tell farm (and city) wives how to prepare and preserve food, and how best to feed their families.

To get its vast store of information into farmers' hands, the Department of Agriculture uses the nation's oldest radio program, the popular Farm and Home Hour. It employs a corps of news and bulletin-writing "information men" large enough to staff several big daily newspapers. It publishes and distributes hundreds of thousands of pamphlets every year on an encyclopedic scale of subjects, more than any other government department. It maintains an intricate network of telegraph and telephone lines to gather and report market information. It employs thousands of experts to help it predict the outturn of crops, and hundreds of other experts to predict prices. All told, the Department spends about two billion dollars a year.

The Farm Bloc

Farmers got their federal farm program and they maintain a steady stream of cash benefits by the everlasting application of tremendous political pressure, and by continually making demands in excess of expectations. With all their demands, they have been effective political strategists. Although many of their demands have arisen from the world-wide agricultural depression, they have been smart enough never to buck the tide too long. (Other pressure groups might well take a leaf from their book, for the farmers have the smartest pressure groups of all.)

In reality, farmers have three sets of forces working for them in Washington: The farm bloc in Congress, which often runs ahead of the others;

the farmers' own organizations, which are big-time businesses and not hay-seedy; and the Department of Agriculture itself, which has political and social motives of its own for helping farmers. In combination, they are virtually irresistible.

The farm bloc in Congress is not a majority of either the House or the Senate, yet by voting as a unit on big issues, it has molded the pattern of recent history. It is against big business, and generally against labor, and against city folks where their interests and those of farmers conflict. It is first, last, and all the time for farmers.

Its leading members are mostly old congressional hands—wily politicians and resourceful parliamentarians. Three-fourths of all the committees of the House and Senate are headed by men from agricultural states, with the South predominating in chairmanships of power. These men want to stay in Congress, and because the principal business of their constituents is agriculture, they serve their constituents well—by enacting legislation favorable to farmers, and by pressuring the executive branch of government for pro-farmer policies.

Farmer Organizations

The farmers' organizations are greatly respected and much feared by Congress, from which all farm benefits flow, and by the Department of Agriculture, which directs the flow. The reason is simple. The farm vote is vital to party victory. About five-sixths of the nation's farm population belongs to the farm organizations—representing perhaps as many as 18 million voters, but probably closer to 15 million. So the leaders of the farm organizations (who have their jobs to keep) speak politically with mighty voices. Organized business has no comparable leather lungs. Labor is just developing them. And other groups merely whisper.

Five organizations of farmers maintain offices and full-time staffs in Washington. Together they do a thorough job of pulling and hauling Congress, the Department of Agriculture, and the administration in general. They are never halted in their march toward their objectives—they are merely delayed.

Biggest, smartest, and most powerful is the American Farm Bureau Federation. The Farm Bureau, as it is called, is comparatively young, having gotten going in the 20's as an outgrowth of the early field forces of the Department of Agriculture, with which it still has umbilical connections. It has been hand in glove with the administration. Before Wickard, it frequently dictated major policy to the Department of Agriculture. But now it appears to be slipping. The Farm Bureau is mainly responsible for the big-money trend of the farm program, and probably more of its members proportionately have benefited from the program than mem-

188

bers of other farm organizations. Its executive management is top-heavy with Southerners who pressure the powerful southern bloc in Congress. Its president is Edward A. O'Neal, an arm-waving, loud-talking, soft-soaping southern Democrat, a genius at turning the heat on Congress.

The Farmers Union is the leftist organization of farmers, mainly in the wheat-growing states. It is a force among the agricultural liberals in Washington, especially effective on farm legislation of a drastic reform character. It is effective in lobbying for trade-baiting legislation and for plans, both administrative and congressional, for aiding farmers' cooperatives. Its Washington work is operated with little fanfare by M. W. Thatcher, a persuasive ex-accountant whose farming experience is mainly in management of big farm marketing cooperatives.

The Grange—the National Grange and Patrons of Husbandry—the oldest farm organization, is basically a fraternal organization of farmers, organized 75 years ago with a background of Republicanism. It is now regaining some of its earlier power under the drive of Albert Goss, its new national master, who was an officer of the Farm Credit Administration earlier in the New Deal. The Grange can, for practical purposes, be considered the administration's "loyal opposition."

The National Cooperative Milk Producers' Federation operates with very little noise, yet its members represent the industry which accounts for almost a fourth of the entire farm income. It is the lone wolf, a trade association in the farm field. Charles Holman is its secretary, one of the most effective lobbyists in Washington.

The National Council of Farmer Cooperatives, "the Co-op Council," is the youngest of the lot. It represents farmers more indirectly than the other groups, for it concentrates on representation of the farm co-ops. Its work in Washington is handled by Ezra Benson, a Westerner, and an almost-tenderfoot in Washington lobbying.

In addition to the five formal farm pressure groups on which farmers rely regularly, "commodity groups" frequently journey to Washington to lobby for some special treatment. The usual technique is for them to sell the scheme they want to members of Congress, who, in turn, help the farmer groups sell it to administrative officials. These commodity groups are usually the leading growers of a specialty crop grown in one locality. Walnuts, prunes, raisins, peanuts, northwestern apples, hops, and others are crops which have been benefited by this method. It usually happens that the growers want the Department of Agriculture to buy up their surplus to boost the price.

The Department of Agriculture is itself an extremely powerful lobbyist for farmers. Its statisticians and economists provide the farm organizations with most facts and figures on which they base their demands. It also provides members of Congress with information suitable for supporting legislation favorable to farmers, or for opposing bills unfavorable to farmers. The Department's lawyers are always available to devise and put in constitutionally legal language a precise plan for carrying out some vaguely-conceived relief scheme wanted by farmers. And, of course, when the President is wavering over the signature of a bill favored by farmers and opposed by others, the Secretary of Agriculture can speak directly into the presidential ear—and frequently does, successfully.

The Department is in perfect position to initiate schemes for helping farmers. It originates an idea, convinces farm leaders of the merits, helps them lobby it through Congress—then administers it with a congressional appropriation of money which permits the Department to hire more employees and further expand its power and influence. The practice is increasing steadily, more than is recognized by farmers themselves.

What It All Means

If you don't fully understand all these complicated goings on in the realm of agricultural politics, you are not the only one. Most agricultural officials don't understand them all. Most politicians have never gotten their arms around the whole thing. Most agricultural experts understand only single aspects.

But it amounts to this: Farmers as a class have gotten themselves married to government, and there is no possibility of either divorce or separation. Or, to put it another way, there has grown up an indissoluble partnership. Farmers contribute votes. Government contributes money (which it gets from the people), and policing, and regulation, and general direction of the broad policies of the whole industry of agriculture. The direction extends clear down to the hog lot and barnyard. The result of the marriage or partnership has been to get more income for farmers. To that extent it has been selfish.

The next result, yet to be accomplished, is to get more total production from the farming industry, more stuff, more of the kinds of things which people need, more consumption, more goods—plenty for all. If this is accomplished, the farmers' movement will have been justified in a broader general interest. It remains to be seen—in the postwar era.

What has happened to agriculture is what the New Deal would like to have happen to all other major industries—marriage with government, partnership, joint supervision, in the hope of getting greater production, wider distribution, larger consumption, more things for more people. That would be fine. The farmer now gets paid well for not doing what he gol durn pleases. Next on the list come the manufacturers. It may pay them. Will it pay the consumers? It may, but that also remains to be seen.

18

Thrones of Labor

WHEN you think of labor you normally think of factories, but in Washington it would be all right for you to think of office buildings. Labor unions don't exactly own Washington, as some people like to say, but they own a lot of very fine expensive real estate here. Some office buildings they own and occupy as national headquarters, some they own and rent to others, and some they finance out of their big reserves and cash balances in Washington banks. They own more real estate than any other group of organized interests. Even the noble temple of the Chamber of Commerce of the United States on Lafayette Square, across from the White House, does not compare in value with the aggregate of labor holdings. Union labor is big business in Washington.

If you prefer to judge labor not by its material holdings, but by its political influence, try this experiment: Go to any average congressman from any average city and tell him that labor doesn't like the way he is voting. Watch him fidget, listen to him explain that he is really a friend of labor. Or try the same thing on almost any official of government, and you will strengthen the impression that organized labor's bark is very loud, exceeded only by the bark of organized farmers.

Labor plays a game, and the opponents are employers. But labor has learned how to use government to run interference. And labor has learned how to persuade the umpire. That's why so many labor unions have moved their headquarters to Washington, where they can be close at hand to press the government into pressing the employers. The game works well.

If you think that labor is hamstrung by the split between the two rival groups, the American Federation of Labor and the Congress of Industrial Organizations, you have another think coming. True, there's not a united front, but behind the front of the leaders there's an essential spirit of cooperation, and it gets things done.

Labor unions have more than 10,000,000 members. These represent more than 20,000,000 votes out of the total of 50,000,000 votes. The numbers are growing, and organized labor thinks it can control the elections in 1944. (So do farmers, but their votes are less controllable than labor votes.) Anyway, the administration in power is taking no chances of losing the labor vote, and that is the main reason why labor looks so big in Washington.

If you happen to retain a remnant of that old idea that an excursion through labor is a sort of slumming expedition, get it out of your head. Labor is not in the pit, it is on the stage. Labor sits on thrones in Washington, to the right and the left of the Topmost Throne, to which it can whisper what to do.

There's another reason why labor plays close to government—a defensive reason. Having gotten government to lean to labor, and having grown big in the process, labor now sees the beginnings of a desire for government to regulate labor organizations. "Trade unions will now be kept constantly under what we term social surveillance," said the Secretary of Labor to the AFofL convention in 1941. That was a note of warning to labor against abuse of new-found privileges. Just as business practices have been regulated, so may labor practices be regulated when the "right time" comes. Just as business complained that the New Deal regulations were "anti-business" so is labor complaining that the threats of regulation are "anti-labor." Union headquarters in Washington are all set to resist regulation.

In addition to the functions of offense and defense, unions now are demonstrating practical interest in a wide variety of subjects which have to do with welfare of the masses—such things as inflation, taxation and housing. So the Washington headquarters of labor unions are gradually taking on the appearances of headquarters for social movements, broadening out beyond the narrower aspects of the labor union movement.

Well Heeled

The three major parent organizations, AFofL, CIO and the Railway Brotherhoods, all operate from Washington. In addition, there are the headquarters of twenty-three AFofL unions, four CIO unions, five railroad, and two independent national unions. Others have research staffs which work with government social agencies on wage-hour, labor relations, social security, and the like.

Unions own about $10,000,000 worth of real estate. One of the finest office buildings in the financial district, the Bowen Building, belongs to the Bricklayers. A block away is the impressive headquarters of the United Mine Workers, which John L. Lewis bought from the University Club and spent some $250,000 refurnishing. Three blocks up Fifteenth Street is another office building owned by the AFofL Electrical Workers.

A second cluster of labor-owned buildings surrounds the AFofL headquarters at Ninth Street and Massachusetts Avenue. Across the street is the Machinists' building, and two blocks away is the Carpenters' building.

The railroad unions wanted to get close to Congress, so their building is just across the street from the Capitol.

There is a growing respect for the size of some of the unions' bank rolls, which often are invested in real estate. The Machinists financed the Longfellow Building on high-toned Connecticut Avenue, just a block north of the Mayflower Hotel. Evalyn Walsh McLean, Washington social leader, owner of the Hope diamond, and author of the book *Father Struck It Rich*, went to the Bricklayers after the bankers said "No," and she borrowed $300,000 to build the Greyhound Bus Terminal at New York Avenue and Twelfth Street, NW. The Bricklayers deposited $300,000 worth of securities with a bank, borrowed the money at 3 per cent and loaned it to Mrs. McLean at 6 per cent.

The Bricklayers have about $5,000,000 in liquid securities, $8,000,000 in net assets. The United Mine Workers have some $4,000,000 in convertible securities and cash, and any time they need more, a $2 per head assessment on UMW members will bring in another million. The Electrical Workers are in the money too. They set aside a round million dollars for expenses of their 1941 convention. Their explanation was that since they have a convention only once every twelve years, they can afford to do things up brown.

Nobody knows exactly how much money all the unions really have, but the House Naval Affairs Committee found that 101 out of 162 AFofL and CIO international unions reported assets of $82,000,000 in 1941.

Wars Help Unions

Wartime is a growing season for union influence. World War I let union leaders come out of basements and saloons and other hide-outs. World War II is moving them more and more into important government councils where policies affecting all the people are decided. This in turn gives labor organizers something else to sell to non-union members—a voice in government.

In World War I, under the drive of Samuel Gompers, AFofL representatives were appointed to such agencies as the Food Administration, Emergency Construction Board, Fuel Administration, Selective Service, Women's Board, and War Industries Board. AFofL delegates were finally given a place in the peace negotiations. Labor in return pledged not to strike in war plants, and not to seek extension of the closed shop during the war.

The result of this recognized status, and especially of the War Labor Board's recognition of labor's right to organize, was that from 1916 to 1920, AFofL membership nearly doubled, rising from 2,050,000 to 4,075,000.

After World War I, industry renewed its resistance to unionization, and union membership slumped. But the NRA pumped new vigor into unionization, and the dormant United Mine Workers under John Lewis, was one of the first to come to life.

Out of the NRA came the National Labor Relations Act. It gave labor the right to organize and bargain collectively without employer interference. By 1936, AFofL membership had jumped to 3,400,000 but even this rate of growth was not satisfactory to some leaders. The big mass production industries—steel, automobile, rubber, textiles—were almost untouched by unions. Lewis led the group which urged that these be organized by industries instead of by trades. AFofL leaders insisted upon organizing along trade lines—Boiler Makers, Machinists, Pattern Makers, Electrical Workers, Teamsters, and the like. So at the 1935 AFofL convention, Lewis and his adherents formed a committee to organize the mass production industries in their own way. The AFofL Executive Council suspended them, and after peace efforts failed, the unions which followed Lewis were expelled. They formed the Committee for Industrial Organization, later called Congress of Industrial Organizations (CIO).

Rivalry and the coming of World War II stimulated both AFofL and CIO to new activities. By 1941, each claimed 5,000,000 members. World War II already is a boon to unions. When peace comes, it will not be surprising if union membership totals 15 million instead of 10 million.

Labor's New Deal

Roosevelt brought with him a new deal for labor. His ace was the National Labor Relations Act.

Next was the Government Contracts Act, which lets the government apply wage and hour standards to companies selling supplies to government agencies. This was followed by the Fair Labor Standards Act, which authorizes the fixing of wage and hour standards for all interstate industries, regardless of whether they do business with the government.

Unions, especially the AFofL, claim parenthood of the Social Security Act with its unemployment benefits, old-age pensions, and the like. This law is one of the biggest evidences of labor's power in Congress. Labor already is making important headway in the government policy-making field. It is continually, and officially, advising the President on government procedure for handling labor disputes. And it is also giving advice on production in war plants, a field usually reserved for management alone.

Government Labor Agencies

When organized farmers wangle a new service out of Congress, it is a matter of course that the Department of Agriculture will administer it. When, in recent years, since Frances Perkins became Secretary of Labor, organized labor got a new law, it joined with Congress and industry in trying to keep administration of that law out of the Department of Labor.

From the beginning of her tenure, organized labor resented Miss Perkins. What happened to the Department of Labor under Miss Perkins illustrates what labor thinks has happened to its representation in government. An army of more than 19,000 is on the government pay roll administering labor laws. Of these, only 4,000 are in the Department of Labor, and half of the 4,000 are in the Wage-Hour Division, which Congress set up in the Labor Department only after making sure that Secretary Perkins would have no authority over the Wage-Hour Administrator.

Clipping Miss Perkins' wings was a game in which even the President joined. But although she muffed the ball with both labor leaders and politicians, her subordinates were usually loyal, and regarded her as an able and fair administrator.

Two Perkins subordinates whose jobs bring them into contact with labor and industry have learned to work with both. One, Isador Lubin, Commissioner of Labor Statistics, is close to the President and does special war jobs. Lubin has won the respect of members of Congress. The other, John R. Steelman, Director of Conciliation, has walked the tightrope between unions and employers with unmatched skill. Congress likes him. He prefers anonymity, and was upset for fear his service as chairman of the board which granted the union shop in captive mines would give him so much publicity that it might decrease his effectiveness as a silent conciliator.

Many former labor union officials are on the staffs of agencies which deal with labor matters. Numerous others have labor men as advisers. One of the outstanding is Edward McGrady, who kept the Labor Department in good standing as long as he was Assistant Secretary of Labor. Now, he works with the War Department. But by and large, even labor advisers are scarce, particularly at the National Labor Relations Board, and that is one reason why the AFofL has been so critical of that Board.

Influence on Congress

Labor's influence with Congress seems mysterious to some people, but it is really very plain and simple. Organized labor's formula is this: "Elect your friends and defeat your enemies." Labor makes friends with the congressmen, for friendship means support all of the time instead of on certain issues.

Men and women who want to come to Congress know about labor's vote power, so if they are wise, they try to get labor support before starting the campaign. They may go after the AFofL or the CIO or both—and they may get both, for the AFofL-CIO split does not extend to legislative matters. Generally, the legislative aims of the two are parallel.

After a man is elected to Congress, his voting record is sent back home to the unions in his state or district. The unions act accordingly. If he is not a friend, they work for his defeat. If he is a friend and in danger of losing, labor gives him financial support and even sends workers or speakers to help him.

Of the three major labor groups, the AFofL and the Railway Labor Executives are the best electors and the best lobbyists, and the CIO lags far behind. The reasons are easy to understand. The AFofL and Railway groups have been at it longer. They have the know-how. The Railway Labor Executives represent thirty organizations, including five railroad brotherhoods, a CIO affiliate and more than twenty AFofL craft unions. They even elect some men from their own ranks to Congress, among them Senator James Mead of New York. The AFofL has an organization which covers every state in the land. It has twenty-two affiliated unions which are constantly at work with members of Congress. The CIO is younger, and concentrated in a few states, and even in a few areas of the few states.

The major difference in effectiveness is caused, however, by differences in tactics. The AFofL and Railway Labor Executives speak softly, avoid publicity, wave the big stick very infrequently, and even go so far as to visit congressmen when they do not want something. Thus they make real friends, and when a big issue arises and they don't have time for corridor clumping, they just grab the telephone. The word-of-mouth system is still the best way to win votes. All of this work is done so quietly that few people know the names of the AFofL legislative representatives, William Hushing and Paul Scharrenberg.

The CIO does have power in industrial areas, but it uses different tactics to try to influence those who do not come from CIO strongholds. It strains to try to catch up with the AFofL, and often overshoots. It goes dramatic, and uses shot-in-the-arm methods. When troubles arises, CIO makes hurry-up calls upon its unions to send representatives to Washington for a blitzkrieg descent upon congressmen.

The AFofL's attitude toward the use of words either by itself or its friends was best expressed by the late Andrew Furuseth, head of the

Seafarers Union and one of labor's best philosophers. Asked once whether labor should support Henrik Shipstead or the father of Charles A. Lindbergh, Furuseth exploded: "Lindbergh wrote a book. Shipstead has not written a book. Take Shipstead."

The big shots of labor seldom go to the Capitol except for formal hearings. Instead, each union looks out for its own particular interests, and if the bill affects seamen the AFofL and CIO seamen's organizations carry the ball.

The increasing dependence of labor upon the favors of government people in and out of Congress would have saddened Samuel Gompers. He fought to keep labor independent of government. He believed that labor and management should settle their disputes without government interference. He knew, too, that if government helps it can hinder, and pendulums always swing. But the Gompers philosophy is not the Green or the Murray or the Lewis philosophy.

Gompers wanted earnestly to keep labor out of national politics except for electing its friends and defeating its enemies. He did not want a labor party, such as John Lewis and Sidney Hillman have been trying to build. Whether a labor party will emerge from the welter of war and after-war depends upon circumstances not yet foreseeable. So far Roosevelt has succeeded in capturing and holding the labor vote despite John Lewis.

Lewis

John Lewis' middle name is "Llewellyn," and he is a Welshman.

The Lewis power is in large measure due to his own dynamic and sometimes startling personality, and in part to his presidency of the United Mine Workers. The United Mine Workers of America is a sort of model for the whole CIO program. The UMW was born in strife and christened in bloody battle. But today, with very few exceptions, mine owners know that the UMW will see that there are enough miners available to mine coal, and that the miners will even be fined and the money turned over to the operators if an unauthorized strike is called. The owner-worker relationship in the soft coal industry is stable.

The strength of the UMW is tremendous, for without the coal which the miners produce, industrial wheels can't turn. That power begets more power in new fields, as it did in the captive coal mines. In that case, Lewis defied public opinion, but when the dust settled, he had won a union shop in captive coal mines, and that was all he had wanted in the first place. Lewis has lost some battles. He has often guessed wrong. His worst error came in 1940 when he backed Willkie against Roosevelt. But even then his loss wasn't 100 per cent. He promised to resign the CIO presidency if

197

Willkie lost. He did, and as many workers remember that as remember his selection of the wrong horse.

In labor negotiations, Lewis is a sound and fury expert. Some say that the day of sound and fury in labor relations has passed, and that Lewis is a back number. But he is beginning to develop the ability to talk facts and figures rather than blustery threats.

Without Lewis, the automobile, rubber and steel industries would not have been organized into industrial unions by this time. He may guess wrong again, just as he guessed right about those industries. But as long as he remains president of the UMW, a pigeonhole in memory will never hold him.

Green

A lack of aggressiveness got William Green his job as president of the AFofL, for the strong men in AFofL wanted somebody they could lead and direct, instead of follow. And unless some of them become more envious than they are now of Green's $25,000-a-year job, he probably will hold it until he reaches 70 in 1943 and retires.

Green is a worker—sober, honest, trustworthy. He can't believe that any of his friends in the AFofL are working for themselves rather than for him and the AFofL. He isn't brilliant, shrewd, dramatic. He has no publicity sense, no bushy eyebrows to catch attention, no mane to wave for spellbound audiences. He makes a fair speech, but not a spine-tingling one.

The leaders of the big international unions were responsible for Green's original selection, and also have clipped any wings which Green might have begun to sprout to carry him into a place of greater power. These unions are controlling because AFofL is really run by its Executive Council. It can endorse or repudiate practically anything Green does or says without specific authorization. And the Council is bossed by the unions rather than by Green. The Council has restricted AFofL publicity, its directly affiliated membership, and it has let the AFofL build up a treasury of only $1,000,000.

As a consequence, the AFofL did not have the money to hire the organizers to compete effectively with the CIO in unionizing the mass production industries, nor does it have the authority to purge all affiliates of racketeers.

Green feels he has suffered unjustifiably from attacks by writers like Westbrook Pegler who demanded that he get racketeers out of unions. Green is a churchgoer, and is "against sin," even if he is timid about calling some union leaders racketeers. He has a reason to be. The minute he did, the very people who have restricted his power would be after his scalp or his job, and maybe both. He has purged some unions over which he had jurisdiction, but he has left the others alone. Even the AFofL Executive Council would do nothing more than remove the builder of slush funds, President George E. Browne of the Motion Picture Machine Operators, from the Council. It left the rest up to the law and Browne's union.

Hillman

Sidney Hillman is a fox, but an intelligent one—not just shrewd and tricky. He loves to outwit the pack, and he has done so many times. When you read that he is convalescing in some hospital, the chances are that he isn't really ill, but that several packs have converged upon him and he has run to his hole. After the scent from his last doubling-back maneuver fades, he will come out again, with new tricks worked out in his mind.

He has been the President's real labor adviser, and has developed a strong sense of labor's responsibilities in war. This has made some labor men accuse him of representing government rather than labor nowadays, but he feels that labor must serve government or be subjected to a crack-down.

If his past achievements are any indication, Hillman will work his way out of his present dog house. He did it with NRA, and he did it with OPM.

Hillman's ability as a strategist extends to his dealings with employers. When he was beginning to build up the Clothing Workers, his favorite tactic was to let organizers soften employers with strikes, picketing, and boycotting. Then a hint would be dropped that Hillman might be willing to "deal." The result usually was a victory for the union, but it also kept the employer in business. Hillman even sent his own production experts into many plants to build up efficiency so higher wages could be paid and the employer still make a profit.

The Clothing Workers' boss has many enemies. He has weathered many battles, and he doesn't have too many scars. His future depends upon how far the AFofL and CIO get with their recurring demand for their own direct representatives in government.

Murray

A lot of things about Philip Murray are explained by the fact that he first reached prominence as a vice president of the United Mine Workers, of which John Lewis is president, and that he remains basically loyal to the UMW, despite break with its president. But in the spring of 1942, the Steel Workers Organizing Committee, of which Murray was head, became a full-fledged international union and Murray was elected its first president. He then became his own man in a larger sense.

Murray already is not only the president but the real boss of the CIO—

this year. The 1941 CIO convention showed that. Lewis wouldn't even go to it, and if he had he might have been impressed with the fact that the demonstrations for Murray were bigger than the demonstrations for Lewis ever had been.

Lewis' isolationism caused the shift in CIO favor. There were, too, many unions which could not stomach the raiding and brass knuckle methods of A. D. Lewis, John's brother. So the loyalties shifted to Murray, whose big job at the moment is to maintain harmony in the CIO, speak for the CIO, build it up, obtain representation for it in government war agencies.

Murray is a plain and simple man. He dislikes swank, is friendly, humble, religious. He feels more at home at a factory gate, in a mine pit or a worker's kitchen, than in a carpeted office. His major handicap has been physical, for he suffered two strokes in 1941, but at the CIO convention he seemed in perfect health, tore through mountains of work, and ran the whole show. He is nobody's Charlie McCarthy.

Dubinsky

In a class by himself is David Dubinsky of the Ladies' Garment Workers. He and his union, now in the AFofL, are bitter rivals of Sidney Hillman and the Amalgamated Clothing Workers. Dubinsky wants to make New York the style center of the world, and his actions in that direction led to an indictment charging that he and employers conspired to violate the antitrust laws. Dubinsky is particularly adept at publicity, and a trier of new tactics. One of his outstanding achievements is "Pins and Needles," the propaganda play against garment industry sweatshops which he even got government to finance for a while. Now, it is making money for the union.

AFofL Bosses

The men who really run the AFofL are a half dozen or so leaders of strong unions who can and do shape decisions of the Executive Council.

One of the most potent is Dan Tobin, president of the Teamsters. He has fought for years to make his union the biggest in the AFofL, and he will fight to keep anybody from invading his field of authority. When he really gets going, he can buffalo the whole AFofL Executive Council, as he did last year when the AFofL convention voted to reduce the per capita tax paid to the AFofL by its affiliated unions. That meant more money for the Teamsters, who pay Tobin $25,000 a year, and less for the AFofL.

John P. Frey is another dominant personality in the AFofL because of his presidency of the Metal Trades Department. He, too, loves a fight, and

200

never pulls his punches. He hates communists and dislikes strikes, especially when he feels the union is in the wrong. He has even walked through picket lines. His own union, the Molders, has gone 50 years without a strike call. He, like Samuel Gompers, bitterly opposes government wage-fixing, preferring employer-union agreements.

One of the most colorful chiefs is bow-tie Matthew Woll of the Photo Engravers. He was Samuel Gompers' heir apparent, but it turned out that his union was too small and he might be too vigorous, so he didn't succeed to the AFofL presidency. He is actually a doer-of-good, a civic worker, and, surprisingly, a businessman and a capitalist. He makes $15,000 a year through a sideline—the Labor Union Life Insurance Company.

The Building and Construction Trades Department of the AFofL is one of its most powerful units, and it has two leaders high up in labor councils —John P. Coyne, its president, and George Meany, who is secretary-treasurer of the AFofL. Coyne has made quite a record for cooperation with industry as well as government. Meany was put in the No. 2 AFofL spot because some of the Building Trades group thought William Green was about to grab some power, and they wanted a strong man to watch him.

William Hutcheson of the Carpenters is just as strong and tough as they come. It was he who took a poke from John Lewis, and it might well have been the reverse. His union is big, well entrenched, well financed, and one to have on your side if you want to accomplish anything in the AFofL.

CIO Leaders

The leaders of CIO unions are generally younger than those of the AFofL. A frequent criticism of them is that they do not have the experience at handling labor disputes and unions that makes for stability. That is less true than it used to be. They are learning fast. Some of them even take public speaking training. And at their last convention it would have been difficult to see any difference between them and the businessmen you would find at a manufacturers' or a chamber of commerce convention.

James Carey, secretary of the CIO, is a shining example of this element. He is now in his early thirties, and was president of the Electrical, Radio and Machine Workers International Union until kicked out for anti-communism, and for supporting the administration's defense program. His reward was the CIO job, which pays him $7500 a year, twice what he got as the Electrical Union president.

Two other supporters of the defense program even before Russia and Germany went to war were R. J. Thomas of the United Automobile Workers and Emil Rieve of the Textile Workers. Thomas, aided by Walter Reuther, pulled the UAW through its tough fight with the AFofL for the leading spot in the automobile industry. Rieve has weathered similar storms, and his union is particularly adept at transporting flying squadrons of workers from one plant or one town to another to build crack-proof picket lines, and also in building production efficiency in bankrupt plants.

Joseph Curran of the National Maritime Union and Julius Emspak, secretary of the Electrical Workers, both opposed the defense program before Russia started fighting. But their unions are important even if that attitude has reduced their actual influence within CIO.

Harry Bridges doesn't cut much ice when it comes to general CIO policy, but his aggressiveness has made his Pacific Coast Longshoremen one of the most powerful unions in the country. It took him years to do it, but employers now have to telephone his union when they want a crew to unload a ship and hire the men that are sent to them.

In the growing aviation industry, Richard Frankensteen has taken the leadership under the United Automobile Workers of America. Some of his strikes have had bad short-range effects, but the union is growing and when the war is over it will be a force and power that must be reckoned with.

AFofL and CIO Staffs

The top executives of both the AFofL and CIO are the doers, the actors, the people who get out in front. In these times, they often have to have facts and figures instead of bluster, so they have staffs who provide them with the material—a sort of brain trust.

Most of the staff workers prefer obscurity and work quietly for the cause. Typical of the AFofL group is Florence Thorne, who runs the research bureau. She is quiet and unassuming and doesn't want anybody to think she has any influence. She once convinced a series of *Saturday Evening Post* emissaries that they shouldn't write the story of her life because they would merely sacrifice a valuable career upon the altar of publicity. She is a potent intellectual adviser within AFofL.

Boris Shishkin is AFofL's economist, who speaks for Green on special occasions. Robert Watt is an undersized package of intellectual aggressiveness whose ability has forced on him such posts as AFofL representative to the International Labor Office, Chairman of the Federal Board for Vocational Education, and member of the National War Labor Board. Frank Fenton, director of organization, can combine knowledge of the law with practical experience to stop the theorists and hardheaded businessmen who tangle with him.

In the CIO, the organizers are Allan S. Haywood and John Brophy, the latter a former socialist who once tangled with John Lewis because of his political views. Ralph Hetzel, Jr., a youngster, is CIO's economist who has come through with a lot of right things at the right time. Lee Pressman, a Harvard graduate, is CIO's legal spokesman who is one of organized labor's best debaters, even if he does sometimes get his facts confused.

Labor in the News

Labor is often news nowadays, big news, news for the general public and not just news for the workers. That is quite a change from a few years back when the press practically boycotted labor news, and a reporter considered a labor assignment an unpleasant task on the wrong side of the tracks. The reasons for the change are many, but among them is competition. Labor was not getting a good press, so it began to set up its own, and the general newspapers had to carry more labor news or lose circulation.

Labor reflected the newspaper antagonism—a situation of you-hate-me-and-I'll-hate-you. The result was brusque treatment of newspapermen which intensified the feelings of unfriendly reporters and offended those who would have liked to be friendly. That feeling still prevails today in many labor men, and is particularly strong among members of the AFofL Executive Council.

AFofL trade union publications are comparable to business trade publications. Many of their articles deal with technical developments in their crafts. These journals help hold memberships intact, but they do not do much good with the public because it is a case of the union talking to itself.

But the CIO is publicity-wise, public relations conscious, largely because John Lewis is that way. He has a strong sense of the dramatic, is essentially an actor, loves Shakespeare, his own voice, and applause. So CIO has a press agent, one of the best in the business, Len De Caux. He has a good staff of writers and cartoonists, has streamlined CIO publicity, and built up a good press and news service from nothing.

Standing by itself is the publicity achievement of the railroad unions. *Labor,* their official Washington weekly edited by Edward Keating, former Colorado congressman, is probably the best labor newspaper in the country, although there are hundreds of good ones.

Labor's Future

If you are a side lines observer in Washington, not all wrapped up in the tugs of war, your impressions about the future of organized labor are likely to be along these lines:

Labor union membership will continue to grow. Union votes will decide the 1944 election, and will be more or less unified, not split between the two parties. The AFofL and CIO will not merge any time soon, but they will gradually come together, cooperate, and pursue a parallel policy course. More union leaders will be drawn into government, both during the war and after the war. They will help to decide broad policies of industries, working through government committees, to a greater extent after the war. Union discipline over its members and its locals will not be established fast enough to suit the public, and government will impose some regulation upon the unions. It will regard them as semi-public agencies, and will require publicity of their internal affairs, and eliminate some of the criminal racketeering. CIO unions especially will have to learn discipline. A Labor party, a third party, will not be established on any big national scale in 1944. (1948 is too far off for visibility.) Labor's influence in politics and in industrial management policies will suffer occasional setbacks, but over the long pull it will continue to expand.

19

Money Shovelers

O N THE motor roads at the city limits there isn't any such sign as the following, but there might be, and it would not be false advertising:

YOU ARE NOW ENTERING WASHINGTON

Home of the World's Greatest Banker.
Investment Banking, Wholesale and Retail.
All Kinds of Underwriting and Guaranteeing.
Protected by Interlocking Directorates.
Biggest Holding Company in America.
Millions of Satisfied Customers.
More Borrowers than Income Tax Payers.
Own Your Own Home, Farm, or Business.
Either Collateral or Character Loans.
Lowest Rates, Easy Terms.
Do You Need Money? Inquire of Us.

Somewhere within Washington you could find a government agency whose business it is to furnish the money, precisely in accordance with the terms of that imaginary advertisement . . . precisely.

Once upon a time you were supposed to borrow money from some individual who had saved it up, or from some institution, like a bank, which handled the savings of the people in the community. The business of borrowing and lending was supposed to be a private business. Also once upon a time debt was supposed to be akin to sin, and a mortgage on the old home was something you didn't talk about.

Now times have changed. Now government encourages debt, and even puts out great corps of solicitors (called by other names) to get people to go into debt for things they can use, such as homes, farms and electric washing machines. Government stands behind the loans which it promotes, for it either makes them itself, directly, or it guarantees them if they are made by private lending institutions, such as banks, insurance companies and building and loan associations. The system isn't simple and single-track. It works through dozens of different channels and agencies of the government.

People who are emotionally disturbed at the term "socialism," and who "fear" that we are headed toward it, often do not know that in the realm of money-lending, and especially in what is called investment banking, we have already reached the stage of "socialized credit." Some people call it "government capitalism." There are distinctions, but the essential point is that we have it . . . *now*. It is not full and complete. Government capitalism is practiced alongside private capitalism, but it is gradually growing, and in many lines of activity, private capitalism is being gradually replaced.

Once upon a time people were supposed to borrow money or lend money with the sole ultimate idea of making a "profit" on the transaction—at both ends of the line. This motive hasn't disappeared by any means, but now there's another idea on the part of the government as a lender. It is this: Lend primarily with the thought of getting some material thing done that needs to be done, and consider the technical profit as incidental, to be made if possible, but to be foregone if necessary. "Get the money back if we can, but don't bother too much for the present about whether we can, so long as something useful can be done with it immediately." The point is "social need."

Big-Scale Lending

Government lending had its beginnings in the darkest days of the Great Depression during the Hoover regime. What started under the Hoover administration as a gingerly underwriting of private credit agencies, has grown into a full-fledged federal banking business.

There are very few citizens of the United States now who cannot borrow money from their federal government, or in some way share in the billions being shoveled out by the numerous lending agencies. The total of money out on loan by government corporations and credit agencies at the end of 1941 was about $9,000,000,000. Add to this the other commitments and investments of these same agencies and the total comes to more than $15,000,000,000.

Who gets this money? The direct beneficiaries are more than 6 million persons and may exceed 7 million. Included are nearly 5 million home owners, over a million farmers, thousands of flood and drought sufferers, small businessmen, railroads, banks, insurance companies, building and loan associations, drainage districts, and city and county governments. In one way or another the money trickles out to nearly all classes and kinds of people. The number of people who have government loans is greater than the number of those who paid federal income taxes in 1941.

The expansion of government lending was easy, because it was labeled "temporary" or "emergency." Many private bankers who ordinarily would oppose such "government competition" welcomed public assistance in the days when banks were closing, railroad bonds were heading for default, and some insurance companies had doubts of their own solvency.

That temporary phase has evolved into a permanent program. Now a new theory is openly avowed as basic government policy. The new theory is that the private credit system of the past has failed to meet today's needs, and that the federal government itself hereafter must be a main channel through which credit and capital will flow.

The New Dealers who espouse this new line of thought admit that private capital functioned well in the past, despite certain abuses and excesses. But they point out that since 1932 the need has been for new projects of a type that private investors cannot be expected to undertake. They argue that the country, except for war needs, is pretty well built up with respect to hotels, office buildings, railroads, factories and the like. But there is need, they say, for hospitals, schools, roads, bridges, power dams, slum-clearance housing projects and many other such facilities which are essentially non-profit, and which are not suited to the investment of private savings. In some cases, they urge a combination of private capital and public credit, such as government insured Federal Housing Administration loans for homes to be purchased on the easy-payment plan.

Washington Headquarters

In Washington, there is no one big government bank building. The various credit agencies are scattered all over the city. Loans for farmers are centered in the old Southern Railway Building, now full to overflowing with hundreds of employees of the Farm Credit Administration.

The Federal Home Loan Bank Administration once was housed in a new monumental government building in the famous "triangle." But it grew, needed more space, and finally bought the former home of the Acacia Mutual Life Insurance Company, a large office building at the edge of the Capitol grounds. Then the flood of war workers came to Washington, and to make more room for them, hundreds of employees were moved to Park Avenue, New York City. The Federal Housing Administration does business in a rented office building which formerly housed the whole Department of Justice.

The Reconstruction Finance Corporation and subsidiaries have the "swellest" office of all. Just before the big scramble for Washington office space took place, the RFC financed the private construction of the $7,-000,000 Lafayette Building, a streamlined 12-story building overlooking

Lafayette Square. When the building was completed, the RFC leased it, moved in, and began paying rent to help meet the loan to itself.

Jesse Jones

On the top floor of the Lafayette Building, where one can see the White House through the elms and beeches of the park, is a knotty-pine paneled room as big as a ballroom. In it is throned the government's No. 1 banker, Jesse H. Jones, the man who can shovel the most money while sitting down. The would-be borrower has to walk so far from the entrance door to the Jones desk that he has plenty of time to scale down his request from $1,000,000 to $800,000.

Jones is a rich big businessman of Houston, Texas. He owns office buildings, newspapers, banks, hotels, radio stations, and many other things, but he is richer still in personal traits which make a man stand out from the crowd. He stands well above six feet, has silvery hair, blue eyes that any actress would envy. He mixes a simple, amiable nature with the shrewdest business acumen that any Wall Street banker ever encountered. He never reads books, and does not know the professional phrases that New Deal brain men use, but he is far ahead of many New Dealers in sensing the drift of things. For he is a conservative who bends with the trends, rather than buck them. Sensing the tidal wave of the times, he treads a course "just a leetle bit left of center." His heart is conservative, but his head pulls him toward the left and also tells him the dreams of idealists need to be tempered by the wisdom of practical men. He talks the language of the Texas cow country. He seldom uses ordinary profanity, because he knows earthy, barnyard phrases which are more expressive. "Gal" newspaper reporters are apt to feel a bit out of place at his press conferences.

Many left-wingers distrust Jones because he is rich and believes in the old traditional right of a man to earn, save and build a personal fortune. But others thank him for putting business methods into the administration of liberal policies. He is, in effect, the most potent implementer of the New Order of state socialism or state capitalism in the field of banking. Being the "sound" custodian of lending authority that he is, he has been able to get from Congress broad authority that no outright New Dealer could possibly have got. Being the realistic capitalist that he is, he probably thinks he is merely forestalling a revolution. But because of his very successes, he has made the federal government the creditor of such a large segment of the whole national economy that there probably is small chance that government ever will retreat from this dominant creditor position.

Jones has a way of enlisting good "Jones men" to help him. Most important of these men is Will Clayton. Clayton's main assignment is to supervise loans to foreigners and watch the industrial commodity dealings of the government. But he watches everything, and gives Jones the steer on many strategic maneuvers. He is a cotton broker who, from his Texas headquarters, built up a world-wide business, made a huge fortune, with a trader's astuteness that reaches the point of genius. He shrinks from all publicity, but never from the necessity to make quick decisions.

Chairman of the RFC, under Jones, is Charles B. Henderson, who got his start in politics, and as a young man was U. S. Senator from Nevada. He faithfully reflects the Jones philosophy in the conduct of RFC.

Two RFC directors about whom little is heard, Sam H. Husbands and Howard J. Klossner, are the sort of men who are qualified to take over and run the biggest bank in the country. For years the RFC treasurer, Henry A. Mulligan, whom Jones once called a "shrewd, capable, financial genius," has quietly handled most of the RFC's big bond financing transactions.

Probably the most retiring of all of the Jones men is William Costello, who for two or three decades, as confidential assistant, has served as practically an extra pair of hands, eyes and ears for Jesse Jones.

By early 1942 the number of agencies concerned with housing loans and other phases of housing, had multiplied to the point where the President decided to merge the dozen or more such agencies into a newly created National Housing Agency. Among them the FHA, the HOLC, and various offshoots of the old Federal Home Loan Bank System were shifted from Jones' jurisdiction into this new agency. Administrator of the new NHA is John B. Blandford, Jr., professional student of public administration, erstwhile general manager of TVA and recently assistant director of the Bureau of the Budget. Blandford is not primarily a social reformer.

Abner Ferguson, head of the FHA under the 1942 housing reorganization, grew up in this agency as the main understudy of Stewart McDonald, the Jones man who built up FHA. John H. Fahey, Commissioner of the Federal Home Loan Bank Administration, is an ex-businessman, newspaper publisher, man of many affairs in Worcester, Massachusetts.

Of all the head government banking officials, the only one who is at heart an indoctrinated exponent of socialized credit is Dr. Albert G. Black, governor of the Farm Credit Administration. He frankly believes that the time has come when public policy requires the government to assume credit risks which private lenders should not undertake. If this means that farmers borrowing from the government will be forced to fall in line with government crop controls, he can justify that as the price of progress and as a preferable alternative to agricultural chaos.

Who May Borrow?

Who are the borrowers from the numerous government banks? Nearly anybody *may* be, if he has some sort of record for honesty, working ability, and can make a showing that he has a reasonable chance to repay the loan eventually. Study a few cases and you see the scope of the business.

The home owner who somehow was able to get title to his home and then ran into hard times, was able to get the government to take over his mortgage, give him a period of grace, and let him work off the mortgage over a long term of years at low rates of interest. This was the job of the Home Owners' Loan Corporation. It is making no new "distress" loans now, but it or its successor is sure to do the same kind of job when the next depression hits. There were 1,017,827 of such loans between 1933 and 1936, totaling $3,093,000,000. Many mortgages thus taken over have been foreclosed, leaving the government a heavy owner of city real estate.

The thousands of local building and loan associations have their own pet government bank system. This is the Federal Home Loan Bank System, another Hoover idea subsequently expanded by the Roosevelt administration. These associations can hock their mortgages with the Home Loan Banks and get new money at a profitable rate of interest. Such loans are now close to $200,000,000.

The ordinary fellow with a few hundred dollars to pay down can buy a house which has been financed through the Federal Housing Administration. It may, perhaps, be insurance company money, but the FHA insures the insurance company, or the bank, or other lender. If the home purchaser falls down on his payments, as many do, the government pays off the insurance company and takes over the property. So it is a form of government credit, although the money originally advanced comes from private sources. The government through the FHA has put its credit behind nearly $5,000,000,000 of such home mortgages, involving over 4,000,000 home purchasers.

The FHA also has been a boon to big builders, providing insured mortgage money for construction of large-scale low-rent apartment houses. Tenants get the low rents, and the builders and owners get a nice margin of profit.

The railroads are among the principal RFC debtors. For them the RFC has become almost the sole banker in recent years. In many cases, the railroads came to the RFC because private lenders regarded them as too shaky. In other cases, they borrowed from the RFC because they could get lower interest than they could get through the established Wall Street investment houses.

How to Get Loans

The procedure for getting a loan from one of the government agencies is not highly complicated. It is not necessary to go to Washington. Branch offices and local facilities are provided within easy reach of citizens in nearly all parts of the country.

For an RFC loan the thing to do is to go or write to one of the 30 RFC regional offices. Your local bank can tell you about RFC procedure and the address of the nearest branch office.

If you want a loan to build a house under the FHA insurance plan, you deal directly with your local banker, building and loan association, or insurance company loan representative.

If you are a farmer seeking government credit, see your county farm agent, state your needs, and he will tell you what to do.

RFC and Family

The first big plunge into federal lending was made with creation of the Reconstruction Finance Corporation under President Hoover, early in 1932. At first it was intended to lend only to banks, insurance companies, financial institutions, railroads, states, counties and cities, in the belief that this relief at the top would check the depression and start business recovery. But the pressures were too strong to be met with halfway measures. The wave of unrest that swept Hoover out swept in a regime which threw overboard the old inhibitions against government money-lending.

The New Deal in 1933 embraced Hoover's RFC and built it bigger and bigger as the new program of money relief continued to expand. The RFC and its related agencies now constitute the greatest government bank ever conceived. The principal units of the RFC "holding company system" are: Export-Import Bank, RFC Mortgage Company, Federal National Mortgage Association, Electric Home and Farm Authority, Disaster Loan Corporation, Rubber Reserve Company, Metals Reserve Company, Defense Plant Corporation, Defense Homes Corporation, and Defense Supplies Corporation.

When national defense became the main job in Washington, Jesse Jones lost no time getting into the thick of it. With broad, new authority from Congress the RFC moved beyond the loan phase and plunged into the business of building and owning factories and homes, buying and holding supplies and materials, all as part of the war effort. The RFC and its string of special corporations had financed or underwritten up to the end of 1941 about $6,000,000,000 of defense operations, including new plants to fill Army and Navy orders, the piling up of huge stocks of strategic and critical war materials. Jones did a lot of buying, but has been criticized for not doing enough.

Farmers

Outside the Jesse Jones banking sphere, the Roosevelt administration also set up new machinery for direct loans to farmers. A complete government banking institution was created through the Farm Credit Administration to serve nearly all the credit needs of agriculture. Henry Morgenthau was the first head of the FCA before he became Secretary of the Treasury. The FCA now has outstanding about $3,000,000,000 of farm loans of various kinds.

Good farmers, the so-called solvent farmers, can get loans on their farms from the Federal Land Banks and Federal Farm Mortgage Corporation, the loans to be paid off over 30 years. The operating interest rate is 3½ per cent. For these loans, the farm lobby has been able to secure legislation fixing an interest rate below what is needed for the government to break even. This means that each year, the Treasury, out of public tax money, makes up the difference—in effect, subsidizing the farmers' interest rate to the extent of several million dollars a year. The government farm credit system holds the mortgages of more than a million farmers, and the total runs to $2,500,000,000, or about 40 per cent of all the nation's farm mortgages.

Farmers can also borrow from the government to finance their crop production. The cotton or tobacco farmer, for example, can borrow in the spring and agree to pay the loan when he markets his crop. This is done through government directed production credit facilities. Since this type of money-lending was started in 1933 there have been over 1,700,000 such loans totaling over $2,000,000,000.

Loans for Relief

The most New Dealish kind of government farm lending is done through the Farm Security Administration. The FSA frankly tries to set up the down-at-the-heel farmer who wants to be a farm owner instead of a farm tenant or share-cropper. If such a man can show reasonably good character, health and work habits, he can get the government to buy him a farm, provide livestock, tools and seed; in short, start him off with a going farm of his own. In each county where such loans are made in substantial volume, there are government social workers and farm advisers, who spend their time telling the borrower how to farm and telling his wife how to can blackberries and the like, so as to make the farm family a near-self-sustaining enterprise. There are now about $500,000,000 of FSA loans outstanding, and repayments are almost on schedule—a record better than that of many other government lending agencies.

The RFC's Disaster Loan Corporation is another example of government relief lending, although previously the RFC had made certain types of relief loans. The Disaster Loan Corporation was created at the time of the Ohio River flood of 1937. Disaster loans have since been made to New England storm victims and others. Tony the barber got $500 to refit his shop. Jake the hamburger man got $300 to restock his eating joint. Total of such loans has risen to over $10,000,000, to about 9,000 persons.

Electricity and Small Business

In many communities you can buy your electrical appliances with government credit through the Electric Home and Farm Authority. The EHFA, affectionately referred to as "Little Eefa," was originally created to facilitate operation of the Rural Electrification Administration. And it got a boost from the attempt of the TVA and the anti-utility-company forces to have the government finance installment purchases of electrical appliances at low interest rates so the TVA could quickly build up outlets for its power. Finally it was dumped in the lap of the RFC. Now it operates all over the country, through more than 2,000 dealers, has about $8,000,000 of business on its books, and shows a satisfactory balance sheet. Since it was started it has financed more than 100,000 persons for an average of $150 per person. By operating through private dealers and underwriting private lenders, it has escaped any serious attack from private interests.

Farmers now are getting electric lights and power for their farm machinery through government credit provided by the Rural Electrification Administration. Private power companies found this business unprofitable in many sections, due to the heavy expense of stretching lines across sparsely settled areas. So the government puts up the money, assumes the risk, and is prepared to write off part of the cost if the experiment fails to pay out. The REA lends to special farmer cooperatives which it helps to set up. Up to 1942 it had outstanding around $300,000,000 of such loans.

With government lending to all sorts of "little fellows," there grew up tremendous political pressure for loans to the "small businessman." The RFC bucked this pressure for quite a while, but Congress finally authorized such loans. And now the RFC has made nearly 8,000 loans, totaling about $300,000,000, to small businesses. This takes care, for instance, of the gadget manufacturer with 25 employees who may need only $5,000 for new machinery which will permit him to handle a war sub-contract. In many cases the loans are for working capital to carry raw materials needed for business already on the books.

Foreigners too are heavy borrowers from our government banks. The Export-Import Bank has lent money in China, Finland, Chile, Cuba, and a dozen other countries. These loans have been intended to unfreeze foreign trade, spur the flow of American exports, and are, at least theoretically, secured loans. Yet they are largely policy loans calculated to aid in the war effort.

Get the Money Back?

Shift now to the question of repayments. The final record is yet to be seen, for a considerable portion of loans have not become due. Also it happens that the country has been in a generally upward business trend since most of the lending was done, and so there has been no serious test of what will happen to collections when another depression comes.

In some cases, Congress has frankly intended to allow for considerable losses. The Home Owners' Loan Corporation, for instance, was specifically set up to take over home mortgages in cases where hard-up debtors were faced with foreclosure. Actually, the record of HOLC in liquidating its "distress" mortgages has been good. In 1941 it had worked off thousands of foreclosed houses on a rising real estate market. It has reduced its loans outstanding to less than $2,000,000,000, a reduction of more than $1,000,000,000. It has headed off much grumbling among private real estate dealers who fear government .competition, by letting these dealers earn commissions in selling foreclosed HOLC houses. Final appraisal of results will have to wait, of course, until it can be determined what happens when a real estate depression hits.

Another type of loan considered shaky at the outset was the Disaster Loan Corporation loans, but thus far repayments have pleasantly surprised officials in charge of collections. Approximately 80 per cent of such loans due have been paid.

Contrary to what one might expect, it looks as though the RFC's "small business" loans will make a worse showing than the "disaster" loans. In fact, Jesse Jones says there will probably be a substantially larger percentage of losses from industrial loans than from any other class.

Some of these little business borrowers have thrown in the sponge after a hard struggle and after great leniency and wet-nursing by the RFC. So the government has acquired ownership of businesses. The RFC, of course, tries to find buyers for these foreclosed businesses, at the best price obtainable. This is handled through the 30 regional offices of RFC. (If you have the urge to buy yourself a business, you might find it worth while to look over the RFC list of offerings, but you must be prepared to put some fresh capital into the venture.)

Railroad borrowers also have been slow in repayments, at least as measured by total dollar volume of such loans. Out of its total of $460,000,000 of railroad loans, the RFC in 1941 had about $170,000,000 tied up in defaulting railroads. Some other railroads are "solvent" only because of the sufferance of RFC. This is not the whole story, however. In several cases, private investors have been glad to take over from the RFC railroad loans, which they at first refused to touch. And the "threat" of government credit, in other cases, has caused private financiers to shove down interest rates on railroad issues.

Electric appliance loans of the EHFA have been no problem—they have been repaid along with the customers' monthly electric service bills. But the Rural Electrification Administration seems headed for plenty of bad accounts. Congress probably will eventually vote outright subsidies to provide part of the cost of taking electric power to rural areas.

Crop production loans to farmers make a good showing—so good, in fact, that commercial banks complain of unfair government competition in this field.

Long-term farm mortgages of the FFMC and Federal Land Banks are being paid satisfactorily on the average. A further test of these loans is yet to come, when the "up" phase of the business cycle turns into a "down" phase.

If and when defaults on government loans begin to pile up, it probably will be argued by defenders of government banking that over-all social benefits from the loans outweigh the losses.

The RFC as a whole has built up a surplus of over $225,000,000, after setting aside $125,000,000 to meet future losses.

Government Controls the Banks

The billions which government lends must come from somewhere. They come partly from taxes, but largely from borrowings by the government. Oddly enough, the government borrows from banks in order to lend to all sorts of interests which under the old procedure might have been considered potential customers of the banks. Banks lend to government, which then lends to the banks' customers, who then put the money back into circulation within the banks' communities, where the money comes back into the banks as deposits. It's a sort of forced pumping process, with government doing the pumping.

This process has done something to the banking business. Banks tend to rely less on the shavings of interest profit which they formerly made on loans of varied kinds, and more on the shavings of interest profit which they now make by lending to government. Thus government has become the biggest single customer of the banks.

Government formerly regulated the banks, and still does, but now it goes further and practically controls them. They are subservient. They are compelled by a new set of circumstances to do pretty much what government wishes them to do.

The Treasury, through its office of the Comptroller of the Currency, is charged with looking out for the soundness of the national banks. And through the Federal Deposit Insurance Corporation, the Treasury is faced, in effect if not in law, with making good in case of any possible future crash, over 30 billions of deposits. The government now insures deposits up to $5,000. Close to 40 millions of persons thus look to the Treasury to back up their bank accounts. Thus the interests of the government, the banks, and the millions of depositors have been tied up together in a single package.

Banks look the same on the outside as they did ten years ago. They have the same awesome fronts, the same barred windows and tellers' cages. But inside they are different. They look more to government, as an organ grinder's monkey looks to the organ grinder for instructions on what to do. They get paid for following instructions, or "suggestions." The pay is the interest on the money they lend to government by buying the government's bonds. The pay amounts to a subsidy to banks.

They earn the subsidy, for they do all sorts of services without direct compensation. For one thing, they administer the nation's money, which is mainly in the form of bank checks. (The paper money, the currency, which passes from pocket to pocket, is only an incidental fraction of the nation's money.) For another thing, the banks help the government sell war bonds. They pay all the expenses of the clerical hire and overhead for these war bond dealings, and they don't make any money on them. They are merely service stations for the government. They can't rebel and still live. Furthermore, they don't want to rebel, for they are caught in the web of government favors which has been spun for them in the past ten years.

What of the Future?

As a preliminary for looking into the future, look once again to the past. Note that the huge structure of government borrowing, government lending, government banking, grew up fast during the past ten years—not as a pre-planned and intended structure, but merely to meet emergencies which arose from year to year. All the schemes were expediency schemes. There wasn't much thought about making them permanent.

Thus arose a tolerance of government lending, government banking. There were shudders from those people who had always clung to the idea that lending should not be mixed up with politics. They said, and still say, that if the mayor of the town controls the lending policies of the First National Bank of the town, it is bad for the depositors of the bank. They said, and they still say, that if the bank's borrowers control the policies of the bank with their votes, the business of lending will become quite different in the future than in the past.

The business of lending *has* become different. It already *has* become dominated by politics. It *has* become socialized.

Can it go back? No, there isn't the slightest possibility. The whole new system has been accepted. Plenty of people squawk about the principle of the thing, about the spectacle of having politicians dictate the policies under which government lends money direct to the voters, who are thereupon encouraged to vote for the politicians who got them the loans. But many of the same people who squawk on principle have become beneficiaries of the new system in practice. They protest, audibly, less and less.

The war cinches the thing. The war puts government firmly into the driver's seat as the general manager of the people's money, as the social director of the uses to which the people's savings shall be put. There was a time when J. P. Morgan was a symbol of the financial coercion of Wall Street. It was said that Morgan dictated the policies of many key corporations. (And he did.) But Morgan was a pigmy, and has been succeeded by a giant. Wall Street was small potatoes, and has been replaced by Pennsylvania Avenue. Socialistic management of capitalism, long considered a vague bogey for the future, has become an accomplished fact.

Many more billions of government debt in the future are certain. The depression of the 30's accounted for something like 50 billions of debt. The war will ring up more, and make it 125 or even perhaps 150 billions.

Then, postwar, there will be programs for government spending and lending to keep the national economy from going bust during the shift from war conditions to peace conditions. People will go along, and applaud, for it will be an emergency, like the emergency of the early 30's. People will say that statistics of debt don't count, so long as material things are being done, and people are provided with jobs. People will say that this is a new era. So they said in the late 20's. But then there was no strong central government to be responsible for the things which happened to them. Now there is, and people with their votes will *compel* that strong central government to do whatever is necessary to keep the economy running at full blast.

Inflation in the future? Yes, of course. Government will be a heavy borrower, a heavy debtor, despite all the lendings set forth in this chapter. Debtors always want a certain amount of inflation. They want prices to be higher, for higher prices ease the burden of carrying their debts. Government just now deplores inflation in its official publicity, but that's partly a pose. Government really wishes some inflation. It expects inflation gradually, over a period of years, not suddenly. A higher plateau of prices through the 40's is the prospect.

All these things that will come to pass had their inception in the money-shoveling of the 30's.

20

Government the Papa

UNCLES are relatives one step removed. They flash in and out of the family picture, and sometimes are helpful, but usually a bit distant. Often they are merely legendary. Papas are different. They are always close at hand, always on the job, always good for a penny or a dime, always telling the children what to do, for the children's sake.

For many years federal government was an uncle—Uncle Sam. He was once removed from the ordinary little affairs of ordinary little men. When they needed help he would help, but only on a big scale, for he was entirely too busy with Large Affairs to be bothered when a little man needed a job, or a baby needed a pair of shoes. That was a matter for states, or cities, or towns, or local charity groups.

But now federal government has become papa, and has moved into the house of the humblest. As papa he forks out aid on a retail scale, even for baby's shoes. Acting as mama, government tries to see to it that the food is well cooked and has enough vitamins, that the baby gets the right care before and after birth. No person is too small for this papa and mama attention, and if he is poor he has the inside track.

Twenty million wards have been acquired by papa and mama government, mainly in the last ten years. That's one-sixth of the population, and plans are afoot to acquire still another sixth in the next ten years. This will make one-third of the population into direct special charges of the government, with varying degrees of dependency, just as children have varying degrees of dependency on their parents. The relationship is and will be directly paternal, maternal, and filial. The wards have learned and will learn further to hold government directly responsible for what they have, and also for what they have not. This is not a new idea, but the big scale is new. It is different from the former idea, which was that federal government should deal with its citizens indirectly, through other mediums, such as state and local governments. The new idea is national rather than federal. It means first-hand dealings with citizens, rather than second-hand. It means papa, not uncle.

The wards have strings on the government, for they have votes. They

219

like the new close relationship, and they support it with their votes. That's why, regardless of parties and regimes which may come and go, the system of papa-ism in national government is permanent, and perfectly sure to grow further.

The upper two-thirds pay the bill, and government is merely their agent, their institutional social worker, their community chest on a national scale. Some of the upper two-thirds like the system, and some grumble, but enough of them approve to make a clear majority for the system. Permanency does not rest solely upon the lowest third who are the wards, the beneficiaries.

Not one person in ten knows how extensive the system is. People know single phases which have grown up piecemeal, and which are administered piecemeal within government, without complete over-all coordination. Even Washington welfare officials themselves, with their eyes focused on their own particular jobs, often don't know what other welfare agencies are doing—in the government building three blocks down the street. So, you are not alone if you are startled by this recital of the scope of government welfare work. More than twenty government agencies are at work on jobs which relate directly to human welfare, benevolence, aid—the functions vaguely regarded once upon a time as "charity." (The new idea is that it is not charity, but long-range "investment" in human life.)

The fact is that national government provides direct aid services from the cradle to the grave. It is paying billions of dollars to millions of persons —at the rate of about 160 million dollars a month. Here are just a few of the things it does for mothers and children:

Gives to mothers advice and assistance before and after the baby is born, with money payments in many needy cases. Helps feed the children with wholesome vitamin-rich food, and teaches the mother how to prepare it. Helps out on the problems of health all along the span of life, from the young to the old. Fights disease, checks up on medicines, develops new medicines, and promotes the habits and opportunities of health. Builds schools for the children and the youths. Helps to keep the schooling up to a standard. Provides milk and hot lunch for millions of school children. Pays teen-age boys and girls to help them stay in school or college. Gives them vocational guidance and training in regular schools and special schools. Hires youths to work in forests and fields, to study on the side, and sends pay-money to their needy parents or families. Keeps children and youths out of certain jobs which hurt their health.

For adults, government performs these services: Helps find the right job for the right man or woman. Makes jobs and does the hiring on public projects when private jobs are scarce. Helps finance the house, and even some of the things inside it. Sets up poor farmers on small farms, buys them a mule and tools, supervises the family budget and the farm budget. Helps get electricity down the road, and into the house, so some of the work can be done with power. Provides houses at low rent. Keeps women from working at some factory jobs which would injure their health, and even pays for time off during pregnancy. Helps to pay men for time lost when they are hurt or ill, or when their former jobs blow up. Pays old folks so that they can quit work and still exist.

All these are human and individual services. Sometimes they are called "welfare," sometimes "social security," which is a catch-all term, a label attached to many projects.

Government Agencies

The agencies which do these things for people are all mixed up and scattered within the framework of government. They are located where they are for a combination of reasons, which may be historical, or political, or special interest pull. There is much duplication and overlapping, much rivalry and institutional jealousy, and the odd thing is that they work as well as they do. They have coordination and liaison, and now there is the beginning of a movement to get them all assembled, with definite lines of blue-printed responsibility and authority.

There are four main groups of welfare agencies. They are under the Federal Security Agency, the Department of Agriculture, the Department of Labor, and the Federal Works Agency (construction).

Under the Federal Security Agency are the Social Security Board; the U. S. Employment Service; Civilian Conservation Corps and National Youth Administration (in process of being merged); the Office of Education; the Public Health Service; and the Food and Drug Administration.

Within the Department of Agriculture are the Farm Security Administration (formerly known as Rural Resettlement); the Rural Electrification Administration; the Bureau of Home Economics; and the Agricultural Marketing Administration.

Within the Department of Labor are the Children's Bureau and the Women's Bureau.

Under the Federal Works Agency are the Work Projects Administration (WPA); the Public Works Administration (PWA, whose work is being taken over by the whole organization of FWA); the Public Roads Administration; and the Public Buildings Administration.

McNutt

The man who runs the biggest and most important dispensary of federal paternalism, the Federal Security Agency, is Paul V. McNutt. He is not a

221

professional welfare worker, but welfare workers say he does a good job at it. McNutt is instead a professional politician, and he seems to be doing a good job at that, too. His ambition is to fall heir to Mr. Roosevelt's job.

He has political guts, as was well demonstrated when he backed the right of the public to have vitamin-fortified oleomargarine against the opposition of the most powerful individual farmer pressure group in the nation—the organized dairy farmers. That scrap may cost him some day a sizable block of the farm vote, and he knew it.

For all his photogenic personality, Paul McNutt works hard at his welfare work. His comfortable but not imposing office is connected by direct wire with the White House. Around the conference table in his office the heads of his agencies gather every Thursday forenoon for staff conference. There McNutt gives his orders for the week. He is readily accessible, and seldom ruffled despite a steady stream of callers and 50 phone calls a day.

McNutt has what amounts to cabinet status, and if he and his aides have their way, the Federal Security Agency will be a regular government department and McNutt its Secretary before this administration comes to an end. He is also Director of Defense Health and Welfare, which is merely an expansion of his regular work, with the accent on public health and morale during the war. As Director of Defense Health and Welfare, McNutt is running the national nutrition program which began operations by putting the vitamins back in bread; and is now administering the work of the Social Protection Committee which is cooperating with the Army and Navy to suppress prostitution within range of off-duty service men.

The home of McNutt's Federal Security Agency is the Social Security Building, an imposing, brand-new, block-long structure situated on the Mall, four blocks from the Capitol. It is one of the few office buildings in Washington equipped with escalators. McNutt's office on the fourth floor is one of the smaller of the large suite of offices assigned to him. But, outside of McNutt and his immediate staff, no other welfare workers work at welfare there, for the building which was supposed to house them all— including 4,500 clerks temporarily stationed in Baltimore—was taken over for war-emergency work. So now, war workers jampack its offices, and even its halls. And the 4,500 girl-tabulators are still in Baltimore.

Federal Security was set up in 1939 to coordinate the work of seven existing agencies, some New Deal, some pre-New Deal. Mr. Roosevelt said at the time that it was to "promote social and economic security, educational opportunity and the health of the citizens of the nation."

With such a blanket grant of authority, the FSA has been able to go about its chores with ambitious enthusiasm. Virtually every citizen is aided by the operations of at least one of its agencies.

Social Security

Workers are the principal beneficiaries of the biggest of McNutt's agencies—the Social Security Board. It operates a nation-wide free job-hunting service for the unemployed; helps the states administer the system of weekly checks which tide them over jobless periods; and it sends them a monthly pension check after they are old and have retired. In addition, the Board helps states pay for special assistance for the blind and the aged, and for dependent children.

If you lose your job, you take your social security card to the nearest of the 1,500 offices of the U. S. Employment Service and apply for a new job. That means filling in a blank—what work you have done, how much you got for it, and what else you can do. At the same time you apply for unemployment compensation. Thereafter you drop by the office once a week to see if there is a job for you. In about 30 days you get in the mail a compensation check for as much as $20. Each week thereafter another check comes, *after* you visit the Employment Service office. No visit, no check—for you might have found a job in the meantime. The weekly checks will continue for from three to six months, depending on the law of the state in which you live. In some states you have to be fired in order to get the checks. In others you can just quit your job. In some you can get the checks while you are on strike.

The system is an insurance plan—pay check insurance, not job insurance as many believe. Your boss pays part of the premium directly, and indirectly, through your general taxes, you pay the rest. The checks you get while you are out of work come from the kitty in the state capital to which the employers contribute.

Old-age pension checks, which you can get when you quit work after you have reached 65, also come from an insurance system. You and your employer pay the premiums, each paying a percentage of your wages which originally was set at 1 per cent and will gradually increase. Your monthly checks will range from $10 to $85, depending on your previous wages and the number of your dependents. This whole system of easing the shocks of unemployment on both the able and the aged probably is the longest social stride we have taken as a nation. But we were well behind other countries in making it unnecessary for our burnt-out workers to go "over the hill to the poorhouse."

For the youth of the nation, periods of heavy unemployment are a special burden. There's nothing for them to do, even if they have special training—which few of them have. And hard times increase the difficulty of getting the education or training required of today's workers. The depression of the 30's re-emphasized these facts. Some six million out-of-school, out-of-work youngsters couldn't get jobs on WPA or elsewhere. And others didn't have the money to finish their schooling. Theirs was the bleak prospect of hitch-hiking and rod-riding in chase of work and rumors of work. It was an emergency, and the government stepped into it in a hurry with the Civilian Conservation Corps and the National Youth Administration. Together they have helped seven million young men and women, and they have spent a little more than three billion dollars. Under McNutt's direction, they are being merged. And out of the merger will come a permanent system of youth relief directed from Washington.

Some sincere critics claim that this coming system will be federalized education, subject to the evils of state education as it is practiced in the totalitarian countries. Equally sincere boosters say such charges are bosh. They make the counter claim that public support of the CCC and NYA indicates public objection to certain deficiencies of the established public school system. It seems clear that future youth relief policies will plow a furrow carefully between the two—a sort of post-graduate work-relief course in the adjustment from book larnin' to work.

Both the CCC and the NYA operate on a work-relief basis, the CCC with the atmosphere of the summer camp and the great outdoors, and the NYA by taking the made work to the campus. The CCC was first to be organized, and has had general public favor. At one time it operated 1,500 camps, but now that the war has made more jobs for young men, less than 600 camps are in operation. The volunteer, who is between 17 and 23, usually ends up by staying in the CCC for two years, probably because he is taught the value of his work. He gets a sense of usefulness and accomplishment from tree planting, building fire towers, seeding range lands, digging drainage ditches, and helping to fight fires. CCC wages are certainly not the lure, because the boy only sees $12 of his pay each month. Of the $30 he is paid, $10 is sent to his family and $8 is saved for him.

The Army builds the camps, supplies the food, and supervises the "extra-curricular" studying which the boys do after hours. The Departments of Agriculture and Interior pick the camp sites and generally supervise the work. The CCC itself acts merely as a liaison agent.

The NYA has had less popularity, with the young people between 16 and 24 who are eligible, as well as with the general public. Even so, the NYA operates in about 30,000 high schools and colleges; and through "out-of-school programs," in almost every county of the country. Poor public understanding may be part of the reason, as NYAers claim. But the chances are that the fanciful dreaminess of some of the things it has done plays a larger part, for NYA has been guilty of much outright boondoggling.

NYA itself recognizes this. Since last year it has put heavy emphasis on the training of war workers—a really gigantic vocational training program. NYA's "leaf raking," such as the grading of papers and the tutoring of backward pupils, is being de-emphasized as rapidly as possible. The push now is on training apprentices for work in shipbuilding, aviation, the building of machine tools, wood working, automotive work, riveting, welding, electricity, forging, ceramics, and other lines. It may turn out that the merged CCC-NYA will eventually take off the shoulders of both industry and labor part of the job of apprentice training.

Health and Education

Washington welfare work and the New Deal are not synonymous, as many persons loosely think, despite the billions spent since 1932 to put government social work on its present highly personalized and individualized basis. The federal government took an active part in education and public health, even before Roosevelt I.

The Office of Education, now under McNutt's jurisdiction, was established in 1867 as the administrative agency for the land grant college system, and it still supervises the spending of such government money.

The U. S. Public Health Service administers laws enacted as early as 1902, and is one of McNutt's pets, because its work is now so widely accepted. All in all, the Health Service has become a potent force in American medicine through its research, its cooperation with state agencies in the prevention of epidemics, and its fostering of the best of the new things in medical practice. Its crusade against venereal disease is one of the dramas of modern medicine. The first battle was against the hush-hush atmosphere surrounding the subject, for Surgeon General Thomas Parran, the dynamic and courageous head of the Service, insisted that the nation couldn't come to grips with syphilis and gonorrhea until it could talk about them in public. That fight has been won, and since then, in less than three years, 3,500 venereal disease clinics in all 48 states treat more than 400,000 patients a month—and the spread of the diseases now seems checked.

225

Women and Children

Fashions in welfare work are as subject to change as other fashions. Originally it was the style for federal government to do things for all the people, not merely for specified groups. Near the turn of the century a change occurred. Groups of people, classes, began to demand special consideration. Their demands were symptoms of a change in the public's ideas of government. The farmers demanded and got a federal department. So did organized labor. And in the Department of Labor even children got a special agency—the Children's Bureau. But with it, as with most government welfare agencies, the original demands were made by professional social workers. And in spite of the fact that these professionals like to emphasize American backwardness in such things, the Children's Bureau was the first public agency of its kind in the world. It was supposed to work for the welfare of children in all walks of life, but there were so many children that the Bureau had to concentrate on children in the lower-income brackets.

The Bureau is the national maternity nurse and nursemaid, and the steady decline in the death rate of mothers and infants is largely its doing. It is also protector of the child worker in industry, and once the Bureau says an industry is unsafe for children, that, for all practical purposes, is that. Young mothers are now writing for Children's Bureau pamphlets that their mothers swore by, for the Bureau is one of the government's most prolific pamphleteers.

Katharine Lenroot is now Chief of this first government agency to be headed by a woman. Her enthusiasm for the job hasn't waned in her 27 years with the Bureau, and much state legislation and many state organizations in her field of child welfare follow patterns she has drawn.

Soon after Congress decided children in industry needed a federal guardian, the same sort of agency was set up for women—the Women's Bureau. The need developed during the last war when women took over factory jobs vacated by young men who went into the Army. The Women's Bureau is unique in that it does not administer laws. It merely "influences"—influences state legislatures and Congress. Most state and federal laws which affect the working woman are the product of skillful lobbying. This is supposedly not lobbying by the Bureau itself, but by the women's trade unions, the Leagues of Women Voters, the YWCA's, and other women's organizations with which the Bureau cooperates. Mary Anderson, known throughout the labor movement as "Our Mary," has run the Bureau ever since her appointment by President Wilson.

Feeding and Drugging

Government started out to protect all the people from food which might be dangerous to health, or even poisonous. Then it began to tell people what foods were good for them, then how to cook it to get all the goodness out of it, then how to buy it most cheaply. Then government got around practically to buying the food and giving it to people who couldn't afford it, and then, almost finally, to cooking the food. The final step is government subsidy to farmers to grow more of the food that's good for people (as noted in chapter 17, Farmers Go To Town).

The Food and Drug Administration, another of McNutt's agencies, does the protecting. Its field has been extended from food to include drugs and cosmetics, and it inspects the products of more than 50,000 factories.

The Bureau of Home Economics of the Department of Agriculture, under the capable direction of Dr. Louise Stanley, a nutritional chemist, tells people how to buy food economically and how to cook it so its most healthful qualities aren't lost. It also tells them how to buy clothes and cloth to make clothes, how to can and preserve at home, how to plan a kitchen, and how to choose household equipment. Lest farmers think such goings-on unseemly for a bureau of *their* department, Dr. Stanley sees to it that farmers' wives like her work. One such job was the standardization of children's clothes' sizes. The result is that a blouse marked "Size 5" will, in about nine cases out of ten, fit Mrs. Farmer's 5-year-old. The Bureau is doing the same sort of job for women's clothes. Also the Bureau speaks with final authority on certain phases of nutrition and is playing a major part in the present national nutrition program. Dr. Stanley's Bureau obviously practices the economy it preaches, for, on a budget of less than $350,000, it manages to do the research, to prepare, and to distribute about four and a half million of its bulletins a year.

The Food Stamp plan of the Department of Agriculture is considered dramatic by the general public, for it approaches simon-pure state socialism. There are two ideas behind it. One is that people must eat more of the right kind of food whether or not they can afford to buy it. The other is that farmers must sell at a profit all the food they grow. Of course these appear to be incompatible, but there's nothing much new about either point of view. Each has been strongly agitated for years. But mixing the two in one administrative agency of government—and keeping them mixed —is a real triumph in political ingenuity. And that is precisely what the Food Stamp plan does, and is doing for every needy relief family in the United States who takes advantage of the plan. The whole thing appears simple—now that someone thought it up, but the pressure for thinking it up didn't come until federal government quit testing the waters of social welfare and jumped all the way in. Yet, socialistic as the whole thing is, it makes use of one of the most highly competitive of the private-initiative industries—the food trade. In fact, it wouldn't work without the food trade, for it's all done with a system of government stamps that people on relief can use instead of cash at their grocery stores. Thus, without touching the food, or getting into the food business, the government provides both poor relief and farm relief.

Free food for hot school lunches is arranged by the same agency, the Agricultural Marketing Administration, for about 7 million school children. The lunches are cooked by local welfare agencies, which the government helps support in one way or another, and are served, along with penny bottles of milk in many communities, to children who otherwise couldn't afford to eat at noon.

Farmers' Relief

The Department of Agriculture's other experiment in poor relief and farm relief has been a storm center ever since it started. It is the Farm Security Administration, which spends most of its energy helping tenants and share-croppers along the road to farm ownership and self-sufficiency. Farm Security makes loans, by which houses and outbuildings, including privies, are built; mules, seed, and fertilizer are bought; and carefully-made minutely-detailed government farming plans are followed.

Farm Security has never gotten over the effects of public antagonism to its originator and first administrator, Rexford Tugwell. Even though it has helped with cash and encouragement in thousands of pitiable cases of human misery, it is accused of harboring outright "reds" as well as "pinks" on its ample pay roll. And even though it is run by C. B. Baldwin, a young but certainly not overzealous zealot, it is accused of *trying* to do two "radical" jobs for every conservative job it does.

Farmers are the main accusers, especially the American Farm Bureau Federation, which represents the American equivalent of the "landed aristocracy," and the most powerful of the farmer's general pressure groups. The Farmers Union, less potent than the Bureau, is Farm Security's main defender. Thus, Farm Security is in the middle of a political battle for power and prestige, and is, therefore, the one federal welfare agency which now seems more likely to contract than to expand with the years.

The Rural Electrification Administration, also under the Department of Agriculture's somewhat unwilling wing, is dedicated to the job of getting electricity to as many farms as it can. Hate of private electric utilities is poorly concealed by some of its officials. The result has been a long series

228

of headaches for Henry Wallace when he was Secretary of Agriculture, and now for Secretary Claude Wickard. The REA claims it is really aiming at decentralization of industry, and is trying to attract packing plants, canneries, creameries, and similar industries with abundant cheap power, and labor rooted in the soil outside cities. So REA helps farmers organize "electric co-ops," and lends them the money and the engineers to run power lines in farming areas, especially where private utilities haven't found service profitable.

The Future

At present the whole program of government welfare work is a jumble, but two things are clear. One is that localized charity "for sweet charity's sake" has been outmoded as a national practice. The other is that the future direction of government welfare is toward a larger measure of state socialism, direct state responsibility for the welfare of the people.

Localized charity failed early in the depression of the 30's, in spite of the Hoover efforts to stir up local, county, and state responsibility. This failure, perhaps as much as anything else, put Roosevelt in and Hoover out. Roosevelt chose a professional social worker, Harry Hopkins, to do the charity work.

But Hopkins went further than that, and it was then that the pattern of the future was cut. Hopkins almost immediately substituted "work relief" for "charity" in our national vocabulary, and in our national policy. For Hopkins had three ideas which he pushed with vigor: (1) Federal aid to the needy should be based on a policy of liberal outpouring, to *do* the job, not half do it. (2) The outpourings should go direct from government to individuals, short-circuiting the states. (3) The individual should work for his share of the outpourings. These Hopkins ideas, backed by Roosevelt, established the general policy as it exists today. Under that policy, made work, leaf-raking, and boondoggling developed, but the dole was avoided.

All welfare work of the government has been going through changes, changes designed as much as anything else to insure its survival. For, when certain changes are made, politics can be depended upon to maintain the flow of necessary cash. When the appropriations are before Congress, the beneficiaries get busy with lobby pressure, which is directed from Washington by the government welfare agency whose appropriation Congress is considering. Congress rarely cuts, except in wartime.

Thus, the system is self-perpetuating. Blocs of citizens, nurtured by money from Washington, tie themselves to government—and government, nurtured by the votes of these blocs of citizens, ties itself to them. That is both how and why the system has already become entrenched.

The common argument against the system is that government paternalism and maternalism diminishes individual initiative and destroys the will to struggle for one's self. The counter argument, advanced by government and its welfare workers, is that adequate government help tends to *free* the initiative, opens the way for the seizing of opportunities, and fits the individual to do his own struggling.

There's always the danger that the government's welfare movements will run wild, for enthusiastic welfare workers sometimes mix their determination to perpetuate their welfare work with the normal human determination to perpetuate their jobs, their own pay checks. Thus, welfare workers themselves tend to become "vested interests." Long-visioned welfare workers recognize this, and admit the danger to their work as well as to their jobs. But they are inclined to expect corrective developments. They expect, for example, that the taking of more and more income taxes from the pockets of more and more middle-income people will result in more effective squawking against extravagance.

In the long run, expansion is inevitable in the government's help for the unfortunate and the downtrodden. Your children in their day, by their standards, probably will regard the government's welfare work of today as small potatoes.

21

Government the Builder

GOVERNMENT welfare activities are one thing, and government construction operations are another thing, but they are two wings of the same bird. Welfare gives services, and construction gives material things; but they both have the same purpose. The purpose is to round up and put to work the idle and available energies of people, for their own as well as others' benefit.

The Pyramids were public works and served the same purpose in those days as public works in these days. They gave work to men, provided them with a living, and still there was something left over for the generations which followed the builders. So government construction is nothing new.

George Washington and Alexander Hamilton wanted the government to do big-scale building for itself, and they even went so far as to propose that the government borrow money to do it. They were opposed by Thomas Jefferson, the Great Liberal of his day, who insisted on federal economy, small debt, and less centralized responsibility. He was afraid of big government, the power of borrowed money, and the influence of spendings—which shows how the styles of liberal thought change. Henry Clay, the "radical" of his day, wanted and got roads into the wilderness of the West. Congressman Abraham Lincoln wanted canals. "General" Jacob Coxey in the early 1890's wanted roads and actually went to the extreme of proposing to Congress that a whole half billion dollars be spent, but he left Washington disappointed.

Herbert Hoover in the early 20's had a scheme for taking up slack in depressions by having the government do a lot of public works, and he was regarded then by many conservatives as a bit visionary. Senator Robert LaFollette in the early 30's asked the government to spend five billion dollars for public works, and was turned down.

By the standards of their days, these men were dreamers. By the standards of today they were pikers. Roosevelt has gone further than any of them dared.

For a half century our government has built post offices and other public buildings for its own use, and it has dredged rivers and harbors, and these were what people had in mind when they spoke of "public works." Then came the depression of the 30's, and government went to town on all sorts of construction—far beyond the post offices and the rivers and harbors of the past.

In the past ten years, at least 18 billion dollars has been spent by government for construction—more than three times as much as the "preposterous proposal" of LaFollette. Half of all construction in the past decade has been paid for by government—federal, state and local, but mostly federal.

Here are just a few of the things that government builds as normal peacetime projects: Dams, roads, trails, lakes, ponds, apartment houses, bungalows, power plants, electric lines, factories, skyscrapers, sewers, water systems, sidewalks, hospitals, schools, libraries, museums, zoos, ships, airports, draining and dredging projects, playgrounds, tennis courts, stadiums, rock gardens, and excellent privies. Government really didn't start out to do things on this scale. A few insiders in government envisioned it, but Congress did not and the public did not. It started merely to meet an emergency, and then it went further to meet other emergencies, either real or fancied, and when it really got going, people liked it and cried for more. There is hardly a community in the entire country where the mayor, or council, or chamber of commerce, or citizens' federation has not tried to get the federal government to build more, and more, and more. Many of the people who make speeches and write letters to congressmen and the newspapers deploring all this government building, have joined local movements to get a bit of the building for their own communities. Many a mayor is elected to office on the pledge that he "will get more federal works for our town."

Federal building programs usually evolve through three stages: The emergency need for something-or-other is met by the government on an emergency basis. Then the emergency treatment serves its purpose, and is well liked. Then the objective shifts from emergency need to permanent purpose, such as human welfare, and the program becomes an established national practice.

Private enterprise couldn't do the job in the emergency of depression, so government did it—merely to fill the emergency gap. It made jobs, and business, and people liked it. Then came the rationalization of social arguments for government building. Apologies ceased—and temporary expediency became permanent policy.

The result is that we now have what amounts to a government department of public works in a class with the "regular" departments. It is the Federal Works Agency, whose administrator, Brigadier General Philip. B. Fleming, has cabinet status.

Associated together in the works agency under Fleming are the Public Works Administration (PWA) ; Work Projects Administration (WPA) for the lighter public works; Public Buildings Administration (PBA) for construction and maintenance of government buildings; and the Public Roads Administration, for building and maintenance of the federal-aid roads.

Most government building projects are in the "non-profit" class. That is, they would not be profitable to private business—schools, libraries, playgrounds, hospitals, roads. Government's original narrow intention to build only such things is still in existence, but at places the line of distinction has gotten dim.

Conservatives declare the whole business of government building is "socialistic," though they ease off a bit when it comes to including construction of buildings and other facilities used by the government. The conservatives go on to say that most of this gigantic federal expenditure for construction is unnecessary, threatens the finances of the nation and imposes a heavy burden of debt on posterity. The odd thing is that the conservatives reject the principle with their minds and fondle the fruits with their hands. Liberals shun use of the word "spending"—use "investing" instead, and say we are adding profitably to the nation's "plant" and operating facilities.

The advocates of government building argue that it actually is highly "profitable"—not by standards of dollars and cents accounting, but by standards of human welfare. They have said, in effect, that a cow in a good barn yields more milk and makes the good barn more profitable; that a man and his family in a good house with a bathroom yield more in the form of total work, and make the government-built house profitable— beyond the bounds of mere arithmetic. But in reality, the controversy is far behind us. Government building of all the things which government now builds is a *fact*, accepted, rooted, permanent, and headed toward far greater growth.

The money cost of all this construction is a problem which the advocates shrug off. They say people can afford anything for which there are available materials and labor. They put the money costs back in the shadow somewhere—secondary, incidental, to be reckoned with at some time in the future.

Federal Works Agency

The Federal Works Agency, which in peacetime spends about two billion dollars a year, is the federal government's biggest builder. The FWA administers most of the government agencies that build—the public works, the roads, and so on. Other building is done by the Bureau of Reclamation in the Interior Department, which has been erecting dams since 1902, and by the U. S. Army Engineers, who are concerned with construction affecting rivers and harbors, and projects for the nation's defense. Into the FWA in 1939 went the public works agencies of the 30's and the old-line agencies which put up government office buildings and built roads. Already it is a major cog in the nation's war machine. When peace comes, its officials hope it will have an even bigger task of building on an unprecedented scale to create business and jobs to cushion a postwar slump.

The FWA has a division—the Public Works Reserve—which is working in cooperation with the National Resources Planning Board on plans for public works and services which will aid in taking up the slack when men and factories grow idle with the advent of peace. The plan calls for a listing and rating of "necessary public works and services" and contemplates expenditure of five billion dollars or more annually for the years immediately following the war. The program spans five or six years and will be revised steadily to remain projected that far into the future. And in the process of putting these projects into effect, the Federal Works Administrator may become Secretary of Public Works.

Fleming

Brigadier General Philip B. Fleming, boss of FWA, is not a social philosopher who spends his time debating the merits of government spending. He is a doer, an executive, administering a program. In his brisk manner, he can turn down million-dollar requests without alienating the proponents. Fleming, now 54, gray-haired and mustached, is a West Point graduate. He got his government experience as administrator of the Wage and Hour Division in the Labor Department, in its stormy days, and also as executive officer of the PWA. Fleming's office is on the sixth floor of the North Interior Building, a block from the State Department and two blocks from the White House. In winter he likes the glow of a fire in his fireplace.

In this same office Secretary of the Interior Harold Ickes began the spend-build program in 1933 as administrator of the PWA. Ickes built slowly and cautiously at first to keep graft and inefficiency out of public works, but later speeded up.

The typical Federal Works project doesn't start in Washington. It starts in Tuscaloosa, New York City, Birmingham, or some other community where the city government decides a slum-clearance housing program is needed, or the county commissioners propose a new highway. The project is too expensive to be paid for out of local funds. So the community leaders get busy and apply to the appropriate FWA unit or the newly set-up National Housing Agency for a grant of cash to pay most of the cost, or for building directly by the government. The local chamber of commerce votes its endorsement. Details are placed before federal field representatives. Members of Congress support the project—and themselves. Impressive delegations come to Washington with bulging brief cases, though the decentralized system, under which field offices must give initial approval, reduces necessity of coming to the capital. If the project is approved, the local government often floats a bond issue to pay its share of the cost.

The Federal Works Agency early this year had a personnel of 40,000. Through the contracts let to private contractors by the FWA, it makes work for about two million. Its employees are widely scattered both in Washington and out around the country. In Washington the PWA has headquarters in the North Interior Building where the FWA offices are located. WPA is around the corner. The Public Roads Administration is a half mile away, next to the National Press Building, and its laboratories are down the Mount Vernon Boulevard overlooking the new National Airport—which itself was a federal building project. The Public Buildings Administration is just off the Mall, and seven blocks from the Capitol. All these agencies have field offices outside Washington—as many as 53, for the WPA.

WPA and PWA

In 1933, with unemployment still running high, something brand new sprang up in Washington—an agency that made work to keep people employed, did its own hiring and ran its own projects, which were often leaf-raking and frank boondoggling. This was the Federal Emergency Relief Administration, started under Harry Hopkins. Soon, under the goad of public criticism, it became the Works Progress Administration, and now it is the Work Projects Administration. It was quite different from the Public Works Administration, begun by Ickes two years earlier under the National Industrial Recovery Act. Ickes' PWA had been providing made work, but it gave money to cities, states, and other federal agencies in loans and in outright grants to hire private industry to do the building. The WPA was "government in business." It did the building itself. And as it became better organized it did less boondoggling and more of the type of work handled by private industry.

The WPA idea has prevailed, probably will continue. Today WPA holds the record for spending—about ten billion dollars. The PWA, two years older and a more efficient builder, has spent "only" six billion dollars.

The PWA, now headed by Colonel M. E. Gilmore, is being liquidated and its work will be carried on by other sub-agencies of the FWA.

In less than a decade the WPA and the PWA, the essential public works units of the government, have built, or improved, in cooperation with the Public Roads Administration, a half million miles of roads and streets, some of which are major arteries connecting important industrial areas. Some are metropolitan area roads for commerce and tourist travel, and some are farm to market roads. In addition, they have reached across the nation's borders and contributed more than a million and a half dollars toward construction of the Pan-American Highway—and more will be contributed later.

They have developed the nation's airports. For several years more than 85 per cent of the airport construction has been done by WPA—more than 3,000 airport buildings, all over the country.

Practically every community in the nation has had a share of the government's building. In seven years, PWA made allotments for projects in all but three out of the 3,071 counties in the United States. Such things as new schools, community centers, libraries, enlarged and modernized hospitals, and two million privies are of incalculable social and economic benefit to the nation as a whole.

The Dams

But the roads, and airports, and houses, and privies are puny things compared to the *biggest* jobs accomplished by the government in its role of builder—the dams. Nowhere else in the world have such gigantic undertakings been attempted—no one but the government of the United States could consider the erection of structures which dwarf even the Pyramids— the enormous dams flung across a dozen rivers. Americans by the millions are awed by their visits to the dams every year. Boulder Dam alone had an annual "gate" approaching a million, before the war forced the closing of all dams to visitors.

Government has built the five largest masonry dams in the world— Grand Coulee across the Columbia River in Washington, Shasta in the Sacramento Valley of California and Friant in Central Valley of California, Boulder at the Nevada-Arizona border, and Marshall Ford across the Colorado River in Texas. These were built by the Bureau of Reclamation. The TVA network spreads across an area of 41,000 miles in seven states under its own independent authority. And the largest earth-fill dam, Fort Peck, stretches itself across the Missouri River in Montana, the work of the U. S. Army Engineers.

While the crowds stare in amazement at 500-ton gates that open at the touch of a finger to a button, they are subjected to a torrent of statistics from guides trained in showmanship by government the builder. At Grand Coulee they are told that its storage basin holds water enough to supply New York City for ten years; that it will generate three times as much power as the Russians got from the Dneiper Dam before it was blown up in front of the German armies.

Many of the elementary needs of life are provided by the dams. They check the swirling torrents that destroy land, and convert them into sluggish irrigation streams that give life to land; they provide drinking water, and cheap electric power for industry, and for homes by the million.

The dams weren't conceived during the depression. But it was then that government became a mammoth builder. Boulder Dam, tallest in the world, was planned in 1927 by Herbert Hoover. As Secretary of Commerce, he headed a committee of representatives of the seven neighboring states which wanted to stop disastrous floods, and to irrigate farms. Boulder's power sale was to be secondary, and was to pay the cost of construction. Damming of the Columbia River was proposed in a survey ordered by Congress in 1925.

TVA's forerunner was Wilson Dam at Muscle Shoals, started during the first World War to manufacture nitrates. After the war, its power was always the subject of controversy, and made many a front-page newspaper headline. Farm interests wanted it leased for a long period to private industry for the manufacture of fertilizer. The electrical industry wanted a private lease to sell power. Senator George Norris led a successful fight against both proposals and twice obtained congressional passage of bills calling for government operation and power sale at the Tennessee Valley. These bills were vetoed by Coolidge and Hoover. The issues of the drawn-out debate involved more than public power vs. private power, and the laws of 1933 and later years, creating the TVA as it is today, provided for navigation, irrigation, flood control and reforestation as well.

Once the government was in the power business, TVA became the Number One operator in the field. It set yardstick prices to measure the charges of its rivals, the private operators. Then it started to buy up the private operators.

The government agencies which build the dams and other public works are made up of people very much like those in private construction companies. The majority of these people are laborers. But there are also some of the best engineers in the country. To draw up its plans and supervise its construction the FWA has 5,000 architects and engineers. The Bureau of Reclamation has about 3,500. The finest of them get salaries far below what they could make in private industry. John Lucian Savage, the Bureau of

Reclamation's star engineer who has designed the seven greatest dams in the country, makes $8,000 a year, and until recently he made less than that. To big private contractors he probably would be worth about $50,000 a year. In the 40-year-old Bureau of Reclamation the engineers have a strong esprit de corps, and take great pride in their work and in their Bureau.

Public Buildings

Some types of government building have been commonplace for so long that their expansion causes little raising of eyebrows. Since its earliest days, the government has been putting up post offices and other buildings to house government agencies, and the government has been sharing in road building by grants of money to states since 1916. So the appearance of the name of Postmaster General James A. Farley on thousands of modern new buildings throughout the country passed almost unnoticed in the 30's. When the government was seeking new things to build, it was only natural that the established types of government building, entrenched past the point of sharp criticism, should be increased too. So now there are new post offices, new federal office buildings, new custom houses. Such building work is handled by the Public Buildings Administration, headed by W. E. Reynolds.

Congressmen are partial to such building. They can use the dedication ceremonies for campaign speeches to grateful constituents. The Public Buildings Administration has in the last decade spent about half a billion dollars, as much as it had spent during the whole previous century.

Houses

The government goes in just as much for building houses as it does for building dams, power plants, airports, and roads. Until recently, its housing-construction activities were messed up—distributed among sixteen units of the federal government. But in February 1942, these activities were merged by presidential order into a single organization, the National Housing Agency, of which John B. Blandford, Jr., was made administrator. That agency will continue a home-building program under which the government already has constructed more than three hundred thousand private homes in a decade.

For years, social workers had preached about the dangers of slums and had called in vain for government housing for the needy. Then, in the early days of PWA expenditure of funds for useful projects, the practice of making federal loans for housing projects was established. By 1937, there were about 48 major groups of government-built housing projects, and the United States Housing Authority, since then merged into the National

Housing Agency, was doing the building and supervising operations. Under USHA domination, tenants were required to meet certain need tests. One requirement was that only families in the lowest income group could be rehoused in USHA-aided homes. The other was that no family could be admitted to a project built with USHA assistance if its net income were more than five times the shelter rent plus the cost of utilities, unless three or more dependents were in the family.

The theory of operation under the United States Housing Act is that subsidies are paid to bridge the gap between what tenants can afford to pay and the economic rent of the project. The act requires that, in slum clearance, one substandard home must be demolished, closed or repaired for each new dwelling constructed under the program. Even if vacant land is chosen for the new construction, the old buildings have to come down in accordance with the "one for one" provision. Local authorities have thus been provided with a strong weapon for use in battle against slum areas. And that weapon already has been broadly used in elimination of thousands of dangerous, unsanitary, overcrowded dwellings. Such elimination, it is hoped, has reduced juvenile delinquency, crime, preventable sickness and death, and has cut public expenditures for fire, health and police services.

Another 100,000 homes have been built by the government in connection with its war activities. These house defense workers and enlisted men in areas where housing shortages would impede war work. There also is a special category of "defense public works," and "defense highway construction" (under the general direction of the FWA), which will fill wartime requirements not specifically military in character.

The Future

When the war begins to show signs of ending, the government builders will spring into action. They will bring forth great new plans. The plans will be adopted. Government building of the past will be dwarfed by building programs of the postwar future. Expansion will come all along the building front, especially in housing for low-income people, making work for thousands. The postwar era will doubtless be the greatest building era in history.

22

Supreme Court, New Model

YOU can't saunter into the new Supreme Court building as you do into most government buildings. You don't amble in right off the street. You climb—up, up, up the tiers of steps, as if climbing to the portals of heaven. When you gain the top and step into the high-ceilinged entrance hall you are out of breath, but that is not the reason you whisper. There's something about the Supreme Court and its environs that makes people whisper, lest they disturb the processes of deep thought of Great Judges. The air of reverence in the lofty hall is not broken even by the presence of those chromium spittoons, the most expensive of all spittoons in the nation's capital. They are like the Court itself—of very latest model and design.

It's a new building, up across from the Capitol, on the wide avenue with the Library of Congress. It's a new Court, for seven of the nine justices have been appointed by one President under the New Deal. And in the minds of the new justices is a new set of ideas about how a Supreme Court ought to conduct itself in relation to the law-making branch and the executive branch of the government.

The principal new idea is that almost anything done by any legislature (and especially Congress) is OK, provided it does not infringe on civil liberties. Current laws flow from bodies which have recently been chosen by the people, and, therefore, the new laws ought to be given the benefit of the doubt if anyone thinks they conflict with the Constitution, which is the basic law. The Constitution can be construed to make elbow room for new laws. That states it too flatly, but that is the general idea.

You know, of course, that the justices of the Supreme Court are very important men in Washington, that they collectively are supposed to be coordinate with the executive and the legislative. You know that they decide things, and that these usually stay decided for a long time.

You know, too, that the Supreme Court consists of the only nine men in the whole government who are appointed for life and whose continuance in office does not depend directly on the vote of the people or the will of the people. Except in circumstances so unusual that they have never occurred, the Court is answerable only to its own collective conscience.

240

This is important, because it gives these nine men the theoretical opportunity of not listening to elections, not reading the political news, not paying any attention to the ebb and the flow of political life. They may do what they think is best and right and constitutional.

Now it develops that they think it is best and right to read the political news, and to bow when the political winds blow. This has been a policy of the Court not just since the seven new men were appointed by Roosevelt. It became a policy before that. After the elections of 1936, and early in 1937, the Court handed down at least four decisions that could not be reconciled (except by a Supreme Court scholar) with other decisions made by the same men not six months before. It did not overrule the earlier cases, but it "distinguished" the new cases from the old ones so well that any layman or lawyer would consider the old cases quite effectively killed. After the Court received a spur from the elections, it got another kick in the pants which hurried the policy switch. This time it was the "Court packing" plan. And this time, the Court moved ahead of an exceedingly angry President—angry that some New Deal laws had been invalidated by the Court.

The "Court packing" effort did not succeed. That is, the proposed legislation did not succeed in Congress. And yet it *did* succeed, for it raised such a ruckus that the Court bowed and changed its ways of thinking. And that was followed by a series of events, all natural and constitutional, by which vacancies occurred and one President was enabled to appoint the seven new justices who might be expected to carry his New Deal ideas into the judicial game. The seven Roosevelt-appointed justices are: Hugo L. Black, Stanley F. Reed, William O. Douglas, Felix Frankfurter, Frank Murphy, James F. Byrnes, and Robert H. Jackson. Chief Justice Harlan F. Stone was appointed by Coolidge, and Owen J. Roberts, by Hoover.

It is probable that this Court will be with us for some time. The oldest of the justices—Stone—is only 69. Douglas, the youngest, is 43. The average age of the Court is about 56. The "nine old men" are not so old. Since men as a rule retire from the Supreme Court only through death or approaching senility, it is a safe guess that the New Deal will dominate American judicial philosophy for the next quarter century.

The Justices' Job

Supreme Court justices go about their jobs in a quiet and businesslike way. When they convene on the first Monday in October each year, there is no big ceremony, no official blowout. There are no photographers' flash bulbs in the chambers of the Court. The judges start calmly to work by mounting the bench in the high-ceilinged courtroom. They first hear motions to admit lawyers to the bar. Then for a week, they confer and decide which cases they will hear argued orally. The judges have spent nearly all summer studying the petitions for review of lower court decisions.

On the next Monday, after the nine men have hashed over the petitions for review, the Court again climbs upon the bench. This time it hands down the "order list" of cases that will be reviewed in the near future. After the "order list" has been read, the nine men begin hearing argument on cases which were not ready for argument during the previous term. And while an argument is being presented, there's none of the "objection sustained" and "objection overruled" that you hear in the lower courts. All nine judges are free to break into the lawyer's spiel at any point and question him about anything in the case. The lawyer attempts to answer all questions that the judges put to him. When the judges have found out as much as they want to know, the argument is over, and usually about an hour is allowed on each side.

Decisions are usually handed down on Mondays. The Court routine runs about like this: For two weeks, the nine men hear arguments in the Court chamber. Then they get together for a conference on the following Saturday. (They work a six-day week.) As decisions are reached, and all the judges agree, or agree to disagree, the Chief Justice assigns one of the majority to write the decision of the Court. After two weeks of argument, the Court recesses for two weeks to write opinions. Thus by the time decision day has come around, it has been four weeks since the Court handed down its first "order list." Two weeks of hearing argument, and two weeks of decision writing. The process is repeated throughout the term, with new requests for review coming in all the time, and new order lists handed down from Monday to Monday.

Writing Decisions

The Chief Justice picks the judge who will write each opinion. Therefore it is an advantage to have as Chief Justice someone who has had enough experience on the Court to know which judges are strong in which branches of law. On the present Court, anything involving corporation finance is likely to end up with Justice Douglas, something on patents with Chief Justice Stone or Justice Roberts, something on admiralty with Justice Black. The Chief Justice does not assign cases arbitrarily. The decision always follows a discussion during which every justice expresses his opinion on the case. The Chief Justice is chairman of the session, and he starts with the junior member of the Court, the most recently appointed judge. He works up in order of seniority, and expresses his own opinion at the end. After all this, he designates one judge to write the majority opinion. Others may write concurring or dissenting opinions.

In the two weeks that the judges spend writing decisions, they don't lock themselves up in solitary seclusion. They have frequent contacts with their colleagues, sometimes in informal bull sessions, sometimes by written memoranda. After a justice has written a decision on a case assigned to him by the Chief Justice, he circulates copies of the decision to all his confreres. This gives each judge a chance to decide whether to disagree with the decision and write a dissenting opinion, whether to agree with the conclusion, but write a differently worded opinion, or whether to OK the thing as it stands.

No Leaks in Advance

In all this routine, it might seem easy for a decision to leak out in advance of decision day, but as a matter of fact, such a leak has occurred only once. Quite a few people handle the decision, however, before it is read from the bench by the justice who wrote it. After it is written, and before it is circulated to the other eight judges, the decision is set in type and printed. For many years, all printing for the Court has been done by one firm, Pearson's Printing Office. The owner himself actually reads the decision as much as a week or more before it is handed down. But he is the only person in his company who does. To make sure that no leak will come about, he first cuts the decision up into many pieces, having one typesetter set each piece, and holding the final part of the decision to be set with his own hands. He himself assembles the type for the full decision and makes proof copies for the justices. When the proof is returned to the justice who wrote the decision, a number of other persons in the Court building handle it. Messengers carry it, sealed, to the offices of the other justices. The justices' secretaries hand it on to the law clerks, and the law clerks hand it on to the justices. Thus, before the nation hears the decision of its highest court, approximately 37 people have had the text in their hands.

Whenever the justices get together to talk over the cases they have heard, or to decide which ones to admit, they use a high-paneled conference room built especially for the purpose in the marble Court building. What goes on inside the room, no Court attaché will venture to say. No one except the nine judges is present. And the walls and doors are completely soundproof.

Spectators, Salaries and Press

Spectators can get into the Court whenever hearings are going on or decisions are being handed down. It doesn't require a special pass or letter from a congressman. When some big case is expected, the crowd often runs over the 200 available seats, and a long line forms outside the ornate chamber rooms. But even on those days, an average American citizen with perseverance can stick around and see his Supreme Court in action.

The sight is the most impressive court scene in America. The nine men, with the Chief Justice in the middle, sit in front of a huge red velvet curtain and four Ionian marble columns. The whole setting is majestic, including the high-backed chairs, which dwarf even the tallest justice. Whenever they are on the bench, the judges wear their black robes, which are specially tailored for each justice by one particular firm in Albany, N. Y. The average justice should have no trouble in keeping his robes in repair, for the salary of an associate justice is $20,000. The Chief Justice gets $500 a year more.

In the elaborate new Court building, members of the press are treated royally. A comfortable press room occupies a large corner of the ground floor. Telephones, good desks and typewriters are handy. In charge of press relations is a special officer, one of the Court's assistant clerks, who has been in the Supreme Court Clerk's office for 13 years, knows the Court inside out, and is himself a lawyer. He has on file briefs in all cases, so that newspapermen can look over any which are of interest to their papers or news services. On a particularly important decision day, the Court may be covered by 75 or more reporters.

Law Clerks and Legal Research

Supreme Court justices cannot delegate much of their responsibility to assistants, but they can and do get a great deal of help from their law clerks. The clerks are high-ranking young lawyers, just out of law school, who usually stay with a justice for a year or two before going into private or government practice. Justice Holmes inaugurated the custom of taking a new clerk each year from among the brightest graduates of large law schools. During the summer they read and brief the petitions for review of lower court decisions. For the rest of the year they do research jobs. How much more is entrusted to a law clerk depends on the clerk and the justice. Some of the young men carry a great deal of influence. This is especially true with Frankfurter's clerks. Many of the New Deal inner circle—notably Tom Corcoran—and not a few Wall Street legal luminaries began their careers in this fashion. Francis Biddle, the Attorney General, started as law clerk to Justice Holmes. Dean Acheson, who has held the jobs of Under Secretary of Treasury and Assistant Secretary of State, was law clerk to Brandeis. Calvert Magruder, credited with drafting the Wagner Act and now a Circuit judge, served with Brandeis.

Legal research is made almost a pleasure for the justices. Their offices (the proper word is "chambers") are dignified, but luxurious. Each one is equipped with a small but excellent law library, plus a bath, shower and dressing room. The innovation of the bath et al. was bewailed by Justice Holmes, who said the communal men's room in the shabby chambers formerly occupied by the Court was the only place where he could meet his brethren often and discuss cases informally with them.

The Men—Stone and Roberts

Chief Justice Stone and Justice Roberts are the sole survivors of the old Court, but it is a mistake to think of them as a couple of last-ditch defenders of the old regime. Both are sound lawyers. Stone is perhaps the soundest on the Court. Roberts is the more conservative of the two, but neither can be tabbed as a real Conservative, in the sense that Sutherland, Van Devanter, McReynolds and Butler were conservatives. Both are fair-minded—sometimes too fair-minded, think the New Dealers, who believe that the intangibles should be heavily weighted in assessing Good Causes.

They have great influence on the Court. Before the Great Change, they represented the middle-of-the-roaders, sometimes siding with the liberal wing of the Court and sometimes with the conservative. They may still hold the same balance of power. The Court's inherent tendency to cleave in some direction, no matter how politically homogeneous a unit it may appear, is quite likely to afford Stone and Roberts opportunities to cast deciding votes when the two factions of the New Deal—the Black faction and the more moderate Frankfurter faction—have divided.

Stone, as Chief Justice, wields particular influence. He is well fitted to decide which of the associates shall do the work on each particular case. His colleagues on the whole do not love him, but they respect him. He is an egotist of the first rank and his vanity is not mercurial and human, but somewhat cold and pompous. He has a well-developed habit of citing his own opinions. But no one denies that they are good opinions, models of lucid exposition.

Justice Black

Justice Black is a bear for work. An example will illustrate both his extraordinary capacity for work and his thirst for knowledge. He decided one day that he didn't know much about admiralty law, and that he ought to correct the deficiency. (Admiralty, the law of ships, shipping, and the sea, is a highly specialized branch of law.) He sent his clerk out for all the texts on the subject, then sat down and digested them. He read all the

245

Supreme Court decisions in admiralty, and proceeded to badger his judicial colleagues with difficult questions bearing on barratry, bottomry bonds, flotsam and jetsam. He now ranks as an expert in that difficult field.

That's typical of Black. He was never a scholar by trade, but he is generally recognized, even by those who dislike his ideas, as one of the best educated men in Washington. He is also coming to be recognized as one of the Court's great judges. He has made himself that, in the years since he was appointed to the Court.

The odds against Black's carving himself such a reputation were tremendous at the time of his appointment. He was not a graduate of one of the "classic" law schools. He had never been an Ornament of the Bar, or a legal scholar, or even a judge (except for a spell in an Alabama police court). In fact, he had never been much of anything except a politician. Consequently, he was accused on all sides—even by perfectly honest legal lights—of professional unfitness for the job. Some persons were so sure of his legal ignorance that, when he turned out some undeniably good early opinions, they accused him of having had them ghosted, of being no more than a Charlie McCarthy for the bright young New Dealers. The rumored ghosts ranged all the way from Tommy Corcoran to Felix Frankfurter.

He was accused of personal unfitness, too, because of his former membership in the Ku Klux Klan—which he joined for about the same reasons that Franklin Roosevelt belongs to the Masons. That, too, he has lived down. Black has proved himself about the staunchest defender of civil liberties on a Court which is, as a group, notoriously prejudiced in favor of individual freedom. He has written more than his share of the opinions which have extended in practice to Negroes the rights which the Constitution has long granted them in theory.

Black today is the undoubted leader of one faction of the Court. The philosophy which differentiates him and William Douglas from Frankfurter, Reed and Murphy may best be described as "no compromise." Black is even averse to the pleasant practice of "distinguishing" objectionable cases. He usually writes concurring opinions advocating outright overruling.

Personally, he doesn't look it. On his appearance, he might be taken for a rural politician or a small-town clerk—almost anything except a justice of the Supreme Court. He speaks soft and slow, with the slightly whiny overtone sometimes found in the deep South. His private life is prosaic and intensely respectable. His relaxations consist largely of tennis, a rare glass of wine, the raising of his young daughter, and reading, legal and otherwise.

246

Frankfurter

Felix Frankfurter probably typifies the New Court to most Americans. He is popularly supposed to have personally invented the New Deal, and certainly he is one of the few members of the original Brain Trust who have continued in favor. Despite his assumption of the judicial veil, he is still a power in palace politics. Many top-flight government officials, including the President, consult him regularly, and he is probably responsible for many appointments to key administrative posts. He enjoys this. There is a strong streak (not really sinister) of Machiavellianism in Frankfurter, and he enjoys the post of power-behind-the-scenes, so long as he is not so far behind them as to be entirely invisible.

Frankfurter has been on the Court since early in 1939, and for some years prior to his appointment he amounted, in practice, to a tenth justice. During his Harvard years, he exerted great influence upon the trend of judicial opinion, both directly and through his numerous disciples. A good part of his life has been preparation for the day, which he probably regarded as inevitable, when he would be elevated to the high Court. Certainly it was his goal. He once refused to accept a seat on the Supreme Judicial Court of Massachusetts, because he feared it might decrease his availability for the bigger Supreme Court job. He succeeded in making the study of the Supreme Court, and the men who sat on it, almost a separate field of law. He inaugurated the custom of conducting, with one or another of his favorite disciples, periodical surveys of the work of the Court. Just as the German General Staff, in the spring of 1940, probably knew more about the terrain of northern France than did the French themselves, so Frankfurter knew more about the Supreme Court than did the justices of it.

Frankfurter wanted to be the Court's "Great Liberal," to wear the mantle of Holmes, Cardozo and Brandeis. The trouble with this ambition was that Frankfurter found, upon arrival in Washington, that the Great Liberal's chair was comfortably filled by Justice Black. Never one to play second fiddle, Frankfurter promptly set himself up as a rival and somewhat more conservative Great Liberal, attracting Murphy to his banner, and, occasionally, Reed. Generally, Frankfurter and Black have differed more in reasoning than results. Frankfurter, less forthright and blunt than Black, and more given to conforming to judicial precedent, tends to "distinguish" old cases rather than to overrule them. He has also a knack of finding that *Congress* has by statute changed the rule established by some earlier decision of the Court—often seizing upon statutes in which the alleged congressional intent is something less than crystal clear.

Frankfurter likes young people. He has always regarded his bright young men at the Harvard Law School as something in the nature of a family, and nothing has hurt him so much during the past year or so as the knowledge that some of these young men believe that he was considerably more impressive as a professor of law than he has been so far as a justice of the Supreme Court. There are grounds for believing that Frankfurter's opinions may, in the future, tend in the direction of more sound law and fewer purple patches. He is undoubtedly capable of better judgments than he has written so far, and he knows it.

Personally, as judicially, Frankfurter is a puzzling collection of contradictions. His warm friends are probably nearly as many as his warm enemies. He is capable of displaying pettiness and temper, usually when his vanity is offended. On the other hand, there are plenty of examples of kind and unadvertised actions to his credit. He inspires tremendous loyalty among his disciples. They read the same books, hold the same ideals, admire the same philosophers that Frankfurter does. They even have the same ailments. Frankfurter suffers from sacroiliac trouble, an often painful condition which can be relieved by the use of a specially designed chair. To one of his admirers, as a special mark of favor, he once made a gift of one of the chairs.

Douglas

Douglas sees almost eye to eye with Black. The two are rarely separated on a case. Unlike Black, Douglas regards the Court as a stepping stone to positions of even greater influence and consequently he has not put himself as wholeheartedly into the work of the Court as has Black. But he has a special field, in which the rest of the Court members (with the occasional exceptions of Stone and Roberts) follow his lead. An ex-chairman of the Securities and Exchange Commission and Yale professor, he probably knows more about the more rarefied levels of corporation law and finance than any other living man. He threads his way with ease, and even some pleasure, through the most tangled thickets of financial manipulation, separating the bondholding sheep from the stockholding goats with a firm and sure hand. In this field, his mark on the Court will probably be permanent. It is an important field, too. About twenty-five expensive and high-powered Wall Street law firms derive the larger part of their fat incomes from this type of practice. They and their clients do not love Douglas. He has a quizzical skepticism and a prejudice in favor of simple honesty in the handling of other people's money, a prejudice which leads him often to disregard legal forms intended to place a shady transaction just within the law. His decisions have done much to make the law of corporation finance a practical common-sense thing, bearing relation to realities rather than legal mirages.

Douglas has always disliked the personal restraints imposed on him by the necessity of being a justice of the Supreme Court. He was glad to have the prestige, but he hated to be tied down to a judicial job. His friends, knowing this, periodically started campaigns of rumors that he would step down and out of the Court, into a more active administrative post. Doubtless this is what will happen to him some time.

Reed

Of all the justices on the Court, Stanley Reed inspires the least heat pro or con. He lacks equally bitter enemies and passionate admirers. Few can call his opinions outstandingly bad. Probably the bitterest epithet yet hurled at him by a legal commentator is "earthbound precisionist." All agree that he is pedestrian, both in his thought and in his language. But he cannot be dismissed so casually. He is a workhorse, and a capable one. From the solicitor generalship, he came to the Supreme Court with a wide knowledge of the sort of legal problems with which he was likely to be confronted, and he has received a variety of difficult and uninteresting assignments— knotty questions of taxation, federal jurisdiction and the like. Possibly his reputation for dullness has been enhanced by the fact that he is a strong exponent of unspectacular common sense on a Court now dominated by idealistic prima donnas. It is also enhanced by the fact that there are not known to be extant any picturesque anecdotes concerning Reed, any fascinating details of his private life. He is said to be a skilled amateur cook. Beyond this not even the most indefatigable Washington gossip-monger has been able to whip up much human interest in Reed.

Murphy

The case is quite otherwise with Frank Murphy. As the Court's solitary bachelor, he is a perennial subject of talk and speculation, neither of which is abated by the fact that the justice has a pronounced taste for the lighter side of life. He is a squire of many dames, but a suitor of none. He is found at numerous affairs at which alcoholic beverages flow with considerable freedom, but he himself practices complete abstinence. Although a moderately hardworking individual, and one generally regarded as having a purpose in life, his friends include such shining examples of the society rich as Evalyn Walsh McLean and Walter Chrysler, Jr. It is known that Felix Frankfurter is irritated by Murphy's failure to adhere, in his out-of-Court existence, to the Frankfurter standards of judicial decorum. A noticeable coolness has grown up between the two men, which may lead to a legal separation if Murphy remains on the Court. But so far, despite the deep differences of temperament between the two men, Murphy has almost invariably followed Frankfurter's cue on decisions.

This may have been sheer inertia. Despite the length of time he has been on the Court, Murphy has yet to write a significant opinion, and even impartial observers are beginning to suspect that his principal qualifications for elevation to the high Court were: (a) A record of unswerving devotion to the New Deal. (b) Need of a job. (c) The fact that he is a Catholic. A Catholic was needed to fill the place of Pierce Butler. There is strong indication that Murphy doesn't like the Court, or its work, and would like to be back in active politics.

Byrnes and Jackson

Byrnes and Jackson are still somewhat unknown quantities. As a senator, Byrnes was a staunch New Dealer, but that is not a good guide to his legal philosophy. Jackson probably will go along with the more conventional Frankfurter faction of New Dealers. Despite some of the farfetched opinions that he issued, as Attorney General, to oblige the President, he really is a good lawyer. It is not every man who can wind up on the Supreme Court without either a college or a law school degree. But Jackson, after two years at an Albany night school, took the New York bar examination, passed it, and went straight into practice.

How to Become a Justice

As you can see, the backgrounds of the Court's present justices have some things in common. All the present justices at one time or another engaged in the private practice of law. Roberts and Jackson were conspicuously successful. Murphy, Reed and Frankfurter picked up their brief experience of private practice at the beginning of their careers, and never returned to it. Black and Byrnes, like most politicians, have practiced law to fill in intervals while they were out of office and to recoup their fortunes.

Frankfurter and Stone may be said to have established their reputations in academic life, Frankfurter as a professor at Harvard and Stone as dean of the Columbia Law School. Douglas was a shining star on the faculty of the Yale Law School. Roberts taught at the University of Pennsylvania. And Murphy taught law in Detroit at one stage of his career.

Three of the justices—Black, Byrnes and Murphy—have had plenty of experience in down-to-earth politics, all three having been elected to important posts in their home states. Black and Byrnes were United States senators. Murphy was Governor of Michigan. Stanley Reed served a term in the Kentucky legislature. Jackson, Murphy and Stone have been Attorney

General of the United States. Reed was Solicitor General. And Black, Douglas, Frankfurter, Murphy and Reed have military backgrounds of sorts. At least, they were in the Army during the last war—Douglas as a buck private.

Apparently one factor that didn't cut much ice in the selection of the present justices of the Supreme Court is previous judicial experience. Only two of the Nine Middle-Aged Men have judicial experience of any sort, and these in the lowest and most insignificant of courts. Black was a police court judge in Alabama; Murphy did a turn in the Detroit Recorder's Court.

This may prove that every police magistrate has a Supreme Court robe in his briefcase, but more likely it indicates that the pursuit of politics is one path to legal eminence.

The New Philosophy

The Court's new philosophy is that (with several important exceptions) a state legislature is usually right, and that Congress is always right. This is because the legislative bodies are elected by the people, and responsible to them. The Court, which is not, should be extremely hesitant to overturn the will of the people, to indulge in "negative legislation." If state legislatures go unusually loony, and in such a manner as to interfere with the national welfare, it is Congress rather than the Court that should correct the situation. Thus, if state legislatures should seriously threaten to "Balkanize" the United States, to cut it up into unworkable compartments by a series of tax and "health" regulations, whose real purpose is to favor local businessmen at the expense of out-of-staters, it is up to Congress to meet the situation. Congress should pass sweeping legislation which so thoroughly covers the field that it would invalidate the conflicting local legislation. Congress can do this by virtue of its power to "regulate commerce among the several states"—a power to which the farseeing judicial eye has as yet discerned no real boundary.

The exception to this theory which holds that "the legislature is nearly always right" is civil liberties. Where the Court believes that freedom of speech, or religion, or due process of law is being denied, it will give short shrift to the actions of courts and legislatures, state or federal.

There will be plenty of cases that are hard to fit into the new Court's basic philosophy. There will be plenty of disputes in the Court as to the application of that philosophy. There will be plenty of individual variation. It would be impossible, except perhaps in Germany, to assemble nine men who thought exactly alike, and the nine men on the Court are no exception to the generalization.

What Does It All Mean?

Does the change in the Court mean anything to ordinary citizens? Yes, plenty. The lawyers may be aware of the changes before laymen are, but the changes filter down just the same. Don't forget that the Court swings power over the lives of all of us—a power equaled only by that exercised by the President and Congress.

Principally, we'll feel the effect of that power indirectly—through the green lights given to Congress, and, to a lesser extent, to the state legislatures. But also, many a man will go free who might have been hanged if it had not been for the Court's belief that "due process of law" is something more than just a phrase. Other men, with unpopular opinions, will have a better chance to get them off their chests because the majority of the Court believes so thoroughly in Voltaire's credo: "I may disagree utterly with what you say, but I will defend to the death your right to say it."

23

The Business of Politics

YOU read about the *game of politics*, and how Washington *plays politics*, as if politics were a sport, and as if all the players were having a jolly good time at it, full of tricks and wiles and mischief against the other side. Well, of course, it is true. People *do* have a good time playing politics. But the emphasis on *play* is wrong. The truth is that they *work* at politics. Especially in Washington they work very hard.

A politician, a member of Congress, a public official, is a good deal like a sales manager. He takes his work seriously. He thinks about it every minute of the day. He arranges his evening hours to fit it. He thinks about it while shaving. What to do to make a few votes is very much like what to do to make a few sales, and he devotes all his energies to the problem. Usually his living depends upon it. If he manages well, he can get a promotion to a bigger job with more luster and more pay, more power, more influence. And either he or his friends can make some money out of that influence.

Politics is a business. That doesn't mean that it is always sordid, or that all the motives are material. Neither is business always sordid and material. But business is down to earth, practical, corporeal, and so is politics. People often think of politicians as a different breed, but they aren't. They are merely in a different business.

Washington is the national center for this business of politics, just as Detroit is the center for automobiles, Pittsburgh for steel, and Akron for rubber. Washington supplies its customers out around the country, and it collects votes, which are the currency in the business of politics. Votes can be used to make jobs, power, favoritism. If the favoritism is toward you, or your community, or your business, or your class, you call it "good." If it is toward others whom you consider not deserving, then you call it just "favoritism" and let it go at that.

Politics has a soul and plenty of people talk vaporously about that, but it also has a body which many people pretend to ignore. You can understand politics a little better if you do not overlook the physiology, and that's what this is about.

253

Professionals

Those who really make the party system work are the minority who have personal interests at stake on the outcome of elections. If it were not for these it would be hard to maintain the virility of political parties as we have known them. These are the fellows who roll up their sleeves and work furiously night and day for weeks prior to elections. In a population of over 130 millions, more than 1,000,000 professional party workers are active participants in political organizations. With their families and dependents, they constitute a bloc of perhaps 3 to 4 million persons whose fortunes are helped or hurt by any shift of political winds.

Often a youngster just drifts into politics, as he might by chance drift into pharmacy, accountancy, or the cleaning and dyeing business. He gets a toe hold somewhere, and one thing leads to another until he is engrossed in politics.

A person who has an urge to go into politics can do it easily by going to the local committee chairman and saying "I want to help." By systematically doing the jobs assigned to him, he can go up in the party. It is easy to become a member of the precinct, city, or county committee. From this, an aspirant may progress to chairman of the local committee or go on the regional or state committee. A few years of faithful service in these capacities puts him in line for the party's rewards for service. He can get a political appointment, be named a candidate for elective office, or profit in various other ways.

It is not enough to take a hand in politics during the heat of the campaign. The thing to do is to work with the party organization quietly and regularly, day in and day out from one election to the next.

The Lures

The lure for most is simply the lure of the pay roll. The rank and file of party machines are the lowly job seekers who crave only a job in Washington, or in the state capitol, the county courthouse or the city hall as clerk, custodian, guard, charwoman or any other "position."

The leaders, the ones whose names get in the papers, are those who know how to make real money out of politics, or want the distinction and pay of high public office. The most colorful figures in politics are usually the candidates for such offices as governor, senator, or congressman. To these the pay is not distasteful, but the glamour has more pull. It is publicity, the limelight, the chance to strut that urges many of them on.

A considerable number of people go into politics to promote their business interests or increase their professional contacts. These usually work behind the scenes, but they do a lot of the money-raising and the actual contributing to campaign expenses.

Some just naturally take to the game of politics as a duck takes to water. Politics fascinates them, consumes them, and they move on from one campaign to another.

A few sincerely seek to serve their country. But you have to look hard to find those who are ready to make serious personal sacrifices on the altar of the public welfare.

The Party Organization

Washington is not merely the main hangout of party political workers and job holders. It is literally the nerve center of a vast political network which spreads out to every state and touches live cells in every county and town.

The organization for politics is this: The national committee of a party is made up of committeemen and committeewomen from each state who are elected by their state committees. This national committee manages the presidential nominating conventions, handles campaign funds, and decides the main operating policies of the party. The national chairman, elected by the committee, is the big shot of the party hierarchy. Each state has its own central committee, and other committees down the line in counties, townships, cities and precincts.

National political organizations are shockingly inefficient by standards of ordinary business practice. The head man has little authority to give orders to the sub-leaders. The top group has little disciplinary control over the state and local units, and there is often much working at cross purposes within the party ranks.

Nevertheless, a national chairman has ways and means of giving a certain direction to the entire party. The chairman of a party in power has the White House behind him and can wield the patronage lash. The chairman of the minority party has no such backing, but he can marshal a certain following through the influence he has with potential presidential candidates and through his control of campaign funds.

The national committees in recent years have learned the lesson that politics, to be most successful, must be pursued 365 days a year, every year, and not just once in four years, during campaigns. They find that a dollar spent a year in advance of a campaign is worth more than two dollars spent a month before election day.

The Democratic and Republican national committees have spacious office headquarters in Washington. The Democrats for years were located in the

255

National Press Building, but soon after the 1940 election they took over most of one floor of the fashionable Mayflower Hotel. The Republican committee since 1936 has occupied three and a half floors of a small office building at 718 Jackson Place, within a block of the White House.

The committee headquarters are operated by salaried staff specialists. They have publicity directors ($20,000 a year), and executive assistants to the chairman. The work is parceled out among divisions for specialized activities such as research, women's organizations, finance, and contact with youth organizations. Many of the speeches by minority members of Congress which get publicity are based on facts and figures and phrases produced by the national committee headquarters staff. This was especially true during the years when the Democrats conducted a high-pressure campaign to discredit the Hoover administration. The Republicans as a minority party have tried similar tactics but have been less successful. In off years, salaried committee staffs in Washington usually range from 30 to 75 workers, but in election years the pay roll may jump to 1000 or 1500 staff employees during the final weeks of the campaign.

Both parties have special committees in Washington (called Congressional Committees) whose job it is to help elect their candidates for the Senate and House of Representatives. These committees handle substantial amounts of money which are used to help candidates in close districts, and in districts where victory is considered strategically important. In some of the larger states, the central state committees also maintain full-time staffs of political workers modeled on the lines of the national committee set-up. When the campaign gets hot, bigger staffs are recruited. Other states and some big cities and counties set up temporary headquarters with salaried staff workers in campaign years.

Below the national and state committee organizations is an army of county chairmen, county committeemen, district leaders, township and precinct captains and workers. There are approximately 500,000 of these local workers for the two parties together. In addition, there are innumerable special campaign organizations such as the Young Republicans and the Young Democrats, the women's organizations, groups organized along professional lines, certain labor union campaign committees and committees organized on race lines. These special groups, plus the regular party professionals, plus political patronage job holders, make another 500,000 energetic political workers in the two major parties.

These are the 1,000,000 professionals who make a business of politics. They keep the parties alive. They run the campaigns, and they get their reward in the form of jobs, contracts, power, prestige and influence.

Running the Campaign

The party committee organizations generally have to keep neutral in primary election contests within their own parties. Once the candidates are nominated, however, the campaign begins. Usually it starts at low speed, working up steam gradually until the final weeks of the campaign, when full steam is turned on. One of the things political managers fear is a build-up to a peak of enthusiasm too far ahead of election day. The theory is that the tempo should rise steadily up to the very minute when the polls are closed.

Raising the money is one of the first big jobs, of course. The party organization works through all its established connections to get campaign contributions. Each party has old wheel horses who know how to pass the hat in the right places. Early in the campaign the money comes mainly from wealthy contributors. As the campaign warms up, the general public is induced to open its pocketbooks, and toward the end of a campaign there usually are thousands of small contributions pouring into the national, state and local committees.

The job of selling a candidate is largely a job of ballyhoo. Skilled organizers and eloquent stump speakers are important, but in recent years the main effort of the campaign has been to get plenty of radio time at the right hours with radio voices that will click with the public.

On election day, the whole campaign organization concentrates on getting out the votes. The money spent on election day is a major part of the entire cost of the campaign. The public explanation of this is that thousands of men with automobiles must be hired to transport voters to the polls. It is also explained that the party finds it necessary to hire watchers at the polls and men to do innumerable emergency chores. What this amounts to is that thousands and thousands of votes are bought and paid for. On election day in many a county and precinct some trusted party worker is given a roll of "folding money" which is disbursed to voters. Some shiftless fellow with 8 or 10 voters in his family may be paid $20 for his services in transporting voters to the polls. He does transport his family of voters, but if he could not deliver the votes of such a family, his services as a transporter would not be sought.

How Much Money Is Spent?

It is usually said that in each four years the national party organizations spend 50 million dollars, but this is probably an understatement. The Senate committee investigating campaign expenditures for 1940 concluded that the two parties had spent more than 22 million dollars in that year alone. It could easily have been 40 million dollars, for there are all sorts of ways in which interested persons can dish out cash to be spent without any accounting. A large part of the election day money is of that kind. While the national committee must make a rigid public accounting, the state and local committees need not be so careful in their bookkeeping.

The Hatch Act amendments of 1940 impose a limit of 3 million dollars expenditures for any political committee in any one year, but much more than this was spent by both the Republicans and the Democrats in 1940. The limitation was circumvented by the simple device of organizing numerous separate committees, each of which could spend the permitted 3 million dollars.

The Hatch Act also makes it illegal for an individual to contribute over $5,000 to a national political committee, but there is no limit on the amount that a person can give to various state and local committees. Thus by splitting up their contributions between national, state, and local groups, many contributors in both parties gave considerably more than the $5,000 limit.

Hotly contested state and local elections often bring forth colossal campaign expenditures and the handling of such funds often is so roundabout that a public accounting is hard to get. A recent mayoralty contest in New York cost $600,129—that much was officially reported. State-wide contests in New York have been known to cost as much as $1,000,000. Contests in several of the larger states of the country have cost an average of $500,000 or more. For example, the Nye Committee of the Senate found that $442,571 was spent on behalf of Mrs. Ruth Hanna McCormick's ill-fated senatorial aspirations in Illinois in 1930. In the famous battle between Frank L. Smith and William B. McKinley for the Republican senatorial nomination in Illinois in 1926, the Reed Committee of the Senate found that $1,015,618 was spent. In the same year in Pennsylvania the Republican primary fight saw an outlay of $2,265,392. Smith of Illinois and William B. Vare of Pennsylvania, the victors of these two senatorial contests, were denied their seats by a Senate vote, because of the excessive use of money in their campaigns.

Nevertheless in Pennsylvania in 1930 a total of $1,211,698 was spent in a three-cornered primary contest, with James J. Davis and Joseph R. Grundy as the two chief contenders for the Senate. Out in Wisconsin in 1928, as another example, more than $100,000 was spent to get the Republican gubernatorial nomination for Walter J. Kohler. The Kelly-Nash machine in Chicago in the 1936 Democratic governorship contest, spent $600,000 in Cook County alone to man the polls, according to a *Fortune* magazine survey.

State political machines have their own money-raising systems and some of these are highly efficient. When Paul McNutt was governor of Indiana his party rather bluntly let it be known that job holders in the state government were expected to contribute regularly 2 per cent of their pay checks to the state party treasury. This produced plenty of money and enabled McNutt to build up a party organization that was the envy of his rivals.

Politics is Big Business and costs big money.

Who Puts Up the Money?

Political campaign funds come roughly from three classes: (1) Government job holders and job seekers, (2) business and professional men who have interests they want to protect, and (3) large numbers of plain citizens who feel the urge to support or to oust the party in power.

A government job holder on the patronage list who does not make his contribution regularly to the party campaign fund will lose his good standing. The money collectors are usually reasonable in their demands. The chap with an $1800 job and a family to support is let off with a small levy, but that small levy is important. If it does not come through, a note is made of it. The top-flight political job holders, those with $8,000 to $12,000 jobs, and those who happen to have plenty of money aside from their salaries, are expected to be very generous in support of the party.

For years, the Democratic National Committee organized dinners all over the country, at which the faithful party men and women were expected to gather and honor the birthday of Andrew Jackson. These Jackson Day dinners were a roundabout way of prying out contributions to the party funds. In Washington, for instance, those who attended the dinner were expected to pay $100. This covered the cost of the dinner and left a profit per plate of $90 or more. In other cities the charge was $25 per plate for a $2 dinner, and in many small cities a charge of $5 to $10 was made for a $1 dinner.

Since it is illegal to levy party assessments directly on government employees, the Jackson Day dinners were a real lifesaver for the Democratic party money-raisers. They have produced from $200,000 to $400,000 annually for several years.

The second class of political contributors includes businessmen who are especially dependent upon the good will of the party in power—contractors, lawyers and others who find it profitable to have a stand-in with the powers that be. It also includes certain very wealthy men who want no special favors but who think of the outcome of party elections as decisive turning points in the course of the nation's life, with all that this implies with respect to their own large economic interests.

It was easy for Mark Hanna to collect millions from the rich in 1896 to defeat the "wild man," William Jennings Bryan. In 1924 Joseph R. Grundy easily tapped Pennsylvania manufacturers for $700,000 on the prospect that the Republicans would preserve tariff benefits. The tariff sales talk works both ways, however. The Roosevelt administration reduced tariffs on cigarette paper, saving the cigarette companies about $500,000 a year. It also cut the duty on Turkish tobacco, an essential blend for U. S. cigarettes, thus saving American manufacturers about $2,000,000 a year. This may explain why R. J. Reynolds, cigarette manufacturer, "loaned" the Democratic National Committee and other committees $300,000, besides giving the legal limit of $5,000 to the national committee.

It is now illegal for corporations to make political contributions. But party money-raisers have other ways. Democratic National Chairman Farley in 1936 devised a scheme for getting money directly from corporations. He sold advertising in a "Convention Book" at $5,000 a page to large corporations, many of which were doing business with the government. Farley's agents also sold many thousands of copies of this book at $5 each to corporations, some of which did not advertise in it. After the 1936 campaign there were several thousand unsold copies of the book on hand. Farley had President Roosevelt personally autograph these, bound them in leather, and as a "deluxe edition" offered them for sale to corporations and others at $250 each. The Bethlehem Steel Corporation, for instance, purchased $7,500 of the "deluxe" books. The Joseph Schlitz Company sent its check for $10,000. Other breweries and liquor companies, oil companies, radio stations, construction companies, manufacturers of building materials, dredging companies, steamship lines and business machines makers bought one or more of the books. The list of purchasers included all sorts of corporations doing business, directly or indirectly, with the government or subject to regulation by federal agencies. The book produced $1,246,763 for the Democrats. There was evidence that some of the solicitors reminded reluctant advertisers or prospective purchasers of the business they were doing or might do with the government. Such warning, it was said at the time, usually was sufficient to cause the reluctant ones to sign on the dotted line. It was, of course, just a holdup. It violated the spirit, although not the letter, of the corrupt practices act.

The Diplomatic List

Both parties have what they call the "diplomatic list," which is a rich source of campaign contributions. Here is the way it works: In 1936 the Democrats received $33,700 from Anthony J. Drexel Biddle and his wife, and Biddle later became Ambassador to Poland, and still later envoy to numerous refugee governments in London. Doris Duke Cromwell gave

$50,000, and her husband later had a brief career as Minister to Canada. Robert W. Bingham gave $15,000; he was Ambassador to the Court of St. James in London. Joseph E. Davies and his super-wealthy wife gave $17,500, and Mr. Davies became Ambassador to Russia and later to Belgium. The man who was Minister to Egypt, Bert Fish, gave $13,000. Laurence A. Steinhardt, former Ambassador to Russia, now Ambassador to Turkey, gave $10,000. The spectacular Ambassador to France, William C. Bullitt, paid $6,000 to the campaign fund. John Cudahy, who became Ambassador to Poland, paid $3,000, which was only slightly more than the $2,500 contributed by Leo R. Sack, Washington newspaper correspondent, who held only the minor post of Minister to Costa Rica.

This is not a purely Democratic device, of course. The Republicans worked the same strategy for years with equal success. Nor is it a strictly American device. In England wealthy campaign contributors are made peers, barons, knights, and given other honors in return for party subscriptions.

Party Angels

The big contributions for the Republicans have come from a relatively few groups in recent years. The Pews of Pennsylvania and the du Ponts of Delaware have put both their hearts and their money into the Republican cause. One survey shows that since 1933 seven members of the Pew family have thrown a total of $778,602 into Republican election funds, plus other substantial contributions that have not been officially recorded. Congressional reports show that members of the du Pont family during the same period gave the Republicans $734,650. Doubtless there were other substantial gifts not accounted for.

Why such generosity? There are no indications that either the Pews or the du Ponts want to be ambassadors or to garnish themselves with honors of high public office. Both groups have tremendous business interests, however, and work hard to preserve their business enterprises. It seems clear they feared the New Deal trend—thought that the whole American system of private enterprise was endangered, and were willing to risk public criticism by financing the political opposition to the administration in power.

Lining Up the Public

In addition to those who are interested in political jobs and those who want to protect their businesses or their fortunes, there are plain citizens who contribute for no apparent reason except that in the heat of political campaigns, they become emotionally interested in the outcome. It is the business of party campaign managers to arouse the public, and they always

261

succeed in getting large numbers to take sides, with their pocketbooks as well as their hearts.

In the past generations people not directly concerned with the spoils of elections were likely to take sides just because they happened to grow up as Democrats or Republicans. Since 1932, however, "inherited" political allegiance has counted for less. Future historians of political parties probably will set 1932 as a point at which party alignments began to take form on the basis of the "have nots" versus the "haves." This is reflected not only in election results but in the source of campaign contributions. In 1936 John L. Lewis and associated unionists of the new vigorous labor movement known as the Congress of Industrial Organizations, put more than $500,000 into the Roosevelt re-election fund. Lewis subsequently bluntly let it be known that he expected the administration to reward him and his movement for such support.

Political researchers have discovered that in 1928 about 28 per cent of Republican contributions of $5,000 or more came from bankers and brokers, and that in the same year gifts of this size from the same group constituted 25 per cent of Democratic campaign funds—not much difference. But in 1936, of gifts of $1,000 or more from bankers and brokers, $578,910 went to the Republicans and only $42,000 to the Democrats. On the other hand, in 1936, the Democrats got $30,250 from the motion picture industry against only $1,000 for the Republicans. And brewers and distillers gave $73,050 to the Democrats and only $6,650 to the Republicans.

Some men of wealth work both sides of the street, or partners in the same group divide their monetary allegiance. Samuel Insull, utilities promoter, split his contributions in Illinois when he needed an "in" with whatever party came into power. Partners in Morgan & Company regularly have split—some help one side, some the other. Frank Phillips, Oklahoma oil man, donated liberally to both parties in 1932 and 1936. R. R. Deupree, president of Proctor and Gamble, did the same. Years ago Jay Gould of Erie Railroad fame buttered both sides and frankly said, "In a Republican district, I was a Republican. In a Democratic district, a Democrat. In a doubtful district, I was doubtful, but I was always for Erie."

The crumbs of party politics are many, and so are the avid recipients. Many a stalwart ward campaigner is happy to get his $6 to $12 a day for manning the polls on registration, primary, and election days—perhaps $50 in the course of a year. Beyond these minor rewards there are thousands of real but small jobs which look good to party workers. Despite the fact that a majority of federal government jobs are now filled through civil service examinations, there are many thousands of jobs parceled out to the party faithfuls on a strictly patronage basis. And despite the genuine advances in setting up the merit system in government, the fact is that thousands of employees get jobs as political rewards and then are covered over with the mantle of civil service legitimacy by presidential order.

"Committee Clearance"

Years ago the plums of politics were mainly local jobs—postmasterships, internal revenue collectorships, federal marshals, or the city and county courthouse offices. Now there are a lot of new patronage jobs under federal departments and new federal agencies which have spread their organizations out to cover all sections of the country. This great increase in the number of federal patronage jobs during the Roosevelt administration gave Postmaster General James A. Farley, as head of the party's patronage, a great opportunity. He devised a system for political appointments which involved "clearance through the committee."

Young men or women who were candidates for federal appointments usually were asked by the appointing official to whom they made their application, whether or not they had been "cleared by the committee." The applicant who had overlooked this procedure found it desirable, and in many cases necessary, to start at the bottom and get his back-home county committee or precinct committee chairman to OK him. With this certification he proceeded to get the blessing of his congressman or senators or state national committeemen, and with these documents in writing he would find his way to the Democratic National Committee headquarters, and file them with the custodian of credentials of job holders. For straight so-called patronage jobs, this was and still is almost a prerequisite to consideration for a job.

After the political worker comes to Washington and gets settled down into his government job, he is expected to keep his ties with his home town local committee. If he should forget that, he will be reminded of it from time to time. He will be called upon to register for the primaries and to cast his ballot regularly. There is a carefully conceived central organization in the national committee to help office holders vote by absentee ballot in their home states. Whether it is good or bad, this "clearance" plan has the effect of invigorating local political organizations and welding them into the central structure of the national party committee.

The Limelight

The lure of fame, prestige and publicity pulls many men into politics, especially men who have made fortunes in prosaic businesses. Party leaders always know certain successful businessmen who want to "cap their career" with some position of dignity and respectability in public service. Often such men try for a seat in the Senate or seek the governorship of their state. But dozens of them are glad to become some sort of commissioner, or member of a government board, or head of some government executive agency. Once they land in Washington, get in the swim of official life, they usually want to stay on. They are a substantial part of the party organization, both as contributors and as workers in the cause.

The Senate is the magnet for political aspirants who love the dramatic. It is the stage on which the politician can play with the nation as his audience. The pay of $10,000 a year is small considering the expenses that go with getting and keeping the job. The lure is not the money so much as the glamour. Here the star performer can make his name known, can often wield decisive power, and there's the hovering thought that he may become President of the United States. The House of Representatives has the same kind of pull, even though it is not as glamorous as the Senate.

Real Money in Politics

Government has grown so big that it is increasingly good business for businessmen to take part in politics. There may be big money in it, or conversely, it may be costly to stay out. Politics is a major side line for contractors, manufacturers, merchants, radio station owners, insurance agents, air lines, railroads, shipping lines and innumerable others who look to government for favors. Likewise, lawyers, lobbyists, promoters, all sorts of go-betweens who need contact and influence in official quarters, find it pays to take a hand in the game of politics.

For more than 20 years the only visible source of income for Boss Frank Hague of Jersey City has been his $8,000 salary as mayor, but he has acquired a fortune that most men would consider a lucrative reward for a lifetime of successful activity in private business.

The bonding of postmasters and other official custodians is nice business for certain surety companies. Boss Tom Pendergast sold ready-mixed cement in Kansas City, and rival non-political cement companies just didn't have a look-in.

The air lines radically changed their managements after the Roosevelt administration attacked them and outlawed former air mail contracts. They elected officers and directors with Democratic backgrounds or contacts, and most of them got new lawyers who had better standing at Washington.

The big radio broadcasting systems make no pretense of political indifference. They are quick to adjust their top personnel and operating policies to please the government in power.

264

Many expensive homes in Washington today are occupied by men who came to the city with the Wilson and succeeding Republican administrations and remained to take advantage of their experience and contacts in lucrative practice of law. With the advent of the New Deal a new crop of political lawyers made their appearance. Notable among them were a trio of Democratic National Committee members—Robert Jackson of New Hampshire (not the Supreme Court Justice), Arthur Mullen of Nebraska, and J. Bruce Kremer of Montana.

These men had been in the forefront of the fight to nominate and elect Franklin D. Roosevelt. They hung out their shingles as lawyers in Washington and clients appeared as by magic. O. Max Gardner, former governor of North Carolina, and Joseph E. Davies, long active in Democratic politics, also found their services as lawyers in great demand after the inauguration of the New Deal.

A more recent success story is the case of the young brain truster, Thomas G. Corcoran. He got a job during the Great Depression in a minor legal capacity with the Reconstruction Finance Corporation. He learned the ropes, became a power in the New Deal after 1933, and contributed many ideas which found their way into legislation. He worked effectively for the re-election of President Roosevelt in 1936 and 1940, and attained a position where he could name numerous friends to key legal posts in many government agencies.

When Corcoran left the government service after the 1940 election, his salary was $10,000 a year. Due to his knowledge of how the government functions and his influence and prestige with New Deal officials, Corcoran had no trouble finding clients. Seekers after defense contracts and government financial assistance sought him out. He told a Senate committee that fees from four clients totaled more than $100,000 in 1941, and that he was so pressed with work that he could "not afford" to take cases with a retainer fee of less than $5,000.

Charles West, former Ohio congressman, Under Secretary of the Interior and liaison man between the White House and Capitol Hill, likewise found that such connections could be put to profitable use when he left government service. In a lawsuit recently filed against a defense contractor, he placed a value of $700,000 on the services which he claimed he rendered getting business for this contractor.

Lawrence Wood Robert, Jr., of Georgia, is an outstanding example of the contractor's go-between who has done well in politics. He has played the business angles of politics for many years, but his biggest successes came while he was serving as Assistant Secretary of the Treasury and later as Secretary of the Democratic National Committee.

James Roosevelt found a great deal of insurance business rolling to his door when his father became President. In a magazine article he stated that while he was in the insurance business, his individual tax returns showed incomes as follows: 1933—$21,714; 1934—$49,167; 1935—$33,593; 1936—$44,668. When he was charged with profiting from his family connections, he said: "My name got me into a lot of places I might not have got into if my father had not been President. And that is all right, too. If you want to do business with a man you get in to see him by whatever legitimate means you can."

High government officials and their families sometimes make good money writing articles for magazines and in radio broadcasting, using government time and facilities to prepare their material. Mrs. Roosevelt strongly defends her large earnings as a writer, a lecturer and a broadcaster. But Vice President Garner once refused a lucrative offer to go on the air. He said in effect that what he as a private person, John Garner, might say would not be worth a dime, and that what he as Vice President Garner might say was "not for sale."

When billions are being spent by the government as freely as in the past few years, it seems humanly impossible to keep some of the money from sticking to the fingers of favored political insiders. Now and then a case of outright corruption is revealed. On the whole, politicians probably are about as honest as any other large class of people. Often money is made in ways that are morally reprehensible, although "within the law." Many years ago George Washington Plunkitt, a Tammany Hall leader, accumulated a fortune through his political connections. With advance information on plans for municipal improvements, he quietly bought real estate low and later sold it high—sometimes to the city government. He called this "honest graft." He said, "I seen my opportunities and I took 'em."

Everyone a Politician

It may be too much to expect, but it would be helpful if everyone could be a politician, if everyone would spend more time working in politics. You may say this would increase the volume of chicanery in politics. But it wouldn't. It would diminish the volume. The trouble with politics is that the active practitioners pull monkey business when people aren't looking, aren't paying attention, are temporarily indifferent. Shrinking from politics is really a shirking. The reason people shrink is that they regard politics as something dark and mysterious. It may be dark, but it isn't mysterious.

24

Understand Your Congressman

YOU can study the Constitution, and the charts which show organization of the government, and the functions of Congress, and the parliamentary procedure, and the committee assignments, and you still will not know much about Congress. You can read books about the legislative principles, and the theories, and the methods, and you still will not know what makes the wheels of Congress go 'round.

Congress consists of *men*. They are men who grew up with you, or your father, or your children, in your locality, with some of your same environment and antecedents. As you do not consider yourself great, so it is likely that they do not regard themselves as great. They suffer from the limelight of Washington. They find their faults and virtues magnified, so that when they read about themselves they hardly recognize themselves.

Your congressmen are standard butts for gibes by the press and by nearly everyone else who undertakes to portray Washington. The tendency is to think of them as members of the *institution* of Congress and expect them to measure up to some ideal of virtue and wisdom, rather than to think of them as they are—just men, human beings, 531 individuals who happen to have the jobs of legislating.

Remember that being a congressman is a job—and a business. The congressman is alert to do what he can to keep his job, just as the banker or grocer or factory employee is anxious to do what he can to please his customers or his employer. Pure altruism is almost as rare in Congress as it is in private life.

If members of Congress are able men it is a credit to the voters of their districts. If they are dumbbells, it shows that the districts from which they come are not particularly concerned about the type of men they want to represent them. In Congress there are plenty of able men, and plenty of dumbbells, just as there are in all districts and in all segments of life.

Get acquainted with your congressman. Learn how he lives, how he acts, how he reacts to the pressures upon him in Washington. Close study of him will not make him a hero, but it probably will make you less cynical about him. There are reasons why he acts the way he does, and if you understand these reasons you will better understand him, and be more willing to take a hand in the naming of men who are to represent you in the national legislative body.

What a Congressman Gets

The salary of your congressman is $10,000 a year—the same for both senators and representatives. In addition each gets free postage and telegraph service, travel expenses to Washington and back home, and $200 for stationery supplies.

The travel pay of 20 cents a mile looks big, but it does not cover travel expenses for most congressmen. It covers only one round trip each session of Congress. Out of this must come travel expenses for the whole family. And there is no allowance for extra trips home which nearly every congressman has to make during each session.

For clerical help, House members get $6,500 a year and senators get $15,120. There has been considerable criticism of those who put members of their own families on the office pay roll. The fact is that in most cases such family employees do the work required and earn their pay. There are cases where office employees are paid less than the law allows with the difference being kicked back to the congressman, but these are exceptional cases.

If a congressman gets sick, has to have tonsils or appendix removed, he can go to a government hospital, get the best of care, and it's all on the taxpayers. There is no specific authorization for this, but it is the custom. Some refuse to accept this free service, but many have no such scruples.

A congressman who has made a national name for himself and is a good speaker can get good fees on the lecture platform to piece out his income. The range is from $100 to $300 per performance, plus expenses. Only a few find this possible or expedient, and some of them find themselves under suspicion of capitalizing too much on their public position.

While the congressman's $10,000 salary is not as big as it may sound to most people, the fact is that it is more than most congressmen ever earned before coming to Washington. And it is more than most of them ever receive after leaving Washington.

Most new members of Congress have a little money. There are very few poor men and very few millionaires. The Senate used to be called a "millionaire's club" but it certainly is not that now. A good many in both branches are "well fixed," however, and don't need their jobs as a source of livelihood. In the Senate such men are Robert A. Taft, David I. Walsh, Henry Cabot Lodge, Peter G. Gerry, James J. Davis, Harry Byrd and Carter Glass. Some independently wealthy House members are George

H. Tinkham of Massachusetts, James W. Wadsworth of New York, Richard Kleberg of Texas (King ranch fortune), and Jerry Voorhis of California.

Congress provides a fair living, but it is no place to accumulate a fortune. Old timers who have seen them come and go will tell you that 90 per cent of those who leave Congress are worse off financially than when they came. They usually find their scale of living in Washington expensive. They often have to maintain two homes—one in Washington, and one in the home state. And, in addition, they are expected to kick in contributions to dozens of funds.

A majority of congressmen are lawyers. The rest are recruited from all sorts of professions and occupations—businessmen, newspapermen, publishers, farmers, professors, doctors. Many have made a career of political job-holding. The congressman who is retired from Congress finds it hard to resume his former profession or vocation. The common experience is that the man who serves 10 or 15 years in Congress pays for the privilege rather than making anything out of it financially.

Then why do men want to serve in Congress? The pay is attractive at the outset, of course, but there are other inducements. They love the limelight, the game of politics, the satisfactions which come from being able to act on the stage. Some want to do a public service. Nearly all of them aspire to higher honors. They want to be senator, governor, cabinet member, federal judge, or something else that gives them luster, power, or security for old age. The few rich men in the Senate and House are usually just as eager for re-election as the poor men. The rich find in Washington and in the power that goes with the job an extra outlet for their personalities, for they can afford to splurge and mix in the whirl of official life.

Pleasing the Constituency

We don't draft ideal men for Congress. We elect those who want the jobs and are able to win them in spirited contests. It was the theory of the drafters of our federal Constitution in 1789 that the voters would choose able representatives who would use their own discretion in deciding what laws to pass for the best interests of the country. A frankly "representative" government was planned, rather than a pure democracy. The trend has been in the direction of pure democracy. This is the practice if not the theory, and to congressmen the practice is the thing that counts.

When your congressman votes on a controversial bill, he votes the way he thinks most of his constituents want him to vote. His constituents may be wrong. The congressman may have information which makes him want to vote in opposition to what he knows to be the prevailing sentiment in his district. But in a majority of cases he knows that if he doesn't vote the way his voters want him to vote he will soon be out of a job.

It is a good guess that not more than 10 out of 531 congressmen are willing consistently to stand on principle even if they know it may cost them their jobs.

That is human nature. Ask yourself if you would do differently. If you are in business you avoid ruffling your customers. If you work for wages you try to please your boss. Lawyers and doctors play up to their present and prospective clients and patients. Congressmen are the same.

When the Townsend old-age pension movement was at its peak a few years ago a certain conservative congressman became alarmed by the volume of petitions for the plan from his district. He discovered that nearly every businessman in his home town had signed up for the Townsend program. He went home, saw these businessmen, asked them if they really favored the Townsend bill. "Lord, no," they all said, "I just signed because so-and-so is a customer, and I wanted to keep his trade."

You probably have heard the much quoted phrase, "There comes a time in the life of every congressman when he must rise *above* principles." This has been variously attributed to many different congressmen. Actually it was first voiced around the year 1921 by Percy Quin, picturesque rabble-rousing representative from Mississippi. Now it is a stock phrase around the Capitol.

Demagogues

Are there demagogues in Congress? Yes, many of them. Those who refuse to "demagogue" usually are defeated for re-election and their places are taken by someone who does "demagogue." If there is a fault, it is the fault of the voters.

Many Congressmen are not without a sense of humor about their demagoguing. Before times got too serious for such levity, a group of them organized a "Demagogues' Club" which met daily in the House cloakroom. After a legislator made a particularly demagogic speech for home consumption, he was haled into the cloakroom and compelled to make the speech he would like to have made, if it had not been for the necessity of pleasing his constituents. Then he was asked to repeat the Club pledge to "vote for all appropriations and against all taxes" and inducted into full membership. The badge was a safety pin—worn under the coat lapel. Three Speakers of the House and one Vice President have worn that badge.

Take a look at the day-to-day work of a member of Congress. He works hard. In Washington he is on the job from 9 a. m. to 6 p. m. and often longer. Actual attendance at the sessions of the House or Senate is the least of his worries, although the long hours on the floor are exhausting. His main job is to answer letters from constituents. These pour in day after day, an endless stream, asking all kinds of favors. Great care in answering them is required, since every unsatisfactory answer means adverse votes in the next election.

Visitors from home are a ticklish problem for the congressman. Each visitor thinks he should be able to take the congressman's time, but if the congressman played host to all back-home visitors, he would be able to do nothing else. Entertainment of constituents is expensive too. If a constituent and his wife and daughter drop in at the Capitol and the congressman invites them to lunch with him in the Capitol restaurant, it doesn't seem serious when the bill sets him back about $4.00. But when this happens day after day you can see that it makes a big dent in the congressman's bank account. Yet it is hard to escape this. No constituent ever seems to believe it if the congressman says he is "too busy" to give him all the time he wants.

This business of catering to visiting constituents is even more serious for senators than for representatives. Since senators are serving much larger clienteles they must, in self-defense, make themselves less accessible. Don't think your senator is high-hat just because he is hard to find. If he did not hide out a good deal of the time he could not get any work done and would never amount to a hill of beans in the Senate.

The handling of job seekers is a back-breaking job for congressmen for the first year or two after a change of administration. Once the bulk of the jobs are filled, the pressure eases a bit. While the Democrats are in power the Republicans escape this worry, of course. Contrary to the common belief, most congressmen secretly long for a strict civil service merit system so they may be relieved of responsibility for finding political jobs for all their loyal henchmen. "Every political appointment means one ingrate and a dozen enemies."

Applicants for government jobs who ask their congressman for a letter of approval are almost never refused. The writing of such letters is a pro forma performance. The government official to whom the letter is presented usually does not pay much attention to it. If the congressman has a deep, personal interest in the applicant he must do more than write a letter. He will phone the person who has the job to dispense, and follow up by a visit in person if that is necessary. There are enough of these "must" job seekers to constitute a real burden for the congressman.

The drudgery of errand boy chores is endless in the average congressman's office. As friend at court in Washington he is appealed to by constituents constantly to follow through on veterans' claims, delayed farm benefit checks, WPA projects, city airports, NYA school projects, passports, immigration snarls, flood control measures, RFC loans, war contracts, and countless similar matters involving action by the federal government.

In years past, the one standard handout disbursed by congressmen was free seeds. These are no more. But there are many new kinds of handouts which the alert congressman can pass on to his folks back home. Each congressman gets 100 free "Infant Care" booklets each month which he can send to parents of the newly born. The *Agricultural Yearbook* is a favorite for farmers. A booklet on garden flowers is provided for members of garden clubs. And appropriate government booklets or publications for veterans, publishers, city officials, and many other classes of people are available to congressmen who make a business of servicing their constituents.

The franking privilege is of inestimable value in the never-ending campaign for re-election. The congressman writes a speech (or has his secretary write one), gets permission to have it printed as "extension of remarks" in the *Congressional Record*, and then mails out thousands of reprints, postage free. This gives him a head start on any candidate who may try to get his job.

The chores, the correspondence, the daily grief of the congressman would literally leave no time for the big job of legislation, except for the services of competent secretaries, most of whom are men. Only a good secretary can save a congressman from a life of misery. Secretaries of unusual ability have "made" many a member of the House or Senate. One senator is so appreciative of his secretary that he turns over to him his own full salary as senator.

Congressmen cannot settle down in fine permanent homes in Washington. They don't dare make a big investment in a house, for they never know how long they will be here. Mostly they rent apartments or live in hotels, in the "best" section of the city, but not at the swankiest addresses. Those with school-age children have a special problem. They must either move from their home town to Washington in September or shift their children from one school to another in mid-year.

Recesses of Congress are not vacations for congressmen. They usually work harder at home than they do in Washington, and are glad to get back to Washington to escape the pressure. Many a vote against adjournment sine die has been due to the dread of facing the exacting demands of constituents in the home district.

The next primary or general election is always ahead. To most members it is a constant threat, and it colors nearly every vote that is cast. This is especially true as to members of the House, since they all come up for re-election every two years. In the whole membership of Congress probably not more than two dozen are politically so well entrenched that they don't have to worry about the next election.

Re-election costs money. The sum varies greatly, but an outlay by the candidate himself of from $1,000 to $5,000 is not uncommon for members of the House. For senators the cost runs considerably higher. Friends frequently offer cash aid to the candidate, and this is sometimes gladly accepted. But House members try, as a general rule, to avoid contributions. They fear the obligations that such gifts are likely to entail. Senatorial candidates usually take all the help they can get. They need lots of money to campaign over a whole state, and contributions are usually less personal and, therefore, less of an obligation for future favors.

All candidates welcome money assistance from their national party campaign chests. Both major parties always raise such a fund to help candidates in close districts. Such donations of from $1,000 to $5,000 are commonly made for House candidates, and considerably more for Senate seat-seekers. This party chest money goes only to the "regular." Those who kick over the traces of party discipline can't expect help from this source. This is, therefore, a strong pressure for party regularity.

Local political machines bind some congressmen more tightly than does party regularity. Tammany Hall cracks the whip over the heads of most New York City congressmen. Representatives from Chicago are prone to take orders from the Kelly-Nash machine. The Crump organization in Tennessee requires strict accounting from the men it sends to Washington. And the tight state organization in Louisiana lines up its congressmen and votes them en bloc on issues deemed to be important. Adherents to these machines never know when they are to be sidetracked by the bosses and someone else is to be named to take their places. A large majority of congressmen are not in bondage to such political bosses, of course, and are "free" to shape their own political conduct. A few build up their own powerful personal machines. Senators Norris of Nebraska and LaFollette of Wisconsin are good examples.

The bondage to party regularity now is more a matter of "yessing" the White House than kowtowing to the professional party managers. This is due, of course, to recent voting of huge discretionary funds and authority to the President. If a congressman wants to get a government dam built in his district he is apt to feel the screws turned on him unless he votes right on certain issues. The few congressmen who consistently buck the administration's policies get little or none of the big spending projects for their districts. The man who is aching to be named federal judge may have a promise that he is in line for it, but he knows that if he fails to vote the way he is supposed to vote on some major test his chances for the judgeship are apt to fade away.

All of this is done deftly. Seldom does a spokesman for the President say, "Do this, or else—" There are ways of passing the word along, however, and seasoned congressmen know how to hear things which are never said audibly.

When the Democrats are in power the South is in the saddle. The reason is easy to explain. The South, being "solid," sends Democrats to Congress uninterruptedly. Thus, the Democrats on the important committees having the longest record of service are likely to be Southerners. And the almost unbroken rule is that committee chairmanships go to the top man in length of service.

The seniority rule accounts for the fact that Robert L. Doughton of North Carolina is chairman of the powerful House Ways and Means Committee; that Hampton P. Fulmer of South Carolina heads the Committee on Agriculture; that Carl Vinson of Georgia and May of Kentucky are chairmen respectively of Naval Affairs and Military Affairs. Other southern chairmen in the House are Wilbur Cartwright of Oklahoma, Roads Committee; Schuyler O. Bland of Virginia, Merchant Marine Committee; Hatton Sumners of Texas, Judiciary Committee. Still other Southerners head minor committees.

In the Senate there is much the same situation. Some Senate committee chairmen from the South are Tom Connally of Texas, Foreign Relations; Robert Reynolds of North Carolina, Military Affairs; Walter George of Georgia, Finance; Carter Glass of Virginia, Appropriations; Josiah Bailey of North Carolina, Commerce; Kenneth McKellar of Tennessee, Post Offices; Ellison D. Smith of South Carolina, Agriculture.

Long tenure is the sure road to committee promotion. Ability counts little—except the ability to keep in office.

In appraising your congressman, remember that the really constructive work on legislation is done in committee. Your man may render highly valuable service within his committee and never get any public credit for it. Many of those who make the newspaper headlines with sensationalism on the floors of Congress are small potatoes as compared with the hardworking men who struggle with the intricacies of pending bills behind committee doors.

It is possible for new members to acquire influence and prestige without waiting for the lapse of years for a chairmanship. One way is to pick a legislative hobby to ride. Martin Dies of Texas did this with his crusade against "isms." Wright Patman also of Texas always has a hobby. Once it was the veterans' bonus, and then it became the chain store tax bill. John Rankin ("Kilowatt John") rides the "power trust" hobby, and so does Senator Norris of Nebraska. The late Senator Key Pittman agitated the silver issue so persistently that his name became synonymous with silver.

There are other sure but less spectacular ways for a new man to rise to the top in Congress. A veteran leader in the House gave one ambitious young new member these instructions:

First, get yourself the best secretary you can find, so you will not have to be a messenger boy all the time.

Second, keep quiet on the floor of the House until you have had time to get acquainted and see how it is done. Then talk briefly, and only if you have something worth saying, and in your first speeches don't lecture the older members.

Third, study parliamentary procedure. If you know well the rules and practices you have the jump on many members who have served a decade or two and still don't know them.

The main point for the aspiring young congressman is to so conduct himself that the leaders of his party will "adopt" him, spot him for a comer, and push him along.

Much is written about what goes on in the "cloakrooms" at the Capitol. The cloakrooms are institutions—not just places where the congressman hangs his hat and coat on a hook that has his name on it. They are lounges with clublike facilities, just off the legislative chambers, where members smoke, read the newspapers, tell stories, talk, get their lunch, and where party leaders pass around the word as to policy and legislative schedule. Also it is where the party whip does his whipping in lining up the party vote on close contests. Since smoking is not permitted on the floors of House or Senate, the cloakrooms usually are well occupied.

When you first visit the visitors' gallery you are likely to be unfavorably impressed by the smallness of the attendance of legislators on the floor. But if a roll call is ordered, you see the lawmakers pile into the chamber— from the cloakrooms, like bees swarming from a hive. There are separate cloakrooms for Republicans and Democrats in both House and Senate. The public is not admitted. The cloakrooms are the real lobbies of Congress, but "lobbyists" are strictly excluded.

Life on Capitol Hill is really a life apart. Over the years there has grown up a body of traditions, practices, and courtesies which only the initiated can appreciate. Tradition is strong; new ideas are resisted; the status quo is near-sacred. Innovations are few and far between. This refers, of course, to customs and not to legislation. The congressman who messes in a public works project in another man's district is guilty of gross misconduct. A gentleman's agreement as to the handling of legislation is more binding than law. A member forced to be absent on a roll call can ask to be "paired" with someone who would vote the other way and can depend on it that he will be so paired. If the Democrats wrest control from the Republicans, the Republican Clerk, Sergeant-at-Arms, Doorkeeper, and other staff attachés know that they will be taken care of in lesser but fair positions for the duration, and vice versa. And nothing except a grave national emergency can prevent early adjournment of Congress on the day of the opening baseball game of the season.

In the Senate, confirmation of a presidential nominee will be blocked if a senator from the nominee's state asserts on the floor of the Senate that the nominee is "personally obnoxious" to him. Seldom has this rule been overridden.

Heated words exchanged in debate on the floor may appear to strangers to threaten bloodshed. But in many cases the participants off the floor lock arm-in-arm in brotherly mood. In life outside the chamber Republicans and Democrats are as likely to be buddies as are members of the same party. When John N. Garner was Democratic floor leader he and Republican Speaker Nicholas Longworth used the same official automobile, the Speaker's, which Garner called "our car." Ogden L. Mills was another arch-Republican House crony of the Democrat Garner.

An old custom which still prevails in Congress is logrolling—the promise of one congressman to vote for another man's measure in exchange for a return vote on his own pet bill. The large number of Naval posts and harbor projects spread among a great many congressional districts is a bond that ties together enough votes always to insure generous appropriations for these purposes. On various occasions the attempt to cut down the number of Civilian Conservation Corps camps has been logrolled to death by the numerous congressmen affected. Logrolling sometimes reaches huge proportions when proponents of several big, highly controversial measures coalesce and roll all their logs into one big pile.

Don't think your congressman doesn't amount to much just because he seldom if ever sees the President at the White House. Only the top leaders have entree to the President's office, and they see him only on serious public business. The ordinary member can get an appointment for a few minutes at the White House by stating his business, but if he tries to do this more than two or three times during one session of Congress, he probably will be regarded as a nuisance and thereafter sidetracked.

Congressmen can see cabinet members and heads of government agencies as often as they wish. These officials know better than to offend unnecessarily the men whose votes might be needed on their departmental appropriations. But the average congressman doesn't have much time for seeing such officials.

Social life in Washington for a congressman is just what he wants it to be. Very few try to cut a swath in Society with a capital S. Sometimes Mama and the girls get the society bug, and prod a sturdy, homespun congressman into splurging in a serious way, but often he doesn't do it well. Many a congressman will tell you that he wishes he could rear his children in a more "normal" atmosphere than is found in Washington official circles. They say the town "does something" to young minds.

Graft

What about graft in Congress? Those who saw the movie, "Mr. Smith Goes to Washington," may wonder if that was a true picture of Congress. It was clearly an exaggeration, of course. Congressmen have their shortcomings, but the moral level is well above what was depicted in that movie. Many congressmen saw the picture and were pretty sore.

Straight-out graft is rare in Congress. One representative from Indiana was sent to the penitentiary in recent years for selling a postmastership. Another one from California went to prison because of his commercializing of an appointment to the Naval Academy. But such cases are very unusual. Actual bribery probably is as rare in Congress as it is in any other class of citizens.

There are always a number of border-line cases, suggestions of near-graft, smelly circumstances which give rise to much rumor and suspicion. Usually these cases do not get any publicity. But occasionally a congressman fails of re-election because his opponent digs up dirt on him which cannot be adequately removed. It is not illegal for some special pleader to hire as his counsel the brother or son or daughter or cousin of the chairman of a powerful House committee, but it looks bad, and may be unfair to others. Washington police did too thorough a job in one search for crime and produced dictaphone records which cast strong suspicion upon a highly placed member of Congress, but the matter was hushed up. Congressmen frequently are faced with legislative proposals which would help or hurt them financially through the effect on their own investments or connections. Congressmen sometimes use their influence to get legislation or government action that means money to them or their close associates, but this is not so much different from the conduct of the cotton-planter congressman who uses his power to get legislation to boost the price of cotton.

Congressional graft or technically legal misuse of power or position is really too risky to become common practice. Every incumbent must look out for the day when some opponent may face him with charges of corruption. Congressmen are in the public eye, their acts are hard to conceal. Most of them know this and even if tempted to do wrong are usually too smart to risk their political future for the sake of tainted money or unlawful emoluments.

On the whole the 531 congressmen probably are a fair cross section of the people. The rascals and nitwits are overshadowed by the decent and reasonably intelligent members. And in the winnowing process there has come to the top enough men of brains, character and leadership to give a certain dignity to the nation's highest law-making body. It can be made better, but only if the people decide to make it so.

What can you do about your congressman? The question is appropriate, because he *is* important, and there *are* things you can do about him.

First, you can learn to know him. You don't have to get buddy with him, but you can inquire about him, check up on his record, keep tab on his official conduct, and generally appraise him as a man who should be kept in Congress or as one who ought to be replaced.

Second, if you decide he is above the average, you can do a little plugging for him, give him moral encouragement if he shows a disposition to perform his duties under trying circumstances.

Third, if you decide he ought to be replaced, do some serious thinking and work to help find a substitute who would be definitely better.

Fourth, at all times think of him as human, and not as a superman. Meet him halfway in your appraisals of him.

Congressmen are what the people make them.

25

How to Lobby

LOBBYISTS are to Congress what lawyers are to courts.
You can't imagine a court operating with just a judge and a clerk, and with the litigants themselves running in and out, telling their own stories and pleading their own points of law. At least, such a court would be very old fashioned and could not operate in these complex times. Neither could Congress operate as it does without the lobbyists. Their function is an integral part of modern government.

You yourself are doubtless a member of a lobby group, and are represented in Washington by a lobbyist, or two, or three. If you are not, then it shows that you are not a very active citizen. You never get what you really want at the polls. You merely lay the groundwork at the polls and you get what you want by subsequently fighting for it with the men whom you elected at the polls. You as one person haven't much weight, but you plus others who think like you can have a great deal of weight, subject to an *if*—if you combine with others and work for whatever you want. That involves lobbying and lobbyists to promote the cause.

The term "lobby" has a sinister meaning in the minds of most people. To call a man a "lobbyist" is to smear him. To say to you, as is said above, that you engage in lobbying is vaguely supposed to be some sort of insult. But that approach is all wrong. It grows out of too much reading of textbooks and blueprints of government, which don't cover lobbying specifically. And yet they do cover it under another term. The term is the "right of petition." Now, a petition may be a statement of position with a lot of names signed to it, or it may be expressed through an organized movement, and the latter is the effective method. It is the modern way of exercising the right of petition guaranteed by the Constitution.

There are two kinds of lobbying and lobbyists: (a) Good, and (b) Bad. The good kind are those which represent what you think is right. The bad kind represent what you think is wrong, but which some other people think is right. Every cause has at least two sides, your side and the vicious side, and both sides are likely to be represented by lobbyists.

The term "lobby" is a worn-out expression which really doesn't mean

279

what originally it meant. It arose because once upon a time people with causes to sell to Congress caught their representatives or senators in the "lobby" of the House or Senate, "buttonholed" them, and poured pleading or threats into their ears. It isn't done that way any more. Some of it is more likely to be done in the private offices of the members of Congress, sitting at a desk, face to face, talking it over. But even that is minor and incidental. Most lobbying is done by organizing pressures out around the country. Many lobbyists are seldom seen around the halls of Congress, and certainly not in the "lobbies" of Congress.

So the word ought to be "pressure," and lobbyists ought to be called "pressers," or "organizers," for that's what they are.

If you think lobbyists go skulking around the back alleys of Congress with cloaks wrapped about their heads, slipping in and out furtively lest some-one see them, it shows that you have been reading fiction. The truth is that lobbyists have big offices in the best buildings in Washington, and also small offices in some of the worst, but in either case they advertise what they are doing. Usually they tell the world what they are "up to."

This lobbying business pesters members of Congress. It sends swarms of gnats around their heads. This may seem an unwholesome procedure, and every member of Congress has his moments when he prays for peace and relief from gnats, and yet he really doesn't mean it, for the lobbies also send gnats around the heads of other members to make *them* vote right. So it works two ways—this pestering.

How It's Done

Lobbying has been conspicuous in Washington since the First Congress. It has regaled the public with the scandals of *Crédit Mobilier* and the orgies at Pendleton's Hall of the Bleeding Heart, and more recently, with the public utilities battle of 1935 and the pro-war and anti-war pressures of 1941. So powerful are the lobbyists that they are sometimes called the Third House.

In the early days, lobbying consisted chiefly of the efforts of various commercial or business interests to get legislation favoring them. Much of the lobbying was social. Wine, women and song were frequently employed. Blocks of stock were transferred quietly. Actual cash sometimes changed hands either outright or in the form of "kick-backs" on contracts. Poker games were played so that the right man won. The lobbyist worked almost solely on a man-to-man basis with those whom he sought to influence. Such methods caused the word "lobbyist" to become a smear word.

Modern lobbying methods are very different. Man-to-man buttonholing, wining and dining are now regarded as belonging to horse and buggy days.

The modern lobby is far more subtle. Public interest is aroused through the press, the radio, meetings and other propaganda devices. With the way thus paved, the modern lobbyist can more readily approach any member of Congress and be assured of a hearing, since he represents large numbers of constituents who have already expressed their opinions. All members of Congress keep a weather eye upon their own district to spot such oncoming movements.

Throughout the whole campaign on any issue, these public demands are kept at fever pitch. Telegrams and letters flood the offices. Marches on Washington are staged. Delegations call upon congressmen, or appear before committees. No opportunity for publicity is overlooked. Thus the lobbying today is a two-way campaign—with the public and with Congress.

There are professional lobbyists who sell their services to the highest bidder, irrespective of personal convictions. With them, lobbying is a means for making a livelihood. They are mainly the ones who have given lobbying a bad name. On the other hand, some professional lobbyists work for causes upon personal convictions. In addition to these, many strictly non-professionals occasionally or incidentally do lobby work in Washington on legislation which affects their interests.

Sometimes legislation is inspired for the express purpose of creating lobby and propaganda work. Lobbyists may be disappointed if their proposals become law, for that might end their attachment to a pay roll.

Three Classes

The Washington lobbies can be roughly divided into three groups: (1) The permanent group organizations for which lobbying is only one activity out of many, (2) lobbies organized to promote some specific projects or "causes," and (3) special lobbies formed to meet emergency situations.

Outstanding examples of the first type, the permanent, continuing type of lobby organizations are the Chamber of Commerce of the United States, National Association of Manufacturers, American Bankers Association, and Association of American Railroads. These are much more than lobbying organizations, of course. They work constantly to promote the general interests of their memberships in other than legislative matters. But during every session of Congress they inject themselves into congressional fights over measures affecting their interests.

The farmers also have their representative organizations which stand ready to go to bat whenever the welfare of farmers is at stake. The principal general farmer lobbying groups are the American Farm Bureau Federation, the National Grange and the Farmers Union. Often they take opposite sides—engage in spirited tussles over methods as well as principles involved in legislation. Aside from these, there are organizations concentrating on the interests of particular phases of agriculture—cotton, cattle, walnuts, raisins, peanuts, tobacco, and many others.

For years the one top labor union organization was the American Federation of Labor which wielded great power. Now the rival Congress of Industrial Organizations (CIO) is almost equally powerful. Although they clash on many issues, they frequently join forces on lobbying matters which affect all labor alike.

War veterans form another major group for purposes of organized lobbying.

The school teachers' lobby doesn't get much publicity but it is highly effective, mainly because it works through its members in their home localities.

The second type of lobbies includes the dozens which promote certain causes that reflect the interest of their members in principles and programs which may have no direct bearing on the livelihoods of the supporters. The pro-war and anti-war groups are good examples. Others are Birth Control Federation of America, the National Child Labor Committee, and the American Civil Liberties Union.

Women have their own organizations lobbying for peace, temperance, patriotism, and on numerous other subjects of general importance. Such groups include the General Federation of Women's Clubs, the Daughters of the American Revolution, the Women's Peace Party, and the American Association of University Women.

The third type, specialized lobbies formed to meet an emergency or to promote some one project, often are short-lived. They win or lose quickly or the reason for existence disappears. Often they are brought into play by a sudden interest in some one bill in Congress, like the Roosevelt plan to reorganize the Supreme Court, which precipitates a spontaneous coalition of groups. They are likely to be effective, despite their emergency character, inasmuch as they form the channels through which the merits and demerits of legislation can be quickly brought to the light.

Social Lobby

The "social lobby" is largely a game for the women. Women of wealth, official prestige, social position, and a flair for public affairs often play the lobbying game for the kick they get out of the contacts and the appearance of power and influence. Some play the game for pay, some for the love of it, and some because of sincere interest in the cause. In many cases women lobby to help their husbands.

If not overdone, social lobbying can be highly effective. Everyone is apt to be more relaxed and approachable at social gatherings. Good food, good drinks, pleasant surroundings, laughter and gaiety, tend to make a legislator more receptive to suggestions. Naturally there is a certain amount of obligation to the host and hostess. Feminine wiles which would appear foolish in a business office can be fully employed at a social gathering. The diplomatic lobby is largely a "social lobby." All foreign governments lobby for their own interests in one manner or another. These lobbies, directed from the embassies and legations, never overlook an opportunity to court favors for their countries—with Congress, with the departments, with the President, and with the public through the press, the radio, the movies, and lectures. Actual legislative lobbying is seldom done by foreign diplomats themselves. Such work is entrusted to others, usually to paid Americans.

Back Home

The major part of lobbying—the part that is done back home—is carried on through various groups or "cells" in the home districts, and especially in the districts of congressmen who are in key positions to help or hurt the cause.

Lobbying for some causes is often a matter of several years. In such cases, work in the election campaigns is part of the lobby campaign. The Townsend Old Age Pension Plan is a good example of this type of lobby. The technique is to support friends and fight foes in their bids for re-election.

The lobbyist knows, and the congressman knows, that 1,000 active supporters or opponents are more potent than 10,000 voters who are passively for or against him. The stronger the support from back home for any lobby cause, the easier is the work of the lobbyists in Washington.

Delegations which converge on Washington are usually the product of lobbying operations. This may take the form of "marches," as in the cases of the soldiers' bonus, the relief workers and the anti-war groups. It may take the form of witnesses who appear before committees, or groups which call upon congressmen or stage demonstrations such as the hanging of Senator Pepper in effigy on the Capitol grounds. In any case, there is a committee or skeleton campaign group in Washington which heads up activities. Such lobby tactics are always good for much publicity, particularly in the back-home papers. Then, too, delegations whose members spend a few days in Washington return home, not only with increased prestige locally, but with far more incentive to promote the cause and work in election campaigns.

These mass crusades, swarmings of delegates at the Capitol, are used mostly by the high-pressure "cause lobbies." Women seem to work this method better than men. Nothing irritates a congressman, especially a senator, more than to have a flock of super-earnest ladies camping at his door with their campaign demands, but the ladies usually get results.

The large, established, dignified national organizations do not engage in such dramatic "marches" on Congress. They often accomplish the same purpose, however, in quiet ways. One way is to have a convention in Washington, and sick convention delegates on their respective congressmen.

The Course in Congress

The job of lobbying a bill through Congress calls for a wide variety of tactics, but there is a general pattern that is followed in most campaigns. And in watching the course of a campaign, you also get a good look at the progress of a bill through Congress.

After kindling the home fires, the lobbyist looks for a congressman to introduce the bill. The ideal introducer should be: (a) Representative of a region affected by the bill, (b) favorite of the administration in power, (c) a good fighter or a skillful strategist in maneuvering legislation through Congress, and (d) a member of an important committee, such as Rules, Ways and Means or Appropriations, or the one which will have jurisdiction over the bill.

Introduction of the bill should be timed to get the best publicity. And to make sure the introducing speech is right, the lobbyist will provide the introducing congressman with speech material, or perhaps the speech itself. Often, after the speech is delivered, copies of it are mailed around the country to help create pressure on Congress for passage of the bill.

If several congressional committees claim jurisdiction over the legislation, the lobbyist will try to have it considered by the committee which is most favorable. Then begins an important part of the campaign—that of getting a favorable report from the committee. The committee's first step in considering a bill usually is to ask an advisory opinion from the executive department which would have charge of administering it, so the lobbyist does what he can to see that the departmental attitude is favorable. Then the important thing is to get good witnesses to appear at the committee hearings. When the hearings are over, the lobbyist uses all the influence he has to see that the bill is reported favorably on the floor of Congress. Sometimes he gives substantial help in the actual drafting of the committee report. This report and the record of hearings on which it is based are extremely important, for they are a source of information for members of Congress, and are sometimes consulted by the Supreme Court in determining the "intent of Congress."

When the bill has been reported to the House, the lobbyist tries to make sure that the Rules Committee is "sold" on it. Then, if the bill gets immediate right of way in congressional business, the lobbyist's campaign is directed toward the 435 members of the House. The lobby's master mind will estimate the members for and against, and focus his attention where it will do the most good, supplying the bill's friends with ammunition, and working on the doubtful members to vote "aye."

If the bill passes the House, the same rigmarole is necessary for the Senate. And then, if there are differences between the versions of the bill passed by House and Senate, the lobbyist may have to wrangle with a joint conference committee, although he is not allowed to appear directly before it.

The final hurdle, and an important one, is the signature of the President. The lobbyist may encourage a flooding of the White House with telegrams from the public, or he may arrange to have someone with special influence call on the President and give him a clinching sales talk.

The whole procedure varies from case to case, but the outline is fairly standard. Sometimes secrecy is better than publicity. Sometimes it is more effective to get a measure attached as a "rider" to a more publicized bill.

In the course of a legislative lobby campaign, there are numerous lobbies at work on the same bill. It is seldom that a well-organized lobby can operate without arousing lobby forces on the other side. Thus Congress is unofficially provided with a many-sided research agency, for the interplay of forces usually brings out facts and arguments on all sides of the question.

Hints on How

No two lobbying jobs are alike, and lobby tactics must be varied to meet the requirements of each job, but there are some general guides.

One new rule which has come to be accepted in recent years, is that the lobby group at the very outset should try to enlist the help of one or more important government agencies. A great many government departments and bureaus nowadays are in the hands of officials who are skillful lobbyists. The clever private lobbyist can get invaluable help from friendly government officials if he can get them on his side.

There is quite an argument among experts as to whether or not professional lobbyists should appear in person before committees. This depends largely on the personality of the man who presents the case. It is a fact that congressmen much prefer to listen to the testimony of some layman who speaks from first-hand experience, and who is frankly asking for something of benefit to himself or his group, than to listen to a professional lobbyist working for pay. An awkward, bumbling carpet-tack manufacturer who knows his stuff and makes an impression of honesty and sincerity, may carry more weight with the committee than the glibbest, most polished hired advocate.

One common weakness of laymen who try to do their own lobbying is that they are often too scared by a congressman, too timid about going before a congressional committee and emphatically stating their case. This seems to be especially true of businessmen, and the bigger the businessman the more scared he is apt to be. This probably is due to the fact that on many occasions congressional investigating committees have smeared prominent witnesses, have put them on the defensive and given them harmful publicity.

In most cases, however, the lobby group should be able to produce some suave, bold, quick-thinking lay member of the organization who can carry the ball in making a case before a committee. If this cannot be done, then, of course, it is better for the professional advocate to do the job.

Some "Do's"

Here are a few general rules for those who appear before congressional committees:

1. Know your subject thoroughly. Present facts to support opinions. Have the evidence at hand or know exactly where it can be found.
2. Be brief, clear and concise. Committee members are busy people and will appreciate conservation of their time. Have a prepared statement or an outline from which to talk.
3. Keep the attention of the committee at all times, even if you have to stop talking until committeemen finish a private conversation. Speak loudly enough for all to hear, firmly, sincerely, and convincingly.
4. Refuse to be diverted from the main line of arguments by questions or comments. Answer questions to the best of your ability and then resume your own statement where you left off.
5. It is better to present one argument or one angle of your proposition well, than to present several arguments in a slipshod manner.
6. Have copies of your statement for the press.
7. Be courteous. Learn the names of committee members and address them by name in answering questions.

Some "Don'ts"

The lobbyist needs to know how "not to lobby" as well as how to lobby. Here are a few pointers:

286

1. Avoid identical letters or telegrams or canned mail-in cards. These are given far less weight than appeals which seem spontaneous, self-inspired.
2. Don't buttonhole a member of Congress in a corridor. If it is worth seeing him at all, it is worth seeing him in his office.
3. Use care if you hire a professional lobbyist. Some have shady reputations with Congress, and those who claim they can "get to" key members are usually shysters.
4. Don't give long-winded, rambling statements, with too much personal history, to congressional committees.
5. Don't cringe before belligerent congressmen. You have a right to your opinions and a right to express them.
6. Don't resent questioning when you appear before a committee. Even antagonistic questions often help bring out facts.
7. Don't sneer at those who disagree with you. They have a right to their opinions too.

Ballyhoo

Public ballyhoo has become a major part of lobbying tactics. Propaganda is now taking the place of personal influence. "Write or wire your congressmen." "Write or wire the President." These appeals are frequently heard on the radio when some campaigner for a cause pays big money for time on the air to stir up a public following. These organized barrages of telegrams and letters often make officials and legislators angry, but they are not disregarded.

If a senator makes an appeal by radio at night, he is apt to ask his secretary at noon next day how many telegrams he has received, both pro and con. A close check is kept upon them and he knows from past experience that letters will follow the next day in some fairly constant ratio to the telegrams.

At the White House, also, secretaries carefully count and appraise the fan-mail reaction to presidential speeches or public statements. The President beams when letters are unusually numerous and favorable.

Good practical advice is that if you want to add measurably to your influence on government, you can do so by freely and frequently writing or telegraphing your *approval or disapproval* of public utterances of officials and congressmen. These men are your servants, elected to protect your interests. They cannot know your wishes if you do not express them.

Intra-Government Lobbying

The federal government, itself, now maintains the biggest and best lobby of all. It is a two-way lobby—operating on Congress and on the public.

It often out-lobbies the lobbyists. This is the result of the tremendous new powers acquired by the federal government—the money powers, the spending powers, and vast regulatory authority of the Executive and the bureaus, without the checks formerly exercised by Congress. A government propaganda program usually is started by trial balloons—some official makes a prediction or gives a hint in a public speech or press conference.

Every department prints and publishes vast amounts of literature, much of it beautiful in composition and presentation—at the taxpayers' expense, distributed postage-free through the mails. A steady stream of press releases is fed to the press. The radio stations carry programs sponsored by the government.

Thus, government-stimulated public sentiment is used to convince congressmen that the public wants certain things done. Every department has its "liaison men" who work constantly on Capitol Hill. Reluctant congressmen are whipped into line by promises of appointments for themselves or friends, by withholding use of public money in their districts, or threats of campaigning against them in the next election.

Lobbying Is Entrenched

Representatives in Congress are supposed to represent "districts"—all the people in their districts. Senators are supposed to represent "states"—all the people in their states. That's what the blueprints of government call for. Actually it doesn't work that way, because it can't work that way. People of a district or a state are not homogeneous in their interests. They are akin not to everyone else within the geographical subdivision, but to similar people or workers or thinkers in other districts or states. Thus in the evolution of lawmaking by Congress, members of that body tend more and more to become representatives of "interests." These are usually a combination of the interests of some of the home folks (needed to get reelected), and the interests of others, elsewhere, who are not home folks. Lawmaking and government in general tend to become an agglomeration of "special interests," national in scope, even though the promoter of each "special interest" conceives it to be of "general public interest," and honestly thinks so.

Whatever abuses there are in lobbying can be tempered by public knowledge of what the lobbies are doing from time to time—and why, and who. This is a problem of publicity. Newspapers report that Congressman A or Senator B said such-and-such. They would be more accurate if they were to report that Congressman A or Senator B was merely the voice of the X-Y-Z lobby group. Lobbies guide government, and are a part of the governing processes. The more you can know about them from year to year, the more you can know about the realities of government.

Hotbed of Causes

"THERE ought to be a law . . ." says someone. And if enough people think so, they form a little group, and they promote other little groups, and these make up a national group. Before long there is a "movement," and it has an office in Washington, called the "national headquarters." It becomes a "cause," and it battles for a law, a reform, a different attitude by the government and the people toward the object of the cause.

Washington is full of such cause advocates. They are, in the main, a deeply sincere and honest lot of zealots, giving their lives to their pet causes, perhaps making a living at the work, perhaps not. They toil along for years without getting their laws or their reforms, but they contribute their doses of ferment to the public thinking, and most of them make some progress. If they get their pet law, as a few do in the course of time, they move on to some further refinement, for there is never any end to the big and little causes awaiting promotion.

The cause advocates do lobbying with Congress and with the governmental agencies, and they use all the standard tricks of lobbying, ranging from direct approach to the building of fires of sentiment back home, but they are different from the class of lobbyists who work for some material or business objective. For example, child welfare, prohibition, peace, and women's rights are "causes," and different from tariff on textiles, tax on excess profits, and regulation of stock exchanges. The "causes" are likely to be "social," or "sentimental," or "unselfish." There's a twilight zone, for every pressure movement for everything is usually promoted under the claim that it is "unselfish" and ultimately in the "broad public interest," but in a general sort of way the cause workers in Washington are in a separate class from the lobbyists, as discussed in the preceding chapter.

If you feel strongly on some subject, the chances are there's an outfit in Washington which is geared to your feelings and has a membership blank waiting for your signature. That goes if you are for birth control, against cigarettes, for wild life, against narcotics, for land conservation, against steel traps—for or against almost anything. The organizations cover practically every cause under the sun, including health, social justice, child welfare, old-age pensions, municipal improvements, federal economy, veterans' welfare, conservation, international policies, education, prohibition, kindness to animals, and women's rights.

Wanted: Laws and Rulings

The main effort, ordinarily, is directed toward pushing a piece of legislation through Congress or combating measures proposed by others. One of the first steps is to form an executive committee, and put on it as many impressive names as can be corralled. Then the executive secretary—who generally turns out to be practically the whole organization—is chosen, or chooses himself. He (or she) rigs up plans for expanding the membership, writes press releases, prepares statements for delivery before congressional committees, feeds material to members of Congress who are friendly. If he is fortunate enough to have some nationally-known figures on his executive committee, he is only too glad to have them do the speechmaking. He lets them appear before congressional groups and take credit for what he writes in the press releases.

Legislation is not always the prime objective. In this case, the cause depends upon executive rulings from the White House or government departments. Frequently the objective jibes with an executive agency's plans and policies. Then officials of the federal unit work with the causers, more or less openly. Once in a while you come across an organization that is content to work broadly in furthering an ideal by giving its message to the public and expanding the circle of followers. Organizations of that type capitalize mainly on the advantages Washington offers as a publicity center.

Most causes are financed by their membership through monthly, quarterly, or annual dues. Others depend upon free-will contributions which vary from a few cents to thousands of dollars. Small sums are solicited by mail and many organizations send out thousands of "please give" letters. Potential contributors of large sums get the executive secretary's personal attention. Some of the organizations have enthusiastic and wealthy "angels" who pay all bills or, at least, meet deficits which still exist after all other money-raising methods have been exhausted. A few zealots use their own money or serve in executive positions without pay. One thing the cause advancers have in common is the realization that the publication of a "house organ" is necessary. Even when funds are low, a causer will find some way to publish a magazine or handout sheet.

In membership, cause organizations range from those with small bands of dues payers to the large, powerful ones whose mailing lists contain hundreds of thousands of names, some dues payers, most not. Among the largest and oldest cause organizations are those which have dealt with women's rights, prohibition, veterans' welfare and the peace movement. For headquarters, these usually have had buildings of their own, or occupy large suites in office structures. And organizations with common interests tend to maintain headquarters close to each other. Four prominent peace organizations, for instance, are clustered around the State Department, and campaigners for prohibition are bunched within two blocks of the Capitol building.

Big and Little

The offices of the big, powerful groups, usually look like those of average business concerns. They have receptionists, private switchboards, individual offices for executives, large slabs of filing cabinets, and platoons of stenographers. Such layouts are in marked contrast with those of the small-fry organizations. The little fellows, with little standing and not much power, struggle along as best they can, but among them you find real fervor and fanatical devotion.

These small alliances, which far outnumber the large ones, usually have a set-up something like this: The name is a high-sounding, several-worded affair. The address turns out to be that of a third, fourth or fifth rate office building or an old brick residence that has been chopped into low-rent offices. The small, struggling causes are headquartered largely in buildings on H and I Streets, fringing the business section and a few blocks north from the White House. If there's an elevator, it's one of the rattling, bird-cage type and it's run by an old Negro. Down a dingy hall is the office.

You may find headquarters of three or four cause organizations jammed together to keep down costs. One glass panel of a door in the Maryland Building on H Street lists an Anti-Cigaret Alliance, the Esperanto Association of North America, the National Society for Humane Regulation of Vivisection, "World Fair for Washington" and—in the remaining space—the names of three individuals. Inside the door are just three small rooms. Frequently, a lawyer who has achieved only moderate success, or less, doubles in brass as the Washington representative of a cause and thereby gets the right to put a lot of lettering on the door below his name.

As standard equipment, a run-of-mine cause office has an old-fashioned, littered roll-top desk, a picture of George Washington or Abraham Lincoln, wooden shelves with cloth over the front to keep dust off the books, copies of the *Congressional Record*, tied-up batches of House and Senate committee hearings in which the organization has participated, and piles of cause literature.

The occupants of these small offices usually welcome visitors with open arms and gladly answer any questions, except those which bear embarrassingly on the size of memberships. They eagerly offer letterheads bearing long lists of individuals on their executive committees, taking pains to point to at least one "big name."

Except for the large, well-established organizations, few of the cause headquarters are staffed with more than three or four people. Those with one or two are numerous. The "head men" usually are lawyers, with a sprinkling of former newspapermen. Each has his own tale about how he came to be doing what he's doing. The best story along that line is about a salesman broken down by alcoholism who went to a woman friend and told her he was going to end it all. She persuaded him to make just one more try, with the promise that she would figure out something for him to do. She figured out a cause. And he went ahead to a moderately successful career promoting the cause.

Slowed by War

Almost without exception, the causers today have a special professional reason for lamenting the war. They lament it because people pay little attention to their causes and campaigns when the fate of their nation is at stake. But they find consolation in the thought that when peace returns, if they can hang on that long, they again will have the chance to command the attention of legislators and the populace.

It's only natural to assume that crooks would work their way into the field of crusading in Washington. The fact is, however, that among the cause executives there are few slickers on the trail of easy money. Only once in a great while does a get-rich-quick Wallingford show up, make a small killing, or fizzle out and disappear. One cause secretary came to Washington a few years ago and flooded the country with offers to give a membership in his organization, together with a lot of books and pamphlets and a subscription to the official magazine, all for a dollar. When the dollars began coming in he pocketed them and sent nothing in return. He left town and hasn't been heard of since.

Another questionable movement ran its course recently. With a fine idea for making a living, a clever lady came out of the South and tried to tie in with the defense movement by setting up a "patriotic" organization. She offered membership to women at a nominal rate, and gave them the opportunity to buy a $4.50 uniform for $9.50. But when the District Attorney came onto the scene, she closed up shop, and the last echo of the affair was a promotion company's suit to recover some expense money and $42.50 they had given her to buy a fur coat.

None of the crusading groups seems to be further from gaining its ends than the peace advocates. Four of them, all nationally prominent, have headquarters close to the State Department and the White House. They are the Carnegie Endowment for International Peace, the century-old American Peace Society, the National Council for Prevention of War, and the Women's International League for Peace and Freedom. The first two are conservative and academic. The other two have formed the spearhead of the active peace movement. The National Council for Prevention of War had approximately 11,000 paying supporters in 1940. It then operated on a budget of about $77,000, which was less than half what it spent in some of the prewar years. Its expenditures from 1920 to 1940 are estimated at $2,000,000. Also there is the Women's International League for Peace and Freedom, which claims 15,000 members. Before the present war, the League claimed 25,000 members. In times of war, however, organizations like these crawl into their shells and wait for the end of hostilities.

Nearly every cause organization on one side of a major issue has its counterpart on the other side. Those which would have the world lay aside its arms are matched by others which long have campaigned for a building up of the nation's military strength. These organizations include the American Coalition of Patriotic Societies, the National Patriotic Council and the Women's Patriotic Conference on National Defense. Other organizations, most of which were born between the outbreak of World War II and the entry of the United States into the conflict, include the Committee to Defend America by Aiding the Allies, the Committee for Democratic Defense, the Council for Democracy, Fight for Freedom Committee and the American Home Guard, Inc.

Dominating the list of patriotic societies are the solid stand-bys, like Daughters of the American Revolution, Sons of the American Revolution, United Daughters of the Confederacy, and the United States Flag Association. While these are not dyed-in-the-wool "cause organizations," they do battle for causes through legislative and publicity committees. Veterans' organizations are among the oldest causes in the country. They keep experienced representatives in Washington to further the causes of veterans and their dependents. Outstanding in this field are the American Legion, Veterans of Foreign Wars, Disabled American Veterans of the World War, Disabled Emergency Officers of the World War, and United Spanish War Veterans. Aside from working for national defense measures, the patriot-veterans' groups have lobbied successfully for measures dealing with compensation for disabled veterans, more hospital facilities for veterans, bonus legislation, and a variety of other aids to service men and their families.

The most intriguing spectacle in the field of cause activities came last year when a group of leftish organizations switched from the anti-war side of the fence to pro-intervention. When Germany and Russia went to war, they broke rule number one of the successful causer: "Adopt a policy and stick with it, come hell, high water or anything else."

Drys and Women Crusaders

The prohibition forces, who won their first fight during the first World War, are now arousing themselves to take advantage of World War II, and Washington is witnessing a strong revival of their activities. The citadels of the three most potent dry organizations, all located near the Capitol Building, are beginning to look as they did in earlier days. These organizations are the Board of Temperance of the Methodist Church (successor to the once-powerful Board of Temperance, Prohibition and Public Morals), the Woman's Christian Temperance Union and the Anti-Saloon League. The general staff is the National Temperance and Prohibition Council, in which all three groups are represented. At the turn of the year, their workers were energetically going about the business of getting pledges from individual senators and representatives to support a bill aimed at outlawing liquor advertisements, and legislation for prohibition on the wartime United States.

Also set up near the Capitol are the headquarters of the National Woman's Party, which has a small staff in Washington and members in all the states. Its members, successors to the suffragettes who got votes for women, now are aiming at the adoption of a constitutional amendment to provide that: "Men and women shall have equal rights throughout the United States and every place subject to its jurisdiction."

Ranging from one extreme to the other in size and influence are dozens of other cause organizations, such as the League for the Larger Life, the National Council for Mothers and Babies, Birth Control Federation of America, Society for the Prevention of Cruelty to Animals, American Civil Liberties Union, National Old-Age Pensions Association, Chinese National Salvation Association, Criminal Justice Association, National Anti-Steel Trap League, National Committee for the Revision of the Comstock Law, National Negro Congress, National Service Board for Religious Objectors, National Wildlife Federation, People's Lobby, Repeal Associates, World Narcotics Research Foundation, and the American Society for the Hard of Hearing.

All causes have backers who believe in them. All are meritorious in the minds of someone. Furthermore, government has become so complex that

Congress cannot be expected to represent fully and nicely all the fine shades of ideas which people have about public policies. So it has come to pass that cause organizations take over the job of representing various groups and their various ideas of what should be. Thus the cause promoters serve a useful purpose as auxiliaries to the more formal machinery of representative government.

27

Woman Influence

WOMEN are women and also persons, and in both capacities they cut a lot of ice in Washington. When you think of men in Washington, you don't think of them as males, but rather as individuals, even personages. It's the same with women. They have their places in their homes, but they also do much work outside their homes, and they have achieved a great accumulation of that quality known as Influence.

In no foreign capital, not even in countries where the women have been "emancipated," as in Sweden, is there such a large proportion of women of affairs who do things in their own right, not merely as the influencers of men of affairs.

In the average American city women play a great part in the affairs of the community, and a growing part, but usually they are on the fringes of the public work of the community. Here in Washington they are smack in the middle. In the typical community women do not participate to any general extent in directing the business, the industry of the community. Here in Washington women are all mixed in with the running of the business, the industry, which is government and the making of public policies. They rank and work alongside men.

This is not to say that it is a "woman's town." Despite the great growth of woman influence, the women do not have preponderant influence. It is a "man's town." Men occupy the great bulk of positions of public importance, and women are in the minority. Most decisions are made by men, either with or without the collaboration of women, and usually without. Washington is still a "man's world," but the women are coming up.

A situation which has lowest common denominator value in showing the progress of the "woman invasion" of Washington within a single generation is the modern status of women's toilets. Many government buildings a generation ago had only a few rooms for women. The error has been rectified in the newer buildings and the proportion is now 50-50. Once upon a time the Press Galleries of Congress were sacred to men, but when "women newsmen" began to gain admission in numbers, they required a great tearing up of the plumbing facilities in the Capitol Building. After all, these are fair indexes—and basic.

The woman influence in Washington is not of the mistress variety. There are no Pompadours, or du Barrys, or Lupescus. There are private affairs and petty scandals, and people gossip about them as they do in any city, but they are not important by standards of broad public policy. There are no mistresses who are publicly influential. The family life of public men in Washington seems to be reasonably regular, and certainly not of the liberal standards prevailing in many world capitals.

Wives are influential as wives, just as they are everywhere. Plenty of wives run their husbands on unseen wires (or sometimes seen), but on this Washington has no monopoly. The difference here is that the husbands are engaged in public work, and the fortunes of the family depend on how well the public thinks the men are doing. Consequently wives have special reason and license for collaborating on the careers of their husbands. By careful social management, they can woo their husbands' friends, and also enemies.

Women secretaries of public men, considered en masse, probably have more effective influence in Washington than any other group of working women, high or low. They are unseen and unknown to the public, they are practically "anonymous." Yet in the day-to-day operations of public affairs they are powerful, not because they seek power, but because they handle it in routine manner. The extent to which they do it well often is a big factor in the smooth operations of their Big Bosses. Most of them do it well, few are fumblers.

The No. 1 private secretary is Grace Tully, who took over as the President's private secretary when illness overtook Marguerite LeHand, commonly known as "Missy." Another high-up is Malvina Thompson, private secretary and companion to Mrs. Roosevelt. A former Second Lady of the Land, Mrs. Garner, was private secretary to her husband, Vice President Garner. She did a grand job, even if eyebrows of the society ladies did lift a bit at the thought of a Second Lady who continued to be her old self, a working woman.

The social position of stenographer-secretaries has risen tremendously in Washington in recent years. For one thing, more educated young women are going into secretarial work as a career. Besides, the growth in complexity of governmental operations has thrust more responsibility onto the young women who are the "right-hand men" of big public men. Often they determine who gets in and who does not. Often they are the bosses of the time schedule of their bosses. Often they take the rap, seldom do they get full credit, almost never do they get their names in the papers.

Other influential women are leaders of causes, officials, members of Congress, judges, lawyers, career administrators, scientists, writers, diplomats, club leaders, and educators. There are even some feminine examples of that class of persons who, in the masculine realm, are known as "stuffed shirts."

Pioneers

It is only in the last couple of decades that it became "respectable" for women to mix up in politics and to campaign for a cause or reform. There are persons still living in Washington who can remember back to the times when the public was shocked at "women who made spectacles of themselves" by insisting that women should rightfully participate in public affairs, which had been considered the exclusive province of the men. Old Washingtonians remember Clara Barton who nursed the wounded in the Civil War; Dr. Mary Walker, the woman physician who had to get congressional approval when she insisted on wearing pants; Frances E. Willard, the advocate of education for women and of temperance for all, the only woman who is represented in Statuary Hall at the Capitol; Susan B. Anthony, Lucretia Mott and Elizabeth Cady Stanton, who fought for woman suffrage and women's rights; Dr. Anna Howard Shaw, who inherited the Anthony mantle and carried on, to be succeeded by the present "Dean," Mrs. Carrie Chapman Catt.

It was only one generation ago, in 1917, that women suffragettes paraded in front of the White House to demand woman suffrage, and were regarded as "indelicate." For disturbing the peace the leaders were thrown into jail. I was the only reporter who was allowed to visit them that first night in jail, where they played on a wheezy organ such old melodies as "God Be With You Till We Meet Again" with an audience of black faces behind other bars. They told me that regardless of jails the woman cause would progress. It was a sound prediction . . . and how!

The leader of that doughty band, Miss Alice Paul, split with the National American Women's Suffrage Association over the degree of "militancy" women workers for the cause should show, and founded the National Woman's Party in which she is still active. Mrs. Helena Hill Weed, Washington lawyer and daughter of a former congressman, is another of the historic "jailbirds" who proudly wears a pin depicting a cell door.

The less violent wing of the suffrage movement, the "suffragists," had many prominent and influential women in its leadership, many of whom are still active leaders in other movements. There is Mrs. Kate Trenholm Abrams, daughter of President Cleveland's Comptroller of the Currency and granddaughter of the Secretary of the Confederacy, noted as the first prominent southern woman to brave the prejudice and traditions of her family and state (South Carolina) to openly champion the right of women to the vote. She is still in the forefront of many woman movements, notably peace and international cooperation. Mrs. Laura Puffer Morgan turned her energies from suffrage to world peace, and is now the motive power behind the newly formed "Institute on World Organization." Miss Charl Ormond Williams rose in the educational world to become the first woman president of the National Education Association and now is its Legislative Secretary.

The National Woman's Christian Temperance Union was a pioneer in woman influence, and as its Legislative Secretary, Mrs. Lenna Lowe Yost was credited with swinging the organized woman vote to win the fight for the prohibition amendment. Later she was active in Republican party affairs. During the Hoover administration, another woman gained prominence through the attempt to enforce prohibition—Mrs. Mabel Walker Willebrandt, a West Coast lawyer who was the first woman Assistant Attorney General.

These are only a few typical examples of outstanding women who have pioneered.

Mrs. Roosevelt

It was not until the New Deal came in that women really went to town in Washington. They may not have been fully ripe, politically, but they were riper than they had ever been. They were better organized in their own various groups. They had helped to get Roosevelt elected. They set up headquarters for all sorts of causes, worked furiously in public and didn't care who knew it. The old ladylike furtiveness was gone. The jail sentences for suffragettes were well in the past. They took their places on the public stage of Washington and they still hold them. In the center of the stage is Mrs. Roosevelt.

1. She is the First Lady, the wife of the President, which is enough to give any woman a high rank and a reputation, to make her a cynosure of all eyes.

2. Upon this foundation she has built a superstructure, a wide following which results from the personal respect and affection that is felt for her by all who come into personal contact with her. She is well liked. She conveys that comfortable feeling that goes along with warmhearted neighbor women. She is the sort who would feed cookies to neighborhood kids at the kitchen door, or scare up a yard of cheesecloth to lend to a neighbor man for wiping his car. Women like her because she is homey, and also perhaps because she

is no beauty. Even people who disagree impersonally with her views find her personally agreeable.

3. She has energy. All persons who work with her tell tales about how she keeps going continuously and outdoes them all in sustained activity.

4. She has humane interests and impulses which cover many fields, but which are particularly acute in any field having to do with women.

People in Washington from time to time make up lists of the three or four most influential persons in the capital. Always the President heads any list. At times such lists have included a Moley, or a Frankfurter, or a Corcoran, or a Hopkins, or a Nelson, or a Henderson, but they always include Mrs. Roosevelt.

Here are some of the reasons: She is the second-best publicized person in Washington, the President being first. Her personal life is disclosed to the public daily by her own published diary. She is a spokesman for the President. She often spills to the public an idea, a sort of trial balloon, which subsequently develops as an idea sponsored by the President himself. There is no sure way of knowing whether she gives the idea to him, or he gives it to her; it probably works *both* ways. At any rate, the two are seldom out of step in their public positions on issues.

She influences policies within government agencies by her talkings and her writings. All officials keep a close eye and ear on Mrs. Roosevelt in order to know what she is thinking, for they have ample records from the past to show that the President is probably thinking that, too, and she may be merely his mouthpiece. That may or may not be the way it is intended, but that is the way it works out, as any public official will bear witness in private conversation. Officials do not dare disagree openly with the wife of the President. It is impolitic, inexpedient, and dangerous. "It simply isn't done."

With legislation in Congress, it is much the same. Technically, Mrs. Roosevelt keeps hands off current issues in Congress, by refraining from comments which bear directly upon the issue, but any leader in Congress can tell stories of how her writings and talkings have influenced votes, always indirectly, but often effectively. The seasoned leaders of Congress like her personally, but have deep unspoken resentment against her influence on their sheep, which they regard as *their* sheep, not hers.

Mrs. Roosevelt has what is called a "good press." It is of her own making. First, her daily column provides popular reading. Second, she has attracted a corps of women newswriters who report her every publishable thought and comment. They like her, they are sympathetic reporters, and they do their best for her.

She can accomplish things which the President can't, and he can get the political benefit of them when they go right, and not always take the blame for them when they go wrong. She has cultivated good working relations with left-wing organizations, with many enterprises for the poor, with movements for the benefit of women and children, and with Negroes. Usually she does these things more quietly, with less fanfare, than the President could do them.

Mrs. Roosevelt's self-assumed connection with the Office of Civilian Defense was due mainly to her desire to promote the training of women for war work, especially for work on farms. LaGuardia was not sympathetic, and he wasn't doing it, so she jumped in. The burst of public criticism over her part in OCD was the first open general blow-up against her. It was due not merely to the merits of the row over OCD, but also to an accumulation of repressions from the past. The press generally feels that Mrs. Roosevelt should be regarded as a public character, and, therefore, subject to criticism on occasion—for any acts which are public acts. But there exists an unwritten code that the First Lady shall be immune from public criticism, or at least relatively immune. Hence, the repressions in the past, and hence the blow-off over OCD.

Mrs. Roosevelt has brought many women into government. Miss Perkins as Secretary of Labor was brought in by the President himself, but Mrs. Roosevelt's influence helped to keep her in. Women officials in government and women workers below the official class know that she will help them keep their jobs, and climb to higher jobs. She is their friend at court, their queen, their elder sister in the sorority. Most of them worship her. Most of them are starry-eyed and gaga about her. They will claw out the eyes of anyone who intimates that she intrudes herself into too many public matters without authority.

Two former first ladies, Mrs. Woodrow Wilson and Mrs. William Howard Taft, live in Washington. They are respected but they do not try to be influential.

Women Officials

The first woman ever to sit in a President's cabinet, Miss Frances Perkins (whose private married name is Mrs. Paul Wilson) owed her appointment as Secretary of Labor primarily to her long record of conspicuous service in sociological and industrial work in New York State. The Labor post had always been a hard job, even for men. She was a good administrator, and she gave the Department a much-needed house cleaning, but even the most ardent advocates of the woman cause do not claim that Miss Perkins added prestige and distinction to the office.

Other women officials have been given positions—sometimes for merit, but often as rewards for faithful and productive labors in the Democratic party vineyard.

Mrs. Blair Banister, the brilliant and witty sister of Senator Glass, is Assistant Treasurer of the United States. Mrs. Nellie Tayloe Ross was appointed the first woman Director of the Mint, after serving as the first woman Governor of Wyoming. Miss Josephine Roche served in the early days of the New Deal as Assistant Secretary of the Treasury, combining with her record of party loyalty a wide practical experience as a coal mine operator in Colorado.

Women occupy important posts on various boards and commissions. Mrs. Lucille Foster McMillin, widow of a former Governor of Tennessee, succeeded Miss Jessie Dell on the Civil Service Commission. A number of prominent Democratic widows have been taken care of in ingenious ways by a benevolent administration. A special post was created by the State Department, that of decorating our Foreign Service Embassies, for the widow of our former envoy to Canada and Roosevelt kin, Mrs. Warren Delano Robbins. The job of publicizing American ships, as publicity director for the Maritime Commission, was given to the socially-conscious Mrs. A. Mitchell Palmer.

When changes occurred in the original Social Security Board, Miss Mary W. Dewson, warm personal friend of Mrs. Roosevelt and one of the original FDR group, was appointed one of the three members. After serving one term, she was succeeded by Mrs. Ellen S. Woodward from Mississippi, also a Democratic stalwart, who had served as Assistant Administrator of the Work Projects Administration in charge of Women's Activities. Another of the New York group of party workers is Miss Katherine C. Blackburn, who was named Assistant Director of the Office of Government Reports, and who directs the systematic reading of the press for all government agencies.

Among the impressive "firsts" of the Roosevelt administration have been the appointment of women to two major diplomatic posts—Mrs. Ruth Bryan Owen as Minister to Denmark, and Mrs. J. Borden Harriman to Norway. Mrs. Harriman showed up particularly well in the trying days of the Nazi invasion of Norway.

Women in Congress

Most women elected or appointed to Congress are novices in the political game and not many of them have made any deep impression or any real contribution to the congressional scene. Easily the most influential is Mrs. Mary T. Norton, shrewd and capable politician from "Boss" Hague's Jersey City, now serving her eighth successive term in the House. She is the first woman to be elected to Congress from the Democratic party, and is also the first to hold an important chairmanship, that of the powerful Committee on Labor. Mrs. Edith Nourse Rogers came to the House from Massachusetts in 1925, to take the seat of her deceased husband, and has served continuously since that time. Two recent additions to the "widow contingent" in the House are Mrs. Frances Bolton, of Ohio, and Mrs. Katharine Byron, of Maryland; they show signs of becoming political personages in their own right.

The only current woman senator and the only one ever to have been elected to the upper house is quiet and retiring Mrs. Hattie W. Caraway of Arkansas. Originally appointed as a "seatwarmer" to succeed her late husband, she got herself elected and twice re-elected.

The women who have managed to get to Congress without the aid of a husband, deceased or otherwise, are few. The first woman ever elected to the House, Miss Jeannette Rankin, of Montana, who was noted chiefly for her vote of protest against entering the first World War, is now serving a second term and, still true to form, cast the only vote against entering the second World War. Miss Jessie Sumner, ardent anti-New Dealer from down-state Illinois, now serving her second term, is by far the most vocal, energetic and provocative of the women in Congress.

Career Women

Nowhere is there a greater concentration of highly trained women specialists in every field than in Washington. Least showy of the woman groups, these women do the spade work of the government as far as dealing with the day-to-day problems of Mrs. Average Citizen and her family is concerned.

The Women's Bureau, created in 1920 as a recognition of the growing importance of women's problems, has had as its first and only director vigorous and able Mary Anderson.

The Children's Bureau has had three women heads since its establishment 25 years ago. The first chief, Julia C. Lathrop, developed the mechanics of the Bureau and did much to build it up. Her successor and long-time associate, Grace Abbott, was the more practical political force, originating and driving through to enactment the Sheppard-Towner maternity bill. When she retired to become Dean of Women at the University of Nebraska, she was succeeded by her assistant of many years, the present chief of the Bureau, Katharine F. Lenroot, daughter of the former Senator Lenroot of Wisconsin, who has carried on in an unspectacular but highly effective way.

Dr. Louise Stanley, long-time head of the Bureau of Home Economics, is, of course, one of the best-known home economists. The 4-H Clubs, under the Department of Agriculture, are directed by Miss Gertrude Warren. In many of these bureaus there are women whose names and work are familiar through their writings, lectures and radio talks—Miss Miriam Birdseye, senior nutritionist, Agriculture Department; Miss Ruth O'Brien, chief of the Textile and Clothing Division of Home Economics; Miss Ruth Van Deman, head of the Information Section of Home Economics.

Mrs. Ruth Shipley, a veteran of 28 years of government service, is Passport Chief of the State Department. Miss Mary E. Switzer, with 20 years of government service behind her, is Senior Assistant to the Social Security Administrator, Paul V. McNutt, assisting in the administration of the Food and Drugs Act and public health work. The Chief of the United States Information Service is Miss Harriet M. Root, and she has answered more questions about government in the past 10 years than any other one person in the city. Miss Mary M. O'Reilly was Assistant Director of the Mint for many years until her recent retirement.

The U. S. Office of Education has a number of women of national reputation in the educational world, among them the Assistant Commissioner, Dr. Bess Goodykoontz, and Miss Mary Dabney Davis, in charge of Primary Education work. In the Washington schools are many outstanding teachers, some of whom have attained national reputations in their special fields—Miss Anna D. Halberg, an authority on teacher education; Dr. Julia L. Hahn, in the elementary grade work; Miss Maude Aiton, adult education and Americanization; and Miss May Bradshaw, secondary education.

Scientists

Women scientists in the government service, working quietly and unostentatiously, have made great contributions in their particular fields of research, many of them attaining nation-wide or world-wide recognition. Dr. Alice Evans, the discoverer of the source of undulant or Malta fever, has received international honor. She is a victim of the disease, contracted from her close association with the germ, but she has never deviated from her search for a cure.

Another woman scientist with notable achievements to her credit and a score of academic and scientific honors is Dr. Eloise B. Cram, probably the best-known woman parasitologist in the medical world. Dr. Sara E. Branham, senior bacteriologist of the National Institute of Health, also has been the recipient of many national and international honors for her discoveries on meningitis.

In the Department of Agriculture, Dr. Charlotte Elliott has attended the sick bed of many a field of corn and prescribed for it. Dr. Annie May Hurd Karrer has done outstanding work on soil substances and the elements which are poisonous to plants and cattle. Miss Edith Cash is an authority on certain groups of fungi, and her sister, Miss Lillian Cash, specializes on the ills of the potato, while beans and peas have the scientific attention of Specialist Florence Hedges.

A number of Washington women are geographers, naturalists and authors of national and international reputation: Dr. Millicent Todd Bingham, Dr. Margaret Mead, Mrs. William Chapin Huntington, Miss Louise A. Boyd, the only woman on record to have a section of Greenland named after her, and Mrs. William M. Mann, wife of the Director of the Washington Zoo and a collaborator in his studies of animal life.

Temporarily on the Washington scene are scores of women experts working on the defense program: Dr. Helen S. Mitchell, director of nutrition on the staff of the Coordinator of Health, Welfare and Related Defense Activities, on leave from Massachusetts State College; Miss Mary I. Barber, food consultant to the Secretary of War, assigned to the Quartermaster Corps, with the job of seeing that the Army is fed the proper food; Miss Marion E. Maclean, specialist on the chemistry of oils, with special application to the problems of defense, at the Bureau of Standards; Dr. Lucy S. Morgan, with the Public Health Service working on a program of community health education in areas where there are large Army camps, and Mrs. Oveta Culp Hobby, first Director of the Women's Auxiliary Army Corps, with rank of Major.

Women Lawyers

Women lawyers have shared in the general advance of their sex. Miss Stella Akin was appointed Special Assistant to the Attorney General, under Homer Cummings. Miss Genevieve R. Cline is the first woman to be judge of the U. S. Customs Court. The appointment of Miss Grace B. Stiles as Assistant U. S. Attorney for the District of Columbia also broke a precedent.

The U. S. Employees' Compensation Commission has a woman chairman, Mrs. Jewel W. Swofford. Miss Marion J. Harron, of California, sits on the Board of Tax Appeals, and Miss Annabel Matthews is a member of the Processing Tax Board of Review. On the 25-member Board of Veterans Appeal, three women are serving, Mrs. Laura S. Brown, Judge Lucy S. Howorth and Mrs. Carroll L. Stewart. Besides these top judicial posts, women lawyers are sprinkled liberally through the departments and bureaus.

The Washington front is covered by the top-notch correspondents and writers of this country and foreign countries and proportionately has more women writers than probably any other one spot on the globe. The woman influence, however, was negligible until the New Deal. Then for the first time they had their own White House press conference, with the First Lady holding regular weekly conferences when in Washington and making news wherever she was. This necessitated the addition of at least one woman reporter to all the major bureaus and news services. Their numbers multiplied in the Press Gallery and at the President's press conference; they even head several bureau staffs.

Mrs. Esther Van Wagoner Tufty, sister of Governor Van Wagoner of Michigan, heads the Tufty News Service, with an impressive string of Michigan papers. Ned Brunson Harris was chief of the *Minneapolis Journal* Bureau until it closed last year. May Craig has her own chain of New England papers. Lorania Francis assists her husband in running the *Los Angeles Times* Bureau. Ruth Cowan is special correspondent for the Associated Press (AP) assigned to cover Mrs. Roosevelt. Ruby Black, formerly of the United Press (UP), and biographer of Mrs. Roosevelt, now is with the Rockefeller office. Mary Hornaday is the ace woman correspondent of the *Christian Science Monitor* Bureau. Lilian Rixey is a leading member of the Washington bureau of *Life* magazine. Maxine Davis is an active magazine writer and author. Eleanor Ragsdale, of the Newspaper Enterprise Association (NEA), writes widely circulated special articles. Winifred Mallon is a veteran writer of the *New York Times* staff.

One of Washington's four major newspapers, the *Times-Herald*, has a woman publisher, the wealthy and unpredictable Eleanor (Cissie) Patterson, member of the Medill-Patterson publishing clan. Ruth Finney, of Scripps-Howard, and Doris Fleeson, *New York News,* cover political news ably and realistically. Anna Youngman handles editorials and special articles for the *Washington Post* in a keen and analytical way. Martha Strayer, competent feature writer for the *Washington Daily News,* was one of the first to have her own by-line. Mary Haworth writes Washington's most popular local column in the *Washington Post*, devoted to advice on personal problems. America's top woman commentator on the air and political columnist, Dorothy Thompson, is a familiar figure in Washington. Martha Dalrymple, formerly of the Associated Press, now helps to direct the government's public relations with Latin America. Helen Essary writes a locally influential column for the *Times-Herald*. Jackie Martin, ace news photographer, is with the Washington Bureau of the *Chicago Sun*, and is an associate editor of the *Woman's Home Companion.*

Besides the newspaper women, Washington has many women writers. Nationally-known writers such as Mary Roberts Rinehart, Frances Parkinson Keyes, Pearl Buck and Temple Bailey make their home here for at least part of the year. And there are the women who take a prominent part in the social or political life of the city and write their memoirs, and the numerous local authors who turn out books based on the Washington scene—Mathilde Eiker (*The Senator's Lady*), Helen Lombard (*Washington Waltz*), Lella Warren (*Foundation Stone*), May Merrill Miller (*First the Blade*), Lucy Salamanca (*Fortress of Freedom*), Eleanor Pierson (Mrs. Warren Lee Pierson) (*The Defense Rests*), Leslie Ford, who keeps Washington in the *Saturday Evening Post* with her murder mysteries, and others.

Labor Leaders

In the field of organized labor, women leaders are active and influential in various lines. The National Women's Trade Union has been represented for many years by Miss Elizabeth Christman and Miss Mary N. Winslow. As the chief executive of the Teachers' Union, Miss Selma Borchardt has worked for reforms in the working conditions and pay of teachers. Miss Gertrude McNally is Secretary-Treasurer of the National Federation of Federal Employees. The labor interest of the National Catholic Welfare Conference is handled by Miss Linna E. Bresette. Shy and retiring Miss Florence Thorne heads the research staff of the American Federation of Labor.

Joint Congressional Committee

The most potent single "woman bloc" in Washington is the coalition group known as the Women's Joint Congressional Committee—the WJCC. In 1920, when the women no longer had suffrage as a single burning issue, the great national women's organizations got together, chose representatives to sit on the Committee and worked out a legislative program with whose objectives they all could agree. Presenting thus a united "woman front" and claiming to control 10 or 12 million votes, they succeeded in getting the Sheppard-Towner maternity law enacted, and in having the child labor amendment submitted to the states for ratification—both after years of delay and obstruction. They were also largely instrumental in getting the law providing for the independent citizenship of women and the reclassification under the Civil Service Act in 1922.

The membership of the WJCC is impressive, and it shows the scope of women's interests: American Association of University Women, American Dietetic Association, American Home Economics Association, American Federation of Teachers, American Medical Women's Association, American Nurses Association, Inc., American Physiotherapy Association, Association for Childhood Education, General Federation of Women's Clubs, Girls' Friendly Society of the U.S.A., National Board of the Young Women's Christian Association, National Committee of Church Women, National Congress of Parents and Teachers, National Consumers' League, National Council of Jewish Women, National Education Association, National Federation of Business and Professional Women's Clubs, Inc., National League of Women Voters, National Women's Trade Union League, Service Star Legion, Inc., and Women's National Homeopathic Fraternity.

Some of the nationally known women mentioned previously are active in the WJCC and others are these: Miss Helen W. Atwater, Mrs. Saidie Orr Dunbar, Miss Elizabeth Eastman, Mrs. Glen L. Swiggett, Mrs. William Kittle, Mrs. Basil Manly, Miss Agnes Winn, Mrs. Harris T. Baldwin, Mrs. Anne H. Johnstone, and Dr. Julia M. Green.

The peace cause has had many prominent women advocates here since the first World War, among them Miss Dorothy Detzer, able and vocal national secretary of the Women's International League for Peace and Freedom; Mrs. Florence Boeckel, associate secretary of the National Council for Prevention of War; and Miss Mabel Vernon, director of the People's Mandate Committee.

Women's Clubs

The women's clubs of Washington are legion, ranging from the intellectual and those-with-a-purpose to the purely social. There are the usual local clubs for all kinds of civic reforms and philanthropic purposes; the branches of the professional or service clubs, national or international in scope; patriotic, political and educational. Practically all the great national organizations have headquarters in Washington—American Association of University Women, National Federation of Women's Clubs, League of Women Voters, Woman's National Democratic Club, League of Republican Women, and others.

National headquarters of the American Association of University Women see much of such outstanding educators as Dr. Aurelia Mills Reinhardt, Dr. Virginia Gildersleeve, Dr. Meta Glass, Dr. Mary Woolley and Dr. Helen C. White. Dr. Kathryn McHale, general director, and Dr. Esther Caukin Brunauer, in charge of international relations, are authorities in their fields. The AAUW's membership roster includes the name of Mrs.

Franklin D. Roosevelt, as it formerly did those of Mrs. Calvin Coolidge and Mrs. Herbert Hoover. Active leaders in the AAUW and in other Washington organizations are: Mrs. Richard Hogue, Mrs. Wilson Compton, Mrs. John Jay O'Connor, Mrs. Joshua Evans, Jr., Mrs. Philip Sidney Smith, Miss Harlean James, executive secretary of the American Civic Association, Mrs. Helen Duey Hoffman, executive secretary of the Washington Housing Association, Dr. Mary Louise Brown, Dean of Women at American University, Mrs. Lucy Madeira Wing, head of the Madeira School, Judge Fay L. Bentley, of the Juvenile Court, Mrs. Gregory (Charlotte) Hankin, an authority on legal procedure, Miss Margaret M. Hanna, formerly American Consul at Geneva. Dr. Harriet Elliott, only woman appointed to the National Defense Commission, Miss Marguerite M. Wells, president of the National League of Women Voters, Mrs. Harvey W. Wiley, pure-food crusader and active in the National Woman's Party, Mrs. John L. Whitehurst, president of the General Federation of Women's Clubs, Miss Marion Martin, director of the women's division of the Republican National Committee, and Mrs. Howell Moorhead, of the Foreign Policy Association.

A few personalities stand out among Washington women, apart from official life, their careers or the part they take in organized club activities:

Mrs. Alice Roosevelt Longworth, daughter of Teddy Roosevelt but antagonistic to the present Roosevelts, who has been closely associated with the great of both political parties all her life. Mrs. Henry Grattan Doyle, who has served on the Board of Education for 13 years and as its Chairman for 6, and been interested in many civic and humanitarian causes. Mrs. Jean Bennett, who took over the superintendency of the Central Union Mission when her husband, its founder, died, and, in addition, is national president of the Soroptimist Clubs. Miss Mabel T. Boardman, of the American Red Cross. Mrs. Dwight Davis, the former Mrs. Charles Sabin, who is serving as Chairman of the American Red Cross Volunteer Service. Mrs. Jouett Shouse (Catherine Filene Dodd) whose particular interest is in the problems of the training and placement of women in the professional fields. The Army's first woman major, Julia C. Stimson, who as director of the Army Nurse Corps of the AEF in 1918 was decorated with the D.S.M. and given a citation by General Pershing. Another Army nurse who wears the D.S.M., Miss Dora E. Thompson, former superintendent of the Army Nurse Corps. Miss Janet Fish, recently retired Superintendent of Nurses at Emergency Hospital, who won the Legion d'Honneur for her distinguished war service. Mary Mason, known as "Cousin Mary" to women radio fans all over the country. Mrs. Gifford Pinchot, energetic campaigner and individualist.

Scores of prominent women are now directing their energies into the American Women's Voluntary Services and other defense activities: Mrs. Raymond Lee, Miss Anita Phipps, Mrs. Preston Delano, Mrs. Walter Lippmann, Mrs. Archibald MacLeish, Mrs. James Forrestal, Mrs. Donald Church, Mrs. Eugene Meyer, Mrs. G. Howland Chase, Mrs. Alan Kirk and Mrs. Emily Newell Blair.

The present war has raised the military status of women another peg with the recent commission of Army Nurses Julia O. Flikke as colonel and Florence A. Blanchfield as lieutenant colonel.

What Are Women Like?

It is apparent that women are not a unit on any public issue. They are not overwhelmingly Democrats, or Republicans, or conservatives, or liberals, or prohibitionists or anti-prohibitionists, or pro-war or anti-war. They are influenced in their attitudes by their training and backgrounds, just as men are. Women in government now have a "liberal" tinge, but that is true also of the men in government, and is an accompaniment of the New Deal. Another fairly good generalization is that women in public life often have a personal approach to issues, rather than the impersonal approach which men try to cultivate. The personal approach is sometimes a handicap to smooth operations in the hurly-burly of politics and government.

Generally, women have "humane" interests, they are concerned with social welfare and are found in the forefront of movements which have to do with bettering living and working conditions.

The woman influence is a wholesome influence in Washington, and it is likely to be much more potent in the future than at present. Public men doubtless will have to learn to work more with public women . . . and like it.

28

Lawyers' Paradise

THERE is one place where all Washington lawyers in private practice come together. It is not in a lawyers' club. It is not at the local bar association. It is not at the District of Columbia Court House, for most Washington lawyers have little truck with the Court House. It is not in any particular government department, or restaurant, or hotel, or other hangout. It is in the telephone book, the classified section in the rear, the yellow pages.

There they are—seven solid pages, 28 solid columns, 3,000 lawyers, preceded by "Lawn Mowers," followed by "Leather Goods." Further on in the directory come the Patent Attorneys, 600 of them. The total number of Washington lawyers engaged in private practice is somewhere close to 4,000.

Add about 4,000 more lawyers within government, who act as attorneys, legal counsel, legal advisers, legal draftsmen or legal administrators of legal procedures under legal regulations. And add hundreds of others who hold non-legal jobs and dream of the day when they will break out of government, land a few good cases and really practice law.

The grand total of private practitioners and lawyers in government is over 10,000. A city swarming with lawyers. No other American city of comparable size has as many lawyers.

What do those in private practice earn? It is impossible to know definitely. Some make hardly enough for existence, some of them make about $5,000 a year, perhaps 50 per cent $5,000-$10,000 a year. Probably not more than 5 per cent earn over $20,000 a year, though every once in a while you will hear—doubtless correctly—that Lawyer So-and-So took in a $100,000 fee. It is the composite opinion of a number of Washington attorneys that lawyers' incomes are "considerably higher" than the average in other cities.

Walk down the corridor of almost any Washington office building, and you'll think you've wandered into a center for the legal profession, like the Bar Building in New York. You'll see lawyers in every business building of the "uptown" area, within a few blocks of the White House—the National Press Building, Munsey Building, Colorado Building, Washington Building, Investment Building, Woodward Building, Shoreham Building, Union Trust Building, Southern Building, Tower Building, Transportation Building. The signs on the doors read "Lawyer," "Lawyers," "Attorneys at law," "Patent Attorney," "Tax Consultant," "Law Offices," "Legal Counsel."

Some of the lawyers have imposing offices with reception halls and switchboard operators, and some have little cubbyholes without even a clerk. There are plenty of offices where several practitioners share expenses. Some offices are sublet, after regular working hours, to "sun-downers"—government employees by day, legal counselors at night. Even at home addresses are other law offices.

What you won't find in Washington is the kind of "legal factories" that flourish in Philadelphia, Chicago and New York, with ten names on the letterhead and 20 gilded on the door. The largest Washington law firm has no more than 30 attorneys, while New York has a number of "factories" employing more than 100. There is a tendency these days, however, for large outside firms to establish branches in Washington, and many lawyers expect Washington some day to have a number of "law factories."

Most Washington lawyers are not general practitioners. They are specialists, and they practice their specialties within government administrative agencies. They practice what is called "administrative law." Their special fields are taxes, patents, radio, railroad rates, maritime law, and others. They "practice government."

Only a few come under the head of "influence lawyers." Some there are, spectacular on occasion, and when they stick out their necks they get into the news, but actually they form only a small percentage of all Washington lawyers. Mainly the influence men are ex-members of Congress, or politicians who have come to town to play politics and remain to pick up any fruits that drop from political boughs. A handful really have pull, but most who claim it do not have it. And when they have it, their haymaking lasts only a few years. Within this brief period, most of them fail to make a killing. Thereafter they settle down to routine practice of routine cases, or to business getting.

There are, too, some lawyer-members of Congress who keep membership in their firms back home. These local firms may have some close connections with a Washington firm which, in turn, becomes "close to" the Gentleman from Podunk. And most successful lawyers depend on influence to bolster their regular business, and they make a practice of entertaining with dinners, lunches, smokers and golf parties. So "drag" does make itself felt, but lawyers who rely entirely on it are the exceptions.

Overrated, too, are the personal advantages of government alumni who go into private practice. Many of the lawyer specialists in Washington have served an apprenticeship with government, but what they have gained is a knowledge of the ropes, the procedures, the workings of federal agencies rather than favoritism from personnel.

There's another rather widely known group of Washington lawyers who do work with no technical name. It might be called "contact work." It involves systematic "nosing about," "feeling the pulse of things," making acquaintances who can give straight dope on the probable course of public policies. It isn't really legal work, it's intelligence work. Some lawyers of this class are shrewd appraisers of public movements and good judges of political tides.

Tax Specialists

Biggest group consists of the tax lawyers, for tax matters create more differences between individuals or corporations and the United States than any other type of case. More tax cases go to the Supreme Court than any other kind of case. They are 15 per cent of the whole volume of the Court's work. The Bureau of Internal Revenue—a branch of the Treasury—occupies a whole building on Constitution Avenue. There is perennial talk of the simplification of tax laws to make the formalities easier on the taxpayer. Each year many procedures are simplified, or standardized. But each year some new taxes, involving new procedures, are added by Congress. Thus the load of tax complications mounts from year to year. When each new tax law comes along, taxpayers groan, but it means more business for tax lawyers. Within the fraternity each new tax law is called a "lawyers' relief act."

Accountants share much of the tax work. They are specialists in figures, but they also know much about tax law and many of them know more about it than some of the lawyers. Accountants figure the government's share on the books and put it into the records. They are the nurses on the job all the time, assisting the tax lawyers who are the doctors called in when things go wrong. Washington abounds with accountants, practicing taxes.

Patent Lawyers

Second in number, among the capital's legal fraternity, are the patent lawyers. And the practice is an old one. Drama and romance color the history of the Patent Office as well as of individual inventions. During the War of 1812, when the British captured Washington, legend has it that one Dr. Thornton, head of the Office, thrust himself before the cannon of the soldiers who had already burned the Capitol. "Are you Englishmen or only Goths and Vandals?" he yelled. "This is the Patent Office, a depository of the ingenuity of the American nation, in which the whole civilized world is interested. Fire away, and let the charge pass through my body!" The soldiers were so shamed that the depository of ingenuity was spared for posterity, inventors, and the Patent Bar.

Today, 70,000 applications for patents pour in to the Office annually. Some of them come to nothing; others make history. Patenting an invention is like putting up a "Keep Off" sign. For 17 years, the owner of a patent has the right to sue if anyone makes or sells the process or device for which the patent was granted. The idea is simple enough, but getting your monopoly is not so simple. You call in a patent expert to make a search among the 2,500,000 American patents classified and subclassified and sub-subclassified in the Office files, to make sure there hasn't been any "prior use and anticipation of the art." You depend on him to put your verbal and diagrammatic claims to novelty, etc., etc., in shape for the Patent Office Examiner. If he establishes your claims, you get your patent. If someone else has had the same bright idea at the same time, both your representatives plead your causes in "interference proceedings." If the examiner won't grant your patent, your attorney can appeal first to the Patent Office Board of Appeals, and if he is still unsuccessful he can go to the Court of Customs and Patent Appeals.

Some Washington patent law firms are branches of outfits in other cities, some are exclusively Washington. Some get most of their business referred by other lawyers, some are on retainer from large corporations, and some draw business from the general public. The American Patent Law Association has long kicked about the men who advertise as "patent attorneys" but who aren't lawyers. The Patent Bar maintains they should call themselves "patent agents." For many years their alluring notices of fortunes through patents have been sent by mail, and placed in farm journals and popular scientific and mechanical magazines. These advertisements have stirred many a dreamer into patenting an invention, but some of the practitioners who do not advertise feel that the advertising serves the purpose of increasing the quantity of worthless devices. Admission to Patent Office practice has been tightening in recent years and all applicants must now pass an examination.

Undoubtedly the move of much of the Patent Office to Richmond will cause inconvenience, but it will not destroy Washington as the Patent Capital.

Other Specialists

The Federal Communications Bar Association has 285 members—about half of them located in Washington. Federal regulations on radio cover more than 200 closely-printed pages. To run a radio station—whether it be for commercial broadcasting, wireless telegraph and wireless telephone, for ships at sea, for airport ground stations, for police cars, or just for fun— you must be licensed by the Commission. And a license is no more permanent than a permanent wave, for it must be renewed at least every three years. Some renewals, as well as each issuance of a license, mean business for radio lawyers.

For some 200 Washington lawyers who practice before the Interstate Commerce Commission 55 is a lucky number. The Commission just celebrated its 55th birthday, and it administers 55 different laws regulating interstate railroad, motor and water transportation.

Now and then some of the Commission's functions have been taken over by other agencies—airplane regulation by the Civil Aeronautics Administration, telephone and telegraph by the FCC. But others have been added— busses and trucks in 1935, water carriers in 1940—so the specialists haven't suffered.

The ICC has a bar of its own, its Association of Interstate Commerce Commission Practitioners, lawyers and traffic representatives, with headquarters right in the ICC building. Admission to practice before the Commission is stiffer than before any other government agency except the Patent Office. The special bar has about 2300 members—the 200 Washington ICC lawyers plus approximately 1000 other lawyers, and about 1100 trafficmen, who practice ICC matters out around the country.

A handful of Washington law firms specialize in Court of Claims practice. Though Court of Claims lawyers are relatively few in number, their earnings give a substantial lift to the general average of Washington lawyers' earnings.

The Court of Claims, located for years across Pennsylvania Avenue from the State Department, is the special court where you may sue the United States. Claims against the government by contractors who have built things for the government, by Indian tribes, by large taxpayers, run into astronomical figures every year.

The Court of Claims has been called the "Unknown Court." Considering the size of the matters that come before it, and that it is a high court, reversible only by the Supreme Court (and even then on matters of law, not fact), the Court is singularly unpublicized. Many lawyers in general practice know nothing or little about it.

More than 25 coal specialists represent the interests of about 12,000 coal companies before the Bituminous Coal Division. Labor lawyers represent unions before the National Labor Relations Board. The bulk of labor practice is localized in cities throughout the country, but every now and then a case begun in Seattle, Chicago or Pittsburgh ends up in Washing-

315

ton. The general counsels of both the AFofL and the CIO have head-quarters here. The Department of Agriculture benefits lawyers through litigation arising from the operations of the marketing regulations.

Lawyers must be specially admitted to practice before some federal agencies. Some commissions or administrations require more complicated admission forms than others, but in general, admission is perfunctory, and requires little more than a sworn statement that the applicant is in good standing with a local bar.

As might be expected, lawyers' associations mushroom in Washington. There's the Federal Bar Association, composed of lawyers in government employ, the Women's Bar Association of the District of Columbia, the Association of Interstate Commerce Commission Practitioners, the American Patent Law Association, the Washington Bar Association, colored. And a club, the Barristers' Club. The Lawyers' Guild, left-wing organization, started out strong a few years ago with both intra and extra government members, but has become a negligible influence in Washington.

The Bar Association of the District of Columbia, once dominated by the local lawyers or general practice lawyers, now increasingly draws members in federal practice. It is currently trying to merge the various associations within itself, and so create a really strong bar association organized in sections.

Administrative Practice

Most Washington lawyers handling matters before federal bodies function under what is called administrative law. Administrative practice merely means that you take up your business with officials in the executive branch (or in an independent commission) instead of in the judicial branch of the government, that you litigate before an executive bureau or an independent board instead of before judges in a courtroom. Administrative tribunals make regulations that have the force of law and decisions that usually have the force of legal judgments, although sometimes only the basis for getting judgments in court.

The government has been under fire for the growth of administrative law, and the way in which it is handled. About a year ago a majority bill and a minority bill on the subject were up in Congress. The bills were designed to simplify administrative procedure, to make it uniform among the multiplicity of agencies, to have a common tribunal for appeal, to correct some of the abuses such as day-to-day shifts in provisions. The bills came to nothing.

One of the most common criticisms of the extension of administrative law is that it concentrates too much legislative and judicial authority in the executive branch of the government, and that it may tend to create an arrogant bureaucracy. Another criticism is that cases may be decided by subordinate officials on evidence that may have been colored by the reports of government investigators. In favor of more administrative law, the argument is that it prevents clogging of the courts, and that it expedites the handling of many matters that are essentially administrative rather than legal. Whatever the arguments, nearly all the experts agree now that administrative reform is a sleeping issue until the end of the war.

Government Lawyers

The growth of big government in Washington naturally has meant the rapid growth of the number of government lawyers. Just as outside lawyers specialize in certain fields of federal law, so do thousands of government lawyers specialize in the particular laws for which their government agencies are responsible. Executive officials of the government seldom take important action without counsel of their legal advisers. Every executive order must conform to the laws of Congress, and it is the job of the government lawyers to see that executive acts jibe with the law.

There is a lot of court work for government lawyers. Federal district attorneys are directly in charge of handling litigation for the federal government in the district and circuit courts. But in recent years so many complicated special laws have been enacted that district attorneys often are baffled, and call on specialists from the various government departments to help them handle their cases in the federal courts.

Many government lawyers are political or policy lawyers, directly responsible to high officials in charge of determining government policy. In nearly all government agencies, however, there are numerous professional lawyers who take no interest in policy matters, but do technical jobs in drafting orders, rules, and regulations and advising their superiors as to the ramifications of the law. These career men usually are glad to go through life as government lawyers, hoping to work up to the $6,000 to $8,500 range. (Less than one-third ever get there.)

A special committee headed by Supreme Court Justice Stanley Reed made recommendations in 1941 concerning the enrollment and appointment of lawyers in the government service. The Reed report urged the merit system for government lawyers but asked for a separate board to deal with lawyer appointments, and such a board was created.

The system now is this: Lawyers who want government legal jobs may file application with the Civil Service Commission. But actual certification for appointments is supposed to be made by the special Board of Legal Examiners, after a noncompetitive examination. This is the official theory, but in practice employing officers still get their lawyers wherever they can find them. The lawyers in due course may be given civil service status, but many are not.

The confusion as to civil service for lawyers is due mainly to the fact that Congress is suspicious of the special board and has failed to vote money for its operations. Many congressmen think this board is dominated by Harvard influences, and that one effect of its operation would be to load the government with lawyers from Harvard Law School and New York City. It seems likely, however, that efforts to raise the status of government lawyers will bear fruit. The policy now is systematically to recruit the best men graduating from the law schools, to make government service attractive as a career.

More Laws, More Lawyers

Government laws and regulations get more and more complicated. Often the laws of Congress lay down merely general rules, to be applied by the administrative agencies charged with enforcement. Closer and more intimate are growing the relationships between citizens and government. Deeper and deeper into the affairs of citizens the government is going. The zones of frictions and disputes multiply. Wherever there are legal disputes, there also are lawyers. It is no wonder that Washington has become a paradise for lawyers.

29

Trade Association Men

JOE HOLLINGSWORTH of Akron is a manufacturer and he belongs to the local Chamber of Commerce, and through it he is represented in Washington in a general sort of way. Also he belongs to the state manufacturers' association, and through it he is represented in Washington and in a somewhat more specific sort of way. Also he knows his congressmen and his senators, and he sees them three or four times a year, but they are pretty busy and so is he, and they have "Washington ideas" which seem fancy to him, and he thinks they don't represent him especially well.

But Joe Hollingsworth belongs to a trade association, and he calls the executive director by his first name. The association's offices are in Washington, and Joe gets a bulletin every week telling about Washington things in general, and Washington plans affecting his industry in particular. So he feels close to his trade association representative in Washington, and he tells him how he feels about things, and he gets advice in return. The working relations are very close.

In Washington the trade association man is in touch with government men who are working on policies affecting his industry. He tells them things, and they tell him things, and he writes Joe and the other members of the association. That's the way in which Joe is most accurately and specifically represented in Washington. No one ever thinks of calling the trade association man in Washington an ambassador of business, but that's really what he is.

The trade association man goes up to the Capitol now and then and sees some member of a committee which is considering a bill that his industry likes, or perhaps dislikes. He gives the congressman some information on the probable effects. To that extent he's a "lobbyist," but he doesn't spend much of his time at it. Other days he is busy seeing some downtown officials, or statisticians, or government lawyers, about the new regulations which affect his industry. He helps them and they help him to work the thing out. He writes to his members and tells them how things stand. They don't always like it, and sometimes they scold him, and sometimes he scolds them, and takes the part of the government, and tells them they've got to be long-visioned about this thing. Sometimes he lectures his members about "public policy," and "social vision," and the "inevitability" of this or that. Maybe some of them think he is fancy, but most of them take it.

At the end of the year, members of the association meet in convention, have some speeches, some committee meetings, a few drinks, a concluding banquet in the tuxedos which they brought along (the wives are there too), and they re-elect the Washington man, and he goes back to his job. None of the members of the trade association would ever think of calling their man an "economic statesman," and he would be embarrassed if they should, but that, too, is what he really is.

The days are over when a trade association man was just a hail-fellow-well-met. Now he's a hard-working man, with as many bosses as he has members of his association, and one Super-Boss, which is the United States government. He runs a pumping station with a two-way flow of ideas—one from his members to the government, and one from the government to his members. He's a sort of perpetual trouble shooter. He must know his politics, his business practices, and his economic theory. He must keep in touch with the representatives of other industries, and collaborate with them on inter-industry problems. He's a Jack-of-all-trades, and a master of one—that of being a Washington trade association executive.

There are about 150 of these men in Washington. They form a sphere of their own, and they are probably the best-informed small group in the capital. Man for man they know more about what is going on beneath the surface than the average official, or the average member of Congress, or the average newspaperman. They don't blab everything they know, but they know.

How It Works

The trade association is a utilitarian device. It is an organization formed by individual business units engaged in a certain line of work in all parts of the country. The idea is that the association as a cooperative movement can do many things to help the individual businessman which such individuals could not possibly do for themselves. Overhead expenses are usually shared on a pro rata basis—the $10,000,000-a-year business pays about ten times as much as the $1,000,000-a-year business. While the purpose is basically to promote profits, most trade associations of today are farsighted and know that self-interest requires them to fit business policies into public policy. The few which fail to do this generally get into trouble.

Hundreds of industries have professional organization executives outside of Washington, but the number in the capital is continually increasing. As government grows more and more centralized and as government regulation is broadened to cover almost every form of business enterprise it becomes a matter of necessity for businessmen to have someone at the center of regulation who will guide and advise them. And government officials regularly call in these men for consultation and advice on technical and policy matters. The amount of time thus spent by many trade representatives is enormous.

Legislation

Are these men lobbyists? To some extent most of them are. And yet almost none of them are lobbyists as that term is commonly understood. Most of them do undertake to influence legislation and government policies, which is the right of all citizens when their interests are at stake. But they are not "buttonholers." Generally they have the background which permits them to advise key members of their industries as to what to do in order to see that proposed measures deal fairly with them. Thus, if you hear or read that Manufacturer A or Retailer B or Banker C has testified before a congressional committee, you can be pretty sure that some on-the-job Washington trade executive weeks ago organized the presentation of the case for his industry. These Washington trade experts know that congressmen prefer to hear from active principals in an industry rather than from their Washington hired men. They know the lobbying techniques, however, and time and again they turn on the heat in their own way when there seems to be need for it. But this kind of pressure work is a minor part of the activities of the trade representatives. Most trade groups are too small numerically to exercise much voter pressure, and so they must rely mostly on skillful presentation of the merits and the facts of their cases and on educational work at the grass roots.

Antitrust

Antitrust laws have long been a special worry for trade associations. The suspicion lurks in the minds of many government prosecutors that, as one of them puts it, "all businessmen are price-fixers at heart," and that industries are inclined to use their trade associations as devices for price fixing, monopoly and restraint of trade. There is always some basis for this suspicion but there was more basis in the past than now. At various times certain trade groups, a decided minority, have been "caught" and convicted of antitrust law violations. And others have inched close to the borderline, relying on counsel to keep them just barely within the law.

A mitigating circumstance for these borderline cases is that the government's own policy has fluctuated with respect to enforcement of antitrust laws. The Hoover administration undertook to sanction certain intra-industry joint actions through so-called standard trade practices as approved by the Federal Trade Commission and the Department of Justice. Then the Roosevelt regime went whole hog for formal industry cooperation on prices, wages, cost accounting and sales policies. This was the era of NRA codes, set up and policed under the whip and spur of General Hugh S. Johnson.

After the death of NRA, the government turned again to free competition and strict enforcement of the antitrust laws. Then exigencies of war produced another shift in government policy, and industries were in effect invited to "combine" on many activities involving industry-wide collaboration.

The trade associations are vital links in tying industry into the war production program. They act as service channels on policy, information, and coordination—as go-betweens for businessmen and government men. They set up an advisory committee of the American Trade Association Executives, which meets frequently for luncheon and threshes out with some invited government official the many acute problems for industry which have arisen from government activities and especially from war efforts.

Individual industries also have their own advisory committees to consult regularly with war production officials on all matters concerning the industry's part in meeting the wartime requirements. These committees are technically separate from the trade associations, partly because of past skirmishes over antitrust disputes, but actually they utilize the services of the Washington trade executives in much of their work.

The over-all interests of business as a whole are promoted by such national organizations as the Chamber of Commerce of the United States. A large number of trade groups, as constituent members, help to finance and support the work of the Chamber in promoting national policies favorable to the business community. While the Chamber maintains a special service division to assist trade associations, it does not attempt to influence their specific programs and policies.

The National Association of Manufacturers in Washington does for manufacturing the same sort of job that the Chamber of Commerce does for business as a whole. The NAM is manned by men who are doing a creditable job of keeping members informed as to fast-growing developments in the field of business-government relationships.

A "Profession"?

While trade association executives often have conflicting purposes in Washington they are, nevertheless, highly congenial and gregarious. They do not think of their work as a "profession" but in the course of years there have grown up standards and practices which may be regarded as professional ethics and operating techniques.

Each summer at Northwestern University there is a one-week course of instruction which is attended by many trade executives who want to brush up on new ideas and new organization techniques. A certificate of graduation is awarded to those who have done a certain amount of work in these courses.

Trade executives are paid well. Representative salaries range from $7,500 to $25,000 a year. Expenses for maintaining an office and staff are provided by the association. Some of the larger industries require the services of a big staff, with specialists handling certain phases of the association's work.

Along with the growth of trade association work in Washington there has been a corresponding expansion in the coverage of Washington activities by the trade journals. These trade paper men and the trade executives work closely together, feeding each other information and conferring frequently on trends and prospects.

The Men

A few of the trade association men have become public figures and are recognized as leaders of thought in their own right. Such men are Dr. Wilson Compton, secretary-manager of the National Lumber Manufacturers Association; Pyke Johnson, president of the Automotive Safety Foundation, formerly executive vice president of the Automobile Manufacturers Association; Charles J. Brand, executive secretary of the National Fertilizer Association; V. P. Ahearn, executive secretary, National Sand and Gravel Association; and Bond Geddes, executive vice president, Radio Manufacturers Association.

Many other trade association men are of comparable weight and highly effective, and generally know more about the trend of public policies than nine out of ten congressmen. Among them are William L. Daley (once Billy Sunday's publicity man) of the American Publishers Conference, A. M. Ferry of wire cloth, Herman Fakler of the millers, Charles P. Garvin of stationers, Chester H. Gray of highway users, John A. Logan of food chain stores, Hector Lazo of retailer co-ops, Neville Miller of broadcasters, Warren N. Watson of chemicals, Louis B. Montfort of bottle caps, Harold R. Young of retail dry goods, Edgar F. Fowler of small loan companies, Robert C. Hibben of ice cream, John D. Battle of coal, Julian D. Conover of mining, H. C. Berckes of southern pine, and Charles Holman of milk producers.

Scores of interesting stories could be told about things done for the public by those men and by Douglas Whitlock of clay products, John E. Walker of cellulose, George N. Walker of laundries, Arthur P. Hall of aluminum, S. Walter Stauffer of lime, R. H. Rowe of wholesale grocers, John J. Riley of soda pop, A. C. Oliphant of power, M. J. McMillan of cement, John V. Lawrence of motor trucks, Rowland Jones, Jr. of druggists, David R. Craig of retail trade, and Charles F. Baldwin of credit men. And there are dozens of other able trade executives who represent scrap iron, crushed stone, tanning, paint, whisky, petroleum, power, binder twine, slag, oysters, road machinery, restaurants, and almost anything else you use or buy.

New Trend

Even before war, government power and authority was expanding, and businessmen were being drawn closer to government as it took over functions they used to exercise. Now, there are such new questions as how to pool workers and tools and facilities within industries, and even among a number of industries, to get the most war stuff in the shortest time. The trade association executives know many things about their own industries, and a lot of things about other industries too.

A new economy is bound to grow out of the ferment of these times. The way trade association executives and their members conduct themselves now will go far toward determining the position of trade associations in the postwar economy.

30

Think Factories

YOU are familiar with the process of thinking up an idea to be put to work. You do it and you see it done—in the family, the school, the neighborhood, the city, factory, office, and in all other groups of which you are a part. Someone has an idea, and gets to thinking and talking. Others get the idea, and do their own thinking and talking. It is criticized, torn to pieces, put together again in better form, and tried out. Maybe it works and maybe it doesn't. Anyway, that's the way new things start— with ideas and thinking, with crazy plans which gradually become less crazy, and which sometimes even go so far as to work.

It's the same in government. There's no essential difference between the thinking and planning in Washington, and the thinking and planning in your own private affairs, your factory, office or kitchen. It's all human, clumsy, faulty, but moving along toward new things which usually turn out to be better. Government thinking and planning is done on a bigger and broader scale than your own. It is done by groups of men, institutions. They include the researchers, analysts, statisticians, economists, planners, professors, scholars, theorists, and doctors of philosophy. They include the dreamers, who often turn dreams into substance. They represent erudition set to work, imagination harnessed. They are the "think factories."

Thinking is one of the chief activities of government. You can see it, hear it, read it, and you can feel the results in the policies of government. Every policy starts with thinking by the thinkers. Some of these thinkers are amateurs, laymen, and some are professionals, working hard at thinking, as at any job. So this is the story of these professionals, and of the mass production of plans and ideas which pour out from the think factories.

Congress votes the laws, of course. But in many cases, before a bill in Congress gets much public notice, certain idea men have quietly spent years in planning the legislation, working up supporting data, getting the backing of influential persons, and perhaps actually drafting the bill itself. That is the way laws are often made.

The ideas themselves evolve from the past—the confluence of thousands of little thoughts springing from thousands of minds and stimulated by individual human experiences with the successes and failures of our economic and social system. The little thoughts rise up in the minds of persons who seek to improve the system, are treated, tested, agitated, and in due course become big ideas or concrete plans for the future. The process involves research, discussion, and often extensive hearings or investigations by congressional committees or public agencies, and the formulation of theories by professional thinkers. These theories come to light through new books, reports, speeches, espousal by public officials and politicians.

The professional theorists on the pay rolls of dozens of government bureaus and agencies are of many sizes and shapes. Some are officials with big titles, others are second-string officials, many have good salaries but no titles, and many others plug away inconspicuously at small pay, doing the preparatory drudgery for the upper-crust men who get most of the credit for the big ideas.

The top group, the elite of the brain trust, who initiate, plan and organize the researches and studies which later mature into concrete programs of action probably numbers about 100 members. These are the men whose brain power and zeal give life to abstract ideas and often convert them into public policies. Most of the major new legislation of the past ten years was devised by this group.

Thinkers of the Past

Professional thinkers were active in Washington long before Roosevelt. Even Hoover, Coolidge, Wilson and Taft had their idea men, their commissions and expert advisers. In fact, governments of all ages have had their counterparts of what people now call the brain trust.

The Federal Trade Commission Act and Federal Reserve Act of the Wilson administration were preceded by years of work and agitation by the "young liberals" of that era. The Pujo investigation of banking abuses and weaknesses during the Taft administration was a job of analysis by experts, frequently criticized as theorists, but in time it bore fruit in the form of a basic remodeling of our national banking system. Dr. Frank W. Fetter of Princeton University and Huston Thompson of Colorado, both now elder statesmen, were the 1913 counterparts of the Tugwells and Corcorans of the New Deal. The probe of the "power trust" by the Federal Trade Commission in the Coolidge regime was a first skirmish of the reformers who kept up the campaign until they got what they wanted in the Public Utility Act of 1935. The Gifford Pinchot of 1904-08, preaching nationalization of forests, was called radical by the conservatives of his day, but his cause was won and in due course ceased to be regarded as a radical idea. Radicals of the past become the conservatives of the future.

In the Hoover administration, dozens of special commissions were created to study national problems, using university professors, professional economists and students of social organization. Critics sneered at Hoover's "amateurs" as they later poked fun at the New Dealers, but the studies of the Hoover commissions are now being uncovered for reference, and the reports of his Committee on Recent Economic Changes constitute a treasure chest of source material which students will explore for many years to come.

Hoover at heart was more of an idea man and planner than a politician. In the course of his years as Secretary of Commerce and as President, he inspired and directed basic studies of the problems of unemployment, wastes in industry, wastes in distribution, use of public works to soften depressions, housing reforms and street and highway safety. He started movements in the fields of child health, unemployment compensation and old-age pensions which paved the way for later major reforms. Head thinker and planner for much of the Hoover program was Edward Eyre Hunt, clearly the No. 1 brain truster of the pre-Roosevelt period. Many researchers and specialists who contributed to the Hoover studies later served in the New Deal organization. Thinking and planning did not start with the New Deal.

Idea Spree of New Deal

What the New Deal did was to expand tremendously the corps of thinkers and idea men. The Roosevelt regime was committed to change. It encouraged the thinkers to "let their minds be bold." Many of the moves of the early Roosevelt administration were essentially opportunistic rather than parts of a well-coordinated program. The President himself seemed to be bent on experiment, quick to take a chance on new ideas and intent on speed. This attitude was an open invitation to the flock of enthusiastic bright young idea men who moved into the Washington scene.

The think job of 1933 was almost boundless. It covered the whole life of the nation. Questioning of all past traditions and social organizations was the official mood. Here, there, and yonder the new recruits from the universities started digging into the workings of virtually all established institutions. Banks were closed and had to be reorganized, with deposits insured by the government. Drastic new policies for raising the status of farmers were quickly formulated. Gold was pushed from its pedestal and a new policy of "managed-money" was adopted. Reprehensible practices of investment bankers, stock market operators, and giant holding companies

327

were attacked at the roots and far-reaching reforms were scheduled. In like manner, the new group of zealots brought into being major systems of old-age pensions, unemployment compensation, standards for wages and hours, collective bargaining for labor unions, and job relief for the unemployed.

The Brain Trust

One thought that dominated much of the bold thinking of the early stages of the New Deal, was that we live in a man-made economy, and that traditional economic laws are not immutable. The theory of *laissez-faire* was ridiculed, denounced, discarded. But the New Deal thinkers were not a unit, not all working within a fixed pattern. They often worked at cross-purposes. Some of the most vigorous members of the brain trust were nationalistic in their concepts, and were powerful enough virtually to wreck the World Economic Conference of 1933. This was the time when Roosevelt's most trusted monetary adviser was the late Professor George F. Warren of Cornell University, who sold the President the notion that many of the economic maladjustments of the country could be corrected simply by raising or lowering the gold content of the dollar.

The original Roosevelt brain trust came under the leadership of Raymond Moley of Columbia University, and this group charted the main course in 1933-34. The Moley men made history, but many of them later moved out of the Washington arena.

Big names of the Moley phase were Adolf Berle, Charles W. Taussig, Rexford G. Tugwell, Gardiner C. Means, Felix Frankfurter and Samuel I. Rosenman. Taussig went back to the molasses business in New York. Tugwell made a tremendous splash as Under Secretary of Agriculture but was ahead of the times, was squeezed out, and later became Governor of Puerto Rico. Frankfurter, working from behind the scenes, placed hundreds of his protégés in important government positions and in due course was made a justice of the Supreme Court. Berle, who won his spurs as a New Dealer by critical denouncement of orthodox banking practices, was not a one-idea man, and as Assistant Secretary of State he sparked bold and novel ideas for the conduct of foreign affairs. Means, in various unpublicized government jobs, quietly but effectively, continued to plug for his concept of a government-planned and directed national economy. Rosenman, a New York State judge, never held federal office, but has held the President's hand, fed him ideas, inspiration, and suggestions for dealing with many troublesome problems.

Moley and his adherents concentrated on the problem of business recovery. They wanted to correct abuses in the economic system, to repair the existing structure rather than to wreck it or replace it. The ill-fated National Recovery Administration was one of their main undertakings. Within a year or two, however, a more daring and belligerent group with an instinct for "fanging the enemy in the jugular vein," gained ascendancy in White House councils and Moley departed. Those who then came into high influence sought a complete remaking of the American economy.

Critics have complained that the New Deal lacked a fixed philosophy, failed to chart a course and then stick to it. There were grounds for such complaints. There was much flopping around, and often government policies seemed to point in conflicting directions. What certain zealots were doing to curb farm production and raise prices seemed contrary to the needs of the millions being carried on relief by the WPA. Promoters of public ownership in the electric power industry seemed to thwart the SEC and Power Commission reformers who said they wanted to put private investment securities on a sound basis that would invite investor confidence. Government favoritism toward union labor went so far that Chairman Eccles of the Federal Reserve System publicly warned of overreaching by the unions as a threat to business recovery. Then there was the intra-New Deal split over antitrust law enforcement—some insisted on real competition at all costs and others urged the NRA type of government-supervised industry combinations and price fixing. There were many other conflicts.

The TNEC

This policy turmoil was brought strongly to light in the business slump of 1937-38. There was both internal and external demand for some standardization of the product of the think factories. Leon Henderson, Isador Lubin, Thurman Arnold, and a few others got the President to ask Congress for an investigation of the causes of unemployment and the laggard habits of private capital. The Temporary National Economic Committee was created for this purpose. The New Deal sponsors knew pretty well in advance what they expected to reveal, but needed a public forum. In the course of several months of public hearings, the probers hauled over the coals the insurance companies, the investment bankers, the steel industry, the patent monopolies, and other representatives of bigness in business. The hearings were shrewdly staged. There was grumbling from some of the witnesses that it was a frame-up, with no fair opportunity for the "accused" to be heard. The investigators insisted that they were out to diagnose the ills of the economic system and not to punish anyone. At the end they produced tomes of diagnosis and remedial prescriptions. The coming of war in 1939 smothered these TNEC reports, but some day they will be resuscitated and studied, and they probably will furnish footing for government economic planning of the future.

So the New Deal gamut of ideas was run—from rebellion against depression in 1933, through the various phases of monetary tinkering, farm relief, public works, NRA, trust-busting, and TNEC, to the current concepts of a government-supervised economy for war-making purposes, and for adaptation to the postwar economy.

Policing the Planners

Gradually there has come about a greater degree of coordination of the planners and thinkers. The war pressure has expedited this, and will expedite it still further. But even before 1939 the President had centered in his National Resources Planning Board considerable responsibility for relating the thought functions of various groups. The President's uncle, Frederic A. Delano, headed the Board and gave it dignity. Prof. Charles E. Merriam of Chicago University and Prof. Luther H. Gulick of Columbia University were pulled into the NRPB and have recruited other professional planners. The director of the staff, through the Board's busy years, has been Charles W. Eliot II, grandson and namesake of Harvard's famous president, Charles W. Eliot.

The NRPB tries to prod other government groups into coordinating their thinking and studies in accordance with certain sets of ideas which have semi-official White House approval. There is a conscious attempt to decentralize the thinking function and to spur researchers to find fresh and original approaches to problems. But aimless wandering in the realms of research is frowned upon. The top idea men formulate certain hypotheses, toss them out to the various collaborating groups for testing and analysis, and then guide the various studies toward the evolving of concrete plans and specific charts for policy-making.

Early in his term of office Roosevelt stressed the slogan of improving the lot of "the one-third of the people who are ill-fed, ill-clad, and ill-housed." But it was not until later that the NRPB completed an extensive study of the data to support that slogan.

This study, a statistical analysis of family incomes of all classes of American people, was typical of many such jobs done through the NRPB. Several different government departments were asked to prepare studies on certain phases of the problem peculiarly of concern to these separate groups. The Bureau of Labor Statistics, the Department of Agriculture, and the Bureau of the Census, for instance, made their respective inquiries and reports. The Works Progress Administration used many of its white-collar reliefers to help assemble facts and figures. The product of all was sifted and processed by the professionals of the NRPB and then the final report was published.

This same technique has been used time and again, not only by the NRPB but by other government agencies charged with studies to support proposed public policies. The social security program was not launched until after a committee of specialists under E. E. Witte had spent months digging into the intricate problems involved in such a tremendous undertaking. A similar staff of economists and social theorists was used in drafting a much publicized diagnosis of the ills of the southern states. Something of the same sort has been done with regard to problems of national power facilities, transportation, fiscal policy, housing, administrative reorganization of government departments, reciprocal trade agreements and many other problems.

The Raw Material

The product of government thinking is much more than the brilliant cerebration of the star brains. Quantitatively, about 90 per cent of it is apt to be the tedious work of underlings who gather the facts and figures, dig out the countless columns of statistics and correlate them according to instructions and blueprints handed down by the head men of the think factories. Many of these underlings are trained economists and statisticians—expert in the craftsmanship of complicated professional statistical techniques.

Many others are just skilled operators of the new miracle machines which mechanically shuffle, sort, and classify thousands of cards with mysterious holes punched in them. By pressing certain keys you can make one of these machines almost instantaneously jerk out the perforated cards which will show, for example, how many out of 100,000 homeowners have electric iceboxes. And another jerk may show how many of these have their iceboxes paid for. Washington is packed with tons of statistical data on almost every conceivable subject. Hundreds of government employees spend all their time collecting routine statistics and assembling them.

Non-Government Think Factories

Not all of the heavy thinking that shapes public policies is done in government offices. Privately financed and independently operated foundations and institutions regularly make scholarly studies of major economic, social, and political questions that influence the course of national affairs.

The Brookings Institution, organized about 20 years ago by the late Robert S. Brookings of St. Louis, Mo., is an outstanding example. Many New Deal left-wingers do not like the Brookings Institution, think of it as made up of old-fogey economists, but the *New York Times* once called it "as important in the world of economics as the Pasteur Institute is in the world of medicine." This organization has consistently preached the theory of an economy of plenty as against an economy of scarcity, and in the past few years both government and business have embraced much of the Brookings preachments. Its studies of the war debt problem and of America's physical productive capacity have been major contributions. The Institution has turned out men as well as ideas. Many former Brookings staff men and students now play important roles in government. These include Isador Lubin, economic adviser to the President; Leo Pasvolsky, adviser to the Secretary of State; Stacy May, research head of the War Production Board, and Mordecai Ezekiel, adviser to the Secretary of Agriculture. Dr. Harold G. Moulton, the head of Brookings, has a combination of theoretical and practical ability.

The Twentieth Century Fund, started through gifts of the late E. A. Filene, Boston merchant, is doing a job of economic study and analysis somewhat like the job the Brookings Institution is doing. It works closely with government officials, but in its analytical publications it undertakes to bring out constructive criticism and offers facts for guidance of independent students of government. Its main office is in New York but its staff men spend much time in Washington. Frederic Dewhurst, former Hoover adviser, is chief economist.

The National Planning Association is relatively new, but already has established itself as a point of contact between government economic policy planners and leaders of business, labor, and agriculture, who foresee the need for closer collaboration between private enterprise and government in the era that will follow the war. The head of this organization is Charles E. Wilson, president of the General Electric Company, and the Washington staff director is E. J. Coil, former Columbia University professor.

Numerous other well-endowed private foundations make their imprint on nearly all professional thinking and planning that goes on in Washington. Experts from the Rockefeller Foundation, the Carnegie Foundation, the Guggenheim Foundation and the Russell Sage Foundation freely collaborate on all sorts of research jobs. The Institute for Advanced Study at Princeton, N. J., has a staff of super-brains available at call for consultation with government officials who need help on knotty problems.

How Ideas Become Laws

Most idea men are not good at promoting their own causes. They mature their conclusions and trust to others to convert plans into action. Some can sell as well as produce, however.

Thomas G. Corcoran is a good example, and his operations in Washington typify much of the whole process of making laws out of ideas. Corcoran, a Frankfurter protégé from Harvard Law School, had seen Wall Street rascality at close range as an underling in a prominent New York law firm. At the tag end of the Hoover administration, he got a job as lawyer in the Reconstruction Finance Corporation. From that office he branched out, tied up with another astute lawyer, Ben Cohen. These two, collaborating with Frankfurter and James M. Landis (later Director of the Office of Civilian Defense), drafted a special program of corporate and financial reform and systematically went about putting it into effect. It took nearly three years for Corcoran and his associates to formulate, draft, and get enacted what he called his "trilogy"—the law regulating issues of new securities, the law regulating and policing stock exchange transactions, and the law virtually pronouncing a death sentence for public utility holding companies. He did not originate the proposals, of course. They were ideas that had matured after extensive and sensational hearings of the Pecora Senate investigation of Wall Street and investment banking and the Federal Trade Commission's exposé of holding company abuses. The build-up had been done and the time was ripe.

Over a period of many months, Corcoran talked, argued, planned, studied the problem of how to curb the utility holding companies. He relied heavily on Cohen, whose ability as a draftsman of legislation is unsurpassed. Day after day, night after night, Corcoran and Cohen wrestled with a thousand minute problems involved in the whole financial, legal, and political set-up of these corporate giants. They consulted dozens of others, both for practical suggestions and for planting their own ideas with persons whose support would be helpful.

Long before the proposed legislation got into the headlines and before the President himself knew just what he wanted to do, the Corcoran-Cohen team knew precisely what they wanted, and had a bill drafted and ready for introduction in Congress. They knew, moreover, the men in both the House and the Senate who could be relied upon to sponsor their legislation.

Part of their job was to prime President Roosevelt and prod him into assuming leadership in pushing for passage of legislation.

After many months of spade work, the President finally called a White House conference to consider plans for dealing with the utility holding companies. Corcoran and Cohen attended, not as principal sponsors, but as technicians available to answer questions as to details of procedure. By sheer force of thorough preparedness on the subject they easily sold themselves and their program to the President. From that time on they operated as authoritative go-betweens in passing White House ideas to members of

Congress, and in the course of several months of bitter debate at the Capitol, many a wavering congressman swung into line on hearing the charming telephone voice saying, "Corcoran speaking from the White House."

In the early stages they sought little publicity for their cause and took great pains to avoid any personal publicity for themselves, but systematically and quietly they fed their ideas to numerous Washington newspaper writers and especially to certain columnists. These were the days when Corcoran, Cohen, and nearly a dozen other New Deal reformers lived in a big red brick house on R Street in the Georgetown section of Washington, where night after night campaign plans were laid and persons who could be helpful in the cause were fed, entertained, and inspired.

When the campaign in Congress got hot they turned on all the publicity heat they could. They planned public blasts from the President himself at the crucial moments. And when the utilities lobby appeared to be almost able to block the legislation, they engineered a special senatorial investigation of lobbying headed by Senator Black, now a justice of the Supreme Court, and thus were able to reveal enough corrupt practices on the part of one particular utility company to smear the whole cause of the public utilities. The bill squeezed through by a narrow margin and became law.

This story of Corcoran and Cohen, and their campaign for reform legislation on securities, exchanges and utilities, is the story of brilliant brainsters turned lobbyists for a cause. The same technique, with variations to fit the circumstances, has been applied repeatedly by others on other reform causes.

Career Thinkers

Years hence some of the most colorful workers in the think factories will have passed out of mind, but certain quiet, persistent pluggers will get credit or blame for drafting a new set of ideas for our future political economy.

Marriner Eccles is one of the very few idea men who set a course and consistently stuck to it. His name will long survive as one of the main architects of the new economy of the years ahead. Without him as a spearhead, Alvin Hansen, Lauchlin Currie and other exponents of government deficit spending probably would not have won the success they have. Henry Wallace, the Vice President, is one of these persistent planners, despite his conspicuous part in some ill-fated ventures of the first Roosevelt years.

Other thinkers are Milo Perkins, ex-businessman who now heads up the Board of Economic Warfare; Adolf A. Berle, Jr., Assistant Secretary of State; E. A. Goldenweiser and Woodlief Thomas of the Federal Reserve Board. Harold D. Smith, Director of the Bureau of the Budget, is little known to the public but has tremendous influence as the President's incorruptible right-hand man for purposes of internal administrative coordination.

Gardiner Means did the spade work in 1932 for the Berle and Means startling book, *The Modern Corporation and Private Property,* but subsequently modestly side-stepped the limelight. Since then he has worked behind scenes to develop and promote his economic concepts, and he has now seen these concepts largely woven into fixed government policies.

Joseph B. Eastman of the Interstate Commerce Commission, and wartime Defense Transportation Director, has been a professional government thinker for so long that he has almost ceased to have news value. But he is at the top of those who give a high quality of thought and ability to the public welfare without regard for money or personal aggrandizement.

Max Lowenthal is of the same stripe as Eastman, devoting his very great talents to study of the railroad problem, shrinking from publicity and refusing to align himself with militant groups of reformers.

Some of the foremost members of the New Deal professional thinking brigade have moved on up the ladder.

Robert H. Jackson, Jamestown, N. Y., lawyer, started in 1934 as counsel in the Bureau of Internal Revenue, and by sheer hard work, ability, and a capacity for knowing which way the wind blows, became Solicitor General, Attorney General, and finally went to the Supreme Court. William Douglas likewise started from a subordinate post in the SEC and played his cards so well that he became the youngest justice of the Supreme Court since John Marshall. Another who ascended to the Supreme Court by way of ardent work in the New Deal think factory was Felix Frankfurter.

Other examples of professional thinkers and students who worked their way through the think mills to high public office are Federal Circuit Judge Jerome N. Frank, James M. Landis, and Francis Biddle, Attorney General. (Douglas, Frankfurter, Biddle and Jackson all were pushed up the ladder by the clever hand of Tom Corcoran.)

What Are They Aiming At?

New Deal professionals as a class call themselves "liberals" in their concepts of the political economy. Conservatives think they are "reds" or at least socialists. Doubtless some of the group do hope for the demise of private capitalism and the profit system. Some others think this demise is inevitable, although they do not really wish for it. But most of them at heart favor the system of private capitalism, although they nearly all agree that the capitalistic system of the past will have to be radically adjusted to modern conditions, meaning the new New Deal economy.

They are in general agreement on the main New Deal thesis that govern-

335

ment controls must be imposed to break up the concentration of economic power in the hands of private groups. Also there is almost unanimity that huge spendings of borrowed money by the government are all right, and that a steadily growing public debt need not cause much worry. The accepted theory is that the unspent savings of individuals and corporations make for depression, and that the government must spend sums equivalent to these uninvested savings to keep the flow of money from shrinking.

Most practical businessmen scoff at New Deal theorists, call them fellows who "never tried to meet a pay roll," who have a nerve to tell businessmen what to do. And the New Dealers look down on businessmen because, they say, businessmen have been stupid in the past, have not made a success of private enterprise, have not run their own businesses so as to avoid depressions. The two groups operate from opposite poles. Neither seems to understand the other.

The Washington thinkers and planners who have made their mark have learned to mix theory with gumption. Some know enough about the facts of practical business life to know that "what ought to be" is sometimes utterly impossible in practice. Others are smart enough to recognize their lack of business or administrative experience and content themselves with doing the best jobs of research and analysis they know how to do, leaving to others the final decisions and the execution. There are a few who think they know all the answers but don't. Some who have Ph.D.'s from the best universities have exuded erudite books full of all the technical phrases that professors use, know all the signs and symbols of statistical computations and understand the language in papers read to annual meetings of the highbrow learned societies, and still don't know beans about the practical workings of business, politics, and government. They have large educations and small intelligence. Ordinarily these super-educated nitwits could get jobs only as assistant professors in universities. By net appraisal they are generally harmless, but they do cast a cloud on the whole product of Washington professional thinking.

Thinkers for the Future

Both professorial theorists and practical businessmen must face a future in which government will dominate the national economy. This will enhance the status of professional political economists but it will force them to be more than abstract theorists. Likewise it will force businessmen to think of the total economy and learn some of the lessons taught by the graduate schools. When more businessmen are trained to fit their operations into the whole, and more government theorists learn the practical workings of business, then government and business can work together.

This is now beginning to happen in a limited way. It will happen in a larger way. A political Utopia will be realized if and when the Washington brain trust becomes a reserve corps of talent upon which both business and government can draw.

One of the current hopeful signs is that much of the best thinking, private and public, is concentrating on economic planning for the postwar phase. Government thinking and planning may then shift over from adolescence and become of age.

31

Postwar Plans

WASHINGTON thinkers think they can prevent a long deep dark depression after the war. They have plans. They talks in terms of a new order which will be better for every individual, every home, and many businesses. They talk of more goods for more people, more material things. They assume that on top of material betterment will come social and spiritual improvement. Not a slipback after war, but an advance, they say. The plans may or may not work out, but, anyway, this is the story of what the thinkers hope can be done.

Wars usually make inflationary booms, and such booms usually are followed by terrible depressions. But many ace thinkers and planners in Washington, even now in the thick of this war, are spending all their time in figuring out how this "normal" economic cycle can be forestalled. The planners' job is to say what *ought* to be done. They haven't the authority to say what *will* be done. The size of the postwar planning job depends on the extent of the economic dislocations, and that depends on the length of the war. There are not many, however, who look for the war's end before 1944 and, in fact, most plans are based on the assumption that the war may run longer. But even in 1944 there will be 20 to 25 million workers in defense industries and the armed forces—or perhaps more. How to keep these workers fully employed after the war is the key problem.

Inflation

Inflation is feared as a product of the wartime dislocations. Not so much during the fighting, for government will tax heavily, soak up savings through bond sales, regulate prices, and actually ration supplies to consumers to head off severe inflation. The main inflation test will come when the war is over. Then people will have lots of money and will want to splurge—will want to buy the automobiles, radios, appliances, houses and many other things withheld during the war. Demand for many things will temporarily exceed supply. When the war is over people will resist continuance of wartime restrictions. It will be politically difficult to restrain a spending spree that would zoom prices to fantastic heights, and precipitate a crash. The planners know this, and that's why they are so intent on pre-

338

arranged programs which will help to keep things in balance, to lessen post-war adjustments.

How much inflation? Despite present strong curbs many Washington analysts think the average price level of early 1942 will rise 50 to 75 per cent in the next two years. *If* the curbs were to be lifted at the end of the war, they believe prices *could* double or treble the 1942 level.

So the effort is to keep the boom restrained and thus minimize the chances of later collapse.

Full Employment

Postwar plans call for a definite national policy of full employment—jobs for all even if government must make the jobs. War industry workers and the millions in the Army and Navy would not be discharged until other jobs were provided.

Planners say that government in the future must spend whatever is necessary to make full employment for all.

National income is a measuring stick used by government planners in calculating the ups and downs of the national economy. It is the sum total paid out in the form of wages, rents, interest, and other forms of income to recipients. For 1942 the total income of the nation is estimated at 100 to 105 billion dollars. Statisticians figure that a national income of approximately this amount would provide full employment—a job for every adult able and willing to work. The actual amount would need to be adjusted, of course, to the extent that prices rise or fall.

Public Debt

Over-saving by the well-to-do, according to government planners, is responsible for much unemployment. People with surplus incomes tend to hoard money instead of spending it or investing it in ways that create jobs. To the extent that this is done the total national income falls and unemployment follows. This is the prevailing theory among the planners. This is why the planners say the government must spend money to whatever extent is necessary to make up for the savings that do not flow into job-making enterprises.

One obstacle in the way of such national planning is that it means tremendous public debt, and most people instinctively think of debt as a bad thing. But the planners have crystallized their thinking into a formula which tries to overcome this hostility to debt. They say boldly that debt is not a bad thing, since "we as a people owe the debt to ourselves." They insist that every debtor obligation is offset by a creditor asset, and therefore the nation as a whole can continue to build up a public debt without becoming poorer as a nation. The practical test, say these theorists, is whether or not

339

the nation is productive enough and prosperous enough to keep the interest-carrying charges on the debt within manageable limits, and that it's a good "investment" if the debt continuously provides full employment.

Big Government Spending

The main scheme for meeting the postwar crisis, therefore, is based frankly on government expenditures. The aim is not just to throw money out into circulation. Effort is to find ways to spend that will add to the wealth and well-being of the nation. Not only economic wealth, but social benefits as well—things that contribute to the health, morale, education and spiritual assets of the people. It is not easy to write a program that will be acceptable to the public and to Congress. But the planners have tried to do it, and here are some of the things they have in mind:

A large military establishment would be kept intact after the war, although considerable shrinkage from wartime levels is expected. This means especially a large Navy and air forces, with great expansion and improvements of airports, Naval bases, harbors, shipyards, and related facilities. Commercial air lines also would be greatly expanded. The planners take seriously the idea that joint American-British forces will assume major responsibility for world law and order. They say America is sure to "go internationalist" in a big way.

Huge public works are contemplated. The Federal Works Agency has accumulated what it calls a public works reserve—hundreds of large and small projects in the blueprint stage. These public works include power dams, rural electrification, flood control projects, irrigation, drainage projects, transmission lines, highways, bridges, tunnels, elimination of railroad grade crossings, viaducts, by-passes, development of inland waterways. (Note that current policy is to hold back on such activities during war, to save them for postwar.)

A corollary of the public works program involves a major reform in relations between the federal government and local governments. New federal and state legislation will be sought to authorize the rebuilding of many cities and towns. This job as now outlined is too big and complicated for private capital or for local financing. So the plan is for the federal government, at a cost of billions of dollars, to acquire land in urban areas, redevelop it along modern efficient lines, and recover whatever portion of the cost is feasible through rentals to users of the reconstructed areas. Master plans would be advanced by local authorities, subject to the approval of the federal agency. It is hoped, however, that private investment institutions, such as insurance companies and savings banks, can be induced to contribute a certain portion of the original investment, perhaps with the federal government guaranteeing some low rate of interest.

Projects for expansion of social services contemplate expenditure of huge sums of federal money for modernized schools, hospitals, playgrounds, parks, recreational facilities, and more of such services as nursing care, health clinics, and health insurance schemes. As a sort of general underpinning of the whole system, it is proposed that old-age pensions, unemployment insurance, and public support for unfortunate and disabled classes would be greatly extended and perfected.

World Reconstruction

The theory is that many backward and war-ravaged countries will be ripe for much reconstruction and development work when the war is over. Details are vague, but you can get the general idea if you think in terms of a super-world-wide Reconstruction Finance Corporation and a mammoth world WPA program.

Acceptance of the philosophy of abundance on a world-wide scale will be advocated more and more as the reconstruction period draws nearer. This means the full use of all industrial capacity to produce consumer and durable goods to the limit, with lower production costs, lower prices and greater consumption of such goods. The domestic planners have been advocating this for a long time. Now the idea has expanded to cover world-wide postwar planning.

Lower tariffs, freer exchange of goods between countries, and other related developments are envisioned in the 1942 U. S.-British economic agreement, which forms the basis for furthering the philosophy of abundance. That agreement is part and parcel of plans for using wartime capacity of America to help feed, clothe, and house the postwar world; for shifting the armament facilities of this country to peacetime output; and for using the mass-production aptitudes of Americans to promote world-wide reconstruction.

Revitalizing Civilian Industry

Government planners know that government expenditures alone cannot insure a healthy prolonged prosperity. They rely much on the prospect that private industry after the war will have the incentive to produce to meet a reviving market for civilian goods. The fact is that nearly all large corporations and many small ones already are carefully planning ways to improve their products so as to expand their production and markets in the postwar period.

There is no assurance, of course, that normal incentives will operate to cause private capital to provide the extra employment that will be needed when the war economy is liquidated. The government planners have in mind, therefore, some alternatives in case extra stimulants are needed.

341

One of these plans calls for outright government subsidy of private industries operating their own and government war plants which are now producing war goods. Under this plan the principal large industries would be called into conference and told that if they would produce a certain amount of goods in the course of a year at certain reasonable prices, the government would undertake to compensate them in some way for any surplus that they might have left unmarketed at the end of the year. This idea is based, of course, on the much discussed New Deal concept of national economic planning, whereby government supervisors would attempt to integrate total productive capacity with the potential demand of consumers. (A side light is that this sort of planning seems to appeal more to the very large corporations than it does to the small business units.)

The Cost

There are no dependable estimates of what the cost of postwar projects will be. Planners take the view that the cost should not be an obstacle. They argue that in the new economy of the future "the nation can afford anything that it has the man power and material to produce."

The wartime government budget of around 50 billions a year will be shrunk considerably when the main war effort subsides, but federal spendings probably will continue indefinitely at a level of 15 to 20 billions—more than double the peak prewar expenditures.

How raise the billions required for the program now planned? Very high taxes, of course. The planners talk of a compensatory tax system which will more heavily tax the enlarged national income to pay for new projects, but they recognize that the outlay probably will exceed revenues.

The prospect is that the budget will not be balanced for many years. Public debt of 150 billions or more is indicated. Planners say the debt doesn't hurt so long as we don't try to pay it off. In fact, they insist that any attempt to reduce the debt would bring on a depression.

Whether this is good economics is a question on which wise men disagree; the new thinkers believe it is good, the orthodox thinkers doubt it. But no one disputes that spending and deficit financing is "good politics," at least while the spending is flowing. Politicians think usually of the next election, and any system which seems to work at the moment is politically popular. Thus the indications are that Congress *will* vote the money for a great postwar program, regardless of which party is then in power.

Who Are the Planners?

Soon after the 1940 elections President Roosevelt asked his National Resources Planning Board to get busy on plans for the period to follow the war. This Board has done the job, therefore, of prodding many other government agencies into postwar planning. In the NRPB itself the key men are Luther Gulick and John D. Millett. Dr. Alvin H. Hansen of Harvard University and adviser to the Federal Reserve System is the postwar planners' authorized exponent of government debt financing of "full employment." Guy Greer of the Federal Reserve System is taking the lead on ideas for rebuilding our cities. Two indoctrinated Department of Agriculture planners, Mordecai Ezekiel and Louis Bean, are devoting themselves to the postwar planning job. Others are Dal Hitchcock in the Department of Labor; Arthur R. Upgren and M. Joseph Meehan in the Department of Commerce; Adolf Berle, Assistant Secretary of State; and Jacob Baker, Federal Works Agency. The President's economic adviser, Lauchlin Currie, keeps tab on all the planners and helps to keep them coordinated.

Aside from the NRPB, the Board of Economic Warfare has, as part of its charter from the President, the duty of developing plans for meeting postwar dislocations. This function is now subordinated to the prosecution of war measures, but by the end of the war this Board, of which Milo Perkins is the executive head, will take a big part in planning and directing efforts to meet the crisis. Vice President Wallace, chairman of the Board, will have much to say about such plans.

Most of the recognized government postwar planners are at heart favorable to the preservation of our American system of private capitalism and private enterprise. They think they can superimpose a large degree of government spending and direction of the national economy and still keep the essential features of private enterprise intact. Most of them do not really want socialism or any variation of the fascist or totalitarian state, but they recognize that as the area of governmental authority and control is widened, the area of private capitalism is narrowed.

Despite the sincere policy avowals of the planners, it seems reasonably clear that a powerful trend is running in the direction of governmental domination of business and the whole economy. It is part of the big shift of power into the hands of political officials in Washington.

Some of the schemes projected for postwar doubtless seem fantastic at the present time, in the midst of war, and against the background of the orthodox thinking of the past. Some of them may turn out to *be* fantastic. Nevertheless they are the goal toward which our government is working, and within the broad outline as sketched in this brief discussion you can insert the details as they come along within the next year or two.

The economy of the future will be much different from that of the past, and it is toward the new economy that we are now heading.

32

Science Center

HUMAN animals populate our whole country, and they set up a system to govern themselves. They become very much preoccupied with the details of their man-made laws, and with the center in which many of these laws are made and administered—Washington.

· But there is another system of law which is far deeper and more fundamental than the man-made laws—that is the natural law by which the universe and everything in it runs. Men are working at the job of discovery, and what they have learned, compared with what they formerly knew, is amazing. What they seem to be on the point of learning is awe-inspiring.

Washington is best known as a center of politics, of attempted reforms in the social sciences. A fact which is not generally known is that it is also the center of the natural sciences—the hub of scientific knowledge.

The war has made the United States, and particularly Washington, serve the same purpose as the monasteries of Ireland did during the Dark Ages— the preservation of scientific learning of the world.

Once Paris was the city where weights and measures were compared and standardized for the entire world. Germany once held the monopoly on the measurement of colors and dyes. Once Vienna was the medical center of the world. Once Moscow was the center of research on the brain. Today Washington is the leader in all these—and more.

Washington is today the mecca of the world's greatest scientists regardless of their race, religion or nationality, and when the National Academy of Sciences meets in Washington the roll call reveals not only many of the most famous names in American science but also those of such men as Dr. Nils Bohr of Denmark, pioneer in atomic physics research, Dr. Albert Einstein of Germany and Dr. Enrico Fermi of Italy, Nobel Prize winner in physics. During the past 10 years the United States has had the greatest influx of trained brains in the history of any nation in the world.

It is not an uncommon sight to find these men, along with Dr. Merle Tuve of the Carnegie Institution of Washington, Dr. Hans Bethe of Cornell University, Dr. Arthur Compton of the University of Chicago and Dr.

344

Robert A. Millikan of the California Institute of Technology squatting Indian fashion on the lawn of the Bureau of Standards—America's super-university. In one breath they will be exploring the mystery of the heat of stars billions of miles away in space and in the next breath be discussing the particles of the millionths-of-an-inch atoms beyond the range of human vision. It is a cosmopolitan group in which American and English scientists converse with Germans in French. A Chinese astronomer may interpret English to a Russian. Latin American scientists put Portuguese into Spanish and English. And all of them understand each other because science is the one universal language in the world and Washington is the one place where it is now spoken freely.

Many of the scientific researchers have turned to war purposes. Refugees from Hitler have turned on Hitler. They have joined forces with good American scientific brains to beat the common enemy. They are devising new implements of death. And yet the bulk of the scientific work in Washington rolls along toward more constructive ends for the betterment of human living, not only for Americans but for people of the whole world. Scientific research has been called the "yeast of life." If it is, then Washington is the "yeast center."

In Washington some scientists are working at the cracking of the atom, which eventually may provide a new source of power. Others are working on house flies, and have discovered that they can carry the germs of infantile paralysis as well as other diseases. There are experiments designed to curtail or eliminate the common cold, cancer, and many fevers. Much work is being done on the "sulfa" drugs. There are experiments to determine which building materials are best, which shoe leather will wear longest, how best to combat the boll weevil and other insect pests. There are new discoveries which may result in roses as big as soup plates, carrots as long as your arm, and potatoes as big as cantaloupes. There is research to determine how matter is made from light by chlorophyll, and whether it will be possible for future humans to eat grass and thrive on it. Scientists study the weather, and how it is made; they hope sometime to foretell it a long time ahead. Scientists are continually reducing the death rate. They are prolonging the span of human life. They are perfecting airplanes which will fly by themselves (almost). They are finding out new things about foods, and vitamins, and they are preparing for postwar, when America will have to do a lot of feeding of the world.

Your watch, your clock, your fence line, your yard of muslin, your pound of sugar—all are determined by the standards maintained in Washington. Your watch is set by the stars. Your fence line, too. Your yard of anything is set by a platinum bar kept in an air-conditioned vault in Washington.

345

You may think you are master of your future. Perhaps you are, but the automobile and the airplane which your children will drive are being determined by experiments now going on, largely in Washington. Some of the diseases from which you suffer will be unknown to your children. Your children's houses will be better and cheaper, due to Washington research. The roads will improve. The distances will be cut. Heat will come by wire. People may be taller. They will live longer. Food will be more plentiful. You are living today in a crude age. The material conditions of the future will be better, regardless of the trials of the present. Who says so? The Washington scientists say so.

Research

The scientific laboratories of Washington are sprawled out like the catacombs of Rome. It would require months just to walk through them. In some of them, scientists are studying the atom, which is the most fundamental secret of all. It is the particle of matter out of which everything on earth develops. But the atoms, which you could pick by the billions from the dust under your shoe, are composed of still other electrical particles known as protons, neutrons, deuterons, neutrinos and bits of matter. And these hurl themselves around the nucleus of the tiny atom in much the same way as the earth, moon, the planets and the sun speed around in the ceaseless millings of the universe.

Within this ultra-miniature solar system of atomic particles, three scientists, Dr. Merle Tuve, Dr. L. R. Hafstad and Dr. N. P. Heydenburg, whose total ages would not be more than 100, have explored deep inside the atom in the "atomic observatory" of the Carnegie Institution of Washington, hidden in a corner a mile from Washington's famous Connecticut Avenue. They have already discovered the existence of a powerful binding force, or atomic cement, which holds all the particles of matter in the entire universe together. What practical use this discovery will have is anyone's guess and Dr. Tuve and his associates decline to speculate. Their work is pure science, as differentiated from applied science, and they have no more idea of how it can be applied than the Wright Brothers did when they flew the first powered airplane. However, it has helped them in unraveling the first thread in the biggest secret in the world today—the unlocking of the energy of the atom.

Following the clue of a German woman scientist they have actually unlocked some of the energy of the atom, a thing which scientists pooh-poohed for years but now admit is possible. Using Uranium 235, they have produced an infinitesimal "atomic explosion" which, under certain conditions involving other atoms, would cause an explosion great enough to make

346

Washington and most of the area surrounding it a part of the Atlantic Ocean.

When James Watt invented the steam engine more than a century ago, he started the industrial revolution and brought about a new era in the living conditions of the world. Not long ago J. N. "Ding" Darling, the famous cartoonist and a keen scientific observer, declared that if something as vital as the steam engine should be discovered it would remake the history of the world for centuries to come. Scientists in Washington say the answer to that may lie in the practical use of atomic power.

Standards

The National Bureau of Standards is today the only place in the world where master instruments, weights and measures can be adjusted with the precision necessary to insure that when you buy a pound of anything or a pair of shoes the guarantee will mean what it says.

Here in Washington more than 500 men and women are working quietly and efficiently to solve the fundamental problems of how much a pound of sugar weighs, how much energy there is in a volt of electricity and the exact length of a yard, a foot or a mile. With a beam of light they can measure any given piece of material down to a millionth of an inch, using the platinum steel bar in the guarded vault of the Bureau as the standard. Or they can use the international kilogram to measure your sugar, bread or meat. Or, using the standard apparatus buried five floors deep in one of the Bureau's buildings, they can measure a volt, an ampere, or an ohm to a point of accuracy which you could not calculate.

If such figures seem trivial and you are inquisitive about the weight of the earth you can find the answer from Dr. Paul Heyl, a one-armed scientist who can calculate faster in his head than most people can with an adding machine. He has weighed the earth by minute observation of the swing of a pendulum in a small laboratory deep within the Bureau's campus-like grounds on upper Connecticut Avenue. And why measure the weight of the earth? Because as it swings along through space at the rate of more than 2,000 miles per minute, the earth is the yardstick by which every other movement of the universe is calculated. Its weight and its size are two of the fundamentals used by astronomers in measuring the heat and distance of stars trillions of miles away in space. (The weight of the earth, incidentally, is approximately 6,000,000,000,000,000,000,000 tons.)

A life-saving instrument is the Bureau's newest X-ray machine, an instrument stretching three stories high in its special building. This huge tube generates so much energy that it could, if proper precautions were not taken, rapidly destroy the fingers or the entire bodies of the men who operate it.

The small, eager-faced scientist who designed it, Dr. Lauriston S. Taylor, and his coworkers keep at a respectful distance behind five inches of lead shielding, however, as they measure the strength of its X-rays in a tiny thimble set at the bottom end of the tube. With these essential measurements, it is becoming possible for a specialist to take more accurate X-ray pictures, and to treat skin diseases and deep cancer with more effectiveness and safety.

Dr. Lyman J. Briggs, the lanky, perpetual pipe-smoking director of the Bureau, enjoys taking visitors into the laboratories where machines tear a 20-foot steel beam apart as you would break a match, where walls two feet thick are crushed like an eggshell, and steel bars as big as a man's arm are stretched out like taffy—all to see "how they can take it" and establish standards for buildings. He also likes to show his furnaces in which automobiles, airplanes, steel safes, brick walls, and concrete reinforcement pillars can be subjected to terrific heat to find out how fire-resistant materials can be made still more resistant and provide still more human protection. This he calls his "construction work."

The Bureau's scientists are among the world's leaders in radio science. They aided materially in founding today's short-wave broadcasting and television by standardizing radio frequencies up into the megacycles, the scientists' way of measuring very short radio waves. They also devised some of the first directional radio beams used to keep an airplane pilot on his course and land him safely at an airport by "riding the beam in."

The gangling Dr. L. F. Curtiss designed, built, and put into production one of the most valuable robot radio broadcasting sets ever invented. Starting with a dollar alarm clock, he built a tiny machine weighing two pounds which soars aloft 21 miles or more above the earth at the tail of a small balloon. As it goes up it automatically measures the temperature, pressure, and water content of the air and radios this information back to the ground. This device has saved the government hundreds of thousands of dollars in hiring pilots to make weather flights, and besides it can be sent aloft in weather too thick for an airplane pilot to buck.

Food and Life

The Department of Agriculture contains the world's largest research organization, and by the time Vice President Wallace, the first scientist ever to be Secretary of Agriculture, finished that job, the Department was doing things it never thought were possible before. Using a method originated by Dr. Albert F. Blakeslee, biologist of the Carnegie Institution of

Washington, a slim, goateed man who looks every inch a scientist, it has created entirely new species of plants by treating seeds with a gout remedy called colchicine made from the autumn crocus. These are different from anything which ever grew on earth because colchicine increases the number of chromosomes, or heredity determiners. The scientists decline to make any predictions, but do say that it may be possible to increase greatly the size of fruits, vegetables, and flowers.

Agriculture seems to be unrelated to medicine, but the Department's Bureau of Entomology had a new problem proposed to it last year when two Yale University physicians proved that common flies can carry the virus of infantile paralysis from one child to another. And, while insects are man's worst enemies, they are sometimes lifesavers. Dr. William Robinson, a chemist in the Department, discovered recently that the surgical maggots used in treating chronic wound and bone infections secrete a healing substance known as allantoin. With the help of other chemists, he made the drug synthetically and then tried it out with 50 practicing physicians and surgeons. It healed wounds even better than the maggots. Today it is one of America's most effective wartime medical weapons.

That isn't agriculture, as one old-time government bureaucrat complained, but neither is the Smithsonian Institution supposed to be in the farm business. Yet, despite the popular belief that the Smithsonian is just a museum, it is one of the country's important agricultural scientific laboratories. One group of scientists there, among whom has been the pretty and vivacious Dr. Florence Meier Chase, is studying the fundamental problem of how matter is made into light by chlorophyll, the common but mysterious green coloring matter of plants. That is pure science in agriculture. Everyone knows how matter is converted into energy by burning coal, wood, gas and oil. But no one yet knows how the chlorophyll captured the sunlight of other eons and made those sources of today's energy. Dr. Chase and her coworkers may look a little silly wading in a pool of water and skimming off the green scum, but the algae which compose that scum may hold the answer to this basic secret of life.

Health

Illness is the principal liability of any family or the community, and the National Health Survey of 1937, a door-to-door questioning, revealed that on an average day 4,000,000 people are disabled by illness, and during a year more than 1,000,000,000 man-days are lost in industry at a total cost of about $10,000,000,000 per year.

In one of the many efforts to correct this situation, more than 300 scientists are at work in the National Institute of Health, the research division of the Public Health Service, and are risking their lives every day in efforts to conquer disease. More than a dozen have given their lives in this unknown battle. They work with everything from cancer to the common cold and they court death daily, but they would chuckle if you were to call them heroes or heroines. They handle bottles containing billions of germs as casually as you handle the morning's milk. With the accidental breaking of a bottle or a tiny scratch on the finger, their careers are ended. One woman scientist splashed a single drop of infantile paralysis virus in her eye and died three days later.

Courage is something they know almost instinctively. For example, one scientist attempting to find out how leprosy is transmitted, not only worked, ate, and slept with lepers, but also injected himself with the supposedly deadly germs and even drank them continuously for two years. He finally gave up in disgust because he couldn't get the disease, but he had partially eliminated the old Biblical fear of leprosy.

In medicine, our generation is known as the chemical era in the conquest of disease. For centuries medical men have sought for magical remedies to cure disease. Some near-answers may already be found in the "sulfa" drugs—sulfanilamide, sulfapyridine, sulfathiazole, sulfadiazole, sulfaguanadine, and perhaps more later—strange names in the treatment of our ills.

These drugs have cut the pneumonia death rate to less than a third of what it was four years ago and reduced the illness and death rates from such diseases as childbed fever, streptococcic sore throat, blood poisoning and gonorrhea to a fraction of the former figure. This is revolutionary in medicine, but at the National Institute of Health, now located just northwest of Washington in Bethesda, Maryland, Dr. Sanford Rosenthal, a young aggressive scientist, grins at the idea that the chemical treatment of diseases has gotten anywhere. "We're just getting started," says he.

The new Institute laboratories are swarming with men and women in white who are constantly injecting animals, observing them, weighing them —making continuous analyses. On the results of their work, your life and the lives of thousands of others depend. Yet they are just ordinary people who grow flowers, mow the lawn, play bridge or poker, and trim their fingernails.

One of them, Dr. Charles C. Armstrong, recently made a discovery which may be all-important in the fight against infantile paralysis. After years of work, he found that the common white cotton rat could be infected with the paralysis virus, whereas before the rhesus monkey imported from India was the only known animal which could catch the disease. His research not only saved the government money, but also enabled it to continue research when the supply of monkeys was cut off by the war.

350

The Institute is under the Federal Security Agency, another part of which, the National Cancer Institute, is exploring one of the most fundamental mysteries in human life—the cause of cancer and its prevention. Surgery, X-rays, and radium are today's methods of treatment, and they are successful only if the cancerous growth is caught early. But what the Cancer Institute scientists—and they are among the best in the world—want to know is why normal cells suddenly start running wild. The answer, they believe, is in the chemistry of the living cells themselves.

They now have a new instrument for studying those cells—the electron microscope. It was invented by Dr. Vladimir Kosma Zworykin now of the Radio Corporation of America, who came out of a small Russian peasant village to become in America one of the world's authorities on electron optics, or seeing with electrons instead of light rays. With this super-microscope, the cells, a thousand of which would barely cover a pin point, are magnified more than 100,000 times. It makes a dime look a mile wide and a human hair look as thick as a California redwood tree. Cancer cells loom up as big as a sofa cushion and can be studied in such detail that minute chemical particles—the clue to cancer—can be seen inside them.

America's Wings

Aviation today is both the hope and despair of the world. Dr. Orville Wright, a shy little gray-haired man, has admitted that he didn't know what he started when he made the first flight in a powered airplane 40 years ago.

Dr. Wright, now 70 years old, but still spry despite back injuries received in the early days of aviation, is still a member of the National Advisory Committee for Aeronautics, the organization chiefly responsible for the design of most of today's airplanes. The Committee, which has its headquarters in Washington and meets here once a month, operates with three laboratories containing every aeronautical research device known to man, many of which were invented by Dr. Wright and his brother, Wilbur. Its investigations have resulted in today's six-mile-a-minute airplanes, and will bring even faster planes.

Most Americans accept airplanes today with the complacency of a five-year-old child picking up the telephone. But the modern plane is the result of long and hard work by some of the country's smartest scientists. Practically every plane in the air—American, British, German, Russian, Dutch, or Japanese—is modeled after designs of the National Advisory Committee for Aeronautics in its laboratories at Langley Field, Virginia, one of the most interesting places in the world.

Here the scientists and engineers create winds of more than 500 miles per hour—three times as fast as the winds of a hurricane, which are "only"

150 miles per hour—just to study the best possible wing and fuselage design for tomorrow's airplanes. The men who do it, directed by the 200-pound dynamo Dr. George W. Lewis, study these terrific drafts from an air chamber which they enter through two heavy steel doors. As the 8,000 horsepower electric fans throw the air around faster and faster in the wind tunnel, the effect is exactly the same as that of climbing in an airplane at 5,000 feet per minute.

Some of the other tunnels they use in the search for better airplanes are equally uncanny. In a special egg-shaped building, they fly miniature airplanes in a steady air stream. It is a grown-up boy's paradise, but with it the model planes, built precisely to the scale of a full-size airplane, make it possible to test the performance of any plane within half an hour and make corrections for maneuverability which would take a pilot hours of time in the air to figure out.

In another "free flight" vertical tunnel similar models are put through steep power dives and tight spins in a rising column of air. A tiny clock mechanism manipulates the tail surfaces and if the plane doesn't recover from a spin, it isn't a funeral for the pilot. The engineer merely fishes the tiny plane out of the net below, carries it back to his drawing board and figures out what made it crash. As a result of such calculations, it is much harder to crack up an airplane today, for today's plane can be so precisely balanced that if you just let go of the controls and freeze your pants to the seat, the plane will right itself and sail along until the gas runs out.

The NACA engineers don't stop with model planes, however. In their flight-testing laboratory they have three of the nerviest test pilots in existence, who must work for the love of the work because none of them gets more than $5,000 a year and no insurance company will write a ten-cent insurance policy on them.

One of them, given the job of finding how a plane behaved with an unbalanced wing, took it up to 10,000 feet and tugged on the ripcord of the sandbox on the wing. Nothing happened. Someone had forgotten to dry the sand and it had frozen in the sub-zero atmosphere. With more swearing than thought for himself, he grabbed a screwdriver, climbed out of the cockpit and went out along the wing to chisel away at the box. The plane went into a spin, so, with more cursing, he climbed back, brought it out and tried again. At the third attempt, with only a bare mile of air between him and the earth, the sand loosened. The plane lurched and he dropped the screwdriver to grab a handhold as he swung back into the cockpit. He brought it down with all of the scientific data on his instruments intact and then apologized to Dr. Lewis for having lost the screwdriver—that was government property.

Fountainhead of Medicine

There is only one place on earth today where even the most learned physician can get more knowledge than he can digest on any subject in medicine—the Army Medical Library in Washington. It has in its files more than 2,000,000 books, some of them the hand-written texts of 1,000 years ago. And, until the war began, it abstracted every article on medicine from every country and in every language in the world. Any physician has access to this material and can even borrow all but the most precious books and documents through his local librarian. (And many physicians don't know it.) This, however, is only a part of the library. Colonel James E. Ash, a small, bald-headed Army officer who asks nothing more than to be left alone at his work, has prepared the largest collection now in existence of glass slides and descriptive material on diseases. Any physician can get this material at the cost of less than a dollar, and, if he owns a microscope, can take a post-graduate course in medicine in his own office.

Your Boundaries

If you ever get into an argument with your neighbor about the location of your fence line, don't pick up an ax handle and start swinging. The boundaries of the bit of the earth which you live on are fixed by the stars. You can easily fix your property line without any question by having a surveyor tie it in with the master network of boundary lines established by the Coast and Geodetic Survey.

The Coast and Geodetic engineers measured exactly the position of given points by sighting on the stars. They then ran a network of lines across the country. At least every 15 miles they set up a "benchmark" giving the precise location of that point, from which any surveyor can determine a boundary to within a few inches.

They also developed the finest camera in existence today to make aerial maps of the country. It is a two-ton machine with nine lenses which they call their "brownie kodak," and they had to tear the bottom out of a twin-engine Martin bomber to mount it. With one click of the shutter they can photograph 20 square miles of the earth. And, by taking "twin" pictures similar to those in the stereopticons, they make accurate contour maps showing the height of every hill and the depth of every valley. Two men with these pictures and a stereopticon viewer can do as much mapping in a single day as 200 could do on the ground by laborious checking of heights and distances.

The Survey experts also manipulate one of the most complicated calculating machines in existence to figure out exactly the heights of tides throughout the world. Its mechanical brain can absorb 17 different mathematical figures and give the answer in 10 seconds—a job which would require one man working for a year with pencil and paper to do, if he could do it at all.

What Time Is It?

Time today is regulated by four master clocks buried in a vault at the U. S. Naval Observatory, established 60 years ago on the outskirts of Washington, but now in the heart of the city. They were off three-thousandths of a second last year, a fact which the director, Captain J. F. Hellweg, reported in an almost apologetic tone. Few persons ever see these clocks which send the time signals from the Arlington radio station, and fewer yet ever touch them. Their pendulums swing in a vacuum to protect them against the friction of the air, and the area around them is air-conditioned to maintain a constant temperature. The men who tend them check on the earth's time by the movement of the stars. They note the star movements by telescope and simultaneously check the clocks by telescope from a room above the vault.

The only similar timepieces in the world are the crystal clocks of the Coast and Geodetic Survey located in the Department of Commerce building on Constitution Avenue. The heart of a crystal clock is a bit of quartz, which vibrates thousands of times per second and measures time to millionths of a minute. These are so important and valuable that a foreign government placed two of its secret agents aboard a U. S. Navy submarine three years ago in an effort to steal one while the submarine crew was charting some of the unknown waters of the Caribbean Sea.

Much to Learn

Washington has a million secrets. The Patent Office and the National Inventors Council, set up to study war suggestions for inventions, have in their keeping thousands of inventions which they guard jealously. The Army Ordnance Department and Chemical Warfare Service could tell stories which would cause our enemies worry. The Naval Research Laboratory is doing fundamental work on deep-sea diving and high-altitude flying. The National Research Council, housed in the magnificent marble building of the National Academy of Sciences on lower Constitution Avenue, is directing research on nutrition, and half a hundred other projects. The Weather Bureau in its new quarters on M Street is working on data which may replace the present weather forecasts with long-range forecasts to aid farmers in their crop plans several months in advance, and to aid many businessmen too. Dr. C. G. Abbot of the Smithsonian Institution also is working on the problem of long-range weather forecasting. The Carnegie

Institution of Washington is finding out how an unborn baby grows. The Bureau of Mines and the Geological Survey are digging deep into the earth's secrets and coming up with ores which may make the United States independent of foreign sources of such vital metals as magnesium and manganese. These are but a few of many other problems now being undertaken and in many cases solved by Washington's scientists. The men and women doing a vital part in science in Washington do exacting work without complaint and most of them have never heard of an 8-hour day or a 40-hour week. They keep the wheels of science turning and the average of their salaries is less than $3,000 a year. Even the best of them earn less than $8,000. Many Washington bricklayers and carpenters get more per day and per year than the Washington scientists who have spent from four to eight years just in training for their highly specialized jobs.

The Future of America

More than twenty centuries ago in Athens, Greece, there developed the highest culture man had ever known. It produced such men as Socrates, Plato, Aristotle, Hippocrates, Miltiades, Sophocles, Demetrius, Demosthenes, Praxiteles and Xenophon. Dr. E. G. Conklin, the noted historian, believes that these intellects were as far above those of the modern world as our present brainy men are above the intelligence of the African or Australian bushmen.

They developed into the world's leaders in philosophy, science, oratory and military tactics primarily because they had time to think. Every freeman had four slaves to work for him. Today every American has 3,000 horsepower working for him, according to Charles F. Kettering of the General Motors Company, America's modern Edison, and one theory is that men are approaching a stage of cultural development similar to that of the ancient Greeks. When we arrive at this millennium, it will not be because of the work of slaves but from mechanical development and unlimited electrical power, possibly generated from atoms. We have in America today the greatest collection of brains ever assembled in the modern world, the finest instruments and machines ever invented and we are gradually getting the time to do things outside the scope of mere subsistence.

Scientists think that within a generation, despite the present war's handicap, people will be working fewer hours per day, fewer days per week, fewer weeks per year—at necessitous work. They think that people, relieved of drudgery, will have more time for hobbies and constructive pleasures, and will create a culture surpassing that of Athens in its days of greatest glory. If so, it will be due largely to the contributions of science, and it is possible that Washington, being the science center, will be regarded as the Athens of the modern world.

33

G-Men, T-Men, Sleuths

ANYONE who inspects the machinery and methods of government crime chasers will conclude that although Sherlock Holmes was an interesting gent, he is as much out of date as a carriage maker. As a detector of crime he has been replaced by organized teams of law graduates, accountants, chemists, physicists, biologists, psychologists, researchers, and expert file clerks. They are the modern government sleuths. They call themselves "investigators." They just "investigate," and put two and two together. Their work is methodical, systematic, usually plodding, often tedious.

Many of them carry guns and can shoot from the hip, but the more common implements of the trade are the fountain pen and the brief case. False whiskers and dark glasses are mainly fictional, and most of these government agents look more like spic-and-span young salesmen. They know human nature, the habits and conduct of men, and they know what violators of law are likely to do under given sets of circumstances. Their powers of deduction sometimes come from hunches and flashes of genius, but usually they come from an accumulation of details, records, and rules set down in the book.

They don't like to be called "G-Men," which means "government men," a term that originated in the underworld and ascended to the upper world. They don't like to be called "T-Men," which means "Treasury men." They don't think of themselves as detectives, or sleuths, or gumshoe men, and they don't even admit that they are romantic, but the public thinks they are, and so they *are*.

There is no single over-all head of detective work for the entire government. There is no political intelligence agency, such as the Gestapo of Germany, or the OGPU of Russia, or the comparable political sleuth-agencies of many small European states. Such centralization has always been prevented by the American fear of excessive power in the hands of a single detective agency, the fear of a "police state." Instead, the groups work independently, but with a certain amount of cooperation and exchange of information.

In addition to the Big Three sleuthing agencies—FBI, Treasury and Post Office—there are dozens of other investigational agencies, working in practically all government departments. Army and Navy have intelligence branches, which do special work related to war and the preparations for war. Other departments have their own investigators, devoted mainly to detecting petty crookedness within their departmental machinery, checking on their employees, and on people who deal with the departments.

There are no mysteries and very few secrets of operation among the federal detective agencies. They are glad to tell the world how they operate. They advertise their methods. They are not averse to publicity. They operate on the assumption that the more people know about the means by which violators of laws can be detected and caught, the more people will consider it unwise and inexpedient to attempt violations. There are some exceptions to the rule of openness and publicity: The Postal inspectors and the Treasury's Secret Service like to operate in the dark, with the least possible publicity. And all agencies, including the FBI, are reluctant to let the public know all about how they catch spies, except occasionally in arrears.

FBI and Its Agents

Federal Bureau of Investigation agents are detectives of a super police force operating throughout the United States and its possessions and territories. There are more than 3,000 of them and their authority is expanding constantly as federal laws expand. The FBI, a part of the Department of Justice, has found its powers greatly expanded since the entry of the United States into war, for the Bureau now has the authority to arrest and question anyone in order to prevent espionage. This part of their job—spy catching—now draws most attention, but it still is not the FBI's major job. Most of the agents' time is spent on the more tedious and less glamorous job of enforcing the run-of-mine federal laws.

The impact of war was not so much of a shock to the FBI as it was to many other agencies. The Bureau had been operating on an emergency basis for many months and had been preparing for the worst since 1938. The total number of employees, including special agents, expanded from 3,299 in October of 1939 to approximately 8,500 in February 1942. The number of agents alone was expanded more than three times, from 851 to 3,100. Working hours were stepped up, and long before the United States was attacked, the Washington office and all field offices were operating 24 hours a day.

The special agents of the FBI are known in police circles as the "smoothies" of law enforcement. They are scientifically trained investigators

357

and they are deadly accurate in their shooting, but they are also trained as diplomats, and they are the best-dressed group of men in the whole government. The Bureau orders them to dress well and they follow orders, wearing snap brim felt hats and conservative collegiate styles. Intentionally, the agents are different in every way from old-time tobacco-chewing cops. They must be able to meet a Supreme Court justice, a bank president or a Dillinger—all with the same courtesy and effectiveness.

Much of the FBI's success in dealing with criminals is a result of the excellent manners of its agents. Director Hoover would be merciless in dealing with any of his agents who used violence on a suspect, or yelled at him, or threatened to make trouble for a friend or relative. A gunman who has been pushed around by hard-handed policemen under a focused electric light is likely to appreciate the FBI's friendly word and a cigarette before the questioning begins.

Never does the FBI break its word. A man who for the time being held the title of Public Enemy No. 1 was caught at the muzzle of a gun:

"It's the chair for me and I know it," he said to the FBI. "But I want to fix things so my wife won't be scared all her life. Can I make a deal?"

The murderer told where thousands of dollars in loot could be found and in return—well, what in return? No one has ever said. But the night the murderer took that last walk he sent a message to Hoover:

"Just tell him I said 'thanks.' "

An applicant for special agent in the FBI must be between the ages of 23 and 35, a graduate of a recognized school of accountancy with at least three years' experience in commercial accounting, or a graduate of an accredited school of law, or be a college graduate with either extensive experience as an investigator or a "fluent, workable knowledge of a foreign language." In the Bureau, you can find practitioners of practically every trade or profession, from landscape painting to experting on Diesel engines. If an applicant passes these tests and a difficult physical examination his background is examined. The FBI wants to know all about his family and where he went to school and how he got along with his teachers. A drunken father or a silly mother might put him out of the running. He might be refused because he is rude or thoughtless or slow on the uptake. The standards seem almost impossibly high, but there is always a waiting list and the number of agents has more than tripled in the last few years. FBI agents are not protected by Civil Service. If a man makes a mistake which shows a lack of care or intelligence or weakness he is dropped forthwith. An agent who shows unusual ability may win promotion without waiting on seniority. He need never fear to tread on the most important toes.

Most law enforcement officers—like politicians and actors—thrive on publicity, but FBI agents' names seldom appear in newspapers. Only office chiefs are permitted to give information to newspapers. These are the strict orders of Director J. Edgar Hoover to guard against leakage of information, to keep agents from specializing in the spectacular cases which make headlines, and to prevent the agents from becoming so well known that they could not conceal their identity. Hoover is the chief spokesman for the Bureau, and occasionally appears as the author of magazine articles.

Hoover

J. Edgar Hoover is a black-eyed, swarthy, muscular man. He has an utter contempt for criminals as a class. "They're rats," he says, "yellow rats." Hoover is a native of Washington, and worked his way through George Washington University and Law School. He practiced law in Washington, then joined the Department of Justice in 1917. Four years later he became assistant director of the Bureau of Investigation. In 1924, Harlan F. Stone, then Attorney General, determined to reorganize the detective division attached to the Department of Justice. It was a typical political bureau of that day, and although recognized as a pretty sad affair, its misdoings were condoned on the theory that most detective agencies were apt to be like that. Some of the agents were incompetent, some dishonest, some were drunkards, some were blackmailers, and some were good men who had been discouraged by conditions inside the office. Stone had had occasion to ask that a certain investigation be made, and on the advice of a man who knew the ropes, he directed that Hoover be set on the job. The young man was an enthusiast. He worked nights on the records, and he made a convert of Stone. "I want you to take charge of this bureau," Stone told Hoover. "Make it what it should be. You'll have a tough job, but I'll stand by you." Stone's offer was something Hoover cherished, but he tied a string to his acceptance: "If there is to be any politics in the job, I don't want it."

"There will be no politics," said Stone.

There never has been any politics.

Hoover's success is due not merely to his ability as a policeman, but because the FBI is his life. He does not hesitate to delegate authority but he knows the details of every significant case. His check-up system requires a report more than six times a year on every unsolved case, with an explanation. An angry columnist once sneered that Hoover gave others a chance at all the gunplay. His ego was so wounded that he arrested the next public enemy in person. He gave up the practice, however, when the press complained that he was reckless.

359

Hoover is pleasant, courteous, cold, and entirely ruthless. He likes an occasional look at the bright lights, enjoys the company of pretty women, and is not afraid to look on at gambling in the Florida communities where gambling is a source of revenue. The FBI might still be an excellent but unheard-of adjunct to the Department of Justice if Hoover had not had the idea of playing up the sensational exploits of his men during the kidnaping and bank-robbing heyday. He also knows that if a chink were found in his armor a thousand arrows of publicity would be shot through it and he takes no chances. He is completely outspoken in his likes and dislikes, and for that and other reasons has accumulated a fine list of enemies, jealousies and envies. More than once, aspiring politicians have tried to move in on him, on the theory that his enemies were powerful, but the event has always shown that the public and Congress reacted strongly in his favor. His men are intensely loyal to him because of his qualities of leadership. They also know that if one of them were found to be dishonest or subject to influence Hoover would classify him as a "yellow rat" and never rest until the offender was disgraced. He works his men without mercy but he works as many hours as any of them. The crook who kills an FBI man might just as well be dead.

FBI and the Laws

The authority of the FBI to act in crimes formerly the province of local police has grown in the same way that the power of other federal agencies has increased. FBI jurisdiction is limited to crimes against branches of the government and crimes of an interstate nature. And the concept of interstate crime has changed just as much in the last few years as that of interstate commerce. Until 1932 federal laws against crime were inadequate to make the FBI an effective law-enforcement agency. In some cases, agents had no authority to carry weapons or to cross state lines. When Homer Cummings became Attorney General in 1933, he drew up a series of laws which were intended to correct the more glaring defects. Congress was apathetic, but when the Lindbergh baby was kidnaped the country's emotions were stirred, and the adroit Cummings put the bills through before Congress cooled off. Originally an interstate crime was one in which the *action* took place in more than one state. Kidnaping became a federal crime because abductors were seizing victims in one state and carrying them to another. Then authorities went a step further and decided that fleeing from one state to another after committing a crime was sufficient to constitute an interstate crime. The mere presumption that they *might* cross a state border was enough.

Under a recent law, the FBI is empowered to assist local officers in apprehending the perpetrator of any local crime who may have fled across state borders, but in these cases the FBI acts only when called in by the local officers.

Under the Hatch Act, FBI agents are assigned to investigate government employees. This is a sore spot with some government employees who object to the "invasion of their private lives."

The FBI is charged also with catching white slavers but this duty does not appeal to them. They feel that both the slavers and the slaves are ordinarily of the lowest human strata, and a girl rescued today is likely to be wandering down the same old street as soon as she is freed. Now and then an exception is discovered, and the FBI does what it can for the victim. There was, for instance, a little French girl from Montreal who had quite innocently been drawn into a life of prostitution. She was discovered in the course of an inquiry into a high-jacking case. An armory had been robbed of government-owned weapons, a rival mob broken up by murder in order to get the men needed in the exploits planned, a suspected "canary" was shot to death in a hospital bed before he could "sing," and a street battle fought before the gangsters could realize on the loot they had stolen. The girl was found puzzled and frightened and in mortal danger of murder.

"She'd be all right if she had a chance," was the decision of the agents.

"Give her a chance," ordered Hoover.

She is married now, and happy. She has never suspected that agents of the Bureau keep a constant watch over her to see that none of the mob with which she once associated returns to kill her.

In 1941, 68,368 cases were investigated, 6,182 convictions were secured (which was 96 per cent of the cases brought to trial), 2,633 federal fugitives were located and apprehended, 7,102 fugitives from state laws were located for local officers, and the total of savings, fines and recoveries amounted to $8,650,272.

Spies and Saboteurs

The FBI is the coordinating agency for all government departments in detecting spies and saboteurs. In the months before war its feats against espionage were even more daring and brilliant than the romantic doings of FBI heroes in the comic strips and movies. And none was more exciting than the operation for more than a year of a radio station which the Germans thought to be manned by their own spies. The station on Long Island was built largely with Nazi funds. It was set up after William Sebold, a loyal naturalized American, sent word to the Bureau that he had been ordered by the Nazis to transmit spy reports from America to Germany. When the FBI sprung its trap it caught 33 Nazi spies.

Equally important, though less spectacular, was the guarding of American factories important to the war effort. From the fall of 1939 to the declaration of war in 1941, 2,000 industrial plants rated as most important by War and Navy Departments were inspected and suggestions were made for protection against sabotage and espionage. Early in 1942, 12,000 other plants were listed for examination. Within two hours after war was declared, 2,971 aliens considered dangerous were in custody. The Bureau has tried to avoid any injustices to loyal and well-behaved aliens.

Files and Museum

In the FBI files are 33,000,000 fingerprint records and other prints are coming in at the rate of 40,000 a day. Only about 5,000,000 of those fingerprinted are classified as professional criminals—living and dead. The other prints are of past or present members of the armed services, of some government employees, of employees of many industrial organizations and of men and women who place their prints with the Bureau voluntarily. The use of the civilian files is illustrated by the story of a corpse that was recovered from the waters of a western harbor recently. It had been immersed so long that it was utterly unrecognizable. Patient work in the laboratory eventually yielded prints from the swollen and decomposed fingers. The results were a murder story and the inheritance of an estate.

The FBI has branch offices in 56 cities and they are connected by teletype. All day and all night information pours in to be digested. The Bureau's card index is not a dry and dusty affair. It is kept alive, and each day the agent responsible knows precisely the status of his cases in the field.

The pertinacity of the Bureau is almost incredible. In the Mattson kidnaping case in the state of Washington, 24,000 possible suspects were examined and 2,000 finally qualified as suspects. Of the 211 kidnaping cases which were handled before kidnaping ceased to be a criminal industry, only two remain to be cleared and FBI agents are still patiently at work on these. Only one perfect crime was ever reported to the Bureau. Not much may be said of it, for the man and woman who did the killing are influential members of their community, and would inevitably demand huge damages if their identity were hinted at. The Bureau knows when the murder was committed and where and how. But the body was never found and the evidence was not the kind that a court would listen to. But, even now the FBI agents have been "getting up" in the morning with the killers, and "putting them to bed" at night—for seven years.

The Bureau's crime museum in the modern, air-conditioned Justice

Department Building in the Federal Triangle was closed to visitors when the United States entered the war. This was a forced action, for the Bureau almost overnight became too busy to route 1,000 men and women through the museum each day. In the museum is a variety of objects which suggest that crime does not pay. John Dillinger began his professional life as a village tough boy, but his death mask is in the museum, along with his straw hat riddled with bullets and his collar stained with blood, and the cigar he was about to light when the blast started. In the same glass case are the automatic pistols he carried, the tommy gun found in Baby Face Nelson's car when he tried to shoot it out, and the chains with which kidnaped Charles Urschel was lashed in a farm cellar. Pretty Boy Floyd's guns are there, too.

Crime Laboratory

In the Bureau's crime laboratory—never open to the public—a ballistics expert is surrounded by samples of almost every kind of firearm ever used in this country. With his scales and microscope he can tell from what kind of gun a bullet was fired and, if a gun is found, whether it is the right one. Also in the closed-off crime laboratory is Oscar, whom the public never sees. The Bureau is not ashamed of Oscar, who is one of its most efficient and untiring aides, but Oscar often is too busy to be seen. Oscar is a dummy. Today he may be a man of the world, in evening dress. Tomorrow he may impersonate a dockhand. At all times Oscar wears a sour, supercilious air. Agents who have dealt with him have been known to dislike him bitterly.

Oscar is one of the properties used in the training school. He is invariably the murdered man. The pupil-detective is given no advance information. He is ushered into the room in which Oscar lies and told to find out what he can. There may be but a single clue—a torn scrap of paper, a photograph, a broken glass—and that one clue is anything but conspicuous. If the pupil has what it takes he will get at least a sniff of the events that resulted in the dummy's death. If he misses the clue, the miss goes down on the records.

The Bureau's neophytes are put through an extensive course in everything which has to do with crime. They may measure shadows, pick up hairs, sweep tiny bits of dust into little envelopes, cut out the bit of wood on which blood or oil may have fallen, for future inquiry in the laboratory, draw diagrams of the scene and maps of the near-by roads and streets, or watch the flight of birds overhead. The Urschel kidnaping was solved because Urschel, chained in a lightless cellar, noted that an airplane passed over his prison house at approximately the same hour each day. It was the mailplane. The FBI followed its course and found the hoodlums who had lived in the farmhouse.

A pupil in the crime school attends lectures, works with other agents, practices with rifle and revolver and keeps himself fit. He must know enough of practical jujitsu to be able to take care of himself in a rough and tumble, and how to jump from a moving automobile without getting hurt. The FBI men are not often called on to use their weapons, thanks to the estimation in which they are held by their enemies, but the few men who fight back are desperate. In almost every case a "murder rap" is hanging over them, and their one hope of safety is shooting themselves free.

School for Police

Rather than a central federal police system with authority over all local police, the FBI has become an important coordinating agency for local police throughout the country. One of the most important and least known of the Bureau's activities is the National Police Academy. For generations this country's police operated on a hit-or-miss plan. A chief of police had no authority beyond the city line, although he often took it. A sheriff was in presumable responsibility in the non-urban areas. There were state police forces in a few states, with no authority over either chiefs or sheriffs, and no detective organizations or facilities. For the most part the business of state police was to control traffic. In one or two states in which were large bodies of restless workmen, the state policemen were mostly concerned with riots and disorders. New York City had an excellent organization, Los Angeles was beginning to show signs of police intelligence, and Chicago's police knew their own districts with all their peculiarities. In all cities police progress followed an identical line. But in comparatively few cases did the men who ultimately became police chiefs look for or obtain any instruction from other chiefs in other towns.

Director Hoover of the FBI undertook at first to correct one glaring defect of this national lack of system by setting up a clearinghouse of crime statistics. Police chiefs and sheriffs had been depending on the unpleasant portraits occasionally stuck up in post offices and on relaying information about wanted men to areas in which the interested policemen thought they might have taken refuge. The criminal had a distinct percentage in his favor. This was increased as American roads were improved and high power cars came into use. A murderous mob could get away from the scene of a crime with comparative ease. Communications had been bettered coincidentally, but if the mob happened to run in an unexpected direction the wired alarms could not catch up with them. Hoover enlisted the cooperation of police authorities in forwarding information. The Bureau's Uniform Crime Reports are now studied by all men responsible for the maintenance of law and order. Out of this initial effort the National Police Academy grew.

Police chiefs in 461 cities have selected officers to attend the regular sessions of the Academy, which are held at Bureau headquarters in Washington. The men in many instances pay their own expenses. They are taught everything the FBI has learned. The graduates of the Academy return to their own cities to set up classes for their associates. In 56 cities the FBI has established training courses for police chiefs, sheriffs and members of state police forces. The significant inquiries in the FBI laboratory are reported to these police schools.

Elmer Irey of the Treasury

The men of the six enforcement agencies in the Treasury are grouped under the coordination of Elmer Lincoln Irey, who is officially known as the Coordinator of Treasury Agency Services. His men call him "chief," but he does not encourage this. Irey is a quiet, soft-spoken, unassuming man and that title carries a suggestion of sensationalism he deprecates. The men of the Treasury's agencies are "law enforcement officers" and the word "detective" is taboo. Irey heads the Intelligence Unit of the Bureau of Internal Revenue, which keeps an eye and hand on the 2,668 investigators.

Irey is the man who caught Al Capone and sent him to Alcatraz. Another of Irey's extraordinary cases was that of "Waxey" Gordon, who dealt in beer and murder in New York City. The Post Office inspectors were powerless, for Gordon did not use the mails. The FBI gathered information but Gordon transgressed no law that the FBI was set to guard. Elmer Irey's Intelligence Unit in the Bureau of Internal Revenue was called in. They found that "Waxey" lived like a baron of the better sort. He wore $25 silk shirts, had three huge cars, a ten-room apartment, sent his children to exclusive private schools and spent his winters at the most extravagant resorts. Yet he reported a taxable income of only $6,000. Irey's men began a painstaking search of Gordon's records and spending. Gordon went to a federal prison.

The Narcotics Bureau—another of the Treasury's agencies—knew that a group of Orientals in Honolulu was doing a thriving business in opium, but the proof could not be found. Unfortunately for the dope peddlers, they had omitted paying their income taxes. Now they are out of business and in a federal institution and the Treasury has $247,000 it might not have had otherwise. Irey has returned to the government $100 for every two dollars spent on the Revenue Bureau. It was Irey who really broke the Lindbergh kidnaping, for against the wishes of the anxious father he insisted on taking the serial numbers of the bills used for the pay-off. When they began to come into circulation, the FBI mapped the district in which they were distributed, and Hauptmann paid with his life.

365

Irey was born in Kansas City. His father came to Washington when the future chief was a boy and got a job in the Government Printing Office. When young Elmer had completed his schooling he found a job as stenographer in the Post Office Department. Presently he was a postal inspector. In 1919, Daniel Roper, then Commissioner of Internal Revenue, found that he needed smart men to collect the income taxes of a careless people and asked the Post Office for men with experience as investigators. Irey was loaned to Roper as the head of a seven-man unit and Roper refused to give him up. Irey was not long in realizing that the Intelligence Unit might be made into something wider in scope than was originally planned.

Criminals who are otherwise lawproof are often caught through their income taxes as in the cases cited. The Revenue Bureau intelligence men concern themselves only with evasion of taxes. A man may be a gambler, a briber, an accepter of bribes, a crooked politician, but his offenses are none of the Treasury men's business—*unless* he fails to pay his proper income tax. The Treasury agents know plenty of secrets about illegal operations of some taxpayers, but they do not tell any other agents of the government, so long as the right income taxes are paid. Crooks may beat one law, but if they cheat the Treasury out of taxes on illegal gains, then the Treasury agents will be on their necks. Many a criminal has gone to prison for failing to pay his taxes, although court records may show no trace of all his other offenses against the law.

A master bootlegger was caught in New York, not for bootlegging but for lying about his income. Irey's men found suspicious entries in his books, which in turn led to other men. One morning a police whistle blew in New York and Irey's men of the Alcohol Tax Unit moved in from the four corners. A three-story still was found inside what had seemed to be a warehouse, which was equipped to turn out 6,000 gallons of so-called whisky a day. Last year the Alcohol Tax Unit made 23,843 arrests for bootlegging, and the number of cases is on the upgrade because of increased taxes on liquor. Forty-six per cent of the inmates of federal prisons are alcohol tax evaders.

Customs, Narcotics

The Treasury's Customs Bureau, which frowns on all smugglers, and the Narcotics Bureau are natural partners in Irey's coordinated six. Working together they nipped in the bud a poisonous conspiracy to finance a revolution in Honduras by the sale of heroin in the United States. On another occasion the partnership smashed the Lyon-Bacula narcotics smuggling ring. There were in the personnel of the ring the owner of a restaurant on the Rue Boissy d'Anglais in Paris, two South American diplomats, a professional murderer from Italy, a deputy of France, a lovely woman who owned a lingerie shop in London, the head of a gang of organized criminals in New York, and a convict in Alcatraz. They had outlets for morphine and heroin in every principal city in the United States and ran true to fictional form by meeting ships at sea in powerful motorboats and running into hidden inlets where armed gangsters waited for them. Some were killed by others of the gang when the heat was turned on and they might have turned state's evidence.

Secret Service

The Secret Service of the Treasury does two things: It catches counterfeiters and it acts as bodyguard of the President and a few other dignitaries. To guard the President, his family, and in election years the President-elect, the agents have absolute power. A President now and then may trick the Secret Service. Calvin Coolidge managed to get away for one unaccompanied stroll, Herbert Hoover outran the S.S. escort in his fast car once or twice, and Franklin Roosevelt has gotten out for a drive a few times with only a man or two following. These are the exceptions. Congress conferred powers on the S.S. which transcend those of the President himself, when his safety is at stake. When a President tours the country, the cities in which he will make stops are given almost microscopic examination, every minute of his prospective stay is scrutinized in advance, men are planted at strategic points, and if he drives through the streets the S.S. calls in policemen from cities for scores of miles around to make sure that no fanatic can get near enough to do harm.

In its other activity, the battle against counterfeiters, Chief Frank J. Wilson conducts an unending "Know Your Money" campaign of education, and more and more the public is responding in the detection of counterfeits. Fewer counterfeits are afloat now, and the total output is less than ever before in history. There will always be counterfeiters, just as there will always be fools, but it is a fact that no counterfeiter is successful for long.

Postal Inspectors

The Post Office inspectors have performed feats of detection that are not excelled by anything in the records of the FBI or Treasury Intelligence. They have fought gun battles, hidden in thickets, worn disguises, lived up to the best storybook standards ever since the force was created. But they tell no stories, and avoid all publicity. They do not go along with the theory prevailing in the FBI and other sleuthing agencies that one way of curtailing crime is to let the public know how effectively crime is usually detected. The Post Office inspectors will not even admit that they have broken up the

367

widely known "Spanish prisoner racket," but they have, at least temporarily. This is a business that has been a prosperous swindle for 170 years.

Thousands of men—very rarely a woman—in the United States have received letters from the Spanish prisoner. The letters are written on coarse paper and ordinarily with a pencil. The writer is, he says, a Spaniard of good family and at one time possessed of wealth. But he unfortunately mixed himself in politics and was placed under arrest by the men now in power. At the worst he fears that he may be assassinated. Under the "ley de fuga"—the law of flight—his guards may shoot him any day and explain that he tried to get away and so they were justified in killing him. At the best he anticipates years of imprisonment. Fortunately he has made a friend of one of his guards, and this guard will, for a consideration, help him to freedom some dark night. The prisoner, of course, has no money in his possession;

"But when I was warned that I was to be arrested I managed to hide a brass chest containing"—as many thousands of dollars in gold and jewels as seems advisable—"and I will share this with you if you will provide the money with which to bribe my guard. If you will write Señorita So-and-So, who is my beloved niece, she will meet you. Only to her will I reveal the hiding place of the money."

The sucker is always required to bring his money to the foreign city in which the swindle is being operated. He is made to feel that he can watch and guard his interests at every point. If he takes the bait, he meets the girl, turns over the money with which to bribe the guard, and then is left sucking his thumb in an unknown town. The police never take any interest in his plaint. It is not often that he dares complain, for to do so would reveal that he had planned to break the law, suborn an official of the state and rescue from imprisonment a public enemy.

The most the Post Office inspectors will say of their recent exploit is that they found the "powerhouse" with a card index system and five letter writers and a complete equipment of handsome nieces and venal guards and cashbooks, showing that Americans either do not read the newspapers, or they do not retain what they read.

"Crime Does Not Pay"

When amateurs in any line go up against professionals, the amateurs are likely to get licked. That's one of the difficulties in trying to evade laws. The violator is usually an amateur. He may think he is good at avoiding detection, but he is up against a set of professionals on the other side, and in practically all cases it develops that they know more about the game than he does. The big or little crook, professional or amateur, is always

368

stupid, but he doesn't always know this until he has had time to think, and jail is a good place to think.

The slogan, "Crime does not pay," may sound like a lecture or a sermon, but it is merely an observation of fact, based on statistics which are available everywhere, especially in Washington. Evasion of federal laws is particularly inexpedient.

34

Jews in Government

IT'S AN artificial issue—this issue of "Jews in Government"—but it *does* exist, and so it should be discussed factually, not hushed. The best antidote for any unwholesome fanning of the flames of prejudice and discrimination is the truth, presented frankly.

As a practical measure stick, remind yourself that 4 per cent of the population of the United States are Jews. Thus 4 per cent is "proportional."

Washington as a city is not a "Jewish city," for only about 3 per cent of the population is Jewish. This is far less than the proportion in most other big eastern cities. New York, for example, has 28 per cent of Jews. Most of the old Jewish residents of Washington have been here for several generations. They are in business, or the law, or perhaps the government, and up until 1933 nobody paid any particular attention to the question of who were Jews and who were not. It wasn't considered an item of any particular significance.

In 1933 two things happened: Hitler came into power in Germany, and gave momentum to the world-wide propaganda crusade against Jews. Also the New Deal came into power in the United States, and brought into government a large number of Jews. The two events, coming simultaneously, made the issue.

What are the facts? It isn't easy to know, for statistics are not available. Government keeps no record of its employees, as to who are Jews, who are Methodists, who are Catholics, or German-Americans, or Italian-Americans, or English-Americans. Government as an employer is satisfied with the fact that its employees are citizens, and keeps no record of their religious affiliations or national or racial antecedents. Thus it is impossible to prove anything about Jews in government, on the basis of government statistics. This makes it easy for agitators to claim that excessive proportions of government workers are Jews, and it also makes it hard to refute the claim.

But any experienced Washington observer who has eyes and ears is in position to know the approximate truth. My own observation and opinion is that the number of Jews in government is probably not in excess of the proportional 4 per cent, considering the average in all government agencies.

But it is also my observation that men who are Jews occupy positions which are very influential within government. It would appear that of the total weight of influence within government, Jews have more than 4 per cent. This may be interpreted as either a crack at the Jews, or as praise for them and their ability. It is meant as neither. It is meant as merely a factual observation.

The next question is whether there is cohesive "Jewish influence." Is there anything about the influence of Jews in government which is "Jewish," which adheres to any Jewish pattern of thought, feeling or tradition? If there were, it would be bad, for we do not want our government policies determined by influences which are excessively Jewish, or Methodist, or Catholic, or Harvard, or Californian. I have made some studies to see whether Jews stick together in their attitude on public policies. Are they a clique, or cabal, or a group, or a philosophical unit in their influence on government policies? They are not. They are split wide open among themselves. They don't agree on everything any more than non-Jews do. They cuss each other out, as do others. They don't gang socially among themselves. They don't gang together philosophically. They are diverse. Thus it becomes clear that there is no such thing as a "Jewish influence" within government. There isn't any deep dark mysterious "Jewish plot" or even any "Jewish unity."

Concentration

But that isn't the whole of the story. The rest of the story is that Jews have become concentrated in a few government agencies where they *are* disproportionate, and where they are conspicuous for their numbers, and where they have close and intimate contact with the public, and where they tend to create the public impression that Jews are in the ascendant in government.

These agencies are: The Securities and Exchange Commission; the Department of Labor, especially the Wage and Hour Division; the National Labor Relations Board; the Social Security Board; and some offices of the Department of Justice. In some of the offices of these agencies the Jews are so numerous that it is no wonder that the public which deals with them gets the idea that Jews are quite as numerous in the whole government. By any standards of administration, public or private, this is an error, and it needs to be remedied by the reduction of the proportion of Jews in these offices. Inherently it may not be wrong, but it looks wrong to have any public offices manned by people of any particular group.

Note also that the agencies in which Jews are disproportionately numerous and conspicuous are "friction agencies." They are established under laws of Congress to do certain reform jobs. People who are subjected to reforms of any kind usually do not like the reforms. They are rubbed the wrong way by the reforms themselves. They may transfer their irritations over the reforms to the Jewish officials who apply the reforms, just as people squawk about the traffic cop when they mean to complain about the inconveniences of heavy traffic. This claim that people transfer their objections from the cause to the administrators of the cause is made by Jews themselves, in a defensive spirit. Perhaps it is so. Nevertheless, it seems shortsighted for any group, especially any minority group, to permit its members to become so dominant in any governmental function, and this observation has nothing to do with anti-Semitism.

In certain professions or occupations within government, the Jews are undoubtedly disproportionate, higher than 4 per cent. These occupations are: Lawyers, economists, statisticians.

One reason is that Jews have found it difficult to get private employment, especially since 1933, when anti-Semitism began to spread out from Nazi Germany. Intelligent and well-educated young Jews just out of universities (notably Harvard and Columbia) found private jobs barred to them, but not government jobs, so they took what they could get. They preferred government jobs to no jobs at all. Thus the situation is a circle of cause and effect. Another factor is this: Jewish immigrants of the first and even the second generation were inclined to steer clear of the lofty aspirations of participating in the government of their new land. Succeeding generations do not feel that way about it, however. They feel like taking part in any activities, including government, to which their abilities entitle them.

As for the abilities of Jewish officials and employees of government, their average rating is unquestionably high. This is the observation of all fair and impartial observers. It is commonly said by Jews that they *must* work harder than non-Jews, to make up for the prejudice against them. At any rate, the Jews in government are hard workers, zealous for their jobs and particular causes. They are inclined to be intense, passionate and aggressive in their work.

Jews in government are mainly "big city people." It is usually true that big city people, regardless of whether they are Jews or non-Jews, have approaches to social and economic problems which are different from the approaches of small city, small town or country people. They think and deal in terms of teeming masses, rather than in terms of individuals and small groups. They have "city ways" of living, and "city ways" of thinking. They do not recognize that there are differences between big city and small town ways. Sometimes this makes them clumsy in dealings with the great numbers of people who are small city, small town, rural, individualistic, stalwart, or even hick. Of course it is true that the entire New Deal is pretty heavily manned by big city men and big city ways and big city thinking, and this applies to both Jews and non-Jews.

The Jews in government are mostly "liberal," and on the average they are probably more "liberal" or more "humanitarian" than are non-Jews. They are "New Dealers," like non-Jews within the New Deal, but they are probably a little more "New Dealish" or "leftish" than the average of New Dealers. Conservative Jews are not welcomed in the New Deal any more than are conservative non-Jews. A few Jews in government are communist fellow travelers, but most are not—most are merely "liberal."

If the squeeze against young Jews continues in private business, the result probably will be to force a greater number of them into government in the future. This is already the outlook. Many young Jews are taking civil service examinations, passing them with high ratings, making themselves eligible for government appointments. In due course they will be hired, because government personnel administrators follow the civil service requirements of accepting the best-by-test. The policy is neither Semitic nor anti-Semitic. It is the normal grinding of the civil service system.

Sentiment in Congress

Still, the subject of public sentiment against disproportionate representation of any minority group will remain, and this sentiment is expressed most clearly through Congress. Suspicion of Jews in government exists in Congress in far higher degree than is warranted by the proportion of Jews in government. It exists even among members of Congress who are not actually anti-Semitic. They are merely opposed to too many of any one group. The feeling often shows up on issues which are not labeled as Jewish in open debate, but which are clearly understood among members of Congress as involving the "Jewish question." (Also the "Negro question" is closely related in the minds of many members of Congress, especially the southern members.)

For example, a conference report on a civil service bill was rejected by the House in October 1940, just before the national elections, because it proposed to eliminate photographs from civil service records. Such photographs tended to show that certain applicants were Negroes or Jews. Southern members rose in protest. The bill was subsequently presented without this provision and accepted. Later the Civil Service Commission, by its own executive authority, abandoned photographs and substituted fingerprints as identifications. These identify persons, but not races or groups.

In other ways the question of Jews often pops up in legislative processes. In hearings before appropriation subcommittees, government administrators are often asked by congressional committee members how many Jews are employed in their agencies. In some cases they are advised not to employ any more Jews. There is no authority for such advice from members of Congress, but it carries an implied threat when it comes from members who sit on committees that vote the money. In one case Congress refused to vote money for a Board of Legal Examiners to recruit lawyers for government service, and the motive for the refusal grew out of the fact that the plan was written by one high-placed Jew and was to be administered by another young Jew. In other cases Congress has talked against "New Yorkers" in the civil service, and it was understood in Congress that this term was a synonym for Jews.

The motives in Congress are sometimes hard to determine. There is a small amount of actual anti-Semitism, especially in the attitude of some southern members. But in many cases, perhaps most cases, the motives are not anti-Semitic, but are merely due to a desire to keep the civil service "balanced."

Discrimination

In some government agencies there is no doubt that discrimination exists against Jews for employment. It is hard to prove, but is known to exist. In some cases charges of discrimination have been made, but have not been supported by the facts and circumstances. The Committee on Fair Employment Practice was set up in OPM to combat discrimination against Negroes and Jews by government war contractors, and it has extended its interests into the sphere of checking against discrimination within the government. Its inquiries to date suggest that there is no mass discrimination. Those cases where it does exist are balanced out by other cases in which Jewish applicants get their share of jobs, or more than their proportionate share.

Some Jewish leaders themselves have taken a quiet but stiff stand against the employment of too many Jews by government. In one case a high Jewish official was asked by Jewish leaders not to send New York Jewish employees to act as field agents, especially in the South. It was argued that to refrain from doing so was to "refrain from drawing lightning." On the other hand, non-Jewish officials within government, acting under the direction of the President, are trying to get various agencies to employ more Jews, and thus to counteract the discrimination which has been subtly practiced against them in the past, and to make the practice accord with the preaching of equal rights for all minorities.

The whole subject is very much tangled and illogical. Anti-Jewish prejudice and propaganda have done their part, and in some ways they are assisted by Jewish hypersensitiveness. This latter is understandable, and it is not to be wondered at, and yet there are times when it is one of the unfortunate entangling influences.

Non-Jews, the 96 per cent of the population, should recognize that Jewish citizens are citizens, entitled to participate in government with the same rights as all other citizens. Furthermore, it is practically desirable and relaxing to recognize the fact that Jews in government are not unified in their social and economic philosophies, that their ideas are quite as diverse as those of any other group of citizens.

Jews, the 4 per cent, should give thought to the fact that under the normal workings of government in the current regime they have either achieved the abolition of discriminations against them on employment, or are well on the way to achieving it. The next step for them is to avoid, in so far as they can, an excessive loading of the government with Jewish citizens. If there were to be such an overloading, it would cause muttering from citizens who are not anti-Jewish, but who resent on general principles any over-representation in their government, or even in certain agencies, with the people of *any* one group.

If such restraints and good sense are shown by the 96 per cent and by the 4 per cent, then perhaps eventually this issue can be dissolved, and become what it ought to be—no issue whatsoever.

35

Wonderland of Pamphlets

ELECTRIC signs on rooftops are supposed to advertise something. Ordinarily they are used to attract business, to draw customers. Government has all the customers it can handle, and normally it does not use electric signs, but there is one exception. High in the air atop an eight-story building, visible from train windows as you pull into Washington's Union Station from the North, is a huge electric sign which reads "GOVERNMENT PRINTING OFFICE." It is the biggest printing plant in the world. It is the job printer for the biggest publisher, which is the United States Government.

Specify any subject, and the government has something on it in print. Is it toads, fishing worms, rest rooms for women, or knots in rope that interest you? The government has pamphlets on them. Do you want to know about famous trees, anemia in dogs, divining rods, mountain lion trapping, common colds, baby rearing, getting rid of bats in buildings, the cannibalistic habits of the corn earworm, caviar, poison ivy, or how to build your house? The government can tell you in a pamphlet. Maps to guide you through hills and creeks of your environs? The government has 'em. How to save the apparently drowned? Treatment for frostbite? Cost of going to college? Termites? Recipes? White rats? Simple plumbing repairs in the home? Government can tell you.

Canaries, earth's magnetism, mopsticks, camp stoves and ancient America. Sex education for the young, dog tricks, furniture, earthquakes, and officers of the Confederate Navy. Where to establish a cheese factory, and faculty inbreeding in land-grant colleges. How to make air-raid shelters. How to make good privies for country homes. Dams, mittens, child adoption, and Jewish people in Palestine. Woodpeckers, roadside planting, handling of riots, recreation, eclipse of the sun, American battlefields in Europe, the effects of alcohol and tobacco. Government has them all in print, and sixty thousand other subjects. How to live, how to work, how to make things, how to raise children, how to sleep—ask government and get a pamphlet.

This business of dispensing wisdom has been going on for a long time. Even back in 1862 there was a government document telling husbands how to treat their wives. It was the annual report of the Commissioner of Agriculture, and in it were nine pages on the "Hardship of Farmers' Wives." Farmer husbands were sternly enjoined to dig the potatoes for the wife, to get the winter wood supply "piled up cosily," and to help with the house work on washday. The report then added this useful information:

"Unless made otherwise by a vicious training a woman is as naturally tasteful, tidy and neat in herself, and to all her surroundings, as the beautiful canary, which bathes itself every morning, and will not be satisfied until each rebellious feather is compelled to take the shape and place which nature intended."

That, in 1862, was a forerunner of the farmers' bulletins of today, but the style has changed so that many of the bulletins nowadays are devoted to telling farm wives how to treat their husbands so as to make the most of them.

People think the government knows everything about everything, and each year they write thousands of inquiries, most of which can be answered by sending a copy of some pamphlet on the subject. Here are some of the more interesting inquiries:

From Long Island: "Please send me information on what you intend to do with the dust bowl area. Are you going to try to fix it up or sell it? I will be glad to get all the information you can give me."

From Massachusetts: "Could you give me the address of some turkey farm? I need some nice long feathers from the turkey's tail. They should be fairly straight and about 12 inches long. I use them to clean my oboe."

From Ohio: "Please send me your bulletin on bedbugs. Hope you send it in an envelope, but send it anyway."

From Texas: "I shall appreciate any literature on the care and rearing of babies and how to receive the same in large quantities."

Truckloads of mail bags containing government bulletins, pamphlets and booklets go into the Washington Post Office every day for distribution to millions of citizens. Some are sold, most are free for the asking. Many cost 5 cents or 10 cents, which is supposed to be printing cost plus a percentage. Around 25,000,000 copies of documents are sold every year. Six or seven times that number are given away free. The free documents have replaced free seeds of former years as the things which members of Congress may send to their constituents to curry favor.

Documents have become the standard vehicles by which government bureaus and agencies may advertise themselves or their work. Some documents are bright and cheery, most are dull. A farmer who, as chairman of his AAA committee, receives bushels of official documents, once remarked wistfully, "You don't reckon they could put just a few jokes in these things, do you?" Thousands of citizens, especially in small towns and rural regions, make a practice of getting their names on all the government mailing lists that they can, for this swells their mail and gives them a sense of importance. Besides, as one man said, "Government documents are all good and solid." Another remarked that the only fault he had to find with them was they "don't have no advertising matter in them to read."

Superintendent of Documents

The Superintendent of Documents, who supervises the outpouring of pay-for pamphlets, does the biggest mail-order publishing business in the world. He also runs an office in Washington which handles a vast amount of over-the-counter sales to people in the capital.

Among the most unusual bits of printing for sale is a copy of *School Life* which has as an insert a reproduction of a photograph of President Franklin D. Roosevelt autographed "to the pupils and teachers of the United States." The document is the first autographed photograph ever sent out by the Superintendent of Documents.

President Roosevelt is one of the GPO's paying customers. Ordinarily he can get almost any government publication just by asking for it, but specific provisions of law prohibit the giving away of certain items to anybody, and if he wants them he must buy them like anybody else.

The Superintendent of Documents is a real man, more than six feet tall, with a booming voice, a spectacular memory, and about half a century of work with government publications to his credit. His name is Alton P. Tisdel. He started at the bottom, dusting off books in stock. He works about ten hours a day and nobody can remember when he took a vacation.

Boss of the Government Printing Office, of which the office of the Superintendent of Documents is a part, is Augustus E. Giegengack. He came to the job with an impressive record as a progressive commercial printer, having supervised mechanical production of the *Stars and Stripes*, AEF newspaper, during World War I. By installing modern equipment and stepping up efficiency, he has lowered the costs and improved the appearance of government documents.

The biggest continuing job of the plant is getting out daily issues of the *Congressional Record*. Typed copy of what members of Congress have said in the Senate and House chambers during the day is received around midnight. By eight o'clock all 45,000 copies are printed and delivered.

Job printing for the various government agencies—the production of office forms and such material—amounts to approximately 4,000,000,000 pieces annually. The departments pay the GPO, with Congress appropriating the money to the departments.

The cost of printing pamphlets has raised many squawks on Capitol Hill from time to time, and whenever a new one springs up publications experts bring out their figures on the cost. They estimate that if the government answers inquiries by individual letter, the cost per letter is 75 cents. The cost of a pamphlet to answer some often-asked questions is put at less than 5 cents. Many of the pamphlets now issued were originally inspired by a flood of questions from the public.

The literary style of government writers, though sprightlier than it used to be, still tends to be stodgy. The appearance of documents has been spruced up by the increased use of illustrations, and improvements in typography.

The publishing house of Uncle Sam has a fine and efficient printing plant, but it lacks an advertising department and an editorial board. Sometimes a government publication comes into being simply because there's some unexpended money in a bureau's till. If someone in authority decides to run off a publication, there's no one to say "No." Often federal agencies send batches of words into print to impress Congress and the nation at large with their importance—to pave the way for larger appropriations. That's on the order of propaganda. Nevertheless, the publications tinctured with propaganda are far outnumbered by those which deal forthrightly and objectively with their subjects. Fear that a powerful propaganda machine might be built up accounts, in part, for the absence of a centralized peacetime coordination of the federal agencies' output of reading matter. There's a feeling that "coordination" might become "dictation."

Regardless of the continuous controversy over the question of whether government engages in propaganda in its routine pamphlets, one big fact stands out: People seem to like the pamphlets, for they buy a lot of them.

· · · · · ·

(If you would like to know more about publications for your own use, turn to the section headed "How to Get Government Pamphlets," later in this book, page 483. There you will find practical tips on procedure in obtaining, either free or at nominal cost, a wide range of publications—maps, baby care books, home and household aids, health, texts of laws, vacation suggestions, and even movie films.)

36

Tourists See the Sights

WASHINGTON is the greatest sight-seeing city in the world, the rubbernecker's dream come true. In normal times, four million people come every year to the capital, the nation's history factory since 1800. They find it jampacked with buildings where occurred the events they read about at school. Cluttered with houses where these days' men with headline names and newsreel faces brush their teeth and growl about the toast. Bulging with big stone structures which incase thousands of Uncle Sam's hired hands during working hours. Splattered with embassies and studded with statues. Green grass and trees grow all around. The city green and white.

All this puts a hankering to see Washington in the mind of anybody who has a suitcase, a little spare time and enough loose change to make the trip. The camera-lugging, guidebook-buying throng that rides into Washington in each peacetime year outnumbers the capital's residents four to one. It equals the combined populations of New Orleans, Minneapolis, Cincinnati, Newark, Indianapolis, Houston, Seattle, Rochester and Denver, with some thousands to boot.

This year, though the hankering to sight-see in the capital remains, it is harder to satisfy. Vacations are fewer and shorter, auto tires are scarce, the family car must be conserved, and hotel rooms in Washington are at premium. Nevertheless, hundreds of thousands still come to look at Washington's landmarks, and the capital still maintains its position as No. 1 sight-seeing city.

Peddling food, lodging, city transportation and gimcracks to the normal horde of 4,000,000 is one of Washington's "export businesses." The exports are the memories and impressions which tourists take back home. The business involves the money spent while those memories and impressions are being formed. Sight-seers spend, on an average, at least ten dollars each while in the capital. That mounts up to the total of at least $40,000,000 in a normal year.

The People

The mass of four million tourists contains as many kinds of people as there are in the thousands of home towns from which they come. Overweight gents. Lads who peer twice at the price of a blue-plate lunch before ordering. Grand dames who have toured the world. Girls who are making their first trip away from home. Children and babes.

Twosomes (many of them honeymooners) and family groups are in the large majority. And there are high school students, under the chilling watch of chaperoning teachers. Assorted tourists bound together by the money-saving opportunities of the "everything-included tours." Newsboys, sent traveling by the youth-molding fancies of publishers. Workers who take to the joint vacation idea as a means of whittling costs. Unattached men and boys (a minority) who are going it alone. Unaccompanied women and girls (numerous) who are seeing the sights within the security of organized tours.

Those who get the least return for what they spend are the pompous folks who waddle up to desks in top-priced hotels. They hire limousines with uniformed chauffeur-guides. Setting themselves in the middle of dignity, they ride stiffly up Connecticut Avenue and the length of Pennsylvania Avenue. They do little looking—people might think they were looking.

Not so with the common herd. Arriving on the banks of the Potomac in family cars, as four-fifths of them do in the average year, they drive up and down the city, back and forth, gawking all the while, contributing to Washington's notorious traffic jams. Those who want nothing to do with aimless driving and traffic jams either pile on the rubberneck busses or hire the licensed guides who stand on street corners, waiting to sell their knowledge of the city.

Thousands come to Washington with no thought of driving their own cars on the streets, or riding busses, or hiring guides. They are those who fasten themselves upon friends or relatives residing in the capital. Result: Tired Washingtonians—trudging at the elbows of people they met casually in other cities, entertaining distant relatives and people whose names are at the tail-end of their Christmas card lists.

Apart from all that, most tourists who come to Washington have definite and fairly accurate ideas about what they are going to see. Credit this to the space Washington commands in papers and magazines and on the movie screen. No other city in the world is more photographed or more written about. Most sight-seers, therefore, are just soaking up details. Getting closely acquainted with things about which they have advance knowledge.

The man from Boise, sitting right behind the bus driver, sees that the Washington Monument looks just like he thought it would look. The Kansas City lady in the seat across the aisle had been seeing pictures of the Capitol Building ever since she was six, which was forty years ago.

The Sights

The National Museum, under control of the Smithsonian Institution, attracts the most sight-seers. It normally draws at least 2,700,000 a year, according to the count kept by guards at the doors, with their clicking counting machines. Counts made at other buildings and memorials show the comparative popularity with tourists. Here are some recent annual totals: Lincoln Memorial, 1,600,000; Mount Vernon, 1,500,000; Congressional Library, 1,000,000; Washington Monument, 950,000; Bureau of Engraving and Printing, 425,000. No count is kept at the Capitol and, during the national emergency, the White House is not open to visitors in general. It should be noted, also, that the Washington Monument total is held down by the limitations of the elevators. And the Japanese cherry blossom crowds, who pour in every spring, are impossible to count. But anyone who has seen the cars packed bumper to bumper around the Tidal Basin and Speedway knows that the numbers run well into the hundreds of thousands in an average year.

A few tourists go up in the air and look down on the capital as though it were a giant picture spread out on the floor. The helium-filled blimp "Enterprise" (now taken over by the Navy) normally carries 6,000 passengers a year when operating commercially on its 20-minute sight-seeing trips. Another 18,000 do their aerial sight-seeing in airplanes.

Those people get a panorama of a metropolitan area of over 1,000,000 people, without a skyscraper, centered in a saucer between rolling hills, with the Potomac River a silver ribbon in the middle. Near the river are massive, squatty buildings spread for almost two miles between the Capitol and the Lincoln Memorial. With the exception of the two-story temporary war buildings, they are six-story structures, each covering about a city block. Most of them are on the river side of Pennsylvania Avenue. On the other side of "The Avenue" spreads the central business section. As the tourist looks northward he sees office buildings giving way to apartment houses, the area of fashionable residences, embassies, the suburban belt and, finally, the Maryland countryside. Net impression of Washington, seen from the air: It looks as though it had been plopped down in the middle of the woodland growth, with trees and grass showing through between the buildings. A flat city which sprawls over the ground, not rising toward the sky as does New York. A city with few factories and tall smoke stacks. A city dominated by one building—the Capitol.

If you look from the Capitol toward the north, south, east or west, you will see that it stands at the intersection of four thoroughfares which divide the city into four quadrants or sections, Northeast, Northwest, Southeast, Southwest. A set of numbered streets paralleling the north-south axis runs to the east from the Capitol and another to the west. Similarly, one set of streets designated by letters parallels the east-west axis on the north and another set parallels it on the south. This gives each of the four sections its own set of lettered and numbered streets. That is why Washington street addresses have to be written with N E, N W, S E, or S W after the street names.

In the Northwest section are the main business sections, top-flight hotels, apartment houses, old mansions, government workers' boarding houses and above-the-average homes. The Northeast and Southeast quadrants are distinctly middle-class. The Southwest area is loaded with the big government structures, and railroad yards, and meat-packing warehouses, and that glamorous quarter, the fish wharf, where tony people go to smell the smells which are not tony.

The Sights in 1791

What would your great-great-great-grandfather have seen if he could have viewed this region from an altitude of a thousand feet, back in 1791, when George Washington, acting on authority of Congress, selected it as the site for a custom-built capital? He would have seen these things: Georgetown, then a 50-year-old Maryland town and now a part of Washington, to westward. The little farm home of David Burnes, owner of quite a bit of the land, on a plot near where the Washington Monument and White House now stand. Seven miles down the Potomac—Alexandria, up and coming port for ocean-going and coast-plying vessels, home town of the First President. Goose Creek, later renamed Tiber Creek, flowing near the base of Jenkins Hill on which the Capitol later was erected. Marshes reaching back from the river, occupying the area over which dirt has long since been piled to form the great stretch of green which is the Mall. And a wide expanse of river waters where now stand the Jefferson and Lincoln Memorials and the Tidal Basin with its rim of cherry trees. That was the way these parts looked when Washington hired Pierre Charles L'Enfant, a French engineer, in 1791, to lay plans for the capital.

L'Enfant's mind held a great dream: A city of half a million, a capital that would be able to hold its head high among all the world's capitals. More than a century before anybody was to get caught in a horn-tooting traffic jam, he laid plans for streets 100 feet and more in width, avenues even wider. And a great thoroughfare 400 feet from side to side. Today's map of Washington shows how closely L'Enfant's layout was followed. The streets running north and south, east and west—a gridiron. Major avenues running at angles from various centers, giving the effect of huge wheels on top of the gridiron.

L'Enfant was dismissed in 1792, but his assistant who succeeded him carried on his ideas. The work of transforming those ideas advanced very slowly, however. The place was a mess in 1800 when the federal government moved from Philadelphia to set up shop in the new capital city. (There were fewer than 200 federal employees, including everybody from the President on down, at that time.)

A member of Congress from Connecticut, John Cotton Smith, wrote a letter showing just how much of a mess the city was: "One wing of the Capitol only had been erected, which, with the President's House a mile distant from it, both constructed with white sandstone, were shining objects in dismal contrast with the scene around them. Instead of recognizing the avenues and streets portrayed on the plan of the city, not one was visible, unless we except a road, with two buildings on each side of it, called the New Jersey Avenue. The Pennsylvania Avenue . . . was nearly the whole distance a deep morass covered with elder bushes."

Spaces between the few scattered houses, wrote Congressman Smith, were covered with scrub oak bushes. "The roads in every direction were muddy and unimproved. A sidewalk was attempted in one instance by a covering formed of the chips hewed for the Capitol. It extended but a little way and was of little value; for in dry weather the sharp fragments cut our shoes, and in wet weather covered them with white mortar."

Secretary of the Treasury Wolcott added this:

"You may look in almost any direction, over an extent of ground nearly as large as the city of New York, without seeing a fence or any object except brick kilns and temporary huts for workers."

Even many years later, pigs wallowed and grunted in the mud of streets which long remained unimproved.

Architecture

Now it is even more years later, and like capital cities of the Old World, Washington displays the work of top-notch architects and landscape artists. The government buildings naturally attract the most attention, much admiration and plenty of criticism. Those which are not jammed closely against others generally show good lines, as also do the federal buildings erected for non-office purposes. It's this business of wadding big office structures of uniform height close to each other that has produced some unhappy effects. Architects explain this by saying that designers of office buildings in the Triangle group on the Mall had to make concessions to the idea that all buildings in that group were to be viewed as a unit. Also, they had to sacrifice quality of exterior design to obtain a maximum of well-lighted working space in the comparatively low structures.

As the thing works out, it is impressive, like the Paris that was built centuries ago, and the Rome that was built more centuries ago, and the Moscow that was built by the czars. But the façades lack human charm, and the people who work behind the façades do not have places to park the cars which brought them to work. That is the curse of Washington. Visitors oh-&-ah over the beauties which their home towns do not afford, but they do not see the half-efficiency of the governmental machinery which must try to operate behind these architectural fronts borrowed from other nations and other times.

Touring through the residential sections, the tourist has an opportunity to see just about everything that ever came from the drawing boards of home-designing architects. The succession of architectural fads and fancies through almost a century and a half is displayed. On top of all that is the fact that wealthy cosmopolites, deciding to "build in Washington," introduced almost every foreign type of architecture except the African's hut and the Eskimo's igloo. A flashy pink stucco job on the Italian order stands alongside a staid be-columned take-off on the colonial style. A glass-brick-streamlined "modern" is next-door neighbor to a monstrosity in brick with a narrow driveway which dates it back to the horse and trolley era. And all around the town are relics of the 80's and 90's, the years when architects plastered exteriors with a great variety of ornamental gewgaws, the years when the band saw was king. The capital's residential architecture is a scrambling of the good, bad and the indifferent, with a preponderance of the bad and the indifferent. The suburban areas, with their twentieth-century styles, are like those which rim most of the nation's large cities.

Church architecture, following traditional lines, is high grade, topped by the uncompleted Episcopal Cathedral of St. Peter and St. Paul and the Catholic Shrine of the Immaculate Conception, also far from finished. A good deal of the rest shows nothing to brag about. Apartment-house architecture is run-of-mine.

Incongruities

Tourists who do not get off the beaten tracks go away without seeing the incongruities which abound in the capital. Dingy and squalid buildings are only a traffic light away from some of the city's finest structures. Negro homes are within two blocks of the mansions of Dupont Circle. Solid blocks of homely shop buildings line both sides of Pennsylvania Avenue a block west of the White House. Beer joints, penny arcades, the home of the Gayety burlesque, and pool halls are just up the street from the magnificent building which houses the archives of the United States. Cheap hotels and rooming houses rim the pristine Supreme Court Building. Railroad trains clack along near some of the newer government buildings south of the Mall but have the good grace to dive into a tunnel just before they reach the Capitol.

Nor are such incongruities all that the tourists who "go by the book" or take only scheduled tours fail to see. Here are just a few of the things they miss: The old Georgetown water front to which eighteenth-century ships came from across the seas, now the abode of warehouses, coal yards, and gravel companies. Old forts which circle the capital, from one of which (Fort Stevens) President Lincoln watched a Civil War battle. The United States Naval Observatory, where the goings and comings of the stars and planets are observed "officially." Washington's little Chinatown on H Street. The great hall of the old Pension Office Building (now filled with desks and girl clerks) in which presidential inaugural balls were held between 1885 and 1909. The Octagon House which served as the executive mansion for President Madison and his wife Dolly while the White House was being restored after it was set afire by the British troops in 1814. The subway which hauls senators between the Capitol and their office building. Small stone gatehouses which were on the Capitol grounds until 1874, now in the Mall. Augustus Saint-Gaudens' famous statue over a grave in Rock Creek Cemetery, known as "Grief" because Mark Twain declared it represented all the woes of humankind. (Now a few Washingtonians visit it and call it "Hope.")

"Doing the City"

The efficient and most economical way to "do the city," unless a guiding friend or relative is at hand, is to ride the sight-seeing busses on tours which parade the capital's more obvious glories at from $2.00 to $3.25 per tour. The bus companies offer several tours, each requiring from two hours to four and a half hours. They are timed to enable tourists to cover two routes each day, one in the morning, one in the afternoon—or three, if an evening tour is taken. One company, handling approximately 50,000 passengers a year, signs up business at desks in hotel lobbies and calls at the hotels for its customers. Another specializes in providing chartered busses for groups attending conventions in Washington, parties organized by travel bureaus in other cities and others who come to the capital "in the mass" to reduce expenses. Smaller bus lines, limousines in sight-seeing service, and taxicab drivers handle the rest.

Tourists waiting at a bus terminal for a tour to begin look like nothing else but what they are. They fidget. They tinker with adjustments on their cameras. They glance at bus company literature and then stuff it into purses and pockets. They do little talking, trying to hide their self-consciousness from passers-by, for ordinary men and women like to be tourists but don't like to *seem* to be tourists.

The bus pulls up. "This bus for the tour of government buildings," announces the starter. Like children bossed around by their parents, the ticket holders get into their seats. Ahead of them is a typical Washington tour (as it was before the war closed a number of public buildings to visitors) : The ever-wagging tongue and ever-pointing forefinger of the lecturer. Miles of buildings sliding past the windows. Bus riding punctuated with stops at government structures. Stops which mean much walking down long corridors, around rooms, up and down stairs.

As the bus gets under way, the lecturer tilts his badge-fronted cap, braces himself. Then he begins his spiel by asking each passenger to speak up and tell the folks the name of his or her home state. In one busload there may be people from a dozen states. First comes the White House, living place of every President except Washington. Likenesses of them and their wives, done in oil. Rooms full of relics. High ceilings. Main attraction is the East Room, hall of state functions, weddings, funeral ceremonies ever since the days of John Adams.

On to the Bureau of Engraving and Printing, there to see sheets of blank paper become spending money. A snicker at the lecturer's stock gag: "Don't forget to bring me back a sample."

Then up the Mall toward the Capitol, stopping to go through the Smithsonian Institution buildings which house the National Museum exhibits. Everybody takes a gaze upward at Lindbergh's "Spirit of St. Louis" plane, slung from the ceiling. Women hasten to the large room where costumes of the Presidents' wives are displayed on wax figures. Men wander around areas devoted to machinery and transportation. Other exhibits, seen by the few who are not slaves to the bus schedule: Textiles, coins, naval and military history, firearms, medical and dental history, power, foods, wood industries and mineral technology.

Tiring legs and hot feet climb aboard the bus. The lecturer announces: "Next stop is the Capitol. One hour to go through the interior." The elderly couple from Louisiana take stock. She says her feet ache. He tells her his eyes are blurry. The lecturer prattles: "The Capitol is 750 feet long and half as wide. The corner stone was laid in the year 1793 and . . ."

The voice begins to sound something like the motor—ceaseless, monotonous. The motor finally stops, but the voice continues. "We are now on the Capitol Plaza. You will enter the door at the head of the main steps in the center of the building. You will not be permitted to take pictures of the interior. Please stay with the guide assigned to your group."

Going up the Capitol steps, the comment is: "Here's where the Presidents are inaugurated." Inside, under the great dome, another voice, another pointing arm, more statistics, more details, more listening, walking—walking—walking—listening—paintings—statues—with stone-floored corridors in both directions.

The group jostles through a narrow door into the old Supreme Court Chamber. "We will next enter the chamber where the Senate is in session. We will remain five minutes." Twelve senators are at their desks. Eighty-four are not. Disappointment. "Don't they ever do any work?" Outside again, and the guide takes pains to tell the tourists that senators and representatives work long hours in committee rooms and at their offices. "They really do most of their work there."

Then more looks at enormous paintings and statues of famous people. Dates, names, masses of information. Then a look at the House in session and the party returns to the bus.

Over to the Library of Congress, with the Declaration of Independence under protective yellow glass, the Constitution of the United States, the Gutenberg Bible and the Magna Charta (all taken off display until the war's end).

Tired feet plod out of the building. The bus again. The Californian wishes out loud that he was back in his hotel. "Hotel. Name your hotel," spouts the lecturer. "The tour is concluded and we will take you to where you are stopping. If you wish to purchase tickets for the grand double tour to Georgetown, Arlington National Cemetery, Alexandria and Mount Vernon, leaving at two o'clock this afternoon, I have them on sale."

The Tours

The Mount Vernon tour attracts the most sight-seers. One company sells 500 tickets for it every week during a normal summer season. Running a close second is the tour of the government buildings. Others rank as follows:

Third: The general tour labeled "Seeing All of Washington Beautiful"—taking the tourist past the prime residences, the "fashionable shopping center" and the Lincoln Memorial.

Fourth: The religious tour of the Franciscan Monastery, the National Shrine of the Immaculate Conception at the Catholic University, and the

National Episcopal Cathedral (with the Scottish Rite Temple and the Soldiers' Home thrown in).

Fifth: Short tour of Arlington National Cemetery, Fort Myer and Georgetown.

Sixth: "Washington at Night"—along the city's streets and avenues, around the Tidal Basin (famous for its cherry blossoms), along the river and ending at the gilded Library of Congress.

Seventh: The interiors of the new government buildings—including the Supreme Court Building, Folger Shakespeare Library, Department of Justice (with the FBI), the Archives Building and the new National Art Gallery (donated by Andrew Mellon).

In addition, out-of-town tours run to historic areas in Maryland and Virginia, all linked with the national capital by early nineteenth-century happenings and personages. Many of them have ties with the earliest of colonial history.

Thirty-six miles across Maryland from the capital is Annapolis, colonial and present seat of Maryland's government and home of the United States Naval Academy. In Virginia, Fredericksburg, 55 miles distant, is close to battlefields of eighty years ago—The Wilderness, Chancellorsville and Spotsylvania. Charlottesville, 116 miles from Washington, was well known to Monroe, Jefferson and their associates, and is near the homes of those famous Virginians. Richmond, 108 miles from Washington, capital of Virginia, is filled with historical interest. Williamsburg, deeper in Virginia, was the colonial capital of Virginia, and has been restored to its appearance of long ago. Also, in the same region, are Yorktown, where Cornwallis surrendered, and Jamestown, site of the first permanent English settlement in America. Westward from Washington, the touring busses move through beautiful valley country where Civil War history was made, and along the crest of the Blue Ridge Mountains on Skyline Drive. The fields of Antietam, the first and second battles of Bull Run and other major encounters are scattered over areas within an hour or so's ride from Washington. Eighty miles distant, up north in Pennsylvania, is the Gettysburg National Military Park.

What They Like

One day I questioned several tourists who were resting their aching muscles in lobbies of three medium-priced hotels which cater to sight-seers about what they liked about Washington.

A grocer from Minneapolis was most interested in the homes of former Presidents and political notables.

A high school teacher from Pueblo, Colorado, "was just thrilled" at seeing the house near Twentieth and I Streets, N. W., where Peggy (O'Neale) Eaton lived as the glamour girl of Andrew Jackson's day when she played hob with national affairs.

A housewife from Wichita, Kansas, liked the interior furnishings of the Lee Mansion at Arlington and the Mansion House at Mount Vernon.

An oboe player from Boston was "intensely interested" in the Music Division in the Library of Congress.

A meter-reader from Pittsburgh remembered the Surratt House where conspirators laid plans for Lincoln's assassination (in the six hundred block of H Street, N. W., now the heart of Chinatown).

A 15-year-old girl from Litchfield, Illinois, liked the ride to the top of the Washington Monument, and the chance to see women members of Congress on the floor of the House.

A librarian from Oklahoma City was glad she had seen the house on M Street in Georgetown where Washington and L'Enfant did the work of planning the capital city.

A shoe dealer from Bridgeport remembered the houses noted for connection with men who were close to Presidents, such as the "Little Green House on K Street" (scene of goings on during the Harding administration), the Blair House (where Jackson's henchmen manipulated the "Kitchen Cabinet"), Tayloe House (residence of Senator Mark Hanna when he was the power behind the McKinley administration), and the "Red House on R Street" (where Tom Corcoran and Ben Cohen drafted much of the early New Deal legislation).

A retired merchant from Portland, Maine, told me he had a weakness for statistics and produced the evidence to prove it. He pulled out a notebook filled with figures, big and little, which he had collected from guidebooks and bus lectures. This is the sort of thing he had jotted down:

Pennsylvania Avenue is six miles long and 166 feet wide from building line to building line. The assessed value of the Capitol and improvements on its grounds: $37,500,000. Head-to-toe measurement of the Lincoln Statue in Lincoln Memorial: 19 feet. The bodies of 229 men who lost their lives in the sinking of the *Maine* are buried beneath the mast of their ship at Arlington National Cemetery. The Commerce Department Building is 1,050 feet long and occupies nearly eight acres. The top of the Capitol dome is 285 feet above ground level on the plaza side. The Library of Congress contains six million books and pamphlets, 3,000,000 maps, charts and musical compositions. Washington has 700 parks, ranging in size from a few hundred square feet to Rock Creek Park (1,800 acres) and the Mall (one mile long and an eighth of a mile wide).

An elderly citizen from Sacramento looked as if he was sorry he had come. "Sure, Washington is a fine city and an interesting place. But it isn't the Washington I knew thirty years or so ago before I went out to the Coast. Everything's changed. There's a filling station at Connecticut and N Streets where the British Embassy used to be. A government building where Poli's Theatre stood. Old Center Market is gone and a Federal Triangle building covers the spot. Old Chinatown on Pennsylvania Avenue near the Capitol is torn down. Office buildings and apartment houses where fashionable people had their mansions. Restaurants, shoe stores and the like where there used to be saloons, musty and with sawdust on the floor, along the north side of Pennsylvania Avenue. Fancy steel and concrete stands out at the ball park instead of the wooden seats where real fans saw Walter Johnson and Ty Cobb when they were rookies. Office buildings in place of the fine old residences which once surrounded Lafayette Park opposite the White House. A noisy, overcrowded city instead of a place that was sleepy and quiet like a village. It's all a lot different than when I knew it. It's too dressed up. Wonder what it'll look like thirty years from now."

37

Scads of Schools

WASHINGTON is a "college town" without a "campus atmosphere." If the average city the size of Washington had as many as 25,000 students above the high school rank, as Washington does, you'd see and feel the influence of the college life far more than you do in Washington. Truth is that Washington has a great volume of schools, colleges and universities. Quantitatively it is a big educational center, but qualitatively it is not a great educational center. Whatever intellectual life the city has comes primarily from government and politics, and not from the educational institutions within it.

Father George Washington would be greatly disappointed. He left some shares of stock as a nest egg for the creation of a truly great federally supported university in the capital city, but the stock became worthless, and the project never really got going. Others have had the dream of making Washington the great educational capital of America, but their dreams evaporated, and the educational capitals of this nation already seem to be established elsewhere.

Girls' schools do well in Washington, because for generations the papas and mamas of upper-income level have had the idea that the atmosphere of Washington imparted some sort of special polish to their daughters of the debutante class. The girls got ahead faster in the home-town society after being "finished" in Washington, where they were exposed to historical sights, and where they had the educational opportunity of pouring tea for real live statesmen.

Night schools also do well, because young government workers can support themselves while going to school at night. Relatively few young men and women come to Washington and devote their full time to college study. They do not come to Washington to study, and work on the side. They come to work, and they study on the side. When government employment rolls rise sharply, college attendance also rises sharply. In the past two years the influx has been heavy. Many of the new arrivals have been part-time students from large swarming schools such as the College of the City of New York and Brooklyn University. The night school faculties are relatively good—better than in most night schools—for in general they consist of qualified men who also work for the government by day and teach on the side at night. Some of them are particularly good in law, in economics, and in government administration.

Most Washingtonians send their children to the public schools, which are of average quality, but generally satisfactory. Only a few Washingtonians of the upper crust send their children to the private schools, whose students come mainly from out of town.

Universities and Colleges

The largest university in Washington is coeducational George Washington, which has 7,500 students in its regular courses, and about 2,400 more in summer and special work. About half of the enrollment consists of night students (or late afternoon and evening), and the University was a pioneer in classes for people who go to school after working hours.

Georgetown University, founded in 1789, is the oldest collegiate institution in Washington, and the oldest Catholic college in the United States. The enrollment is 2,500 men, with about 80 women in the School of Nursing.

The Catholic University of America, with a student body of about 2,500, ranks high in theology. It is located three miles north of the Capitol, adjoining the U. S. Soldiers' Home grounds, and in the section called Brookland, which has become a center of Catholic religious and educational activities.

American University, coeducational, was planned to be the leading Protestant institution of learning in America, but has so far fallen short of its goal. A few years ago it almost went off the educational map. Today it is on the comeback trail and its School of Social Sciences and Public Affairs located in downtown Washington is largely responsible.

For Negroes, the world's largest and highest-ranking educational institution is the federally supported and coeducational Howard University. It was founded in 1867 with five students. Now it has more than 2,400 students, draws approximately $2,000,000 annually in congressional appropriations and is administered by the Federal Security Agency. It is located on a high hill, above the city's largest Negro section. At one time its faculty was composed almost entirely of white men, but now nearly all the professors are Negroes.

The Graduate School of the Department of Agriculture, though not formally a university, is organized on an academic basis, has 3,400 students, a curriculum of more than a hundred courses and a faculty of 125. Some of its courses are truly "graduate," and some are elementary. It offers no

393

degrees, but the quality of the teaching is high. Two-thirds of the faculty are federal officials who were professors before they entered the government, and all but 300 of the students are government workers. Classes are held at night, and all expenses are met from fees paid by the students.

The University of Maryland, about twenty miles from the White House, is not actually a "Washington school," but its "campus atmosphere" and its low state-institution fees attract many students from the capital's environs. It is coeducational, has 5,500 students in its regular sessions and 1,400 in summer sessions, and ranks as an average state university.

The capital has two full-fledged women's colleges, both Catholic. The larger and older is Trinity, located just down the street from Catholic University, and the newer is Dunbarton College of Holy Cross, established in 1935 and affiliated with Catholic University.

Two coeducational teachers' colleges are located in Washington, one of them for Negroes. Wilson Teachers College, for whites, has an enrollment of 450. Miner Teachers College, for Negroes, is near Howard University and has approximately 600 students.

Unique among the nation's schools is Gallaudet College, a federally supported coeducational school for the deaf and speechless, located in northeast Washington. Its 200 students have come from all over the world, and they are granted degrees in the liberal arts and sciences under an act signed by President Lincoln in 1864.

Specialized Schools

Washington has dozens of specialized schools that draw heavily from the thousands of government workers who study when they're not working. They teach mainly law, accountancy, economics and business administration. Special schools preparing for foreign service examinations naturally locate in the capital. In Washington, also, are "civil service schools" which advertise their abilities to give instruction, in classes or by home study, to those who want to get a running start for civil service examinations leading to government jobs. Scattered around the city are schools that deal out instruction in scores of other lines, such as hotel work, electrical engineering, speech culture, art, drama, engineering, fashion modeling, poise, efficiency, drafting, aviation, and psychiatry.

Development of the federal government always presents the problem of training administrators and Washington is the laboratory for this training. One experimental method adopted by the National Institute of Public Affairs is the "interne system" under which students come to Washington and work in governmental agencies to get first-hand training.

Every year in September, hundreds of young girls, daughters of rich and socially prominent families, flutter into Washington. They come from all over the country to attend the finishing schools and junior colleges clustered in and around the capital. They come ostensibly to obtain knowledge, but there's more to it than that. They and their parents have been intrigued by the idea of going to school in a city loaded with foreign diplomats, senators and representatives, grand dames, cosmopolites and other social luminaries that shine in the center of national government. The men and women who run the girls' schools capitalize on that idea. Some of them, in their catalogues, go to the extreme of emphasizing social advantages above educational facilities. Others stress the benefits of studying in the Washington environment, knowing that the lure of the capital's glamour will take care of itself.

Many of the young ladies suffer violent disillusionments after they've been on the scene a while. They may have expected to be invited right off the bat for luncheon with at least an under secretary of one of the major embassies. They may have anticipated the thrill of a rhumba with the military attaché representing a South American country.

But that doesn't mean that the youngsters completely miss out on the capital's social splash. No matter from what part of the nation a girl comes, there's almost certain to be at least one well-established family in Washington that knows her folks back home. That situation provides a short cut. Also, members of Congress, acting more or less in their own political interests, provide another type of social aid. Soon after the school year opens, alert senators and representatives, or their wives, ask the executives of girls' schools in Washington for names of students whose homes are in the states or congressional districts they represent. Then, largely for the effect it will have on prominent families back home, they invite each girl to dinner, a dance or an evening at the theater. Some schools do not wait to be asked for the names. They send them along to Capitol Hill as soon as student registration is completed. "There's a problem, of course," one executive admitted, "when a girl's senator or representative is a bachelor; but fortunately, most of them are married, and their wives are glad to help entertain the girls."

Some of the private girls' schools in Washington give a high school education and stop there. Some are primarily high school, but with college preparatory work. The junior colleges offer the equivalent of two full years of college work.

By educational standards, girls' schools in and near Washington are average or better. One authority, recently mulling over the list, ranked only two as being below average. The courses cover the range ordinarily found in schools of the type, with the exception that those dealing with social sciences, civil government, citizenship and history are emphasized. This enables school officials to use their location at the seat of government as a strong selling point. Several of the schools take full opportunity to make use of the government as a "laboratory."

As a center of boys' schools, Washington is not so notable as it is for its showing of girls' schools, but there is a group of boys' schools in and around Washington. They don't put heavy emphasis on the social side. A number of them specialize in preparation for West Point and Annapolis.

· · · · ·

Washington educational facilities as a whole—colleges, universities, night schools, special schools, girls' schools, boys' schools—suggest that the city has an educational glow, but not many bright piercing lights.

38

Society Swirl

O H, la de da. R.S.V.P. Remember today the Guckenall tea. Hurry here, and hurry there. Cocktails 5 to 7. Dinner Friday, 8:30. Reception May 17 to meet General and Mrs. Whoom. Black ties, white ties, and cleaners' bills. Mr. and Mrs., with the extra man for Miss. Here, my dear, is the Minister of Buffland, whom of course you know. In the corner there, talking to those two pretty girls, is the noted economist, Sir Gardner Whittletree. (He likes potato chips.) That little woman in the green gown is the wife of the man who wrote the book about the Atlantic Ocean. . . . I forget the name. Three parties in an afternoon. Two dinners out next week. Make a round of calls again, and drop the cards. A round of calls to keep the record straight. Daughter Jean comes out next year. Cocktails Tuesday, cocktails Wednesday. Stay till the time the mob has left, the stragglers make more buzz. Seat him halfway down the table, for he isn't entitled to be higher. Jam, cram the week full. Gotta go there, for they are important. Big party, little party, see and be seen. Oh, la de da.

"In Washington you meet such interesting people."

"You meet such *interesting* people."

"But, my dear, you meet SUCH interesting people."

You hear it said again and again, from year to year, again and again. You hear it said by newcomers to Washington, and by some of the old-comers. They must make social hay in the precious time while hubby's name shines in the newspapers. They live for it, they work for it, they give a big lot of their time to it. It is part of their careers—to meet the interesting people.

That's why society is so big in the pattern of Washington. That's why the per capita consumption of society in Washington is greater than that of any other city. It's a major occupation. It may be an exaggeration to say that society is the warp and the woof of governmental activity, but it is not a preposterous exaggeration.

In other cities, in your city, society is incidental to the life of good citizens of the upper or middle class. It is on the rim of their interests. They take it on the side, to garnish the other things of life. But in Washington, to most people of comparable upper class, society is a main course. It's a must. Some like it, some don't, but, still, it's a *must*. And so they strive, and run, and plan to make it hum. Through it they make contacts, and through contacts they climb, even to better jobs with more publicity, so that they become known back home and out around the country as Somebodies.

This is the American court, and these are the American courtiers.

Washington is the only city in the world where . . .

. . . Ordinary tourists may attend parties given by important officials.

. . . An obscure embassy attaché with feathers on his headdress is more sought after at an official reception than a famous scientist.

. . . People cram a breakfast party, a wedding, a funeral, a tea and a dinner into one day as a matter of course.

. . . Newcomers are expected to make the first calls.

. . . Hostesses send their calling cards around by messenger.

. . . Every third person at an official cocktail party is on the make.

You may have the personality of a mouse, the income of a country school teacher, and the soporific effect of chloroform, and still count for something in Washington society. In the city on the Potomac, where government is the biggest business, official position is more important than charm, money or background in winning friends and influencing people. Even an attaché of an embassy, who at home eats in the kitchen with his cook, finds that because he has a handle to his name he is listed in the Social Register.

In Washington society, a senator who can hardly speak the King's English is labeled, not uncouth, but "rugged" and "too picturesque." After all, it's expedient to overlook idiosyncrasies when someone can give you a boost up in the world. Knowing the "right people" may lead to all sorts of agreeable results—at the most, passage of a certain bill by Congress—at the least, a better job for the son-in-law.

Someone called Washington the "eatingest, drinkingest, gossipingest place in the world," and it is true. Ambassadors, senators, lobbyists, and an assortment of bizarre characters who help make up society, skip from function to function with incredible agility. To an obbligato of popping champagne corks, the elite and the would-be elite gather around flower-laden tea and dinner tables to exchange the latest gossip or push their pet projects. No wonder that jaded cosmopolites who have lived all over the world maintain that in social swirling no other city approaches Washington.

What the war has done is to change some of society's habits. Black-tie-and-tuxedo dinners have supplanted the white-tie-and-tails which began to get the bum's rush during the defense boom swirl in the middle of 1941.

Very elaborate diplomatic functions are out the window, although many embassies are still entertaining on a smaller scale. The White House no longer observes its official calendar of social events. It was canceled in the fall of 1941 with the proclamation of a full emergency. But capital society is undismayed, and if the quality of social gadding is somewhat diluted, the lack is made up by the increase in quantity.

Official Society

Capital society is a pyramid, with the President at the top. The hierarchy of lesser officials who come below him range from the Vice President down to the Assistant Deputy Third Assistant Postmaster General. Titular leaders of Washington society are always the President and his Lady. Their invitations have the authority of a royal command. To decline, except in case of illness or great emergency, is distinctly not etiquette. Thus capital hostesses wait until the First Lady has announced her schedule of entertainments before setting the dates for their own parties. In an average year, the nightmare of every hostess is to have the lion of her party drop out of a dinner because a reception at the Executive Mansion is announced for that evening. This year, with state functions called off, hostesses can plan their calendars for the whole season without fear of official competition.

The White House is the only residence in America where royalty is entertained at tea one day and the inmates of a girls' reform school the next. During a normal year, over 3,000 invitations for meals alone are sent out. Ever since the days when Abigail Adams used to hang the family wash in the East Room, the White House has been, from time to time, the scene of mass entertaining, depending on how democratic the various occupants were. When Andrew Jackson was inaugurated, the crowd which flocked inside the Executive Mansion was so great that cups and plates were smashed and many guests made exit through the windows. On the historic January day that Franklin D. Roosevelt took the oath of office for the third time, some 4,000 were invited to the White House reception. Farmers from near Hyde Park mingled in the stately rooms with New York shopgirls who had helped to campaign. The Roosevelt hospitality is so extensive that some complain the White House isn't exclusive any more. It's true that the President and Mrs. Roosevelt have dined social workers almost as much as social registerites.

High point in the peacetime social calendar, and most glamorous event of the season, has always been the White House reception for members of the diplomatic corps. War times have interrupted this event, but when things quiet down again, society will very soon forget there was ever a lull. At this state reception, foreign chiefs of missions from all over the world gather, with their wives, daughters and staff members. When the diplomats appear in all the glory of their official uniforms, an American present might wonder whether he has not accidentally walked smack into a Graustarkian operetta. The British Ambassador resembles a Christmas tree laden with ornaments as he moves about under pounds of gold braid. His colleagues are equally impressive, with their cockaded hats sporting white feathers.

Gourmets sigh that the fare served at this brilliant gathering and the other state receptions is far less lavish than the costumes of the guests. In the big dining room, beneath a portrait of Lincoln, a long table is set up with platters of modest cookies, salted nuts and bonbons. Enormous silver bowls hold a wine punch, which, weak as it is, is welcomed. (In the prohibition era, only a large ice cooler and pitchers of water graced the dining room.) Even the unpretentious cookies are an innovation, for in the Coolidge and Hoover administrations the guests at receptions were offered nary a crumb. The sumptuous fare of the Taft era—lobster salad and champagne—had been discontinued by the Wilsons.

During a regular winter season in normal times, the colorful diplomatic party is only one of a series of state receptions held at the White House. Members of the Supreme Court, Congress, the Army and Navy, and the heads of the various government agencies are all feted in turn at large receptions. Many of the guests appear in rented tails, but some forego that much elegance, and black ties and even ordinary business suits are spotted in the crowd.

Oldest of the social events on the White House calendar is the dinner for members of the Cabinet. It, like the other state functions, has been discontinued during the war. (It dates back to the latter part of the eighteenth century, when President Washington used to ask his cabinet officers and their wives to dine with him.) In turn, the Cabinet gives an annual dinner for the Chief Executive—one of the few occasions on which the President attends a social function outside the White House.

Though pomp and circumstance are customarily kept to a minimum in a democracy, receptions at the Executive Mansion are still impressive. Half an hour before the starting time, 9 o'clock, guests begin to assemble in the long East Room with its three sparkling chandeliers and full-length oil paintings of George and Martha Washington. The company is lined up strictly according to protocol, with top-flight officials heading the procession, and lesser lights at the tail end. Just as the big grandfather's clock in the hall chimes 9, the scarlet-coated members of the Marine Band strike up "Hail to the Chief"—signal for the President to appear. He makes his way from the dining room to the Blue Room, escorted by an aide and followed by the First Lady and members of the Cabinet.

In the Blue Room, one of the three state sitting rooms on the main floor, the President receives his guests. This elliptical room has been called the most beautiful in the White House. The walls, the heavily-brocaded window draperies reaching to the floor and the upholstery of the chairs are all a soft, deep blue. As he waits for the line to start, the President may set his watch by the gold clock on the mantel presented by Napoleon to Lafayette, and by him to George Washington.

While the Secret Service men keep their eyes cocked, the guests file past to shake the presidential hand. More than an hour has passed before the last dignitary greets his host. Several times during this endurance test the President takes time out to rest. While the line is held up, he sips a glass of water and exchanges banter with his aides. Finally the line is finished and the hand-shaking job is done.

The guests wander off to take a twirl about the polished floor of the long East Room, where the Marine Band has adjourned to play for dancing, or they stop for a chat with friends in the crowded hall, and then begin to straggle home. Those lingering are gently prodded on their way by the various military and naval aides on duty at all big White House parties. The aides have a system all their own for getting rid of people who are inclined to stay too long. They stand around and stare intently at those remaining, until the guests take the hint.

"At Homes"

Typical of the democratic spirit of official entertaining in Washington are the "at homes" of the wives of officials. These functions are the capital's greatest free-food institution.

In the old days, when all official ladies were "at home" every week, sight-seeing busses would drive up and disgorge hungry tourists eager to see inside an official's home. Worn out with dispensing hospitality on such a mass scale, the wives a few years ago got together with Mrs. Roosevelt and agreed to rotate the functions. Now official hostesses are "at home" only two or three times a year. Each group is allotted a particular day.

During prohibition days, the diplomatic open houses were jammed to the window sills, because diplomats were the only people who served liquor legally. To cut down the crush somewhat, the embassies and legations issued unofficial cards, but visitors still were admitted without them.

Famous in the annals of Washington society is a little old woman who attends nearly every Cabinet "at home" and crams food from the buffet into a knitting bag. She has been getting her supper this way for years.

She is the widow of an Army officer who died many years ago, and once had "at homes" of her own. Now she is as inevitable a fixture at the parties of others as the caterer's thin sandwiches.

The Cave Dwellers

In the avalanche of official entertaining which gives Washington society most of its character, ordinary residents are sometimes lost in a shuffle of politicos and diplomats. The socially high-rank natives who live in Washington from administration to administration, symbols of permanency in a shifting sea of transients, are called "cave dwellers." Many of their caves are magnificent old homes, built when Washington was a muddy village. Few officials ever see the inside of Tudor Place, the Georgetown home of Armistead Peter. It is one of the most perfect examples of Georgian architecture in America. The same family has lived there through the generations since Martha Custis, granddaughter of Martha Washington, came to Tudor Place in 1805 shortly after her marriage to Thomas Peter. Only when a daughter of the house makes her debut or marries are Tudor Place and many other "caves" opened to more than a small circle of intimates.

One of the finest of old Washington homes, Decatur House, is still lighted only by gas. When the owner, Mrs. Truxtun Beale, entertains at a reception, one somehow expects the guests to appear in knee breeches and powdered wigs. They would be much more in keeping with the lofty ceilings, bare polished floors, and softly gleaming crystal chandeliers and wall sconces. The architect of the mansion, which is across Lafayette Park from the White House, was Benjamin Latrobe. His water-color plans are still at Decatur House, as well as the sword of the man who built it, Admiral Stephen Decatur. It was in 1819, just after Decatur had concluded his brilliant Mediterranean campaign against the Corsairs, that the mansion was built. After his death in a duel a year later, Decatur House passed to other hands, and the huge garden at the rear was at one time used as a slave market.

Café society is practically non-existent in Washington. Instead of basking in the glare of photographers' flashlight bulbs in local night spots, people much prefer to gather at private dinner parties. Then, too, Washington's favorite indoor sport is conversation, and an orchestra makes too much competition for a busy tongue.

Embassies Entertain

Most sumptuous settings for capital dinner parties are furnished in normal times by the more than 50 embassies and legations which adorn the capital. In wartime the entertaining is more informal. Along polite Massachusetts Avenue and on Sixteenth Street are the palatial, red-carpeted, marble-floored homes of chiefs of foreign missions.

Largest and swankiest is the great pile of red brick which houses his Britannic Majesty's Ambassador. The Embassy, modeled after the work of Sir Christopher Wren, was built at a cost of close to $1,000,000, and stands on a plot of ground donated to the British government by Harry Wardman, the one-time English carpenter who became Washington's biggest real estate plunger of the 20's.

Lovers of pomp and circumstance thrill at formal dinners at the British Embassy. They love the factotum, resplendent in Highlander costume, kilts, red coat and fur busby, who greets them at the foot of the curving marble staircase. Upstairs, they may sip their cocktails in a drawing room with pillars of yellow marble and mirror-lined walls. At dinner they are impressed by the footmen, one for every two guests, wearing scarlet livery, knee breeches, and white cotton gloves.

More prized by many than an invitation to the White House has been a bid to the annual garden party at the British Embassy, held in honor of the King's birthday, but discontinued "for the duration." Several garden parties were held in the beautiful grounds of the Embassy, however, for British relief. Heretofore, each June, some 1,000 of the elite palpitated with excitement at receiving a much-sought-after gold-crested invitation to this function. For days preceding the big event, tea tables buzzed as ladies pondered whether to wear long, sweeping dresses, British style, or "go American" in street-length frocks. When the eagerly anticipated afternoon arrived, society swarmed over the green lawn of the Embassy, some of the women trailing flowered chiffons, while many of the men imitated Ascot and sported pearl-gray toppers. Wine punch and strawberries and cream were served in true British garden party fashion, while everyone exclaimed over the rose gardens and the swimming pool.

It took the historic visit of the King and Queen, in June 1939, to raise excitement over British Embassy garden parties to a peak of frenzy. Before the arrival of the royal couple, members of the smart set thrilled to receive invitations issued in the names of Their Majesties to an outdoor reception. Every woman in society had been breathless with fear she'd be left off the list. Many called up the Embassy to request they be sent an invitation. A few hours after the cards were out, a storm broke from official quarters. Among the hundreds asked, only the dozen or so members of the Senate Committee on Foreign Relations and the House Committee on Foreign Affairs, and a few socialite solons were included, leaving out many a furious congressional couple.

"It's our impression the royal pair are supposed to be making an official tour, not a social one," snapped the wives of senators. "If J. P. Morgan and Mrs. Cornelius Vanderbilt are invited to come down from New York for the party, why shouldn't we be asked, too?"

The angry women appealed to Mrs. John Nance Garner, wife of the then Vice President. Upshot was that Mr. Garner invited the British Ambassador, Sir Ronald Lindsay, down to the Senate for lunch and a little chat, and the next day the ladies received their invitations.

Never before or since the day of the famous garden party has Washington seen such an outcropping of gray toppers and monocles. Even the most blasé members of society forgot their dignity and shoved and pushed to get a good look at the King and Queen. Guests outdid themselves in sweeping curtsies and low bows, though the official wives had decided after a conclave that to bend the knee to royalty wouldn't go over well with the folks back home. They just shook hands, American fashion.

Climax of all social entertainments ever to take place in Washington was the dinner given by the President and Mrs. Roosevelt in honor of the King and Queen. Eighty guests sat at the long table centered with the great gold epergnes of the Monroe dinner service, dripping with their clusters of golden grapes. Earnest New Dealers as well as sophisticated diplomats were in the company. Mountaineers and country school teachers, members of the Soco Gap Square Dancers, did American folk dances for the royal couple and were presented to them when the program was over. It was as exciting an experience for the King and Queen as for the country visitors.

Although the British Embassy signifies diplomacy at its fanciest, it is the Latin Americans in Washington who have done the most lavish entertaining. Ten or twelve years ago, the Latin Americans were distinctly bush leaguers in Washington's diplomatic society. But more recently, due to official good neighborliness, bigger expense accounts and higher-grade diplomats, the Latin American embassies and legations have become very much the vogue. They serve the most staggering buffets and have the most all-inclusive guest lists of any in the capital. When the Ecuadorian Ambassador gave a reception at a local hotel, the line of guests waiting to greet him overflowed all the way down a long hall. More than 200 uninvited guests once showed up at a soiree at the Mexican Embassy and passed unnoticed in the throng.

People still talk of the gala ball the Cuban envoy gave when his country's strong man, Colonel Batista, visited Washington. Though it was autumn, the embassy garden blossomed with masses of flowers planted there for the evening by a local florist who later put in a bill for $2,000. On two

404

floors were bars, an orchestra, and groaning buffets. Champagne and Latin gallantries flowed until morning.

At some dinners given by the Spanish Embassy you may have your after-dinner coffee in a patio with flowers and a fountain. For Turkish Embassy tea parties, the chef prepares exotic little sugar pastries. Soviet hospitality is so lavish that even Daughters of the American Revolution attend out of curiosity.

Washington's newest embassy building, and the only one done in modern style, is that of the Venezuelan government. The long, low building of white stone has windows outlined in chromium, which glitters in the sun. Rare orchids were flown up from Venezuela especially for the housewarming.

Congressmen

As for members of Congress, very few of them play a part in the glitter side of Washington society. Chairmen of important committees, administration spokesmen, or the independently wealthy are the only ones greatly sought after. Most must live on their salaries ($10,000 a year), and their wives are too busy with home and children to play the high society game. Some rent apartments in unfashionable sections, others have roomy homes in non-chic suburbs. Many of the women center their social activities about the Congressional Club, an organization founded by and for wives of members of Congress. The Senate Ladies Club meets to sew and chat, and once a year members are entertained by the wife of the Chief Executive. Younger members of the congressional set have two clubs—Daughters of the Senate and Daughters of the House.

Principal woman member of Congress to combine an active social life with her duties in the House is Mrs. Edith Nourse Rogers of Massachusetts. Socially registered, comfortably off, lively gray-haired Mrs. Rogers finds time to go to many a dinner, and her own dinners are noted for their good food. Also in demand are two Massachusetts couples, Senator and Mrs. Henry Cabot Lodge, and Representative and Mrs. Richard Wigglesworth. Others from Congress popular in society are Senator and Mrs. Warren Austin of Vermont, Senator and Mrs. Peter Gerry, and wealthy Senator Theodore Green of Rhode Island. Though Representative Joseph Martin, House Minority Leader, doesn't smoke, drink, play cards, or stay up after midnight, he is a much-sought-after congressional bachelor.

Young Thomas Eliot, Representative from Massachusetts, and his wife give baseball parties at their home in suburban Seminary Hill, Virginia. The grandson of Harvard's famous President Charles Eliot, and one of the authors of the social security bill, Tom Eliot is also an authority on baseball and can entertain guests by quoting batting averages from 40 years ago.

Senator Arthur Capper, though in his seventies, is fond of dancing. Mrs. Charles Dewey, charming wife of the wealthy Representative from Illinois, has written cook books. Aged Senator Glass was seen at parties much more frequently after his marriage to an attractive Virginia widow. Senator and Mrs. Millard Tydings of Maryland entertain and are entertained frequently. Mrs. Tydings' father, Joseph Davies, former United States Ambassador to Russia, married as his second wife the wealthy Mrs. Marjorie Post Close Hutton, Post Toasties heiress.

Vice President, Cabinet and Court

Since the President seldom dines outside the White House, a great deal of gadding about may fall to the lot of the Vice President. He (fortunate soul!) need never repay any invitations. Etiquette authorities maintain that his mere presence at a party gives sufficient prestige and honor for a hostess. Former Vice President and Mrs. Garner were social recluses. They refused all invitations and went to bed with the chickens. Their successors, Mr. and Mrs. Wallace, enjoy society and are frequently seen at private parties and charity affairs. When Mrs. Wallace came to Washington from Iowa, she wore glasses, had her hair in an unexciting bun at the back of her neck, and didn't care much for clothes. Now her graying hair is carefully waved, she has discarded the glasses, and has been named the best-dressed woman in official life.

Washington's most notable social hermit is hard-working Secretary of State Cordell Hull. He and his wife make no engagements for the evening, as he could not, in his position, accept some and decline others. Mrs. Hull faithfully represents him at diplomatic parties, however.

Justice Frank Murphy, although ascetic in that he never smokes or drinks, nevertheless is a sociable soul. He is the only bachelor on the Supreme Court, and is one of the capital's most popular "extra men."

The Holy Protocol

The Chief Justice of the United States Supreme Court and a foreign ambassador never meet at dinner—because protocol experts have never decided who outranks whom. Whether the envoy or the Chief Justice should be placed at the right of the hostess is not as trivial a problem as it sounds, for in Washington the wrong dinner table seating may result in an international incident. As the personal representative of the head of his government, an ambassador would take a slight to him as an insult to his country.

Almost a decade after it occurred, capital residents still talk of the feud which arose between Mrs. Nicholas Longworth and Mrs. Edward Everett Gann over who should rank higher. The battle raged for weeks, with nobody daring to invite the two to the same dinner table.

A very thick book could be written on the thorny subject of diplomatic protocol. Social secretaries and State Department experts follow a mass of traditions, some based on common sense, others on rules laid down in the Treaty of Vienna back in 1815. The Vice President is, logically enough, second only to the President in the official hierarchy. Following him come the Chief Justice or foreign ambassadors, the Speaker of the House, the Associate Justices and/or foreign ministers, the Cabinet, senators, representatives, and so on. Subdivisions in officialdom go on indefinitely and there are several schools of thought on nearly every questionable point. American officials are roughly ranked according to which of the three divisions of the government they represent—executive, judicial or legislative. This custom explains why a Supreme Court justice outranks a senator. The Secretary of State precedes other cabinet members because foreign affairs was the first cabinet post to be created by the infant American republic. The other cabinet officers follow in the order in which their posts were set up, with the Secretary of Labor bringing up the rear.

Wherever a foreign statesman or diplomat is concerned, the State Department will advise on correct seating. When it's a question of American government officials, hostesses must struggle with the problem themselves.

Calls, Calls and Calls

As peculiar to Washington as protocol is the system of making calls. In most American cities, the calling card is as passé as the reticule, but in the capital it flourishes like the green bay tree. Newcomers in official circles are expected to make the first call on their superiors in rank, instead of waiting, as is the custom in most places, for others to make the approach. A foreign envoy can spend the entire first month after his arrival in a dizzy round of card-leaving on other envoys and important American officials or influential private citizens.

Calling in these circles is done by rule and rote and is about as impersonal as driving a tractor. The usual procedure is to hand your engraved pasteboard to a servant at the door and then depart immediately. Calls are supposed to be returned within 24 hours. Busy hostesses sometimes send their cards around via their station wagon, or even by telegraph messenger.

Mark Twain's wisecrack about the weather—"everybody complains but nobody does anything about it"—is applicable to Washington's calling system. Yet, ponderous and bothersome as it is, the custom serves one useful purpose in that it's the first step in getting the many newcomers acquainted. In recent years, in keeping with greater informality everywhere, people have succeeded in paring calling to a minimum.

Social Citizens

A colorful capital character who came to Washington many years ago is Mrs. Edward Beale McLean. Daughter of the late Thomas F. Walsh, who struck it rich out West, Evalyn Walsh McLean has been one of Washington's most lavish hostesses for more than 20 years. A few years ago she sold one of her two magnificent town houses, turned the other over to the Red Cross, and retired to historic Friendship. Then early in 1942, that estate was sold to the government for the construction of low-cost housing. She then moved to a Georgetown mansion, which she immediately christened "Friendship."

Mrs. McLean is noted for her parties, and for owning the Hope diamond, the blue gem which legend says brings ill luck. Her dinners at the old Friendship were reminiscent of the lavishness of a more extravagant era. Friends bidden by telegram to dine "informally" at Friendship found these "informal" affairs to be seated functions for 100.

Mrs. McLean does not now, nor has she ever, held an official position, so she is free to entertain whom she pleases, when she pleases. With dowagers from the smart set she will ask labor leader John L. Lewis. Senators on the opposite side of the fence politically forget their squabbles in the gay atmosphere of her drawing room. The British Ambassador may find himself seated next to Walter Winchell.

In super-social Washington, the most prosaic event furnishes an excuse for a party. A woman with a farm near town invited senators and diplomats to a supper celebrating the classification of her herd of cows. City dwellers with gardens give wisteria and dogwood parties in the spring, leaf-raking parties in the fall. Senator Guffey of Pennsylvania was host at a "bas relief" tea when an artist completed a piece of sculpture for his garden.

But it took glamorous "Evie" Robert, Washington's *enfant terrible*, to stage a party for a horse. The wife of Lawrence Wood Robert, Jr., former secretary of the Democratic National Committee, took over an entire stable to entertain in honor of her favorite mount, St. John the Baptist. Capital dignitaries were invited to bring their pets, and ambassadors arrived with their dogs or horses. The quadrupeds were served hamburgers and carrots while the prizes were awarded by two bipeds, Mrs. Alice Longworth and Mrs. J. Borden ("Daisy") Harriman.

Mrs. Eleanor Patterson or "Cissie" as everyone from ambassadors to printers calls her, is publisher of the *Washington Times-Herald*, and a member of the Chicago Medill-Patterson families. She is a grandmother, still glamorous, and Washington's only woman publisher. She is also part owner of the *New York Daily News*, which her brother, Captain Joseph Patterson, owns and publishes. Part of her income is from the *Chicago Tribune*, owned by her cousin, Colonel Robert McCormick.

Mrs. Patterson was the first Washington publisher to expand the society page, hiring social registerites at large salaries to cover in detail intimate dinners and teas. Readers from ambassadors to government clerks loved it, and the other papers followed suit.

"Cissie" has a marble palace on Dupont Circle but spends most of her time at the Dower House in near-by Upper Marlboro, Maryland. Her traveling between Washington and her ranch in Wyoming and her Long Island estate is done in her private car, the Ranger. Slender, auburn-haired, with the figure of a 16-year-old, Mrs. Patterson can turn on the charm when she wishes but among the newspaper fraternity she is noted more for sudden hiring and firing of her employees. In favor one day, they may be out on the street the next, and on the third day they may be back again at a higher salary.

Clubs

The Sulgrave Club, a former private home on Dupont Circle, is one of Washington's two swankiest clubs. There gather the intimates of several wealthy sets, a sprinkling of diplomats, and the "right" congressmen. The other smart rendezvous, the 1925 F Street Club, is less sedate and still retains the atmosphere of the private home it was when its owner, Mrs. John Gross, lived there.

During the summer, the smart set which frequents the Sulgrave Club and 1925 F Street moves out across the District line to the Chevy Chase Club in suburban Chevy Chase, Maryland. Of the many country clubs on the outskirts of Washington, Chevy Chase Club is the only one which "rates socially." People will stay on the waiting list for years before being admitted. Ambassadors, justices, generals, admirals, and top-flight cave dwellers play golf on the rolling links and plunge into the swimming pool. They take their ease on the lawn as white-jacketed Negroes scurry back and forth with mint juleps. Photographers are not welcomed on this sacrosanct property, which was originally a fox-hunting preserve.

Now that war has brought new hordes to Washington, social secretaries find their eligible lists overcrowded with men. In contrast with the men-to-women ratio for the whole city (in which women outnumber men), society is overburdened with unattached males. Some of them are the remnants of defense $1-a-year men who have stayed on and who still have not brought their wives to Washington. Many are young men who are "doing their bit" as aspiring administrators. Together, they provide party planners with extra men at a dime a dozen. But before Washington's defense and war boom, the extra man still was at a premium in the higher society circles. So great was the demand for the unencumbered male that musty unmarried gentlemen and immature young men who toiled at some humble government job during the day could count on an invitation to dine out five nights a week.

．　．　．　．　．

So it goes, so it goes in Washington society. Glitter, and glamour, and busyness. Hard-working hosts and hostesses. Frivolous on the surface, deeply serious underneath. Social haymaking, the chance of a lifetime. Mama wants papa to get elected, so mama can make the grade in Washington. Broken hearts of those who fail to climb the rungs they think they rate. The society column, which exercises great influence over political conduct. All this helps to make Washington a dizzy city, and it also helps sometimes to shove the work of government into the background.

39

Guide for Social Climbers

SOCIAL climbing is a common occupation which is recognized in others, but never exists in one's self. You, of course, are not a social climber, but many others are, and for the sake of others there ought to be a guide to climbing in Washington.

Social climbing as a Washington institution is second in popularity only to those two other well-known capital pursuits—gossiping and lobbying. The city has long been a magnet for the rich and socially ambitious who flock from all over the country, attracted by glittering stories of plushy embassies and cabinet tea parties. Wives, widows and daughters of self-made men who were known in their home towns by a penchant for dropping food on their vests come to the capital to make good in glamorous surroundings. If their money is backed by brass and brains, and a well-developed flair for publicity, they stand a good chance of wining and dining live senators here.

The Washington 400 (or 4000) care little where the dollars come from if there are plenty of them. Brewery or baking-powder backgrounds can be overlooked and a high-pressure campaign can put over any fortune—if it is second generation. Charm, which opens many doors, is not always a requisite for muscling your way into Washington society, for charm implies a sense of humor, and those engaged in storming the social battlements are usually a grim and dogged lot.

Getting Celebrities

Bagging a name is an approved method of starting up the social ladder. Among the various kinds of bait the ambitious dangle before those they hope to impress, the most tempting is the aristocracy. There are few women in this Capital of Democracy who aren't impressed by titles. Even the nobility is divided into compartments according to rank and nationality, with the English most solid. A British baronet is worth three White Russian princes. A genuine British duke causes more excitement than Balkan royalty, and is harder to get. Dukes are only for those who have "arrived." Others must often content themselves with Baltic barons.

One wealthy Washington spinster dined out a whole season on the strength of having entertained an Earl and Countess for an entire forty-eight hours. Dowagers who hitherto had never even bothered to answer her invitations scurried around to leave cards.

Even a Viscount, provided he lives up to what Americans expect from the aristocracy, can spend a season in Washington and never pay for a dinner. He need be only terribly, terribly British, or the Continental kind who bows from the waist and sharply clicks his heels.

If the snaring of royalty prove too difficult, the next best bait consists of nationally known celebrities. Painters, novelists, pianists, and even a harmonica player, if he is as famous as Larry Adler, can be classed as lures. Of course, there are authors and authors, and writers of proletarian books are not much in demand among the smart set. Noel Coward, however, would make the career of any social climber who could snag him for a week-end, for he is identified with smart groups in New York and Palm Beach. Yet if the Pulitzer Prize winner, Willa Cather, were to come to town few climbers would bestir themselves. After all, Miss Cather has never been featured at an Elsa Maxwell party.

The way Washington climbers wring every ounce of celebrity value out of even mediocrities would do credit to a Hollywood press agent. Visiting second-string book reviewers from out of town are startled to find that their hostesses have passed around the word that they are "famous authors." Third-rate baritones, especially if foreign, are the pet prey of Washington hostesses. These women are forever arranging cozy musicales at which the guests squirm about on small gilt chairs while the baritones thunder away at "Carmen." The maestros, according to their hostesses, are always just about to be snapped up by Hollywood or by the Metropolitan, but somehow this doesn't always follow.

Should there be a dearth of available tenors and smart scribblers, Washington climbers have a fertile field to fall back on right at home. One reason they choose the capital is because, abounding as it does in ambassadors, senators and congressmen, it is a celebrity hunter's dream territory. Among the local lions, diplomats have the greatest snob appeal. Even a humble attaché may some day be an ambassador, and it is satisfying to be able to call an envoy by his first name. Then, too, members of the diplomatic corps have such an interesting air of being full of state secrets. Many have entertainment allowances which permit them to repay social obligations—something of a novelty among the masculine contingent of Washington.

Diplomats are also fun to have around because they work every minute at being agreeable, and not even a major international disaster can shut off their supply of small talk.

Bachelor diplomats are showered with invitations from people they don't even know, mostly ambitious mothers with marriageable daughters. Social secretaries put the attachés at the top of their lists of available men because, while most of the Americans must leave a dance early in order to be at work the next morning at 9, the diplomats can stay on and give the belles a whirl. Making contacts is supposed to be part of their job, and, except in super-special war times, they don't have to show up at their chanceries until mid-morning.

The common or garden variety of American is sought after if he's a political celebrity, but is harder to "come by." Unlike the diplomat, charm is not a part of his stock in trade. Then, too, he is more wise to the ways of social climbers. Supreme Court justices, cabinet members, and senators are the most angled-after members of officialdom, but the majority work too hard to be bothered with numerous cocktail parties. They also receive enough invitations to be able to pick and choose. Former Chief Justice Charles Evans Hughes, who restricted his dining out to Saturday nights, was often booked up in November for parties the following April.

The real climber keeps on doggedly trying, for official titles dress up the dullest dinner and "read well" in the papers next day. Even the most color-less senator, who eats his way stolidly through a meal without addressing a word to his partner, is supposed to lend a certain cachet to parties given by the socially ambitious. "Mention that Senator Jones was at my party" whispers Mrs. X to a gossip columnist. "It will help me."

Methods of Approach

Rich and socially insecure newcomers usually try to storm Washington by one of two methods. The first method is based more on money than on brains, and entails financial splurging. Devotees of the first group conduct their campaigns on the theory that anybody will come to a party if the food and liquor are good. They throw incredible soirees where champagne cascades and orchids decorate the tables. Half their guest list is made up of people they've never met. Such an all-out effort implies a certain lack of imagination and usually only the bores among the social registerites and officialdom bother to attend such functions. The few wits who may show up are apt to be fringy folk who haven't the money or position to make the grade themselves. The subtle climber would never make the mis-take of one rich divorcee newly arrived from Portland, and determined to storm the citadels. In speaking of a forthcoming party she was giving she said naïvely, "I do think I've got a lot of really smart people coming *this time.*"

The second method, employed by the really clever climber, is to concentrate exclusively on the "right people." These are the ones who are "smart," of assured background, or solid official position. This system requires patience and it may be several years before the newcomer "belongs," yet it pays dividends if he or she really aims at the inner circles. Such climbers must display imagination and ingenuity. In planning dinners, they should know which people are congenial or would like for more devious reasons to be brought together at the same table. The clever climber can manipulate things so that Mrs. X, a thoroughly established widow on the hunt for a political husband, can know she will sit next to rising young Representative Y.

The very fastest way to climb socially is through charitable work. Mrs. Climber is generally quite willing to buy a box for one of the pet charities of a social leader, who in turn must extend Mrs. Climber an invitation. Collecting funds for the Community Chest is one tried and true way of meeting the smart women who head the local charities. If the socially ambitious will shoulder the dirty work, all the better. Another way is to sign up for war relief work. One woman was heard to say, "Yes, I'll help, but I'd much rather work in the Walsh mansion, because the chances of making contacts are so much better."

The social climber who wants to take the church route to the inner circles will find one of the most fashionable congregations at historic St. John's Church on Lafayette Square across from the White House. Supreme Court Justice Owen J. Roberts teaches a Bible class there and Mrs. Cordell Hull occasionally attends services. President Roosevelt and his family worship at St. Thomas' Church in the Dupont Circle sector. Society weddings of Catholics frequently take place in big St. Matthew's Cathedral just off Connecticut Avenue.

The ambitious mama with a debutante daughter will not consider the latter's preparation successful unless she gets into the Junior League. Membership is not a sign of great social arrival, but it is a "must" for the striving young girl. To this society social welfare group belong the "nice" girls from the "nice" families in the upper brackets. But no matter how rich mama is, she can't buy her way into the League. Admission depends on family background, pleasant personality and the energy necessary to complete the hours of social work required for entrance. Though Junior Leaguers of Washington mingle more with the residential group than with the glittering transients of official and diplomatic society, for a debutante who wants to lay a firm basis of friendships among the "right people," the League is the organization at which to aim.

Society Page and Social Register

You don't need a press agent to crash the society pages, but a knowledge of the machinery of society reporting is a help to any climber.

The society editors in the nation's capital are a busy lot. In no other city of similar size is so much space devoted to chitchat and coverage of every sort of gathering. All four of the local papers employ special staffs to handle the social news. Each society editor has several assistants, as well as two or three columnists who cover particular groups such as Army and Navy, residential, diplomatic, smart, not-so-smart.

One Washington publisher, in despair over a survey which showed his big-league political writers were not as widely read as he hoped, said, "I've decided that the Washington public cares only for society and the comic strips."

Society reporting in the nation's capital is a good deal less trivial than it sounds. Not only social leaders, suburban housewives and debutantes scan the social columns, but cabinet officers, diplomats and even hard-bitten newspapermen and newspaperwomen as well. After seeing who is dining with whom, it sometimes is possible to figure which way the political wind is blowing.

Attachés of South American legations sometimes ring up society editors to ask that such-and-such a dinner they are giving be mentioned. Such notices are copied in the papers of the home country and boost the diplomats' careers. One embassy official was recalled because of an item in a society column. The gossip writer reported that the official had made derogatory remarks to the effect that his country's ambassador squeezed the pennies when giving dinner parties.

All Washington society editors work twelve hours a day at a job which requires them to be a combination drudge and social butterfly. In the morning they assemble stories and plan the make-up and in the afternoon and evening trot out to cocktail parties and dinners. Half the town's great call them by their first names and they are invited everywhere.

Margaret Poe Hart, a descendant of Edgar Allan Poe, is society editor of the *Washington Star*, and has years of training in society and straight news reporting. Like that newspaper in general, the society column follows a rather formal style.

Hope Ridings Miller, society editor of the *Post*, is Texas born, a college graduate with a Master's degree in English and a Phi Beta Kappa, and is one society editor who is allergic to adjectives.

Betty Hynes is society editor of the *Times-Herald*. She has also been dramatic editor of that newspaper and editor of its woman's page.

Several socially prominent women are employed as Washington society columnists. They usually concentrate on the intimate details of small dinners and teas given by their friends among the smart set. An exception to this rule is Evelyn Peyton Gordon, who writes of the whole range of society in her column for the *Washington Daily News*. Though once a capital debutante herself, she likes to kid society, and refuses to take it as seriously as do some of her colleagues.

Washington's gossipiest column of the Winchell variety is "These Charming People" in Cissie Patterson's spicy *Times-Herald*. The author, Igor Cassini, is the grandson of a Russian ambassador to Washington in the McKinley administration. Igor gained international notoriety some years ago when a group of Virginians who objected to innuendoes in his column abducted him from a dance, stripped him and smeared his torso with cold road oil.

The three biggest newspapers build circulation by devoting space to the non-chic as well as the Social Register, and no item is too unimportant to be placed somewhere in their columns. The social climbers and the obscure are all included.

If the ambitious only knew this they wouldn't pull such boners as did one rich widow who came to town determined to crash the inner circles. A society reporter, meeting her at dinner one night, wrote her up in the usual complimentary style and was surprised to find in her mail the next day a check for $50 as "just a simple expression of your kindness in mentioning me." The check was returned with a polite note. You can't buy your way into Washington society columns.

When a climber begins to go coy on the press, it is a sign she is "arriving." A few become so exclusive they won't even speak to a reporter over the telephone. Others refuse to give their dinner lists for publication, but are careful to invite one of several Social Register columnists who they know will next day describe the party down to the last hors d'oeuvre. These writers are, of course, "not invited as newspaper people, but as intimate friends." One columnist who concentrates on the smart set is often told, "I'll give you my list if you'll put it in your column, so it will sound as though you'd been there. But I don't want it used anywhere else on the page."

When a climber has really "arrived," she is listed in the Social Register. The New York committee which decides whose names shall be listed between the cardboard covers moves in mysterious ways its wonders to perform. In applying for membership, the ambitious matron must arm

416

herself with letters from three registerites, preferably long-time residents of Washington. The committee then consults its capital agent, whose identity is kept secret. Money alone is not enough to guarantee admission, and multiple divorces, newspaper notoriety and scandals are distinct handicaps. Yet many are admitted to the Washington Register who would never make the grade in other cities. In the capital, official position is taken into account and cabinet officers, senators and diplomats are automatically included. That's why even the late Huey Long, who was far from being part of Washington's "smart society," was included in its sacrosanct pages. Conversely, many welcomed in the capital's social circles are not listed in the Register.

Backstage Ropes

One of the best ways for a climber to get a foothold in Washington society is to hire one of the capital's well-known social secretaries. The most prominent of these are women of assured social standing themselves, and will work newcomers into gatherings of their own. If the clients are not too boorish, they usually can catch hold and begin to make their own way. After the climbers are introduced, the social secretary can still be of great help in advising on the "right" people to invite to select functions.

Some of these secretaries have specialties. Most of Washington's large coming-out parties are handled by Mrs. Wallach Merriam, herself a social registerite. The debutante who places herself in Mrs. Merriam's hands is likely to be included in the other younger set parties she arranges, which is most of them.

Two of the best known embassy secretaries are Miss Irene Boyle, who has handled many of the British Embassy's social matters, and Miss Rebecca Wellington, who helped steer the German and Italian Embassies in the days before their guest lists dwindled away. Miss Anne Squire has guided several Supreme Court justices' wives, and has written a book called *Social Washington*, which is a useful handbook for any hardworking society newcomer, for it lists Washington's social customs and gives some "do's and don'ts" of advice. Several of the embassy secretaries are now advising such agencies of the government as the State Department and the Rockefeller organization.

Not all social secretaries have specialized. Mrs. Loring C. Christie, widow of the former U. S. Minister to Canada, and Mrs. Nathan C. Wyeth both handle general matters, as do the sisters Anne and Mary Randolph. Miss Anne Randolph took care of the social affairs of Andrew Mellon when he was Secretary of the Treasury.

After a climber has learned the ropes, she can be her own social secretary. And she might well take a hint from one leading Washington hostess who keeps not only a tremendous file of guests, but has subdivisions labeled "smart," "music loving," and "intelligentsia." She entertains on such a big scale that she maintains not just one, but several social secretaries.

Besides leaving cards at embassies, the climber in normal peacetime also may enjoy the thrill of depositing a pasteboard at the White House. This is supposed to be done early in the autumn immediately after the First Lady returns for the winter. Any woman may also call on wives of Supreme Court justices, cabinet members and congressmen on their days "at home."

A certain type of climber will stop at nothing. One woman whose name has become legend in the capital's social annals pursues her prey so relentlessly that they have small chance of escape even by the white lie method. One of her victims was maneuvered into being her guest of honor at a luncheon for fifty. It took place in May and some of the most prominent women in town were surprised to find each other among those present. Comparing notes, they discovered that their hostess had invited all of them the previous December for a date five months off.

But then you are not interested in all this, because, of course, *you* are not a social climber.

40

Tales of the Town

EVERY community has its stories which people tell, and retell, and pass on to succeeding generations, often with embellishments. Washington has thousands of stories about the Great, the near-great, and the unknown. A few of the stories are recorded here. Most of these stories are old, and have been told a thousand times. Some have been twisted a bit to conceal the real identities, but all are true, and all are peculiarly typical of those qualities and attitudes which Washington has in exaggerated proportions.

Babies and Birds

When winter nights come to Washington the starlings also come. Thousands of the birds roost in the trees along Pennsylvania Avenue and make life hazardous for pedestrians, especially for men with new hats. Many methods have been used to frighten them away, and all have failed. A bureau of the Department of Agriculture once installed smoking smudge pots high in the trees, where they hung like huge wasps' nests. Nicholas Longworth, then Speaker of the House, was riding down the Avenue one day with John Garner, then Minority Leader. Said Jack to Nick, "What are those big black things in the trees?" Said Nick to Jack, "Those are smudge pots for the starlings." "Oh," said Jack, "and who is going to teach the birds to sit on 'em?"

Alibi

Government agencies sometimes make announcements which embarrass the White House or the State Department, and if the embarrassment is great, they are asked to amend or retract the statement. The Maritime Commission pulled a diplomatic boner about ships to Archangel, and subsequently retracted it under White House orders. Admiral Jerry Land of the Maritime Commission told this story:

In the lobby of the Mayflower two men were sitting talking, and a couple of women approached. Said one man to the other, "Say, look at that homely woman." Said the other, "Why, that's my wife." Said the first man, "Oh, no, I didn't mean that young woman. I meant that ugly old woman with her." Said the other man, "That's my mother."

. . . A very long pause . . . Then the first man mumbled, "I never said it."

Bedtime Story

Saintly old Justice Brandeis always took a nap after lunch during his summer vacations in a cottage on Cape Cod, and often asked a member of his family or some visiting friend to read something aloud to put him to sleep. A house guest one summer was Richard Boeckel, a Washington journalist. He had bought a book to read on the train, and he read it aloud to the Justice to put him to sleep. But the aged and learned Justice did not doze in the first five minutes, as was usual, or even in the next half hour. He did not go to sleep for an hour and a half—only when the book was read to the end. The book was *Gentlemen Prefer Blondes*.

How to Live Long

Old Mike was a messenger at the entrance door of the Attorney General, but he never carried messages. His sole duties were to receive callers, take their hats and coats, and open the door leading to the private office of the Attorney General. That he did and nothing more. One day a caller asked him how he kept his health in spite of advancing years. He explained his secret: "When I leave this office at the end of a day and go to my home, I do not do as some public men do. I leave all my official cares behind."

Incognito

Building guards have their own ideas about who is a well-known man. A few years ago the Department of Justice, which is headed by the Attorney General and which includes the subordinate FBI, required cards or credentials for anyone entering the building at night. The Attorney General came back to his office late one evening, did not have his identification card and was refused admission. "But I am the Attorney General," he expostulated, and the guard replied, "You can't get in without a card, and that goes flat, and I wouldn't care even if you said you were J. Edgar Hoover himself."

Intrusion

Press conferences with the Secretary of State have always been regarded as sacrosanct, and intrusion of others, even other officials of the State Department, is completely taboo. But there was once an exception to the rule. During a press conference of William Jennings Bryan, while he was

Wilson's Secretary of State, newsmen were startled when suddenly there burst into the room two Assistant Secretaries of State, the Legal Adviser of the Department, the Chief of the Division of European Affairs, and the Chief of the Division of Far Eastern Affairs. They came all at once, out of breath, and one said, "Yes, Mr. Secretary, did you ring?" Mr. Bryan said he had not, but all the intruders insisted he had. The Secretary found that he had been sitting on the edge of his desk, on a whole row of push buttons.

Confidential

Press releases of government departments are marked with the advance date of publication, and the more important bear a notation in red ink by rubber stamp, "CONFIDENTIAL, HOLD FOR RELEASE." One day some years ago all newspaper offices received a release bearing this extra-extra cautionary warning against accidental premature publication. The proper editors took it, and scrupulously observed the release date. The copy was from the Department of Agriculture's Bureau of Home Economics, and contained the recipe for a new cake.

Look the Part

People have the erroneous habit of thinking that important men *look* important. At a conference of state governors in Annapolis more than 20 years ago a Washington reporter was waiting for the Massachusetts delegation headed by Governor Coolidge, who was conspicuous at that time because he had broken the Boston police strike. The delegation finally arrived, and there was a lot of buzzing and how-do-you-do. The big man in the middle, taking handshakes right and left, obviously was the Governor. To make sure, an AP reporter sidled up to a little man on the edge of the newly-arrived crowd, nudged him with an elbow, and asked him whether he could point out Governor Coolidge. "Yes," replied the little man, "I am Mr. Coolidge."

How to Get News

There were rumors that Secretary Blank was about to resign. The rumors were circumstantially correct, and most of the newspapermen believed them and wrote dispatches in July that he would quit in August. One newspaper-man wrote, however, that he would not resign in August. Later, when asked how he knew, he said he had read a society item which said that the Secretary's daughter would make her debut at Christmas time. The Secretary did resign—but after the debut at Christmas time.

Steam Roller

One of the most common terms heard in the halls of Congress is "steam roller," and here is the way it originated: It was June 1908, in Chicago, and the Republicans were in convention there, trying to nominate a successor to President Teddy Roosevelt. Teddy wanted Taft, who had been his Secretary of War. Other party leaders wanted the nomination to go to one of their own pet state sons—Uncle Joe Cannon, Charlie Fairbanks, Charlie Hughes, Philander Knox, or Joe Foraker. The decision lay in the seating of delegates from eight states. The National Committee was to decide on the seating. The National Committee met and decided on the seatings from two states, Alabama and Arkansas, which were keys to the decisions in the others. The meeting was covered by Oswald F. Schuette of the *Chicago Inter-Ocean*, now a counselor of public relations in Washington. As he dashed back to his office to write the story he saw in front of the convention hall a steam roller. He wrote in his lead that the Roosevelt-Taft forces had flattened the opposition like a steam roller. Next day the convention echoed with shouts of "steam roller." Politicians ever since have talked of "steam roller." The term has been added to the language. The newspaper reporter who added it didn't know at the time that he was adding it.

Money Breeds Money

Andrew Carnegie was a guest at a peace society banquet at which President Taft was the chief speaker. Carnegie sat at the end of the table, where a press table adjoined at right angle, and a newspaperman spent the time talking to Mr. Carnegie, who spent his time playing with a nickel on the tablecloth. In the middle of the address of President Taft, the nickel slipped from Mr. Carnegie's fingers and fell to the floor. The newspaperman tried to catch it, but missed. Mr. Carnegie shoved back his chair, made a commotion which interrupted the speaking President, dropped to his hands and knees, dived under the table, and came up with the nickel—plus a dime.

Richly Unconscious

When Andrew W. Mellon came to Washington to be Secretary of the Treasury he was regarded as a "mystery man" because he had none of the attributes of a politician. To dispel the mystery, the *New York Times* commissioned a Washington writer to make a study and prepare an article on Mr. Mellon, on the character, temperament and spirit of the man. The writer prepared a list of 20 questions, with the understanding that the answers were not to be used in print at the time, but were to serve merely as background illumination. Sitting in his quiet office at the Treasury Mr.

Mellon answered most of the questions without embarrassment, but when he came to one, he stopped, looked out the window, then spoke with the hesitancy, almost a stutter, which was his mannerism. The question was this: "What have you to say about being a rich man?"

"Why . . . I . . . I . . . don't know what to say. I . . . I . . . suppose I am . . . what they call a rich man . . . They tell me so . . . I'm not particularly conscious of it . . . I don't use money . . . for myself . . . I don't spend much . . . on myself . . . I have always . . . just worked . . . done what needed to be done . . . in business . . . I didn't try to make money . . . especially . . . I'm not interested in it . . . in money . . . I don't care . . . but . . . well . . . I . . . I can't think of anything to say about it."

Wolf, Wolf

Before the nation's gold was stored at Fort Knox, protected by soldiers and electric rays, it was kept in a vault in the basement of the Treasury Building in Washington, protected by some steel doors and a burglar alarm. The alarm got out of order, and finally became so bad that it went off two or three times a day for no apparent reason at all. During the two weeks that it was on a rampage, the clerks in the Treasury and pedestrians on the street became accustomed to it. They didn't even run to the vaults to catch the burglars. They merely remarked, "Well, someone is stealing the gold again."

Finnigin to Flannigan

One of the most beloved residents of Washington, more widely known than most cabinet members or senators, is a serious-minded and kindly philosopher of life who is famous as a professional humorist-lecturer, writer, radio performer. His name is Strickland Gillilan. But he complains that people can't remember his name. They call him "Finnigin." He fought against it for years, but finally accepted it, for he made Finnigin. It was on a mean February afternoon in 1897. Gillilan was a young cub reporter on the *Daily Palladium* of Richmond, Indiana. There wasn't any news, and the printers were yelling for copy, so he grabbed a piece of laundry wrapping paper and scribbled a six-stanza poem, and called it "Finnigin to Flannigan." The last two lines were "Off agin, on agin, gone agin—Finnigin." It was a poem in Irish dialect, and since the printers didn't like either poems or dialect, he thought they would throw it away. But they didn't. They set it up, and printed it, and the town of Richmond chuckled and roared, and called him "Finnigin." He doctored the poem a bit and sent it to the old humor magazine, *Life*, which paid him $9 for it. Since then millions in many lands have read the poem and belly-laughed. Parents have recited it to their children, children have spoken it as a piece at school. Says Strick Gillilan, "I didn't write 'Finnigin,' it just kinda wrote itself."

Gold In Them Thar Bulletins

Many years ago a couple of government geologists named Schrader and Brooks spent a summer in Alaska doing a bit of mapping, and while they were there they found a gold rush in progress on the beaches at Nome. So they made a study of the geological formations of the region, including the Yukon country, then returned to Washington and wrote a bulletin called "A Preliminary Report on the Cape Nome Gold Region, Alaska." It showed that a prehistoric beach had existed in the country back of Nome, and that it should contain more gold than the newer beach at Nome. The bulletin was printed and distributed free. Several years later, a greater gold rush started, in the back country, just where Schrader and Brooks had said the gold would be—in their free government bulletin.

Rough Riders

Theodore Roosevelt's "Rough Riders," of the Spanish-American War, got their name inadvertently from a newspaper correspondent, Richard V. Oulahan, who was then a young reporter for the Washington Bureau of the *New York Times*, and who later, before his death, became "dean" of the Washington correspondents. Theodore Roosevelt was then Assistant Secretary of the Navy (as was later his cousin Franklin). Teddy Roosevelt told Dick Oulahan, in strict professional confidence, that he intended to muster a regiment of western horsemen as cavalry to fight in Cuba. Oulahan was authorized to write the story in advance, to be held for release. He wrote it, and submitted it to Teddy, who edited it. Once he penciled out the term "rough riders" which Oulahan had injected as a way of characterizing the regiment. Twice he edited out the same term. He didn't like it. The third and final reference was carelessly overlooked. The story was published. The headwriter of the *Times* had seized upon the single "rough rider" term remaining in the story, and had brought it from the tail end to the heading. "Rough Riders," read the heading. "Rough Riders," read the news stories for days thereafter. "Rough Riders" they became.

Fame

Herbert Hoover, Jr., son of the former President, has always been modest, has always shrunk from the limelight that goes along with members of the family of any President. Several years ago he and his wife went for vacation to an isolated Canadian lodge in the far north. When he signed the register, the clerk asked whether he happened to be related to the "Great Hoover." Young Hoover, always anxious not to sponge off the reputation of his father, fumbled a bit on reply, but the clerk added hastily, "Hoover, the great G-Man, you know." Young Hoover, feeling relieved, said he was no relation. The clerk said, "Well, we are glad to have you, anyway, but we always like to know when we are entertaining the relatives of celebrities."

Secret Mission

During the first World War, the Governor of the Federal Reserve System was W. P. G. Harding, and he was a key figure in the control of the fiscal policies of the United States and the world. One day there was an unusually important and secret meeting of the Gold Export Committee, which reporters were watching from the outside. Governor Harding slipped out, somewhat furtively. A reporter followed him, thinking he might be going to the British Embassy to close a world agreement on gold. Instead, Governor Harding walked down F Street and turned into a movie palace which was showing Charlie Chaplin.

The Moving of General Grant

Headquarters of a peace organization, the Women's International League for Peace and Freedom, for years were on 17th Street across from the State, War and Navy Building, in an historic old structure which bore a plaque saying that in that house had resided General U. S. Grant while serving as Secretary of War. One day the peace organization had to move, and the moving was done by an old Negro porter who had long been a fixture of the office. When the moving was finished, someone discovered that he had removed the plaque from the old building and screwed it onto the face of the new building. He finally took it back, but only after much grumbling that "General Grant, he belong to us No'the'ners."

Diplomacy

A young man studying for the diplomatic service was one of the guests at a select musicale given by the British Ambassador. Everyone rose at the opening anthem, "God Save the King." In the solemn moment of reseating, the young man sat on the front edge of his collapsible chair. It skidded on the slick ballroom floor and he descended with a great clatter. All heads turned, but he was on the floor, invisible. He thought fast and stayed there, until all heads had turned back to the stage. That was his start in a successful career as a diplomat.

Who's New?

Homer Joseph Dodge, a Washington newspaperman, covered the Treasury through numerous administrations, from Taft on. But when Morgenthau first took over, Dodge was temporarily off that beat. At the first conference which Dodge attended after that, Morgenthau noticed the sharpness of his questions and said, "You're new around here, aren't you?" To which Dodge replied: "No, Mr. Secretary, *you're* new."

Tip from the Court

The late Justice Harlan of the Supreme Court lectured law students at Georgetown University, and sometimes he discussed the principles involved in pending cases. A Washington brokerage firm got one of its junior partners to study carefully all pending cases which might have market effect, and to enter the law class. One night the Justice outlined the principles involved in an important pending case, and carried it to a logical conclusion. The broker's lawyer took a night train to New York, and got his firm to play the market to fit the expected decision. Sure enough, the decision came down from the Supreme Court the following Monday, but the firm lost heavily in the market, because the decision was contrary to the advance speculation. At the bottom of the printed opinion was a single line which read: "Mr. Justice Harlan dissents."

Lifelong Ambition

Irene Chamberlain was a government clerk on a small salary. She supported her aged mother, and so she had no spare money. But her ambition for years had been to take a trip to Europe "with good clothes." The mother finally died, and Irene started scrimping and saving for the trip. It took her four years, but finally she had enough to sign up for an all-expense tour, and to buy a trunkful of pretty clothes. Her friends advised her to buy clothes on the other side, but she said no, she wanted them to wear both ways. On sailing day it rained. On the way over she was seasick the entire time, and kept to her cabin. In Rome she fell ill, and died. Friends in Washington sent for her body and luggage. When her trunk was returned and opened, it was found full of new clothes, never unpacked. In her suitcase was found a postal card, addressed but unmailed, which said, "My lifelong ambition has been fulfilled."

Accidents Sometimes Happen

During World War I a Washington reporter wrote himself a loose "think piece," all about how German propaganda and Irish propaganda were similar. The story got a bigger play than he had intended, and became the sensation of the week. Both German and Irish citizens denounced the story and the reporter. Even he thought he had gone too far, and looked forward to getting fired. Two weeks later Sir Roger Casement was arrested in Ireland, charged with conspiring with Germans on arms and propaganda. Until then the reporter had never heard of Casement, but he received credit for knowing in advance. He got his pay raised and a citation for "meritorious reportorial enterprise."

The Top Rung

Francis X. Gharrity was a policeman, but the ambition of his life was to become a Washington newspaperman. So he applied once a month to Washington news bureaus for a job which he never got. But during a flu epidemic reporters became so scarce that a news bureau hired him to telephone crop reports from the Department of Agriculture. He was happy. He had climbed to the top. A week later he was stricken with the flu and taken to a hospital. He called in a fellow reporter and asked that if he died, he be given a newspaperman's funeral. He died, and six newspapermen knocked off work and carried his body to the grave. They called him Frank, and never quite knew his last name.

Genteel Atmosphere

J. D. Bowers was city solicitor of Dubuque, but in the first World War he wanted to serve his country, so he came to Washington as examiner of contracts for the War Department. He was made a lieutenant colonel, and wore his uniform although it was a little tight around the neck. He and his wife liked the genteel atmosphere of Washington better than Dubuque, so after the war he got an appointment as attorney in the Department of Commerce. He is still there, although he doesn't like the New Deal ideas, and he wishes he had run for mayor of Dubuque in 1920. His close friend did, and later became governor, as Bowers says he might have done. He is active in his neighborhood's citizens' association.

Their All for Daughter

Mr. and Mrs. J. Harrison Pogue brought up their only daughter to be a lady. They sent her to the best schools, took pains that she should associate with the best people, and protected her from ordinary young men. They introduced her to Washington society at the age of 19, and she was soon engaged to a young Boston blueblood. While the young man was visiting here, the parents went into debt to throw a series of elegant parties. They were not religious people, but they joined a church. At the end of the year the daughter was married to the young blueblood in the church by the Bishop, and went away to live. The parents immediately sold their house, paid their debts, got a divorce, and disappeared from Washington. The daughter is doing very well.

Career

George Watson at the age of 18 went in for a career of foreign service. In 1920 he became a student in the Georgetown School of Foreign Service, and studied subjects which would fit him for the managership in China for the Standard Oil Company, or National City Bank, or something. Foreign trade, he said, would make this nation great. Julius Klein said so and Secretary Hoover said so. After graduation George got a job in the Bureau of Foreign and Domestic Commerce at $1200 a year. It was for training. He would work up and out, to China or Java. George is still with the Bureau. He compiles information on trade opportunities. He has never been abroad, but he attends all free evening lectures on foreign trade. His work is satisfactory and he is protected by civil service. His pay is $2040.

Turn of the Wheel

Years ago, when Bob Maguire was 23, and two years out of the University of Idaho, he had a government job and when the section chief left, Bob got the section chief's job. This was quite a step up, but he was equal to it. He didn't like the girl secretary who was assigned to him, and he ordered her sent back to the stenographic pool. She was angry at the demotion, at the hurt to her pride. She warned her young boss that he'd rue the day. He dismissed the incident as the raving of an hysterical woman.

Years passed. Bob Maguire rose through the merit ranks of government and became an assistant to a cabinet member. It was an "earned job." But a new cabinet member became his chief, and rumors arose that Bob was to be fired. The rumors proved to be correct. He was fired. The only clue to the reason was the fact, unearthed by friends, that the girl-secretary whom he had sent back to the stenographic pool more than 20 years before, had risen in life and had become the wife of the cabinet member who had fired him.

Poll Tax

Phil Campbell was a congressman from Kansas. In the days of Uncle Joe Cannon, he became whip of the House, chairman of the Rules Committee, and a great power in Congress. Congressman Phil Campbell had to spend so much time in Washington that he bought a house in which to live. It was on a hill, across the Potomac from Washington, and on Virginia soil. Naturally he paid Virginia real estate taxes. In the Virginia tax bill there was an item of $1.50 for poll tax. Phil paid the whole bill via secretary without noticing the poll tax item. Then, as usual, he ran for reelection back in Kansas. His opponent dug up the Virginia poll tax bill, had it photostated, distributed it to Kansas voters as proof that Phil Campbell of Kansas was really a legal resident of Virginia. At Campbell's final rally in the campaign his opponent induced Phil's own band, as a final number, to play "Carry Me Back to Ole Virginny." Phil was defeated in Kansas and lived successfully thereafter in Virginia.

Scholar of the Press

A visiting San Francisco businessman was a luncheon guest at the famed round table of the National Press Club. He displayed much knowledge of geography, literature, history, fauna, Shakespeare and the Bible. When he was joshed for seeming so learned, although "only a businessman," he confessed that he had just been reading a book. Turning to a silent farmerish-looking newspaperman to his left, he poured out a torrent of talk about the book, saying that it contained the lore of the centuries, that it was called *What Do You Know?*, and that it was written by someone named George W. Stimpson. "You ought to read it," he urged. The other replied, "I have, I wrote it, I'm Stimpson."

Tainted?

Edward Carl was a nonpolitical career man in the Bureau of Foreign and Domestic Commerce when Hoover was Secretary of Commerce, and he was often consulted by Hoover in the routine of departmental work. When Hoover got to be President, Carl got the reputation of being "close to Hoover," although he never saw Hoover as President and was not close to him. The Democrats came along and Carl was fired on the grounds that he had been close to Hoover. For eight years he did not have a government job. Then he was called back into service to take a position similar to that from which he had been fired. He proved to be competent, so he was consulted often by Jesse Jones. Now he is worried lest at some future time the Republicans come in and he be fired for being close to Jesse Jones.

Government Competition

Gus Barlow was head of a news bureau, got $100 a week, and had two assistants. When the defense program came along, the government started hiring good newspapermen as publicity agents. The government hired Barlow's $60 a week assistant for $100 a week, and then hired his $40 assistant for $100. Barlow took pride in maintaining his bureau, and good reporters were scarce, so he cut his own salary to $80 a week, and hired one man at $80. He cussed the government's "prodigal salary policy," saying it would wreck the Washington news corps if it continued. Then the government offered him $120 a week as a publicity man. He sighed twice and took it.

Delegated Responsibility

Almost the last of the colorful Indian chiefs who used to file into Washington and tell the troubles of their tribes to the committees of Congress was Quanah Buller, of Oklahoma. One of the problems that troubled the administrators of Indian groups was the fact that they were a little loose in the matter of marriage. Many braves, it was reported, had more than one wife. The representatives of the White Father admonished their leaders against this. The Chairman of the Senate Committee on Indian Affairs was particularly disturbed when he was told that Quanah Buller himself had two wives. He told Buller that he must go back to Oklahoma and get rid of one of those wives. The next year when the Chief appeared the Chairman questioned him.

"Did you get rid of one of those wives?" the Chairman asked.

"No," said Quanah.

"This will never do," the Chairman thundered. "You go back home and you tell one of those women that she will have to go back to her people."

"You tell 'um," said Quanah.

Duke and a Drink

The Duke of Windsor, while Prince of Wales, had at least one drink in America during the days of American prohibition. It happened at the National Press Club, in Washington. He was a guest, and he was engaged in the ordeal of shaking the hands of a long receiving line of newspapermen and their dressed-up wives. Jimmy, the Press Club steward, had been instructed earlier in the day to scurry up a good bottle of scotch for the Prince, and to make perfectly sure that it was fit for human consumption. Jimmy obeyed orders, and made himself the testing ground for determining absolutely that the scotch was nonpoisonous. To make sure he took enough himself to show up any possible traces of poison. By the time the test was completed, the receiving line was in full swing. Edging up behind the line to the Prince of Wales, he nudged him a good sound nudge, and muttered, "Hey, Prince, how'd yuh like to have a drink?" The Prince said he'd be delighted, and the receiving line was suspended. Later the Club membership got into an awful row over the issue of whether Jimmy, the steward, should be fired for not letting the official committee extend the invitation. Jimmy pleaded that he was the only living person who was in position to assure the Prince that the scotch was nonpoisonous. He was not fired, and the Prince was not poisoned, but lived thereafter to be King and Duke.

Southern Point of View

Southerners have their own way of looking at things. It was so after the "War Between the States." And it was so later at the turn of the century, when the statue of General Sherman was erected at the south front of the Treasury. General Sherman rode a horse, and the horse and rider were set upon a high pedestal, as you see them today, where Pennsylvania Avenue, after a straight sweep from the Capitol, bends an elbow to get around the Treasury. In those days Lyman J. Gage was Secretary of the Treasury. He presided at the unveiling of the monument to Sherman on horseback. He knew, of course, that Sherman was the man who had devastated Georgia from Atlanta to the sea, and who was hated by all true Southerners. So he timidly asked a southern newspaper correspondent, who was present at the unveiling, what he thought of the monument. The Southerner hesitated, then slowly replied, "Well, Mr. Secretary, from the north side where we stand, you see General Sherman as a soldier and gentleman, but from the south side all you can see is a horse's hind end."

False Face

When the war spirit first hit Washington a rule was established in the War Department that every employee had to wear a badge bearing his name and his photograph in miniature, like a passport photo. One clerk decided to become a bit of an experimenter, so he removed his own photograph from the badge and substituted another which he had clipped from a magazine. For three whole weeks, it served to pass the outer guards and inner guards. Then a deskmate happened to notice that the face on the badge was that of Adolf Hitler.

No Laughter, Please

The mace is the symbol of the dignity of the House of Representatives. When disorder occurs this fasces-formed and heavy baton, with the beak of the American eagle at its top, is supposed to be carried erect by the Sergeant-at-Arms and presented before unruly members with a stern and formal order to keep the peace in the name of the House. On one occasion when two members had squared off and the Speaker called for the mace, the Sergeant-at-Arms was not present and a newly appointed young deputy who had not yet been instructed in the handling of the

431

mace, was called upon to perform the duty. Grasping it like one carrying a quarterstaff, he dashed down the aisle where stood the embattled members and truculently advancing the eagle's beak cried: "If you don't stop, I'll peck you."

It Can Happen Here

A boy, part Indian, part white, was raised on an Indian reservation, and as a youth went to Topeka, Kansas, where he drove a hack. The hack had a high seat, and a light to the right, and a light to the left. By these two lights, while waiting for fares, the youth read law books. Eventually he was admitted to the bar, got into politics, and became Vice President of the United States. His name was Charlie Curtis.

41

and also . . .

Meet Fifty-Five Big Men

HERE are additional details about public men, many of whom are discussed elsewhere in this book.

These sketches cover the principal men who are running the government during war—not all the important men, but the most prominent, the most influential men in Washington. You may wish to pick out and read only those in whom you are especially interested.

Some interesting facts showed up in arrears, after these sketches were written:

Parentage: Their origin is predominantly middle-class, not "rich" and not "poor." Of the 55, only 7 were born with golden spoons in their mouths. These are Morgenthau, Stimson, Rockefeller, Stettinius, Harriman, Welles and Wayne Taylor. Some others have become wealthy, or relatively wealthy, but they were not born that way.

Income stratum: Figures are not available on the worldly goods of all of these men, but a good guess is that the average wealth or income is what might be called "upper middle." The average is not "wealthy," but is far above average.

Age: The average age is 52.4. None is under 30. (Rockefeller at 33 is the youngest.) Between 30 and 39, there are three. Between 40 and 49, there are 17. Between 50 and 59, there are 23. Between 60 and 69, there are ten. Between 70 and 74, there are two.

Education: Of the 55, 44 have gone through college. Five others attended college, but did not finish. Total who went to college, 49. More than one half of those attending college earned all or part of their expenses while in school. Only six did not go to college, and they might be regarded as constituting an "honor roll" of men who got high in government without college education. They are Jesse Jones, Steve Early, Lowell Mellett, Milo Perkins, William Knudsen and Sidney Hillman.

Harvard: Of the 49 who went to college, 13 went to Harvard, which seems like an extraordinarily high percentage for any one school.

Naturalized citizens are four—Knudsen, Hillman, Frankfurter, Currie.

Careers: Generalizations are a bit dangerous, but a few impressions seem warranted. Very few started out to be government officials. They

434

got into their present positions as a consequence of a series of career incidents at some stage of their lives. These incidents gave them a bend toward a line of work or interest which landed them finally in their present jobs. In one way or another most seem to have worked up to their present posts —step by step progress—with some sort of notable distinction before they came to government.

Career civil servants: Only five of the group can be said to be career civil servants in the sense that they have devoted most of their adult lives to governmental work—J. Edgar Hoover, Sumner Welles, Daniel W. Bell, Harold D. Smith, and John B. Blandford, Jr.

The men in this list are executive or administrative officials, not legislators and not judges (with one or two exceptions). A complete picture would cover Congress and the Courts, but the current interest now is mainly in the executives.

Look over this list and note that very few of these men were known to the general public ten years ago. Most of our national leaders come up from obscurity within a decade, and also go back to obscurity. It is quite probable that the President of the United States ten years hence, and a dozen cabinet members then, are NOT in this list.

Henry Agard Wallace: Vice President; Chairman, Board of Economic Warfare. Age 53. Born on Adair County (Iowa) farm. Father was agricultural teacher, editor, and Harding's Secretary of Agriculture. Left farm as baby. Iowa State College, 1910. Associate editor Wallace's *Farmer*, 1910-24; editor, 1924-33 (Wallace's *Farmer* was merged with Iowa *Homestead*, 1929). After years of experimentation, developed high-yielding hybrid corn. Broke with Republicans over farm and tariff policies, supported Al Smith, Roosevelt. Secretary of Agriculture, 1933-40; inaugurated crop restrictions, soil conservation payments. Elected Vice President, 1940. Appointed chairman Board of Economic Warfare, 1941. Originally a weak administrator, but learned and improved. Serious, tense, looks worried, preoccupied, ill at ease; essentially a thinker and dreamer, but obstinately persistent. Deeply religious, moody, shy. Nervous laugh. Inquiring mind of wide range, delving into comparative theologies, mysticism, astrology, plant genetics, agricultural economics, postwar prospects, Spanish and Portuguese languages. Ever-ready experimenter; frequently tries out diet theories on self. Exercises diligently: tennis, boomerang-throwing, paddle ball, walking. Medium build, rumpled hair.

Cordell Hull: Secretary of State. Age 70. Born Overton County, Tenn., amid feuding kinsmen, son of farmer-timberman. Attended National Normal University (Ohio), 1889-90. Graduated Cumberland University Law

435

School, 1891. Member Tennessee legislature, 1893-97. Circuit judge, 1903-07 (still called "Judge"). Member U. S. House of Representatives, 1907-21; 1923-31. In House noted for doughty opposition to protective tariffs; author of federal income and inheritance tax systems. Chairman Democratic National Committee, 1921-24. U. S. Senator, 1931-33. Service as Secretary of State, since 1933 (longer than any other in history), marked by inauguration of reciprocal trade agreements; evangelical zeal in behalf of new world order through economic, military disarmament. Idealistic about international collaboration. State Rights Democrat of Jefferson school, has kept aloof from New Deal domestic controversies. Inwardly tough-minded, will of flint, relentless enemy. Outwardly suave, kindly (almost gentle), courteous, easy to approach, uses salty language. Lives simply. High-pitched, rasping voice. Plays croquet. Thin, angular, strong face, white hair.

Henry Morgenthau, Jr.: Secretary of the Treasury since 1934. Age 51. Born New York City, son of rich lawyer-financier, Wilson's Ambassador to Turkey. Abandoned study of architecture, preferring farming to managing father's real estate holdings; spent two years on Texas ranch; took agricultural course, Cornell, 1912-13. Bought 1,400 acre Dutchess County (N. Y.) farm, 15 miles from Roosevelt's Hyde Park, 1913. Has made farm pay its way. Naval lieutenant, World War I. Publisher *American Agriculturist*, 1922-33. Chairman, Governor Roosevelt's Agricultural Advisory Commission, 1929-33; New York Conservation Commissioner, 1931-33. Brought to Washington, 1933, to head up new Farm Credit Administration; moved to Treasury as sponsor of new "managed-money" theories. Has directed most extensive, diversified fiscal program in history. Once contemptuous of bankers, now more tolerant. More interested in humanitarianism, social reform than money. Aspires to be known as good administrator. Idolizes Roosevelt. Taciturn, reserved, shy, suspicious. Forgets names. Tall, baldish, pince-nez glasses. Sensitive face. Farm his hobby.

Henry Lewis Stimson: Secretary of War. Age 74. Born New York City, patrician family, father noted surgeon. Andover. A.B., Yale, 1888; A.M., Harvard, 1889; Harvard Law School, 1890. Commenced practice of law in New York with Elihu Root, his lifelong idol. U. S. District Attorney, 1906-09. New York Republican gubernatorial nominee, 1910. Secretary of War, 1911-13. Field artillery colonel with AEF, 1917-18. Coolidge's special representative to Nicaragua, 1927. Governor General, Philippines, 1927-29. Secretary of State, 1929-33. Sought to halt Japanese invasion of Manchukuo; authored "Stimson Doctrine" of non-recognition of territory acquired by aggression. Leader in movement to halt Nazi menace; fought American neutrality legislation. Drafted to promote American defense, 1940. More policy-maker than administrator; impatient with routine details. Dislikes political manipulation. Orthodox conservative. Precise, scholarly. Austere, difficult to approach. Meticulously courteous, stiff in conversation. Inspires devotion in staff, friends. Despite age, sticks close to job, arising 6 a.m. daily. Regularly rides, swims, plays deck tennis. Victorian cut to clothes. Smallish; gray hair, mustache.

Francis Biddle: Attorney General. 56 years old. Direct descendant Edmund Randolph, first U. S. Attorney General. Life spent around Philadelphia. Fatherless at 6. Identifies self as one of "poor branch" of Biddle family, but managed to graduate from Groton, 1905; Harvard, 1909; Harvard Law School, 1911. Oliver Wendell Holmes' secretary, 1911-12. General law practice, 1912-39. Special assistant U. S. District Attorney, 1922-26. Abandoned Republicanism, supported Roosevelt, 1932. Chairman National Labor Relations Board, 1934-35. Chief counsel, TVA investigation, 1938-39. U. S. Circuit Appellate judge, 1939-40. U. S. Solicitor General, 1940-41. Attorney General, since August 1941. Avid to preserve civil liberties during this war. Complains liberals must be more realistic, constructive. Once wrote a novel. Civic-minded. Genial but reserved. Precise, clipped accent. Tall, slender, round face, wide mustache, broad smile. High forehead, receding hair.

Frank Comerford Walker: Postmaster General. Born 56 years ago, Plymouth, Pa., son of storekeeper. At 3 taken to Butte, Montana, by family seeking opportunities in mining country. Gonzaga University (Spokane, Wash.), 1903-06; law degree Notre Dame University, 1909. Assistant prosecutor Silver Bow County, Mont., 1909-13. Member Montana legislature, 1913. Anaconda Copper numbered among law clients. Became Roosevelt devotee when latter was campaigning for Vice Presidency. Migrated to New York, 1925, to assist uncle with movie house chain, which netted him modest fortune. One of original Roosevelt-for-President backers, $10,000 contribution. Democratic National Treasurer, 1932. Had major hand in early New Deal patronage distribution. Drafted to coordinate recovery agencies as director of President's Emergency Council, 1933-35. Succeeded Farley as Postmaster General, 1940. One of Roosevelt's warmest friends, most loyal supporters, not politically ambitious. Performs many delicate, confidential missions for President. Shrewd businessman, politically smart. Quiet, diffident. Tight-lipped. Shuns publicity. Chunky, heavy-jawed.

437

Frank Knox: Secretary of the Navy. Age 68. Born in Boston, son of corner grocer. Taken to Grand Rapids, Mich., at 7. Sold newspapers, did odd jobs to assist family. Worked way through Alma (Mich.) College, 1898. Rough Rider in Cuba, Spanish War, 1898. Reporter, city editor, circulation manager, *Grand Rapids Herald,* 1898-1901. With $1500 purchased half-interest in decrepit *Sault Ste. Marie News,* 1901. Michigan State Republican Chairman, 1910-12. Sold Soo *News* for $50,000; founded *Manchester* (N. H.) *Leader,* 1912; later merged with *Manchester Union,* which he still owns. Enlisted at 43 in World War I, fought in France, came back lieutenant colonel. Unsuccessful candidate for New Hampshire Republican gubernatorial nomination, 1922. Publisher Hearst Boston newspapers, 1927-31; general manager all Hearst newspapers, 1928-31. Left $152,000 annual salary with Hearst in policy disagreement. Publisher, part-owner *Chicago Daily News,* since 1931. Republican vice presidential nominee, 1936. Broke with Republicans to support Roosevelt foreign policy; appointed Navy Secretary, 1940. Driving executive. Shrewd business judgment. Prudent manager. More doer than deep thinker. Given to hyperbole in oratory. Blustery, talkative, amiable. Medium height, corpulent. Pleasant large face; pince-nez glasses, reddish hair.

Harold LeClaire Ickes: Secretary of Interior. Age 68. Born Blair County, Pa., son of planing mill manager. At 16, on mother's death, went to live with Chicago aunt. A. B., Chicago University, 1897. Newspaper reporter, 1897-1901. Studied law, Chicago University, 1907. Tried law practice, achieving financial independence through marriage. Most of life given to aggressive but unsuccessful support of reform candidates of all parties, battling Insull, traction, other Chicago "vested interests." YMCA worker in France, 1918-19. Backed Roosevelt in 1932, his first winner. Wanted Indian Affairs commissionership, but through Hiram Johnson's support landed Interior post, 1933. Directed six-billion-dollar public works program, 1933-39. Administered coal, petroleum regulations. With young second wife, started rearing second family at 64. Constantly quarrels with New Deal associates, Congress, press, industry. Belligerent, contentious, acid-tongued. Called New Deal's "Donald Duck." Tireless hater. Given to intemperate statement. Diligent administrator, but fusses with details; distrustful of other men. Pungent, earthy, witty phrase-maker. Proud of his prose style. Lives on near-by big Maryland farm, raises dahlias, sells poultry, eggs, and pigs. Thick-set, round-faced.

Claude Raymond Wickard: Secretary of Agriculture. Born 49 years ago on 380-acre Carroll County, Indiana, corn-hog farm, which grandfather hewed out of wilderness century ago. Began farming with father. Graduated agricultural course, Purdue, 1915. Acclaimed "master farmer of Indiana," 1927. Awarded 10 gold medals for farming excellence. State Senator, 1932. Assistant chief AAA corn-hog section, 1933-35; chief, 1935-36. Director North Central Division, Agricultural Conservation Program, 1936-40. Under Secretary of Agriculture, February 1940; Secretary, September 1940; first real dirt farmer to sit in Cabinet. Solid, practical. Called good administrator. Proud of farming ability; modest about all else. Wishes name were "Andrew Jackson Wickard," as was father's, grandfather's. Talks simply, farm language; decisive, resonant voice with Indiana twang. Describes beliefs as "common sense." Unpretentious. Smiles easily, hearty laughter, jolly. Stocky, medium height; kewpie weather-bronzed face, thinning hair.

Jesse Holman Jones: Secretary of Commerce. Age 68. Born in Robertson County, Tennessee, son of farmer. At 19 went to Dallas, Texas, managed uncle's lumber business. Moved to Houston, made millions in lumber, office buildings, hotels, apartments, banking, newspaper, radio. Member American Red Cross Council, World War I. Finance director, Democratic National Committee, 1924-28; staged presidential (Al Smith) convention, Houston, 1928. Named RFC Director by President Hoover, 1932; Chairman RFC, 1933. Federal Loan Administrator, 1939. Secretary of Commerce, 1940. Handled over 6 billion dollars of war industry loans, 1941-42. Promoted Will Rogers Memorial; Woodrow Wilson Birthplace Foundation; San Jacinto Battle Grounds Monument; Texas Centennial Exposition. Prides himself on administrative skill; works long hours and loves it. Likes power, seeks responsibility, popular with Congress. Good storyteller, picturesque language; enjoys bridge; seldom exercises, occasionally plays golf. Dislikes tobacco smoke. Huge frame, silver hair, blue eyes, soft voice.

Frances Perkins: Secretary of Labor. First woman ever named to Cabinet. Born 60 years ago, Boston, daughter of twine manufacturer, who was classical scholar. Graduated Mount Holyoke College, 1902, majoring in biology, chemistry. Family prejudice against women working caused rejection of proffered chemist's job, turned her to Boston social work, 1902-04. Taught chemistry at Chicago girls' school; drifted back to social work at Hull House. Determining on welfare worker's career, studied economics, sociology, Pennsylvania University; M.A., Columbia, 1910. Married Paul C. Wilson, 1913, still her husband. Spent next 20 years in various welfare jobs improving working conditions in New York factories. Member New York State Industrial Board, 1923-33 (chairman, 1926-29). New York Industrial Commissioner, 1929-33. Appointed Secretary of

Labor, 1933. Has played inconsequential part in recent labor movements. Labor Department now restricted chiefly to administering humanitarian legislation. Fair administrator. Politically inept. Antagonized both wings of union labor. Welfare worker outlook. Sentimental. Brisk, humorless, energetic. Speaks with broad "a's." Noted for tricorne hats, large brown eyes. Close friend of Mrs. Roosevelt.

General George Catlett Marshall: Chief of the General Staff, U. S. Army. Age 61. Born at Uniontown, Pa. Graduated Virginia Military Institute, 1901. Honor graduate, U. S. Infantry-Cavalry School, 1907. Graduated from Army Staff College, 1908. Commissioned second lieutenant, U. S. Army, 1901. Promoted through grades to major general, 1939. Served in Philippines, in China and with A.E.F. in France. Was second man ashore when first contingent of American troops landed in France in 1917. On general staff of First Division overseas for more than a year. Chief of Operations of First American Army, and noted for strategic handling of troops in Meuse-Argonne offensive. Aide-de-camp to General Pershing and continued to serve with him until 1924. Assistant commandant, Infantry School, 1927-32. Senior instructor to Illinois National Guard, 1933-36. Commanding general, Fifth Brigade, 1936-38. Chief, War Plans Division, General Staff, July-October, 1938. Acting Chief of Staff, July 1-September 1, 1939. Chief of Staff, with rank of full general, since 1939. Chosen over 34 other brigadier and major generals to be Chief of Staff. Awarded nine decorations by six countries. Has remarkable memory. Boyhood ambition was to be a soldier. Unable to obtain appointment to West Point because his father was a Democrat in Republican Pennsylvania. Hard worker, on job at eight in the morning. Likes horseback riding, tennis, dancing and canoeing. Six-footer and lean.

Admiral Ernest Joseph King: Commander in Chief, U. S. Fleet. Age 63. Born at Lorain, Ohio. Son of railway mechanic. Began naval service as midshipman in Spanish-American War. Graduated from Naval Academy, 1901. Commissioned ensign, 1903. Advanced through grades to full admiral, 1941. Assistant chief, Bureau of Aeronautics, 1929-30; chief, 1933-36. Student, War College, 1932-33. Commanding Aircraft Battle Force, U. S. Fleet, 1938-39. Member, General Board, Navy Department, 1939-40, then named Commander in Chief, Atlantic Fleet. Appointed Commander in Chief, U. S. Fleet, December 1941, later given duties and authority formerly held by Chief of Naval Operations. Awarded Distinguished Service Medal twice in recognition of successful salvaging of S51 and S4, submarines which sank off Atlantic Coast. Also awarded Navy Cross. While holding rank of captain and in his forties, learned to be an aviator at Pensacola Air Station and piled up hundreds of flying hours as a pilot. Dubbed "Dolly" at Naval Academy. Recently called "The MacArthur of the Navy." Strict disciplinarian—"toughest man in the Navy." Excellent tactician. Cool. Likes walking and golfing. Tall, square-shouldered, firm of step. Piercing blue eyes.

Harry Lloyd Hopkins: President's alter ego, closest personal, political friend. Born 52 years ago, Sioux City, Iowa, son of harness maker. Worked way through Grinnell College, 1912. Aspiring to be social worker, went immediately to New York on teacher's advice. From supervisor of poor in slums, rose through various welfare jobs to direct unemployment relief in New York State, 1931-33. Came into New Deal as Federal Emergency Relief Administrator, 1933-35. Works Progress Administrator, 1935-39. Secretary of Commerce, 1939-40; knocked out of job by illness. President's emissary to London to perfect lend-lease arrangements, February 1941; later to Moscow for Stalin conversations. Gets paid as lend-lease supervisor; does all sorts of jobs. Lives, sleeps, eats in White House. In youth registered as Socialist. Thinks in Roosevelt groove. Deep human sympathies. Streak of stubbornness. Easy talker, caustic. Gregarious. Likes horse racing. Suffers recurrent stomach ailment. Looks frail, cadaverous.

Donald Marr Nelson: Chairman, War Production Board. Born 53 years ago, Hannibal, Mo., son of locomotive engineer. Fired furnaces to pay way through Missouri University, 1911. Aspired to Princeton Ph.D. to qualify as chemistry professor. To get money for this, he taught chemistry, 1911-12; took job for year as Sears Roebuck chemical engineer, 1912, remained 30 years. Became manager men-boys clothing department, 1921-1926; general merchandise manager, 1926-30; vice president in charge of merchandising, 1930-39; executive vice president at $70,000 yearly, 1939-1942. Gave helping hand to NRA, 1933. Returned to Washington, 1940, to organize airplane procurement. Shifted to coordinate all defense purchases under NADC and OPM, 1940-41. Executive director SPAB, 1941-42. Possesses greater authority over business, industry, than any man in American history, except Roosevelt. Wise in ways of business and government. Concentrates on job at hand, leaves theorizing to others. Executive drive; invites responsibility. Kindly, even-tempered, tolerant. Soft spoken; measured, precise in use of words. Pipe smoker. Allergic to exercise. Tall, husky. Rimmed glasses give beaming, unlined face, slight owlish look. He's not politically dumb—he knows that he has a job which could make him or break him.

Leon Henderson: Director of Price Administration. Age 47. Born Millville, N. J., son of glass factory worker. Performed multitude of odd jobs, including minding babies, for schooling. Rose from private to captain of ordnance, World War I. Graduated Swarthmore, 1920. Taught economics, Pennsylvania University, 1919-22; Carnegie Institute of Technology, 1922-23. Deputy Secretary of Commonwealth, Pennsylvania, 1924-25. Fought "small-loan sharks" for Russell Sage Foundation, 1925-34. Economic adviser, NRA, 1934-35. Democratic National Committee economist, 1936. WPA economist, 1936-38, attracting attention by forecasting 1937-38 business slump. Executive Secretary TNEC (anti-monopoly committee), 1938-39; SEC Commissioner, 1939-40. NDAC price adviser, 1940. Made price-civilian supply czar, April 1941. Pugnacious, explosive, self-assertive personality. Courageous, quick-minded, skilled statistician. Government spending advocate, monopoly foe, noisy. Given to long, wordy discourses, earthy vocabulary. Works long hours. Chain cigar smoker. Unkempt in dress. Walks with strut. Squatty, huge paunch, chunky shoulders, broad chest, dark complexioned, black heavy hair.

Sidney Hillman: Labor adviser to the President. Born 55 years ago, Zagare, Lithuania, son of small grain merchant. Educated to be rabbi. Served ten months in jail as result of abortive 1905 revolution against Czar. Fled to U. S. via England, at 20. Sears Roebuck stock clerk 18 months. Apprentice cutter Hart, Schaffner & Marx. His part in 1910 strike against that company won him influential friends, started career as labor leader. President Amalgamated Clothing Workers of America since 1915. Organized 95 per cent of men's clothing industry. In 1920's established for his unions unemployment insurance, old-age pensions, cooperative housing, worker controlled banks. Industry conscious; used union funds to assist distressed employers. Served as NRA labor adviser, 1933-35. Helped organize CIO, 1937. Labor adviser NDAC, 1940. OPM co-director, 1941. WPB labor director, 1941-42. Cautious, undramatic, analytical. Impatient with dogma. Favors that which will work. Little round-faced fellow, bespectacled, curly-haired.

William Loren Batt: United Nations chairman of material requirements. Age 56. Born Salem, Ind., son of railroad shopman. Learned machinist trade outside school hours; soled own shoes until he left college. Mechanical engineering degree, Purdue, 1907. Officer of Hess, Bright Manufacturing Co., when it was absorbed by S.K.F. Industries, 1907-19. General manager latter, 1919; president since 1923. Installed first ball bearings on railroad train. First American to head International Committee for Scientific Improvement, 1939. Chairman Business Advisory Council, 1939-40. Deputy director industrial materials, NDAC, 1940. OPM deputy production director, 1941. SPAB materials director, 1941-42. Member Harriman Mission to Moscow, 1941. Was the hardest driver in the early defense production set-up. Early critic of "business as usual." Exercised restraint on manufacturers' opposition to New Deal. Dynamic, forceful, blunt. Speaks rapidly, with gestures. Amusing storyteller. Hobby: tinkering with old watches, clocks. Large, compact, broad-shouldered; deep-set, black eyes; black shiny hair.

Emory Scott Land: Chairman, Maritime Commission. Age 63. Born Canon City, Colorado, son of prospector-cattleman. Moved to Wyoming as youth. Graduated University of Wyoming, 1898. Made last-minute winning touchdown in 1900 Army-Navy football game. U. S. Naval Academy, 1902. Massachusetts Institute of Technology, 1907. Advanced through ranks as Naval constructor. Attached to Admiral Sims' staff in World War. Awarded Navy Cross. Learned to fly at 50 (Charles A. Lindbergh is a cousin). Assistant chief, Navy Aeronautics Bureau, 1926-28. Promoted to Rear Admiral, Chief, Navy Construction and Repair Bureau, 1932-37. Resigned from Navy, appointed Maritime Commissioner, 1937; chairman since 1938. Directing biggest shipbuilding program in history. Hard-driving administrator. Blunt, outspoken, with seafaring man's colorful vocabulary. Nicknamed "Jerry" in youth after famed football player. Until recently officiated regularly at collegiate football games. Walks two miles to office daily. Fond of dancing, tennis, bridge. Small, spare, wiry. Looks ten years younger than age.

Paul Vories McNutt: Federal Security Administrator. Age 50. Born Franklin, Indiana, son of country lawyer. Graduated in same class with Wendell Willkie, Indiana University, 1913. Harvard Law School, 1916. Never practiced law. Taught law at Indiana University, 1917-25, except for year spent as officer in Army training camps in this country. Dean Indiana University Law School, 1925-33. National Commander, American Legion, 1928-29. Governor of Indiana, 1933-37; played machine politics, but won praise for budget balancing, reorganizing state government. U. S. High Commissioner to Philippines, 1937-39. Federal Security Administrator, since July 1939. Intent on being Roosevelt's successor. Political opportunist, thick-skinned. Disliked, but respected by inner circle New Dealers. Politically shrewd, skillful. Trigger smile, good stump speaker, spectacular stage presence. Joiner. Addicted to detective mysteries; golfs in middle nineties. Called Adonis of American politics. Tall, broad-shouldered;

florid cheeks, flashing eyes and teeth; jet-black brows, prematurely white mane.

Sumner Welles: Under Secretary of State. Born 49 years ago, New York City, son of financier. Groton; Harvard, 1914. Embassy secretary, Tokyo, 1915-17; Buenos Aires, 1917-19. Assistant chief, Latin-American Division, State Department, 1920-21; chief, 1921-22. American Commissioner to Dominican Republic, ending U. S. military occupation, 1922. Next few years carried out several missions in Latin-America. Once defended U. S. intervention below Rio Grande; later reoriented Monroe Doctrine into "good neighbor" policy, coined that phrase. Assistant Secretary of State, 1933; later Ambassador to Cuba to ease out Machado regime. Reappointed Assistant Secretary of State, directing Latin American relations, 1933-37. Under Secretary since 1937. Consulted with chiefs of European belligerents in vain effort to find peace solution, 1940. Chiefly responsible for present solidarity of Western Hemisphere. Storybook career diplomat. Solemn, reserved, socially aloof, impeccably proper, accomplished linguist, wealthy (both himself, and wife). Calculating. Speaks deliberately, decisively. Can be cutting, frigid. Shuns Washington mansion for imposing Maryland estate on the Potomac River. Well-dressed, carries stick. Tall, stiffly erect, trim; vague blond mustache, clear blue eyes.

Milo Randolph Perkins: Executive director, Board of Economic Warfare. Born 42 years ago, Milwaukee, Wisconsin, son of dentist. High school graduate. Migrated to Houston, Texas, when father inherited run-down farm there. Burlap bag salesman at 19, year he married. Sales manager at 23. Three years later struck out on own, King-Perkins Bag Co., subsequently netting him $20,000 annually. Developed enthusiasm for New Deal as member NRA bag code authority. Volunteered services to government 1935, sold out business, assisted Wallace. Subsequently Farm Security Assistant Administrator; president Federal Surplus Commodity Corp. Devised successful food stamp plan; expanded school lunch program. Economic Warfare Board director, since 1941, coordinating U. S. foreign trade with military exigencies, planning for postwar period. Passionate to solve riddle of "want in midst of plenty." Talks economics in street-corner language. Natural-born salesman. Hard-working, volatile. Publicity shy. Average build, strong, sharp features.

Edward Reilly Stettinius, Jr.: Lend-Lease Administrator. Age 41. Born Chicago, son of match manufacturer who was later J. P. Morgan partner. Attended Pomfret (Conn.) School; University of Virginia, 1919-24, where he headed undergraduate YMCA. Commenced work with General Motors in overalls as shop mechanic; later personnel manager. Upped to assistant to G. M.'s President Sloan. General Motors Vice President, in charge industrial and public relations, 1931-34. Served in NRA. Member of Commerce Department's Business Advisory Council. Vice chairman U. S. Steel Finance Committee, 1934-35; chairman, 1936-38. Urged signing unprecedented U. S. Steel-CIO union contract. Chairman of U. S. Steel, 1938-40. Chairman War Resources Board, 1939. NDAC raw materials director, 1940; OPM priorities director, 1941. Lend-Lease Administrator since fall 1941, with duties similar to those of his father in first World War, who was Allied Purchasing Agent, later Assistant War Secretary. Calm, confident, reserved, ambitious. Handsome, erectly tall, silver haired. Spends free time on 500-acre Virginia stock farm.

William Averell Harriman: Lend-Lease expediter. Born 50 years ago, New York, son of famed railroad financier. With brother inherited $100,000,000. Groton; A.B., Yale, 1913. Spent year at Oxford. Worked for Union Pacific Railroad. Founded W. A. Harriman & Co., investment banking, 1920 (merged with Brown Bros., 1931). In 1920's undertook to develop steamship lines. Financial interests include aviation, shipping, publishing, telegraph, banking, railroads. Served as director of more than 50 corporations. Chairman of Union Pacific board since 1932; inaugurated streamlining that road. Hugh Johnson's right-hand man in NRA. Thrice chairman Commerce Department's Business Advisory Council, serving as liaison between Roosevelt and big business. Director industrial materials, OPM, 1940-41. Named to expedite war aid to Britain, February 1941. Headed American mission to Moscow, September 1941. Unostentatious. Famed as 8-goal international polo player, now breeds polo ponies. Tall, lithe, dark, collegiate appearance.

William Signius Knudsen: Lieutenant General, directing War Department industrial production. Age 63. Born Copenhagen, Denmark, son of customs inspector. Attended Danish schools, government technical institute. Came here at 20, shipyard riveter, railroad shopman, 1899-1902. Advance from storeroom keeper to superintendent Buffalo bicycle factory, 1902-13. Developed assembly line production for Ford Motor Company, 1913-21. General manager, Mathews & Ireland Manufacturing Co., 1921-23. Vice president, Chevrolet Motor Co., 1923. Executive vice president (1933-37), president (1937-40) General Motors Corp. Left $300,000-a-year job to direct defense production under NDAC, 1940-41. Co-director OPM, 1941-42. Great production man, shrinks from red tape, political manipulation. Modest. Simple, direct, easygoing, amiable. Loves charts, blueprints. Wears hat in office while thinking. Writes memoranda, letters in long hand for typing. Soft Danish accent; simple words, syntax of his own. Homely wit. Likes dancing. Plays piano, accordion, xylophone. Huge physique, cropped mustache, twinkling blue eyes, gray hair.

Felix Frankfurter: Close political adviser to the President. Age 59. Born Vienna, Austria. Father was rabbi, later small fur merchant. Brought to United States at 12. Earned money for education. New York City College, 1902. Harvard Law School, 1906. Assistant U. S. Attorney (under Henry L. Stimson), 1906-10. Law officer, War Department, 1911-14. Law professor, Harvard, 1914-39. During World War I, assistant to Labor and War Secretaries, Chairman Labor Policies Board. Attached to American delegation, Paris Peace Conference. Outspokenly claimed Sacco-Vanzetti trial unfair. Declined appointment to Massachusetts Supreme Court, 1932. Among chief early Roosevelt advisers; framed legislation, placed dozens of his law school students in important posts. Not consulted, did not approve Roosevelt Supreme Court enlargement plan. Appointment to Supreme Court, 1939, overwhelmingly lauded by bar. One of Harvard's most stimulating teachers, firing students with enthusiasm. Aggressively liberal; warm humanitarian. Bubbling energy. Tireless letter writer. Fond of polysyllabic words. Argumentative. Sense of humor. Merry manner. Small, stocky figure. Pince-nez glasses, bulging forehead, thin gray hair. Hobby: civil service improvement.

Samuel Irving Rosenman: Last of original brain trusters to remain in Roosevelt confidence. President relies heavily on his judgment—calling him in when trouble brews. Assists in assembling fireside chat material. Born 46 years ago, San Antonio, Texas, son of immigrant merchant. Taken to New York at 7. A.B., Columbia, 1915 (with highest honors). First lieutenant in Army, 1917-18. LL.B., Columbia Law School, 1919. Private law practice, 1920-32. Doorbell ringer for Tammany Hall. Won N. Y. Assembly seat in 1922-26. Bill Drafting Commission, 1926-28. Met Roosevelt during 1928 gubernatorial campaign—served as legislative expert. Counsel to Governor, 1929-32. Acted as liaison man between Roosevelt and Tammany Hall. Behind-scenes worker and right-hand assistant in Roosevelt campaigns of 1932, 1936, 1940. Helped organize original Roosevelt brain trust. Achieved ambition to become New York Supreme Court Judge at 45, salary of $25,000 a year until 1948. Liberal judge—not radical. Ability to clarify the obscure. Good researcher. National leader in Jewish educational and social activities. Vivid sense of humor. Retiring, self-effacing.

Dislikes exercise, loves picnics, outdoor frolics, good food. Short, chubby, large jowls and heavy hair. Has many friends, apparently no enemies. Idolizes Roosevelt.

Harold Dewey Smith: Director of Budget. Born 44 years ago on Haven, Kansas, farm. Served in Navy as apprentice seaman, 1918. Aspired to be electrical engineer; obtained B.S., University of Kansas, 1922. Employment with Detroit Governmental Research Bureau, 1924, changed career. Acquired public administration degree, University of Michigan, 1925. Municipal consultant, League of Kansas Municipalities, 1925-28. Director, Michigan Municipal League, 1928-37; director Bureau of Government, University of Michigan, 1934-37. Named Michigan Budget Director by Gov. Frank Murphy, 1937-39. Reorganized Michigan State government; installed Michigan's first effective budget system. Became first U. S. professional budget director in 1939, sponsored by Murphy. Roosevelt's business manager; chief coordinator of departments. Gradually executing reorganization of federal government. Serious-minded, methodical career man. Quiet, mild-mannered, pleasant. Personally thrifty: cuts 12-year-old son's hair; makes household repairs; but leaves home budget to wife. Hobby: woodworking. Speaks slowly, with deliberate precision. Medium height, slightly chubby, stooping shoulders; bespectacled; graying hair.

Isador Lubin: Commissioner of Labor Statistics, close presidential adviser, one of most influential fact-and-figure men in government. Born 46 years ago, Worcester, Mass., son of immigrant merchant. Graduated Clark College, Worcester, 1916. Economic statistician in first World War with Food Administration and War Industries Board. Assistant professor of economics at Universities of Missouri and Michigan. Brookings Institution fellow, 1923-26. Consultant to various congressional committees. Appointed Commissioner of Labor Statistics in 1933. Participated in virtually all New Deal undertakings to solve unemployment, combat monopoly. Most of time works as one of Roosevelt's "interpretive economists," preparing "fever charts." Less given to theoretical experiments than most New Deal economists; more faith in free enterprise. Tolerant. Friendly. Chops wood for exercise. Small, wiry, bespectacled.

Lauchlin Currie: President's economic adviser. Born 39 years ago, West Dublin, Nova Scotia, son of Scotch parents. Graduated London School of Economics, 1925. Came to U. S. to teach economics and finance at Harvard, 1925-34; meanwhile acquired doctor's degree, Harvard, 1931. Brought to Treasury by Dr. Jacob Viner, 1934, to assist currency studies, working with Marriner Eccles. Went with Eccles to Federal Reserve Board as assistant director of research, 1934-39. Ardent advocate Eccles-Hansen public spending theory; proposed, unsuccessfully, huge replacement of railroad rolling equipment with government loans as cure for 1937-38 recession. Presidential administrative assistant since 1939. Flew to China (first airplane trip) as Roosevelt emissary to work out monetary agreement, 1941. Now undertakes, correlates economic studies for President. More thinker than administrator. Quiet, studious. Quick-minded, precise. Once termed "an inflexible unenthusiast." Goes sailboating on holidays. Soft spoken. Professorial appearance. Small, slender, wiry; bespectacled; prematurely gray.

Wayne Coy: Asst. Director, Bureau of the Budget. Age 38. Born Shelby County, Indiana, son of railroad station agent. Worked way through Franklin (Ind.) College, 1926. Young Republican leader at college. Country newspaper editor several years. Aggressively supported Paul McNutt for Governor, 1932. Assistant secretary to Gov. McNutt, in charge pardon, parole work, 1933-34. Director Indiana unemployment relief, director state welfare department, 1934-35. Indiana PWA Administrator, 1935-36. Hopkins called him "best state relief director," made him WPA midwest regional director, 1936-37. Administrative assistant to High Commissioner McNutt in Philippines, 1937-39. Assisted carrying out executive reorganization act as member U. S. Budget Bureau staff, 1939. Assistant Federal Security Administrator, 1939-41. Presidential assistant, general choreman, trouble-shooter, since April 1941. Great ability to reconcile differences. Keen analyst, diagnostician of difficult situations. Clear, concise manner of speech commands attention. Ingratiating, persuasive, quiet, very modest, tight-lipped. Unimpressive appearance; small, frail, grim face, black eyes, black mustache. Most "anonymous" Roosevelt assistant.

Stephen Tyree Early: Secretary to President. Born 52 years ago, Crozet, Va., son of railway mail supervisor. Collateral descendant, General Jubal Early. Graduated Washington, D. C., high schools. Reporter, Washington staff, United Press, 1908-13; Associated Press, 1913-17; 1921-27. As reporter became Roosevelt intimate when latter was Assistant Secretary of the Navy. Machine gun captain; executive officer, *Stars and Stripes* (AEF publication), 1917-19. Roosevelt's advance representative in 1920 vice presidential campaign. Publicity director, U. S. Chamber of Commerce, 1920-21. Achieved six-minute AP scoop on Harding's death. Paramount Newsreel Washington representative, 1927-33. From March 4, 1933, has directed administration's relations with press, radio, motion pictures. Acts as Roosevelt spokesman, frequently interpreting presidential mind. Largely responsible for happy press relations at White House. Quick tempered; acts tough on occasion. Inwardly kind, warmhearted. Works hard, plays hard. Golfs in low eighties. Likes deep-sea fishing, horse racing. Robust, stocky, keen blue eyes, graying hair.

Lowell Mellett: Roosevelt's general handyman. Born 58 years ago, Elwood, Ind., son of small-town newspaper editor. Left school at 13 to work on *Muncie* (Ind.) *Star* at $5 weekly. Newspaperman in Indianapolis (where long friendship with Roy Howard started), St. Louis, Cincinnati, New York. Editor *Seattle Sun,* 1913-15. With United Press in Washington, London, France, 1916-19. Managing editor *Collier's Weekly,* 1920. Editor Scripps-Howard *Washington Daily News,* 1921-37: manager Scripps-Howard *Alliance,* 1925-37, resigning because he disagreed with Scripps-Howard criticism of New Deal. Director National Emergency Council, 1937-39. Director Office of Government Reports since 1939; administrative assistant to President since 1940. Has daily access to presidential ear. Evangelical political reformer. Very reserved, self-effacing, soft-spoken, deliberate manner. Has three-green, nine-tee golf course at his Virginia home. Smallish figure, graying hair.

Robert Porter Patterson: Under Secretary of War. Age 51. Born Glens Falls, N. Y., son of lawyer. Union College (Schenectady), 1912; Harvard Law School, 1915. Practiced law, New York City, until 1930. Served on Mexican border, 1916; advanced to major in World War, in division with Stimson; awarded D.S.C. for "extraordinary heroism." U. S. District judge, 1930-39. U. S. Circuit Appellate judge, 1939-40. Doing kitchen police, in blue denim, at Plattsburg Training Camp when named Assistant Secretary of War, July 1940. Under Secretary since December 1940. New Deal's biggest spender, supervising billions of Army purchases. Caused lifting of conservative eyebrows when he drafted original property seizure bill. First-rate, fast-moving, concise administrator. Reserved, judicial temperament. Candid. Dislikes publicity, making speeches. Uncanny memory for faces, names. Hobbies: Civil War military history, Oliver Cromwell's life, improvement of 70-acre dirt farm. Voice has ring of command. Medium height, slender, square-shouldered, erect. Long face.

James Vincent Forrestal: Under Secretary of Navy. Born 50 years ago, Beacon, N. Y., son of minor politician. Worked way through school: Dartmouth one year; Princeton, 1911-15. Financial reporter, *N. Y. World,* 1915. Bond salesman, William A. Read & Co. (later Dillon, Read & Co.), 1915-

17. Naval aviator, training in Canada, 1917-18. Headed Dillon, Read bond department, 1919-23; partner since 1923; vice president, 1926-38; president, 1938-40. In 20's, helped direct $150,000,000 Dodge automobile financing. Sponsored by Harry Hopkins for presidential administrative assistant, June-August 1940. Navy Under Secretary since August 1940. Went to England 1941 to coordinate Naval equipment uniformity. Alert administrator. Quick, cold, skeptical mind. Quiet, pleasant, suave. Shuns publicity; declines to return *Who's Who* questionnaire. Fond of boating. Trim, youthful appearance; medium height; chunky shoulders; nose flattened in amateur boxing bout.

Brigadier General Lewis Blaine Hershey: Director of Selective Service. Age 49. Born on farm near Angola, Ind. Attended one-room schoolhouse, Fremont (Ind.) High School; three months course in pedagogy at Tri-State College, Angola. Started teaching in country school at 17. Joined Indiana National Guard as private 1911, subsequently elected lieutenant. Service on Mexican border, 1916. Course at Indiana University in further preparation for teaching interrupted by American entry in World War. Went to France as captain in Field Artillery near end of war. Attended French artillery school. Commissioned captain in regular army, 1920. Instructor in military tactics at Ohio State University and Fort Bliss. Army War College, 1934. Two years in Hawaii. Executive officer Joint Army-Navy Selective Committee, 1936-40, doing spade work planning for "next war" draft. Appointed deputy director Selective Service, 1940. Homespun manner; midwestern accent; noted for Lincolnian anecdotes. Study of psychology his only hobby. Big, stoop-shouldered, red hair. Looks like dirt farmer.

Joseph Bartlett Eastman: Director of Defense Transportation. Born 60 years ago, Katonah, N. Y., son of clergyman. Graduated Amherst, 1904. Spent next year in Boston settlement work, meeting Louis D. Brandeis, who influenced his entire life. Under Brandeis aegis, abandoned law studies, commenced career devoted to public utility regulation. Secretary, Boston Public Franchise League, 1906-13. For Brandeis dug out facts on financial manipulation in famed New Haven railroad case. Represented street railway employees in wage arbitration cases, 1913-15. Member Massachusetts Public Service Commission, 1915-19. On Brandeis recommendation, named member Interstate Commerce Commission, 1919, serving ever since. Frequently critical, in sizzling dissenting opinions, of railroad financing. Advocates coordinated federal regulation for all interstate transportation, railroad unification, despite labor objections. Serious economic, financial student.

Keen, reflective mind. Mild mannered. Pleasant spoken. Inquiring eyes. Keeps to self. Lives in bachelor simplicity.

James McCauley Landis: Director, Office of Civilian Defense. Born 42 years ago, Tokyo, Japan, son of American missionary. Mercersburg Academy, 1914-16. Served year overseas with British YMCA, 1917-18. Developed lucrative tutorial system to get money for education. Topped his class, Princeton, 1921. Bachelor and doctor of law, Harvard, 1924-25. Law clerk to Justice Louis D. Brandeis, 1925-26. Assistant and professor of law, Harvard, 1926-34. Collaborator with Felix Frankfurter on book, *Business of Supreme Court.* Under Frankfurter sponsorship helped draft New Deal securities and stock exchange acts. Member Federal Trade Commission, 1933-34. Member Securities Exchange Commission, 1934-35; chairman 1935-37. Dean Harvard Law School, 1937-42. Member President's Emergency Board on national railway strike, 1938. Special Labor Department trial examiner in Harry Bridges deportation case, 1939 (exonerated Bridges). Took job in 1942 to clean up Civilian Defense mess. Competent legal technician. Realistic New Dealer. Very solemn and earnest, hightensioned. Kindly. Slender, blond, long-jawed.

William Joseph Donovan: Coordinator of Information. Age 59. Born Buffalo, N. Y., son of railroad yardmaster. Worked way through Columbia University (A.B., 1905; LL.B., 1907). Corporate law practice with offices now in Buffalo, New York City, Washington. Colonel of famed "Fighting 69th" in World War I; awarded all three American medals for valor in action. Republican candidate for New York Lieutenant Governor, 1922. Federal District Attorney, 1922-24. Assistant U. S. Attorney General, 1924-29. Sponsored advisory antitrust opinions. Helped manage Hoover's 1928 campaign, but failed in desire to be Attorney General. New York GOP gubernatorial nominee, 1932. Has traveled widely, keeping abreast military developments throughout world. Made 25,000-mile flying tour European-African war fronts in 1940-41 as official observer. Helped inspire Slav resistance to Hitler. Now assembles over-all intelligence for Roosevelt strategists; combats Nazi-Fascist propaganda. Calmness, mild manners belie "Wild Bill" nickname. Serious-minded. Temperamentally loves mystery, intrigue. Apostle of vigorous life. Stocky, sleek, good-looking.

Nelson Aldrich Rockefeller: Coordinator of Inter-American Affairs. Age 33. Born Bar Harbor, Me., second son of John D. Rockefeller, Jr. Earned spending money as boy in Rockefeller tradition. Graduated Dartmouth, 1930. Spent year in India, chatted with Mahatma Gandhi, while on fellowship abroad won for scholastic merit. Served business apprenticeship in Chase National Bank, other Rockefeller interests. Concentrated on family real estate and Venezuelan oil holdings. Latter aroused enthusiastic interest in Latin America. Mastered Spanish to facilitate his trips to Venezuela. President of Rockefeller Center since 1938. Drafted in summer of 1940 by Roosevelt, on urging of Harry Hopkins, to weld Americas, halt spread of Axis sphere of interest south of Rio Grande. Conscientious, steady. Friendly, with sense of humor. Museum of Modern Art, his hobby. Broad-shouldered, wavy blond hair, somewhat collegiate attire and manner. Scion of richest family, but you'd never know it.

Byron Price: Director of Censorship. 51 years old. Born on farm near Topeka, Indiana. Worked way as newspaper reporter, odd jobs, through Wabash College, 1912. Few months with United Press. With Associated Press since 1912, rising to Washington Bureau chief, 1927-37, then executive news editor in charge entire AP report, until drafted to direct censorship, 1941. Came out of World War I as captain of infantry after eight months in France. Dislikes any form of censorship. Unlike most newspapermen, keeps desk clear of papers. Able executive. Quiet, but determined. Collects paper match covers, first editions of Mark Twain and Indiana authors. Gridiron Club performer for years. Heavy-set, handsome features, white hair.

Archibald MacLeish: Director, Office of Facts and Figures. Age 50. Born Glencoe, Ill., son of Scotch immigrant who became prosperous Chicago merchant. Hotchkiss School; Yale, 1915; law degree Harvard (Frankfurter protégé), 1919. Entered World War I as private, came out captain after year in France. Harvard Instructor, 1919-20. Practiced law in Boston 3 years; abandoned it to write poetry. Lived in Europe, writing, 1923-30. Associate editor *Fortune* magazine, 1930-38. Curator Nieman Foundation for Journalists, Harvard, 1938-39. Congressional Librarian appointment, 1939, protested on ground he lacked technical qualifications, was leftist in his views. Named OFF director, over-all supervision American war propaganda, 1941. Authored 15 books of verse, including Pulitzer Prize winning *Conquistador* (1933); also much prose, several radio plays. Noted literary lecturer. Staunch pleader for rights of man. Great personal charm; quiet. Long face with quick boyish grin. Looks younger than age. Spends free time on Conway, Mass., farm.

Brigadier General Philip Bracken Fleming: Federal Works Administrator. Age 54. Born Burlington, Iowa, son of assistant bank cashier. University of Wisconsin, 1905-07. Graduated No. 1 in class, West Point Military Academy, 1911. Assigned Army Engineers Corps, advanced through ranks. Commanded Fort Benjamin Harrison during World War I. Senior instructor and graduate manager athletics at West Point, 1926-33. Executive deputy Public Works Administrator, 1933-35. In charge of controversial Passamaquoddy construction, 1935-36. Coordinator Resettlement Administration, 1936-37. Army district engineer, St. Paul, 1937-39. Wage-Hour Administrator, 1939, until put in charge of all federal public works, 1941, as FWA Administrator. Known as able administrator, one of Roosevelt's most dependable trouble-shooters. Indifferent to ideologies. Organized and participated in amateur theatricals on Army posts. Human, sociable, dashing sense of humor, always well-groomed. Gray hair and mustache, black brows make him impressive figure.

John Bennett Blandford, Jr.: Administrator, National Housing Agency. Born 44 years ago, New York City. Father was in publishing business. Interrupted mechanical engineering course, Stevens Institute of Technology, to serve as World War I naval aviator; graduated, 1919. Abandoned engineering, 1922, for municipal administration. Staff of National Public Administration Institute, New York, 1922-23. Assistant to city manager, Petersburg (Va.), 1923-24. Director of research, Newark (N. J.) Chamber of Commerce, 1924-26. Director, Cincinnati Governmental Research Bureau, 1926-31. Member of President's Emergency Committee for Employment, 1931. Director, Public Safety, Cincinnati, 1931-33. Assisted TVA Chairman Arthur E. Morgan, 1933-34. Coordinator and Secretary TVA Board, 1934-37; general manager, 1937-39, credited with bringing order out of confusion. Assistant U. S. Budget Director, 1939-42. Hailed by Roosevelt for "amazing administrative ability," named to head merger of 16 housing agencies, February 1942. Quiet, unhurried, decisive. Impatient with red tape. Indifferent to publicity. Very affable, jovial. Likes outdoors, smokes cigars. Drives open car year round; seldom wears hat. Short, stocky; round face, thinning hair.

Leo Thomas Crowley: Alien Property Custodian, and Chairman, Federal Deposit Insurance Corporation. Born 52 years ago, Milton Junction, Wis., one of nine children. Attended University of Wisconsin for short period; father's death ended his schooling. Grocery clerk; then commenced lifelong association with General Paper and Supply Co., Wisconsin; became its president. President, State Bank of Wisconsin (now defunct). Chairman, Wisconsin Banking Review Board, 1931-34, instituting banking reforms. Chairman, Wisconsin Governor's Executive Council, 1933-34. Wisconsin

N.R.A. director, 1933-34. Chairman, Federal Deposit Insurance Corporation since 1934, continuing in that post though he became Chairman of Board of Standard Gas and Electric Co. in 1939. Receivership for some $7,000,000,000 of enemy property added to his jobs, March 1942. Decorated by Pope Pius XI with Order of St. Gregory for philanthropies. Hard working, calm, even tempered. Reticent. Allergic to tobacco smoke. Dresses well. Tall, bulky, pink-cheeked and white-haired.

John Edgar Hoover: Director, Federal Bureau of Investigation. Born 47 years ago, Washington, D. C., son of minor federal employee. After high school worked as Congressional Library messenger; studied law in evenings. LL.B., George Washington University, 1916; LL.M., 1917. Entered Justice Department, 1917. Special assistant Attorney General, 1919-21. Assistant director, Bureau of Investigation, 1921; director since 1924. Built FBI from understaffed, inefficient, demoralized group into one of finest law enforcement agencies in world. Now charged with combating subversive fifth column groups. Cold-minded, indefatigable administrator; works at high speed; frequently joins agents in field. Strict disciplinarian. Dramatic, spectacular. Publicity smart. Shuns politics. Convincing talker. Keeps trim riding electrical horse. Collects Chinese antiques. Seldom reads detective stories. Thickset, medium height; hard black eyes; wiry-haired.

Thurman Wesley Arnold: Assistant Attorney General in charge of antitrust enforcement. Age 51. Born Laramie, Wyoming, son of country lawyer —small cattle rancher. A.B., Princeton, 1911; law degree, Harvard, 1914; M.A., Yale, 1931. Practiced law, Chicago, 1914-17. AEF lieutenant, 1917-18. Practiced law, Laramie, 1919-27. Law lecturer, University of Wyoming, 1921-26. Only Democrat in Wyoming legislature, 1921. Mayor of Laramie, 1923-24. Law dean, University of West Virginia, 1927-30. Law professor, Yale, 1931-38. Legal consultant to several New Deal agencies before appointed to antitrust job, 1938. Most vigorous trust buster of all time. Expanded staff, tightened enforcement, aiming at labor unions, physicians, as well as business. Acclaimed for two books satirizing capitalism, government. Breeziest Washington official. Mixture of roistering practical joker, serious thinker. Restless. Impetuous. Deliberately picturesque. Dress disheveled. Garrulous, argumentative, loud voice; talks rapidly, leaving sentences unfinished. Vocabulary colorful, Rabelaisian. Puckish wit. Large, paunchy; yellowish complexion, dark mustache.

Marriner Stoddard Eccles: Chairman, Board of Governors, Federal Reserve System. Born 51 years ago, Logan, Utah, son of Scotch immigrant who amassed fortune in lumber, sugar, insurance. Attended Brigham Young College, 1905-09, working summers in lumber mills. Mormon missionary in Scotland, 1910-12. At 26 took charge family fortune on father's death, directing banks, various industrial, agricultural enterprises. Organized First Security Corp., comprising 26-bank chain in Utah, Wyoming, Idaho; its president, 1927-34. Republican turned New Dealer; he urged government spending as depression solution when Roosevelt was promising budget cutting. Such views brought him to Treasury as Secretary's assistant, 1934. Named Federal Reserve chief several months later; reorganized system. Emerged as foremost advocate of deficit spending, easy-money during depression; saving, high taxes, restricted credit in boom times. Clashes frequently with Treasury. Talks economic, monetary theories on all occasions. Dry, tense, evangelical in speech. Genial, but no mixer. Shoots ducks; golfs casually. Small, spare, beetle-browed; alert, dark, bright eyes; wan, fleeting smile.

John Roy Steelman: Director, U. S. Conciliation Service. Born 42 years ago, Thornton, Ark., son of struggling farmer. Served few months in Army after leaving high school, 1918. Next ten years waited table, logged, peddled books, worked as sawmill hand to attend four colleges: A.B., Henderson Brown College (Ark.), 1922; A.M., Vanderbilt University, 1924; Ph.B., 1925, Harvard University, 1926; Ph.D., University of North Carolina, 1928. Professor sociology and economics, Alabama College (Montevallo), 1928-34. Attracted attention Labor Secretary Perkins when she visited Alabama College to speak; named U. S. Conciliation Commissioner for Southern States, 1934-36. Directing Conciliation Service since 1937, settling major strikes in recent years, such as Allis Chalmers, Vultee Aircraft, captive coal mine. Friendly, warm personality. Vigorous. Did not leave office for 60 hours on one occasion. Inveterate telephoner; suffering paralytic crimp in left wrist and palm holding instrument; now uses device which leaves hands free. Talks worker's language. Tall, husky. Lively eyes.

William Hammatt Davis: Chairman, War Labor Board. Age 62. Born Bangor, Me., son of mining engineer. Taken to Kentucky as child. Followed patent lawyer brother to Washington. Attended Corcoran Scientific School, 1896-98. Worked way as stenographer through George Washington University Law School, 1901. Patent Office examiner, 1902-03. Commenced law practice in New York; now heads prominent firm of patent attorneys. Handled War Department contracts as $1-a-year man, 1917-19. Deputy Administrator, national compliance director, NRA, 1933-34. In last five years made labor mediation his avocation, serving in increasingly important roles. Vice chairman, chairman National Defense Mediation Board, 1941-42.

Sympathetic with labor's aims. Calm, precise, patient. Dry, salty humor, seldom smiles. Studies atomic physics as hobby; said to understand Einstein's theories. Founded art gallery. Stocky; bespectacled bulldog face; tousled head of graying hair.

Adolf Augustus Berle, Jr.: Assistant Secretary of State. Born 47 years ago, Boston, son of clergyman. Infant prodigy. Entered Harvard at 15, graduated with honors in three years, 1913. A.M., Harvard, 1914. Youngest man to graduate from Harvard Law School, 1916. Practiced in Brandeis' Boston law office, 1916-17. Served in military intelligence, 1917-18. Attached American delegation, Paris Peace Conference; resigned in protest over Versailles Treaty. Practiced law in New York, 1919-23. Worked in Henry Street Settlement, 1923-25. Finance lecturer, Harvard Business School, 1925-28. Professor corporation law, Columbia, 1928-38. In original Roosevelt brain trust. Special counsel, RFC, advising on railroads, taxation, bankruptcy legislation, 1933. Counselor, U. S. Embassy, Cuba, 1933. New York City Chamberlain, 1934-37. Chairman New York City Planning Commission, 1937-38. Assistant Secretary of State since 1938, attending that year Lima Pan-American Conference. General behind-scenes worker for President. Much interested in postwar reconstruction. Skillful analytical economist. Sharp mind and pen, glib public speaker. Ball of energy. Zealous for social reform. Cocky, short, slender; thin, boyish face.

Wayne Chatfield Taylor: Under Secretary of Commerce. Born 48 years ago, Chicago, of a wealthy family. Yale, 1916. Learned banking with Central Trust Co., of Illinois, 1916-20. Came out of World War an Army captain. Associated with several investment banking houses, 1920-32. Vice president Field, Glore & Co., 1927-31. Came into New Deal as executive assistant to George Peek, then AAA Administrator, 1933-34. Assistant to Peek as Foreign Trade Adviser, 1934-35. Vice president, Export-Import Bank, 1935-39. Assistant Secretary of Treasury, 1936, resigning in 1939 because of differences with Morgenthau over foreign loans. Previously assisted negotiation of Tri-Partite Currency Agreement of 1937. National Treasurer, American Red Cross since 1939. Toured Europe for Red Cross, 1940. Commerce Under Secretary since November 1940. Methodical administrator. Facile, open mind; wise in ways of finance, foreign trade. Reserved, quiet, congenial. Likes hunting. Golfs in seventies. Medium, stocky; bespectacled.

Daniel Wafena Bell: Under Secretary of the Treasury. Born 50 years ago; Kinderhook, Ill., son of farmer, later carpenter. Worked way through business school, 1910-11. Took Civil Service examination to keep schoolmate company; passed with high mark, appointed $700 year stenographer-bookkeeper in Treasury Department in Washington, 1911. Tank Corps private, 1918-19. Accountant in charge of foreign loans, 1919-20. Executive assistant to Assistant Secretary of Treasury, 1920-24. Studying nights, graduated National University of Law, 1924; took course in higher mathematics, Southeastern University, 1927. Assistant Commissioner of Accounts and Deposits, 1924-31; Commissioner, 1931-35. Acting Budget Director, 1934-39. Appointed Under Secretary of Treasury, 1940. One of outstanding career men in government; has refused big jobs outside government. Nonpolitical. Modest, quietly genial. Medium height, stocky. Bright sparkling eyes, black hair, looks boyish, likes golf. Called "Danny" throughout Washington, from President down.

James Lawrence Fly: Chairman, Federal Communications Commission. Born 44 years ago on farm in Dallas County, Texas. Worked his way through high school; graduated U. S. Naval Academy, 1920. Resigned from Navy, 1923. Graduated Harvard Law School, 1926. Private practice in New York, 1926-29. Special assistant to U. S. Attorney General in antitrust cases, 1929-34. General Counsel, Electric Home and Farm Authority, 1934-35. Solicitor TVA, 1934-39. Won acclaim for successful defense in Supreme Court of TVA constitutionality. Named FCC chairman, 1939, to reconcile radio broadcasting controversies. Has feuded with broadcasters, warred on newspapers owning radio stations. Crusading New Dealer. Foe of red tape. Hard worker. Fixed in opinions. Blunt in speech. Extremely pleasant socially; convivial. Plays good game of tennis. Southern drawl. Tall, spare; sorrel thinning hair; sandy complexion.

Charles Fahy: Solicitor General. Born 49 years ago, Rome, Ga., son of merchant. Notre Dame University one year. Georgetown Law School, 1914. Practiced law in Washington, 1914-24. Awarded Navy Cross for overseas exploits as naval flyer, including crack-up. Health forced him to leave Washington, 1924, for Santa Fe, New Mexico, where he practiced law, dabbled in Democratic politics until 1933. First assistant solicitor, Interior Department, 1933. Member Petroleum Administrative Board, 1933-34; chairman, 1934-35. National Labor Relations Board general counsel, 1935-40, winning 18 Supreme Court cases under Wagner Act, including five testing its constitutionality. Assistant Solicitor General, 1940-41. Journeyed to London, 1940, to work out destroyer-naval base agreement. Solicitor General since November 1941. Hard-working, able lawyer, who prepares cases thoroughly. Earnest. Quiet, mild-mannered. Speaks very softly with southern accent. Medium height, slender; small, round face, large nose, small black mustache. Looks frail.

Dialect of Washington

SOMETIMES the jargon of Washington, the lingo, the shoptalk, is puzzling. Here are some expressions commonly heard in daily conversations in the capital.

The Hill: Capitol Hill, or Congress.

Downtown: The executive end or branch of the government, as contrasted with the Hill, the legislative branch.

The River: The Potomac.

The Bay: Chesapeake Bay, week-end retreat for Washingtonians.

The Triangle: Triangle of fine new marble buildings (actually Indiana limestone) bounded by Pennsylvania Avenue on the north, Constitution Avenue on the south, 15th Street on the west.

The Ellipse: The park between the White House and Washington Monument, which is not an ellipse, but a perfect circle.

The Plaza: The park between Union Station and Capitol, full of fountains.

The Tidal Basin: Inlet of Potomac River, bordered with Japanese cherry trees, and a wall where Negroes sit and fish with worms.

The Mall: The big, wide, straight park from the Capitol to the Lincoln Memorial.

Foggy Bottom: The low-lying portion of Washington, formerly a swamp and dump pile neighborhood, near the region now occupied by the Lincoln Memorial, Navy Building, Munitions Building, Federal Reserve Building, along west end of Constitution Avenue.

The Blossoms: Japanese cherry tree blossoms that bloom around the Tidal Basin in April or May, when visitors come in droves.

The Calendar: Schedule of the day's business in House and Senate.

Career men: Long-service executives in government departments, who stay on and on while administrations come and go.

The Avenue: Pennsylvania Avenue, from the Capitol to the White House and State Department.

Embassy Row: The embassy section of either Massachusetts Avenue or 16th Street.

458

The country: That portion of the United States located beyond the District of Columbia.

The administration: A term used by political writers when they mean to designate vaguely a sphere of influence focusing vaguely in the President and the party.

Clearance: The go-signal for getting a government job, especially the OK given by a member of Congress or a political committee to indicate that the applicant is a partisan "regular."

Freshman: A new senator or representative.

Cloakroom: Retiring room adjoining the floor of the Senate chamber, also the House chamber, where members of Congress may go to smoke, gossip, or wash their hands, and where the public is not admitted. Each party has its own rooms in both Senate and House.

The aisle: Center aisle in House and Senate chambers, which is supposed to separate Democrats from Republicans.

The gallery: Place from which visitors to Congress look down.

The Little Congress: Loose organization of congressional secretaries (who are often smarter than their bosses).

Public interest: Term used by every politician to support his ideas.

Special interest: Term applied by politicians to the other side from his side.

Squirrel cage: Term applied to the House chamber by the press gallery.

Logrolling: "You vote for my bill and I'll vote for yours."

Horsetrading: Logrolling.

Lame duck: Formerly a member of Congress whose term extended beyond his defeat at the polls, now applied broadly to ex-members and ex-officials who hang around Washington after being defeated or fired.

Recess: Time off by Congress, when members go home to put their political fences in shape.

Party man: (1) An unswerving supporter of the party. (2) A chap who likes parties. Sometimes simultaneously both (1) and (2).

Blind partisan: Anyone who stands by his party, right or wrong, and who is usually charged by members of the other party as being unreasonable and wrong.

Fat cat: Heavy contributor to party campaign fund.

Left: A loose word used to designate anyone or anything regarded as "liberal," "radical," "pink" or "red"—by any shade or degree.

Right: A loose word used to designate anyone or anything regarded as "conservative"—by any shade or degree.

The Chief: (1) The President, a term used by White House intimates and close advisers. (2) The boss of a government unit, no matter how small he may be.

459

Press conference: A scheduled meeting at which a swarm of newspapermen go into the office of an official and ask him questions which he tries to answer. It is wholly unofficial, but it is the nearest thing under the American system to the questioning of ministers in the House of Commons under the British system.

White House spokesman: A member of the White House secretariat, usually Steve Early. The term is never applied to the President. The President's statements in press conferences are classifiable into three groups:
(a) Direct quote—attributed to the President, and with quotation marks.
(b) Indirect quote—attributed to the President, without quotation marks.
(c) Background—"off the record," not to be attributed to the President or the White House, but for use by the correspondent as perspective, or as "reliable speculation," or perhaps on his own authority.

Handouts: Mimeographed press releases, issued by government agencies and press agents.

Black sheets: Carbon copies of news stories exchanged between news correspondents as a labor-saving device.

Shoe leather, or Leg work: Energy used by newspapermen in digging up news facts.

Startling disclosures: What lots of people around town knew but didn't recognize as startling before it got into the papers.

Spot news: News with "today" in it.

Well-informed quarters: Quarters, either well informed or not so well informed.

Highest authority: The government authority who told something to the person who tells it to you.

Official denial: A denial made with tongue in cheek, received with lifted eyebrow, and believed by no one in the know. Usually a device for getting out of a publicity hole.

Off the record: Information or explanation not to be published, or at least not to be attributed to the man from whom it came. Loosely used.

In confidence: Not to be printed, or repeated to more than three or four people.

Courtier: Anyone who strives to be socially intimate with members of the President's family.

Violet: A public man who shuns publicity. (Rare.)

Washingtonian: Anyone who has lived in Washington since last month.

Cave dweller: Member of an old Washington family that doesn't have social truck with anyone who has been in the capital less than fifty years.

Cousins: A general term applying to friends from back home who are seeing the sights and staying for a few days at your house.

Alphabeticals: Gov't agencies designated by their initials, such as WPA, USHA, RFC, etc.

The Little Red House: The big red brick house on R Street, Georgetown, where Tommy Corcoran and Ben Cohen lived, with a fraternity of other Frankfurterians.

Boll weevil: A bore, a pest, not peculiar to Washington, but common in Washington.

Stuffed shirt: Stuffed shirt—same in Washington as elsewhere.

Immunity: The privilege of freedom from arrest accorded diplomats and members of Congress under certain circumstances, useful mainly in getting away with overtime parking and other traffic violations.

Mayor of Washington: Chairman of the House of Representatives Committee on the District of Columbia.

Open house: A chance to get good food and drink for nothing, and to cultivate social intimacy with The Great.

Jimmy's: Jimmy La Fontaine's gambling house across the border in Maryland.

Midnight oil: Electric lights till 11.

Five grand: Five billion dollars.

To strike a blow for liberty: To have a drink. (First used by former Vice President Garner in setting up intimate conferences at the end of the day at the Capitol.)

Publicity hound: Man who craves mention in print—same as elsewhere.

Pork barrel: Gov't appropriations for back home.

Watch dog: The Comptroller General, the chief auditor, who scans federal expenditures for errors and irregularities, and plays hob with expense accounts of government people.

Brass hats: High Army officers.

Gold braids: High Navy officers.

Tradesmen's entrance: Door of the State Department used by the economic men, as distinguished from the door used by diplomatic men.

In conference: Busy, can't be bothered, mebbe got somebody in with him.

Official: Any gov't man who is important enough to get his name in the papers.

Gov't clerk: Any gov't employee, any private in the civil service.

Sundown job: Job held by gov't employees after hours, as "sundown taxi driver," "sundown lawyer," etc.

Sick leave: Time off by government workers for either sickness or other leave which can be made to look like sickness.

Reclassification: Promotion in the government service, shift to a higher civil service grade with higher pay.

CAF: Clerical, Administrative and Fiscal, denoting classification of civil service jobs, as distinguished from "professional," which is of higher rank.

C.J.: The Chief Justice.

V.P.: The Vice President.

Jesse James: Jesse Jones.

H.H.: Harry Hopkins.

Sam: Sam Rayburn. Also Sam Rosenman.

Palace Politics: Game played by White House insiders, object being to get closer to the President.

GPO: Government Printing Office.

GOP: Republican Party, the "Grand Old Party."

Iffy: Term used by Mr. Roosevelt to characterize hypothetical questions.

Wilsonian: Term used by New Dealers to designate the old school, "just a little bit liberal."

Protocol: Etiquette for official ranking, especially diplomatic etiquette.

Donald Duck: Harold Ickes.

Mr. Big: Mr. Roosevelt.

Jimmy: Son James Roosevelt.

Eleanor: Mrs. Roosevelt.

Henry: Either Henry Wallace or Henry Morgenthau, depending on context.

To serve the government: To get a government job.

Returned to private life: Fired from public job.

The Next President: A term used by friends of Henry Wallace to designate Henry Wallace.

The Year 1: A New Deal term for 1933.

Parasite: Term popularized by President Roosevelt in early 1942 to describe idle socialites and others who ought to get out of Washington to make room for government employees during war. Subsequently used by everyone to describe anyone whom Washington might well spare, resulting in an accumulation of suggestions which, if applied, would depopulate the city.

Each Agency and Its Job

THIS list of government agencies is for reference. You can look up any department, bureau, commission, board, or other agency, and get a condensed line on what it does—in a nutshell. If you are confused about the agencies which are known as "alphabeticals," this list will be helpful. Also there's a separate list of "alphabeticals" at the end. Bear in mind that the designation of certain agencies by initial letters is merely a matter of common usage, not of official recognition. Fuller explanation of what each government agency does, in legal and formal language, may be obtained from the *Congressional Directory* or the *U. S. Government Manual.*

Many of these government agencies have branch offices in your own home city or nearest big city. You can look them up in your telephone book, under "United States Government." (Look under "U.") Plenty of people do business with their government without ever coming to Washington. Sometimes the branch offices in the field are more alert and quicker in their service responses than are the headquarters in Washington.

In the continuing war reorganizations from month to month, a few of the agencies are being shifted or consolidated, but the chances are that more than 90 per cent of them will remain as reported here. The work of many of the agencies listed is explained in greater detail in some of the preceding chapters.

Aeronautics, National Advisory Committee for: Represents leading government and private agencies in the field, serves without pay and carries on basic aeronautic research at Langley Field, Va., Moffett Field, Calif., and Cleveland, Ohio. Has developed the world's largest wind tunnels.

Agricultural Adjustment Administration . . . AAA (under Department of Agriculture): A huge control mechanism which pays farmers to keep down production of things we don't need, to increase production of things we do, and to carry out soil-building practices.

Agricultural Chemistry and Engineering, Bureau of (under Department of Agriculture): Offers advice on farm buildings, houses, drainage, soils, etc.—directly or through the Agricultural Extension Service.

Agricultural Conservation and Adjustment Administration (under Department of Agriculture): Supervises the work of the Agricultural Adjustment Administration, the Sugar Division, the Federal Crop Insurance Corporation, and the Soil Conservation Service.

Agricultural Defense Relations, Office of (under Department of Agriculture): The go-between agency for farmers and the over-all war production program.

Agricultural Economics, Bureau of . . . BAE (under Department of Agriculture): A fact-finding, statistical, and planning agency for the Department which also assists state and county land-use planning committees of public employees and representative farm people.

Agricultural Extension Service (under Department of Agriculture, in cooperation with state agricultural colleges): Extends the combined agricultural wisdom of Washington and the state colleges through county agricultural agents, home demonstration agents, and 4-H Club leaders.

Agricultural Marketing Administration . . . AMA (under Department of Agriculture): Directs purchase and distribution programs, both domestic and abroad under lend-lease and territorial food programs; market news, inspection and grading services; administration of more than 40 regulatory and market control Acts of Congress; marketing agreements; and other related services in the marketing and transportation of agricultural commodities.

Agricultural Research Administration (under Department of Agriculture): Brings together under one administrator the work of the Bureaus of Animal Industry, Dairy Industry, Plant Industry, Agricultural Chemistry and Engineering, Entomology and Plant Quarantine, Home Economics, the Office of Experiment Stations and the Beltsville (Md.) Research Center.

Agriculture, Department of: The biggest and most complex department. Most of its agencies are grouped under the Agricultural Marketing Administration, Agricultural Conservation and Adjustment Administration, and the Agricultural Research Administration. Department includes the Agricultural Adjustment Administration, Agricultural Extension Service, Agricultural Marketing Service, Farm Security Administration, Federal Crop Insurance Corporation, Farm Credit Administration, Forest Service, Soil Conservation Service, Commodity Credit Corporation, Commodity Exchange Administration, Rural Electrification Administration, Office of Agricultural Defense Relations, and the Bureaus of Agricultural Economics, Animal Industry, Dairy Industry, Entomology and Plant Quarantine, Home Economics, Plant Industry, and Agricultural Chemistry and Engineering.

Alien Enemy Control Unit (under Department of Justice): Coordinates the activities of the Department in controlling the movements of alien enemies.

Alien Property Custodian, Office of (under Office for Emergency Management): Takes over and administers alien property for duration of the war.

American Battle Monuments Commission: Issues AEF guidebooks and histories and maintains the eight European cemeteries where lie 30,907 American soldiers of World War I.

Animal Industry, Bureau of (under Department of Agriculture): Does research, inspects packing houses, and helps states and counties to wipe out animal ailments.

Antitrust Division (under Department of Justice): Enforces the antitrust laws and some thirty other acts of business regulation.

Apprenticeship, Federal Committee on (under Department of Labor): A clearinghouse for information on the subject. Helps to set uniform apprenticeship standards.

Architect of the Capitol: Gives the grand old building expert care, is responsible for the design and upkeep of other important government buildings.

Archives, The National: Guards government records, old and more recent, in a beautiful and bombproof building. Many are microfilmed for further safety. Includes phonograph records and movies, shown in a small theater to groups upon request. Will supply photostat copies of documents at cost and assist scholars doing research. Also publishes the Federal Register of decisions and rulings made daily by the administrative agencies of the government.

Bituminous Coal Division (under Department of the Interior): Administers a code of minimum and maximum prices, fair trade practices and labor relations for the soft coal industry.

Bonneville Power Administration (under Department of the Interior): Handles the electricity generated at Bonneville Dam.

Botanic Garden, United States: Federal greenhouse near the Capitol run by Congress.

Budget, Bureau of the (under Executive Office of the President): Draws up the annual budget for the government. Congress appropriates the money. Before requesting additional money the agencies must first ask the Budget Bureau. The Bureau is increasingly influential in determining the policies and organization of government.

Censorship, Office of: Censors communications leaving the country by mail, cable, radio or any other means of transmission. Also helps the press and radio to withhold information of value to the enemy.

Census, Bureau of the (under Department of Commerce) : Collects figures on population, unemployment, manufactures, agriculture, mines, business, housing, and state and local finances. Statistics are also available annually or currently on automobile fatalities, births, deaths, crime, prisoners, the insane, cotton, cottonseed, divorce, and other items. There is a census of manufactures each two years, agriculture each five, and religious bodies each ten. Full comparative data are available on state and local governments. Upon request will verify the date of your birth.

Children's Bureau (under Department of Labor) : Administers social security grants for free services provided through local welfare offices and public health clinics for crippled children, maternal and child health, and child welfare work. Also administers the child labor provisions of the Fair Labor Standards Act.

Civil Aeronautics Administration . . . CAA (under Department of Commerce) : Sponsors the Civilian Pilot Training Program, establishes federal airways, radio beams and other air navigation facilities, has helped to develop airports, improve commercial plane design, and increase air safety. Recommends and administers the safety regulations proclaimed by the independent Civil Aeronautics Board.

Civil Aeronautics Board . . . CAB (under Department of Commerce, but performs its functions independently of the Secretary) : The high command of civil aviation which prescribes the safety regulations administered by the CAA, investigates accidents and can suspend air safety certificates. Regulates the rates and competing services of airlines.

Civil Rights Unit (under Department of Justice) : Investigates complaints of violations of the civil rights listed in the first ten amendments to the Constitution.

Civil Service Commission, United States: Central personnel office serving virtually all federal departments and agencies, with registers of eligible job seekers who have passed open competitive examinations. For notices of exams, watch the post office billboard or write the Commission to be notified of openings in your type of work.

Civilian Conservation Corps . . . CCC (under Federal Security Agency) : Offers unemployed youth 17-23 a healthful outdoor life, useful work on soil conservation, forestry and parks, and $30 a month, most of which must be sent home for support of their families.

Civilian Defense, Office of . . . OCD (under Office for Emergency Management) : A total-war agency that plans the protection of civilian life and property and coordinates the work of state and local civilian defense councils.

Coast and Geodetic Survey (under Department of Commerce) : Charts airways and seaways, gets its basic data by measuring inland mountains as well as sounding ocean depths. Studies earthquakes, investigates earth's magnetism for radio engineers, and owns a machine which tells any tide, anywhere, at any time.

Coast Guard, United States (under Treasury Department in peace, and Navy in war) : A part of the U. S. military forces, prevents smuggling and enforces customs, navigation and other laws governing the operation of marine craft. All but a few small craft now taking part in Naval operations.

Combined Raw Materials Board: Set up by the President and the British Prime Minister to plan the best and speediest expansion and use of raw material resources for the United Nations.

Combined Shipping Adjustment Board: Dovetails the work of the British Ministry of War Transport and the shipping authorities of our government.

Commerce, Department of: Includes the Bureau of the Census, Coast and Geodetic Survey, Civil Aeronautics Administration, Bureau of Foreign and Domestic Commerce, Inland Waterways Corporation, Patent Office, National Bureau of Standards, Weather Bureau, Reconstruction Finance Corporation, Electric Home and Farm Authority, RFC Mortgage Company, Federal National Mortgage Association, Disaster Loan Corporation, Export-Import Bank of Washington, Defense Plant Corporation, Rubber Reserve Company, Metals Reserve Company, Defense Supplies Corporation and War Damage Corporation.

Commodity Credit Corporation (under Department of Agriculture) : Makes commodity loans to farmers in the AAA program. Congress, which sets the amount which may be loaned, thus can help control farm prices for those crops of which there is a surplus.

Comptroller of the Currency (under Treasury Department) : Supervises national banks and the issuance and redemption of Federal Reserve notes and Federal Reserve Bank notes.

Conciliation Service, United States (under Department of Labor) : Has settled more strikes than any other government agency.

Congress: Makes the laws.

Court of Claims, United States: The court in which you may sue the government.

Council of National Defense: Consists of the Secretaries of War, Navy, Interior, Agriculture, Commerce and Labor, but not very active as a body.

Court of Customs and Patent Appeals: Specialized appellate court of five

467

judges designed to speed the settlement of disputes in customs and patent matters.

Criminal Division (under Department of Justice): Prosecutes all violations under the Selective Training and Service Act, the Neutrality Act, the espionage, sabotage, foreign-agent, and export-control laws.

Customs, Bureau of (under Treasury Department): Collects the duties (tariff).

Dairy Industry, Bureau of (under Department of Agriculture): Knows all there is to know about cows and milk.

Defense Communications Board (under Office for Emergency Management): A wartime set-up which coordinates telephone, telegraph, radio-telephone, radiotelegraph, broadcasting and cables.

Defense Health and Welfare Services, Office of (under Office for Emergency Management): Coordinates health, medical, welfare, nutrition, recreation and related activities affecting national defense. Also makes available to states and localities the services of health and welfare specialists to aid in planning and carrying out state and local programs. Handles the problem of adequate recreation for men in the armed services.

Defense Homes Corporation (under National Housing Agency): Finances housing projects for defense workers.

Defense Plant Corporation . . . DPC (under Department of Commerce): Finances new arms and munitions plants, for lease or sale to private industry, or for government ownership and operation.

Defense Supplies Corporation (under Department of Commerce): Acquires critical war materials in any way it can.

Disaster Loan Corporation (under Department of Commerce): Lends money to citizens of towns struck by hurricane, flood or other disaster.

Economic Warfare, Board of: Looks after the international economic relations of the country. Wages war by use of economics, decides what is to be exported and to whom, and what is to stay at home.

Education, Office of (under Federal Security Agency): Administers grants-in-aid to the states for home economics, for training disabled adults to earn a living, and for vocational schools which train youngsters and adults for war industries. Clearinghouse for all kinds of educational information.

Electric Home and Farm Authority (under Department of Commerce): Finances the sale of gas and electric home appliances through dealers.

Emergency Management, Office for . . . OEM (under Executive Office of the President): A wartime agency, practically a part of the Presidency, acting for the President in supervising many wartime activities.

Employees' Compensation Commission, United States: Compensates federal workers injured in line of duty.

Employment Service, United States . . . USES (under Federal Security Agency) : Assists in maintaining a system of public employment offices in the states, and increasingly important in placing workers made idle by conversion to war production in jobs in defense industries.

Engraving and Printing, Bureau of (under Treasury Department) : Makes paper money, stamps and bonds.

Entomology and Plant Quarantine, Bureau of (under Department of Agriculture) : Fights bugs and pests. Sometimes stops your car on the road to see whether you have any.

Export-Import Bank of Washington (under Department of Commerce) : Makes loans to Western Hemisphere nations. Uses good money to help make these nations good neighbors.

Facts and Figures, Office of . . . OFF (under Office for Emergency Management) : Aims at widespread and accurate understanding of the war effort. Also sets policy for other agencies on government war information and helps clear Cabinet speeches for policy.

Farm Credit Administration . . . FCA (under Department of Agriculture) : Makes long and short-term loans to the solvent farmer, through local cooperative associations backed by chains of federal agricultural banks. Has a chain of banks and expert advice for farm cooperatives. Charters federal credit unions and makes emergency crop and seed loans.

Farm Security Administration . . . FSA (under Department of Agriculture) : Offers live-at-home farm plans, guidance, and small loans and grants in one package to farm folks stranded by drought, war, or other causes. Runs camps for migratory workers in harvests, makes tenant purchase loans, operates cooperative communities for displaced share-croppers and Dust Bowlers.

Federal Bureau of Investigation . . . FBI (under Department of Justice) : Chases crime and criminals, and teaches police how to do it.

Federal Communications Commission . . . FCC: Licenses new and old radio stations and allots wave lengths. FCC technicians eliminate static and FCC investigators eliminate illicit or fifth column stations. Also regulates interstate telephone and telegraph lines.

Federal Crop Insurance Corporation (under Department of Agriculture) : Insures against loss by insects, fire, drought or disease. Premiums paid in kind.

Federal Deposit Insurance Corporation . . . FDIC: Insures deposits in member banks (which means nearly all) up to $5,000 per individual depositor. Inspects and to some extent controls the policies of banks.

Federal Farm Mortgage Corporation (under Department of Agriculture) : A financial backlog for the government's agricultural banks and may sell guaranteed bonds up to two billion dollars.

Federal Home Loan Bank Administration . . . FHLBA (under National Housing Agency) : Consolidates functions in connection with financing home ownership and construction carried on by the Federal Home Loan Bank System, Federal Savings and Loan Insurance Corporation, Home Owners' Loan Corporation and United States Housing Corporation.

Federal Housing Administration . . . *FHA* (under National Housing Agency) : Insures mortgages on approved residential properties providing easier terms, lower down payments. Also insures new construction in certified defense areas.

Federal Power Commission . . . *FPC:* Licenses dams on federal rivers, which means most of them, and regulates the gas and electric companies which cross state lines, including their rates and stock issues.

Federal Public Housing Authority . . . *FPHA* (under National Housing Agency) : Consolidates agencies and personnel engaged in constructing housing with public money. Includes functions formerly vested in United States Housing Authority. Supervises defense building done under Defense Homes Corporation—except on Army and Navy reservations, which are under the jurisdiction of the War and Navy Departments.

Federal Reserve System: A self-supporting chain of twelve banks for bankers. Issues new currency, regulates the bank reserves required for issuance of credit, the discount rate at which brokers borrow, and the legal gold reserve required for issuance of currency. Will also consider loan applications from industry and trade.

Federal Savings and Loan Associations (under National Housing Agency) : Authorized by Congress to provide local thrift and home-financing institutions in which people could invest their funds and to provide sound and economical home financing.

Federal Savings and Loan Insurance Corporation (under National Housing Agency) : Insures the safety of savings in thrift and home-financing institutions.

Federal Security Agency . . . *FSA:* Includes Social Security Board, National Youth Administration, Civilian Conservation Corps, the Office of Education, Public Health Service, Food and Drug Administration, St. Elizabeths Hospital, Freedmen's Hospital, Howard University, and Columbia Institution for the Deaf.

Federal Trade Commission . . . *FTC:* Issues cease-and-desist orders against violators of the antitrust laws and those guilty of misleading advertisements, unjustified price discriminations, allowances and other discriminatory practices. Calls "fair trade practice conferences" for the self-policing of business.

Federal Works Agency . . . *FWA:* A super-agency including Work Projects Administration, Public Works Administration, Public Roads Administration, Public Buildings Administration and the Public Work Reserve.

Fine Arts, Commission of: Advises Uncle Sam on esthetic matters from the design of a monument to the head of a coin.

Fish and Wildlife Service (under Department of the Interior) : Protects and promotes hunting and fishing, whether for money or for fun, throughout the United States and its possessions and the waters off our shores. On request will supply information on obtaining fingerlings from a federal hatchery, the state fishing and hunting seasons, and many other items of outdoor life.

Food and Drug Administration (under Federal Security Agency) : Administers the Food, Drug and Cosmetic Act of 1938, inspects factories, seizes and analyzes samples, watches for misleading labels (not advertising, which comes under the Federal Trade Commission).

Foreign Agricultural Relations, Office of (under Department of Agriculture) : Does liaison work between Agriculture, State, Lend-Lease and Board of Economic Warfare on matters pertaining to import and export of farm-&-food commodities.

Foreign and Domestic Commerce, Bureau of (under Department of Commerce) : First established to promote foreign trade, now serves the home market with branch offices where businessmen can get current information on regulations and services originating in many government agencies.

Foreign Funds Control (under Treasury Department) : Regulates transactions in foreign exchange and foreign-owned property.

Forest Service (under Department of Agriculture) : Manages two hundred million acres of federal forests. Also does economic and technical research in forest products.

General Accounting Office . . . *GAO:* Congress' watchdog over federal expenditures. Settles all accounts in which the United States is concerned, either as debtor or creditor. Includes the office of the Comptroller General of the United States.

General Land Office (under Department of the Interior) : Has no more homesteads to offer but supervises grazing, range development and engineering surveys on the huge remaining public domain. Issues the official map of the United States.

Geographical Names, United States Board on (under Department of the

Interior) : Official authority on what name the government will call your town, but can't prevent the local citizens from calling it anything they please.

Geological Survey (under Department of the Interior) : Has discovered deposits of minerals on the public lands, vital to war production and other industry. Also tells the Army where underground water is available for new camps.

Government Printing Office: . . . GPO Largest on earth. Run by Congress and required to earn its own expenses—which it does.

Government Reports, Office of . . . OGR (under Executive Office of the President) : Makes current, over-all reports of federal activities for the President and the public. Reports are altogether factual, statistical and often innocently dull. Includes the United States Information Service and the Division of Press Intelligence which digests press comments for the benefit of federal officials.

Grazing Service (under Department of the Interior) : Regulates use of enormous federal range lands in the West, except for the national forests, where grazing is regulated by the Forest Service.

Home Economics, Bureau of (under Department of Agriculture) : Aunty Sam, the headquarters of the professional homemaker. Has done important research on national nutrition.

Home Owners' Loan Corporation . . . HOLC (under National Housing Agency) : An emergency relief agency set up during the depression to grant long-term mortgage loans at small interest to those who needed money quickly to keep or recover their homes. Lending authority has expired.

Immigration and Naturalization Service (under Department of Justice) : Patrols the borders, admits no refugees except those who come in under quota or as temporary visitors, and deports undesirables. Citizens are naturalized through state and federal courts; ask at the county court house.

Indian Affairs, Office of (under Department of the Interior) : Tries to help Indians be Indians by encouraging native industries, arts, crafts, agriculture, tribal organizations and traditions. A complete government for Indians on reservations, who have no state or county public services.

Information, Coordinator of: Collects and analyzes all information and data bearing upon national security by means of short wave and other facilities and prepares intelligence reports for the President, Army, Navy and other departments. Not a public information agency.

Information Service, United States . . . USIS (under Office of Government Reports) : On request will supply any desired information about any federal service or activity, free of charge. Also central information and contact service for visitors to Washington. Operates branch office in New York City.

Inland Waterways Corporation (under Department of Commerce): Earns its keep with federal barge lines on the Mississippi, and on the Warrior River in Alabama. Charged with development of inland transportation facilities.

Inter-American Affairs, Office of the Coordinator of (under Office for Emergency Management): Plans and carries out programs to strengthen commercial and cultural bonds between the nations of the Western Hemisphere.

Interior, Department of the: Includes Bureau of Mines, Office of Indian Affairs, Grazing Service, National Park Service, Fish and Wildlife Service, Petroleum Conservation Division, Bituminous Coal Division, Division of Territories and Island Possessions, Puerto Rico Reconstruction Administration, U. S. Board on Geographical Names, Geological Survey, Bonneville Power Administration, General Land Office, Bureau of Reclamation, Office of Petroleum Coordinator for National Defense, Office of Solid Fuels Coordinator for National Defense, and Division of Power.

Internal Revenue, Bureau of (under Treasury Department): Gathers all the revenue except customs, and small profits earned by federal business.

International Boundary Commissions, United States, Alaska and Canada, and United States and Mexico (under Department of State): Permanent commissions which iron out any differences that may arise regarding respective boundary lines. Also conduct technical investigations of all boundary problems which require an engineering solution.

Interstate Commerce Commission . . . ICC: Sees to it that reasonable and non-discriminatory rates for interstate rail, bus, truck and shipping lines are maintained. Also issues licenses and prescribes and enforces safety regulations.

Inventors Council, National (attached to the Department of Commerce): Composed of noted inventors, it evaluates all inventive ideas. Works in close collaboration with the Army and Navy. Passed judgment on 40,000 inventions in first year of operation. This is the place to send your bright ideas for new weapons of war.

Joint Defense Production Committee—United States and Canada: Set up "for the specific purpose of most effectively coordinating capacities of the two countries for the production of defense material." Works with other joint bodies in the fields of military strategy, primary materials, and general economic relations.

Joint Economic Committees—United States and Canada: Seeks ways to promote efficient use of combined resources of the two countries for war production, at the same time studying ways to reduce postwar economic dislocations.

Joint Mexican-United States Defense Commission: Set up in January

1942 to study joint defense problems and to propose solutions to the two governments.

Justice, Department of: Includes Immigration and Naturalization Service, Federal Bureau of Investigation, Bureau of Prisons, Bureau of War Risk Litigation, and the following divisions: Antitrust, Tax, Claims, Lands, Criminal and Customs.

Labor, Department of: Includes Wage and Hour Division, United States Conciliation Service, Children's Bureau, Women's Bureau, Bureau of Labor Statistics, Division of Labor Standards, and Division of Public Contracts.

Labor Statistics, Bureau of . . . BLS (under Department of Labor): Issues very detailed reports on prices and rents, wages, hours, and employment, and the cost of living in general.

Lend-Lease Administration, Office of (under Office for Emergency Management): Strengthens U. S. defenses by providing agricultural commodities and implements of war to America's allies—on the cuff.

Library of Congress: Can be used by anybody, but only congressmen and some government agencies are supposed to take out books. Lends talking-books, translates letters into Braille, and through local libraries lends Braille volumes to the blind. An active cultural center which gives concerts, collects and records American folk songs, and maintains a staff of consultants to answer questions in person or by mail. Includes the Copyright Office and houses the Constitution, Declaration of Independence, and Magna Charta (which have been taken off display until war's end).

Maritime Commission, United States: Looks after merchant marine, has trained many seamen, and stepped up many sleepy shipyards. In wartime can take over all commercial ships for national use.

Material Coordinating Committee—United States and Canada: Established to speed exchange of information between the two governments relating to supplies of strategic raw materials required for war production.

Metals Reserve Company (under Department of Commerce): Acquires, carries and sells strategic materials necessary for the war program.

Mines, Bureau of (under Department of the Interior): Studies mines and minerals, makes helium for dirigibles, and during wartime, licenses the manufacture or possession of explosives. Also does safety research and educational work and makes rescues after mine accidents.

Mint, Bureau of the (under Treasury Department): Coins silver and buys gold (at the Philadelphia, Denver, San Francisco and New Orleans Mints, and the New York and Seattle Assay Offices).

Munitions Assignments Board: Gives advice on all assignments of munitions among the United Nations in accordance with strategic needs at the time.

Narcotics, Bureau of (under Treasury Department): Chases dope peddlers across state lines and catches marijuana merchants for failure to pay a federal tax. Drug addicts are treated by the Public Health Service.

National Academy of Sciences: Established in the time of Lincoln, it conducts scientific research on specific subjects at the request of the government departments. Includes the National Research Council.

National Capital Park and Planning Commission: Plans the parks and playgrounds, and preserves the natural scenery in the District of Columbia.

National Gallery of Art (under the Smithsonian Institution): The gift of the late Andrew Mellon and houses his great collection, with others.

National Housing Agency . . . NHA: Over-all agency for the various housing activities of the government, including both financing and construction. Contains the Federal Home Loan Bank Administration, Federal Housing Administration and Federal Public Housing Authority.

National Institute of Health (part of Public Health Service, under Federal Security Agency): A center for cancer and other medical research operated by the Public Health Service on the outskirts of Washington.

National Labor Relations Board . . . NLRB: Protects labor's right to organize, as set forth in the Wagner Act. Not a conciliation or mediation board. Holds elections in plants where different unions claim jurisdiction.

National Mediation Board: Founded under President Coolidge to assure railway labor the right of collective bargaining. The act provides for a cooling-off period before railway strikes.

National Park Service (under Department of the Interior): Supervises operations of national parks and also helps states and cities, on request, to plan parks. Issues free recreation map of the United States upon request.

National Research Council: Part of the National Academy of Sciences.

National Resources Planning Board (under Executive Office of the President): Cooperates with your State Planning Board and the rest of the federal government in looking as far ahead as possible. Has already prepared and sent to Congress detailed plans for full employment after the war.

National Youth Administration . . . NYA (under Federal Security Agency): Offers part-time employment for secondary school and college students, age 16-24, and training on work projects to out-of-school youth. Pays young people while they learn war industry trades.

Naval Observatory (under the Navy Department): Broadcasts the correct time, and studies the stars, but no longer shows them to Washington visitors once a week.

Navy Department: Runs the Navy and the Marines, and, in time of war, the Coast Guard. Now greatly expanded in caring for administrative tasks entailed in expanding the fleet to two-ocean Navy.

Permanent Joint Board on Defense—United States and Canada: Set up by President Roosevelt and Prime Minister Mackenzie King to study sea, land and air problems involved in the defense of the northern half of the Western Hemisphere.

Petroleum Conservation Division (under Department of the Interior): Administers the Connally law prohibiting interstate shipment of oil produced in excess of quotas set by the states. Also studies ways of preventing the waste of oil and gas resources.

Petroleum Coordinator for National Defense, Office of the (attached to Department of the Interior): Sees that all federal activities concerned with production, refining, transporting and marketing of this all-important war fuel pull together.

Pan-American Union: An international center in Washington providing a solid background of scholarship, precedent and good manners in the progress toward hemispheric solidarity.

Patent Office (under Department of Commerce): "Adds the fuel of interest to the fire of genius." Operates at a small annual profit.

Plant Industry, Bureau of (under Department of Agriculture): Adapts and improves useful plants from the rest of the world. Operates research farm at Beltsville, Md., near Washington.

Post Office Department: Runs the postal system.

Power, Division of (under Department of the Interior): Studies defense power needs and centralizes responsibility for the power phases of the work of the various bureaus of the Department, including the Bonneville Power Administration, Bureau of Reclamation, Office of Indian Affairs, National Park Service, and the Division of Territories and Island Possessions.

Power Policy Committee, National (attached to Department of the Interior): Coordinates federal power policies for war as well as for peace. Interested long-range in wider use of electricity at cheaper rates.

President, Executive Office of the: Includes the Office for Emergency Management, Bureau of the Budget, Office of Government Reports, and the National Resources Planning Board.

Price Administration, Office of . . . OPA (under Office for Emergency Management): Tackles the thankless but important task of keeping prices relatively stable, protecting consumer interests, and even rationing consumer goods.

Prisons, Bureau of (under Department of Justice): Looks after the federal prisons which look after the federal prisoners.

Procurement Division (Treasury Department): Chief buyer for government's non-military needs. Issues the Federal Standard Stock Catalog.

Public Assistance, Bureau of (under Federal Security Agency): Administers grants by the federal government to states for old-age assistance, aid to dependent children and to the needy blind.

Public Buildings Administration . . . PBA (under Federal Works

Agency) : Builds, maintains and operates the government's buildings everywhere.

Public Health Service (under Federal Security Agency) : Gives direct medical care to federal prisoners, to merchant seamen, and to federal employees on the job. Aids state and local public health officials to set up more clinics and hospitals with federal grants. Leads national drives against syphilis, cancer, pneumonia and other diseases, and for better maternal and child care.

Public Roads Administration . . . PRA (under Federal Works Agency) : Helps build and improve the nation's highways with federal-state-aid funds and technical assistance. Also eliminates or reconstructs dangerous grade crossings.

Public Work Reserve (attached to the Federal Works Agency and co-sponsored by the National Resources Planning Board) : Set up to help cities, counties and states develop a reservoir of public projects to absorb postwar unemployment, at the same time using the nation's full capacity to provide needed public services and facilities.

Public Works Administration . . . PWA (under Federal Works Agency) : Supervises construction of bridges, schools, and other civic projects, partly from federal funds. It has handled a total of 34,000 projects.

Puerto Rico Reconstruction Administration (under Department of the Interior) : A miniature New Deal for the island, complete with slum clearance, soil and forest conservation, etc.

Railroad Retirement Board: . . . RRB A social security system providing annuities, pensions and unemployment insurance for railroad workers.

Reclamation, Bureau of (under Department of the Interior) : The world's greatest dam construction agency. Grand Coulee, biggest dam and hydro-electric project on earth, will irrigate an area larger than Delaware when completed. The electricity is essential in making aluminum—which is essential to meet the war plane production program.

Reconstruction Finance Corporation . . . RFC (under Department of Commerce) : The greatest financing corporation on earth. Includes the Metals Reserve Company, Rubber Reserve Company, Defense Supplies Corporation, Export-Import Bank of Washington, Defense Plant Corporation, War Damage Corporation, and Disaster Loan Corporation.

RFC Mortgage Company (under Department of Commerce) : A financial backlog for FHA insured mortgages. Has also made some loans on its own account.

Red Cross, The American National: Gives volunteer aid to the sick and wounded in time of war. In time of peace relieves suffering caused by famine, fire, floods and other great calamities.

477

Roosevelt Library, Franklin D., at Hyde Park, N. Y.: Keeps the President's papers where the public and posterity can see them.

Rubber Reserve Company (under Department of Commerce): Built a rubber stockpile before the war in the Pacific, and is still adding to it.

Rural Electrification Administration . . . REA (under Department of Agriculture): Lends money to rural electric cooperative associations to build power lines in areas not already served. Has helped to double the number of farm homes electrified since 1935. Has developed mobile Diesel generators to plug breaks in power circuits.

Scientific Research and Development, Office of (under Office for Emergency Management): Brings the country's best scientific minds to bear on war production.

Secret Service Division (under Treasury Department): Protects the President and his family and the President-elect and his family. Suppresses counterfeiting and investigates certain other crimes against the Treasury.

Securities and Exchange Commission . . . SEC: Compels "full and fair disclosure" of the facts when new securities are issued. Regulates trading in stocks and bonds, and regulates public utilities to prevent violation of the holding company laws.

Selective Service System . . . SSS: Administers the draft.

Smithsonian Institution: Runs the National Museum of sciences, arts, industries and history, the National Gallery of Art, and the zoo. Also engages in research on many subjects, from the American Indian to rocket ships and solar radiation. James Smithson, an Englishman who never set foot in the United States, gave the money to found the Institution more than 100 years ago.

Social Security Board . . . SSB (under Federal Security Agency): Four main jobs are administering of: Old-age and survivors insurance (old-age benefits to workers and wives over 65, and surviving dependents); public assistance (grants to needy aged, dependent children and the blind); unemployment insurance; and public employment offices. Only the first is handled in Washington. Public assistance, unemployment insurance and employment offices are operated jointly with the states.

Soil Conservation Service (under Department of Agriculture): Redesigns farms to control erosion, with help from the CCC. Does not pay farmers to practice conservation farming, but tries to convince them by demonstration that conservation pays. Functions chiefly through aid to locally organized Soil Conservation Districts.

Solid Fuels Coordinator for National Defense, Office of (attached to Department of the Interior): Recommends necessary steps to keep a ready and adequate supply of solid fuels at reasonable prices for military, industrial and civilian purposes.

Standards, National Bureau of (under Department of Commerce): Keeps the standard weights and measures, references and working standards used in the sale of a pound of sugar or the design of a bomber; tests anything from a baby carriage to a steel beam, on request of other government agencies or private industry. Encourages industry to raise standards of quality, to label goods adequately, and to reduce the number of unnecessary shapes and sizes.

State, Department of: Looks after foreign affairs and includes following divisions and offices: European Affairs, Near Eastern Affairs, Far Eastern Affairs, Passport, Visa, Protocol, American Republics, Philippine Affairs, Commercial Treaties and Agreements, International Communications, Cultural Relations, Foreign Service Personnel, Translating, and Communications and Records.

Superintendent of Documents, Washington, D. C.: The man from whom you order government publications.

Supreme Court of the United States: Highest court in the land.

Tariff Commission, United States: Investigates and reports on the workings of tariffs imposed by Congress. Special reports on various commodities have considerable research value.

Tax Appeals, United States Board of: Not final—decisions may be reviewed by appellate courts, and U. S. Supreme Court.

Tennessee Valley Authority . . . TVA (main offices at Knoxville, Tenn.): Started as a "yardstick" to measure private utility rates but now demonstrates how the public can harness a great river for maximum usefulness. Dams are coordinated for flood control, navigation and power, and also for soil and forest conservation. Important war unit in producing power for aluminum.

Territories and Island Possessions, Division of (under Department of the Interior): Coordinates federal activities in Alaska, Hawaii, Puerto Rico, and the Virgin Islands and (through the U. S. High Commissioner) in the Philippines. Also operates the Alaska railroad.

Transportation, Office of Defense (under Office for Emergency Management): Fits all domestic transportation facilities—railroad, motor, inland waterway, pipe line, air transport, and coastwise and intercoastal shipping—to war needs.

Travel Bureau, United States (under Department of the Interior): Free federal travel bureau for all citizens and for good neighbors desiring to visit this country. On request will send information on American resorts, parks, forest recreational areas, etc.

Treasury, Department of the: Manages the national finances and includes the following divisions and bureaus: Procurement, Secret Service,

Coast Guard (in time of peace), Comptroller of the Currency, Customs, Engraving and Printing, Internal Revenue, Mint, Narcotics, Monetary Research, Tax Research and the Fiscal Service.

Veterans Administration: Handles pensions and hospitalization of America's ex-soldiers.

Wage and Hour Division (under Department of Labor): Administers the minimum wage and maximum hour provisions of the Fair Labor Standards Act of 1938.

War Department: Runs the Army. Also operates the Panama Canal, river and harbor development, and flood control.

War Damage Corporation (under Department of Commerce): Set up in December 1941 with a capital of $100,000,000 to compensate property owners in continental United States for losses by enemy attacks.

War Labor Board, National . . . NWLB (under Office for Emergency Management): Settles labor disputes in war industries after direct negotiation and Department of Labor conciliation fail to do so.

War Production Board . . . WPB (under Office for Emergency Management): Directs the entire war production program. Has priorities and subcontracting field offices in about 120 cities. Makes final decisions on all matters involved in converting the country to war production. Includes the Secretaries of War, Navy and Commerce, Lieutenant General in charge of War Department Production, Director of the WPB Labor Division, Price Administrator, Chairman of the Board of Economic Warfare and the Special Assistant to the President.

War Relocation Authority (under Office for Emergency Management): Provides work corps in which persons forced to move from military areas may voluntarily enlist for duration of the war. Sets its own wages and work conditions.

War Shipping Administration (under Office for Emergency Management): Controls operation, purchase, charges, requisition and use of all U. S. merchant shipping, "for the successful prosecution of the war."

Weather Bureau (under Department of Commerce): Studies and forecasts weather.

Women's Bureau (under Department of Labor): Administers no laws. Just studies its comprehensive subject.

Work Projects Administration . . . WPA (under Federal Works Agency): Provides work for the jobless. Employs only American citizens of 18 years or older, who are able to work and certified for relief by local welfare offices.

Zoological Park, National (under the Smithsonian Institution): A first-rank zoo in the nation's capital.

Commonly Used Abbreviations

AAA—Agricultural Adjustment Administration
AMA—Agricultural Marketing Administration
BAE—Bureau of Agricultural Economics
BLS—Bureau of Labor Statistics
CAA—Civil Aeronautics Administration
CAB—Civil Aeronautics Board
CCC—Civilian Conservation Corps
DPC—Defense Plant Corporation
FBI—Federal Bureau of Investigation
FCA—Farm Credit Administration
FCC—Federal Communications Commission
FDIC—Federal Deposit Insurance Corporation
FHA—Federal Housing Administration
FHLBA—Federal Home Loan Bank Administration
FPC—Federal Power Commission
FPHA—Federal Public Housing Authority
FSA—Farm Security Administration or Federal Security Agency
FTC—Federal Trade Commission
FWA—Federal Works Agency
GAO—General Accounting Office
GPO—Government Printing Office
HOLC—Home Owners' Loan Corporation
ICC—Interstate Commerce Commission
NHA—National Housing Agency
NLRB—National Labor Relations Board
NWLB—National War Labor Board
NYA—National Youth Administration
OCD—Office of Civilian Defense
OEM—Office for Emergency Management
OFF—Office of Facts and Figures
OGR—Office of Government Reports
OPA—Office of Price Administration

PBA—Public Buildings Administration
PRA—Public Roads Administration
PWA—Public Works Administration
REA—Rural Electrification Administration
RFC—Reconstruction Finance Corporation
RRB—Railroad Retirement Board
SEC—Securities and Exchange Commission
SSB—Social Security Board
SSS—Selective Service System
TVA—Tennessee Valley Authority
USES—United States Employment Service
USIS—United States Information Service
WPA—Work Projects Administration
WPB—War Production Board

How to Get Government Pamphlets

WHEN you know how to go about it, you can get information on practically everything from the United States Government.

First of all, if you know what you want and how much it costs, the procedure is simple. Send your order with check, cash or money order, to the Superintendent of Documents, Washington, D. C. Don't send stamps. If you intend to become something of a steady customer, you can buy coupon books, each containing 20 coupons, for one dollar apiece, and forward coupons enough to cover each purchase. If you know what you want, but don't know the price, send at least five dollars with your order and the balance will stand to your credit, or you can get the balance back by requesting it. It might be well for you to see in advance whether the public library in your city has a copy of the publication you have in mind before you send in your order. You can't return the book and ask for your money back. And the Superintendent of Documents will not send things out COD.

If you don't know what you want, read on here for a while, and you may get some ideas.

Some of the printed publications are for sale, others are for free distribution. A few are both for sale and free. If you write your congressman or to the federal agency which issues these, you get them for nothing until the free supply runs out. But the price of these bulletins usually is only five or ten cents, anyway. Outside of the printed publications, nearly all the federal agencies have a lot of mimeographed bulletins for free distribution. If you write to the agency dealing with the subject in which you are interested, it will give you an idea of what it has on hand along that line. The law doesn't allow an agency to put your name on a list to receive free copies of future publications as they are issued, but some departments will place your name on a list to receive notices of its new publications, both free and for sale. And the Superintendent of Documents has thousands of special mailing lists, with more than a million names on them, of persons who have a continuing interest in some subject or group of subjects. These persons are sent special notices of new publications of interest to them.

You can keep posted on what the Government Printing Office is offering for sale by writing to the Superintendent of Documents and asking that your name be placed on the mailing list for the "Weekly List of Selected United States Publications." It's free. Some fifty thousand people take it. If you want to get a list of all the government publications issued for sale, subscribe to the "Monthly Catalog of United States Public Documents." The subscription price is $2 a year. On this same list are included many of the free publications.

Before you go in for any current listings, however, it would be a good idea to catch up on what the government has already printed. This is easy, because the Superintendent has prepared dozens of price lists, any of which you can get from him for nothing. Each gives titles, descriptions and prices of publications dealing with a specific subject. Each of these lists has a number. You pick out the list dealing with your particular interest and ask for it by number. These lists are kept well up to date. List 50, covering American history and biography, for instance, has been revived twenty-seven times. It includes approximately 1,000 items.

As a start here are the available price lists of publications:

10. Laws (Federal)
11. Foods and Cooking
15. Geological Survey (Geology and Water Supply)
18. Engineering and Surveying
19. Army and Militia
20. Public Domain
21. Fishes
24. Indians
25. Transportation and Panama Canal
28. Finance
31. Education
32. Insular Possessions
33. Labor
35. Geography and Exploration
36. Government periodicals for which subscriptions are taken
37. Tariff
38. Animal Industry
41. Insects
42. Irrigation, Drainage, Water Power
43. Forestry
44. Plants
45. Roads
46. Agricultural Chemistry and Soils and Fertilizers
48. Weather, Astronomy and Meteorology

484

Price List 73 deserves special attention, because its subjects are sure to include one or more that will interest you.

Annual reports submitted to the President by the department heads, and to them by subordinate bureau chiefs, sometimes have something valuable for a reader with a special interest. But be prepared to encounter batches of statistics. The reports come out around the end of the year.

If you want some information which is not listed as a printed document or given in one of the special reports, write to the federal agency which you think would be responsible for the subject. If you don't know which agency to ask, write to the U. S. Information Service, Washington, D. C., and they'll get the information for you, without charge. The U. S. Information Service, headed by Miss Harriet M. Root, is a unit of the Office of Government Reports and compiles current directories and reference material relating to the government. It maintains files of government documents and publications and publishes the *Digest of the Purposes of Federal Agencies* as well as the more extensive *United States Government Manual*. The service maintains a branch office at 521 Fifth Avenue, New York City. The Washington office handles between 900 and 1,000 requests for information daily, two-thirds of them coming over the phone. A big part of its job is telling inquirers where they can reach people working in the government.

485

Every reader must blaze his own trail through the wonderland of government publications, but the following suggestions may help you to get started on your own trail-blazing. The publications for which no price is given may be obtained from the issuing agencies. Where a price is listed, the document is for sale by the Superintendent of Documents.

The War

Victory (weekly, 75 cents a year) carries information relating to war-production progress and official announcements of the Office for Emergency Management. OEM also issues *War Against Waste,* dealing with conservation and substitution of materials. The *Reference List of National Defense Publications* (Office of Government Reports) lists a selection of bulletins and articles prepared by federal agencies. The Office of Civilian Defense issues the following booklets on air raid precaution (one per person): *Blackouts, Air Raid Warning System, What to Do in an Air Raid, Handbook for Air Raid Wardens* and *Handbook of First Aid.* *Selective Service,* a monthly bulletin, is distributed in limited numbers by the Selective Service System. For the *Selective Service Regulations,* revised, write Superintendent of Documents for price. The *Training Within Industry Program* (Labor Division of the War Production Board) outlines principles and policies of the issuing unit. *How Inventors Can Aid National Defense,* 1941, (Department of Commerce) explains the purpose of the National Inventors Council and suggests procedure for submitting inventions. *The Soldier's Handbook* (35 cents) is what its name indicates, but contains much information a civilian can use. *Effective Use of Women in the Defense Program* (10 cents) is a Department of Labor publication. *Workers Needed for National Defense* (weekly, Civil Service Commission) contains job announcements. *Defense Employment and Training for Employment,* 1941, (Office of Government Reports) contains information on employment opportunities and training in both the civilian and military phases of the war program. *Food for Freedom* leaflets (Department of Agriculture) assist farmers and others in producing the foods to help win the war.

Official Reference Books

The *Congressional Directory* (two editions a year, $1.25 each) is loaded with information about members of Congress and other officials in Washington. It tells whom to see about what, gives telephone numbers and addresses, with brief autobiographies. The *United States Government Manual* (three editions a year, $1 a copy) is the most complete account of what each government agency does, including Congress and the courts.

If you simply want a useful list of federal agencies, you can get it for nothing from the U. S. Information Service. Digests of government expenditures and activities by states and counties and an *Informational Handbook* describing federal activities for the country as a whole are available without charge from the same source. The biggest bargain in statistics about our nation is the *Statistical Abstract of the United States,* revised, which has just about everything except the ages of actresses and baseball scores. Write Superintendent of Documents for price. *The Government of the United States,* a chart issued by the Office of Government Reports, shows principal agencies of the federal government and their subdivisions.

Laws

As soon as the President signs a measure passed by Congress, the text is printed. You can get them all by spending three dollars for a year's service of the printed sheets. Or you can stick to laws on one subject and buy special compilations. (See *Price List 10* in the preceding.)

Vacations

National Forest Vacations (10 cents) is just the thing if you like trees, birds and such things when you take time off. Free maps and folders showing campgrounds, trails, fishing spots and the like in any national forest are sent free by the U. S. Forest Service, Department of Agriculture. The same service concerning national parks is offered by the National Park Service, Department of the Interior. The U. S. Travel Bureau of the Department of the Interior will supply folders and pamphlets on public and private resorts. It also has a free *Map of Recreational Areas in the United States,* showing state and national parks, public forests, and the facilities each affords. Other items: *Scenic Resources of the Tennessee Valley* ($1); *Sport Fishing in Alaska* (5 cents); *Forest Trail Handbook* (15 cents); *Basic Photography* (35 cents); *Handbook for Recreation Leaders* (20 cents).

Natural Resources

To Hold This Soil (45 cents) deals with the soil, its history, its abuse and what is being done to save it. It is well illustrated. *Forests and Human Welfare* (Tennessee Valley Authority, Knoxville, Tenn., free) and *New Forest Frontiers* (Forest Service, Department of Agriculture, 30 cents) are good. *Our National Resources* is well worth a dime. Small, free folders on the great dams in the West are obtainable from the Bureau of Reclamation, Interior Department.

There's a lot of good reading about natural resources in the annual reports of the Secretary of the Interior (75 cents). More detailed information is in annual reports of the heads of the Department's bureaus. (Note *Price List 20.*)

Agriculture

The government puts out more books and pamphlets on agriculture than on any other subject. You could fill a book the size of this one with descriptions of them. *Price List 46* gives a lot of titles. If you are one of those who dream about turning farmer, ask the Department of Agriculture for *Planning a Subsistence Homestead* and *Selecting a Farm*. The Department has other bulletins that will guide your every step as you go along, and it will send you on request a list of all its publications. The annual yearbooks of the Department are gold mines of information. Some recent features: *Climate and Man* (1941, $1.75), *Farmers in a Changing World* (1940, $1.50), *Food and Life* (1939, $1.50) and *Soils and Men* (1938, $1.75).

Hearth and Home

All over this land are homes which have been planned or improved by folks who have poked their noses into government publications on housing. There are a lot of helpful ones, notably the FHA technical bulletins (10 cents), especially *Principles of Planning Small Houses*. Others in *Price List 72: Small Houses* (10 cents), *Light Frame House Construction* (40 cents), *How to Judge a House* (10 cents), *Care and Repair of the House* (15 cents), and *Rammed Earth Walls for Buildings* (5 cents). Blueprints on farmhouse plans, sold by county agents at prices that vary according to states, are among the best and cheapest you can get.

Mrs. Housewife, whether she's in the city or out in the country, can get more information from the Department of Agriculture than the devoted guidance of any mother in the world could impart. *Home Canning of Fruits, Vegetables and Meats* went without charge to 650,000 people during the 1937-39 period. *Diets to Fit the Family Income* hit the 450,000 total. Next in popularity among the Farmers' Bulletins are *Stain Removal from Fabrics, Homemade Bread, Cake and Pastry, Roses for the Home,* and *Farm Poultry Raising*. Leaflets which have passed the 100,000 mark also include *Eggs at Any Meal, Good Food Habits for Children, Ice Cream Frozen without Stirring,* and *Cooking Beef According to the Cut*.

For tips on economical buying, send for the *Consumers' Guide*, a twice-monthly magazine (monthly June through Sept.) issued for sale and to a limited free list by the Consumers' Council Division of the Department of Agriculture. Five cents for single copies; 50 cents a year.

Babies

Best seller of all government publications is *Infant Care*, one of the child-care series of the Children's Bureau, Department of Labor. Since its first edition in 1914, approximately 2,500,000 copies have been sold at ten cents each, and more than 10,000,000 other copies have been given away. Booklets in the child-care series, like the Farmers' Bulletins, can be obtained free of charge by writing to the agency issuing them or to your congressman so long as the free supply lasts, or from the Superintendent of Documents for the purchase price. *Prenatal Care* has a record of more than 1,000,000 copies sold. Free distribution totals more than 4,000,000 copies. *The Child from One to Six* is credited with a total distribution of more than 4,500,000 copies.

Much of the tremendous distribution of these Children's Bureau bulletins is due to bulk purchases by commercial and other organizations. Only ten copies may be sent free of charge in answer to an individual request. All large quantities must be purchased. State health departments buy them in bulk and many department stores keep copies on hand for presentation to layette-buying parents. One member of Congress used to do his bit by having his secretary watch the birth notices in home-town papers and send copies to parents who had new babies.

Health

A large portion of the federal publications on health and medical care, such as are named in *Price List 51*, are intended for physicians and laboratory workers. Child health is covered by the Labor Department's child-care series. Nutrition of children and adults is thoroughly dealt with in Department of Agriculture pamphlets, notably in *Food Fads, Facts and Fancies*. Don't overlook the Farmers' Bulletins on how to get rid of poison ivy and ragweed. And at 5 cents each, you can get: *The Home Medicine Cabinet, Common Colds, Leonard's Appendix—And How It Burst, What to Know and What to Do About Cancer.*

House and Senate Documents

Among the congressional documents are some of the most interesting books in America. They don't get a wide circulation, because they are tagged formally and coldly with numbers and names of investigating committees, and they are never given a tumble by book reviewers in newspapers and magazines. The best way to spot what you want is to watch newspaper accounts of congressional activities, particularly those of committees, and then—later on—write to your senator or congressman, or to the Superintendent of Documents, to see what has been printed in connection with the activities that interest you.

Maps

The government goes in heavily for expert and accurate map making. Maps are the only exception to the cardinal rule that all government publications which are for sale can be bought only from the Superintendent of Documents. While all federal maps are listed in *Price List 53*, some of them may be purchased from the issuing agency. You can get a free circular from the Geological Survey, Department of the Interior, giving descriptions and prices. Their topographic maps show a large amount of detail, because each of them covers just about fifty square miles. They can give you a good acquaintance with any section of the country, useful for fishing or hiking trips, or for driving back-country roads full of interest and free from traffic. They're priced at ten cents each, and available only from the Geological Survey.

The rural free delivery maps sold by the Post Office Department also are rich in detail, scaled one inch to the mile. Transportation maps, showing railroads, highways, canals, air lanes, dredged channels and pipe lines are sold by the Superintendent of Documents. Maps of Central America are sold by the Military Intelligence Division of the Army. If you roam around in a boat once in a while, you can get charts and navigation aids covering inland rivers and coastal areas from the Lighthouse Service and the Coast and Geodetic Survey, respectively. The Survey will send a list on request. It also prepares maps and charts for aviators. *Practical Air Navigation* ($1) is issued by the Civil Aeronautics Administration. The Public Roads Administration issues federal highway maps, but those distributed at filling stations are better for ordinary driving purposes. Department of Agriculture maps show types of soils, farming areas and forest regions. Census Bureau maps (15 cents) show minor civil divisions, such as townships. Your local Weather Bureau office can tell you about daily weather maps (subscription, 30 cents a month). Official maps of the United States are prepared by the General Land Office, and sell for $3.50. But they're big and you need a lot of wall space for one of them.

Federal Writers' Project

The *American Guide Series*, with a book for each state and many cities, is the prize product of the WPA writers' project. The books forming this series cover "every major motor highway mile by mile, with descriptions of

490

towns and villages, inland and coastal waterways, and recreation areas along the route, the historic shrines, architectural monuments, contemporary and historical points of interest." These books and other products of the project, strictly speaking, are not government publications. With the exception of the Washington guidebook and one or two others, they were not published by the Government Printing Office and are not listed by the Superintendent of Documents. Ask your bookstore about them.

Periodicals

The government issues approximately one hundred printed periodicals. Subscriptions for most of them are handled by the Superintendent of Documents. Oldest and best known is the *Congressional Record* ($1.50 a month; single copies from three cents up, depending on size, which in turn depends upon how much talking was done in Congress on the day covered by the copy). Of the 45,000 copies printed daily, most go to "folks back home" whose names have been placed on the list by members of Congress.

Some other periodicals: The *Federal Register* (daily, $12.50 a year) which presents administrative rulings and decisions of executive agencies of the government. *Survey of Current Business* (monthly, $2 a year), *Federal Reserve Bulletin* (monthly, $2 a year) which can be purchased at offices of the Federal Reserve Board. *Monthly Labor Review* ($3.50 a year), *The Child* (monthly, $1 a year), *Soil Conservation* (monthly, $1 a year), *Education for Victory* (ten issues annually, $1 a year), *Public Housing* (monthly, $1 a year). *Examinations for the United States Civil Service* is a bulletin issued periodically, usually weekly, by the Civil Service Commission, giving details on forthcoming examinations.

Keep in mind that in the matter of publications as in everything else these days, prices are subject to change without notice.

Films

More than four hundred government-made films are available without any charge except to cover shipping expenses. Geared to national defense interests are the 16mm. sound films distributed to schools, clubs, civic groups and other non-profit organizations. They are obtained through the Washington office of Office for Emergency Management, which is the producing agency, and through the YMCA motion picture bureaus in New York, Chicago, San Francisco and Dallas. These run from seven to twenty minutes each and include: *Building a Bomber, Aluminum, Defense Review No. One, Defense Review No. Two, Homes for Defense, Power for Defense* and *Army in Overalls.* These OEM films also are for sale. The Department of Agriculture, which distributed *The River,* has the largest list of government films, with most subjects pertaining to farming and the home. The Department of the Interior, with the next largest list, issues reels dealing mainly with scenic beauties of the land. Others are issued by the Public Health Service, the Army and the Navy. To get information on films, write to the Office of Government Reports, and it will tell you where you can get the reels.

Other Books to Read

THIS book covers Washington broadly, as a whole, with many subjects, and with as much detail on each subject as space allows. If you want more details on certain subjects, you may read other books which are suggested in the following list.

This list is not a bibliography on Washington, for that would be voluminous. It is not a record of source material for this book, for practically all of the material for this book has been gathered fresh from current sources.

Some of these books are obtainable from your bookstore, or the publishers, or your local library. A few are out of print, but you can get them at a library.

Government Directories

Congressional Directory, revised and reissued at each session of Congress. Superintendent of Documents, Washington, D. C., $1.25. Essential for anyone who deals all the time with Washington and wants to know names, addresses and telephone numbers of all officials, members of Congress and diplomats, and the functions of governmental agencies. It covers all branches of the government, but goes strong on Congress, with detailed information on committees, congressional districts, and biographies of all members of Congress, written by themselves.

United States Government Manual, issued in revised form every four months (February, June, September) by the Office of Government Reports. Order from Superintendent of Documents, Washington, D. C., $1 a copy, or from state branches of the OGR. It is the best all-around book for average persons who must deal with government. It goes more heavily on the executive branch than on Congress or the courts, and it lists the names of top personnel in each agency, without their addresses. It lists all regional branches of government agencies with whom people out through the country often deal.

World Almanac

The World Almanac, published every year by the *New York World-Telegram.* You can get it at bookstores and newsstands for 60 cents. This contains more information per square inch than any other book published, anywhere. It has the well-known and little-known facts about everything, including Washington, government and politics. Every working reference library should have it.

WPA Guides

Washington, City and Capital, by the Federal Writers' Project of the WPA, Government Printing Office, 1937. This is the biggest and most detailed compendium of everything about everything in Washington. It is out of print, but your library probably has a copy. (Also look up the WPA book on your own state or locality; ask a bookstore.)

Washington, City and Capital (revised, 1942), by the Federal Writers' Project of WPA, published by Wilfred Funk, Inc., 1942. This is a shorter version of the earlier giant book of the WPA. It is a handy guide to the history, landmarks, government agencies, and buildings in Washington.

The Presidency

The American Presidency, by Harold J. Laski, Harper and Brothers, 1940. This is an erudite study of the institution of the Presidency, and it advocates more power for the President. The author is professor of political science at the University of London.

Roosevelt: Dictator or Democrat? by Gerald W. Johnson, Harper and Brothers, 1941. This is a pro-Roosevelt study of the President done by an editorial writer for the *Baltimore Sun.* He pitches the book toward the millions who voted against Roosevelt in 1940, and he aims to assure them that Roosevelt is a true democrat who has struck a compromise between revolution and old concepts.

New Deal

The Roosevelt Revolution: First Phase, by Ernest K. Lindley, The Viking Press, 1933; *Half Way With Roosevelt,* by the same author, The Viking Press, 1936, revised edition, 1937. Lindley is a Washington newspaperman who has covered Roosevelt since the days when he was governor of New York, and is often called Roosevelt's "unofficial biographer." He is on the sympathetic side but is essentially objective. In these two books he reviews the policies of the New Deal in its early and middle stages.

After Seven Years, by Raymond Moley, Harper and Brothers, 1939.

This is an intimate story of the origins of the New Deal, written from notes kept by the author at the time. Moley was leading brain truster in the early days, but broke with Roosevelt within a year after he took office. Later he wrote this book, which in many places is critical of the President and other New Dealers. It gives valuable background on the origins of New Deal ideas.

Remaking America, by Jay Franklin (pseudonym of John Franklin Carter), The Riverside Press, 1942. The author is an extreme New Dealer. In this book, he surveys the paternalism and public spending of the 30's, and supports the broad program on the basis that it saved the nation from grasping private interests, and prepared the social and economic structure for the shocks of World War II.

Mrs. Roosevelt

This Is My Story, by Eleanor Roosevelt, Harper and Brothers, 1937. A candid autobiography of the First Lady.

Eleanor Roosevelt: A Biography, by Ruby Black; Duell, Sloan and Pearce, 1940. This is a sympathetic story of Mrs. Roosevelt written by a Washington newspaperwoman and friend of the First Lady. It shows Mrs. Roosevelt as once a shy and solitary young woman who evolved into a forceful character. The book also is interesting for some of its glances at the day-to-day workings of the White House.

White House

The White House: A Biography, by Charles Hurd, Harper and Brothers, 1940. This book by the White House correspondent of the *New York Times* tells the story of the White House and the men who have lived in it since early days and up to Roosevelt.

Preparations for Defense

Your Business Goes to War, by Leo M. Cherne, Houghton Mifflin Company, 1942. A solid, informational and long analysis of ways and means by which businessmen can adjust to the overall program of total war. The author is executive secretary of the Research Institute of America.

Business as Usual: The First Year of Defense, by I. F. Stone, Modern Age Books, 1941. The author, a newspaperman, Washington editor of the *Nation,* traces the lags and bottlenecks of war preparation to the business habits and psychology of businessmen, especially the $1-a-year men. He also argues for decentralization of defense production and greater local enterprise as a builder of democratic processes for postwar.

Confusion on the Potomac: The Alarming Chaos and Feuds of Washington, by Carlisle Bargeron, Wilfred Funk, Inc., 1941. Another study of the first year of defense, written colorfully by a Washington newspaperman. He lays most of the blame for laggardness upon the New Dealers for not drawing in abler businessmen to help.

Army

The New Army of the United States, prepared by the War Department, Government Printing Office, 1942. For sale by the Superintendent of Documents, Washington, D. C. The official version of the set-up and functions of the War Department and all branches of the Army, written for civilians, and revised since the March reorganization of the Army.

What the Citizen Should Know About the Army, by Harvey S. Ford, W. W. Norton, 1941. An explanation of the workings of the Army before the latest reorganization of March, 1942. It describes and illustrates various weapons and tactics. It is written for laymen by the assistant editor of the *U. S. Field Artillery Journal.*

Navy

The United States Navy, prepared under the direction of the Committee on Naval Affairs of the Senate, Government Printing Office, 1941. For sale by the Superintendent of Documents, Washington, D. C., 15 cents. The official story of the Navy's history, present organization, its bases, men, ships and planes—with illustrations.

Fighting Ships of the U.S.A., by Lt. Victor F. Blakeslee, Random House, 1941. A good, short explanation of the operation of the Navy today, written for civilians by the present chief of the Script Division of the Navy's Office of Public Relations. Illustrated with color drawings of planes and ships and men in action.

What the Citizen Should Know About the Navy, by Hanson W. Baldwin, W. W. Norton & Company, revised edition, 1942. The widely-read military expert for the *New York Times* explains for laymen the meaning of sea power, the operations of the fleet, and the organization of the Navy Department. He stresses air power.

State Department

Inside the Department of State, by Bertram D. Hulen, Whittlesey House, McGraw-Hill Book Co., 1939. The story of the growth of the Department (with emphasis on the period since World War I), some famous Secretaries, and the present operations. The author is State Department reporter for the *New York Times,* and the book is regarded as authoritative.

Hull

Cordell Hull, A Biography, by Harold B. Hinton, Doubleday, Doran & Company, 1942. The life of the Secretary of State, from his birth in 1871 to the time of America's entry into World War II.

Politics

Behind the Ballots, by James A. Farley, Harcourt, Brace & Company, 1938. The former Postmaster General and political manager for Roosevelt has written a book which is incidentally a biography but mainly a frank revelation of the attitudes and activities of professional politicians. It is good reading for anyone who wants to know how politics really operate.

Supreme Court

The Supreme Court of the United States, Its Foundation, Methods and Achievements: An Interpretation, by Charles Evans Hughes, Columbia University Press, 1928, revised edition, 1936. The former Chief Justice attempts to help people who are not legal scholars to understand the origin of the Court, the principles upon which it was based, and the results of its work.

Government Agencies

The American Government, by Frederic J. Haskin, Harper and Brothers, 1941. This was first published in 1911, and has been revised five times since then. It is an explanation of government agencies, telling what they do and something about their history, with interesting sidelights thrown in. The author is a prominent Washington newspaper syndicate editor.

The Press

Washington Dateline: The Press Covers the Capital, by Delbert Clark, Frederick A. Stokes Company, 1941. The most recent and most complete book on the Washington press. It is chiefly informational, but occasionally expresses judgments and is sometimes critical of methods of newsgathering, writing, and of government influence. The author is manager of the Washington Bureau of the *New York Times.*

The Washington Correspondents, by Leo C. Rosten, Harcourt, Brace & Company, 1937. A factual study of Washington newspapermen based on the answers to questionnaires. Of primary interest to newspapermen and journalism students.

Crime

Farewell, Mr. Gangster!, by Herbert Corey, D. Appleton-Century Company, 1936. This is a story of the FBI, with a lot of the detective-thriller appeal, but with a factual approach to problems of crime detection. It demonstrates the operation of the Bureau by showing how some of the big-name gangsters of the 20's and 30's were captured. It has current significance especially in showing the techniques used now in spotting spies and saboteurs.

Social Guide

Social Washington, by Anne Squire, (revised edition) 1941. Privately published, and on sale in bookstores. A convenient handbook which tells the Washington hostess the rules of protocol, whom to seat next to whom, the peculiar social usages of the nation's capital, and ends with some advice in the form of "do's" and "don't's" of Washington society. The authoress is a professional Washington social secretary.

Diplomats

Washington Waltz, by Helen Lombard, Alfred Knopf, 1941. The story of recent diplomatic turbulence and machinations is told bluntly in this book by the wife of a former anti-Vichy French military attaché in Washington.

Civil War Washington

Reveille in Washington, by Margaret Leech, Harper and Brothers, 1941. A charming story of Civil War Washington, filled with human touches on Washingtonians of the period.

Hoover Days

Washington Merry-Go-Round, by Robert S. Allen and Drew Pearson, Horace Liveright, Inc., 1931. *More Merry-Go-Round,* by Robert S. Allen and Drew Pearson, Horace Liveright, Inc., 1932. These two books set the pace for a run of books in the late Hoover days which dished out bits of scandal, pulled the sheets off public officials, and provided a feast for those who wanted to read "inside" Washington secrets.

Mirrors of 1932, (published anonymously) by Ray Thomas Tucker, Brewer, Warren and Putnam, 1931. A series of sharp personality sketches of the possible candidates in the 1932 political race for President. It is especially interesting in retrospect for the 1932 slant on men.

Guide Books

There are a number of good 25 cent and 50 cent pocket guide books to the city, and probably the best thing to do when you visit Washington is to go to a bookstore, or newspaper stand, or drug store, and look over the selection. There are also some good higher-priced guide books and picture books on the capital:

And This Is Washington!, by Eleanor Early, Houghton Mifflin Company, 1934. Pocket size. This draws the history of landmarks and buildings into the text colorfully and conversationally, and gives the user some perspective on the capital.

What to See and Do in Washington, by George W. Seaton, Prentice Hall, Inc., 1941. The author is an experienced traveler who suddenly "rediscovered" Washington in a trip which he made to the capital. His book includes tips on restaurants, hotels, and some helpful hints on how to see things most economically.

How This Book Was Written

I spent five years trying to get someone else to write this book. I was too busy, and besides, I didn't know enough. I pestered all sorts of people who I thought could do it. They wouldn't, but they liked the idea, which was this:

People need to know more than just one or two or three facets of Washington. They need to know something about *all* of the intricate phases, for the few phases in which any one person is directly interested are influenced by the other phases. Washington is like a big pie, cut into many wedges, each wedge with a different filling, each flavoring the others and being flavored by the others. People should taste them all if they want to know the pie.

The trouble with doing the book was (and is) that no one person is wise enough to know *all* about *all* the pieces of pie. He may know five or ten, but he can't know fifty. And that's what Washington is—fifty subjects or more.

So no one wanted to tackle such a big job, and neither did I. But, finally, I did—under pressure of the thought that the need for knowing and understanding Washington was getting more urgent.

Here's how it was done: Late in 1940 I started, putting together what I knew, uncovering what I didn't know, getting some picked collaborators to contribute on subjects which they knew well, or which they could dig up. All through 1941 and well into 1942 we labored, we gathered, doing reporting, assembling, boiling down, selecting, discarding. The book is a product of one mind, but the job could not have been done except for the prodigious amount of digging by my excellent corps of coworkers.

Chief assistant for the job was my son, Austin H. Kiplinger, a good reporter, a good editor, a good workman. He was loaned to me by the *San Francisco Chronicle*.

In all, thirty-one men and nine women assisted. Some of these are members of my own immediate staff of newsgatherers, engaged in the week-to-week job of watching and reporting Washington. Some are newspaper correspondents who have specialized on the subjects which they contributed herein. Some are magazine writers. Several are authors of books, authorities on their subjects. More than half are journalists, working currently in Washington, and so it is essentially a journalistic book. Here are the co-workers:

Joseph H. Baird
Leila Wilson Bathon
H. O. Bishop
Joseph W. Bishop, Jr.
Eva H. Boothby
Bernard M. Bour
Katherine A. Brake
Harold Brayman
S. A. Colton
Herbert Corey
Robert G. Covel
Watson Davis
Homer Joseph Dodge
William Atherton DuPuy
Carter Field
Corinne Frazier Gillett
Evelyn Peyton Gordon
O. S. Granducci
Frank C. Hanighen
Dudley Harmon

Oliver Hoyem
Bertram D. Hulen
E. Louise Johnson
Austin H. Kiplinger
LaVerne C. Kiplinger
Jerry Kluttz
Daniel W. Kops
Ernest K. Lindley
Stephen J. McDonough, Jr.
Warren D. Mullin
James B. Reston
J. Lacey Reynolds
Archie T. Robertson
John E. Ryerson
Frederick Shelton
Ira L. Smith
Dorothy D. Walsh
Franklyn Waltman
Donald S. Warren
Clarence M. Wright

Every reader has a right to know about the writer:

I am a journalist, the reporter type, aged 51. Product of Ohio—Bellefontaine and Columbus—the public schools, the State University. My grandfather and father were carriage makers who thought the horseless carriage would never amount to much, and so became victims of technological unemployment, which is why I am a journalist instead of a carriage maker. Really never wanted to be anything except a newspaper reporter. Became one in Columbus, and shifted to Washington in 1916 for the Associated Press. Founded a system of Washington newsletters on a shoestring in the early 20's, and have been at it ever since. Those are the essential facts about the writer.

The book is reportorial, because it is written by a reporter. It is not meant to be ideological; it does not seek to sell any particular point of view.

There is no pretense of being complete in all details on all subjects. The problem of squeezing fifty subjects made omissions necessary. The discarded notes, memoranda and manuscript fill a whole filing cabinet, and would make a dozen books.

The book deals with the basic phases of Washington in the transition from war to peace and in the first stages of war. Naturally there are rapid changes—in men, in functions, in details. To catch them all is like trying to make a plaster cast of a dragonfly on the wing. But the changes which occur in Washington after this book is written do not change the general outline of Washington. New men with new duties are like new cogs, but the machine as a whole runs on.

The book is written for *people*. If the people know what's going on, they can be trusted to think straight, and to guide straight. It is desirable that people not look *up* to Washington excessively, for the habit numbs the brain. And it is equally desirable not to look *down* too much on Washington, for that's a way of using only one eye. The aim of this book is to help people to look Washington square in the face, on a level, with both eyes, and see inside it as it really is.

Washington is not a diamond sitting on a piece of velvet, as some people like to think of it. Instead, it is a collection of tools or implements to be handled and inspected. People can grab hold of them, see how they are put together, and how they may be used to make a better system. I hope this book may serve as a bit of a practical training course—on the *use* of the tools of Washington.

W. M. Kiplinger

Washington, April, 1942

502

Index

Daley, William L., 323
Dalrymple, Martha, 306
Dams, government-constructed, 236-237
Darling, J. N. "Ding," 347
Daughters of the American Revolution, 282, 293, 405
Daughters of the Senate, Daughters of the House, 405
Davies, Joseph E., 261, 265, 406
Davis, James J., 258, 268
Davis, Mary Dabney, 304
Davis, Mrs. Dwight, 309
Davis, Maxine, 306
Davis, William H., 455-456
Dean, William H., 154
Death rate, reduced, 226, 345, 350
Debt, public, 217, 336, 339-340, 342
Decatur House, 402
De Caux, Len, 203
Decisions, Supreme Court, 242-243
Defense, national, 211
  books on, 495-496
Defense Commission, 36, 38
Defense Health and Welfare, 222, 468
Defense organizations, 293
Defense program, women in, 305, 310
"Defense public works," 239
Delano, Frederic A., 330
Delano, Mrs. Preston, 310
Dell, Jessie, 302
Demagogues' Club, 270
Democratic party
  in the South, 274
  organization, 255-256, 259
Democratic process, 6, 15, 17, 87, 269
Depression, 3, 6, 13, 123, 179, 180, 206, 232, 329, 338
Detzer, Dorothy, 308
Deuel, Wallace R., 80
Deupree, R. R., 262
Dewey, Mrs. Charles, 406
Dewhurst, Frederic, 332
Dewson, Mary W., 302
Dickerson, Earl, 152
Dies, Martin, 275
Digest of the Purposes of Federal Agencies, 485
Dillinger, John, 363
Diplomatic list, 260-261
Diplomatic lobby, 283
Disabled American Veterans of the World War, 293
Disabled Emergency Officers of the World War, 293

Disaster Loan Corporation, 213, 214, 468
Discrimination
  against Jews, 374-375
  against Negroes, 149-151, 374
Disease, chemical treatment of, 350
"Distress" loans, 210, 214
District of Columbia (*see also* Washington)
  cost of running, 117-118
  government of, 115-117
Dive-bombing, 60
Dneiper Dam, 237
Documents
  congressional, 489-490
  federal, *see* Pamphlets, government
  Superintendent of, 378, 479, 483
Dodd, Catherine Filene, 309
Dodge, Homer Joseph, 426
Dollar-a-year men, 10, 152
Donovan, William J., 75, 79, 80, 81, 451
Doughton, Robert L., 109, 274
Douglas, William O., 15, 241, 242, 246, 248-249, 250, 251, 335
Doyle, Mrs. Henry Grattan, 309
Drinking in Washington, 99-100, 128
Dubinsky, David, 200
Duggan, Laurence, 71
Dunbar, Saidie Orr, 308
Dunbarton College of Holy Cross, 394
Dunn, James Clement, 71
Du Ponts, 261

Early, Stephen T., 18, 24, 77, 110, 166, 434, 448-449, 460
Eastman, Elizabeth, 308
Eastman, Joseph B., 335, 450
Eccles, Marriner, 329, 334, 454-455
Economic planning, *see* Economy, planned
Economic Warfare, Board of, 343, 468
Economy
  planned, 31, 33, 43, 325-337, 338, 342, 343
  of scarcity, 181, 182, 332
Economy, national, 335-337
Education
  government in, 225
  government standards for, 220
  Office of, 225, 304, 468
  in Washington, 392-396
    Negro, 158, 393, 394
Eiker, Mathilde, 307
Einstein, Albert, 344
Electric co-ops, 229
Electric Home and Farm Authority, 213, 215, 468
Electric utilities, private, 228

Electron microscope, 351
Eliot, Thomas, 405-406
Ellington, Duke, 107, 158
Elliot, Charles W., II, 330
Elliott, Charlotte, 305
Elliott, Harriet, 309
Embassies, 417
  entertaining at, 402-405
Emergency Management, Office for, 84, 468
Employment
  full, 339, 340, 343
  government aid in, 220
Emspak, Julius, 202
En Guardia, 82
Engert, Cornelius Van H., 71
Engraving and Printing, Bureau of, 387, 469
Espionage, 361-362
Essary, Helen, 306
Evans, Alice, 304
Evans, Mrs. Joshua, Jr., 309
Evening Star, 129
"Ever-normal granary," 184
Expansion
  Army, 46-47
  of building programs, 239
  government, 9, 18, 324
  of government lending, 206-207, 216
  industrial, 32
  of labor's influence in politics, 204
  Navy, 54-55, 60
  of planning corps, 327
  postwar
    of Navy and air forces, 340
    of production and markets, 341
    of social services, 341
  production, 40, 179
  State Department, 64, 66
  of Washington population, 123
  of welfare activities, 230
Expenses, White House, 24-26
Export-Import Bank, 214, 469
Ezekiel, Mordecai, 332, 343

Fahey, John H., 209
Fahy, Charles, 457
Fair Employment Practice, Committee on, 374
Fair Labor Standards Act, 194
Fakler, Herman, 323
Fan-mail to government officials and Congress, 287
Farley, James A., 238, 260, 263
Farm bloc, 187-188

Farm Credit Administration, 186-187, 212, 469
Farm and Home Hour radio program, 187
Farm Security Administration, 185-186, 212-213, 228, 469
Farmers
  aid to, 327
  demands of, 11, 179-180
  loans for, 207, 212, 228-229
  organizations of, 188-190
  program for, 183-184
  revolution of, 178-179
  and science, 187
  under government control, 178, 183
Farmers' lobby, 178, 189-190, 212, 281-282
Farmers Union, 189, 228, 281
Father Struck It Rich, 193
Fauset, Crystal Bird, 153
Favoritism, 253, 329
Federal agencies, 463-480
Federal Bar Association, 316
Federal Bureau of Investigation, 357-365, 469
  applicants to, 358
  crime laboratory, 363
  files and museum, 362-363
  and the laws, 360-361
Federal Communications Bar Association, 314-315
Federal Communications Commission, 80, 469
Federal Deposit Insurance Corporation, 216, 469
Federal Farm Board, 179
Federal Farm Mortgage Corporation, 212, 215, 470
Federal Home Loan Bank Administration, 207, 210, 470
Federal Housing Administration, 207, 210, 470
Federal Land Banks, 212, 215
Federal Reserve Act, 326
Federal Security Agency, 221, 222-223, 470
Federal Trade Commission, 84, 333, 470
Federal Trade Commission Act, 326
Federal Works Agency, 221, 233-234, 235, 237, 340, 471
Fenn, H. K., 84
Fenton, Frank, 202
Ferguson, Abner, 209
Fermi, Enrico, 344
Ferry, A. M., 323
Fetter, Frank W., 326
Fight for Freedom Committee, 293

515

Set in Linotype Old Style No. 1
Format by A. W. Rushmore
Manufactured by The Haddon Craftsmen
Published by Harper & Brothers
New York and London